ELIJAH M. JAMES
Dawson College

MICROECONOMICS

SECOND EDITION

PEARSON

Toronto

Vice-President, Editorial Director: Gary Bennett
Editor-in-Chief: Nicole Lukach
Acquisitions Editor: Claudine O'Donnell
Marketing Manager: Leigh-Anne Graham
Supervising Developmental Editor: Suzanne Schaan
Developmental Editor: Toni Chahley
Project Manager: Richard di Santo
Manufacturing Coordinator: Susan Johnson
Production Editor: Susan Bindernagel
Copy Editor: Dawn Hunter
Proofreader: Susan Bindernagel
Compositor: Cenveo Publisher Services
Permissions Researcher: Natalie Barrington
Art Director: Julia Hall
Interior and Cover Designer: Anthony Leung
Cover Image: Shutterstock

Credits and acknowledgments borrowed from other sources and reproduced, with permission, in this textbook appear on the appropriate page within text, and on page C1.

10 9 8 7 6 5 4 3 2 1   CKV

Library and Archives Canada Cataloguing in Publication

James, Elijah M.
    Microeconomics / Elijah M. James.—2nd ed.

Includes bibliographical references and index.
ISBN 978-0-13-801095-9

    1. Microeconomics—Textbooks. I. Title.

HB172.J345 2011a   338.5   C2011-906261-5

ISBN 978-0-13-801095-9

Dedicated to the memory of Winston "Georgie" Carter whose kindness and loyalty will never be forgotten; to the memory of my late cousin, Hurdle Jacobs, who always believed in me and whose acid humour never ceased to make me laugh; and to my dear brother and friend, Warren Scotland (Scottie), who epitomizes the true meaning of friendship.

Brief Contents

Contents

Preface

Writing textbooks does not necessarily get easier with each revision. When a textbook is well received, great effort must be expended in trying to retain and even improve on its strengths and eliminate its weaknesses. It is a constant challenge to incorporate in the new edition the changes suggested by users of the previous edition. Additionally, explanations and passages that students find difficult or unclear must be reworked and simplified.

The primary objective of *Microeconomics*, Second Edition, has remained unchanged, namely, to assist beginning students in economics to understand the fascinating subject of economics and to motivate them to make a serious study of it. In the process, I hope that the book will convey the power and excitement of economic analysis.

Microeconomics, Second Edition, continues to use students' intuitive knowledge of economics as a stepping stone to present basic economic concepts, ideas, and principles. The dialogical approach that proved to be quite successful in engaging students in the previous edition has been retained in this new edition. Like its predecessor, this book is completely interactive. Our survey of students who have used the previous edition revealed that this is one of the features of the book that students find helpful. Many claimed that this approach has actually taught them how to answer questions.

Revisions, additions, extensions, and deletions have been made in order to improve the book and increase its appeal. Where pruning was necessary, it was done without robbing the student of *essential* material. In preparing this second edition of *Microeconomics*, I made a concerted effort to ensure that students continue to find this book easy to read and understand. Much would be lost if this book that was designed specifically to be student-friendly were placed beyond the readability comfort of the very people for whom it was written. It is hoped that such a tragedy has been averted.

As is the case with its predecessor, *Microeconomics,* Second Edition,is written specifically for students taking their first course in economics. Such a course should provide a solid foundation in economic ideas and principles, and in the basic tools used to analyze economic behaviour. Economics is an interesting and important subject, and those who make a serious study of it often find it useful in their personal lives. Such a course should also encourage and motivate students by presenting the subject in a manner they consider relevant. This textbook tries to achieve these objectives. Words and diagrams are the main tools used in presenting economic ideas to students. No mathematics beyond elementary algebra is used in this book, and even then, math is used sparingly or relegated to MyEconLab, where instructors and students who need to use it can find it. Care has been taken to ensure that the use of mathematics facilitates rather than impedes the learning of basic economic concepts and principles.

This book recognizes that many students will not continue their formal study of economics beyond this introductory level. This fact is demonstrated in the material covered in the text.

Responding to Students' Needs

This text is specially designed to help students succeed. Before writing this book, I conducted a survey to determine the features that students find most helpful in textbooks. In writing this new textbook, I incorporated students' expressed needs as follows:

1. **A preview of what is to be learned.** The student survey revealed that students want to know what they will learn in a chapter before reading the chapter. Each chapter begins with clearly stated Learning Objectives in the form of numbered statements of what students should be able to do after studying the chapter. **NEW!** Each of the major sections in the book is associated with a learning objective, and this theme carries through to the **Key Points to Remember**, and the **Problems and Exercises**.

2. **Assess Your Knowledge questions.** As indicated earlier, most students taking their first course in economics have some knowledge of the subject. Many students will be motivated to test their knowledge of the material in the chapter even before studying the chapter. Short self-test questions at the beginning of each chapter provide this opportunity. Answers are provided on MyEconLab.

3. **In-text explanations of graphs.** Students expressed a desire for graphs to be explained within the text. In this book, detailed explanations of all graphs are given within the text. Thus, graphs become an integral part of the explanation being offered or of the concept or principle being presented. **NEW!** All of the key graphs in each chapter have been placed on quad paper.

4. **Concept citation.** According to the survey, students want basic concepts and ideas to be emphasized in the text. This is done in *Microeconomics*, Second Edition. **NEW!** At the beginning of each major section, a key concept or idea is expressed, and this key concept or idea is tied to a learning objective for the chapter.

5. **Definitions and important terms emphasized in the text.** Students indicated that they want definitions and important terms to be accentuated in the text. In this book, all important terms are bolded and the terms and definitions are repeated in the margin. Important material or principles are highlighted because students often highlight material that they consider to be important. **NEW!** The Second Edition of *Microeconomics* also includes a complete glossary at the end of the book.

6. **Review.** Students want a textbook that contains a review of the material studied. Review is an important component of this book. At the end of each chapter, students are asked to review the learning objectives with a view to determining the extent to which they have accomplished the objectives. Additionally, this section contains key points for students to remember. **NEW!** In keeping with the organization of major sections in each chapter by learning objective, we have also organized key sections in the chapter review by learning objective.

7. **Important terms collected at the end of each chapter.** Students have identified this as a desirable feature of a textbook. In *Microeconomics,* Second Edition, a section at the end of each chapter entitled Economic Word Power satisfies this need. Under Economic Word Power, all economic terms introduced in the chapter and included in the margins are listed alphabetically with page references to where they are defined in the chapter.

8. **Questions that challenge comprehension of the material.** The survey revealed that students want the textbook to contain review questions that challenge their understanding of the material they have studied. Accordingly, each major section of the

book is followed by key Reading Comprehension questions, in which students are asked to answer questions based on the material contained in the preceding section and its associated learning objective.

9. **Problems and Exercises.** Students want a textbook that allows them to practise problems and exercises based on the material covered in the text. Responding to this expressed need, *Microeconomics,* Second Edition, contains a Problems and Exercises section in which students can practise applying key concepts in the book. The problems and exercises are grouped into three categories: Basic, Intermediate, and Challenging. Answers to these are not given in the text, but students can consult their instructors for the answers. **NEW!** Basic questions are now tied to the learning objectives in the chapter.

10. **Self-assessment and use of economic resources on the internet.** An important aspect of the teaching–learning relationship is self-assessment. This textbook contains a Study Guide that uses multiple-choice questions as an effective way for students to assess themselves. Answers are provided in the textbook. In addition, the Study Guide contains another set of Problems and Exercises, the answers to which are on MyEconLab. With access to an unlimited number of study questions on the MyEconLab, students have an opportunity to strengthen any weaknesses revealed by the self-assessment. MyEconLab also includes Economics Online Exercises that list websites where students can augment their study of the material in the chapter.

What's Different about This Book?

This question has been partially answered by the 10 points outlining the responses to students' expressed needs and by the dialogical approach taken in this book. However, other differences remain between this and other introductory economics textbooks.

1. *Microeconomics,* Second Edition, draws on the strengths of its predecessors (*Economics: A Problem-Solving Approach; Microeconomics: Basic Concepts, Questions and Answers;* and *Introduction to Economics*). The text is easy to read and understand, it is student friendly, and it focuses on basic principles and concepts that students at the introductory level need to know.

2. This book employs a results-oriented *learning-by-objective* (LBO) approach. Learning objectives are established at the beginning of each chapter, and at the end of the chapter, the objectives are reviewed to determine whether students accomplished those objectives.

3. Graphs are large and clear and are *fully integrated* and explained in the body of the text rather than being curtained off in potentially distracting boxes outside the main body of the text. Thus, all graphs form an integral part of the explanation of the concepts and ideas they are used to represent or depict. Graphs illustrating key concepts are also presented on quad paper to enhance student understanding.

4. A huge number of interesting microeconomic topics can be included in an introductory economics text. For example, this textbook contains an entire chapter on the economics of information in which such topics as asymmetric information, adverse selection, and moral hazard are presented at an elementary level that is suitable for comprehension by introductory students. To keep this book within a reasonable length, I have chosen topics with care. The result is a text that covers a suitable range of microeconomic topics that are relevant to present-day students.

5. Most microeconomics textbooks, in discussing the short run and the long run use terms that imply a period of time. *Microeconomics,* Second Edition, on the other hand, defines these concepts, not as periods of calendar time, but rather as situations in which firms may find themselves. This approach removes the potential confusion of associating the short run with a relatively short period of time and the long run with a relatively long period of time.

6. Many of the students who will use this book are business students. Business and economics share a close relationship. In fact, many business decisions are grounded in economics. Business examples, called Business Situations, are scattered throughout the book to give students an opportunity to apply the economic theory they are learning to a variety of business situations.

7. *Microeconomics,* Second Edition, uses visual aids liberally to complement verbal explanations. This feature will be particularly helpful to students whose first language is not English.

8. *Microeconomics,* Second Edition, uses colour *judiciously* and *effectively* to enhance understanding of graphs and charts. For example, in demand-supply graphs, the downward-sloping demand curve is always shown as a blue curve, while the upward-sloping supply curve is always shown as a red curve.

Organization of the Book

This book is divided into six parts. Part I introduces the subject matter of economics and discusses the economic problem. It also deals with the important topic of demand and supply. Part II deals with elasticity, applications of demand and supply, and consumer choice. Part III incorporates the theory of production, and the costs of production. Competitive markets, monopoly, monopolistic competition, and oligopoly are treated in Part IV under market structure and pricing. The labour market and unions, markets for other factors of production, and income distribution and poverty constitute Part V, while Part VI discusses other microeconomic issues: international trade and trade policy, environmental protection and government regulation, and the economics of information.

New to the Second Edition

In **Chapter 1,** the material on the importance of understanding economics has been substantially rewritten to include more recent events; a new section on where economists work and what they do has been included in this edition; the concept of time as a resource has been included; leadership has been added as an example of entrepreneurial ability; and the concept of financial capital has been further clarified. A short list of Canadian entrepreneurs and the companies and products associated with them has been added.

In **Chapter 2,** the discussion on opportunity cost has been expanded and more examples have been added. More relevant examples are used in **Chapter 3**. For example, USB flash drives, Blu-rays, and iPhones replace older examples, and profit has been v explicit as a motivator for producers. We have also added a new mathematical appendix, in which the basic demand/supply model is presented algebraically.

In **Chapter 4** the discussion on the factors affecting price elasticity of supply has been substantially expanded. Perishability has been given greater emphasis, and the cost of increasing output is now included in the discussion. Measures of elasticity of demand for certain items have been included. A list of items with different elasticity coefficients has been added to the discussion.

A discussion of alternatives to rent control and minimum wage legislation has been added to **Chapter 5**. The effect of a tax on buyers is now added to the discussion on the effects of excise taxes, and an analysis of the effects of price changes on consumer and producer surplus have also been added to this chapter.

Chapter 7 now encompasses Chapter 10 from the previous edition. The discussion of the various forms of business organization has been shortened and organizational structure and business financing have been omitted from this edition. The concept of sunk cost is now included in **Chapter 8**, and a new business situation box has been added.

In **Chapter 9** we have refined the definitions of market structure and differentiated product, and supported these definitions with examples. We have also clarified key terms in **Chapter 10**. The potentially confusing term *monopolistic* firm has been replaced by the terms *monopoly* or *monopolist*. This chapter also boasts more Canadian examples.

In **Chapter 11,** the discussion of game theory has been expanded to include the Prisoner's Dilemma. In **Chapter 12** the concept of featherbedding has been clarified with appropriate examples.

We have added a brief discussion of the effect of the 2007–2009 recession on Canada's exports to **Chapter 14**. A section on Tariffs and Trade Policy Issues is also included in this edition.

Chapter 15 has a new discussion of the carbon tax and cap and trade, as well as the Copenhagen Accord and the Cancun Agreement.

Pedagogy

- **Learning Objectives:** Each chapter starts with a list of learning objectives directly related to the key concepts presented in the chapter. These learning objectives are in turn tied to each major section of the book, associated reading comprehension questions, and key elements of the chapter review.
- **Assess Your Knowledge:** These questions at the beginning of each chapter cover the main objectives of the chapter and can be used to review for tests and exams. Answers to these questions are provided on the MyEconLab.
- **Key terms:** Key terms are bolded within the text and defined. The terms and definitions are repeated in the margins as well. Terms are also listed with page references at the end of each chapter in the section entitled Economic Word Power, and all terms are included in the comprehensive glossary at the end of the book.
- **Business Situation boxes:** These brief vignettes give students an opportunity to apply economic theory to a variety of business situations. Each business scenario is followed by a question about the relevance of the example to the chapter topic. Answers to the questions are found in an appendix at the end of the book.
- **Highlighted sections of the text:** These are used to emphasize important concepts.
- **Figures:** All figures are explained in the body of the text and thus form an integral part of the concepts and ideas they are used to represent or depict.
- **End-of-chapter materials:** These sections provide students with multiple opportunities for review (Key Points to Remember), Problems and Exercises for instructors to assign, and opportunities for student self-assessment (embedded Study Guide).

Supplements

A comprehensive supplements package accompanies the text.

Instructor's Resource CD-ROM [013282416]: This resource CD includes the following instructor supplements:

- **Pearson TestGen** is a testing software that enables instructors to view and edit the existing questions, add questions, generate tests, and distribute the tests in a variety of formats. Powerful search and sort functions make it easy to locate questions and arrange them in any order desired. TestGen also enables instructors to administer tests on a local area network, have the tests graded electronically and have the results prepared in electronic or printed reports. TestGen is compatible with Windows and Macintosh operating systems, and can be downloaded from the TestGen website located at www.pearsoned.com/testgen. Contact your local sales representative for details and access.

- The **Instructor's Resource Manual** is designed to help the instructor make the best possible use of his or her limited time. Each chapter includes a list of important terms and concepts introduced in the chapter, the objectives of the chapter, a brief overview of its contents, and teaching suggestions and possible topics for class discussion. The Manual also contains solutions to the Problems and Exercises. The Instructor's Manual is available for downloading from a password-protected section of Pearson Education Canada's online catalogue (www.pearsoned.ca/highered). Navigate to your book's catalogue page to view a list of those supplements that are available. See your local sales representative for details and access.

- **PowerPoint Presentations** reflect the main topics featured in the text, along with graphic depictions of important economic ideas discussed in the book.

- The **Image Library** contains all of the numbered figures and tables in the textbook.

The moment you know.
Educators know it. Students know it. It's that inspired moment when something that was difficult to understand suddenly makes perfect sense. Our MyLab products have been designed and refined with a single purpose in mind—to help educators create that moment of understanding with their students.

MyEconLab delivers **proven results** in helping individual students succeed. It provides **engaging experiences** that personalize, stimulate, and measure learning for each student. And, it comes from a **trusted partner** with educational expertise and an eye on the future.

MyEconLab can be used by itself or linked to any learning management system. Visit MyEconLab to learn more about how it combines proven learning applications with powerful assessment.

MyEconLab—the moment you know.

For more information on MyEconLab, please visit www.myeconlab.com.

Technology Specialists. Pearson's Technology Specialists work with faculty and campus course designers to ensure that Pearson technology products, assessment tools, and online course materials are tailored to meet your specific needs. This highly qualified team is dedicated to helping schools take full advantage of a wide range of educational resources, by assisting in the integration of a variety of instructional materials and media formats. Your local Pearson Education sales representative can provide you with more details on this service program.

CourseSmart for Instructors. CourseSmart goes beyond traditional expectations—providing instant, online access to the textbooks and course materials you need at a lower cost for students. And even as students save money, you can save time and hassle with a digital eTextbook that allows you to search for the most relevant content at the very moment you need it. Whether it's evaluating textbooks or creating lecture notes to help students with difficult concepts, CourseSmart can make life a little easier. See how when you visit www.coursesmart.com/instructors.

CourseSmart for Students. CourseSmart goes beyond traditional expectations—providing instant, online access to the textbooks and course materials you need at an average savings of 60 percent. With instant access from any computer and the ability to search your text, you'll find the content you need quickly, no matter where you are. And with online tools like highlighting and note-taking, you can save time and study efficiently. See all the benefits at www.coursesmart.com/students.

Pearson eText. Pearson eText gives students access to the text whenever and wherever they have access to the internet. eText pages look exactly like the printed text, offering powerful new functionality for students and instructors. Users can create notes, highlight text in different colours, create bookmarks, zoom, click hyperlinked words and phrases to view definitions, and view in single-page or two-page view. Pearson eText allows for quick navigation to key parts of the eText using a table of contents and provides full-text search. The eText may also offer links to associated media files, enabling users to access videos, animations, or other activities as they read the text.

Acknowledgments

This new edition of *Microeconomics* has increased my indebtedness to instructors, colleagues, and students whose comments, suggestions, and questions have contributed significantly to improving the quality of the book. To them I say a heartfelt thank you. In this regard, I would like to single out Worku Aberra of Dawson College in Montreal and Sandra Wellman of Seneca College in Toronto. No one has contributed more to this edition than they have, and I am greatly indebted to them. Ahmad Banki and Charles-Albert Ramsay have pointed out areas where clarification was needed, and I thank them sincerely. Matlub Hussain continues to be generous with his comments and suggestions. Thank you, Mat.

My students at Concordia University, John Molson School of Business, McGill University, John Abbott College, and particularly Dawson College continue to influence my writing. By their questions, they demanded clarity and precision. Without their contributions, the tone of the book would have been vastly different. I thank them from the bottom of my heart. During the preparation of this second edition of *Microeconomics*, I received invaluable support and encouragement from Koren Norton. Thank you, Koren! I am in your debt.

Just when I thought I had done the most incredible job with this second edition, I was summoned back to the drawing board by the reviewers. Their comments, constructive criticisms, and suggestions were discerning, incisive, and occasionally even caustic. The result? A much improved textbook. I owe them a debt of gratitude. They are:

Mohammad Akbar, Kwantlen Polytechnic University
Aurelia Best, Centennial College
David Desjardins, John Abbott College
Derek Heatherington, Champlain Regional College
John Pirrie, St. Lawrence College
Vitaly Terekhov, Marianapolis College
Russell Turner, Fleming College
Carl Weston, Mohawk College

The skills and professionalism of the Pearson team that worked on this book must be acknowledged. It is tempting to believe that Pearson Canada once again went out of its way to assemble the best possible team for project, including Acquisitions Editor, Claudine O'Donnell; Developmental Editor, Toni Chahley; Project Manager, Richard di Santo; Production Editor, Susan Bindernagel; and Copy Editor, Dawn Hunter.

Finally, I would like to thank my children, Ted and Andrea, for their unwavering support and sacrifice throughout the years. You have given so much and have required nothing in return. You are both terrific and I love you beyond measure. Connie, I am still thinking of ways to thank you for your unparalleled support. My indebtedness to you is so great that I am beginning to think that I will never be able to thank you enough. I must agree with Robert Byrne that "The purpose of life is a life of purpose." I thank you all.

Elijah M. James

To the Student

How to Study Economics

The study of economics requires time and serious concentration. Study habits vary from student to student, and what works for one student may not work for all. This course in economics is designed to provide you with some insight into the functioning of an economy and into some of the policy issues that are being hotly debated.

Interest in economics varies. Some students aspire to a career in economics, while others are concerned merely with acquiring a basic understanding of the subject. Whatever your interest might be, here are some general guidelines that you will find helpful as you study this book.

1. Study the Assess Your Knowledge section to determine your prior knowledge.

2. As you read through the various sections of the text, make sure that you are equipped with paper and pencil to make your own notes. Do not rush through the material. You are learning economics, not reading a story book.

3. Practise drawing the diagrams on the basis of the arguments presented. This way, you will learn much more than if you merely tried to study the completed diagram as it is presented in the book.

4. As concepts are presented, try to provide examples, if possible, from your own experience. Your ability to provide examples is a measure of your understanding.

5. The Reading Comprehension questions at the end of each major section are designed to assess your comprehension of the material covered in the section. Try to answer all of these and then check the accuracy of your answers in MyEconLab.

6. Make sure that you understand the terms and concepts introduced in each chapter by reviewing them in the Economic Word Power section at the end of each chapter.

7. The Problems and Exercises are designed to help you to apply what you have learned. Try to work through as many of these as you can.

8. Form study groups if you can. By discussing economics (answering questions and solving problems) in groups, your understanding will be enhanced.

9. Finally, a Study Guide is included in the text. Use the questions for self-assessment. Answers are provided at the end of the book for your guidance.

Chapter

1

The Subject Matter of Economics

Learning Objectives

After studying this chapter, you should be able to

1.1 Explain the importance of understanding economics

1.2 Discuss economics as a profession

1.3 Discuss the subject matter of economics

1.4 Define resources, classify them into categories, and discuss the incomes derived from each category of resources

1.5 Explain the scientific method and discuss economic methodology

1.6 Identify positive and normative economics and explain why economists sometimes disagree

1.7 Recognize different types of variables and cause-effect relations

1.8 Distinguish between microeconomics and macroeconomics

1

Assess Your Knowledge

MyEconLab

Answers to these questions can be found on MyEconLab at **www.myeconlab.com**.

1. Identify two topics that you would expect to study in economics.
2. Identify one resource that is not scarce.
3. Why do people have to make choices?
4. Can someone make a choice without giving up something?
5. Identify two social science disciplines.

LO 1.1 Explain the importance of understanding economics

Why Study Economics?

Why is having an understanding of economics important?

These are indeed exciting times to be studying economics. Recent events have turned the spotlight on the economy and on economists. News about economic matters can be read in the newspapers, heard on the radio, and seen on television; all over the internet and the World Wide Web, a great deal of information exists on important economic topics. Governments, large corporations, small business enterprises, and consumers are turning to economists for answers to our economic problems.

Whether it is forest fires in California, the H1N1 virus, unusually frequent federal elections in Canada, accusations of price fixing among the gasoline companies, a tsunami in Samoa, government bailouts of failing companies, the so-called *economic stimulus*, or violent protests in Egypt, they all are related in some way to economics. Economics is involved directly or indirectly with whether you decide to go to summer school or take a vacation in the Dominican Republic, to purchase a used car for transportation to and from school or take public transportation, to live at home with your patents or rent an apartment close to school, or to purchase some U.S. dollars to shop in the United States this weekend. On April 14, 2010, and again on October 14, 2010, the Canadian dollar rose above the U.S. dollar in value. On November 4, 2010, the Canadian dollar was on par with the U.S. dollar, and on January 24, 2011, one Canadian dollar was worth 1.0054 U.S. dollars. Why did these changes occur and who benefits from them? The fact is, economic issues and problems are all around us; we cannot escape them.

Economic analysis can shed light on these and many other issues that are of great significance for many of us because they affect our lives in important ways. Once we accept this simple fact, then economic understanding assumes great importance.

Let us consider the following benefits derived from understanding economics.

Understanding the Economy and Society Understanding the operation of our economic system enables us to improve its performance and helps us to deal with many of the problems that our country faces. The economy is such an important part of society that it is impossible to understand society without a basic knowledge of economics. Our relationships with one another, our environment, the manner in which our collective wealth is distributed, the types of work we do, and the amount of money we earn are all related to our economy. Our lives are shaped by the myriad economic decisions that have been made in the past by others and that are being made by us today. A decision to build more warplanes instead of providing more educational and health facilities will affect us not only today but also for a long time in the future.

The better our understanding of our economy and our society, the better the control that we are likely to have over our destiny. It can be argued that the recent global and economic crisis would have been longer and more severe if economists did not have such a good understanding of how the economy works.

Understanding World Affairs   Change is occurring rapidly in the world. Just pick up a newspaper, turn on the radio or television, or go to a news agency on the internet, and you will get an idea of the many important changes that are taking place in the world. The political face of the Middle East has already assumed a different appearance, and the war in Afghanistan still rages on. Many countries of the world are engaged in important negotiations, and North Korea continues to defy the United Nations sanctions by testing its missiles. The economy of Zimbabwe was in shambles with an estimated unemployment rate of 95% in 2010 and an estimated inflation rate of 231 000 000% in 2008. After Zimbabwe abandoned the Zimbabwean dollar in 2009, the rate of inflation fell dramatically to about 5.3% in July 2010.

The G-20—finance ministers and central bankers from a group of 19 countries and the European Union—holds meetings to discuss global economic stability. Their deliberations are important because they hold significant economic power. According to the *African Sun News,* as of August 27, 2010, about 15 African countries were at war or were experiencing postwar tensions. Among other factors at the root of these wars were the rich natural resources owned by each of these countries. Thus, the cause of many of these wars was economic in nature. Portugal, Ireland, Greece, and Spain have all recently experienced economic difficulties. Economics as a discipline may be able to offer some solutions. Our way of life has been changed drastically by terrorist threats, and national security is now on the list of top priorities for most countries. During January and February 2011, demonstrations, protests, and social unrests in Tunisia, Egypt, Yemen, Bahrain, and Libya, engaged the world's attention. Economics will help us to understand many of these important world events and how they affect our country, our governments, and us as individuals.

Being an Informed Citizen   As consumers, it is important for us to know how to spend our income so that we can derive maximum satisfaction from our purchases. It is also important for us to use our labour services and other resources wisely. Not only should people be wise consumers, but as citizens in a democracy, they must also be able to visualize and evaluate the consequences of different courses of action to determine which ones are most likely to lead to improvements in economic and social well-being.

What are the issues involved in the federal government's decision to run a deficit during a period of severe economic slow-down? Will such a policy achieve its intended goal? Did our government make the right decision in its dealings with the automakers? Will Canadians benefit from this arrangement? What are the costs? General Motors offered $3000 to anyone who scrapped an old car and bought a new one. Was General Motors' offer of this $3000 scrap incentive a wise economic move? During the global recession, the Bank of Canada lowered its interest rate drastically. Was that policy initiative a good one? Can the government do anything about unemployment? Should Canada pursue a policy of protectionism as a means of supporting its domestic industries?

Can subsidies to farmers be justified on economic grounds? In an election, citizens often vote for a party on the basis of its political platform, which, to a significant degree, contains issues and intended policies that are essentially economic in nature. A knowledge of economics enables citizens to replace emotional judgment with reasoned analysis in the decision-making process.

Thinking Logically   One of the most important reasons for studying economics is that it develops a particular way of thinking and making decisions. Good decision making requires a careful evaluation of the benefits (advantages) and costs (disadvantages) associated with the decision or the choice. Actually, economic analysis is, to a large extent, an exercise in logic and thus helps to sharpen our common sense.

Getting Personal Satisfaction   People may have a more personal reason for studying economics. Because the study of economics can be intellectually exciting and stimulating, it yields great personal satisfaction. If you happen to become a great economist, you could end up being the president or chief executive officer (CEO) of a corporation, or an economic consultant to one of our levels of government, with an annual salary in the six-figure range.

Reading Comprehension

The answers to these questions can be found on MyEconLab at www.myeconlab.com.   MyEconLab

1.   Present an argument to support the claim that economics is worth studying.

2.   If you were to purchase a car, what benefits would you consider? What costs would you consider?

3.   Describe a recent world affair that you believe to be related to economics.

 LO 1.2   Discuss economics as a profession

Economics as a Profession

Where do economists work and what do they actually do?

Economists are employed in many different places, including the following:

- Private firms, such as banks, insurance companies, large manufacturing companies, unions, and telephone companies
- High schools, colleges, and universities
- Government departments and government agencies
- Research institutions
- Nonprofit organizations
- Independent consultancies
- International organizations and agencies, such as the United Nations, the World Bank, and the International Monetary Fund

You may even find economists serving as ministers of government.

Let us turn to the second part of the question: What do economists actually do? Certainly, you have a good idea of what your economics instructor does. But what other kinds of jobs do economists do? A large corporation, such as Wal-Mart, General Motors, Costco, or your telephone company, might hire economists to estimate the demand for its products or to figure out what effects a change in price will have on its profits. A bank might employ economists to forecast interest rates or the demand for loans. The federal government might hire economists to determine the effects of certain taxes on the government's revenue and on the level of economic activity within the country. Finally, a union might employ economists to study matters relating to wages and employment. Economists serve as presidents, vice-presidents, general managers, and executives of a wide variety of organizations. Clearly, economists can add value to an organization in a variety of contexts.

Reading Comprehension

The answers to these questions can be found on MyEconLab at www.myeconlab.com.   MyEconLab

1.   What opportunities exist for economic graduates?

2.   What kinds of work do economists do?
3.   Why might an electrical power generating company hire an economist?

LO 1.3 Discuss the subject matter of economics

What Is Economics All About?

What do we mean by scarcity? Isn't Canada a land of plenty?

We live in a world where our wants vastly outstrip the means available to satisfy those wants. Society wants automobiles, homes, clothes, computers, entertainment centres, schools, roads, food, telecommunication systems, health services, books, symphony orchestras, amusement parks, libraries, and so on. Indeed, our wants seem to be limitless. But the means available to satisfy all these wants are severely limited. Suppose every Canadian is given a month to list all the things that he or she would like to have, not considering cost. At the end of the month, the lists are collected, and the economy embarks on a massive production effort to produce everything on all the lists. Will the Canadian economy be capable of producing all the things on those lists? The answer is emphatically and resoundingly "no." We just don't have enough factories, natural resources, machinery, and workers to produce all the things we would like to have. **Scarcity** is the situation that exists when resources are inadequate to produce all the goods and services that people want. So although Canada is a land of plenty (we are well-endowed with resources, and we have a relatively high standard of living), we still have the problem of scarcity.

scarcity the situation that exists when resources are inadequate to produce all the goods and services that people want

Now we know what scarcity means, but what does that have to do with choice?

If we could have everything that we want, then we would not have to choose. We would simply take it all. If you have $200, you cannot purchase a Kindle wireless reading device

Figure 1.1	Scarcity Forces Choice

Scarcity —Forces→ Choice

that costs $200 and two jackets that cost $100 each. You are confronted with scarcity and you will have to choose between the Kindle and the two jackets. Your parents have a strict budget of $10 000. They cannot take the Caribbean cruise that costs $10 000 and buy you that red used car for $10 000. They are confronted with scarcity and must therefore choose between your dream car and their cruise. Guy Laliberté can afford to spend several millions of dollars as a space tourist, but he cannot physically attend a hockey game at the same time that he is in space. Even people as wealthy as Laliberté and Bill Gates face scarcity and are forced to choose, since they have a limited amount of time. We see, therefore, that choice is a direct result of scarcity. Figure 1.1 highlights the relationship between scarcity and choice.

Does society as a whole also have to make choices?

Yes. For the same reason that individuals must make choices, society as a whole must also make choices. Society is equally confronted with scarcity and must therefore choose between different alternatives that are available. Society must choose between more schools or more hospitals, better roads or more recreational facilities, more submarines or more environmental protection, and so on. As long as scarcity exists, choices must be made.

BUSINESS SITUATION 1.1

John Adams owns a corner grocery store. He has just obtained a loan of $25 000 from his bank. He is thinking of using this money to increase the size of his stock.

What element of economics does this situation illustrate?

The answer to this Business Situation can be found in Appendix A.

What is economics?

We have indicated that scarcity and choice are at the heart of economics. They are the most basic economic concepts. In fact, economics has everything to do with the way we choose among available alternatives—the way we use our scarce means to satisfy our unlimited wants. We can define economics this way: **Economics** is the social science that studies how people use limited means to satisfy their unlimited wants.

economics the social science that studies how people use limited means to satisfy their unlimited wants

Economics reminds you that you cannot have everything you want. You cannot go to a movie and study for your economics test at the same time. If you think that the movies will benefit you more than studying for the test, then you will give up studying for the test. Conversely, if you believe that studying for the test will benefit you more than going to the movie, then you will give up going to the movies. Economics is at work in your decision.

What is a social science?

social science any discipline that studies human behaviour

A **social science** is any discipline that studies human behaviour. Many disciplines study different aspects of human behaviour. Psychology deals with the mental characteristics associated with a particular kind of behaviour; sociology is the study of society and its institutions; anthropology studies the origin and development of humans as social beings; and political science is concerned with the nature and functions of the state and the way we are governed. All these disciplines, along with economics, are social sciences. These disciplines often overlap. For example, economics and political science both study the functions of the state, but they may do so from different perspectives.

Reading Comprehension

The answers to these questions can be found on MyEconLab at **www.myeconlab.com.**   MyEconLab

1. Why do individuals, businesses, and governments all have to make choices?

2. Economics is the study of scarcity and choice. Do you consider this to be an adequate definition of economics?
3. Would you personally be confronted with scarcity if you could buy all the goods and services you want?
4. What makes economics a social science?

LO 1.4 Define resources, classify them into categories, and discuss the income derived from each category of resources

resources the things used to produce goods and services

goods tangible things that satisfy wants

services intangible things that satisfy wants

Resources

What are the limited means referred to in the definition of economics?

Limited means are the things that are needed to produce the items to satisfy our wants. They are more generally referred to as **resources** or factors of production and include trees in British Columbia, rivers in Quebec, lakes in Ontario, parliament buildings in Ottawa, the oil sands of Alberta, potash in Saskatchewan, the productive efforts of human beings all over Canada, time, factories, highways, nuclear power plants, and all things used in the process of production.

Figure 1.2 shows that resources produce not only goods and services to satisfy consumer wants, but they also produce other resources that can, in turn, be used to produce goods and services.

For example, we use trees to produce paper, rivers for navigation and fishing, buildings as dwellings and warehouses, human effort to operate machines and to load and unload trucks, and nuclear power plants to generate electricity. We produce factories and then use them to produce shoes and clothing.

What is the difference between goods and services?

The main difference between goods and services is that **goods** are tangible things (you can touch them) that satisfy wants, and **services** are

Figure 1.2	Resources Produce Goods, Services, and Other Resources

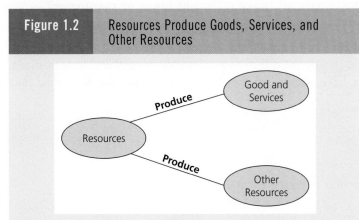

Water is an important resource that Canada is well endowed with.

commodities goods and services together

bads things that are unwanted and do not give any satisfaction

intangible things that satisfy wants. Examples of goods are computers, iPads, television sets, shoes, and textbooks. Examples of services are teaching, banking, transportation services, and garbage collection. Goods and services both give satisfaction and are therefore wanted. Goods and services are collectively referred to as **commodities**. Such items as garbage and pollution that are unwanted and do not give any satisfaction are called **bads**. People are willing to pay money to obtain goods and services; they are also willing to pay money to get rid of bads.

Does the economy produce bads?

Yes, but not deliberately. That is, people do not use the economy's resources with the main objective of producing bads, but in the process of producing goods and services, bads are sometimes produced. For example, in the process of producing automobiles, steel, and many other products, our factories spew out large amounts of environmental toxins. And even in driving our cars and heating our homes, we pollute the environment. We see, therefore, that human activity often results in the production of bads.

Are all resources scarce?

No. Not all resources are scarce; a few resources are available in sufficiently large quantities to satisfy our wants for them. Air and sunlight come readily to mind. They are abundant, not scarce. Of course, air and sunlight are scarce to miners trapped in a mine. We don't have to economize on the use of limitless resources; consequently, economics does not focus on them. Canada is fortunate in that it has large amounts of different types of resources, yet they are insufficient to allow us to produce all the goods and services that we desire.

Is there any way to classify all these different types of resources?

We can classify resources in many ways. For example, we could use a two-way classification and divide them into resources that are scarce and those that are abundant. Alternatively, we could classify them into two categories: natural and human-made. However, economists have chosen to classify resources into the following four categories:

1. Land
2. Labour
3. Capital
4. Entrepreneurial services or entrepreneurship

As you continue your study of economics, you will find that some terms do not have quite the same meanings as they have in everyday language. This will seem strange at first, but you will get accustomed to it.

land all natural resources

Land   All natural resources are referred to as **land**. It includes much more than the solid portion of the earth on which you can grow crops, erect a building, or use as a parking lot. In economics, any non-human resource that is made available by nature is called land. Thus, land includes minerals embedded in the earth; fish in the seas, rivers, and lakes; the vast expanse of oceans; the natural waterfalls; wildlife; oxygen in the air; time; and even the space within which economic activity takes place. The term *natural resources* is often used as a synonym for land.

labour human physical and mental efforts

Labour   **Labour** as a factor of production refers to human physical and mental efforts that people contribute to the production process. It is not difficult to visualize the labour expended by craftspeople as they mould materials into works of art, farmers as they cultivate their crops, or assembly-line workers as they contribute to the production of an item. But the services rendered by sales representatives, lawyers, teachers, doctors, musicians, and actors are all classified under the category of labour.

capital produced means of production

Capital   **Capital** is any produced means of production, that is, any manufactured item that can be used to produce goods and services or other resources. Buildings, roads, manufacturing plants, equipment, and tools are examples of capital, or *capital goods* as they are also called. Actually, there are different types of capital. The physical manufactured resources listed above are called *real capital*. Businesses invest in these capital goods to produce things. **Human capital** refers to the education, training, skills,

human capital education, training, skills, health, and so on, that improve the quality of labour

health, and so on, that improve the quality of labour. Skilled, educated, experienced, and healthy workers are more productive than unskilled, uneducated, inexperienced, and unhealthy workers. Thus, many businesses are willing to invest in their workers to increase their human capital. People take the time to build their human capital to improve the quality of their labour. Students at colleges and universities at all levels are building their human capital as they pursue their studies. They are making an investment in themselves.

Entrepreneurship   The mere existence of land, labour, and capital will not cause the production of goods and services to take place. Someone must make the decision to organize these human and non-human resources into the production process. The individual who brings these factors of production together and organizes them into production is called an *entrepreneur*. **Entrepreneurship** (or entrepreneurial services) is the organization of land, labour, and capital into the production of goods and services.

entrepreneurship the organization of land, labour, and capital into production; the risk-taking aspect of business decision making

Entrepreneurs come up with innovative ways of doing things, are willing to assume the risks associated with their decisions, and are risk-takers. Entrepreneurial skills include managerial skills, organizational skills, decision-making skills, innovative skills, leadership skills, and risk-taking.

Canada has many entrepreneurs. You may be familiar with some of their products. The following is a short list of some of Canada's entrepreneurs and the company or product with which they are associated:

Entrepreneur	Company or Product Association
Jason Goncalves	Permabrand Corporation
Scott Abbott	Trivial Pursuit
J. A. Bombardier	Snowmobile
Tim Horton	Tim Hortons
Heather Reisman	Chapters/Indigo
Edwin Mirvish	Honest Ed's
Christine Magee	Sleep Country Canada
Sam Sniderman	Sam the Record Man
Denise Meehan	Licks
Henry Woodward	Electric light bulb
Linda Lundstrum	Fashion designer

How can we discuss capital without including money?

financial capital money, as opposed to real capital (machinery, equipment, tools, etc.)

In economics, we distinguish between money and real capital. In everyday language and in many areas of business, money and capital are used synonymously. **Financial capital** is defined as funds available to purchase real capital. They are tangible assets that can be used as money. In economics however, the emphasis is on real capital, which refers to the productive agents produced by people to be used in conjunction with other productive factors to produce goods and services. So, to be inclusive, we could say that there are really three types of capital: real capital (machines, tools, etc.), human capital (education, training, etc.), and financial capital (money).

What incomes are generated by the factors of production?

rent income from land

wages and salaries income from labour

interest and dividends income from capital

profit income from entrepreneurship

The factors of production generate incomes for their owners. For example, if you sell your labour services by taking a part-time job while you are at college or university, your employer will pay you for your labour services. Landowners receive income from their land if they use it or if they lease it out to others. The income generated by each category of resources has a special name. Owners of land receive **rent**, and owners of capital receive **interest and dividends**, while those who provide labour services receive **wages and salaries**, and individuals with entrepreneurial skills obtain **profit**. The incomes derived from the four categories of resources are summarized in Table 1.1.

Note that resources are the source of all income. If we total all the rent, wages and salaries, interest and dividends, and profits in an economy, we obtain total income in

Table 1.1	Factors of Production and Their Earnings
Factors	**Earnings**
Land	Rent
Labour	Wages and salaries
Capital	Interest and dividends
Entrepreneurship	Profits

that economy. Thus, if we use R to denote rent; W to denote wages and salaries; i to indicate interest and dividends; and π to denote profits, we obtain the following equation for total income:

$$\text{Total income} = R + W + i + \pi$$

For example, if rent amounts to $80 billion, wages and salaries add up to $500 billion, interest and dividends add up to $40 billion, and profits total $100 billion, then total income is $80 + 500 + 40 + 100 = $720 billion.

Reading Comprehension

The answers to these questions can be found on MyEconLab at www.myeconlab.com.   MyEconLab

1. Scarcity of resources is an economic reality. What are these resources and how are they broadly classified?

2. Give two examples each of land, labour, capital, and entrepreneurship.
3. What is the difference between real capital and financial capital?
4. Why can oil revenues from Alberta tar sands be classified as rent?

LO 1.5 Explain the scientific method and discuss economic methodology

Economics and the Scientific Method

In the definition of economics introduced earlier, the word *science* was used. What is science?

science or the scientific method a particular method of acquiring knowledge that includes observation, measurement, and testing; also refers to the knowledge acquired through the process

The word *science* conjures up images of people in white laboratory coats, test tubes, spacecraft, microscopes, and telescopes. But when we speak of science, we are referring to a particular method of acquiring knowledge that includes observation, measurement, and testing. **Science** can be defined as a branch of study, especially one concerned with facts, principles, and methods. Science refers not only to a method of acquiring knowledge but also to the knowledge produced by the approach. For our purposes, we define science or the **scientific method** as follows:

> The scientific method or approach is the systematic investigation and observation of phenomena and the formulation of general laws or tendencies there from, after testing and verifying hypotheses.

We can discuss the main elements of the scientific approach under the headings of observation and measurement, hypotheses, and verification.

Observation and Measurement   One of the basic tasks of scientists is to observe and record facts about the phenomena they are investigating. This is the descriptive or empirical aspect of science. To facilitate this aspect of their work, scientists use certain technical terms that have very precise meanings. The development of such a particularized vocabulary is an important step in the development of any field of scientific inquiry.

hypothesis a statement of suspected relationships among two or more variables

Hypotheses   The process of observation often leads to ideas, hunches, or guesses about relationships among the things observed. A **hypothesis** is a statement of suspected relationships among two or more variables or factors. It does not state some fact that is already known but something to be tested. For example, consider the following two statements:

Statement 1: The average grade of students who took economics last term was 70%.

Statement 2: Students who attend classes regularly and do their homework will get better grades than those who don't attend regularly and do no homework.

The first statement is not a hypothesis; it merely expresses a fact that is already known. The second statement, however, is a hypothesis because the statement expresses a relationship among students' performance in economics, their attendance, and whether or not they do their homework. Hypotheses should be stated in a verifiable manner so that they can be confirmed or disproved.

Verification   Verification through testing is the heart of the scientific procedure. Once scientists have formulated their hypotheses, they proceed to test these hypotheses to determine the extent to which they are supported by empirical evidence. Relating questions to evidence sets scientific inquiry apart from other types of inquiry.

To what extent does economics follow the scientific approach?

Economics is not a science in the same sense that physics, chemistry, and biology are sciences. Such disciplines as chemistry and biology are called *natural* sciences. Physicists, chemists, zoologists, and biologists can conduct controlled laboratory experiments. They deal with the physical and material world, such as minerals, gases, liquids, and plants. Social scientists, such as economists and sociologists, deal with people and therefore cannot conduct experiments in traditional laboratories. No laboratory instruments can measure human behaviour with any degree of precision. Nevertheless, economics follows the scientific procedure as faithfully as do the natural sciences. In attempting to explain economic phenomena, economists follow the scientific approach. They gather information, analyze it, and select what they consider to be the most relevant facts. They formulate and test hypotheses and thus arrive at general statements or laws concerning economic phenomena. Economics, therefore, has a legitimate claim to be considered a science.

What methodology do economists use in studying economic phenomena?

The factors involved in studying real-world economic events are often quite complex. The scientific economist comes to grips with these complexities by constructing models. An **economic model** is a simplification of the real economy or some aspect of it, and it consists only of the factors that appear to pertain most to what is being studied. Details that do not pertain directly to the question being studied are simply stripped away in the model. The principle of stripping away irrelevant detail is often referred to as the principle of Occam's razor, named after the fourteenth-century philosopher William Occam.

economic model a simplification of economic reality

Economists use models in much the same way that engineers use them. An engineer who has the job of building a bridge would, most likely, design a model before building the real thing. The model allows the engineer to study certain aspects of the bridge before it actually exists. For example, the model bridge could give information about how the actual bridge would look, how it would accommodate traffic, and what modifications might be necessary to make it safe. Similarly, economists construct and use economic models to understand how the real economy works. Several economic models will be introduced and used in this book.

What are the parts of a model?

An economic model can be expressed verbally, mathematically, or graphically. Whatever form an economic model takes, it has the following components:

- Definitions
- Assumptions
- Hypotheses
- Predictions

definition a set of words that explain the meaning of a term or concept

Definitions   All economic terms used in the model must be clearly defined. A **definition** is a set of words that explain the meaning of a term or concept. Economists have developed an impressive number of terms and concepts that form a part of the specialized language or *jargon* of the discipline. You have already encountered a few of these terms (land, capital, scarcity, rent). As you work through this book, many of the other terms and concepts that are a part of the economist's vocabulary will become familiar to you. The main purpose of the set of definitions in a model is to identify the variables of the model so that measurement can be facilitated. For example, if the term *interest rates* were used in an economic model without any clear definition, it would be difficult to determine whether the reference was to long-term rates, short-term rates, mortgage rates, or interest rates on loans or on savings deposits.

assumptions statements of the conditions under which a model will work

Assumptions   An economic model is intended to explain the economy or some aspect of it under certain conditions. These conditions are stated as **assumptions**. Assumptions, then, are statements of the conditions under which the model is supposed to work. Basically, we usually make two types of assumptions in economics. One type of assumption relates to what motivates economic behaviour. For example, we assume that consumers are motivated by the desire to maximize their satisfaction, whereas businesses are motivated by the desire to maximize their profits. Another type of assumption made in economics is aimed at simplifying the complexities of the actual economy so that the task of the economist is made much easier. For example, if economists are not currently concerned with an economy's external trade relations, they may simplify their analyses by assuming that the country does not engage in trade with the rest of the world. Abstractions of this nature are necessary because of the complexities of the actual economy. Admittedly, economic assumptions are sometimes quite unrealistic, but often what is lost in realism is more than compensated for in understanding.

ceteris paribus other things being equal; allows for the investigation of the effects of one variable while assuming that others remain constant

An assumption of particular importance in economics is the **ceteris paribus** assumption, which is a Latin phrase that means "other things being equal." This assumption allows economists to investigate the effects of one variable while assuming that others remain constant. Suppose we are interested in finding out the effect of a fall in the price of iPhones on the quantity of iPhones that people will buy. Some of these factors include peoples' incomes and their preference for iPhones over other types of smart phones. We can hypothesize that if the price of iPhones falls, people will buy more of them. If we observe that a fall in the price of iPhones is accompanied by an increase in the quantity purchased, can we conclude that the increase in quantity purchased results from a fall in price? Is it not possible that the increase in quantity purchased results from an increase in income or some other factor?

To determine how a change in one factor affects other factors, we must find some way of isolating the effects of other factors. In the above example, we must isolate income, preference, and other factors (except the price of iPhones) that can affect the quantity of iPhones that people will purchase. We can accomplish this task by using the ceteris paribus assumption. This assumption allows us to keep other factors constant while we examine the effects of the factor that currently interests us. Thus, we can investigate how a change in price affects the quantity purchased by assuming that income, preference, and all other factors except the price of iPhones remain unchanged throughout the process of investigation. We can emerge with such a statement as "If the price of a product falls, other things being equal, the quantity purchased will increase."

Hypotheses   We have already mentioned hypotheses in an earlier section. You will recall that they are statements about suspected relationships among factors. Hypotheses greatly advance our knowledge of economics because they can be tested and shown to be true or false. Economists have formulated a number of important hypotheses, many of which will be introduced throughout this book. When hypotheses are tested and determined to be correct, we can summarize the results into economic theories. An *economic theory* is a summary statement of what we believe to be true about the operation of an economy or some part of it.

Predictions   Testing a hypothesis results in the ability to predict. If the predictions of the model are consistent with the facts, we can predict with some degree of certainty (though not with perfect certainty) what will happen in the economy. Economic predictions usually take the form of "if you do this, then such and such will result." An economic prediction should not be confused with an economic forecast. An **economic prediction** is a statement about the general direction of a variable resulting from the fulfillment of certain conditions. An **economic forecast** is the assignment of a future value to a variable. The following examples should help to illustrate the difference between the two concepts.

> *Economic prediction:* If the government lowers personal income taxes, total spending on consumer goods and services will rise, other things being equal.
> *Economic forecast:* By next spring, the rate of unemployment will fall to 7%.

economic prediction a statement of the general direction of a variable resulting from the fulfillment of certain conditions

economic forecast the assignment of a future value to a variable

Can we determine the "goodness" of an economic model?

Yes. The whole purpose of an economic model is to help us explain some aspect of economic reality and to predict certain outcomes. An economic model that does this well is a good model. If model A explains and predicts economic phenomena better than the competing model B, then model A is judged to be better than model B. For example:

> **Model A's prediction:** If peoples' wages and salaries increase by 10%, they will increase their purchases of goods and services by 8%.
> **Model B's prediction:** If peoples' wages and salaries increase by 10%, they will increase their purchases of goods and services by 5%.
> **Reality (from actual observation):** When wages and salaries increase by 10%, people increase their purchases of goods and services by 7.5%.

Under these circumstances, we would accept model A as the better model.

If an economic model fails to explain what we observe (that is, economic reality), then it may be rejected. At one time, greater attention was paid to the realism of the assumptions of a model than to the model's power of prediction. It is now generally accepted that the "goodness" of a model should be based primarily on its ability to explain and predict.

The use of high-speed computers has enabled economists to manipulate huge amounts of data in an incredibly short time. Thus, it is now relatively easy to test economic hypotheses against observed phenomena. The branch of economics that deals with the use of statistical methods to test economic hypotheses is called **econometrics**. This has become such an important branch of economics that most schools require their economics majors to take at least one course in economic statistics or econometrics.

econometrics the use of statistical methods to test economic hypotheses

Reading Comprehension

The answers to these questions can be found on MyEconLab at www.myeconlab.com.   MyEconLab

1. What are the fundamental elements in scientific inquiry and to what extent do economists follow the scientific approach?

2. What is an economic model? Why do economists find it useful to construct models?

3. What are the components (parts) of an economic model?

4. Explain the role of assumptions in economic models.

LO 1.6 Identify positive and normative economics and explain why economists sometimes disagree

Positive and Normative Economics and Disagreement among Economists

What is the difference between positive economics and normative economics?

An understanding of the difference between positive statements and normative statements will help you to understand the difference between positive economics and normative economics. **Positive statements** are statements about some fact. They express what is, was, or will be, and they can be verified. Verification is achieved by referring to the relevant facts. An example of a positive statement is "There are 50 students in your economics class." This is a positive statement even if the actual number of students in your economics class is only 35. The point is that it is a statement about some fact—the number of students in a class. Note that a positive statement can be true or false. Because a positive statement relates to facts, it can be verified or disproved by checking it against the facts. The statement "An increase in average income levels will lead to higher consumption levels" is an example of a positive economic statement.

positive statements statements about what is

Normative statements, conversely, are value judgments or statements of opinions about what ought to be. They cannot be tested for verification by referring to facts because there are no facts. An example of a normative statement is "Every student at college or university should take at least one course in economics."

normative statements statements about what ought to be

Obviously, normative statements are not scientific because they cannot be subjected to empirical testing. This does not suggest that the scientific economist is never concerned with normative issues. In fact, concern with the normative aspects of economics is a major focus of disagreement among economists, as you will see shortly. Even though value judgments are not scientific, they are nevertheless important.

positive economics
explains or describes how
the economy works

Now that you are familiar with the difference between positive statements and normative statements, it is easier to understand the distinction between positive economics and normative economics. **Positive economics** explains or describes how the economy actually works and the behaviour of economic units. Positive economics attempts to explain what will happen under certain conditions, but it does not explain what the economic situation ought to be. It does not seek to make any judgments about whether the result of any economic action is good or bad. The concern of positive economics is to describe the economic system as it is and how it actually works. What causes the price of oil to rise? What was the economic impact of the terrorist attack of 9/11? Why has the value of the Canadian dollar risen or fallen in terms of the U.S. dollar? How will an overall increase in taxes affect the Canadian economy? Such questions relate to positive economics.

normative economics
explains how the economy
should work

Normative economics is concerned with explaining how the economy should work. It attempts to judge whether economic outcomes are good or bad and to what extent they can be improved. Should the Government of Canada lend or give money to Air Canada to prevent it from going bankrupt? Should the provincial governments reduce their tax on gasoline? Should governments grant subsidies to farmers? Should the government reduce the tax on cigarettes to reduce the amount of smuggling? Should Canadian banks be allowed to merge? Should the Canadian government have offered greater financial assistance to Haiti following the earthquake on January 12, 2010? Normative economics deals with answers to such questions. Note that the issues of normative economics are policy oriented.

Not surprisingly, normative economics relies heavily on positive economics. Let us consider the following normative economic issue: Should Canada remain a part of the North American Free Trade Agreement (NAFTA)? We could conceivably answer this question on the basis of emotion, but an answer based on an economic analysis of the situation would be preferable. What are the likely benefits of this agreement? What are the costs? Answers to such questions will help up to answer the normative question about the trade agreement.

Why is there so much disagreement among economists?

There is much more agreement among economists than disagreement. This fact may surprise you in view of all the stories of disagreement among economists. Physicists disagree among themselves; so do biologists, geologists, and chemists. Scientists don't always see eye to eye. But let us see why economists disagree. Economists have different values, and they judge economic situations and events differently. When economists are asked to make judgments about some economic action, they may try to be objective, but their objectivity might be coloured by their own moral sentiments. One economist might argue that cigarette smoking is bad for your health; hence, a heavy tax should be imposed on cigarettes to discourage smoking. Another economist might take the position that there are other products that are also hazardous to your health and dangerous to your life—why single out cigarettes? The same economist might argue, moreover, that if people want to smoke cigarettes, it is their business and that the government has no right to interfere with a person's lifestyle; such intrusions should be resisted.

It is not only on normative issues, however, that economists disagree. They disagree on the positive, scientific aspects as well. Often, different explanations exist for how the economy actually operates, and it is not always clear which explanation is best. In other words, economists may disagree over the appropriate model of the economy. It would seem that it should be easy to settle the disagreement simply by confronting the theory with the empirical data. Unfortunately, the available data might not be such as to allow for definitive conclusions.

Economists may disagree even though they use the same economic model. They may agree on the qualitative aspects but disagree on the quantitative aspects. For example, two economists might agree that a fall in interest rates will result in an increase in investment. They might disagree, however, over the magnitude of the increase, one claiming that the increase will be negligible, and the other claiming that the increase will be significant. Again, this type of disagreement can be prolonged because of the inadequacy of relevant data.

Reading Comprehension

The answers to these questions can be found on MyEconLab at **www.myeconlab.com**.   MyEconLab

1. What is the difference between positive and normative economics?
2. Give two examples each of positive and normative statements. Give one example each of positive and normative economics.
3. Do you agree with the statement that normative propositions have no place in scientific economics? Give reasons for your opinion.
4. George Bernard Shaw joked, "If all economists were laid end to end, they would not reach a conclusion." Is this a fair assessment of disagreement among economists? Why or why not?
5. Economists disagree over normative economics but not over positive economics. Is this statement true or false? Explain.

LO 1.7 Recognize different types of variables and cause-effect relations

Variables and Cause-Effect Relations

What is a variable?

The work of economists consists largely of establishing relationships among different factors that can have an effect on economic behaviour. When they construct models, they use variables. In fact, an economic model is a system of relations among economic variables. A **variable** is anything that can change and assume different values under different circumstances. In simpler terms, a variable is anything that changes. Examples of economic variables are prices, income, consumer spending, interest rates, exports, imports, government spending, taxes, total production, the number of people unemployed, the unemployment rate, and the level of savings. A **constant**, as opposed to a variable, is anything that remains unchanged. If in the course of analysis we *assume* that government spending does not change, then that variable becomes a constant. Whether or not we consider something to be a variable or a constant depends on what we are investigating.

variable anything that changes

constant anything that remains unchanged

What is the difference between an endogenous variable and an exogenous variable?

When economists construct models to explain real-world economic phenomena, some variables used will be explained within the model, while others will be determined by

endogenous variable a variable whose value is determined within a given model

exogenous variable a variable whose value is determined by factors outside a given model

factors outside the model. An **endogenous variable** is one whose value is determined within the model. An **exogenous variable** is one whose value is determined by factors outside the model. The exogenous variables affect the endogenous variables. Let's look at an example to show the difference between endogenous and exogenous variables. Suppose we are trying to determine students' grades in an economics class. We could say that students' grades depend on their attendance of classes, suggesting that the more classes they attend, the better will be their grades. In this case, students' grades and their attendance are endogenous variables. But we know that their grades will also be affected by the amount of time they spend studying economics, whether or not they do their assignments, whether they pay attention in class, and so on. All these variables other than their attendance are exogenous variables.

A set of variables labelled endogenous and another set labelled exogenous do not exist. Whether a particular variable is endogenous or exogenous depends on the problem being studied. Needless to say, we cannot determine whether or not a particular variable is endogenous or exogenous without a model.

What is the difference between stocks and flows?

stock a quantity existing at a particular time

flow a change in a stock over time

An important distinction should be noted between stocks (or stock variables) and flows (or flow variables). A **stock** is the quantity of anything existing at a particular time. You may have a stock of five Blu-ray movies beside your Blu-ray player. That's the quantity that exists at that time. As time progresses, your stock of Blu-ray movies will likely change. A **flow** is a measure of the change in the stock over time. If you decide to purchase one Blu-ray movie each month, then the flow would be one Blu-ray movie per month. Note that a flow is a rate and has a time dimension: It is measured per unit of time (per day, per week, per month, per year, etc.). A stock has no time dimension: It is measured at a particular time (on October 11, 2012; at 11:30 a.m. on November 6, 2011; etc.). Note also that stocks and flows are both variables. Examples of stock variables and flow variables are given in Table 1.2.

Is correlation the same as causation?

No. They are not the same, and we must be careful not to confuse them. Two variables can be correlated, which means only that they move together. The fact that variables are correlated does not necessarily mean that a change in one causes a change in the other. The change could be a chance occurrence, or it could be the effect of a third variable. If you obtained a good grade on an economics examination that you wrote on a rainy day, you would not conclude that the good grade was the result of rain. If it can be

Table 1.2	Examples of Stocks and Flows
Stocks	**Flows**
• The balance in your savings account	• The monthly deposits to your account
• The amount of money in your wallet or purse at this moment	• The amount you spend each week for lunch
• The amount of equipment owned by a firm on April 14, 2005	• The amount a firm spends each year on equipment
• The number of people who watched the presidential debates in the United States on a particular night	• The number of people who watch *Dr. Phil* on TV each week
• The number of cars produced on November 1, 1981	• The number of cars sold in Canada each year

determined that a change in one variable causes a change in another, then we know that changing one will change the other. This conclusion may not hold if only a correlation exists between the variables. We must remember the age-old warning that correlation does not imply causation.

What is the post hoc fallacy?

post hoc fallacy the erroneous conclusion that one event causes another simply because it precedes the other

When two events occur in sequence, it is tempting to conclude that the first event caused the second to occur, which may not be the case. This erroneous conclusion is called the post hoc, ergo propter hoc fallacy (**post hoc fallacy**), which is a Latin phrase meaning, "after this, therefore because of this." This fallacy is also referred to as sequential fallacy. Let us assume that you began to read your economics textbook and then it began to rain. If you concluded that it rained because you started to read your textbook, then you would have fallen into the post hoc fallacy. It could very well be that you were planning to go out with your friends, but you listened to the weather forecast and heard that rain was expected, so you decided to read instead of going out. In that case, you would be reading because of the expected rain.

Reading Comprehension

The answers to these questions can be found on MyEconLab at www.myeconlab.com.　　MyEconLab

1. Give an example of each to show that you understand the difference between endogenous and exogenous variables.
2. Give an example of each to show that you understand the difference between a stock variable and a flow variable.
3. Give an example of the post hoc fallacy.
4. A seller of stained glass windows noticed that when she lowered the price of her windows, she sold a greater quantity of windows. Is anything wrong in concluding that the increase in sales was due to the lower price? Explain.

LO 1.8 Distinguish between microeconomics and macroeconomics

Microeconomics versus Macroeconomics

What is the difference between microeconomics and macroeconomics?

microeconomics the branch of economics that studies the behaviour of individual economic units

price theory another name for microeconomics

macroeconomics the branch of economics that studies the behaviour of broad economic aggregates

Economics is divided into two main branches: microeconomics and macroeconomics. **Microeconomics** studies the behaviour of individual economic units and focuses on the allocation of resources. It concerns itself with what determines the composition of total output and analyzes such topics as the behaviour of consumers and firms, the determination of relative prices, and the distribution of the economy's output among various groups. Microeconomics is also called **price theory**. An investigation into the causes of changes in the price of gasoline would be a microeconomic study.

　　Macroeconomics studies the economy as a whole rather than the individual units—the whole flock, so to speak, rather than the individual sheep that make up

income and employment theory another name for macroeconomics

that flock. Macroeconomics concerns itself with the total or aggregate behaviour of consumers and producers, and it analyzes such topics as inflation, unemployment, and economic growth. Macroeconomics is also called **income and employment theory**. A study that attempts to explain the causes of severe unemployment in Canada would be a macroeconomic study. A thorough understanding of the operation of the economic system requires knowledge of both microeconomics *and* macroeconomics. Both study choices that individuals, businesses, and governments make, and the effects of those choices on our economic lives.

Reading Comprehension

The answers to these questions can be found on MyEconLab at **www.myeconlab.com.**   MyEconLab

1. What is the difference between microeconomics and macroeconomics?

2. To which branch of economics (microeconomics or macroeconomics) is a study of the recent global economic crisis more closely related?

3. Why should we study both microeconomics and macroeconomics?

BUSINESS SITUATION 1.2

A company is contemplating the introduction of a new product. To do so will require a loan. Among the factors to consider are the following:
- The price at which the product will be sold
- The level of economic activity and how it will affect the sale of the product
- The quantity of the product to produce
- The general level of interest rates that will affect the company's ability to repay the loan

Which of these considerations relate to microeconomics and which relate to macroeconomics?

The answer to this Business Situation can be found in Appendix A.

Review

1. Review the learning objectives listed at the beginning of the chapter.
2. Have you accomplished all the objectives? One way to determine this is to answer the Reading Comprehension questions at the end of each section. They will help you assess the extent to which you have accomplished the learning objectives
3. If you have not accomplished an objective, review the relevant material before proceeding.

Key Points to Remember

1. **LO 1.1** A knowledge of economics is important because it enables us to understand the economy, society, and world affairs; it helps us to be better informed citizens and to think logically.It gives great personal satisfaction.
2. **LO 1.2** Economists are employed in almost every facet of economic life. They are employed in industry, govern-

ment, and education. Economists are also self-employed as consultants.

3. **LO 1.3** Scarcity is a fact of life. It is the situation that exists when the means to produce all the things that society would like to have to satisfy all wants are insufficient. Everyone faces scarcity—the rich, the poor, everyone.

4. **LO 1.3** Economics can be defined as the study of scarcity and choice. It is the social science that studies how people make choices in the face of limited resources and unlimited wants. Economics, psychology, sociology, political science, and anthropology are all social science disciplines.

5. **LO 1.4** All the various resources can be classified into four categories. Land refers to all natural resources, such as minerals in the earth, rivers, lakes, and so on. Labour refers to human effort, such as the work of farmers in cultivating land and the services provided by sales representatives. Capital refers to manufactured items, such as machinery, factories, and tools that businesses use to produce goods and services. Human capital refers to education, training, skills, and experience that enhance the quality of labour. Entrepreneurship refers to the organization of land, labour, and capital into the production process. Money is financial capital as opposed to real capital.

6. **LO 1.4** Owners of land earn a form of income called rent; owners of labour earn wages and salaries; owners of capital earn interest and dividends; and providers of entrepreneurial services earn profits. Any form of income can be traced back to its source—a resource. The sum of the incomes derived from resources is total income.

7. **LO 1.5** Economics is a science in the sense that it deals with facts and principles, and follows a particular method of inquiry. It follows the scientific approach of observation, measurement, and verification by confronting theory with empirical evidence. Because of the complexities of economic phenomena, economists construct economic models, which are simplifications of reality.

8. **LO 1.6** Positive economics deals with how an economy actually functions, while normative economics deals with how an economy should function. Economists disagree about normative economics because they have different values. They disagree about positive economics because they may use different models. They may also disagree over quantitative aspects.

9. **LO 1.7** Variables can be classified as endogenous (determined inside a model) or exogenous (determined by factors outside a model). They can also be classified as stocks (existing at a particular time) or flows (change per unit of time).

10. **LO 1.7** Correlation between two variables does not establish a cause-effect relationship between them. A post hoc fallacy is the error of concluding that one event caused another because it preceded the other.

11. **LO 1.8** Microeconomics examines the behaviour of individual economic units, while macroeconomics examines the behaviour of broad economic aggregates. Both microeconomics and macroeconomics help us understand economic behaviour and the functioning of the economic system.

Economic Word Power

Assumptions (p. 13)
Bads (p. 8)
Capital (p. 9)
Ceteris paribus (p. 13)
Commodities (p. 8)
Constant (p. 17)
Definition (p. 13)
Econometrics (p. 15)
Economic forecast (p. 14)
Economic model (p. 12)
Economic prediction (p. 14)
Economics (p. 6)
Endogenous variable (p. 18)
Entrepreneurship (p. 9)
Exogenous variable (p. 18)
Financial capital (p. 10)
Flow (p. 18)
Goods (p. 7)
Human capital (p. 9)
Hypothesis (p. 11)
Income and employment theory (p. 20)
Interest and dividends (p. 10)
Labour (p. 9)
Land (p. 9)
Macroeconomics (p. 19)
Microeconomics (p. 19)
Normative economics (p. 16)
Normative statements (p. 15)
Positive economics (p. 16)
Positive statements (p. 15)
Post hoc fallacy (p. 19)
Price theory (p. 19)
Profit (p. 10)
Rent (p. 10)
Resources (p. 7)
Scarcity (p. 5)
Science (p. 11)
Scientific method (p. 11)
Services (p. 7)
Social science (p. 6)
Stock (p. 18)
Variable (p. 17)
Wages and salaries (p. 10)

Problems and Exercises

Basic

1. **LO 1.1** A proper study of economics is quite time-consuming. Do you think studying economics is worth the time involved? Explain why or why not.

2. **LO 1.2** Give three reasons why a career as an economist might be of interest to a student.

3. **LO 1.3** What do economists mean when they describe something as being scarce?

4. **LO 1.3** If you won $50 million in the lottery, would you personally still have an economic problem?

5. **LO 1.3** Scarcity is an economic constraint. Discuss.

6. **LO 1.4** Indicate the category of resources to which each of the following belongs:
   a. A freezer in a supermarket
   b. A hospital
   c. Fish in a lake
   d. Mineral deposits in northern Ontario
   e. The services provided by a neurosurgeon
   f. The driver of a taxicab
   g. The risk taken by an individual who buys resources to establish a business

7. **LO 1.4** Beside each resource category in column 1 of Table 1.3, place the income category associated with the resource category.

Table 1.3	Resources and Associated Income
Resource Category	**Income Category**
Land	_____
Labour	_____
Capital	_____
Entrepreneurial ability	_____

8. **LO 1.5** Economics is an interesting subject. Unfortunately, it cannot be studied scientifically. Discuss briefly.

9. **LO 1.6** Give two reasons why economists might disagree.

10. **LO 1.7** Using S for stock and F for flow, indicate whether each of the following is a stock or a flow:
    a. The amount of money a bus driver earns per week
    b. The number of students who were in class at 11:30 a.m. on Wednesday
    c. The amount of money in your purse/wallet at this moment
    d. Your average expenditure per week in the cafeteria
    e. The total annual sales of a furniture manufacturer
    f. The total value of merchandise in a department store on February 1, 2011, at 10:30 a.m.

11. **LO 1.8** It has been observed that the price of gasoline sometimes fluctuates greatly. A study has been launched to determine the possible causes. To which of the main branches of economics would such a study fall?

Questions in the Intermediate and Challenging Sections cover several different concepts, and have not been organized by learning objectives.

Intermediate

1. Would personal computers still be scarce if all computer manufacturers produced so many computers that to sell them, they had to lower the price to $100?

2. Economics cannot be a science. If it were, economists would not disagree to the extent that they do. Discuss.

3. Alberta and Ontario both have relatively high average incomes; Newfoundland and Labrador and Prince Edward Island have relatively low average incomes. Do you think that scarcity of resources can help to explain these income differentials?

4. Economists can increase the usefulness of a model by including every conceivable variable. After all, the greater the number of variables, the more useful the model. Discuss.

Challenging

1. I have a model that explains students' grades in economics. The model states that regular attendance improves students' grades. One student attends every class, yet his grades have not improved. Does this observation invalidate my model? Explain.

2. One of your friends is contemplating taking either an economics course or some other course. What arguments could you use to persuade him or her to take the economics course? For each argument, indicate whether it is positive or normative and give reasons.

3. Write up a list of five social, economic, or political problems or issues facing Canada today. For each problem or issue, discuss its economic aspects (if any). What role can economics play in helping us to understand the problem or issue, or in finding solutions?

4. In constructing a simple model of the Canadian economy, an economist assumed that only two kinds of goods are produced and that all the goods are used within Canada. Can such a model have any use at all in terms of explaining certain economic events in Canada?

┌───┐
MyEconLab Visit the MyEconLab website at **www.myeconlab.com.** This online homework and tutorial system puts you in control of your own learning with study and practice tools directly correlated to this chapter's content.
└───┘

Study Guide

Self-Assessment

The answers to the Study Guide questions can be found in Appendix B.

What's your score?

Circle the letter that corresponds with the correct answer.

1. A knowledge of economics is important because
   a. It guarantees perpetual employment
   b. It ensures that we will always make decisions that are in our own self-interest
   c. It helps us to understand many of the issues that affect our lives directly and indirectly
   d. All of the above

2. Today, economists work:
   a. Only as civil servants in government offices
   b. Only in profit-seeking organizations
   c. Only in certain large corporations
   d. In practically every aspect of business and government

3. Scarcity exists
   a. When things are available only in small quantities
   b. When resources are insufficient to produce all the desired goods and services
   c. Only among poor people who cannot afford to buy the things they want
   d. In underdeveloped countries but not in advanced countries

4. Choice is a direct result of
   a. Ambition
   b. Scarcity
   c. Extravagance
   d. None of the above

5. Choice is a matter of free will and is quite unrelated to economics.
   a. True
   b. False

6. Which of the following is the primary concern of economics?
   a. How people vote in an election
   b. How people make choices when faced with scarcity

c. The mental processes involved in making a decision regarding the purchase of an expensive item
   d. None of the above

7. Which of the following aspects of human behaviour *most* concerns the economist?
   a. The methods used to select leaders in a society
   b. The public's attitude toward certain social issues
   c. The behaviour of individuals and groups engaged in using scarce resources
   d. The behaviour of people trying to understand the origin of civilization

8. Economics is
   a. An exact science
   b. A social science
   c. A physical science
   d. Not a science

9. Economists work on the premise that
   a. Resources are unlimited but wants are limited
   b. Resources are limited but wants are unlimited
   c. Both resources and wants are unlimited
   d. Both resources and wants are limited

10. Factors of production are
   a. All the factors that must be considered when making a decision to start a business
   b. The monetary costs involved in setting up a business to produce goods
   c. Gifts of nature, not anything that we produce
   d. Things that can be used to produce goods and services

11. Things like cigarettes and alcohol are
   a. Not goods because they are harmful
   b. Goods because they are scarce
   c. Goods because people want them
   d. Goods because the government has not placed a ban on their use

12. Illegal substances and chemicals, and goods smuggled into a country, are classified as
   a. Bads because they are illegal
   b. Bads because taxes are not paid on them

c. Goods, provided that they are wanted
d. Goods because someone produced them

13. Economists classify resources into the following categories:
    a. Available, scarce, expensive, and natural
    b. Land, labour, capital, and entrepreneurship
    c. Artificial, financial, human, and manufactured
    d. Natural, imported, limitless, and personal

14. Capital generates a type of income known as
    a. Money
    b. Interest
    c. Profit
    d. None of the above

15. The scientific approach involves
    a. Total reliance on values and moral sentiments
    b. Observation, measurement, and testing of hypotheses
    c. The formulation of theories without confronting theory with evidence
    d. All of the above

16. An economic model is
    a. An exact replica of a real economic situation, faithfully reproducing every single detail
    b. Always expressed graphically because graphs are easy to read and understand
    c. A simplification of a real economy or some aspect of it, with irrelevant details omitted
    d. None of the above

17. Economists construct models in order to
    a. Impress non-economists
    b. Prevent entry into the economics profession
    c. Make it easier to understand how the economy works
    d. Introduce as many variables as possible into their analyses

18. Assumptions
    a. Have no place in scientific economics
    b. Simply complicate the economic reasoning process
    c. Convert positive statements into normative statements
    d. Indicate the conditions under which a given model is intended to work

19. The Latin phrase ceteris paribus means
    a. No changes should be made because all is well
    b. Sometime in the future
    c. The outcome is certain
    d. Other things being equal

20. An economic hypothesis is
    a. An assumption about how the economic system actually works
    b. An assumption about how the economic system ought to work
    c. An expression of suspected relations among economic variables
    d. A statement that is generally accepted but cannot be proved

21. The main difference between positive statements and normative statements is that
    a. Positive statements can be verified by testing, while normative statements cannot be verified
    b. Positive statements are always true, while normative statements may be true or false
    c. Positive statements are a part of economic study, while normative statements are not
    d. Positive statements are based on emotion, while normative statements are based on facts

22. Disagreement among economists is due to
    a. The fact that economics is not a science
    b. The fact that economic models are often expressed verbally instead of mathematically
    c. The fact that some economists just don't understand the complexities of modern mathematics used in economic models
    d. The fact that economists have different values, or they may use different economic models to explain the same economic phenomenon

23. The values of exogenous variables
    a. Are determined inside the given model
    b. Have no effect on variables within the given model
    c. Are predetermined by factors outside the given model
    d. Are of no concern to the economist

24. Endogenous variables are those variables whose values
    a. Are determined within the given model
    b. Have no effect on variables within the given model
    c. Are predetermined by factors outside the given model
    d. None of the above

25. The main difference between a flow and a stock is that
    a. A flow has a time dimension while a stock does not
    b. A stock has a time dimension while a flow does not
    c. A flow is a variable while a stock is a constant
    d. None of the above

26. Two variables, A and B, are related in such a way that when A rises, B also rises. From this we can correctly conclude that
    a. The increase in B is caused by the increase in A
    b. A and B are influenced by a common factor
    c. There is a correlation between A and B
    d. None of the above

27. Microeconomics
    a. Deals only with small changes in economic variables, while macroeconomics deals only with large changes in economic variables
    b. Is scientific in its approach, while macroeconomics is not
    c. Deals with the behaviour of individual economic units, while macroeconomics deals with the behaviour of broad economic aggregates
    d. Deals only with the positive aspects of economics, while macroeconomics deals only with the normative aspects of economics

28. Considering both microeconomics and macroeconomics, the tools of microeconomics are more useful when predicting
    a. The rate of increase in the average level of all prices
    b. The effects of investment on total income and total employment
    c. The effects of changes in the money supply on national output
    d. The price that will maximize a firm's profits

Problems and Exercises (Use Quad Paper for Graphs)

Answers to these questions can be found on MyEconLab at www.myeconlab.com.

MyEconLab

1. Look through one or more recent newspapers and highlight four headlines that deal with economics. Then, on the basis of your findings, complete Table 1.4, indicating (1) the name of the newspaper, (2) the date of publication, (3) the headlines selected, and (4) the economic issue being addressed.

Table 1.4	Newspaper Information		
Name of Newspaper	**Date Published**	**Headline**	**Economic Issue**
_____	_____	_____	_____
_____	_____	_____	_____
_____	_____	_____	_____
_____	_____	_____	_____

2. Indicate what might be the scarce element in each of the following situations. (For example, time is the scarce element preventing you from attending an economics class at 8:30 a.m. and sleeping in until 9:00 a.m. that same day).
    a. A farmer is unable to produce more corn and more wheat at the same time.
    b. A retailer is unable to carry larger inventories (stocks) of both computers and DVD players.
    c. Tiger Woods cannot play golf at 2:30 p.m. today and appear live as a guest on a popular television program.
    d. You cannot buy all your required textbooks for this term at the same time.
    e. Your parents must choose between taking a cruise and buying a new refrigerator.

3. Indicate whether each of the following should be classified as land, labour, capital, or entrepreneurship.
    a. Oil deposits in Alberta
    b. Highway 401 between Montreal and Toronto
    c. The services provided by administrative assistants in an insurance company
    d. Wildlife in the Prairie Provinces
    e. Forests in British Columbia
    f. Banff National Park in Alberta
    g. The Great Lakes of Canada and the United States
    h. John Henry's efforts in acquiring labour and capital to establish a manufacturing plant
    i. The services provided in establishing and running an electronic boutique
    j. Chemical fertilizer used by Ontario farmers in growing their crops

4. Canada is well endowed with a wide variety of natural resources, a highly skilled and educated adult population, and vast amounts of capital goods. In what sense are these resources scarce in Canada?

5. Indicate whether each of the following types of income would be classified technically as rent, wages and salaries, interest and dividends, or profit.
    a. The compensation (payment) that administrative assistants receive for their services
    b. The money Josh pays each month for living accommodation in an apartment building
    c. The payment Susan receives from her part-time job at the supermarket
    d. The annual amount that a Canadian bank pays its shareholders
    e. The amount of money that Mr. Johnson receives each year for the use of his parking lot
    f. The money that Mr. Johnson pays his parking lot attendant
    g. The net income that John Henry receives for his effort in acquiring labour and capital to establish a manufacturing plant
    h. The net earnings of $200 000 received by a group of innovators for developing and marketing a product

6. In Table 1.5, rearrange the items in the second column, and place the correct arrangement in the third column so that they correctly match the items in the first column.

Table 1.5	Factors and Earnings	
Column 1	**Column 2**	**Column 3**
Labour	Rent	_____
Land	Wages	_____
Entrepreneurship	Interest and dividends	_____
Capital	Profits	_____

7. Categorize each of the following as either positive or normative statements:
    a. An increase in the price of oil will result in higher prices for other products.
    b. If the price of oil rises, people will buy less oil.

c. The government should impose a ceiling on the price of gasoline.

d. The sale of cigarettes should be illegal.

e. Lower interest rates on mortgages will increase the purchases of new homes.

f. Interest rates should be kept as low as possible so that the economy can produce more jobs.

8. Indicate whether each of the following falls under the heading of positive economics or normative economics:

a. A study of the relationship between investment spending and the rate of interest

b. The observation that when average income rises, consumers increase their purchases of most goods and services

c. The conclusion that the amounts of money allocated to education and health in Canada are much too small

d. The assertion that hockey and baseball players should never go on strike, because they earn enough money

e. A program designed to reduce poverty based on the opinion that poverty levels are too high

f. A description of how the money supply affects the performance of the economy

g. The notion that taxing the wealthy to give welfare payments to the poor is unfair

h. The assertion that the accumulation of debts is bad both for individuals and for governments

9. Classify each of the following as a stock or a flow:

a. The annual salary of your economics professor

b. The number of washing machines owned by the Quick Clean Laundromat on December 30, 2011

c. The annual interest payable on a bank loan

d. The number of new homes available for sale in November 2012

e. The quantity of merchandise sold each month by a department store

f. The unpaid balance on a bank loan as of February 23, 2010

g. Consumers' expenditure on goods and services over a six-month period

h. The number of workers who showed up for work at 7:30 this morning

10. Indicate whether each of the following falls under microeconomics or macroeconomics:

a. A study of the relationship between employment and total production

b. A model explaining why, on average, actors earn more than doctors

c. An explanation of the factors that affect total spending in the Canadian economy

d. A theory explaining how the level of investment spending affects aggregate employment

e. A model explaining how many workers a firm should hire to produce a desired volume of output

f. An explanation of the effect of a tax on cigarettes on the price of cigarettes

g. A model showing that when the price of gold rises, the price of silver also rises, other things being equal

h. A model that explains why the prices of home computers have fallen over the past few years

Learning Objectives

After studying this appendix, you should be able to

1A.1 Use functional notation to express relationships among variables

1A.2 Use graphs to show relationships among variables

1A.3 Define and calculate the slopes of linear and non-linear curves

1A.4 Calculate the percentage change in variables

Assess Your Knowledge

MyEconLab

Answers to these questions can be found on MyEconLab at **www.myeconlab.com**.

1. Why are graphs so useful in studying economics?
2. If one line is relatively steep while another is relatively flat, which one has the bigger slope?
3. The price of an item rises from $15.00 to $18.00. Calculate the percentage increase in the price.

LO 1A.1 Use functional notation to express relationships among variables

Functional Notation

Do we need to know a great deal of mathematics to understand introductory economics?

Advanced courses in economics do require a good knowledge of mathematics. However, in this book, you will not be required to know a great deal of mathematics, so you need not fear the mathematics. Graphs are used liberally in this book, but they are explained in simple and understandable terms. The production possibilities diagrams that you will study in Chapter 2 are examples of the use of graphs in economics. In this book, you will learn the basic principles and concepts of economics, and they will be presented by using words, examples, and graphs that help to clarify the ideas. Even when *simple* mathematical tools are used, words, not mathematics, will be the main communication medium. You can therefore feel comfortable with the mathematics you already know.

What exactly is a function?

functional notation a mathematical tool for expressing relations among variables

function an expression of a relation among variables

Economics involves establishing and studying relationships among variables. Such relationships can be expressed by using a **functional notation**, which is a very convenient mathematical tool. A **function** expresses a relationship among two or more variables. Consider the following statement: "The amount of money that people spend on consumer goods and services depends on their income." Another way of expressing the same idea is as follows: "The amount of money that people spend on consumer goods and services *is a function of* their income." Both statements mean exactly the same thing—namely, if income changes, the amount of money that people spend on consumer goods and services will change (other things being equal, of course). We have used the concept of a function to express a relationship between the amount of money that people spend on consumer goods and services (i.e., consumption) and their income.

How can functional notation be used to express the idea that consumption depends on income?

The first step in using functional notion is to symbolize (i.e., use symbols instead of words). Let us use C to denote the amount of money that people spend on consumer goods and services, and y to denote income. Note that the use of these symbols has already simplified our task of expressing the relationship between the variables of interest to us. Instead of writing "the amount of money that people spend on consumer goods and services," we simply write C, and instead of writing "income," we simply write y. The idea that consumption depends on income can now be expressed as

$$C = f(y)$$

and is read "$C = f$ of y" or "consumption is a function of income" or "consumption depends on income."

> **Example:** When air fares increase, people take fewer vacations in foreign countries. We can use the functional notation to express this idea. Let us symbolize as follows:
>
> $$A = \text{air fare}; \ V = \text{number of vacations}$$
>
> We can now express the idea in the functional form as follows:
>
> $$V = f(A)$$
>
> which means that the number of vacations depends on airfares.

What is the difference between a dependent variable and an independent variable?

We'll answer this question with reference to the first example above, in which consumption depends on income. Hence, in the above function, C is the **dependent variable**. The variable on which it depends is called the **independent variable**. The dependent variable, then, is the variable that we are trying to explain, and the independent variable is the one that provides the explanation. In economics, it is customary to modify the form of the above functional notation. Instead of using f, we replace it with the dependent variable. The above function would therefore appear as

$$C = C(y)$$

How is functional notation written when there is more than one independent variable?

Quite often, we need to express the idea that one variable depends on two or more other variables. For example, suppose we want to express the idea that consumption depends not only on income but also on the rate of interest. Using C for consumption and y for income as before, and using r to symbolize the rate of interest, we can express the idea as

$$C = C(y, r)$$

Note that the independent variables, y and r, are separated by a comma, with no space between them.

dependent variable the variable that is being explained

independent variable the variable that provides the explanation; it causes changes in the dependent variable

Reading Comprehension

The answers to these questions can be found on MyEconLab at **www.myeconlab.com**.　　MyEconLab

1. What is the main use of the functional notation in economics?

2. What is the difference between dependent and independent variables?

3. How is the functional notation used when the idea involves more than one independent variable?

LO 1A.2 Use graphs to show relationships among variables

The Use of Graphs

Why are graphs used in economics?

You have probably heard that a picture is worth a thousand words. The same can be said of graphs. Graphs are indeed an effective way of showing relations among variables. They add clarity to ideas that we try to express—they actually *show* the changes that take place. For example, when population growth takes place in a country, we can use a graph to show the growth in population. This type of graphic, visual presentation makes concepts and ideas come alive.

How do we plot points on a graph?

Let us begin at the beginning, as it were, with an elementary introduction to the use of graphs. Consider the diagram shown as Figure 1A.1. The two lines (called *axes*) intersect at a 90-degree angle. The point of intersection is called the **origin**. We give this point a value of 0 and from it measure all distances. Note that the two intersecting lines divide the plane into four quadrants, numbered as shown in Figure 1A.1. In quadrant II, the x value is negative; in quadrant III, both x and y are negative; and in quadrant IV, the y value is negative.

origin the point of intersection of the vertical and horizontal axes

Suppose we want to plot the point for the $x = 3$ and $y = 4$, usually indicated as (3, 4). First, we locate the value 3 along the x axis. Then, we move vertically up to the value 4 measured along the y axis. This locates the desired point (3, 4). Now consider Table 1A.1, which gives values of x and y. We can plot these values on a graph, such as Figure 1A.2. Note that points will appear in quadrants II, III, or IV only when a negative value is involved.

In general, economic variables have either positive values or a value of zero. For most of our graphs, therefore, we will need only the first quadrant. Most graphs will appear without the negative parts of the axes.

| Figure 1A.1 | Axes, Origin, Quadrants, and a Point on a Graph |

How do we graph data contained in tables?

Once we know how to plot points on a graph, we can graph data contained in tables. The process is exactly the same. Suppose we have the information shown in Table 1A.2 for income and consumption in a hypothetical economy for a year.

From this table, we can see that as income increases, consumption also increases; however, we cannot quite see it *at a glance*. Let us graph the information contained in Table 1A.2. This is done in Figure 1A.3.

When income is 0, consumption is 30. This is represented by point A on the graph. When income is 20, consumption is 40. This is shown as point B on the graph. When income is 40, consumption is 50. This is point C on the graph. The other combinations of income and consumption are plotted in the same way and illustrated by points D, E, F, and G on the graph. By connecting the points, we obtain a graph that shows clearly and easily that as income rises, consumption also rises.

| Table 1A.1 | Values of x and y |

x Values	y Values
1	−3
2	4
−3	2
4	1

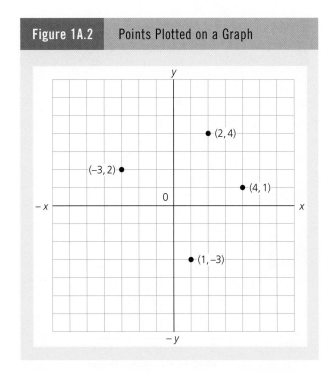

Figure 1A.2 Points Plotted on a Graph

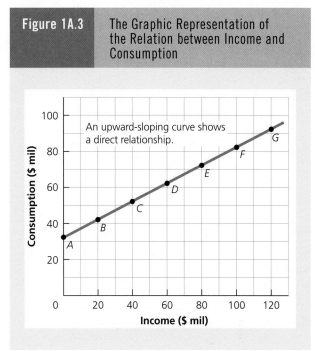

Figure 1A.3 The Graphic Representation of the Relation between Income and Consumption

Table 1A.2	Income and Consumption Data for a Hypothetical Economy
Income ($ mil)	**Consumption** ($ mil)
0	30
20	40
40	50
60	60
80	70
100	80
120	90

direct relation the relation that exists between variables that increase or decrease together; the variables move in the same direction

inverse relation the relation that exists between variables such that as one increases, the other decreases, and vice versa; the variables move in opposite directions

How are direct and inverse relationships shown on graphs?

Consider the following statement: "As the rate of interest rises, people save more; as the rate of interest falls, people save less." Here we have two variables: the rate of interest and the volume of saving. They rise and fall together. When variables move up or down together, we say that there is a **direct relation** between them. A graph showing a direct relationship between two variables is upward sloping, like the graph in Figure 1A.3. Variables that are likely to have a direct relationship are people's height and their weight; age and experience; level of education and income; and class attendance and grade.

Now consider the following statement: "The faster a person travels, the less time it takes to cover a certain distance." Here we have two variables: speed and time; when one increases, the other decreases. They move in opposite directions. When variables move in opposite directions, we say that there is an **inverse relation** between them. A graph showing an inverse relationship between two variables is downward sloping, like the graph in Figure 1A.4.

What are some typical graphs used in economics?

The graph shown in Figure 1A.4 is a good example of the graphs used in economics. Some other examples follow. Consider the relationship between the rate of interest and the level of investment. As the rate of interest falls, the level of investment increases. Investment here refers to expenditure on manufacturing plants, equipment, buildings, and so on—real capital investment. We can get a very clear picture of this relation by using a graph. Note that these two variables move in opposite directions; in other

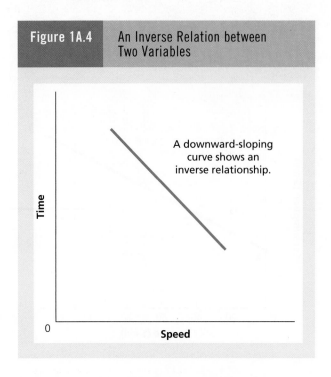

Figure 1A.4 An Inverse Relation between Two Variables

A downward-sloping curve shows an inverse relationship.

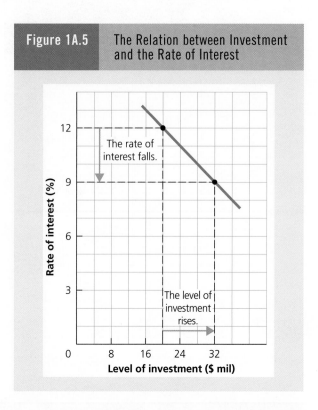

Figure 1A.5 The Relation between Investment and the Rate of Interest

The rate of interest falls.

The level of investment rises.

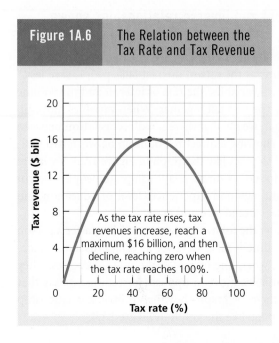

Figure 1A.6 The Relation between the Tax Rate and Tax Revenue

As the tax rate rises, tax revenues increase, reach a maximum $16 billion, and then decline, reaching zero when the tax rate reaches 100%.

words, there is an inverse relation between the rate of interest and the level of investment. This inverse relation is illustrated graphically by the downward-sloping (falling) curve shown in Figure 1A.5. This figure shows that as the rate of interest falls from 12% to 9%, the level of investment increases from $20 million to $32 million. Two very popular graphs in economics are ones that show (1) the relation between the price of an item and the quantity of that item that people would be willing to buy, and (2) the relation between the price of an item and the quantity of that item that firms would be willing to sell.

A graph might show a relationship starting at zero, rising to a maximum, and then falling to zero. Such might be the case between tax revenue and tax rates, as shown in Figure 1A.6.

When the tax rate is zero, the government receives no tax revenue. As the tax rate increases, tax revenue rises, reaching a maximum of $16 billion at a tax rate of 50%. But as the tax rate continues to rise, it may be that the incentive to earn extra income decreases and so tax revenue falls. If the tax rate increases to 100%, no one will willingly earn any income because it would all be taxed away. The government's revenue from income tax would be zero if no one earns any income.

In economics, we also encounter relationships that start at a certain point, fall to a minimum, and then rise. An example of such a relationship is the cost of making photocopies, shown in Figure 1A.7.

As the number of copies increases from zero, the cost per copy falls. At a volume of 1000 copies per day, the cost per copy is minimized at $0.03 per copy. But as the volume

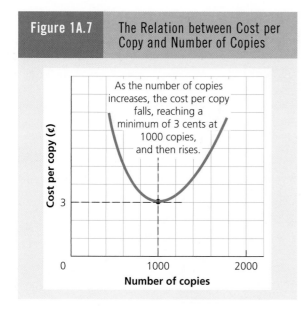

| Figure 1A.7 | The Relation between Cost per Copy and Number of Copies |

As the number of copies increases, the cost per copy falls, reaching a minimum of 3 cents at 1000 copies, and then rises.

increases beyond 1000 copies per day, the cost per copy rises, perhaps because the photocopy machine is pushed beyond its most efficient operating capacity.

Quite often, it is necessary to graph data that are unrelated. For example, no relation exists between inflation and the distance a person travels each day. Such a situation is shown in Figure 1A.8.

In Diagram A of Figure 1A.8, the rate of inflation is 1.5% whether the distance travelled is 20, 40, 60, or 80 km per day. The graph is therefore a horizontal straight line. Consider now the situation shown in Diagram B. The price of fish in Canada has no effect on the number of briefcases sold in an Australian department store each month. When the price of fish changes, the sale of briefcases remains the same, namely, 40. There is no relationship between the two variables, so the graph is a vertical line.

What is the difference between a concave and a convex curve?

concave curve a curve bowed outward from the origin

Students often confuse these two concepts. A **concave curve** is bowed outward, as shown in Diagram A of Figure 1A.9, while a **convex curve** is bowed toward the origin, as shown in Diagram B of Figure 1A.9.

convex curve a curve bowed toward the origin

Are other types of graphs used in economics?

bar graph a vertical or horizontal graph with categories on one axis and the value assigned to each category measured on the other axis

Two other types of graphs are quite commonly used in economics: bar graphs and pie charts. A **bar graph** is a vertical or horizontal graph with categories on one axis and the value assigned to each category measured along the other axis. Let us look at the information contained in Table 1A.3. It shows sales for a firm for the first six months of the year.

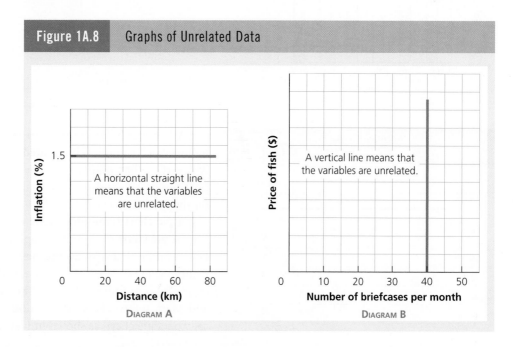

| Figure 1A.8 | Graphs of Unrelated Data |

A horizontal straight line means that the variables are unrelated.

A vertical line means that the variables are unrelated.

Diagram A

Diagram B

Figure 1A.9	Concave and Convex Curves

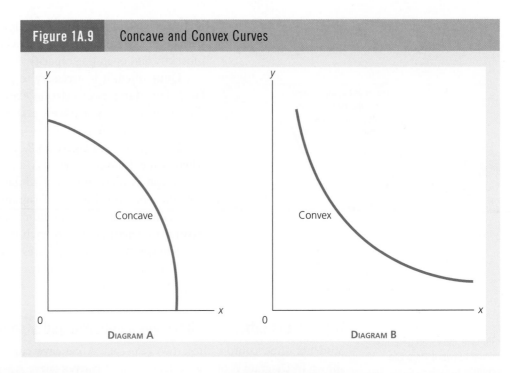

DIAGRAM A

DIAGRAM B

pie chart a circular graph whose pieces add up to 100%

Figure 1A.10	A Bar Chart for Sales from January to June

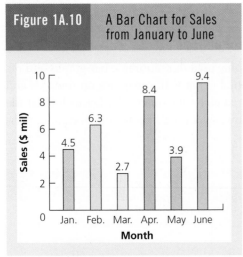

Figure 1A.11	A Pie Chart for Payroll Shares

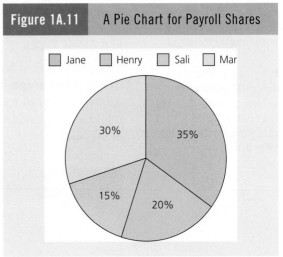

Table 1A.3	Sales for the Period January to June 20XX

Month	Sales ($ mil)
January	4.5
February	6.3
March	2.7
April	8.4
May	3.9
June	9.4

A bar graph can be used to effectively show these sales figures. Such a graph is illustrated in Figure 1A.10. This graph is a vertical bar graph, with the category of month on the horizontal axis, and the sales value assigned to each month on the vertical axis.

A pie chart is another useful device for showing information. A **pie chart** is a circular graph whose pieces add to 100%. Let's assume that a small business has four employees: Jane, Henry, Sali, and Mark. The share of the payroll going to each employee is as follows: Jane (35%), Henry (20%), Sali (15%), and Mark (30%). This information can be presented graphically on a pie chart, as shown in Figure 1A.11.

BUSINESS SITUATION 1A.1

Table 1A.4	The Relation between Number of Calls and Number of Orders	
Number of Calls per Quarter		**Quarterly Sales ($)**
15		250 000
20		300 000
23		320 000
25		350 000
32		400 000
35		425 000

A sales manager observes that the more calls her salespeople make on potential clients, the larger the orders from clients. She gathered the data shown in Table 1A.4. She wants to motivate her salespeople to make more calls by illustrating this link between calls and sales in a graphic manner.

How can she show this relation?

The answer to this Business Situation can be found in Appendix A.

Is there any limitation to the use of graphs?

Yes, there is. Clearly, the economist can make good use of graphs in presenting certain economic relations. Despite their great advantage, however, the use of graphs is limited to cases with few variables. As the number of variables increases, our ability to graph relations among them decreases. How would we graph the idea that consumption varies with current income, the rate of interest, and consumer expectations? This is indeed a formidable, if not impossible, exercise. Models that involve relations among several variables are usually presented verbally or algebraically rather than geometrically or graphically.

Reading Comprehension

The answers to these questions can be found on MyEconLab at www.myeconlab.com.   MyEconLab

1. Discuss the importance of graphs in the study of economics.
2. If two variables are directly related, what would a graph depicting the relationship look like?
3. If two variables are inversely related, what would a graph depicting the relationship look like?
4. Explain the difference between a concave and a convex curve.
5. Discuss the limitation to the use of graphs in economics.

LO 1A.3 Define and calculate the slopes of linear and non-linear curves

The Slope: Concept and Measurement

We understand the terms *upward sloping* and *downward sloping*, but what is slope?

slope (of a curve) the steepness or flatness of a curve; the upward or downward inclination of a curve

In your study of economics, you will find the concept of a slope and its measurement of the utmost importance. Economists are interested in knowing the rates at which the curves they draw rise or fall. Measuring the slopes of these curves provides the answer. The **slope** of a

Figure 1A.12 The Relation between Income and Consumption

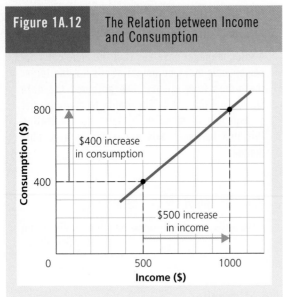

curve refers to its steepness or flatness; it is the upward or downward inclination of the curve. Suppose you observe or believe that as people's incomes rise, they spend more money on consumer goods and services. You could show this relationship on a graph, as depicted in Figure 1A.12. The relationship is similar to the one shown in Figure 1A.3 on page 31.

Consumption is measured along the vertical axis while income is measured along the horizontal axis. The graph shows that as income rises, consumption also rises. It would be interesting and useful, however, to know the degree to which consumers respond to changes in their incomes. We could say, for example, that a $500 increase in income (from $500 to $1000) results in a $400 increase in consumption (from $400 to $800). The slope of the line gives us that information. The slope provides information on the steepness or flatness of the curve and is measured by the ratio of the vertical distance (rise) to the horizontal distance (run).

Consider Figure 1A.13. Because the curve is a linear curve (that is, a straight line), it has the same slope at every point. The slope of the line in Figure 1A.13 is

$$\text{Slope} = \frac{\text{Vertical distance}}{\text{Horizontal distance}} = \frac{AC}{BC}$$

The slope, then, is the change in the y value divided by the change in the x value when y is on the vertical axis and x is on the horizontal axis. The change in the y value can be written as Δy, while the change in the x value can be written as Δx. The symbol Δ is the Greek letter *delta*, used here to mean "a change in." Thus,

$$\text{Slope} = \frac{\Delta y}{\Delta x} = \frac{\text{Rise}}{\text{Run}}$$

In Figure 1A.13, $\Delta y = 8 - 4 = 4$; $\Delta x = 6 - 3 = 3$; therefore, the slope of the line in Figure 1A.13 is $4 \div 3 = 1^1/_3$.

Let us calculate the slope of each line shown in Figure 1A.14. First, consider Diagram A. If we move from point A to point B, y falls from 9 to 4. Hence, $\Delta y = -5$. At the same time, x rises from 2 to 5; so $\Delta x = 3$. Therefore,

$$\text{Slope} = \frac{\Delta y}{\Delta x} = \frac{-5}{3} = -1\tfrac{2}{3}$$

If we move from point B to point A, y rises from 4 to 9. Hence, $\Delta y = 5$. But x falls from 5 to 2; so $\Delta x = -3$. Therefore,

$$\text{Slope} = \frac{\Delta y}{\Delta x} = \frac{5}{-3} = -1\tfrac{2}{3}$$

Figure 1A.13 The Slope of a Straight Line

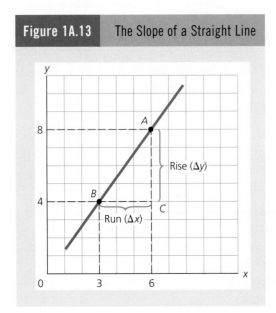

A declining curve has a negative slope.

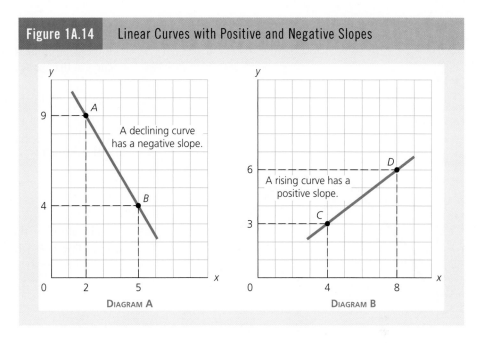

Figure 1A.14 Linear Curves with Positive and Negative Slopes

DIAGRAM A

DIAGRAM B

Let us now consider Diagram B. If we move from point C to point D, y rises from 3 to 6. Hence, $\Delta y = 3$. At the same time, x rises from 4 to 8; so $\Delta x = 4$. Therefore,

$$\text{Slope} = \frac{\Delta y}{\Delta x} = \frac{3}{4}$$

If we move from point D to point C, y falls from 6 to 3. Hence, $\Delta y = -3$. At the same time x falls from 8 to 4; so $\Delta x = -4$. Therefore,

$$\text{Slope} = \frac{\Delta y}{\Delta x} = \frac{-3}{-4} = \frac{3}{4}$$

A rising curve has a positive slope.

There seems to be some relationship between inverse relations and direct relations and slope. Is that the case?

If two variables have an inverse relation, the slope of the curve showing that relationship will be negative. The curve will be downward sloping. If two variables have a direct relation, the slope of the curve showing that relationship will be positive. The curve will be upward slopping.

We can calculate the slopes of linear curves, but what about non-linear curves?

A non-linear curve has a different slope at each point on the curve. We can calculate the slope of a non-linear curve at any point on the curve if we know the following fact:

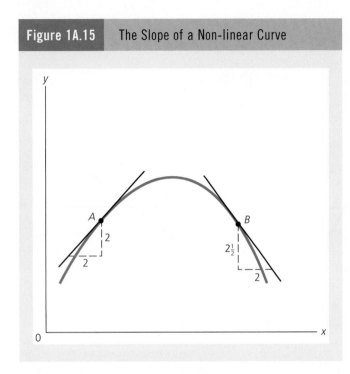

The slope of a non-linear curve at a particular point is the slope of the straight line drawn tangent to the curve at that particular point..

Figure 1A.15 shows a non-linear curve. Tangent lines are drawn at points A and B on the curve. The slope of the curve at point A is the slope of the tangent line at A, which is

$$\frac{\Delta y}{\Delta x} = \frac{2}{2} = 1$$

The slope of the curve at B is the slope of the tangent line at B, which is

$$\frac{\Delta y}{\Delta x} = \frac{-2\frac{1}{2}}{2} = -1\frac{1}{4}$$

Reading Comprehension

The answers to these questions can be found on MyEconLab at www.myeconlab.com.   MyEconLab

1. What is the meaning of slope?
2. How is the slope of a straight line measured?

3. How is the slope of a non-linear curve measured?
4. It is meaningful to talk about the slope of a straight line, but not the slope of a non-linear curve. Explain.

LO 1A.4 Calculate the percentage change in variables

Percentage Change

What is the importance of percentage change in economics?

In economics, it is often necessary to calculate the percentage change in a quantity. Percentages often give us a clearer sense of the magnitude of the change and facilitate comparisons of the size of change. For example, is an increase in price from $115 to $135 relatively larger or smaller than an increase from $120 to $140? In each case, the absolute increase is the same, namely, $20, but the relative or percentage change in price may be different.

Is there a formula that we can use to calculate percentage change?

There is. If x is the original quantity and x_1 is the new quantity, the formula for calculating the percentage or relative change from x to x_1 is

$$\frac{100(x_1 - x)}{x}$$

In words, this means that we subtract the original quantity from the new quantity, multiply the result by 100, and divide by the original quantity. The following illustrative example will demonstrate how the formula is used.

Example: The price of an item increased from \$90 to \$95. What is the percentage increase in the price of the item?

Solution: The original price (x) = \$90 and the new price (x_1) = \$95.

The percentage change in price is

$$\frac{100(x_1 - x)}{x} = \frac{100(95 - 90)}{90} = \frac{100 \times 5}{90} = 500 \div 90 = 5.56\%$$

Let us now answer the question raised at the beginning of this section: "Is an increase in price from \$115 to \$135 relatively larger or smaller than an increase in price from \$120 to \$140?"

The percentage increase in price from \$115 to \$135 is

$$\frac{100(x_1 - x)}{x} = \frac{100(135 - 115)}{115} = \frac{100 \times 20}{115} = \frac{2000}{115} = 17.39\%$$

The percentage change in price from \$120 to \$140 is

$$\frac{100(x_1 - x)}{x} = \frac{100(140 - 120)}{120} = \frac{100 \times 20}{120} = \frac{2000}{120} = 16.67\%$$

Therefore, an increase in price from \$115 to \$135 is relatively larger than an increase in price from \$120 to \$140. Note that the absolute differences between the prices were the same, that is, \$20, but they are not meaningfully comparable. The percentage changes, conversely, are comparable.

The formula used for an increase in a variable applies also to a decrease. For example, if the population of a small town fell from 2000 to 1500 over two years, what was the percentage change in the population?

In this example, x = 2000 and x_1 = 1500. The percentage change is

$$\frac{100(x_1 - x)}{x} = \frac{100(1500 - 2000)}{2000} = \frac{100 \times -500}{2000} = -25\%$$

The population fell by 25%.

It should be clear that a 10% increase on \$1500 is significantly different from a 10% increase on \$150 000. A 10% increase on \$1500 is \$150, whereas a 10% increase on \$150,000 is \$15 000. Although the percentage change is the same (10%), the magnitudes are different.

Is there also a formula for expressing one number as a percentage of another number?

Yes. Suppose we know that a household has an income of \$3000 per month and spends \$800 a month on rent. What percentage of this household's income is spent on rent? We can use the following formula to answer this question.

To express one number, x, as a percentage of another number, y, we divide the first number by the second number and then multiply the result by 100. Thus, x expressed as a percentage of y is

$$\frac{x}{y} \times 100$$

Can we do an example?

Let us assume that the population of a certain small country is 80 000. Assume also that 16 000 of these people are more than 60 years old. Express the number of people over age 60 as a percentage of the total population.

In the example above,

$$x = \text{population over } 60 = 16\,000$$
$$y = \text{total population} = 80\,000$$

$$\frac{x}{y} \times 100 = \frac{16\,000}{80\,000} \times 100 = 20\%$$

Thus, we know that 20% of the population is over 60 years old.

Reading Comprehension

The answers to these questions can be found on MyEconLab at www.myeconlab.com.   MyEconLab

1. Explain the importance of the concept of percentage change in economics.

2. Explain how you would convert a ratio into a percentage.

BUSINESS SITUATION 1A.2

A businessperson can invest $100 000 at 7% interest annually or he can purchase inventories that he can resell for $107 500. Before making a decision, he consults his accountant.

What advice should his accountant give?

The answer to this Business Situation can be found in Appendix A.

Review

1. Review the learning objectives listed at the beginning of the appendix.
2. Have you accomplished all the objectives? One way to determine this is to answer the Reading Comprehension questions at the end of each section. They will help you assess the extent to which you have accomplished the learning objectives.
3. If you have not accomplished an objective, review the relevant material before proceeding.

Key Points to Remember

1. **LO 1A.1** A function expresses a relationship among two or more variables. Functional notation is a very efficient way of expressing relationships among variables. Because much of economics has to do with relations among variables, functional notation is a very useful tool.
2. **LO 1A.1** If A and B are two variables, and if changes in B cause changes in A, then A is a function of B, written as

$A = A(B)$. Here, A is the dependent variable (the variable we are trying to explain), and B is the independent variable (the variable that provides the explanation).

3. **LO 1A.2** Graphs allow us to depict relations among economic variables clearly and vividly so that the relations can be seen at a glance. A rising curve shows a direct relation between the variables under consideration, a declining curve shows an inverse relation, and a vertical or horizontal line shows that the graphed variables are not related—changes in one have no effect on the other.

4. **LO 1A.3** The slope of a straight line is measured by the ratio of the vertical distance to the horizontal distance (rise over run). A straight line has a constant slope. The slope of a non-linear curve at a point on the curve is the slope of the straight line drawn tangent to the curve at that point. The slope is different at every point on a non-linear curve. A rising curve has a positive slope, while a declining curve has a negative slope.

5. **LO 1A.4** Percentages allow us to compare the relative magnitudes of changes in variables. They give a clear sense of the magnitudes involved.

Economic Word Power

Bar graph (p. 33)
Concave curve (p. 33)
Convex curve (p. 33)
Dependent variable (p. 29)
Direct relation (p. 31)
Function (p. 28)
Functional notation (p. 28)
Independent variable (p. 29)
Inverse relation (p. 31)
Origin (p. 30)
Pie chart (p. 34)
Slope (of a curve) (p. 35)

Problems and Exercises

Basic

1. **LO 1A.1** Use functional notation to express each of the following relations:
   a. Coffee consumption (C) depends on the atmospheric temperature (T).
   b. Students' academic performance (P) is a function of their professors' qualifications (Q).
   c. If the quantity of personal computers (Q) sold increases, the quantity of ink cartridges (I) sold will also increase.
   d. An increase in the number of immigrants (M) migrating to Canada will cause the quantity of furniture (F) bought to increase.
   e. An increase in income (y) in Canada will cause an increase in exports (x) from the United States.
   f. The rate of interest (r) influences the use of credit cards (C).
   g. Tax revenues (T) vary with the level of income (y) and the tax rate (t).

2. **LO 1A.1** Use words to express the idea contained in the following notation: $N = N(P,r,y)$ where N is the number of international trips, P is the price of airline tickets, r is the rate of interest, and y is income.

3. **LO 1A.1** For each of the relations in Question 1, indicate the dependent variable and the independent variable(s).

4. **LO 1A.2** Use graphs to show the relationship that you would expect to find between each of the following variables:
   a. The price of grapes and the quantity of grapes bought
   b. The duration of a deep freeze in Florida and the quantity of oranges brought to the market
   c. The rate of interest and the amount of money people put in their savings accounts
   d. The number of students attending a college and the quantity of textbooks bought and sold at the college bookstore

5. **LO 1A.2** Referring to Question 4, indicate whether each relationship is direct or inverse.

6. **LO 1A.2** What kind of graph would you use to illustrate each of the following?
   a. The monthly rainfall for 2010
   b. The proportion of total sales attributable to four retail outlets
   c. A comparison of the populations of 10 different countries
   d. The percentage of total sales attributable to five different products sold by a company

7. **LO 1A.2** Indicate whether each of the following is true or false:
   a. An upward-sloping straight line has an increasing slope.
   b. If two variables are directly related, the graph showing the relationship between them will be upward sloping.

c. A downward-sloping straight line has a negative but constant slope.

d. Concave curves are never used in economics.

Questions in the Intermediate and Challenging Sections cover several different concepts, and have not been organized by learning objectives.

Intermediate

1. Consider Figure 1A.16.
   a. Calculate the slope of line *A* at point *P*.
   b. Calculate the slope of line *A* at point *Q*.
   c. Calculate the slope of line *B* at point *R*.
   d. Calculate the slope of line *B* at point *S*.
   e. What can you conclude about the slope of a straight line at different points on the line?

Figure 1A.16   The Slope of a Straight Line

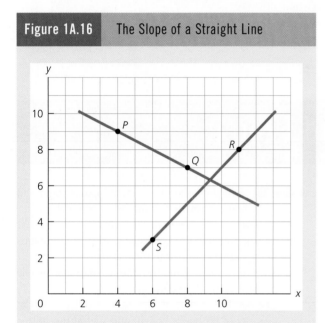

2. Consider Figure 1A.17.
   a. Calculate the slope of the curve at point *A*.
   b. Calculate the slope of the curve at point *B*.
   c. What can you conclude about the slope of a non-linear curve at different points on the curve?
3. Carefully explain the procedure for obtaining the slope of a non-linear curve at a point on the curve.
4. The population of a certain town grew from 150 000 to 195 000 in 10 years. During the same time, the population of another town grew from 250 000 to 320 000. Calculate the rate of growth in each town.
5. At a hockey game, the spectators consisted of 11 000 men and 7000 women.
   a. What was the ratio of women to men?
   b. What percentage of the total spectators were women?

Figure 1A.17   The Slope of a Non-linear Curve

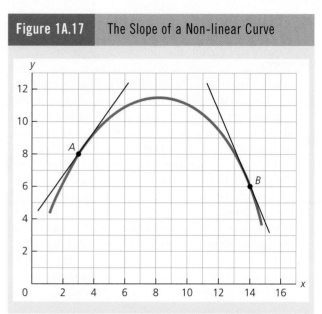

Table 1A.5   Total Cost and Quantity

Q	TC
0	$4 + 2(0) = 4 + 0 = 4$
1	$4 + 2(1) = 4 + 2 = 6$
2	
3	
4	
5	
6	

Challenging (Use Quad Paper for Graphs)

1. a. Between 2007 and 2011, average house prices in one province rose from $180 000 to $205 000. During the same period, in another province, average house prices rose from $235 000 to $260 000. Under these conditions, will average house prices in both provinces ever be equal?
   b. Draw a diagram to illustrate what is happening here.
2. The relationship between total cost (*TC*) and total quantity produced (*Q*) is given by the equation $TC = 4 + 2Q$.
   a. Complete Table 1A.5 by calculating *TC* for each quantity produced.
   b. With *TC* on the vertical axis and *Q* on the horizontal axis, graph the data contained in the completed table. Let us refer to the graph as a cost curve.
   c. At what value does your graph cut the vertical axis? That is called the intercept.
   d. Use your graph to calculate the slope of your cost curve.

MyEconLab   Visit the MyEconLab website at visit **www.myeconlab.com.** This online homework and tutorial system puts you in control of your own learning with study and practice tools directly correlated to this appendix's content.

Study Guide

Self-Assessment

The answers to the Study Guide questions can be found in Appendix B.

What's your score?

Circle the letter that corresponds with the correct answer.

1. The statement that the volume of production is a function of the state of technology means that
   a. Changes in the volume of production will cause changes in the state of technology
   b. Changes in the state of technology will cause changes in the volume of production
   c. The volume of production defines the state of technology
   d. We cannot know the state of technology without first knowing the volume of production

2. The expression $Q = Q(P)$, where Q represents quantity and P represents price, means
   a. Quantity must always be multiplied by price
   b. Price and quantity are equal
   c. If price changes, quantity will also change
   d. If quantity changes, price will also change

3. In the expression $Q = Q(P)$,
   a. P is the dependent variable and Q the independent variable
   b. Both Q and P are dependent variables
   c. Both Q and P are independent variables
   d. Q is the dependent variable and P the independent variable

4. In the expression $I = I(y, r)$, I is
   a. The lead variable
   b. The independent variable
   c. The product of y and r
   d. None of the above

5. If a change in one variable has no effect on another variable, a graph showing the relationship between them will be
   a. A straight line through the origin
   b. Impossible to draw
   c. Either vertical or horizontal
   d. Drawn cutting both axes

6. The statement that changes in the volume of output (Q) and the state of technology (T) will cause changes in the cost of production (C) can be expressed as
   a. $C = C(Q + T)$
   b. $Q = Q(C, T)$
   c. $C = C(Q, T)$
   d. $C = Q + T$

7. Graphs enable us to show
   a. Inverse relations but not direct relations
   b. Direct relations but not inverse relations
   c. Both direct and inverse relations
   d. Dependent but not independent variables

8. When we say that two variables are directly related, we mean that
   a. One is derived from the other
   b. One is a multiple of the other
   c. They appear side by side in functional notation
   d. Both variables change in the same direction

9. A downward-sloping curve means that the variables are
   a. Inversely related
   b. Directly related
   c. Not closely related
   d. None of the above

10. When interest rates fall, businesses invest more. This relationship between investment and the rate of interest would be shown on a graph as
    a. An upward-sloping curve
    b. A downward-sloping curve

c. A vertical line

d. A horizontal line

11. A graph of two unrelated variables

    a. Can be a vertical or a horizontal line

    b. Cannot be drawn

    c. Can only be a vertical line

    d. Can only be a horizontal line

12. The difference between a convex curve and a concave curve is that

    a. One is horizontal and the other is vertical

    b. A concave curve is linear while a convex curve is non-linear

    c. A convex curve is linear while a concave curve is non-linear

    d. None of the above

13. Bar graphs and pie charts

    a. Are useful in statistics but not very useful in economics

    b. Are just embellishments that add nothing to data presentation

    c. Are effective and vivid means of presenting data

    d. Can be used only when the data involve percentage changes

14. One serious limitation of using graphs in economics is that

    a. They are too difficult to understand

    b. They can be used only when several variables are involved

    c. Our ability to use graphs decreases as the number of variables increases

    d. None of the above

15. The concept of slope refers to

    a. Only straight lines

    b. Only non-linear curves

    c. Both linear and non-linear curves

    d. Concave curves but not convex curves.

16. The slope of a line can be measured by

    a. The ratio of the vertical distance to the horizontal distance

    b. The ratio of the horizontal distance to the vertical distance

    c. The difference between the vertical distance and the horizontal distance

    d. The sum of the vertical and horizontal distances

17. An upward-sloping curve has

    a. A negative slope

    b. A positive slope

    c. Zero slope

    d. None of the above

18. A linear curve always has

    a. A positive slope

    b. A negative slope

    c. A constant slope

    d. A variable slope

19. The formula for calculating percentage change from x to x_1 is

    a. $\dfrac{100(x - x_1)}{x}$

    b. $\dfrac{100(x_1 - x)}{x}$

    c. $\dfrac{100(x - x_1)}{x_1}$

    d. $\dfrac{100(x_1 - x)}{x_1}$

20. Percentages are useful because

    a. They are easy to calculate

    b. They facilitate comparisons of relative changes in variables

    c. Numbers always give more information than do words

    d. None of the above

Problems and Exercises (Use Quad Paper for Graphs)

Answers to these questions can be found on MyEconLab at www.myeconlab.com.　　MyEconLab

1. Use functional notation to express each of the following statements:

    a. The level of saving (S) depends on the rate of interest (r).

    b. If the money supply (M) changes, the rate of interest (r) will also change.

    c. Changes in income (y) will cause changes in the demand for money (Md).

    d. If the demand for money (Md) changes, the rate of interest (r) will change.

    e. Changes in income (y) and the rate of interest (r) will cause the level of investment (I) to change.

2. In each of the following functions, identify the dependent and independent variables:

    a. $C = C(P, i)$

    b. $Q = Q(p, y, T)$

    c. $x = x(R, y)$

    d. $y = y(r, W)$

    e. $I = I(y, r, E)$

3. In each of the following relations, indicate the dependent and independent variables:
   a. If the price (P) of computers changes, the quantity (Q) that people will buy will also change.
   b. Changes in the quantity (Q) of VCRs that people will buy are due to changes in the price (P) of VCRs and people's income (y).
   c. A change in the average income (y) of Canadians will result in a change in the amount of imported goods (M).
   d. Changes in income (y) and the rate of interest (r) will cause investment (I) to change.
4. a. Construct a table with hypothetical values to show the relation you would expect between the rate of interest and the frequency of use of credit cards. (Use six different rates.)
   b. Plot the information from your table on a graph.
5. Draw graphs (without plotting) to illustrate the relationship you would expect between the following pairs of variables:
   a. Class attendance and grade in your economics course.
   b. The price of movies and movie attendance.
   c. Air fare and vacations abroad.
   d. Income and the amount of income tax a person pays.
6. Table 1A.6 contains information on combinations of corn and wheat that a farmer can grow on a given area of land.

Table 1A.6	Combinations of Corn and Wheat
Corn (tonnes)	**Wheat** (tonnes)
0	20
1	16
2	12
3	8
4	4
5	0

   a. With wheat on the vertical axis and corn on the horizontal axis, draw a graph showing the various combinations of corn and wheat that the farmer can grow.
   b. Calculate the slope of your graph.

7. Table 1A.7 shows combinations of two goods, x and y, that an economy can produce. With y on the vertical axis and x on the horizontal axis,

Table 1A.7	Combinations of X and Y	
Combinations	**X**	**Y**
A	0	15
B	1	14
C	2	12
D	3	9
E	4	5
F	5	0

   a. Plot the curve from Table 1A.7.
   b. Calculate the slope at point D on the graph.
8. With reference to Figure 1A.18, calculate the slope of the curve at points A and B.

Figure 1A.18	A Slope Calculation

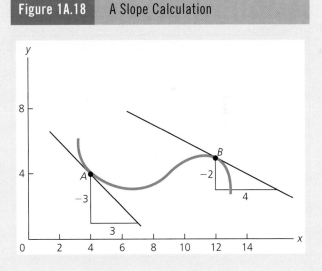

9. Table 1A.8 contains data on total income and government spending for a hypothetical economy for 1985, 1990, 1995, and 2000.
   a. Calculate the percentage change in total income from 1985 to 1990, from 1990 to 1995, and from 1995 to 2000. Complete column (3).
   b. Express government spending as a percentage of total income for each year shown in the table and complete column (5).

10. In 2000, the number of students enrolled in economics at a certain Canadian college was 1500. This figure grew to 2500 by 2004. At the same time, the number of economics professors increased from 10 to 15.

   a. Calculate the percentage change in the number of students enrolled in economics over the period 2000 to 2004.
   b. How does the percentage change in the number of economics professors compare with the percentage change in the number of students enrolled in economics?
   c. Express the number of economics professors as a percentage of the number of economics students in 2000 and 2004.

Table 1A.8	Hypothetical Data for Total Income and Government Spending			
Year (1)	Total Income ($) (2)	% Change (3)	Government Spending ($) (4)	Government Spending as % of Total Income (5)
1985	12 400 000	_____	3 500 000	_____
1990	15 000 000	_____	3 750 000	_____
1995	20 500 000	_____	5 637 000	_____
2000	24 900 000	_____	5 851 500	_____

Chapter 2

The Economic Problem: Scarcity and Choice

Learning Objectives

After studying this chapter, you should be able to

2.1 Explain the relationship among scarcity, choice, and opportunity cost

2.2 Discuss and use the concepts of production possibilities schedules and production possibilities curves

2.3 Discuss and illustrate graphically shifts in the production possibilities curve

2.4 Explain the fundamental economic questions and classify them as microeconomic or macroeconomic issues

2.5 Construct a circular flow model and explain the flow of goods, services, and resources in the economy

Assess Your Knowledge

MyEconLab

Answers to these questions can be found on MyEconLab at **www.myeconlab.com**.

1. Think of cost as whatever you give up when you make a choice. On graduation from high school, you decided to go to college instead of going to work. Using this concept of cost, what did the decision to go to college cost you?

2. Which of the following will enable a country to produce more goods and services?
   a. An increase in the country's workforce
   b. A general increase in the prices of goods and services
   c. Neither a nor b
   d. Both a and b

3. What is a firm?

4. What is economic growth?

LO 2.1 Explain the relationship among scarcity, choice, and opportunity cost

Scarcity and Choice Again

Is there still more to say about scarcity and choice?

Yes, there is. We have already established a relationship between scarcity and the necessity to choose. But there is more to the concept of choice or choosing than you might expect. When you are asked to make a choice between two things, you naturally think of taking one of them. That's how most people see choice—the act of taking. But think about it this way. If you were confronted with a choice between a two-week vacation in Paris and an expensive new television set, and you chose the television set, then you actually gave up the vacation in Paris. If you choose to go to a movie with your friends, you must give up something that you could have done during that time—something like studying economics. If you choose to attend a class at 8:30 a.m., you must give up some extra sleep that you could have enjoyed. The point should be clear: you cannot choose without giving up something.

Let's state it another way. The television set that you chose cost you the vacation in Paris. Going to the movies with your friends may have cost you a better grade on your economics test. And what is the cost of attending your 8:30 a.m. class? That's right! It's the extra sleep that you could have had.

Is there a technical term for the alternative that is given up when we choose?

opportunity cost the next-best alternative that is sacrificed when a choice is made

Not surprisingly, there is. It is a very important economic concept called opportunity cost or alternative cost. **Opportunity cost** is the next-best alternative that is sacrificed when a choice is made. Note that this cost is not necessarily expressed in terms of money but rather in terms of whatever is sacrificed or given up.

If Canada decides to buy new submarines instead of spending the money on health care, then the opportunity cost of the submarines would be the loss of the health services that could have been bought instead. If you decide to go to the movies, the admission ticket is part of the opportunity cost, but if you buy dinner at a restaurant before the movie instead of having dinner at home, then the money you spend for dinner is not part of the opportunity cost. You would have had dinner anyway.

We can measure opportunity cost per unit of the alternative chosen. If John gives up 10 kilograms of potatoes in order to get 20 kilograms of corn, then the opportunity cost of the 20 kilograms of corn is 10 kilograms of potatoes. This means that the opportunity cost of 1 kilogram of corn is 0.5 kilograms of potatoes. If John has to give up 20 kilograms of corn in order to get 10 kilograms of potatoes, then the opportunity cost of 10 kilograms of potatoes is 20 kilograms of corn. This means that the opportunity cost of 1 kilogram of potatoes is 2 kilograms of corn.

We can see from this example that opportunity cost is what we give up divided by what we get in its place.

$$\text{Opportunity cost} = \frac{\text{What we give up}}{\text{What we get}}$$

In John's case, the opportunity cost of corn is

$$\frac{10 \text{ kilograms of potatoes}}{20 \text{ kilograms of corn}} = \frac{0.5 \text{ kilogram of potatoes}}{1 \text{ kilogram of corn}}$$

On the other hand, the opportunity cost of potatoes is

$$\frac{20 \text{ kilograms of corn}}{10 \text{ kilograms of potatoes}} = \frac{2 \text{ kilograms of corn}}{1 \text{ kilogram of potatoes}}$$

Example: In order to get 3 more Blu-ray movies, you have to give up 6 USB flash drives. Calculate the opportunity cost of Blu-ray movies.
Solution:

$$\frac{\text{What we give up}}{\text{What we get}} = \frac{6 \text{ USB flash drives}}{3 \text{ Blu-ray movies}} = \frac{2 \text{ USB flash drives}}{1 \text{ Blu-ray movie}}$$

The opportunity cost of a Blu-ray movie is 2 flash drives.

A relationship seems to exist among scarcity, choice, and opportunity cost. Is there?

Most certainly. We are forced to choose only because of scarcity; and whenever we choose, we incur a cost, that is, an opportunity cost. Figure 2.1 illustrates the relationship well.

Can you give a practical example of the use of the opportunity cost concept in real life?

We make all kinds of decisions in our daily lives. Should I take a part-time job while I am in college? If scheduling conflicts prevent me from registering for both economics and mathematics, which one should I take? Should I skip my economics class today? Let's see how the concept of opportunity cost can help us to arrive at a decision regarding attending (or not attending) an economics class. Let us assume that you have already arrived at school. You attend classes because you believe that you will derive certain benefits from

| Figure 2.1 | The Relationship among Scarcity, Choice, and Opportunity Cost |

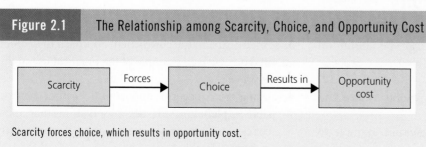

Scarcity forces choice, which results in opportunity cost.

doing so. What are these benefits? Possible benefits are a good attendance record that will improve your grade; better understanding of how the central bank tries to control interest rates (that's what is being discussed in class and you've always been fascinated by it); and being with your friends who are also taking the course. But attending class also has costs associated with it. These may include playing a game of cards with some friends, going to the nearby mall, or taking this last opportunity to watch that movie that you've been waiting to see. Notice that these costs are what you will give up by attending the class. They are the opportunity cost of going to class.

To make the decision, you weigh the benefits against the costs. If, in your own subjective evaluation, the benefits of going to class outweigh the costs, then you will decide in favour of attending the class. If, in your estimation, the costs outweigh the benefits, then you will decide against attending the class. This is the cost-benefit approach to decision making. The **cost-benefit approach** is an analysis in decision making that involves the comparison of costs and benefits. The decision rule is simple: if the benefits outweigh the costs, then do the activity; otherwise, don't.

cost-benefit approach an analysis in decision making that involves the comparison of costs and benefits

Can we apply this approach to more complicated decisions?

This way of thinking, using the concept of opportunity cost, can be applied to the simplest decisions as well as to very complex decisions involving the expenditure of a great deal of money. Let us consider the decision to go to college or take a full-time job. David has just completed his secondary-school education. He can get a job that pays $25 000 per year. However, he would like to go to college to obtain a diploma. This will take two years. Tuition, books, and other things, such as transportation and supplies, that are directly related to attending college will cost $35 000 for the two-year period. What is the full cost to David of a diploma? How should David decide whether or not to go for the diploma?

If David makes his decision on the basis of the $35 000 only, he would severely underestimate his cost. The full cost of his degree must include the $25 000 per year (or $50 000 for the two-year period) that he could have received as salary from his employment. That is the opportunity cost. Thus, the full cost of the diploma is ($35 000 + $50 000) = $85 000. To decide whether or not to go for the diploma, David must consider the benefits of having a diploma. These may include a higher-paying job, better working conditions, greater job security, and the prestige of having a college diploma. If these benefits outweigh the $85 000 cost, then David would sacrifice the job and attend college. Otherwise, he would take the job for $25 000 per year.

Reading Comprehension

The answers to these questions can be found on MyEconLab at www.myeconlab.com.   MyEconLab

1. What is the relationship among scarcity, choice, and opportunity cost?
2. Define opportunity cost and give an example to demonstrate your understanding of the concept.

3. Briefly explain the cost-benefit approach to decision making. Give an example of the practical use of this approach.
4. Using the concept of opportunity cost, give a possible explanation for the observation that most college students prefer late morning classes to early morning classes.

LO 2.2 Discuss and use the concept of production possibilities schedules and production possibilities curves

Production Possibilities

What are production possibilities?

An economy's production possibilities show its potential to produce goods and services with the resources at its disposal. Let us construct a simple model to explain an economy's production possibilities. Assume that our hypothetical economy devotes all its resources to the production of only two goods: smart phones and personal computers. Several possible combinations of smart phones and personal computers are illustrated in Table 2.1.

Table 2.1	A Production Possibilities Schedule Showing Constant Cost	
Possibilities	**Number of Smart Phones** (000 000)	**Number of Computers** (000 000)
A	15	0
B	12	1
C	9	2
D	6	3
E	3	4
F	0	5

If the economy uses all its resources to produce only smart phones, it can produce a maximum of 15 000 000 smart phones (possibility *A*). If it uses all its resources to produce only personal computers, it can produce 5 000 000 computers (possibility *F*). Between these two extreme cases are many combinations of smart phones and computers that the economy can produce. For example, Table 2.1 shows that the economy can produce 12 000 000 smart phones and 1 000 000 computers (possibility B); or it can produce 3 000 000 smart phones and 4 000 000 computers (possibility *E*). Note that for every 1 000 000 computers produced, the economy has to give up 3 000 000 smart phones. Thus, the opportunity cost of 1 000 000 computers is 3 000 000 smart phones. In this example, the opportunity cost remains constant throughout.

Table 2.1 is referred to as a **production possibilities (p-p) schedule**, which is a tabular representation of an economy's production possibilities. It shows the various combinations of goods and services (in this case, smart phones and computers) that an economy can produce with a given state of technology if it uses all its resources.

Note that the economy can produce 6 000 000 smart phones and 1 000 000 computers; but in so doing, it will not be using all its resources. Note also that if it is producing 6 000 000 smart phones, it cannot at the same time produce 4 000 000 computers. Why not? Because it does not have enough resources.

production possibility (p-p) schedule a table showing various combinations of goods and services that can be produced with full utilization of all resources and a given state of technology

What is a production possibilities curve?

The information contained in the production possibilities schedule can be shown on a graph. With smart phones on the vertical axis and computers on the horizontal axis, we can plot all six combinations of smart phones and computers represented by possibilities *A* to *F* in Table 2.1. This is done in Figure 2.2. The curve shows the maximum

production possibilities (p-p) curve a graph showing all combinations of goods and services that can be produced if all resources are fully employed and technology is constant

number of smart phones and the maximum number of computers that this hypothetical economy can produce with given technology at a particular time. The curve is a **production possibilities curve (p-p curve)** or production possibilities frontier (p-p frontier), which is a graphical representation of an economy's production possibilities. It shows all combinations of commodities that can be produced if all resources are fully employed and technology is constant.

The curve in Figure 2.2 is linear (a straight line) because we have assumed a constant opportunity cost; each unit of computers costs exactly the same quantity of smart phones. In other words, the production of computers could be traded off for the production of smart phones at a fixed rate of three smart phones for one computer. A linear production possibilities curve illustrates constant opportunity cost.

Figure 2.2	A Production Possibilities Curve Showing Constant Opportunity Cost

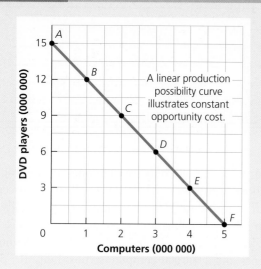

Are production possibilities curves always linear?

No. In fact, in the real world, we are unlikely to encounter situations of constant opportunity cost in production. Constant opportunity cost in production would occur only if all resources were equally efficient in all uses. This clearly is not the case. Some human resources, for example, are better equipped to perform technical work than mental work; and some parcels of land are more suitable for agricultural purposes than are others. In reality, resources are not all equally efficient in all lines of production. Some resources will produce smart phones more efficiently than they will computers. As we continue to shift resources from smart phone production to computer production, we are likely to experience increasing cost. This happens because these resources are likely to become less efficient in the production of computers. For example, it may be relatively easy at first to shift workers from smart phone production to computer production. As the process continues, however, it will become increasingly difficult to find smart phone workers who are efficient in computer production. After all, the number of excellent workers in the production of smart phones who are just as efficient in computer production is limited. For this reason, p-p curves are unlikely to be linear.

BUSINESS SITUATION 2.1

A manufacturer of neckties has a given amount of money that can be used to produce silk ties and polyester ties. Producing more silk ties is possible only at the expense of polyester ties.

What tool can this manufacturer use to illustrate this trade-off situation?

The answer to this Business Situation can be found in Appendix A.

What is the likely shape of a production possibilities curve?

Table 2.2 will help to answer the question. We retain the assumptions that the economy uses all its resources and that it has a given technology.

Table 2.2	A Production Possibilities Schedule Showing Increasing Cost	
Possibilities	Number of Smart Phones (000 000)	Number of Computers (000 000)
A	15	0
B	14	1
C	12	2
D	9	3
E	5	4
F	0	5

Table 2.2 shows that if the economy produces 15 000 000 smart phones it cannot produce any computers. To produce the first 1 000 000 computers, it must shift resources from smart phone production to computer production. In so doing, the quantity of small phones produced falls to 14 000 000. The economy has to give up 1 000 000 smart phones for 1 000 000 computers. To produce another 1 000 0000 computers, the economy must give up 2 000 000 smart phones this time. (The quantity of smart phones falls from 14 000 000 to 12 000 000.) So the opportunity cost of the second 1 000 000 computers is 2 000 000 smart phones. The third 1 000 000 computers can be obtained at an additional cost of 3 000 000 smart phones. According to Table 2.2, the fourth 1 000 000 computers cost 4 000 000 smart phones, and the fifth 1 000 000 computers cost 5 000 000 smart phones. Table 2.3 summarizes the cost of computers in terms of smart phones.

Clearly, as the economy increases its production of computers, the cost of additional computers (in terms of smart phones) rises. Just about any productive activity that you can think of will display increasing opportunity cost.

Is there a name for this phenomenon of increasing cost?

law of increasing opportunity cost the phenomenon of increasing unit cost as an economy increases its production of a commodity

Economists refer to this phenomenon of increasing cost as **the law of increasing opportunity cost**, which states that as an economy increases its production of a commodity, the cost per unit of production rises.

Table 2.3	The Opportunity Cost of Computers in Terms of Smart Phones
Computer	Opportunity Cost in Smart Phones
First 1 000 000 computers	1 000 000 smart phones
Second 1 000 000 computers	2 000 000 smart phones
Third 1 000 000 computers	3 000 000 smart phones
Fourth 1 000 000 computers	4 000 000 smart phones
Fifth 1 000 000 computers	5 000 000 smart phones

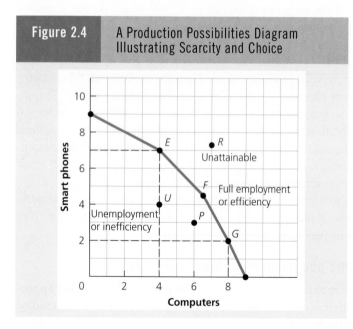

Figure 2.3   A Production Possibilities Curve Showing Increasing Opportunity Cost

A concave production possibility curve illustrates increasing opportunity cost.

Figure 2.4   A Production Possibilities Diagram Illustrating Scarcity and Choice

We have established that production will display increasing cost, but we still have not answered the question: What is the likely shape of the production possibilities curve?

We can answer that right now. Let us plot the information in Table 2.2 on a graph. The resulting graph is shown as Figure 2.3.

Note that the horizontal segments *QB*, *RC*, *SD*, *TE*, and *UF* are all equal, representing equal increases in units of computers. The vertical segments *QA*, *BR*, *CS*, *DT*, and *EU* represent the units of smart phones that must be sacrificed to obtain the additional units of computers. Thus, to increase the production of computers from 1 000 000 to 2 000 000 (*RC*), the economy must give up 2 000 000 smart phones (*BR*). To increase the production of computers from 2 000 000 to 3 000 000 (*SD*), the economy must give up 3 000 000 smart phones (*CS*); and to increase the production of computers from 4 000 000 to 5 000 000 (*UF*), the economy must give up 5 000 000 smart phones (*EU*). Note that *EU* > *DT* > *CS* > *BR*. This means that the opportunity cost of a unit of computers increases as the economy increase its production of computers. A curve that is bowed outward like the curve in Figure 2.3 is said to be concave. A concave production possibilities curve illustrates increasing opportunity cost. Because of the prevalence of increasing opportunity cost, the p-p curve is likely to be concave.

Now we know that the production possibilities model can be used to illustrate opportunity cost. Can it be used also to illustrate scarcity and choice?

Consider the production possibilities diagram in Figure 2.4. All points on the curve, such as *E*, *F*, and *G*, represent combinations of smart phones and computers that the economy can produce with full employment of all available resources and with its current state of technology. Therefore, points on the p-p curve represent full employment.

Notice that once the economy is operating on its p-p curve, it cannot increase its production of one commodity without reducing its production of some other commodity. Economists use the term **productive efficiency** to describe this situation. Such points as *U* and *P*, which lie below the p-p curve, represent unemployment of resources. An economy that is operating below its p-p curve is not producing its maximum output of goods and services. Economists use the term **productive inefficiency** to describe an economy in which it is possible to produce more of one commodity without producing

productive efficiency the situation that exists when an economy cannot increase its production of one commodity without reducing its production of some other commodity

productive inefficiency the situation that exists when it is possible to produce more of one commodity without producing less of some other commodity

less of some other commodity. Such a point as *R* represents a combination of smart phones and computers that lies beyond the economy's productive capacity. Such a combination is currently unattainable. The diagram illustrates scarcity. If the economy is operating at point *E*, producing seven units of smart phones and four units of computers, and decides to increase its production of computers to eight units, it can do so only by reducing its production of smart phones, moving from point *E* to point *G*. The necessary reduction in the production of smart phones is a result of scarcity, as is the fact that combination *R* is unattainable. With more resources, the economy could conceivably attain combination *R*. Scarcity forces the economy to choose among various production alternatives that are available. With full use of its resources and given technology, the economy must choose among points along the p-p curve.

free lunch the additional output produced without sacrificing the production of any other good or service

Can the economy ever be in a situation where it can produce more of one item without giving up any of another item?

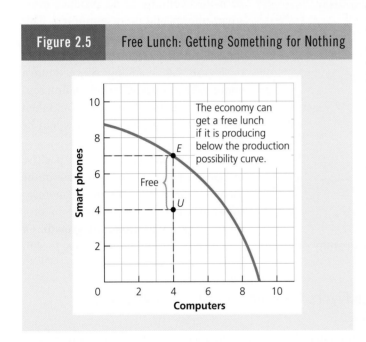

| Figure 2.5 | Free Lunch: Getting Something for Nothing |

That is an interesting question. Let us answer it with the help of Figure 2.5. Assume that the economy is operating at point *U*, producing four units of smart phones and four units of computers. At *U*, there is unemployment. By using unemployed resources, the economy can move to point *E* on the p-p curve, producing seven units of smart phones and still four units of computers. Thus, the economy produces three additional units of smart phones without sacrificing any computers. The economy manages to obtain three smart phones at zero opportunity cost. This is a case of a **free lunch**—getting something for nothing or, more formally, having additional output produced without sacrificing the production of any other good or service. Because the increased output associated with the move from *U* to *E* does not involve sacrificing any output, we can conclude that the opportunity cost of unemployed resources is zero.

Reading Comprehension

The answers to these questions can be found on MyEconLab at **www.myeconlab.com.**   MyEconLab

1. What does a linear p-p curve tell us about opportunity cost?
2. Explain why p-p curves are more likely to be concave than linear.

3. State the law of increasing opportunity cost.
4. Define the following:
   a) Productive efficiency
   b) Productive inefficiency
5. In economics, there is no way of getting something for nothing (no free lunch). Do you agree? Explain fully.

Shifts in the Production Possibilities Curve

How will an increase in the quantity or quality of resources, or an increase in technology, affect an economy's p-p curve?

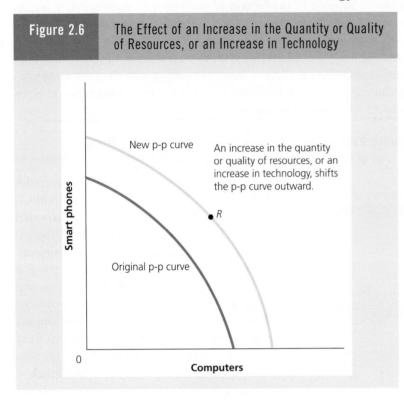

| Figure 2.6 | The Effect of an Increase in the Quantity or Quality of Resources, or an Increase in Technology |

New p-p curve

An increase in the quantity or quality of resources, or an increase in technology, shifts the p-p curve outward.

• R

Smart phones

Original p-p curve

0

Computers

economic growth an increase in the economy's productive capacity

Let's look at Figure 2.6. Point *R* lies beyond the original p-p curve and is therefore currently unattainable. It represents a combination of smart phones and computers that this economy cannot produce with its available resources and its current state of technology. Should technology advance or should the quantity or quality of its resources increase, then the economy could produce more smart phones and more computers. This would result in a new p-p curve lying to the right of the original curve as shown in Figure 2.6, enabling the economy, conceivably, to attain a combination represented by point *R*. Point *R* would then lie on the new p-p curve, and would be attainable.

The outward shift of the p-p curve in Figure 2.6 represents an increase in the economy's productive capacity. Economists sometimes refer to this increase in productive capacity as **economic growth**. Of course, a decrease in the quantity or quality of resources will cause the p-p curve to shift inward, to the left.

The new p-p curve in Figure 2.6 is parallel to the original curve. Is this usually the case?

The parallel shift of the p-p curve implies that the increase in the quantity or quality of resources or the technological advance that caused the curve to shift affected the production of smart phones and the production of computers to the same extent. It will more often be the case that technology and changes in the quantity and quality of resources will affect different industries differently. For example, the introduction of robotics into the manufacturing of automobiles will affect that industry while having no impact on agriculture.

How will the production possibilities curve relating to the manufacturing industry and the fishing industry be affected by technological advance in only manufacturing or only fishing?

If the technological advance occurred only in the manufacturing industry, then the ability to produce manufactured goods would increase while the ability to produce fish and fish products would remain unchanged. The p-p curve would shift out in a non-parallel

Figure 2.7	A Technological Advance in Only One Industry

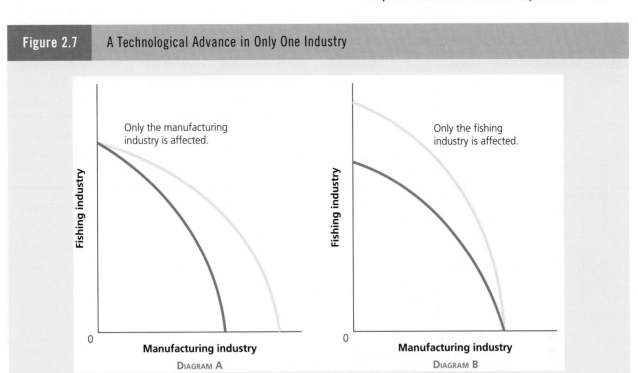

Diagram A: Technological advance in manufacturing only

Diagram B: Technological advance in fishing only

manner, as shown in Diagram A of Figure 2.7. Similarly, if the technological advance occurred only in the fishing industry, then the growth attributed to the technological advance would occur only in the fishing industry. The p-p curve would again shift out in a non-parallel manner, as illustrated by Diagram B of Figure 2.7.

Does an increase or a decrease in actual production shift the economy's production possibilities curve?

No. Only a change in the quantity or quality of the economy's resources or a change in technology will shift the p-p curve. A shift in the production possibilities curve means that the economy's productive capacity has changed. If, for example, new resources are discovered but not yet used, the p-p curve will shift to the right, because the economy now has the potential to produce more goods and services, even though it is not using that potential. If, however, existing resources that were previously not used are now being utilized, then actual production will increase, but the economy's p-p curve would not shift because there would be no increase in the economy's productive capacity.

How does an economy's decision to increase its current production of capital goods at the expense of consumer goods affect its p-p curve in the future?

The decision to produce more capital goods and fewer consumer goods means that the economy is sacrificing current consumption while building up its capital stock. With a

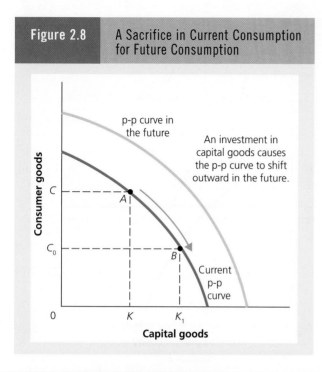

Figure 2.8 A Sacrifice in Current Consumption for Future Consumption

larger capital stock in the future, the economy would be able to produce more capital goods *and* more consumer goods. In other words, the economy's p-p curve will shift out to the right in the future. Figure 2.8 illustrates the point. Let us assume that the economy decides to move from point *A* to point *B*, reducing its production of consumer goods from $0C$ to $0C_0$ and increasing its production of capital goods from $0K$ to $0K_1$. Because of the increase in capital resources in the future, the p-p curve would shift out in the future, enabling the economy to produce both more consumer goods and more capital goods.

Reading Comprehension

The answers to these questions can be found on MyEconLab at **www.myeconlab.com.**   MyEconLab

1. Give three examples of specific events that would cause Canada's p-p curve to shift out to the right.

2. How can economic growth be illustrated on a p-p diagram?
3. Explain why a fall in prices will not shift an economy's p-p curve.
4. Explain why p-p curves are unlikely to shift in or out in a parallel manner.

LO 2.4   Explain the fundamental economic questions and classify them as microeconomic or macroeconomic issues

Fundamental Economic Questions

What are the fundamental questions of microeconomics?

The fundamental microeconomic questions can be stated quite briefly as

- What?
- How?
- For whom?

What does the "What" refer to?

What refers to what goods and services will the economy produce and in what quantities. Will the economy produce automobiles, houses, grapes, milk, computers, musical instruments, television sets, oil, electricity, roads, and so on? In what quantities will it produce them? Because of the ever-present problem of scarcity, more of one thing means less of some other thing. If more hospital beds are provided, fewer classrooms might be the consequence. What to produce and how much are important decisions that every economy has to make.

What does the "How" refer to?

Once the decisions have been made regarding the types and quantities of goods and services that will be produced, a decision has to be made regarding how the goods and services will be produced. How will apples be harvested? Will it be done manually or with the help of specialized machinery? What method of production will be used in producing automobiles? Will robotics be used instead of labour for certain activities? *How* refers to the method of production that will be used in producing the goods and services that have been decided on. The economy's scarce resources can be combined in many ways to produce goods and services. The economy must decide which to use.

What does "For whom" refer to?

For whom refers to who gets the goods and services after they have been produced. Once the "what" and the "how" questions have been addressed, a decision must be made regarding the distribution of the goods and services among the various members of the community. Should all the available goods and services produced be divided equally among all members of society, or should some people get a larger share than others?

What are some of the important issues of macroeconomics?

The list of macroeconomic problems and issues is arbitrary, but we can identify five issues that are fundamental to macroeconomics.

aggregate output the total volume of goods and services produced in the economy

Aggregate Output   First, macroeconomics is concerned with **aggregate output**, the total volume of goods and services produced in the economy. This is an important issue because our standard of living is directly related to the volume of goods and services that our economy produces. The standard of living refers to the volume of goods and services available for consumption. If a society can keep the total output of goods and services close to the economy's potential, its citizens will be better off. Closely associated with the volume of goods and services produced are fluctuations in the total output of goods and services. Economists refer to these alternating periods of ups and downs in aggregate production as **business cycles**. Economic fluctuations can result in unemployment and inflation—two other important macroeconomic problems that policymakers often have to deal with.

business cycles fluctuations in the aggregate output of goods and services

unemployment the condition that exists when people who are willing and able to work at prevailing wage rates are unable to find jobs

Unemployment   Second is **unemployment**, the condition that exists when people who are willing and able to work at prevailing wage rates are unable to find jobs. If an economy is operating at a high level of efficiency, at a point near to its p-p curve, then unemployment will be low. If the economy is operating at a low level of efficiency and output, then unemployment will likely be high. Clearly, unemployment is tied to people's income and hence to their ability to purchase the goods and services required to satisfy their wants. Why does our economy often fail to generate full employment?

inflation a sustained increase in the average level of prices over time; a persistent increase in the cost of living

Inflation   The third crucial macroeconomic issue is the problem of **inflation**: a sustained increase in the average level of prices over time. In your lifetime, you have noticed that a dollar does not buy as much as it used to 10 years ago. Your parents have noticed even more substantial losses in the value of a dollar. When the dollar loses

Economic growth enables Canadians to enjoy high living standards.

value or purchasing power, it means that the cost of living rises. The **cost of living** is the amount of money you have to spend to obtain goods and services. Inflation is a persistent increase in the cost of living. Most people dislike inflation because they realize that they have to spend more money to acquire a given amount of goods and services.

Some countries have lived with rates of inflation of 200% and higher. In general, developed countries tend to have low inflation, while developing counties tend to have high inflation. It is reported that the rate of inflation in Zimbabwe in 2008 was 24 000%. In Canada, we have not had to cope with inflationary situations of the magnitude that many developing countries experience. Yet economists are aware of the dangers of high rates of inflation and are constantly seeking a better understanding of the inflationary process.

cost of living the amount of money that must be paid to obtain goods and services

Economic Growth   Fourth is economic growth. The Canadian economy has experienced economic growth over the past several decades. Our economy is now producing more goods and services than it did in the 1960s and 1970s; consequently, our standard of living has increased. Economic growth requires not only that we use our resources efficiently but also that we increase our productive capacity over time. What are the factors that contribute most to economic growth? What can be done to achieve and maintain a prolonged period of economic growth? Clearly, economic growth has important benefits, but what are the costs? These are important questions that macroeconomics tries to answer.

The International Economy   Last is the international economy. The Canadian economy does not exist in isolation. In fact, almost every economy in the world is affected by factors outside its own borders. The world economies have become more interdependent than ever before. Trading blocks have been formed and new trading blocks continue to be created. Globalization is now an economic reality. How do events in the rest of the world affect the Canadian economy? For example, when the price of crude oil hits a record high, does it have any effect on the Canadian economy? Will Canadian businesses be able to compete with businesses elsewhere in the world? Will Canadian producers be able to find markets in the rest of the world? Macroeconomics tries to find answers to such questions.

BUSINESS SITUATION 2.2

On October 27, 2006, Toronto-based Maple Leaf Foods Inc. blamed its third-quarter loss of $22.3 million in part on the higher Canadian dollar.

How might a strong Canadian dollar adversely affect Maple Leaf Foods?

The answer to this Business Situation can be found in Appendix A.

Reading Comprehension

The answers to these questions can be found on MyEconLab at **www.myeconlab.com.**   MyEconLab

1. What are the fundamental microeconomic questions?

2. What do the following microeconomic questions refer to: what? how? and for whom?

3. Identify four important macroeconomic questions or issues and explain briefly why each is important.

4. Why would ordinary Canadians be interested in the cost of living?

LO 2.5 Construct a circular flow model and explain the flow of goods, services, and resources in the economy

The Simple Circular Flow Model

What is the circular flow model?

Businesses (we can call them firms) purchase resources (land, labour, capital, and entrepreneurship) and use them to produce goods and services for sale to their customers. The sellers of the resources receive income in the form of rent, wages and salaries, interest and dividends, and profits, which they use to purchase goods and services from the firms. The expenditures of the firms' customers accrue to the firms as their income or revenue, which they use to purchase resources; and the process continues. This flow of resources, goods and services, expenditures, and income between sectors of the economy is referred to as the **circular flow**.

Can the circular flow model be illustrated by a diagram?

Let us make the following simplifying assumptions:

1. The economy consists of only two sectors: households and firms. **Households** make decisions about what resources to sell and what goods and services to buy. **Firms** make decisions about what resources to purchase and how the resources will be used to produce goods and services for sale to the households.

2. All the economy's resources are owned by the households.

3. Money is used in all exchanges. That is, firms use money to buy the factors of production, and households use money to buy goods and services.

4. The income received by households is spent in purchasing goods and services, and the income (revenue) received by firms is spent in purchasing resources.

Figure 2.9 illustrates the circular flow model. The sale of resources and the sale of goods and services take place in markets. A **market** is a mechanism that facilitates the buying and selling of resources and goods and services. You probably think of a market as a place where people buy and sell things. For example, you may have purchased your new Nike or Brooks running shoes in a market, and you purchased your last movie ticket in a market. Similarly, firms, such as the Bay, buy labour services in a market. But a market is not necessarily a geographic location. Today, many buying and selling activities take place without any physical meeting of the buyers and sellers. A great deal of buying and selling is done via airmail, telephone, and the internet. Let's study Figure 2.9.

circular flow an economic model that shows the flow of resources, goods and services, expenditures, and income between sectors of the economy

households the economic sector that makes decisions about what resources to sell and what goods and services to buy

firms the economic sector that makes decisions about what resources to purchase and how the resources will be used to produce goods and services

market the mechanism that facilitates the buying and selling of resources and goods and services

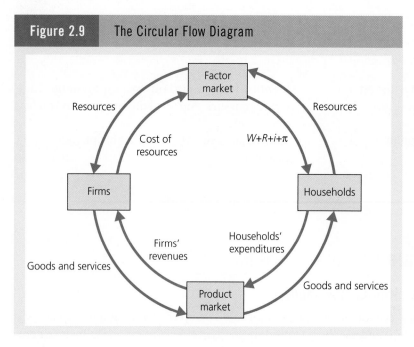

| Figure 2.9 | The Circular Flow Diagram |

We can begin with the households because we have assumed that they have the resources. You will notice that resources flow from the households to the factor market. The direction of flow is indicated by arrows. The **factor market**, also called the **resource market**, is the market in which factors of production are traded (bought and sold). For example, firms buy steel and raw materials and labour services in the factor market.

Firms buy and households sell resources in the factor market. After the exchange of resources for money, we see a flow of resources from the factor market to the firms, and a flow of income from the factor market to the households. The flow of income from the factor market to the households consists of wages (W), rent (R), interest and dividends (i), and profits (π).

factor market or resource market the market in which factors of production are bought and sold

product market or goods and services market the market in which goods and services (products) are bought and sold

Now the firms have resources and the households have income (money). By the process of production, the firms convert the resources into goods and services, which they sell to households in the **product market**, also called the **goods and services market**, the market in which goods and services are bought and sold. For example, consumers buy clothes, vacations, furniture, and automobiles in product markets. You will notice a flow of goods and services from the firms to the product market, and a flow of expenditures from the households to the product market.

Firms sell and households buy goods and services in the product market. After the exchange of goods and services for money in the product market, we see a flow of goods and services from the product market to the households, and a flow of income (revenues) from the product market to the firms.

Note that the roles of buyers and sellers are reversed in the product and factor markets. In the factor market, the sellers are the households, while the buyers are the firms. In the product market, the sellers are the firms, while the buyers are the households.

What is the difference between real flows and money flows?

Let us look again at Figure 2.9. Look specifically at the flow of land, labour, capital, and entrepreneurship from households to the factor market, and at the flow of these resources from the factor market to the firms. Look also at the flow of goods and services from the firms to the product market, and at the flow of these goods and services from the product market to the households. Such flows are referred to as **real flows** and are the flows of real, physical goods and services, such as Blackberries, laser jet printers, refrigerators, and medical services, and resources such as plastic, water, machinery, and raw materials. Because of the way in which this diagram is arranged, these flows happen to be the outer flows in this model.

real flows flows of real, physical goods and services and resources

Look now at the flow of expenditure from the firms to the factor market, and at the flow of income (rent, wages and salaries, interest and dividends, and profits) from the

money flows flows of income and expenditures in monetary terms

factor market to the households. Look also at the flow of expenditures from the households to the product market, and at the flow of income or revenues from the product market to the firms. Such flows are referred to as **money flows** and are the flows of income and expenditures in monetary terms. Examples of money flows are $600 a week on groceries for a family, $6000 a year for college fees, $5000 a week that a firm spends in wages and $100 000 a year for office space. Because of the way in which this diagram is arranged, these flows happen to be the inner flows in this model. In this particular model, the money flows are the values of the real flows, or alternatively, the real flows are what can be bought with the money flows.

Reading Comprehension

The answers to these questions can be found on MyEconLab at **www.myeconlab.com.**   MyEconLab

1. Explain the roles of households and firms in the factor market and the product market. Give one example each of a product market and a factor market.

2. In the real world, earning a profit is associated with firms. Why, in the circular flow model, do households earn profits?

3. Distinguish between real flows and money flows. Give an example each of a real flow and a money flow in the circular flow model.

Review

1. Review the learning objectives listed at the beginning of the chapter.
2. Have you accomplished all the objectives? One way to determine this is to answer the Reading Comprehension questions at the end of each section. They will help you assess the extent to which you have accomplished the learning objectives.
3. If you have not accomplished an objective, review the relevant material before proceeding.

Key Points to Remember

1. **LO 2.1** Because of scarcity, we are forced to choose, and when we choose, we give up something. Whatever it is that we give up when we make a choice is referred to as opportunity cost.
2. **LO 2.2** Productive efficiency is the term used to describe the situation that exists when the economy is operating on its p-p curve. Productive inefficiency describes the situation that exists when the economy is operating below its p-p curve. A point beyond the p-p curve represents an unattainable combination of goods and services.

3. **LO 2.2** If an economy is operating below its p-p curve and then moves to a point on the curve, it will produce additional commodities without having to give up any output. The additional output will be obtained at zero opportunity cost to the economy. That is the case of a free lunch.
4. **LO 2.3** The p-p curve will shift if the quantity or quality of resources or the level of technology changes. An outward shift of the p-p curve is referred to as economic growth.
5. **LO 2.4** The fundamental questions of microeconomics are (1) what goods and services are to be produced and in what quantities? (2) how will the goods and services be produced? That is, what method of production is to be employed in producing goods and services? (3) who will get the goods and services that the economy produces?
6. **LO 2.4** Important macroeconomic questions include the following: What are the factors that determine the volume of goods and services that the economy produces and why does the economy sometimes experience wide fluctuations in aggregate output? Why does the economy

often fail to generate full employment? What causes inflation? What are the factors that contribute to economic growth? What is the relationship between the domestic economy and the international economy?

7. **LO 2.5** The circular flow model is an economic model that shows the flow of resources, goods and services, expenditures, and income between sectors of the economy. Households are the economic sector that makes decisions about what resources to sell and what goods and services to purchase. Firms are the economic sector that makes decisions about what resources to purchase and how to use them to produce goods and services.

Economic Word Power

Aggregate output   (p. 59)
Business cycles   (p. 59)
Circular flow   (p. 61)
Cost of living   (p. 60)
Cost-benefit approach   (p. 50)
Economic growth   (p. 56)
Factor market or resource market   (p. 62)
Firms   (p. 61)
Free lunch   (p. 55)
Households   (p. 61)
Inflation   (p. 59)
Law of increasing opportunity cost   (p. 53)
Market   (p. 61)
Money flows   (p. 63)
Opportunity cost   (p. 48)
Product market or goods and services market   (p. 62)
Production possibilities (p-p) curve   (p. 52)
Production possibilities (p-p) schedule   (p. 51)
Productive efficiency   (p. 54)
Productive inefficiency   (p. 54)
Real flows   (p. 62)
Unemployment   (p. 59)

Problems and Exercises

Basic

1. **LO 2.1** If you did not give up anything, you did not choose; hence, you did not incur any opportunity cost. Discuss.

2. **LO 2.1** Name an opportunity cost associated with each of the following choices:
   a. You decided to go to Europe during your vacation.
   b. You chose to purchase a used car for $8000.
   c. You watched a two-hour movie on television.
   d. You decided to eat out at a restaurant.
   e. You chose to spend two years at college.

3. **LO 2.2** Table 2.4 has information about an economy that produces only books and cartons with its available resources.

Table 2.4	A Production Possibilities Schedule for Books and Cartons	
Combinations	**Books** (000)	**Cartons** (000)
A	0	10
B	1	9
C	2	7
D	3	4
E	4	0

a. If the economy is producing only cartons and then decides to produce 1000 books, what is the opportunity cost of the 1000 books in terms of cartons?
b. On the basis of the data contained in the table, draw the economy's production possibilities curve.
c. On your diagram, indicate a point of productive inefficiency with the letter *U*.
d. Indicate a point of full employment with the letter *F*.
e. Indicate an unattainable combination of books and cartons with the letter *O*.

4. **LO 2.3** Show how each of the following events will affect a country's production possibilities curve:
   a. A large number of people emigrate from the country.
   b. The country discovers new resources.
   c. A more efficient method of production is discovered but not yet implemented.
   d. Unemployed workers are hired.

5. **LO 2.5** Indicate whether each of the following is true or false as it relates to the simple circular flow model with only households and firms:
   a. Firms sell resources to the households.
   b. The firms' income includes wages, rent, and interest.
   c. Firms sell their output in the product market.
   d. Households sell resources in the factor market.
   e. Households operate only in the product market, buying goods and services.
   f. Firms operate in both product and factor markets.

6. **LO 2.3** An economy is producing only two goods, apples and butter, under conditions of increasing opportunity cost. Use diagrams to illustrate how each of the following will affect the economy's production possibilities curve:

   a. A technological improvement in the production of apples that does not affect butter production

   b. The discovery of new resources that affect the production of apples and butter equally

   c. A technological improvement in the production of butter that does not affect apple production

7. **LO 2.5** Using *P* for the product market and *F* for the factor market, indicate the market in which the exchanges in Table 2.5 are likely to occur.

Table 2.5	Product and Factor Markets
Exchange	**Market**
a. A book publisher sells books to bookstores.	_____
b. A book publisher buys paper from a firm.	_____
c. The government buys furniture from a firm.	_____
d. Businesses borrow money from banks.	_____
e. A government employs new civil servants.	_____
f. Households buy electrical appliances.	_____

Questions in the Intermediate and Challenging Sections cover several different concepts, and have not been organized by learning objectives.

Intermediate

1. In the circular flow diagram in Figure 2.10, the inner flows are money flows, while the outer flows are real flows. The arrows indicate the direction of the flows. *H* represents households and *F* represents firms.

   a. In the spaces below, list the items that make up the inner flow from the factor market to the households.

   _____

   _____

   _____

   _____

   b. On the diagram, label the flows shown by the letters.

2. An economy produces only two goods: capital goods and consumer goods. Its production possibilities curve is shown in Figure 2.11. The economy has a choice of operating at point A or point B. At which point should this economy operate if economic growth is a high priority?

3. Use the concept of opportunity cost to explain why attendance at colleges and universities might increase during periods of high unemployment and job shortages.

4. There would be no need to choose if scarcity did not exist. Discuss.

5. Indicate whether the following statement is true or false and give the reason for your choice: "An outward shift of an economy's p-p curve means that the economy is actually producing a greater quantity of goods and/or services."

Figure 2.10 A Simple Circular Flow Model

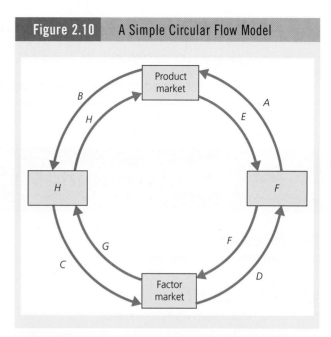

Figure 2.11 A Production Possibilities Curve

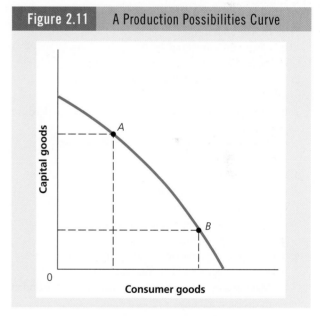

Challenging

1. Explain why, other things being equal, a business executive would be less willing than would his or her administrative assistant to stand in line at a supermarket for 10 minutes. (Hint: Use the concept of opportunity cost.)

2. Use production possibilities curves to illustrate the effect of capital formation now and five years in the future, for two countries, one with a relatively high and the other with a relatively low rate of capital formation.

Study Guide

Self-Assessment

The answers to the Study Guide questions can be found in Appendix B.

What's your score?

Circle the letter that corresponds with the correct answer.

1. Choice involves
   a. Taking something without giving up anything
   b. Giving up nothing
   c. Giving up something
   d. All of the above

2. The opportunity cost of an item is
   a. The market price of the item
   b. The monetary cost of the resources used to produce the item
   c. The profit realized from the sale of the item
   d. None of the above

3. Opportunity cost
   a. Exists in theory but not in practice
   b. Exists in practice but not in theory
   c. Exists both in theory and in practice
   d. Is always zero when it exists

4. The cost-benefit approach to decision making involves
   a. Adding together all benefits and costs
   b. Making sure that opportunity costs are not included in decision making
   c. Reducing opportunity costs to zero
   d. Comparing benefits and costs

5. A production possibilities curve shows
   a. All combinations of goods and services consumed in the economy
   b. The total value of all goods and services produced in the economy
   c. All possible ways of producing goods and services
   d. The boundary between combinations of goods and services that are attainable through production and those that are unattainable

6. A linear production possibilities curve implies
   a. Constant opportunity cost
   b. Increasing opportunity cost

   c. Zero opportunity cost
   d. None of the above

7. A production possibilities curve showing increasing opportunity cost is
   a. Linear and upward sloping
   b. Linear and downward sloping
   c. Convex and downward sloping
   d. None of the above

8. Which of the following will cause a country's p-p curve to shift to the right?
   a. The country acquires more resources
   b. The country increases production by hiring previously unemployed workers
   c. Prices in the country fall
   d. All of the above

9. The phenomenon of rising unit production cost as an economy produces more of an item is called
   a. The law of production possibilities
   b. The law of alternative production
   c. The law of no free lunch
   d. The law of increasing opportunity cost

10. A production possibilities diagram shows all of the following except
    a. Opportunity cost
    b. Price
    c. Scarcity
    d. Choice

11. A situation in which the economy cannot produce more of one commodity without producing less of some other commodity is labelled
    a. Production inability
    b. A state of unattainability
    c. Productive inefficiency
    d. Productive efficiency

Questions 12 and 13 refer to Figure 2.12.

12. According to the diagram, the economy is facing
    a. Constant opportunity cost
    b. Zero opportunity
    c. Increasing opportunity cost
    d. It is impossible to tell

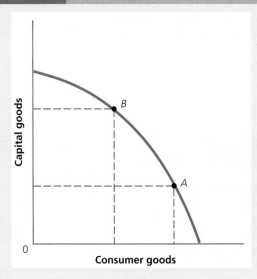

Figure 2.12   A Production Possibilities Curve

c. What determines the level of unemployment in the economy?

d. Why does aggregate output fluctuate?

18. When the dollar loses value
    a. The cost of living rises
    b. The cost of living falls
    c. Most people are better off
    d. Only the poor are adversely affected

19. Which of the following is a true statement?
    a. The factor market is the market in which firms buy goods and services
    b. The product market is the market in which firms sell resources
    c. The product market is the market in which households buy resources
    d. The factor market is the market in which firms buy resources

20. Flows of income and expenditures are
    a. Real flows
    b. Money flows
    c. Normative flows
    d. None of the above

13. If the economy decides to move from point *A* to point *B*
    a. The opportunity cost would be zero
    b. The opportunity cost would be increased production of capital goods
    c. The production possibilities curve would shift to the right in the future
    d. The production possibilities curve would shift to the left in the future

14. The *what* in what, how, and for whom refers to
    a. The price to charge for an item to make the most money
    b. The technology to use to produce goods and services
    c. What to do with the goods and services that have been produced
    d. None of the above

15. The microeconomic questions of *what, how*, and *for whom* arise because of
    a. Scarcity
    b. Poor economic decisions
    c. An overabundance of resources in the economy
    d. All of the above

16. The microeconomic question of *what* refers to
    a. What cost will be incurred in producing goods and services
    b. What method of production will be used in producing goods and services
    c. What resources are available to produce goods and services
    d. What goods and services will be produced and in what quantities

17. Which of the following is not a macroeconomic question?
    a. What determines the aggregate output of goods and services produced in an economy?
    b. What prices should a firm charge for its product to maximize its profits?

Problems and Exercises (Use Quad Paper for Graphs)

1. Table 2.6 shows various combinations of television sets and radios that an economy can produce with a given technology and full utilization of all its resources.

Table 2.6   The Possible Production of Maximum Quantities of TV Sets and Radios

Quantity of TV Sets (000)	Quantity of Radios (000)
0	37
1	35
2	32
3	29
4	20
5	11
6	0

a. On the basis of Table 2.6, complete Table 2.7 showing the opportunity cost of TV sets in terms of radios.

b. Determine whether this economy faces constant or increasing opportunity cost in producing TV sets. Explain.

2. a. Draw a production possibilities curve showing increasing opportunity cost.

   b. On your diagram, indicate a point of unemployment with the letter *U*.

c. Indicate a point of productive efficiency with the letter *E*.

d. Indicate an unattainable production combination with the letter *x*.

Table 2.7	The Opportunity Cost of TV Sets
TV Sets	**Opportunity Cost in Radios**
First 1 000 TV sets	_____
Second 1 000 TV sets	_____
Third 1 000 TV sets	_____
Fourth 1 000 TV sets	_____
Fifth 1 000 TV sets	_____
Sixth 1 000 TV sets	_____

3. An economy produces only two goods: furniture and tours around the country. Assume that the economy operates under conditions of increasing opportunity cost. Use graphs to show how each of the following events will affect the country's production possibilities curve:

   a. A number of immigrants take up residence in the country

   b. A fall in prices causes consumers to buy more goods and services

   c. People migrate to the country but are unable to find work

   d. Research leads to the discovery of a more efficient method of production

   e. Employment increases because firms hire more workers to meet increasing demand for their products

4. Referring to Question 3, draw a production possibilities diagram illustrating the effect of a technological advance that affects only the furniture industry.

5. An economy hires five previously unemployed workers and pays them $400 per week each. What is the opportunity cost of the extra output produced by these five new workers?

6. Table 2.8 shows production possibilities for a hypothetical economy.

Table 2.8	Production Possibilities
Number of Word Processors (000)	**Number of Calculators** (000)
0	15
1	14
2	12
3	9
4	5
5	0

a. What is the table called?

b. Plot the points on a graph and connect them.

c. What is the graph called?

d. Does this economy face constant or increasing opportunity cost?

7. A small country produces only two goods: shoes and corn. Various combinations of maximum quantities of shoes and corn that the country can produce are shown in Table 2.9.

Table 2.9	The Production Possibilities for Corn and Shoes
Quantities of Corn (000 metric tons)	**Quantities of Shoes** (000 pairs)
100	0
90	10
70	20
40	30
0	40

a. With thousands of metric tons of corn on the vertical axis and thousands of pairs of shoes on the horizontal axis, plot the data in the table on a graph.

b. What is the opportunity cost of the first 10 000 pairs of shoes?

c. What is the opportunity cost of the third 10 000 pairs of shoes?

d. What is the opportunity cost of 40 000 pairs of shoes?

8. Complete Table 2.10 by indicating whether each of the following is a major microeconomic or macroeconomic issue.

Table 2.10	Major Microeconomic and Macroeconomic Issues
Issue	**Classification**
What to produce	_____
Fluctuations in total output	_____
How to combine resources in production	_____
Increases in the cost of living	_____
The level of employment in the economy	_____
The distribution of output among consumers	_____

9. Construct a simple circular flow model with only households and firms. Indicate the following:

   a. The product market

   b. The factor market

   c. The flow of resources

   d. The flow of expenditures

   e. The flow of income

   f. The flow of products (goods and services)

Chapter 3

Demand, Supply, and Prices: Basic Concepts

Learning Objectives

After studying this chapter, you should be able to

3.1 Describe the market process and distinguish between demand and quantity demanded

3.2 State the law of demand and explain the shape of the demand curve

3.3 Identify the factors affecting quantity demanded

3.4 Distinguish between a change in demand and a change in quantity demanded

3.5 Distinguish between supply and quantity supplied

3.6 State the law of supply and explain the shape of the supply curve

3.7 Identify the factors affecting quantity supplied

3.8 Distinguish between a change in supply and a change in quantity supplied

3.9 Explain market price determination and the effects of changes in demand and supply

Assess Your Knowledge
MyEconLab

Answers to these questions can be found on MyEconLab at **www.myeconlab.com.**

1. A large segment of the population wants small, fuel-efficient cars. Does this constitute a demand for small, fuel-efficient cars?

2. Indicate whether the following statement is true or false: "The lower the price of an item, the greater the quantity that sellers will offer for sale."

3. Which of the following factors will affect the quantity of an item that people will buy?
   a. The cost of producing the item
   b. The average income of the buyers
   c. The technology used to produce the item
   d. All of the above

4. What is a shortage?

5. If the demand for an item increases and nothing else changes, then we can expect
   a. A fall in the price
   b. An increase in the price
   c. No change in the price
   d. The price to rise and then fall

LO 3.1   Describe the market process and distinguish between demand and quantity demanded

The Market Process

In Chapter 2, we defined a market as a mechanism that facilitates the exchange of goods and services between buyers and sellers. For a market to exist, the following must be present:

- At least one buyer
- At least one seller
- A product (good or service)
- A price

Buyers and sellers are the players in the market. The buying and selling decisions of the players are reflected in their behaviour in the market. This chapter discusses behaviour in markets that are competitive; these markets have so many buyers and sellers that no one can individually exert any influence on the price.

The market process is the process by which buyers and sellers exchange goods and services. In a free enterprise system, such as ours, prices play a crucial role in determining the flow of goods and services between buyers and sellers. You will see shortly that demand and supply are at the heart of the market process.

Demand analyzes the behaviour of buyers. It deals with the buyers' side of the market.

What exactly do economists mean by *demand*?

Think of something for which you are ready to pay a lot of money. Your demand for that thing would be high. If you are not ready to pay any money for something, then you have no demand for that thing. Thus, it is possible to desire or want something without having a demand for it.

Are you saying there is a difference between demand and want?

There is a difference between demand and want. No matter how much you want something, if you are not willing and able to spend money to buy it, then your wants will be ineffective. In economics, demand has a very specific meaning. Let us look at the economic definition of **demand**: the various quantities of a good or service that people are willing and able to buy at various possible prices during a specific period.

We should note the following points in this definition:

1. Demand is not a particular *quantity* that people will buy at a specific price. Rather, it is a series of quantities with their associated prices.

2. Demand is a *flow* rather than a stock concept. It has a time dimension.

3. Demand requires both the willingness and the ability to buy, not just the desire.

demand the various quantities of a good or service that people are willing and able to buy at various prices during a specific period

It sounds as if you are saying that demand is a functional relationship between price and quantity. Is that correct?

That is correct. In economics, demand is a functional relationship between the various possible prices of an item and the various quantities of the item that people would buy. We can show this relationship in a **demand schedule**, a table showing the inverse relationship between price and quantity demanded. It shows the various quantities of a good or service that people will be willing and able to buy at various prices during a specific period, and it is a tabular representation of demand.

Table 3.1 shows the various quantities of USB flash drives per week that people will be willing and able to buy at various prices.

demand schedule a table showing the inverse relationship between price and quantity demanded

So it is the entire schedule that represents demand?

That's right. Demand is not a specific quantity that people will be willing and able to buy at a specific price. It is all the quantities with their associated prices—the entire schedule.

OK. It's clear so far. But what is the name given to a particular quantity that people will be willing and able to buy at a specific price? For example, at a price of $8, people will be willing and able to buy 60 000 flash drives per week. What do we call the 60 000 if it is not demand?

The quantity that people will be willing and able to buy at a specific price is referred to as **quantity demanded**. Thus, at a price of $8, the quantity demanded (not the demand) is 60 000, and at a price of $4, the quantity demanded (not the demand) is 100 000. We will return several times to this very important distinction between demand and quantity demanded. While we are discussing quantity demanded, note the importance of the time period. For example, to say that the quantity of flash drives demanded at a price of $4 is 100 000 is somewhat unclear. To say that the quantity of flash drives demanded at a price of $4 is 100 000 a

quantity demanded the quantity that people will be willing and able to buy at a specific price

Table 3.1	A Hypothetical Demand Schedule for USB Flash Drives
Price of USB Flash Drives ($)	Quantity demanded per week (000 packs)
10	40
9	50
8	60
7	70
6	80
5	90
4	100

week has much more meaning. Buying 100 000 flash drives at $4 each in one week is certainly not the same as buying the same quantity at the same price in a year. The quantities demanded at various prices are per unit of time (per week, per month, per year, etc.).

Are we talking about an individual's demand for an item or the total (market) demand for the item?

It is important to be able to distinguish between individual demand and market demand. Here, we are talking about the total or market demand for a good or service. It consists of all the buyers in the market for that particular good or service. The individual consumer's demand for a good or service is an important microeconomic topic.

BUSINESS SITUATION 3.1

An entrepreneur observed an increase in the number of people buying laptop computers. He concluded that this was evidence of an increase in demand for laptop computers and so thought of increasing his stock of laptops. His economic consultant cautioned that he could be mistaken.

What might the consultant have had in mind?

The answer to this Business Situation can be found in Appendix A.

Reading Comprehension

The answers to these questions can be found on MyEconLab at www.myeconlab.com.   MyEconLab

1. List the four elements that must be present for a market to exist.
2. What is the market process?

3. What is the difference between demand and want?
4. "There can be want without demand, but there cannot be demand without want." Discuss briefly.
5. What is the difference between demand and quantity demanded?

LO 3.2 State the law of demand and explain the shape of the demand curve

law of demand a statement of the inverse relationship between price and quantity demanded

The Law of Demand

It seems logical that as the price of an item falls, a greater quantity will be demanded. Is this characteristic of demand?

In fact, it is. The fact that a greater quantity is demanded at a lower price is so universal that it is called the **law of demand** and can be stated as follows:

> As the price of a good or service falls, other things being equal, the quantity demanded increases; as the price of a good or service rises, other things being equal, the quantity demanded decreases.

Note that the law of demand does not say that if the price of an item falls, the quantity demanded will rise, and vice versa. It says that if the price falls and nothing else changes (other things being equal), then the quantity demanded will rise. So if the price of an item falls, and consumers' incomes also fall, they may not buy more of the item. This would not violate or negate the law of demand, because other things were not equal. This is an important point to remember. Price performs a rationing function, because higher prices discourage people from using scarce goods and services.

Can this response to a price change be explained beyond saying that it makes sense?

The inverse relationship between price and quantity demanded (as price goes up, quantity demanded goes down) has three explanations: (1) the market-size effect, (2) the income effect, and (3) the substitution effect. The specific question that we are trying to answer is this: Why do people buy more USB flash drives as the price falls? Let us examine each of the explanations.

market-size effect the effect on quantity demanded caused by a change in the number of buyers in the market as a result of a change in price

The Market-Size Effect   At a price of $10 per flash drive, some people would not buy any. But as the price of flash drives falls to $9, some of those people will enter the market and purchase some flash drives at the lower price. Thus, as the price falls, more and more people are drawn into the market. In other words, as the price falls, the size of the market increases, thus the quantity of flash drives demanded increases. More people buy the item as its price falls. We can call this the **market-size effect**, a term first introduced in 1994 by your author, Elijah James (1938–).

real income purchasing power

The Real Income Effect   Suppose you have $20 to buy flash drives this week. Suppose also that the price of a flash drive is $10. You will be able to buy two of them with your $20. If the price of flash drives falls to $5, you can now buy four instead of two. Your purchasing power (or **real income**) has increased. Even if you still have only $20, it can now buy more flash drives. When the price of an item falls, other things being equal, the people who buy that item experience an increase in purchasing power or real income, so they buy more—people buy more of the item as its price falls. This increase in quantity demanded resulting from an increase in the buyers' real income is referred to as the real income effect.

The real income effect also works in reverse. When prices rise, other things being equal, peoples' real income falls, so they buy a smaller quantity of the item whose price has risen. The real income effect, which is also called the **income effect**, is the effect on quantity demanded caused by the change in purchasing power resulting from a change in price.

income effect the effect on quantity demanded caused by the change in purchasing power resulting from a change in price

substitution effect the effect on quantity demanded caused by people switching to or from a product as its price changes

The Substitution Effect   When the price of flash drives falls, some people will switch from other items (perhaps external hard drives) that they were previously purchasing but that have now become relatively more expensive. That is, some people will substitute the cheaper flash drive for some other data storage device. This change in quantity demanded caused by people switching to or from a product as its price changes is often referred to as the **substitution effect**.

Figure 3.1 The Demand Curve for Flash Drives

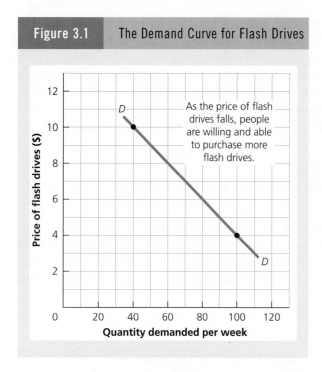

As the price of flash drives falls, people are willing and able to purchase more flash drives.

For these three reasons (the market-size effect, the real income effect, and the substitution effect), we might reasonably expect buyers to purchase a greater quantity of a good or service as its price falls, or alternatively, to buy less as its price rises, other things being equal.

What would be the result if we plot the information in Table 3.1 on a graph?

It has become common practice in economics to measure price on the vertical axis and quantity demanded per unit of time on the horizontal axis. The information in the demand schedule (Table 3.1) is plotted on a graph shown as Figure 3.1. Economists refer to this curve as a **demand curve**, which is a downward-sloping curve that shows the inverse relationship between price and quantity demanded, or the various quantities of a good or service that people will be willing and able to buy at various prices.

It is the inverse relationship between price and quantity demanded (the law of demand) that causes the demand curve to slope downward and to the right, as shown by DD in Figure 3.1.

The concept of demand can be illustrated graphically by a demand curve.

demand curve a downward-sloping curve showing the inverse relationship between price and quantity demanded

Can the demand curve be used to illustrate the difference between demand and quantity demanded?

When we studied the demand schedule earlier, we indicated that a particular quantity that people would be willing and able to buy at a particular price was called quantity demanded, while the entire schedule represented demand. Now let's look at Figure 3.1. At a price of $10 per flash drive, people would be willing and able to buy 40 000. This 40 000 is a quantity demanded at a price of $10. It is a point on the demand curve. Similarly, at a price of $4 per flash drive, the quantity demanded is 100 000. This 100 000 is a quantity demanded at a price of $4 and is another point on the demand curve. We can conclude that quantity demanded is represented by a point on the demand curve, while demand is represented by the entire demand curve.

In the demand curve and also in the demand schedule, the relationship between price and quantity is linear. Does this mean that demand curves are always linear?

No. The linear relationship is used for convenience only. In fact, it's unlikely that demand curves will be linear. People are unlikely to adjust their purchases in constant proportion to changes in price. Figure 3.2 shows a demand curve for cases of soap that is non-linear. When the price of a case of soap is $250, the quantity demanded is 20 cases. When the price falls to $125, the quantity demanded rises to 60 cases, and when the price falls to $50, the quantity demanded increases to 170 cases. At this point, the important thing to note about the shape of the demand curve is that it is downward sloping.

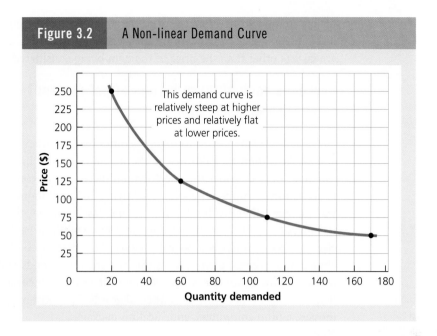

Figure 3.2   A Non-linear Demand Curve

This demand curve is relatively steep at higher prices and relatively flat at lower prices.

Reading Comprehension

The answers to these questions can be found on MyEconLab at www.myeconlab.com.   MyEconLab

1. "A greater quantity of an item will be demanded at a lower price?" Is anything wrong with that statement of the law of demand? If something is wrong with it, restate it so that it is true.

2. Briefly explain each of the following:
    a) The market-size effect
    b) The real income effect
    c) The substitution effect
3. Why does a fall in price increase real income?
4. Why is the typical demand curve downward sloping?

 LO 3.3   Identify the factors affecting quantity demanded

Factors Affecting Demand

What are the main factors that affect the demand for a good or service?

We have seen that when the price of a good or service changes, other things being equal, the quantity demanded (not demand) also changes. This is the law of demand. But we must deal with your question. What are the main factors that affect the demand for a good or service? They are as follows:

- Income
- Prices of related goods
- Tastes and preferences
- Expectations
- Population

Because the factors listed above do not include the price of the good or service under consideration, we can refer to them as *non-price determinants* of demand. *Non-price* means anything other than the price of the item being considered. Therefore, the prices of related goods are included in the category of non-price determinants, because they are factors other than the price of the item being considered.

How does each of these factors affect demand?

Let us deal with each in order.

Consumers' Income   If consumers' incomes increase, they will tend to buy more goods and services than they did before the increase in their incomes. Think about it for a moment. Let's consider the effect that an increase in income will have on the demand for cellphones. Suppose people were buying 3000 cellphones each week when the price was $45 per cellphone. If their incomes increase, they may find that they can now afford to purchase 3500 cellphones at the same price without having to buy less of anything else. As income increases, then, it seems likely that more of a given item will be purchased at any given price. This is the case for most goods and services; hence, economists refer to goods for which demand increases as income increases and for which demand falls as income falls as **normal goods**. For most people, normal goods Blu-ray movies, laptop computers, and vacation packages.

normal goods good for which demand increases as income increases and for which demand falls as income falls

Are some goods not *normal*?

Although most goods are normal goods, for some goods, people do not buy more as their incomes rise. Instead, they may buy less. Let us consider regular ground beef. If the price of regular ground beef is $6.50 per kilogram, at any given level of income, people will buy a certain amount per week. If these people's incomes increase, they may actually reduce their purchases of regular ground beef and buy steaks or lean ground beef instead. Thus, as income rises, people may buy less, not more, regular ground beef. Economists refer to goods for which demand decreases as income increases and for which demand increases as income falls as **inferior goods**. Examples might be drink mixes, such as Kool-Aid (instead of real fruit juices), macaroni and cheese (instead of restaurant dinners), beans (instead of meat), and used clothing (instead of new clothes).

inferior goods goods for which demand decreases as income increases and for which demand increases as income falls

Is it accurate to say that normal goods are necessarily "better" than inferior goods?

Not really. The distinction made between normal and inferior goods does not imply any value judgment about the items. It is better to think of the terms normal and inferior as the economist's jargon for describing buyers' behaviour or reaction to a change in income rather than as descriptions of the goods per se.

How are goods related?

Prices of Related Goods   Goods and services can be related to each other in two main ways: they may be substitutes or they may be complements. One good is said to be a **substitute** for a second good if it can be used in place of the second good. Examples of goods that are substitutes for each other are lemons and limes, sugar and honey, butter and margarine, tea and coffee, and e-readers such as Kindle or Kobo and paper books. Two goods are said to be **complements** if one is used in conjunction with the other (they are consumed or used together). Complementary goods are demanded jointly. If you buy more of one, you are likely to buy more of the other also. Examples of complementary goods (complements) are automobiles and gasoline, Blu-ray movies

substitute a good that can be used in place of another

complements goods that are consumed (used) together

and Blu-ray players, computers and flash drives, flashlights and batteries, and coffee and cream.

Think about goods that are substitutes (perhaps Pepsi and Coke). If the price of Pepsi were to increase, people would tend to switch to a substitute (Coke, for example). Hence, the demand for Coke would increase. In general, if the price of an item increases, the demand for its substitute will increase.

Let us now consider the case of complements and think of coffee and cream. If the price of coffee falls, people will buy more coffee and, as a consequence, the demand for cream will tend to increase. In general, if the price of an item falls, people will tend to purchase more of an item that is its complement.

Can we claim that all goods are related?

That claim would be difficult to justify. Some goods are neither substitute goods nor complementary goods. For example, we would not expect any relationship between automobiles and oranges, computers and winter jackets, or cellphones and baseball bats. Goods, such as those just listed, that are not related are said to be **independent goods**. If the price of cellphones increases, we can hardly expect it to have any effect on the demand for baseball bats.

independent goods goods that are not related

BUSINESS SITUATION 3.2

An office supply store sells computers and USB flash drives. One of the store's suppliers of computers has offered the store a large quantity of computers at a 30% discount on the regular cost.

How might this store use its inexpensive computers to boost its sales of flash drives?

The answer to this Business Situation can be found in Appendix A.

The more you like something, the more of it you will buy at any given price. Right?

Tastes and Preferences   That's correct. Tastes and preferences refer to people's "liking" for things. For example, a more favourable attitude toward exercise is an increase in taste (or preference) for exercise. People will "buy" more exercise (more people will pay to use gym facilities) if their preference for exercise increases. If health concerns about eating meat cause people's tastes to change from meat to vegetable diets, then it is obvious that the demand for vegetables will increase. Businesses spend millions of dollars in advertising in an attempt to influence people's tastes and preferences in favour of their products. By so doing, these firms are trying to increase the demand for their products.

Expectations do influence behaviour, but what kind of expectations are we discussing?

Expectations   Expectations are future oriented. In this particular context, we are discussing price and income expectations. People's expectations regarding the course of future prices will affect present demand for goods and services. If people expect the price of an item to rise, they are likely to increase their purchases of that item now to

As Canada's population grows, the demand for most goods and services also grows.

avoid paying the expected higher price in the future. They may even stock up on the item and thus postpone paying the ensuing higher price for as long as possible. Conversely, if the price of an item is expected to fall, people will attempt to delay their purchases of the item now to take advantage of the lower future price.

That's clear. How about expected future income now?

People's expectations about future changes in their incomes will also affect the present demand for goods and services. If people expect substantial raises in their salaries sometime in the near future, they are likely to buy more goods and services even before the increase in income materializes. If people expect decreases in their income (resulting from loss of employment, for example), they are likely to buy fewer goods and services. Thus, the demand for an item will increase if future income is expected to rise and fall if future income is expected to fall.

So with expectations, people respond to expected changes in future prices and expected changes in future incomes, rather than to actual changes in prices and income. Is that correct?

That is absolutely right. You have grasped the idea.

Now, this is common sense. The more people a market for an item has, the greater the demand for that item will be. Isn't that the idea?

Population   That is the idea. The quantity of an item that people will buy depends on the number of buyers in the market for that particular item. Other things being equal, we would expect the demand for oranges in Toronto, Ontario, to be significantly higher than the demand for oranges in Corner Brook, Newfoundland and Labrador, because Toronto has many more buyers than does Corner Brook. If the number of buyers increases, the demand for an item will increase.

Reading Comprehension

The answers to these questions can be found on MyEconLab at www.myeconlab.com.   MyEconLab

1. List the main factors that are likely to affect the quantity of home movies rented in a month.
2. What are normal goods? Give three specific examples of normal goods.
3. What are inferior goods? Give three specific examples of inferior goods.
4. What is the difference between substitutes and complements in consumption? What effect will a decrease in the price of inkjet printers have on the demand for inkjet cartridges?

LO 3.4 Distinguish between
a change in demand
and a change in
quantity demanded

A Change in Demand versus a Change in Quantity Demanded

The terms change in demand and change in quantity demanded are used differently. Are they different concepts?

Yes, they are different concepts and we should be careful not to confuse them. When economists speak of demand, they are referring to the entire demand curve or schedule. It follows, then, that if demand changes, the entire demand curve will shift (that is, change its position). Suppose the demand for flash drives was as shown in the first two columns of Table 3.2, but that the demand for flash drives increases because the government has introduced a new program that makes it less costly for people to own computers.

Table 3.2	A Demand Schedule Showing an Increase in Demand	
Price of Flash Drives ($)	Original Quantity Demanded per Week (000 packs)	New Quantity Demanded per Week (000)
10	40	60
9	50	70
8	60	80
7	70	90
6	80	100
5	90	110
4	100	120

Figure 3.3 An Increase in Demand

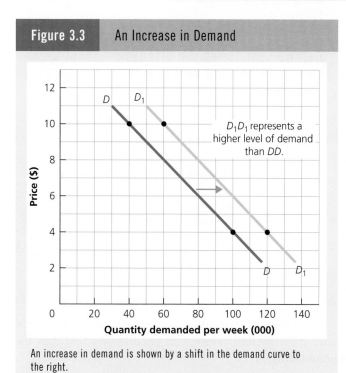

D_1D_1 represents a higher level of demand than DD.

An increase in demand is shown by a shift in the demand curve to the right.

As a consequence of the government's program, we will obtain a new demand schedule showing that a greater quantity of flash drives will be purchased at each price. The new quantities are shown in the right-hand column of Table 3.2. Notice that people buy more flash drives not because of a fall in the price of flash drives, but because they are buying more computers. This is an increase in the demand for flash drives.

What would a graph of these demand schedules look like?

We can plot these two demand schedules on the same graph to illustrate the shift in demand brought about by the government's program. Figure 3.3 shows this.

An increase in demand is shown by a shift in the demand curve to the right. Is that correct?

DD is the original demand curve; D_1D_1 is the new demand curve. The increase in demand is shown

| Figure 3.4 | A Decrease in Demand |

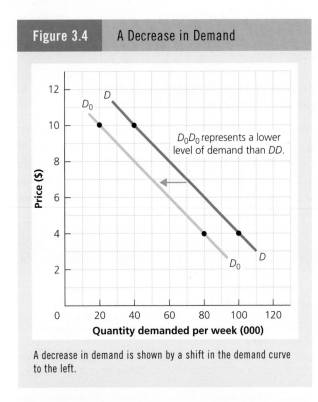

$D_0 D_0$ represents a lower level of demand than DD.

A decrease in demand is shown by a shift in the demand curve to the left.

| Figure 3.5 | A Change in Quantity Demanded |

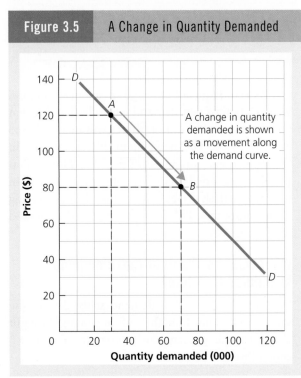

A change in quantity demanded is shown as a movement along the demand curve.

demand shifters the non-price determinants that shift the demand curve

by shifting the entire demand curve to the right of the original demand curve. The location of the demand curve has now changed. Note that at any given price, a greater quantity is purchased. A decrease in demand for flash drives (caused perhaps by the development of a better data storage device for computers) would mean that at any given price for flash drives, a smaller quantity would be purchased. This decrease in demand would be represented by a leftward shift in the demand curve, as shown in Figure 3.4, where the demand curve shifts from DD to $D_0 D_0$.

So a change in demand is shown by shifting the entire demand curve, either to the right (for an increase) or to the left (for a decrease). How do we show a change in quantity demanded on a graph?

A change in quantity demanded refers to the change in the quantity that would be bought as a result of a change in price. Let us examine the demand curve for cellphones shown in Figure 3.5.

At a price of $120 for cellphones, the quantity demanded is 30 000 per week. If the price falls to $80, a quantity of 70 000 per week will be demanded. This change in quantity demanded is represented by a movement along the same demand curve from point A to point B in Figure 3.5.

Can we summarize the discussion about a change in demand versus a change in quantity demanded?

A change in the price of the commodity under consideration will not cause a change in the demand for the commodity; it will cause a change in quantity demanded, shown as a movement along the demand curve. Only a change in a non-price determinant can cause a change in the demand for that commodity. Such factors as a change in income, a change in taste, a change in population, a change in the price of a related good, or a change in expectations will cause a change in demand—that is, they will cause the entire demand curve to shift.

Table 3.3 presents a convenient list of the major factors that cause the demand curve to shift. These non-price factors that shift the demand curve are called **demand shifters**.

Table 3.3	Demand Shifters: Non-price Factors That Change the Location of the Demand Curve
Demand Shifters	**Illustrative Examples**
1. A change in income	An increase in income increases purchasing power. The demand for most goods (normal goods) will increase, but the demand for inferior goods (used tires, for example) will decrease.
2. A change in the prices of related goods	An increase in the price of Coke will increase the demand for Pepsi because related goods of they are substitutes. A decrease in the price of computers will increase the demand for disks because they are complements.
3. A change in tastes and preferences	A successful advertising campaign for eggs increases the demand for eggs because it changes buyers' tastes in favour of eggs.
4. A change in expectations	The announcement of the imposition of a tax on DVDs produces expectations of higher future prices and this increases the current demand for DVDs.
5. A change in population	An increase in the number of immigrants entering Canada increases the demand for furniture.

Can you provide graphs showing the effects of some of the demand shifters?

Yes. Let's do so in Figure 3.6.

Figure 3.6	The Factors That Shift the Demand Curve (Demand Shifters)

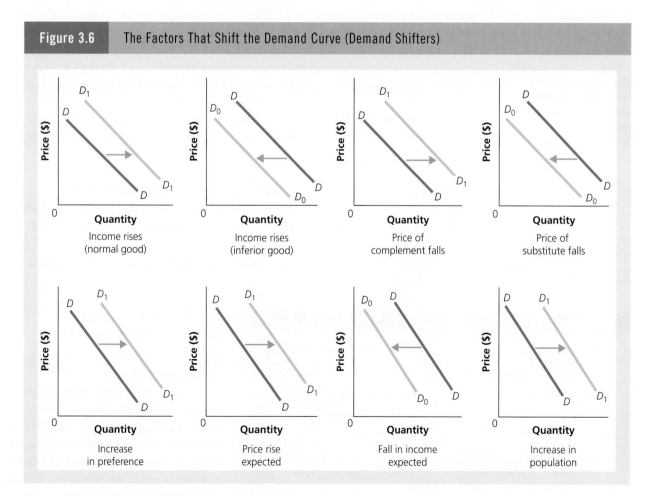

Reading Comprehension

The answers to these questions can be found on MyEconLab at www.myeconlab.com.   MyEconLab

1. With the help of an appropriate diagram, explain the difference between a change in demand and a change in quantity demanded.
2. How is an increase in demand illustrated on a graph? How is a decrease in demand illustrated on a graph?
3. Other things being equal, people buy more of an item as its price falls. Is this an increase in demand? Explain briefly.
4. List three factors that will shift the demand curve to the left.

LO 3.5 Distinguish between supply and quantity supplied

Supply

Demand **has a particular meaning in economics. Does** *supply* **also have a particular meaning?**

Yes, supply has a particular meaning in economics. Producers are motivated to sell goods and services by the price they will receive. The higher the price, the more they will be willing to produce and sell. Supply, like demand, is a functional relationship between price and quantity. We can define **supply** as the various quantities of a good or service that sellers are willing and able to offer for sale (place on the market) at various prices during a specific period.

supply the various quantities of a good or service that sellers are willing and able to offer for sale (place on the market) at various prices during a specific period

As in the case of demand, supply refers not to a specific quantity that will be sold at some particular price, but to a series of quantities and a range of associated prices.

In the same way that we can have a table showing a functional relationship between price and quantity demanded, so too we can have a table showing the relationship between price and quantity supplied. Is that right?

supply schedule a table showing the direct relationship between price and quantity supplied

Yes, that is right. Let's construct such a table right now. Of course, you know what such a table is called.

Table 3.4	A Hypothetical Supply Schedule for USB Flash Drives
Price of Flash Drives ($)	**Quantity Supplied per Week** (000)
10	80
9	70
8	60
7	50
6	40
5	30
4	20

Yes. It's called a supply schedule. Is that correct?

Right again. Table 3.4 shows a supply schedule for USB flash drives.

We can define a **supply schedule** as a table showing the direct relationship between price and quantity supplied. It shows the various quantities of a good or service that producers will be willing and able to sell at various prices during a specific period, and is a tabular representation of supply.

Reading Comprehension

The answers to these questions can be found on MyEconLab at www.myeconlab.com.   MyEconLab

1.   What do economists mean by supply?

2.   What is the difference between supply and quantity supplied?

3.   What is a supply schedule?

LO 3.6 | State the law of supply and explain the shape of the supply curve

law of supply a statement of the direct relationship between price and quantity supplied

supply curve an upward-sloping curve showing the direct relationship between price and quantity supplied

The concept of supply can be illustrated graphically by a supply curve.

The Law of Supply

There is a law of demand. Is there also a law of supply?

Table 3.4 shows that at a price of $10 per flash drive, producers will be willing to offer 80 000 of them for sale. As the price falls, they are willing to offer smaller quantities. Note that price and quantity supplied move in the same direction, that is, a direct relationship exists between them. This direct relationship between price and quantity supplied is called the **law of supply** and is stated as follows:

> As the price of a good or service falls, other things being equal, the quantity offered for sale decreases; as the price of a good or service rises, other things being equal, the quantity supplied increases.

According to the law of supply then, there is a direct relationship between the price of a product and the quantity supplied.

Why will producers offer more for sale as price rises?

Producers are motivated by profit. The main reason that producers will be willing to offer more for sale at a higher price is that higher prices serve as an incentive for producers to offer greater quantities and thus earn more profit. This is the function of price as a production motivator. Increases in price can also entice new producers into the market.

The following example will help to explain how producers respond to an increase in price. Suppose farmers have a certain amount of land on which they produce wheat and corn. If the price of wheat increases, farmers will find it profitable to shift land out of corn production and into wheat production. Also, it is conceivable that some farmers who were not previously producing wheat will now become wheat farmers. Hence, the quantity of wheat produced increases.

What would be the result if we plot the information in Table 3.4 on a graph?

Plotting the data in Table 3.4 on a graph results in Figure 3.7. The graph is called a **supply curve**, which is an upward-sloping curve showing the direct relationship between price and quantity supplied. It shows the various quantities of a good or service that producers are willing and able to offer for sale at various possible prices.

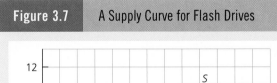

| Figure 3.7 | A Supply Curve for Flash Drives |

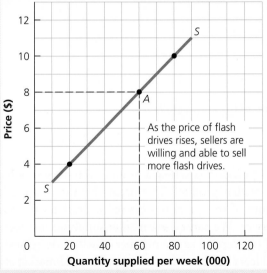

As the price of flash drives rises, sellers are willing and able to sell more flash drives.

As price rises, the quantity supplied rises.

It is the direct relationship between price and quantity supplied that causes the supply curve to slope upward, as shown by *SS* in Figure 3.7.

Can the supply curve be used to illustrate the difference between supply and quantity supplied?

The entire supply curve represents supply, while a point on the supply curve represents quantity supplied at some specific price. In Figure 3.7, for example, the quantity supplied at a price of $8 is 60 000, represented by point *A* on the supply curve. The supply is represented by the entire supply curve.

Reading Comprehension

The answers to these questions can be found on MyEconLab at www.myeconlab.com.   MyEconLab

1. State the law of supply.
2. Explain how price serves as a production motivator.

3. What is a supply curve?
4. Use a graph to show the difference between supply and quantity supplied.

LO 3.7   Identify the factors affecting quantity supplied

Factors Affecting Supply

What are the main factors that affect the supply of a good or service?

We have seen that the quantity of a good or service that producers are willing and able to offer for sale depends on the price of the good or service. In other words, the price of a good or service affects the *quantity supplied*. The main factors that affect the supply of a good or service are

- Number of producers
- Prices of related products
- Technology
- Expectations
- Cost of inputs

How does each of these factors affect supply?

Let's examine each one in turn.

Number of Producers   The number of producers selling a product will obviously have some effect on total market supply of that product. This occurs because the market supply of a good or service is the sum of the quantities offered for sale by all of the individual sellers of that good or service. We can expect market supply to increase as the number of sellers increases, and to decrease as the number of sellers decreases. If, however, the average output of producers increases significantly, the total market supply can increase even if the number of producers decreases.

Are goods related in the same way in supply as in demand?

substitutes (in production) goods that are produced as alternatives to each other

complements (in production) or joint products goods such that the production of one implies the production of the other

Prices of Related Products　Yes, in pretty much the same way. You will recall our discussion of substitutes and complements on the demand side. As you suspect, goods can be substitutes or complements in production. Goods are **substitutes in production** (or production substitutes) if they are produced as alternatives to each other. Examples of substitutes in production are lettuce and tomatoes (a farmer can produce one or the other on the same piece of land), and leather bags and belts (both can be produced with the same type of resources). Goods are **complements in production** or **joint products** (or production complements) if they are produced together; the production of one implies the production of the other. Beef and hides are a classic example of goods that are complements in production.

How does a change in the price of a substitute in production affect the supply of a product?

Let us consider the case of lettuce and tomatoes. If the price of lettuce increases, the supply of tomatoes will decrease as producers shift from tomato production to lettuce production. In general, if the price of a production substitute increases, producers will tend to reduce the supply of the item in question.

If two items are complements in production, an increase in the price of a production complement will increase the supply of the item in question. Is that correct?

That is correct. Let us consider beef and hides. If the price of beef rises, the quantity of beef supplied will rise but so will the quantity of hides as more cattle are slaughtered. In general, if the price of a complement in production rises, other things being equal, the supply of the good in question will increase, and if the price of a complement in production falls, the supply of the good in question will also fall.

It's not quite clear how changes in technology affect supply. Can you explain?

Technology　Producers use inputs (factors of production) to produce goods and services. An increase in technology makes existing factors (inputs) more productive, and introduces new types of inputs that are more efficient than older types. Hence, an improvement in technology causes an increase in supply.

Expectations　If producers of a certain item expect its price to rise in the future, they might begin now to expand their productive capacity and thus increase their present output levels of that particular item. This is particularly so in the case of products that cannot be stored easily. However, it is quite possible that expectations of a higher future price may lead producers into building stocks now so that they will have a larger quantity to sell at the future higher price. Such action will, of course, reduce current supply to the market. Therefore, generalizations should not be made about the effect of expected price changes on supply.

It seems as if the price of inputs affects the cost of production. Is this the case?

Cost of Inputs　That is the case. Payment for factor inputs represents a significant part of production costs. The higher the prices of these inputs, the greater the costs of production will be, and the less will be produced. If wages rise, for example, other things being equal, the ability of businesses to produce an item will be reduced; thus, the supply will fall. A reduction in input prices will, of course, cause the supply to increase.

Reading Comprehension

The answers to these questions can be found on MyEconLab at **www.myeconlab.com**.   MyEconLab

1. List three factors that will cause an increase in supply.
2. Give three examples of production substitutes.
3. What are joint products? Give two examples of joint products.

4. Explain how expectations can influence the quantity of an item offered for sale.
5. What is the relationship (if any) between cost of production and the prices of inputs?

LO 3.8 Distinguish between a change in supply and a change in quantity supplied

A Change in Supply versus a Change in Quantity Supplied

We studied the distinction between a change in *demand* and a change in *quantity demanded*. Does this distinction apply to supply?

Yes it does, and it should facilitate our understanding of the difference between a change in supply and a change in quantity supplied. When we speak of supply, we refer to the entire supply curve or schedule. It follows, then, that if supply changes, the entire supply curve will shift. Earlier in this chapter, we looked at a hypothetical supply schedule for flash drives. We reproduce that supply schedule here in the first two columns of Table 3.5. Let us now suppose that the supply of flash drives increases because of a

Table 3.5	A Hypothetical Supply Schedule for Flash Drives	
Price of Flash Drives Supplied ($)	Original Quantity Supplied (000)	New Quantity Supplied (000)
10	80	100
9	70	90
8	60	80
7	50	70
6	40	60
5	30	50
4	20	40

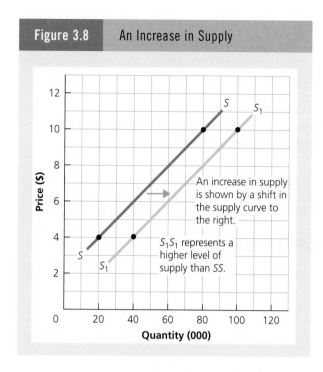

Figure 3.8   An Increase in Supply

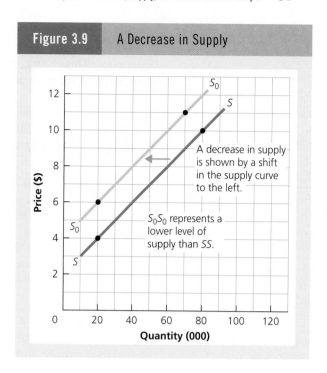

Figure 3.9   A Decrease in Supply

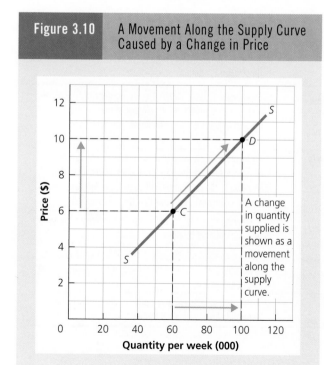

Figure 3.10   A Movement Along the Supply Curve Caused by a Change in Price

reduction in the cost of producing them. We will obtain a new supply schedule showing that a greater quantity of flash drives will be supplied at each price of flash drives. The new quantities supplied are shown in the right column of Table 3.5.

What would these supply schedules look like on the same graph?

Let's plot them and see. In Figure 3.8, SS is the original supply curve; S_1S_1 is the new supply curve. The increase in supply is shown by shifting the entire supply curve to the right of its original position. The location of the curve has now changed. Notice that at any given price of flash drives, a greater quantity is supplied. A decrease in supply would mean that at any given price of flash drives, a smaller quantity would be supplied, and would be represented by a leftward shift in the supply curve, as shown in Figure 3.9. The supply curve shifts from SS to S_0S_0.

Is a change in quantity supplied represented by a movement along the supply curve, as in the case of a change in demand?

Yes. A change in quantity supplied refers to the change in quantity that would be offered for sale as a result of a change in price. Let us examine the supply curve in Figure 3.10.

At a price of $6 for this item, producers will be willing and able to sell 60 000 units of this item per week. If the price rises to $10, a quantity of 100 000 units per week will be supplied. This change in quantity supplied is represented by a movement along the same supply curve from point *C* to point *D* in Figure 3.10.

Can we summarize the discussion about a change in supply versus a change in quantity supplied as we did with demand?

A change in the price of the commodity under consideration will not cause a change in the supply of the commodity; it will cause a change in quantity supplied. Only a change in a non-price determinant can cause a change in the supply of that commodity. Such factors as a change in the number of producers, a change in the price of a related good, a change in technology, a change in expectations, or a change in input prices will cause a change in supply—that is, they will cause the supply curve to shift.

supply shifters the non-price determinants that shift the supply curve

The major factors that cause the supply curve to shift are conveniently collected in a list in Table 3.6. These non-price factors that shift the supply curve are sometimes referred to as **supply shifters**.

Table 3.6	Supply Shifters: Non-price Factors That Change the Location of the Supply Curve
Supply Shifters	**Illustrative Examples**
1. A change in the number of producers	An increase in the number of manufacturers of DVD players increases the supply of DVD players. If many of the firms producing jeans go out of business, the supply of jeans falls.
2. A change in the prices of related goods	An increase in the price of lettuce reduces the supply of turnips because they are production substitutes. An increase in the price of refined cane sugar increases the supply of molasses because they are joint products.
3. A change in technology	The invention of high-speed computers increases the supply of computational services.
4. A change in expectations	Suppliers expect an increase in the price of coffee so they reduce present supplies with the intention of selling at the future higher price.
5. A change in the price of inputs	A substantial increase in the price of steel reduces the supply of chairs with steel frames.

Can we graph the effects of the supply shifters?

Yes. Figure 3.11 shows the effects of some of the supply shifters.

Figure 3.11	The Factors That Shift the Supply Curve (Supply Shifters)

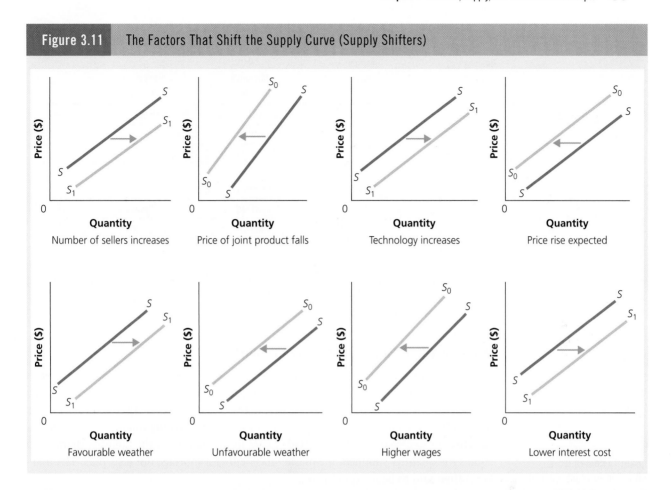

Reading Comprehension

The answers to these questions can be found on MyEconLab at www.myeconlab.com. MyEconLab

1. What is the difference between a change in supply and a change in quantity supplied?
2. What effect will an increase in the price of an item have on the supply of that item?
3. Mention three factors that will shift the supply curve to the right.
4. How is an increase in supply shown on a graph? How is a decrease in supply shown?

LO 3.9 Explain market price determination and the effects of changes in demand and supply

Determination of Equilibrium Price

Are we going to bring the buyers and sellers together?

Certainly—and this is the perfect time to do it; by so doing, we will see how market forces determine the price of a good or service. To help with the explanation, Table 3.7

Table 3.7	Hypothetical Demand and Supply Schedules for Flash Drives, and Market Price Determination			
Price of Flash Disks ($)	**Quantity Demanded (000 packs)**	**Quantity Supplied (000)**	**Market Condition**	**Pressure on Price**	
10	40	80	Surplus	Downward	↓
9	50	70	Surplus	Downward	↓
8	60	60	Equilibrium	None	—
7	70	50	Shortage	Upward	↑
6	80	40	Shortage	Upward	↑
5	90	30	Shortage	Upward	↑
4	100	20	Shortage	Upward	↑

reproduces the hypothetical demand and supply schedules shown in Tables 3.1 and 3.4 (pages 71 and 82), respectively. We also show the market condition at each price-quantity combination and the effect on price.

What do you mean by market condition?

market condition the relationship between quantity demanded and quantity supplied

shortage or excess quantity demanded a situation in which quantity demanded exceeds quantity supplied

surplus or excess quantity supplied a situation in which quantity supplied exceeds quantity demanded

Market condition describes the situation of the market in terms of the relation between the quantity demanded and the quantity supplied. If the quantity demanded (Q_D) exceeds the quantity supplied (Q_S), a **shortage** (or **excess quantity demanded**) exists in the market. Conversely, if the quantity supplied exceeds the quantity demanded, a **surplus** (or **excess quantity supplied**) exists in the market. If the quantity demanded equals the quantity supplied, the market has neither a shortage nor a surplus. The market is then said to be in equilibrium.

We can summarize market conditions as follows:

1. If $Q_D > Q_S$, a shortage exists.
2. If $Q_D < Q_S$, a surplus exists.
3. If $Q_D = Q_S$, the market is in equilibrium.

Then we can use Table 3.7 to illustrate market conditions. Right?

That's right. Let us first consider the situation when the price is $4. At this price, buyers are willing and able to purchase 100 000 flash drives a week, but producers are willing and able to offer only 20 000 for sale. There will therefore be a shortage of 80 000 flash drives. At a price of $9, for example, buyers are willing and able to purchase only 50 000 flash drives a week, while sellers are willing to offer 70 000. There will therefore be a surplus of 20 000 flash drives in the market. Let us now consider a price of $8. At this price, buyers are willing to purchase 60 000 flash drives per week, and sellers are willing to offer 60 000 for sale. At this price, there is neither a surplus nor a shortage.

What happens when a market has a surplus or a shortage?

At any price other than $8, market forces are set in motion to raise or lower the price. Consider a price of $10. At this price, as the supply schedule shows, sellers are willing to put 80 000 on the market, but buyers are willing to buy only 40 000. A surplus or excess quantity supplied will result. Sellers will then attempt to dispose of this surplus by lowering the price. As the price falls, a greater quantity will be demanded. The price will settle at $8 because, at this price, the market will be cleared.

> Whenever a surplus exists in the market, it will exert a downward pressure on the price.

If the price happens to be $6, buyers will be willing to purchase 80 000 flash drives, but sellers will be willing to offer only 40 000 for sale. A price of $6 results in a shortage or excess quantity demanded. Unhappy with the shortage and wanting more flash drives, buyers will bid up the price. Sellers then will offer greater quantities at the higher prices. The price will again settle at $8 because, at this price, the quantity demanded equals the quantity supplied.

> Whenever a shortage exists in the market, it will exert an upward pressure on the price.

Note that the price of $8 is the only price that will prevail in the market. There will be no tendency for this price to change.

Is there a special name for this price?

equilibrium price the price at which quantity demanded equals quantity supplied; there is no tendency for this price to change

Indeed, there is. The price at which quantity demanded equals quantity supplied is referred to as the **equilibrium price**, and the quantity traded (exchanged) at this price is called the **equilibrium quantity**.

> Competitive market equilibrium occurs when the quantity of the product demanded equals the quantity supplied at a specific price.

equilibrium quantity the quantity traded (bought and sold) at the equilibrium price

Figure 3.12 Equilibrium Price and Quantity

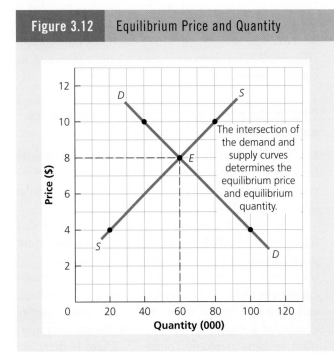

The intersection of the demand and supply curves determines the equilibrium price and equilibrium quantity.

Can market equilibrium be illustrated graphically?

The market equilibrium condition is illustrated graphically in Figure 3.12. The demand curve *DD* and the supply curve *SS* are drawn from the schedules in Table 3.7. The two curves intersect at *E* to give an equilibrium price of $8 and an equilibrium quantity of 60 000.

Is the equilibrium price the price that makes buyers and sellers most happy?

This is a popular, but false, conclusion. It is more likely that neither buyers nor sellers will be completely satisfied with the equilibrium price. The buyers would prefer to pay a lower price for their flash drives, and the sellers would prefer to sell their flash drives at a higher price. But the buyers are purchasing all they want to buy at that price; and the producers are selling all they want to sell at that price.

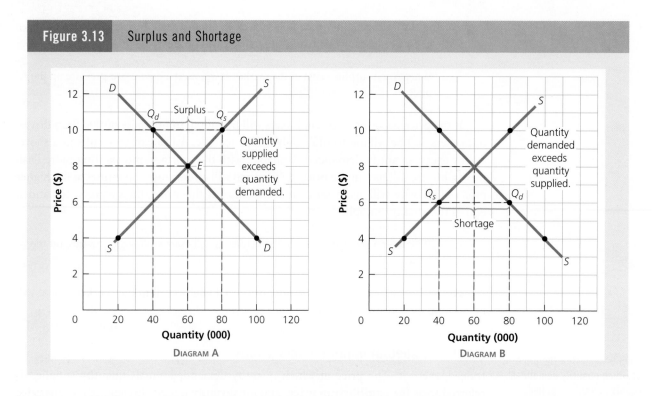

Figure 3.13 Surplus and Shortage

DIAGRAM A

DIAGRAM B

A change in demand, other things being equal, shifts the demand curve and changes the equilibrium price and quantity.

Can surpluses and shortages also be illustrated graphically?

The answer is yes. Let's look at Figure 3.13. In Diagram A we see that at a price of $10, the quantity supplied is 80 000, while the quantity demanded is 40 000. A surplus of (80 000 − 40 000) = 40 000 exists, as indicated in Diagram A. This surplus will cause the price to fall to the equilibrium level of $8. Look at Diagram B. At a price of $6, the quantity demanded is 80 000, while the quantity supplied is 40 000. A shortage of (80 000 − 40 000) = 40 000 exists, as indicated in Diagram B. This shortage causes the price to rise to its equilibrium level of $8.

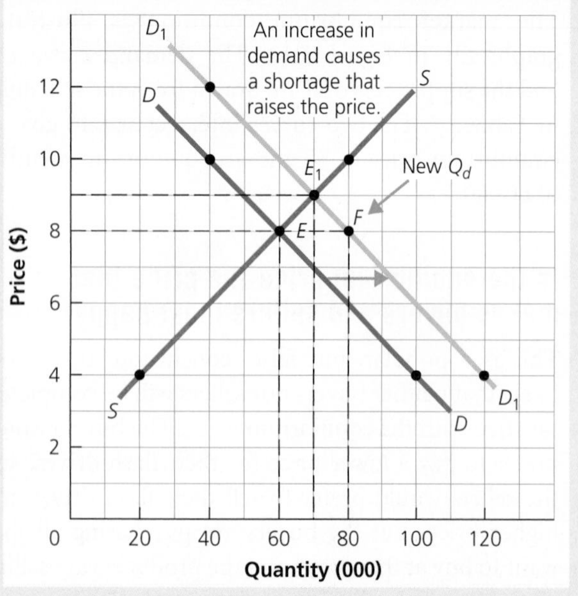

What is the effect of an increase in demand on equilibrium price and quantity?

Let us assume that the demand for flash drives increases because more people own computers and therefore require flash drives. Let us analyze the situation with the help of Figure 3.14.

The original demand and supply curves in this figure are DD and SS, respectively, and the equilibrium price and quantity are $8 and 60 000, respectively. An increase in demand is shown by a shift in the demand curve from DD to D_1D_1. With this new higher demand, and with the initial price of $8, the new quantity demanded is 80 000 (point F), while the quantity supplied remains at 60 000 (point E). There is therefore

Figure 3.14 The Effect of an Increase in Demand

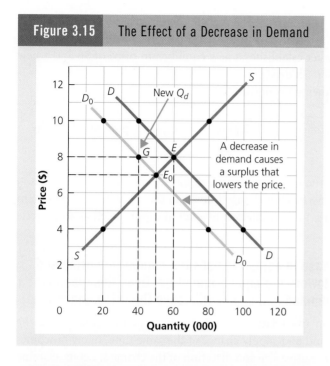

Figure 3.15 The Effect of a Decrease in Demand

a shortage (excess quantity demanded) of 20 000 flash drives. The shortage will exert upward pressure on the price. The market establishes a new equilibrium price of $9 and a new equilibrium quantity of 70 000. The result can be stated by the following proposition:

> An increase in demand, other things being equal, will cause the equilibrium price and quantity to increase.

Note that although the quantity bought and sold increases, supply does not increase; the location of the supply curve remains the same. There is, however, a movement along the supply curve SS, from point E to point E_1—an increase in quantity supplied.

Will a decrease in demand lower the equilibrium price and quantity?

Yes, but let's do the analysis. In Figure 3.15, the original demand and supply curves are DD and SS, respectively, and the equilibrium price and quantity are $8 and 60 000. Now let's suppose that a new data storage device causes the demand for flash drives to fall. This fall in demand shifts the demand curve to the left of its original position, from DD to D_0D_0. With this new lower demand, and with the initial price of $8, the new quantity demanded is 40 000 (point G), while the quantity supplied remains at 60 000 (point E). There is therefore a surplus (excess quantity supplied) of 20 000 flash drives. This surplus will exert downward pressure on the price. The market establishes a new equilibrium price of $7 and a new equilibrium quantity of 50 000.

The result can be stated by the following proposition:

> A decrease in demand, other things being equal, will cause the equilibrium price and quantity to decrease.

Note again that although the quantity demanded and supplied fall, supply does not decrease; the location of the supply curve remains the same. There is, however, a movement along the supply curve SS, from point E to point E_0.

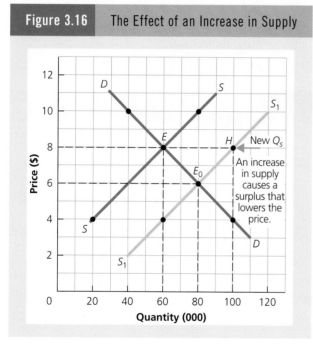

Figure 3.16 The Effect of an Increase in Supply

What is the effect of an increase in supply on equilibrium price and quantity?

Suppose the supply of flash drives increases because of a technological improvement in the production of flash drives. We can analyze the effect of this change with the help of Figure 3.16. The initial demand and supply curves are DD and SS, respectively; the equilibrium price is $8, and the equilibrium quantity is 60 000. An increase in supply is shown by shifting the supply curve to the right of its initial position, from SS to S_1S_1. At the initial price of $8, the new quantity supplied is 100 000 (point H), while the quantity demanded remains at 60 000. The market therefore has a surplus of flash drives. This surplus will exert a downward pressure on the price as sellers compete to sell their flash drives. The market establishes a new equilibrium price of $6 and a new equilibrium quantity of 80 000 flash drives.

We can now state the following proposition:

> An increase in supply, other things being equal, will cause the price to fall and the quantity to rise.

A change in supply, other things being equal, shifts the supply curve and changes the equilibrium price and quantity.

Note again that although the quantity demanded has increased, demand has not; the location of the demand curve has not changed. Instead, there has been a movement along the demand curve, from E to E_0. The effect of a fall in supply is left as an exercise for you.

When demand and supply both change, equilibrium price and quantity can be affected in a variety of ways.

Now, we know that an increase in demand raises the equilibrium price and that an increase in supply lowers the equilibrium price. Does this mean that a simultaneous increase in demand and supply will leave the price unchanged?

Not necessarily. It depends on the relative size of the increase in demand and the increase in supply. When demand and supply change at the same time, many outcomes are possible, depending on the relative size and direction of the changes. Let us examine six of the possible outcomes. Figure 3.17 will help us with the analysis. In each case, DD and SS are the initial demand and supply curves, respectively, and $8 and 60 000 flash drives are the equilibrium price and quantity, respectively.

Figure 3.17 The Effects of Changes in Demand and Supply

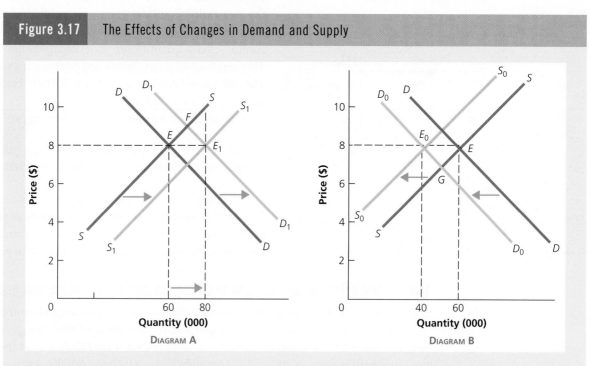

Diagram A: An increase in demand and an increase in supply of the same size leave the price unchanged but increase the quantity.

Diagram B: A decrease in demand and a decrease in supply of the same size leave the price unchanged but reduce the quantity.

Figure 3.17	The Effects of Changes in Demand and Supply (*cont'd*)

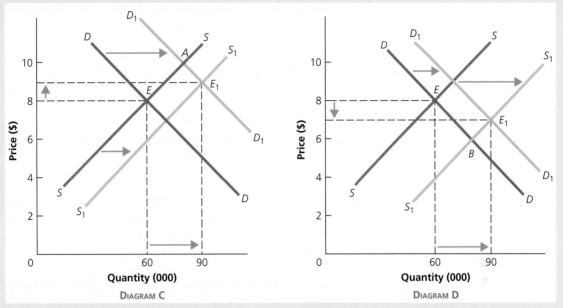

Diagram C: A relatively large increase in demand and a relatively small increase in supply raise both price and quantity.

Diagram D: A relatively large increase in supply and a relatively small increase in demand lower the price but increase the quantity.

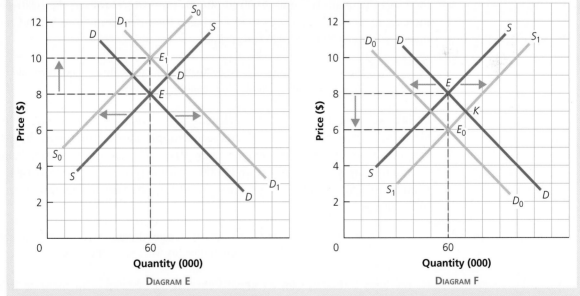

Diagram E: An increase in demand and an equal decrease in supply raise the price but leave the quantity unchanged.

Diagram F: An increase in supply and an equal decrease in demand lower the price but leave the quantity unchanged.

The Increase in Demand Is Equal to the Increase in Supply In Diagram A of Figure 3.17, the increase in demand from DD to D_1D_1 raises the equilibrium price from $8 to $9 and increases the equilibrium quantity from 60 000 to 70 000 (point F). The increase in supply from SS to S_1S_1 lowers the price back to $8 but increases the quantity from 70 000 to 80 000 (point E_1). We can conclude that

> If demand and supply increase equally, the equilibrium price will remain the same but the equilibrium quantity will increase.

The Fall in Demand Is Equal to the Fall in Supply   In Diagram B, the decrease in demand from DD to D_0D_0 lowers the price from $8 to $7 and reduces the quantity from 60 000 to 50 000 (point G). The decrease in supply from SS to S_0S_0 raises the price back to $8 but lowers the quantity even further to 40 000 (point E_0). Thus,

> If demand and supply decrease equally, the equilibrium price will remain the same but the equilibrium quantity will fall.

The Increase in Demand Is Greater than the Increase in Supply   Diagram C shows that the relatively large increase in demand, from DD to D_1D_1, raises the price from $8 to $10 and increases the quantity from 60 000 to 80 000 (point A). The increase in supply from SS to S_1S_1 lowers the price from $10 to $9 and increases the quantity further from 80 000 to 90 000 (point E_1).

> If the increase in demand is larger than the increase in supply, both the equilibrium price and quantity will rise.

The Increase in Supply Is Greater than the Increase in Demand   Diagram D shows that a relatively large increase in supply, from SS to S_1S_1, lowers the price from $8 to $6 and increases the quantity from 60 000 to 80 000 (point B). However, the relatively small increase in demand, from DD to D_1D_1, raises the price from $6 to $7 and raises the quantity from 80 000 to 90 000 (point E_1).

> If the increase in supply is larger than the increase in demand, the equilibrium price will fall, but the equilibrium quantity will rise.

An Increase in Demand and an Equal Decrease in Supply   An increase in demand alone raises the price, and a decrease in supply alone also raises the price. In Diagram E, the increase in demand from DD to D_1D_1 raises the price from $8 to $9 and increases the quantity from 60 000 to 70 000 (point D). The decrease in supply from SS to S_0S_0 raises the price from $9 to $10 but reduces the quantity from 70 000 to 60 000 (point E_1).

> If an increase in demand is matched by an equal decrease in supply, the equilibrium price will rise, but the equilibrium quantity will remain the same.

An Increase in Supply and an Equal Decrease in Demand   An increase in supply alone lowers the price, and a decrease in demand alone also lowers the price. In Diagram F, the increase in supply from SS to S_1S_1 lowers the price from $8 to $7 and increases the quantity from 60 000 to 70 000 (point K). The decrease in demand from DD to D_0D_0 lowers the price further to $6 and reduces the quantity back to 60 000 (point E_0).

> If an increase in supply is matched by an equal decrease in demand, the equilibrium price will fall, but the equilibrium quantity will remain the same.

Can we summarize these results in a table?

That's a good idea. Table 3.8 summarizes the results.

Note that sometimes the effect on price is uncertain. For example, if demand and supply both increase, the price might rise, remain the same, or fall; it depends on the relative size of the change in demand and supply. But in this case, the effect on quantity is unambiguous. Quantity will increase. The effect of changes in demand and supply on price is certain, while the effect on quantity can be uncertain. For example, if demand increases and supply decreases, the price will definitely increase, but the quantity might increase, remain the same, or decrease. It depends again on the relative size of the changes.

Table 3.8	The Effects of Simultaneous Changes in Demand and Supply
Change in Demand and Supply	**Effect on Price and Quantity**
1. Demand and supply both increase equally.	Price remains the same but quantity increases.
2. Demand and supply both decrease equally.	Price remains the same but quantity decreases.
3. The increase in demand is greater than the increase in supply.	Both price and quantity increase.
4. The increase in supply is greater than the increase in demand.	Price falls but quantity increases.
5. Demand increases and supply decreases equally.	Price increases but quantity remains the same.
6. Demand decreases and supply increases equally.	Price falls but quantity remains the same.

Reading Comprehension

The answers to these questions can be found on MyEconLab at www.myeconlab.com.   MyEconLab

1. Define the following terms:
   a) Shortage
   b) Surplus
2. What is the effect of a shortage on price? What is the effect of a surplus on price?
3. Define *equilibrium price* and *equilibrium quantity*.
4. The equilibrium price is the price at which demand and supply are equal. Is this statement correct?
5. What is the effect of an increase in demand on price, other things being equal?
6. What is the effect of a decrease in supply on price, other things being equal?

Review

1. Review the learning objectives listed at the beginning of the chapter.
2. Have you accomplished all the objectives? One way to determine this is to answer the Reading Comprehension questions at the end of each section. They will help you assess the extent to which you have accomplished the learning objectives.
3. If you have not accomplished an objective, review the relevant material before proceeding.

Key Points to Remember

1. **LO 3.1** Demand refers to the various quantities of a good or service that people are willing and able to buy at various prices during a specific period. Demand is a functional relationship between price and quantity demanded and can be represented by a table called a demand schedule or by a graph called a demand curve. Quantity demanded is the amount that will be demanded at a specific price.

2. **LO 3.2** The law of demand states that, other things being equal, as the price of an item rises, the quantity demanded will fall; and as the price falls, the quantity demanded will rise. Because of this inverse relationship between price and quantity demanded, the demand curve is downward sloping.

3. **LO 3.3** The main factors that affect the demand for a product are income, prices of substitutes and complements, tastes and preferences, buyers' expectations about future prices and future income, and the number of buyers.

4. **LO 3.4** A change in the price of a product will cause the quantity demanded of that product to change and is illustrated by a movement along the demand curve from one point to another. A change in a non-price determinant will cause demand to change—this is illustrated by a shift in the entire demand curve.

5. **LO 3.5, 3.8** Supply refers to the various quantities of a good or service that sellers (producers) are willing and able to offer for sale (i.e., place on the market) at various prices during a specific period. Supply can be represented by a supply schedule or by a supply curve. Quantity supplied is the amount that will be offered for sale at a specific price.

6. **LO 3.6** The law of supply states that as the price of an item rises, other things being equal, the quantity supplied will also rise; and as the price falls, the quantity supplied will fall. Because of this direct relationship between price and quantity supplied, the supply curve is upward sloping.

7. **LO 3.7** The factors affecting supply include the number of producers (sellers), the prices of related products, technology, sellers' expectations, and the prices of inputs (cost of production).

8. **LO 3.9** The equilibrium price is the price at which quantity demanded and quantity supplied are equal. The equilibrium quantity is the quantity that will be bought and sold (traded) at the equilibrium price. The intersection of the demand and supply curves determines the equilibrium price and quantity. The equilibrium price is not necessarily the best price for buyers or sellers.

9. **LO 3.9** A change in demand, other things being equal, will cause price and quantity to change in the same direction as the change in demand. A change in supply, other things being equal, will cause price to change in the opposite direction—and quantity to change in the same direction—as the change in supply.

Economic Word Power

Complements (in production) or joint products   (p. 85)
Complements   (p. 76)
Demand   (p. 71)
Demand curve   (p. 74)
Demand schedule   (p. 71)
Demand shifters   (p. 80)
Equilibrium price   (p. 91)
Equilibrium quantity   (p. 91)
Income effect   (p. 73)
Independent goods   (p. 77)
Inferior goods   (p. 76)
Law of demand   (p. 72)
Law of supply   (p. 83)
Market condition   (p. 90)
Market-size effect   (p. 73)
Normal goods   (p. 76)
Quantity demanded   (p. 71)
Real income   (p. 73)
Shortage or excess quantity demanded   (p. 90)
Substitute   (p. 76)
Substitutes (in production)   (p. 85)
Substitution effect   (p. 73)
Supply   (p. 82)
Supply curve   (p. 83)
Supply schedule   (p. 82)
Supply shifters   (p. 88)
Surplus or excess quantity supplied   (p. 90)

Problems and Exercises

Basic

1. **LO 3.1** Use a demand curve to illustrate the difference between demand and quantity demanded.

2. **LO 3.3** Mention three factors that will increase the demand for a normal good.

3. **LO 3.6** What is the meaning of an upward-sloping supply curve?

4. **LO 3.7** With the help of a supply curve, explain the effect of rising costs on the supply of an item. Do rising costs also affect quantity supplied? Explain briefly.

5. **LO 3.9** Draw hypothetical demand and supply curves for iPods in Canada. Show how each of the following events will affect the equilibrium price and quantity of iPods in Canada:
   a. A successful advertising campaign by producers of iPods
   b. Technological advance in the production of iPods
   c. A fall in the price of a portable media player that is a close substitute for an iPod
   d. The government offering tax incentives to all producers of portable media players, including iPods
6. **LO 3.9** Consider apples and oranges to be substitutes as fruits. Unusually cold weather in Florida destroys a large portion of the orange crop. What would you expect to happen to the price and quantity of the following?
   a. Oranges
   b. Apples
   c. Orange juice

Questions in the Intermediate and Challenging Sections cover several different concepts, and have not been organized by learning objectives.

Intermediate

1. Indicate whether the following statement is true (T) or false (F): "An increase in demand implies an increase in quantity demanded, but an increase in quantity demanded does not necessarily imply an increase in demand."
2. Use demand and supply curves to show that an increase in demand, other things being equal, results in a shortage that forces the equilibrium price up. Indicate the shortage on your diagram.
3. Use demand and supply curves to show that an increase in supply, other things being equal, results in a surplus that forces the equilibrium price down. Indicate the surplus on your diagram.
4. Suppose you are given the following information: In 2007, partly because of media publicity, people's interest

in physical exercise increased. Gym membership soared. Sales of exercise equipment skyrocketed, and many new gyms were opened. By 2010, it became extremely expensive to operate a gym because of increases in rent, heating, and electricity costs.
   a. Use a demand-supply diagram to show what happened to the demand for gym time.
   b. What effect did this demand shift have on the equilibrium price of gym time?
   c. Show the effect of the increase in cost in 2010 on the supply curve.
   d. What effect did this supply shift have on the price of gym time?

Challenging

1. During the ice storm in Eastern Ontario and Quebec in 1998, the prices of candles, flashlights, and batteries rose considerably. Some people claimed that the price increase was immoral because the higher prices could not induce a larger output; they merely gave extra profits to the sellers who just happened to own the highly demanded items. These people argued that prices should be prevented from rising or that the government should intervene to prevent unjust profits. Do you agree with this analysis? If so, why? If not, why not?
2. The tuition fee at Success College (a fictitious college) in 2000 was $10 000 per year, and in that year 6000 students enrolled. In 2010, when the college raised its tuition fees to $14 000 per year, 8000 students enrolled. Clearly, when the price (tuition fee) rose, the quantity of students increased. Can we then conclude, on the basis of this information, that the demand curve for places at Success College is upward sloping? Explain.
3. The price of gas rises and you immediately notice a line-up at the pumps. Is this a violation of the law of demand? If not, what possible explanation can you offer for this phenomenon?

MyEconLab Visit the MyEconLab website at www.myeconlab.com. This online homework and tutorial system puts you in control of your own learning with study and practice tools directly correlated to this chapter's content.

Study Guide

Self-Assessment
The answers to the Study Guide questions can be found in Appendix B.

What's your score?
Circle the letter that corresponds with the correct answer.

1. There is a demand for an item provided that
   a. People want the item
   b. People are able to purchase the item
   c. People are willing to purchase the item
   d. People are willing and able to purchase the item

2. In economics, demand refers to
   a. The amount of money that buyers spend on an item during a specific period
   b. The amount of an item that people will buy at a particular price
   c. The various quantities that people are willing and able to buy at various prices during a specific period
   d. All of the above

3. A demand schedule shows
   a. The demand for a good or service at a particular price
   b. Various quantities of a good or service demanded at various prices
   c. The relation between price and income when all other things remain equal
   d. People's preference to have more income than less

4. Demand can be represented by
   a. A demand curve
   b. A point on a demand curve
   c. A price-quantity combination in a demand schedule
   d. All of the above

5. The law of demand states that
   a. Price will fall as demand rises
   b. People will always buy more of a good or service when its price falls
   c. Quantity demanded will fall as price rises, other things being equal
   d. Demand will exist as long as people have money to buy things

6. Which of the following helps to explain the law of demand?
   a. The fact that demand and quantity demanded are related
   b. The fact that price is a production motivator
   c. The idea that buyers operate under consumer sovereignty
   d. The substitution effect

7. The demand curve is
   a. Upward sloping, showing a direct relationship between price and quantity demanded
   b. Upward sloping, showing an inverse relationship between price and quantity demanded
   c. Downward sloping, showing an inverse relationship between price and quantity demanded
   d. Downward sloping, showing an inverse relationship between income and quantity demanded

8. Which of the following is likely to increase the demand for cellphones?
   a. A fall in the price of cellphones
   b. A general increase in income
   c. Expectations of a fall in the price of cellphones
   d. All of the above

9. A normal good is
   a. A good of normal price and quality
   b. A good for which demand increases as price increases
   c. A good for which demand increases as income rises
   d. A good that causes abnormal people to exhibit normal behaviour

10. Tide and ABC are substitutes as detergents. If the price of ABC rises, other things being equal,
    a. The quantity of ABC demanded will fall
    b. The demand for ABC will not be affected
    c. The demand for Tide will increase
    d. All of the above

11. Cameras and batteries are complements. If the price of cameras falls, other things being equal,
    a. The demand for cameras will increase
    b. The quantity of batteries demanded will fall
    c. The demand for batteries will rise
    d. The demand for batteries will fall

12. An increase in the price of Kindle wireless reading device, other things being equal, will
    a. Increase the supply of Kindles
    b. Increase the quantity of Kindles supplied
    c. Reduce the demand for Kindles
    d. All of the above

13. Which of the following will not shift the supply curve for an item?
    a. A change in the price of the item
    b. An improvement in technology
    c. A change in production costs
    d. A change in the number of sellers

Questions 14–16 refer to Figure 3.18.

14. At a price of $8,
    a. There is a shortage that will exert upward pressure on the price
    b. Demand will increase to move the price to its equilibrium level

Figure 3.18   Demand and Supply

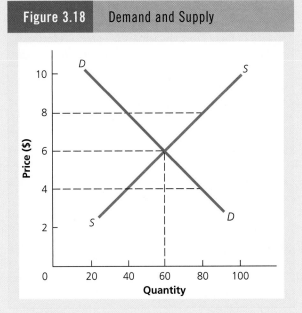

c. An increase in demand

d. A fall in demand

19. If demand and supply increase simultaneously, we can predict that
    a. Equilibrium price and quantity will rise
    b. Equilibrium price will rise, but equilibrium quantity will fall
    c. Equilibrium price will fall, but equilibrium quantity will rise
    d. Equilibrium quantity will rise, but equilibrium price might rise, fall, or remain the same

20. If demand increases and supply decreases at the same time, we can predict that
    a. Equilibrium price will rise, but equilibrium quantity might rise, fall, or stay the same
    b. Equilibrium price and quantity will fall
    c. Equilibrium price will fall, but equilibrium quantity might rise, fall, or stay the same
    d. Equilibrium quantity will rise, but equilibrium price might rise, fall, or stay the same

Problems and Exercises (Use Quad Paper for Graphs)

Answers to these questions can be found on MyEconLab at www.myeconlab.com.   MyEconLab

1. Table 3.9 shows a hypothetical demand schedule for pizza per week in a small Canadian community. Fill in the third column with numbers to show how this schedule will be affected by a rapid movement of people into the community. You have to make up your own numbers.

Table 3.9   A Hypothetical Demand Schedule for Pizza

Price ($)	Original Quantity Demanded	New quantity Demanded
5	6000	_____
6	5000	_____
7	4000	_____
8	3000	_____
9	2000	_____
10	1000	_____

Draw a demand curve based on the data contained in the first two columns of Table 3.9. On the same diagram, draw the new demand curve resulting from the movement of people into the community.

2. Indicate whether the events in the left-hand column of Table 3.10 will affect the quantity demanded or the demand for the item specified in the middle column. Complete the third column. The first one is done as an example: If people expect the price of novels to rise, the demand for novels will increase as people will buy more novels now to avoid paying the higher future price. Because

---

c. Quantity supplied is greater than quantity demanded; this will lower the price

d. The market has reached the highest price

15. At a price of $4,
    a. Demand is greater than supply
    b. The quantity demanded is greater than the quantity supplied; price will rise
    c. There is a surplus that will force the price up
    d. There is a shortage that will shift the supply curve to its equilibrium position

16. At a price of $6,
    a. Buyers and sellers are completely happy
    b. Buyers are willing to buy more, and sellers are willing to sell more
    c. Buyers are buying all they want to buy at that price, and sellers are selling all they want to sell at that price
    d. Buyers will adjust the amount they want to buy, and sellers will adjust the amount they want to sell until both are completely happy

17. In the market for a normal good, an increase in the average income of buyers, other things being equal, will
    a. Increase demand and raise both equilibrium price and quantity
    b. Increase demand and lower both equilibrium price and quantity
    c. Reduce demand and raise equilibrium price and quantity
    d. Reduce demand and lower both equilibrium price and quantity

18. Which of the following will lower equilibrium price and quantity, other things being equal?
    a. An increase in supply
    b. A decrease in supply

Table 3.10   Events and Effects

Event	Item	Concept affected
a. Expectations of a higher price for novels	Novels	Demand
b. An increase in the price of apple juice	Orange juice	
c. An increase in income	Airline tickets	
d. An increase in the price of personal computers	Printers	
e. A fall in the price of personal computers	Personal computers	
f. Expectations of a higher price for colouring books	Crayons	

expectations are a non-price determinant, it is the *demand* (rather than *quantity demanded*) that will be affected.

3. With reference to Question 2, draw graphs to illustrate how each of the events in column 1 will affect the demand for or quantity demanded of the item in column 2.

4. In Table 3.11, you are given the demand and supply schedules for a particular item.
   a. Plot the demand and supply curves from these schedules.
   b. Indicate the equilibrium price and the equilibrium quantity.
   c. On your graph, show the effect of an increase in demand on the equilibrium price and the equilibrium quantity.
   d. On a new diagram, reproduce the demand and supply curves from (a), and show the effect of an increase in supply on the equilibrium price and equilibrium quantity.

Table 3.11   Demand and Supply Schedules

Price ($)	Quantity Demanded	Quantity Supplied
10	60	100
9	70	90
8	80	80
7	90	70
6	100	60
5	110	50

5. Explain, with the help of demand and supply graphs, the effect that each of the following events would have on the equilibrium price and quantity of oranges:

a. Consumers believe a claim that oranges can cure acne.
b. A new machine is developed that will automatically pick oranges more efficiently than previous methods.
c. The price of grapefruit (a substitute for oranges) increases.
d. Average income increases.

6. Use demand and supply diagrams to show the effect of the following events on the equilibrium price and quantity of shoes:
   a. A decision to eliminate the sales tax (that consumers pay) on shoes.
   b. An announcement that the price of shoes will increase by at least 25% within the next month.
   c. The immigration into Canada of a large number of people.
   d. The invention of a machine that greatly reduces the cost of manufacturing shoes.

7. The ABC Moving & Storage Company has the demand for storage bins indicated in Table 3.12.

Table 3.12   The Demand for Storage Bins

Price per Bin per Month ($)	Quantity of Bins Demanded per Month
50	500
45	550
40	600
35	650
30	700
25	750
20	800

The company has 625 storage bins available and currently charges $25 per month for each bin. It cannot obtain more bins.
   a. What problem does the ABC Company face in its current pricing policy?
   b. What might the company do to solve this problem?
   c. Suppose ABC increases its price. What effect will this price increase have on the demand for ABC bins?
   d. Now suppose other storage companies increase their prices while ABC price remains unchanged. What effect will this have on the demand for ABC bins?

8. Use demand and supply analysis (with graphs) to explain how each of the following events will affect the market (i.e., equilibrium price and quantity) for air travel:
   a. A decrease in landing fees.
   b. A marked increase in terrorist activity.
   c. Expectations of increases in the incomes of households.
   d. A substantial increase in the prices of bus fares.
   e. A big discount for round-trip train travel.

3A

Elementary Mathematics of Demand and Supply

Learning Objectives

After studying this appendix, you should be able to

3A.1 Appreciate the mathematical approach to studying demand, supply, and equilibrium price and quantity determination

3A.2 Define the demand function and use functional notation to express demand

3A.3 Define the supply function and use functional notation to express supply

3A.4 Solve demand and supply equations to determine equilibrium price and quantity

3A.5 Use demand and supply equations to calculate the shortage or surplus at a particular price

3A.6 Use demand and supply equations to calculate the effect of a change in demand or supply on equilibrium price and equilibrium quantity

Assess Your Knowledge

MyEconLab

Answers to these questions can be found on MyEconLab at **www.myeconlab.com**.

1. What does a demand equation represent?
2. What does a supply equation represent?
3. What does it mean to say that an equation is linear?
4. If $x = 2$ and $y = 3$, what is the value of $2x + 3y$?

LO 3A.1 Appreciate the mathematical approach to studying demand, supply, and equilibrium price and quantity determination

The Mathematical Approach to Market Analysis

What is the purpose of the mathematical approach to demand-supply analysis?

The main purpose of this elementary mathematical approach to demand-supply analysis is to provide you with another type of tool that can be used to analyze demand, supply, and market price determination. You will have an opportunity to apply the functional notation introduced in Appendix 1A earlier in this book. The algebraic approach can give greater precision and is often easier than a tabular or graphical analysis.

Does this approach require a great deal of mathematical dexterity?

Not at all. No mathematics beyond elementary algebra is used. The actual mathematics used in more advanced economic analysis is much more complex and sophisticated than the simple algebra used here, but even this rudimentary presentation will give you a bit of the flavour of a mathematical approach to economic analysis.

Reading Comprehension

1. How will you benefit from learning a mathematical approach to studying economics?

2. "Only sophisticated mathematics is useful in the study of economics." Do you agree with this statement?

LO 3A.2 Define the demand function and use functional notation to express demand

demand function an equation expressing the relationship between price and quantity demanded

THE DEMAND FUNCTION

What exactly is a demand function?

A **demand function** is a mathematical way of expressing the relationship between quantity demanded and the factors that affect quantity demanded. The demand function for a commodity can be expressed as follows:

$$Q_D = Q(P, Y, P_r, T, E_x, Po) \qquad \text{Equation (1)}$$

where Q_D = quantity demanded

P = price of the commodity

Y = income

P_r = prices of related goods

T = tastes (preferences)

E_x = expectations

P_o = population

The effect of each of the independent variables (the variables in the bracket) on quantity demanded was discussed in Chapter 3 in relation to demand and supply.

In the demand schedules and the demand curves in Chapter 3, we expressed quantity demanded as a function of price alone. Now we have so many variables other than price in the demand function. How do we deal with them?

That is a very important question. To simplify the demand function shown above, let us assume that income, the prices of related goods, tastes, expectations, and population are constant. That is, let's treat them as exogenous variables. The demand function now becomes a relation between price and quantity demanded and may be expressed as the simpler demand function shown in Equation (2):

$$Q_D = Q(P) \qquad \text{Equation (2)}$$

The independent variables in Equation (1) that have been assumed constant are called *shift parameters* (remember *demand shifters*?). If they change, they cause the demand curve to shift. According to the law of demand, the relation between price and quantity demanded is an inverse one. If we assume a linear relationship between price and quantity demanded, then we can express the demand function as follows:

$$Q_D = a - bP, a > 0, b > 0 \qquad \text{Equation (3)}$$

The value of a represents the quantity demanded at a price of zero, and $-b$ represents the slope of the demand function, which is appropriately negative since the demand curve is downward sloping (that is, it has a negative slope). A demand function, for example, could take the form of an equation such as this:

$$Q_D = 10 - 2P \qquad \text{Equation (4)}$$

What are the differences among a demand schedule, a demand curve, and a demand function?

They are all very closely related, but they are *technically* different. They all show the relationship between price and quantity demanded. But the demand schedule is a tabular representation, the demand curve is a graphical representation, and the demand function is an equation.

Reading Comprehension

The answers to these questions can be found on MyEconLab at www.myeconlab.com.   MyEconLab

1. What is a demand function? How is it different from a demand curve?

2. Why does the demand equation have a negative sign before the price variable?

3. Suppose demand is expressed as a functional relationship between price and quantity demanded. List three exogenous variables in this relationship.

LO 3A.3 Define the supply function and use functional notation to express supply

supply function equation expressing the relationship between price and quantity supplied

The Supply Function

What exactly is a supply function?

A **supply function** is a mathematical way of expressing the relationship between quantity supplied and the factors that affect quantity supplied. The supply function for a commodity can be expressed as:

$$Q_S = Q(P, N, P_r, T_e, E_x, P_i) \qquad \text{Equation (5)}$$

where Q_S = quantity supplied
P = price of the commodity
N = number of sellers
P_r = prices of related goods
T_e = technology
E_x = expectations
P_i = prices of inputs

Can we simplify this function as we did with the demand function?

That is exactly what we are going to do. If we assume that the number of sellers (N), the prices of related goods (P_r), technology (T_e), expectations (E_x), and input prices (P_i) are constant, then we can express the supply function as follows:

$$Q_S = Q(P) \qquad \text{Equation (6)}$$

The independent variables in Equation (5) that have been assumed constant are also called *shift parameters* as in the case of demand (remember *supply shifters*?). If they change, they cause the supply curve to shift. A direct relation exists between price and quantity supplied. As in the case of the demand function, let us assume a linear relationship between price and quantity supplied. We can express the supply function as follows:

$$Q_S = c + dP, d > 0 \qquad \text{Equation (7)}$$

where c is a constant and d is the slope of the supply function. The positive slope means that the supply curve is upward sloping. A supply function could be of the following form:

$$Q_S = -5 + 3P \qquad \text{Equation (8)}$$

Assuming that the price is expressed in dollars, the negative sign here means that unless the price is above $1.67 ($5 ÷ 3), sellers will not offer the product for sale.

Reading Comprehension

The answers to these questions can be found on MyEconLab at www.myeconlab.com.   MyEconLab

1. What is a supply function? How is it different from a supply curve?

2. Why does the supply equation have a positive sign before the price variable?

3. Suppose supply is expressed as a functional relationship between price and quantity supplied. List three exogenous variables in this relationship.

LO 3A.4 Solve demand and supply equations to determine equilibrium price and quantity

Market Equilibrium

Can we use equations to present a model of market price determination?

Yes, we can. To determine equilibrium price and quantity, we must bring the demand and supply functions together in a model of price determination. The demand and supply equations give us two equations in three unknowns (Q_D, Q_S, and P). We know that equilibrium in supply and demand analysis occurs when the price is such that there is neither a shortage nor a surplus in the market, hence the equilibrium condition is

$$Q_D = Q_S \qquad \text{Equation (9)}$$

This equation completes the model and allows us to obtain a unique solution. The complete model is

$$Q_D = a - bP \qquad \text{Equation (10)}$$
$$Q_S = c + dP \qquad \text{Equation (11)}$$
$$Q_D = Q_S \qquad \text{Equation (12)}$$

By solving this system of equations for P and Q, we will obtain the market equilibrium price and quantity.

Can we solve the demand and supply equations given in Equations (4) and (8)?

Let's do it. The system of equations that we need to solve is as follows:

$$Q_D = 10 - 2P$$
$$Q_S = -5 + 3P$$

Since in equilibrium $Q_D = Q_S$, we have

$$10 - 2P = -5 + 3P$$

Solving for P, we have $-5P = -15$, so $P = 3$.

Substituting $P = 3$ in either of the equations, we obtain

$$Q_D = 10 - 2(3) = 4 \qquad \text{or} \qquad Q_S = -5 + 3(3) = 4$$

Hence the equilibrium price is 3, and the equilibrium quantity is 4.

Shortage or Surplus

Can we use these equations to determine the shortage or surplus at any given price?

Yes. Let us examine the market condition at a price of $2. At this price, the quantity demanded is as follows:

$$Q_D = 10 - 2P = 10 - 2(2) = 6$$

and the quantity supplied is

$$Q_S = -5 + 3P = -5 + 3(2) = 1$$

Since the quantity demanded (6) is greater than the quantity supplied (1), there is a shortage of $(6 - 1) = 5$.

Let us now examine the market condition at a price of $5. At this price, the quantity demanded is

$$Q_D = 10 - 2P = 10 - 2(5) = 0$$

and the quantity supplied is

$$Q_S = -5 + 3P = -5 + 3(5) = 10$$

Since the quantity demanded (0) is less than the quantity supplied (10), there is a surplus of $(10 - 0) = 10$.

EFFECTS OF A CHANGE

Can we use this algebraic model to determine the effect of a change in demand on equilibrium price and equilibrium quantity?

Yes, we can. Let us use the following demand and supply equations:

$$Q_D = 10 - 2P \text{ and } Q_S = -5 + 3P$$

Now let us suppose that demand increases by 2 units. This means that the quantity demanded increases by 2 units at each price. Thus, the new demand equation becomes

$$Q_D{}^1 = 12 - 2P$$

The supply equation remains

$$Q_S = -5 + 3P$$

We can calculate the new equilibrium price and new equilibrium quantity by solving the two equations:

$$Q_D{}^1 = Q_S: 12 - 2P = -5 + 3P$$

$$-5P = -17$$

The new equilibrium price is $-17 \div -5 = 3.4$.
The new equilibrium quantity is $-5 + 3(3.4) = (-5 + 10.2) = 5.2$.

What about a change in supply?

This can be done in a similar way. Using the same demand and supply equations as before, we can analyze the effects of an increase in supply on equilibrium price and on equilibrium quantity. Let us assume that supply increases by 3 units. This means that the quantity supplied increases by 3 units at each price. Thus the new supply equation becomes

$$Q_S{}^1 = -2 + 3P$$

The demand equation remains

$$Q_D = 10 - 2P$$

We can calculate the new equilibrium price and equilibrium by solving the two equations:

$$Q_D = Q_S{}^1: 10 - 2P = -2 + 3P$$
$$-5P = -12$$

The new equilibrium price is $-12 \div -5 = 2.4$.
The new equilibrium quantity is $-2 + 3(2.4) = -2 + 7.2 = 5.2$.

Reading Comprehension

The answers to these questions can be found on MyEconLab at **www.myeconlab.com**.   MyEconLab

1. The demand and supply equations are given as
    $$Q_D = 90 - 6P; Q_S = -20 + 5P$$
    Quantity demanded is in units and price is in $. Calculate the equilibrium price and the equilibrium quantity.

2. Referring to the demand and supply equations in Question 1, calculate the shortage or surplus at a price of $8.

3. Referring to the demand and supply equations in Question 1, calculate the shortage or surplus at a price of $12.

4. Referring to the demand and supply equations in Question 1, calculate the new equilibrium price and quantity following an increase in demand of 11 units.

Review

1. Review the learning objectives listed at the beginning of the appendix.
2. Have you accomplished all the objectives? One way to determine this is to answer the Reading Comprehension questions at the end of each section. They will help you assess the extent to which you have accomplished the learning objectives.
3. If you have not accomplished an objective, review the relevant material before proceeding.

Key Points to Remember

1. **LO 3A.1** The algebraic approach to demand and supply analysis can give greater precision to the analysis and is sometimes easier than a tabular or graphical approach.
2. **LO 3A.2** A demand function is a mathematical expression of the relationship between quantity demanded and the variables that determine quantity demanded. By assuming that all influences on quantity demanded, except the

price of the item under consideration, are held constant, we can reduce the demand function to a simple functional relationship between price and quantity demanded.

3. **LO 3A.2** Influences on quantity demanded that have been assumed constant are called shift parameters.

4. **LO 3A.2** If the relationship between price and quantity demanded is represented by a table, it is called a demand schedule. If it is represented by a graph, it is called a demand curve; and if it is represented by an equation, it is called a demand function.

5. **LO 3A.3** A supply function is a mathematical expression of the relationship between quantity supplied and the variable that determine quantity supplied. By assuming that all influences on quantity supplied, except the price of the item under consideration, are held constant, we can reduce the supply function to a simple functional relationship between price and quantity supplied.

6. **LO 3A.3** The influences on quantity supplied that have been held constant are called shift parameters.

7. **LO 3A.4** The market equilibrium price and quantity are determined by solving a system of equations consisting of the demand equation, the supply equation, and the equilibrium condition.

8. **LO 3A.5** By using a given price in the demand and supply equations, we can determine whether there is a shortage or a surplus at the given price.

9. **LO 3A.6** The effect of a change in demand or supply on equilibrium price and equilibrium quantity can be easily calculated by using the algebraic approach.

Economic Word Power

Demand function   (p. 104)
Supply function   (p. 106)

Problems and Exercises

Basic

1. **LO 3A.4, 3A.5** You are given the following demand and supply equations:

$$Q_D = 600 - 2P$$
$$Q_S = 300 + 4P$$

a. Calculate the equilibrium price and quantity.
b. Calculate the shortage or surplus at $P = 40$
c. Calculate the shortage or surplus at $P = 60$

2. **LO 3A.4** The demand and supply curves are given as

$$P = 12 - 2Q_D \text{ and } P = 4Q_S$$

Find the equilibrium price and quantity.

3. **LO 3A.4** Solve each of the following equations to determine the equilibrium price and the equilibrium quantity:

a. $Q_D = 32 - 3P$
   $Q_S = -12 + 8P$
b. $Q_D = 60 - 3P$
   $Q_S = -40 + 7P$
c. $Q_D = 900 - 20P$
   $Q_S = -100 + 30P$
   $Q_D = 50 - 4P$
   $Q_S = -10 + 8P$

4. **LO 3A.4** You are given the following demand and supply equations:

$$Q_D = 130 - 3P$$
$$Q_S = -20 + 12P$$

a. Complete the demand and supply schedules in Table 3A.1 on the basis of the demand and supply functions.

Table 3A.1	Demand and Supply Schedules	
Price	**Quantity Demanded**	**Quantity Supplied**
5	0	
10	0	
15	0	
20	0	

b. From the demand schedule, determine the equilibrium price and quantity.
c. Solve the demand and supply equations for P and Q and compare your answer with the answer obtained in part (b).

5. **LO 3A.4** The demand and supply equations in the market for a certain item are:

$$Q_D = 28 - 2P$$
$$Q_S = 5P$$

a. What are the equilibrium price and quantity?
b. Set up demand and supply schedules based on these equations for these prices: $7, $6, $5, $4, $3, $2, and $1.
c. Use your demand and supply schedules to plot the demand and supply curves.

6. **LO 3A.4** The market demand and supply equations are as follows:

$$Q_D = 18 - 2P$$
$$Q_S = -3 + 5P$$

a. By selecting prices ranging from $1 to $6, plot the demand and supply curves.

b. Solve the equations for the equilibrium price and the equilibrium quantity.

7. **LO 3A.6** Referring to the demand and supply equations in Question 6, calculate the new equilibrium price and equilibrium quantity after an increase in demand of 7 units.

MyEconLab   Visit the MyEconLab website at visit **www.myeconlab.com.** This online homework and tutorial system puts you in control of your own learning with study and practice tools directly correlated to this appendix's content.

Chapter **4**

Elasticity

Learning Objectives

After studying this chapter, you should be able to

4.1 Understand the concept of elasticity of demand and how to measure it

4.2 Identify different degrees of elasticity and their graphs

4.3 Interpret the elasticity coefficient

4.4 Distinguish between elasticity and slope

4.5 Explain the relationship between elasticity of demand and total revenue

4.6 Identify the factors that affect elasticity of demand

4.7 Discuss cross-price elasticity and income elasticity

4.8 Understand the concept of elasticity of supply and how to measure it

4.9 Identify the determinants of price elasticity of supply

4.10 Understand the uses of the elasticity concept

Assess Your Knowledge

MyEconLab

Answers to these questions can be found on MyEconLab at **www.myeconlab.com.**

1. When the price of a product changes by 5%, quantity demanded changes by 2% in the opposite direction. Will a 5% increase in the price raise or lower total expenditure on this product?

2. Indicate whether the following statement is true or false: "If a product has a large number of very close substitutes, an increase in its price will cause a relatively small fall in the quantity that people will buy."

LO 4.1 Understand the concept of elasticity of demand and how to measure it

elasticity a measure of the sensitivity of one variable to a change in some other variable

The Meaning of Elasticity of Demand

Is elasticity another aspect of demand and supply?

The concept of elasticity is an important aspect of the demand-supply analysis presented in Chapter 3. **Elasticity** is a measure of the sensitivity of one variable to a change in some other variable. We have established that a change in the price of an item will tend to change the quantity demanded. But just how large will this change in quantity be in relation to the change in price? That depends on the steepness of the demand curve. How does a change in the price of a good or service affect a producer's total revenue? The concept of elasticity will help us to answer such questions.

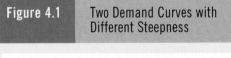

| Figure 4.1 | Two Demand Curves with Different Steepness |

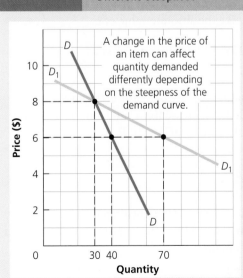

A change in the price of an item can affect quantity demanded differently depending on the steepness of the demand curve.

Can we use a graph to show that the effect of a change in price on quantity demanded depends on the steepness of the demand curve?

We certainly can. Let us consider Figure 4.1. The demand curve *DD* is much steeper than D_1D_1. Let us first focus on *DD*. A fall in price from $8 to $6 increases quantity demanded by 10 (from 30 to 40). Let us now focus on the demand curve D_1D_1. The same fall in price (from $8 to $6) increases quantity demanded by 40 (from 30 to 70).

What is elasticity of demand?

Elasticity of demand is a measure of the degree to which quantity demanded responds to changes in one of the variables that can affect quantity demanded. For some goods and services, a small change in price has a great effect on quantity demanded. For others, a small change in price has no appreciable effect on quantity demanded. The **price elasticity of demand** is the degree to which quantity demanded responds to a change in price. It measures the percentage change in quantity demanded as a result of a given percentage change in price.

price elasticity of demand the degree to which quantity demanded responds to a change in price

We often refer to this concept as own price elasticity of demand to distinguish it from cases where changes in the prices of related goods (substitutes and complements) affect the demand for a good or service.

Is there a formula that we can use to calculate the own price elasticity of demand?

Yes, there is.

The Point Elasticity Formula   If we use E_d to denote own price elasticity of demand, we can use the following formula to calculate own price elasticity of demand:

$$E_d = \frac{\text{Percentage change in quantity demanded}}{\text{Percentage change in price}}$$

Or alternatively,

$$E_d = \frac{\text{Change in quantity demanded}}{\text{Original quantity}} \div \frac{\text{Change in price}}{\text{Original price}}$$

You will recall that we used the symbol Δ (delta) to mean "a change in." We can write the above expression for own price elasticity of demand as

$$E_d = \frac{\Delta Q}{Q} \div \frac{\Delta P}{P}$$

where E_d represents elasticity, Q represents quantity, and P represents price.

This formula is sometimes called the point elasticity of demand formula because it measures elasticity at a point on the demand curve. The value obtained for E_d is just a number, like 2 or 5 or ½, and is referred to as the **coefficient of elasticity of demand**. It measures the degree of elasticity or sensitivity of demand.

coefficient of elasticity of demand the number that measures the degree of elasticity of demand

What is the usual sign of the coefficient of elasticity of demand?

Recall that an increase in price causes quantity demanded to decrease, and that a decrease in price causes quantity demanded to increase. Because price and quantity demanded move in opposite directions, E_d always has a negative value. It is common practice in economics to discard the negative sign and express price elasticity of demand as a positive number. In other words, we take the absolute value of E_d.

Can you give an example to show how the formula is used?

Consider the following example:

> **Example 4.1:** Suppose that a reduction in the price of a product from $10 to $8 causes quantity demanded to increase from 1200 units to 1800 units. What is the coefficient of elasticity of demand?

Solution: The formula for E_d is given by

$$E_d = \frac{\Delta Q}{Q} \div \frac{\Delta P}{P}$$

The change in quantity $(\Delta Q) = (1800 - 1200) = 600$. The original quantity was 1200, that is, $Q = 1200$. The change in price $(\Delta P) = (\$8 - \$10) = -\$2$. The original price was $10. By substituting, we obtain

$$E_d = \frac{600}{1200} \div \frac{-2}{10}$$

$$= \frac{600}{1200} \times \frac{10}{-2} = \frac{-5}{2} = -2.5$$

Discarding the negative sign, we obtain $E_d = 2.5$.

Would we obtain the same answer if the price had changed from $8 to $10 and the quantity from 1800 to 1200?

No. The use of this formula can lead to confusion because different values can be obtained for the coefficient of elasticity depending on whether the price increases or decreases, even if the magnitudes of the changes are the same. In Example 4.1 above, we considered a price decrease. Now consider a price increase in the following example. Note that in both examples, the prices and quantities used are identical.

Example 4.2: If an increase in the price of a product from $8 to $10 causes quantity demanded to decrease from 1800 units to 1200 units, what is the coefficient of elasticity of demand?

Solution:

$$E_d = \frac{\Delta Q}{Q} \div \frac{\Delta P}{P}$$

$$\Delta Q = (1200 - 1800) = -600$$

$$Q = 1800$$

$$\Delta P = (10 - 8) = 2$$

$$P = 8$$

By substituting, we obtain

$$E_d = \frac{-600}{1800} \div \frac{2}{8}$$

$$= \frac{-600}{1800} \times \frac{8}{2} = -1.3$$

Again, discarding the negative sign, we obtain $E_d = 1.3$.

For a price decrease, we obtain an elasticity measure of 2.5. For a price increase, we obtain an elasticity measure of 1.3. The use of this formula seems to place us in a dilemma. Is there any way out?

In fact, there is. The reason for the different measures is that we are measuring elasticity at different points on the demand curve. To remedy this situation, economists have refined the above formula so that the same value is obtained regardless of the direction of the price change. Let us now turn to that refined formula.

What is that refined formula?

The refined formula is called the *arc elasticity of demand* formula.

The Arc Elasticity Formula   By taking the average of the two prices and the average of the two quantities, we obtain the following formula for the price elasticity of demand:

$$E_d = \frac{Q_0 - Q_1}{\dfrac{Q_0 + Q_1}{2}} \div \frac{P_0 - P_1}{\dfrac{P_0 + P_1}{2}}$$

$$= \frac{Q_0 - Q_1}{Q_0 + Q_1} \div \frac{P_0 - P_1}{P_0 + P_1}$$

where Q_0 = original quantity demanded, P_0 = original price, Q_1 = new quantity demanded, and P_1 = new price. This new formula is also called the average elasticity of demand formula and can be written as

$$\frac{\Delta Q}{Q_{avg}} \div \frac{\Delta P}{P_{avg}}$$

where Q_{avg} and P_{avg} are average quantity and average price, respectively.

The concept of arc elasticity becomes meaningful when we consider that the formula measures elasticity between two points on the demand curve. We would like to obtain a measure of elasticity of demand that is the same regardless of the direction of the movement along the demand curve. The arc elasticity formula provides us with that measure. By using this formula, we obtain the same value whether the price increases or decreases.

Let us confirm this assertion by calculating the price elasticity of demand for the price and quantity changes in Example 4.2 above:

$$E_d = \frac{\Delta Q}{Q_{avg}} \div \frac{\Delta P}{P_{avg}}$$

$$\Delta Q = Q_0 - Q_1 = 1800 - 1200 = 600$$

$$Q_{avg} = (1800 + 1200)/2 = 3000 \div 2 = 1500$$

$$\Delta P = P_0 - P_1 = 8 - 10 = -2$$

$$P_{avg} = (8 + 10)/2 = 18 \div 2 = 9$$

$$E_d = \frac{600}{1500} \div \frac{-2}{9} = -1.8$$

The price elasticity of demand is therefore 1.8. Now, see if you can verify that the value for the coefficient will remain the same for a price fall from $10 to $8. Note that the value (1.8) obtained for the elasticity coefficient when we use the average formula is about the average of the values obtained for the elasticity coefficients (2.5 and 1.3) in Examples 4.1 and 4.2 above. This is to be expected, because the average formula takes the average of the quantities and the average of the prices.

> Arc elasticity of demand treats the price and quantity as if they were midway between the initial and the new prices and quantities, and then uses the point elasticity at this midpoint.

Reading Comprehension

The answers to these questions can be found on MyEconLab at www.myeconlab.com.　　MyEconLab

1. Define the elasticity concept.
2. What does own price elasticity of demand measure?

3. Explain why the coefficient of price elasticity of demand always has a negative sign.
4. What is the advantage of the average price elasticity of demand formula over the point elasticity formula?

LO 4.2 Identify different degrees of elasticity and their graphs

Degrees of Elasticity of Demand

What are the varying degrees of elasticity of demand?

A change in the price of a product may have no effect whatsoever on quantity demanded. In other words, the same quantity will be bought whatever the price may be. We can say in this case that we have **perfectly inelastic demand**. The demand for a drug prescribed by a physician is probably close to perfectly inelastic.

Conversely, a small change in price may lead to an infinitely large change in quantity demanded. In this case, we can say that we have **perfectly elastic demand**. If 100 sellers in a fruit market are all selling the same type of grapes at the same price, and one of those sellers in the fruit market raises his or her price, quantity demanded from that particular seller would probably fall to almost zero. In that case, the demand for grapes from that seller is probably close to perfectly elastic. You will encounter this situation in a later chapter.

Between the two extreme cases of perfectly elastic and perfectly inelastic demand are three important cases of elasticity of demand. If a given percentage change in price causes a greater percentage change in quantity demanded, then we have **elastic demand** with respect to price. If a given percentage change in price causes the same percentage change in quantity demanded, then we have **unit elasticity of demand**. Finally, if a given percentage change in price causes a smaller percentage change in quantity demanded, then we have **inelastic demand**.

Can we relate the elasticity coefficient to the degree of elasticity?

You are very perceptive. Applying the elasticity formula to find the elasticity coefficient will help us to determine the degree of price elasticity of demand. The five cases are as follows:

1. If E_d is infinitely large (that is $E_d = \infty$), then demand is perfectly elastic.
2. If E_d is greater than 1 but less than infinity (that is, $1 < E_d < \infty$), then demand is elastic.
3. If E_d is equal to 1, then demand is unitary elastic.
4. If E_d is less than 1 but greater the 0 (that is, $0 < E_d < 1$), then demand is inelastic.
5. If E_d is equal to 0, then demand is perfectly inelastic.

Can graphs be used to illustrate these different degrees of elasticity?

Yes. Graphs can be used to illustrate these different degrees of elasticity. We do this in Figure 4.2. The diagrams in Figure 4.2 are intended to serve for comparative purposes only. The units in which the axes are measured will have some effect on the shapes of the demand curves.

Diagram A illustrates the case of perfectly elastic demand, which is depicted by a horizontal straight line. In this case, a very small percentage change in price brings about an infinitely large change in quantity demanded. Diagram B illustrates the case of elastic demand. An increase in price from P to P_1 causes a more than proportional decrease in quantity demanded, as shown by the change in quantity from Q_1 to Q. The case of unit elasticity is illustrated by Diagram C. A change in price from P to P_1 causes a proportional change in quantity demanded from Q_1 to Q. Diagram D shows the case of inelastic demand. A change in price from P to P_1 causes a less than proportional change

---

perfectly inelastic demand a change in price has no effect on quantity demanded

perfectly elastic demand a change in price causes an infinitely large change in quantity demanded

elastic demand a given percentage change in price causes a greater percentage change in quantity demanded

unit elasticity of demand a given percentage change in price causes the same percentage change in quantity demanded

inelastic demand a given percentage change in price causes a less than proportional change in quantity demanded

Figure 4.2	Demand Curves Showing Various Degrees of Elasticity

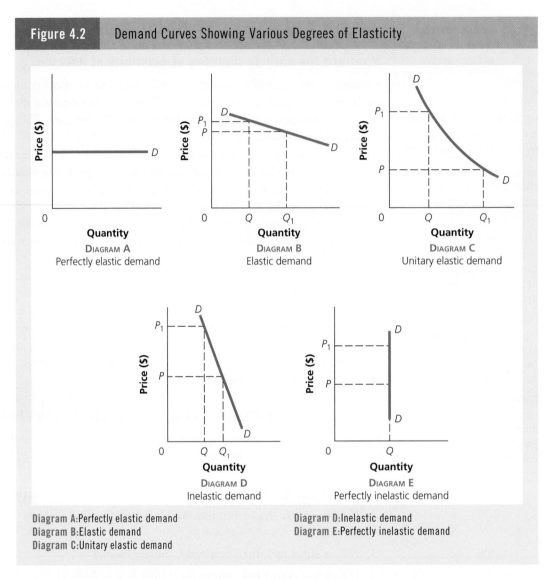

in quantity demanded from Q_1 to Q. Finally, Diagram E illustrates the case of perfectly inelastic demand. A change in price from P to P_1 leaves quantity demanded unchanged at Q units.

Reading Comprehension

The answers to these questions can be found on MyEconLab at **www.myeconlab.com.**   MyEconLab

1. Define each of the following concepts:
   a) Perfectly inelastic demand
   b) Perfectly elastic demand
   c) Elastic demand
   d) Unitary elastic demand
   e) Inelastic demand

2. Explain how the elasticity coefficient can be used to determine the degree of elasticity of demand.

3. What would be the shape (steep or flat) of the demand curve for (a) a product whose demand is elastic? (b) a product whose demand is inelastic?

Interpreting the Elasticity Coefficient

LO 4.3 Interpret the elasticity coefficient

The elasticity coefficient provides us with information about the degree of elasticity. Does it provide us with any more information?

Yes, it does. Previously, we computed the price elasticity of demand by using the average formula and obtained a value of 1.8 for the elasticity coefficient. But what does this number really mean? On the basis of what you learned in the previous section, you will quickly say than a price elasticity coefficient of 1.8 means that the demand for the product is elastic; $E_d > 1$. But it tells us more than that. Let's investigate. We know that

$$E_d = \frac{\%\Delta Q}{\%\Delta P} = 1.8$$

$$\%\Delta Q = 1.8 \times \%\Delta P$$

$$\%\Delta Q = (1.8 \times 10) = 18\%$$

Thus, if the price falls 10%, the resulting increase in quantity demanded is $\%\Delta Q = (1.8 \times 10) = 18\%$. If the coefficient of price elasticity of demand is 1.8, then a 10% change in price causes quantity demanded to change (in the opposite direction) by 18%.

So that means that if the coefficient of elasticity is 2.3, then a 5% fall in price causes quantity demanded to increase by (2.3 × 5) = 11.5%?

You're right. And if the coefficient of price elasticity is 0.7 (demand is inelastic), then a 10% fall in price will cause quantity demanded to rise by only (0.7 × 10) = 7%.

Reading Comprehension

The answers to these questions can be found on MyEconLab at www.myeconlab.com.   MyEconLab

1. Assume that you know that the coefficient of price elasticity of demand for an item is 2.4.
   a) What does this tell you about the demand for the item? (Is it elastic or inelastic?)
   b) By how much would the quantity demanded change if the price were to change by 4%?

2. Assume now that you know that the coefficient of price elasticity of demand for an item is 0.4.
   a) What does this tell you about the demand for the item? (Is it elastic or inelastic)
   b) By how much would the quantity demanded change if the price were to change by 4%?

Price Elasticity along a Linear Demand Curve

LO 4.4 Distinguish between elasticity and slope

A close relationship seems to exist between elasticity and slope. Are they identical?

Elasticity and slope do have a close relationship, but they are not the same. We can demonstrate this by examining elasticity of demand along a linear demand curve. Recall that a linear curve has a constant slope. Let us compute the price elasticity of demand

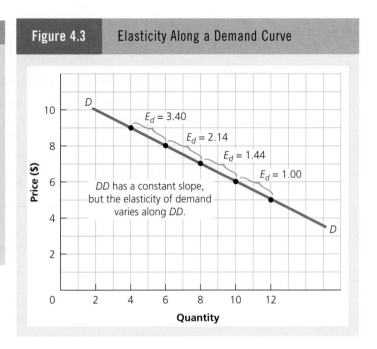

Table 4.1	Demand Schedule and Elasticity	
Price ($) (1)	Quantity demanded (2)	Elasticity (3)
9	4	
		3.40
8	6	
		2.14
7	8	
		1.44
6	10	
		1.00
5	12	

Figure 4.3 **Elasticity Along a Demand Curve**

at each price change shown in Table 4.1. The calculation for the first coefficient only is shown below. The other coefficients are entered in column 3 of Table 4.1 and plotted in Figure 4.3.

$$E_d = \frac{Q_0 - Q_1}{Q_0 + Q_1} \div \frac{P_0 - P_1}{P_0 + P_1}$$

$$= \frac{2}{10} \div \frac{1}{17} = 3.40$$

Note that in Table 4.1, because price elasticity deals with changes in quantity and changes in price, the elasticity coefficients are placed in between the lines rather than on the same lines as price and quantity.

This exercise clearly demonstrates two things: first, elasticity and slope are not identical—the slope of this demand curve is $-\frac{1}{2}$ at every point on the curve (you should verify this); second, the price elasticity of demand varies along a linear demand curve.

> The price elasticity of demand decreases along a linear demand curve as price falls, that is, as we move down the demand curve.

A 5% fall in the price of a $1000 refrigerator is a greater inducement for buyers than a 5% fall when its price is $300.

Reading Comprehension

The answers to these questions can be found on MyEconLab at www.myeconlab.com. MyEconLab

1. What argument can you advance to support the fact that slope and elasticity are not identical?

2. Why is price elasticity of demand higher at higher prices than at lower prices?

LO 4.5
Explain the relationship between elasticity of demand and total revenue

Elasticity of Demand and Total Revenue

What happens to total revenue as the price of a good or service changes?

That depends on the elasticity of demand for the good or service. Total revenue (*TR*) derived from the sale of any product is the price of the product (*P*) multiplied by the quantity sold (*Q*). That is,

$$TR = P \times Q$$

If a seller sells 100 shirts at a price of $15 each, the total revenue received is $(100 \times \$15) = \$1500$. This means, of course, that people spend $1500 on the shirts. Therefore, we note that the sellers' total revenue obtained from the sale of a product is the same as the buyers' total expenditure on that product. If the demand for a good or service is elastic, a fall in its price causes a more than proportional increase in quantity demanded. Hence, total revenue (or total expenditure) increases. Table 4.2 illustrates a case in which the demand for the product is elastic for all price ranges considered. As price falls, quantity demanded increases by a greater proportion than the fall in price, so total revenue increases.

> If the demand for a product is elastic, a fall in its price will cause total revenue to increase; an increase in its price will cause total revenue to decrease.

Table 4.2	A Hypothetical Demand Schedule for a Product with an Elastic Demand		
Price ($)	Quantity Demanded	Elasticity Coefficient	Total Revenue ($)
2.00	70 000		140 000
		5.71	
1.90	90 000		171 000
		4.22	
1.80	110 000		198 000
		3.27	
1.70	130 000		221 000
		2.62	
1.60	150 000		240 000
		2.13	
1.50	170 000		255 000
		1.76	
1.40	190 000		266 000
		1.47	
1.30	210 000		273 000
		1.24	
1.20	230 000		276 000

That makes sense. It would seem to follow that if the demand for a product is unitary elastic, a change in price (increase or decrease) will leave total revenue unchanged. Is that conclusion accurate?

Indeed, it is. In the case of unitary elastic demand, a change in the price of the product causes a proportional change in quantity demanded (but in the opposite direction), leaving total revenue unchanged. Table 4.3 illustrates the case of unit elasticity of demand.

> If the demand for a product is unitary elastic, a change in its price will have no effect on total revenue.

Table 4.3	A Hypothetical Demand Schedule for a Product with Unit Elasticity of Demand		
Price ($)	**Quantity Demanded**	**Elasticity Coefficient**	**Total Revenue ($)**
0.80	60 000		48 000
		1.00	
0.60	80 000		48 000
		1.00	
0.48	100 000		48 000
		1.00	
0.40	120 000		48 000
		1.00	
0.30	160 000		48 000
		1.00	
0.24	200 000		48 000
		1.00	
0.20	240 000		48 000
		1.00	
0.16	300 000		48 000
		1.00	
0.12	400 000		48 000
		1.00	
0.10	480 000		48 000

If the data in the first two columns of Table 4.3 were plotted on a graph, the result would be a demand curve with a constant elasticity of 1.0 ($E_d = 1$). Such a

Figure 4.4	A Demand Curve with Unit Elasticity of Demand

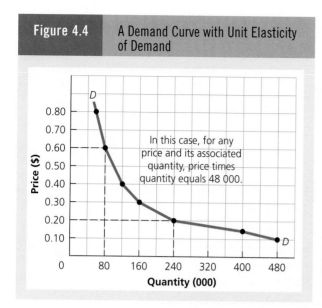

In this case, for any price and its associated quantity, price times quantity equals 48 000.

demand curve would be a rectangular hyperbola conforming to the equation $P \times Q = 48\ 000$, as shown in Figure 4.4.

If the demand for a product is inelastic, will a fall in its price cause total revenue to fall?

Your analysis is correct. If the demand for a product is inelastic, a fall in the price of the product causes a less than proportional increase in quantity demanded; hence, total revenue falls as price falls. The demand schedule for a product with inelastic demand is given in Table 4.4.

If the demand for a product is inelastic, a fall in its price will cause total revenue to decrease; an increase in its price will cause total revenue to increase.

Table 4.4	A Hypothetical Demand Schedule for a Product with Inelastic Demand

Price ($)	Quantity Demanded	Elasticity Coefficient	Total Revenue ($)
0.50	48 000		24 000
		0.52	
0.46	50 000		23 000
		0.46	
0.42	52 000		21 840
		0.40	
0.38	54 000		20 520
		0.35	
0.34	56 000		19 040
		0.30	
0.30	58 000		17 400
		0.26	
0.26	60 000		15 600
		0.22	
0.22	62 000		13 640
		0.18	
0.18	64 000		11 520
		0.14	
0.14	66 000		9 240

Table 4.5		The Elasticity of Demand and Total Revenue	
Price ($)	**Quantity Demanded**	**Elasticity Coefficient**	**Total Revenue ($)**
12	10		120
		6.0	
10	20		200
		2.5	
8	30		240
		1.0	
6	40		240
		0.75	
4	50		200
		0.40	
2	60		120

We noted earlier that the demand for a product can be elastic in one price range and inelastic in another price range. How will total revenue behave in such circumstances?

The basic principle remains the same. If demand is elastic, a fall in price increases total revenue. If demand is unitary elastic, a change in price leaves total revenue unchanged; if demand is inelastic, a fall in price reduces total revenue. As an illustrative example, consider Table 4.5.

As shown in Table 4.5, demand is elastic in the price range from $12 to $8. Thus, as price falls from $12 to $10, total revenue increases from $120 to $200; as price falls from $10 to $8, total revenue increases from $200 to $240. Total revenue remains constant at $240 when price falls from $8 to $6, because demand is unitary elastic between $8 and $6. Within the price range from $6 to $2, demand is inelastic. Thus, when price falls from $6 to $2, total revenue falls from $240 to $120.

Can the relationship between elasticity of demand and total revenue be illustrated graphically?

Yes. Figure 4.5, which is based on Table 4.5, will help you consolidate your understanding of the relation between elasticity of demand and total revenue.

We have seen that if demand is elastic, a fall in price results in an increase in total revenue. Thus, for price decreases within the price range above $8, where the demand is elastic, total revenue rises. This is shown in Diagram B by the rising section of the total revenue curve. If demand is unitary elastic (between $8 and $6 in Diagram A), an increase or a decrease in price leaves total revenue unchanged at $240. This is shown in Diagram B where $E_d = 1$. Finally, if demand is inelastic, a fall in price results in a fall in total revenue. Price reductions under $6 cause total revenue to fall, as shown in Diagram B by the downward-sloping section of the total revenue curve.

Figure 4.5	The Relation between Total Revenue and Elasticity of Demand

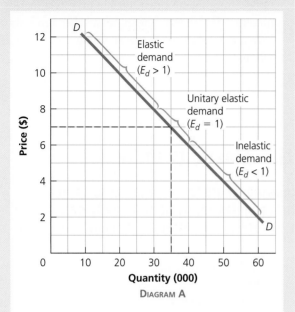

DIAGRAM A

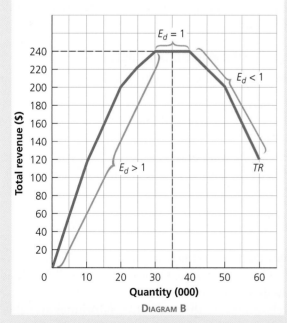

DIAGRAM B

Table 4.6	Elasticity, Price Change, and Total Revenue

Elasticity of Demand	Direction of Price Change	Effect on Total Revenue
Inelastic	Increase	Increase
Inelastic	Decrease	Decrease
Elastic	Increase	Decrease
Elastic	Decrease	Increase
Unitary	Any change	Unchanged

The effect of a price change on total revenue clearly depends on the elasticity of demand. Can we summarize the various results that we have obtained?

The relation between price elasticity of demand and total revenue is summarized in Table 4.6 for quick reference.

Note: The demand for most products is either elastic, unitary elastic, or inelastic. The extreme cases of perfectly elastic and perfectly inelastic demand are rare. You will see in a later chapter, however, that, under certain conditions, the demand for the seller's product can be perfectly elastic.

BUSINESS SITUATION 4.1

The manager of a firm finds out that the demand for her product is highly elastic at the current price.

What price change can she make to increase her total revenue?

The answer to this Business Situation can be found in Appendix A.

Reading Comprehension

The answers to these questions can be found on MyEconLab at www.myeconlab.com.   MyEconLab

1. Explain briefly why an increase in the price of an item with an elastic demand will reduce total revenue, while a fall in its price will increase total revenue.

2. Other things being equal, a fall in price will increase quantity demanded. Therefore, a seller can always increase total revenue by charging lower prices. Discuss.

 LO 4.6 Identify the factors that affect elasticity of demand

Factors Affecting Price Elasticity of Demand

Is there any other way of knowing whether the demand for a good or service is likely to be elastic or inelastic, without actually calculating the elasticity coefficient or observing the effect of a price change on total revenue?

Yes. We can get an idea of the degree of elasticity of demand by considering the factors that affect price elasticity of demand. But before we do so, let us recall that the demand for an item can be elastic in one price range and inelastic in some other price range, as shown in Table 4.5 and Figure 4.5. Note also that the demand for an item can be elastic at a certain time and inelastic at some other time.

What are the factors that affect price elasticity of demand?

The major factors that are likely to affect the price elasticity of demand for a good or service are as follows:

- The availability of substitutes
- The number of uses the item has
- The percentage of income spent on the good or service
- The nature of the product (whether the good or service is a luxury or a necessity)
- The time period being considered

   Let us consider each of these factors.

Substitutes   One of the most important factors likely to influence the price elasticity of demand for a good or service is whether or not substitutes are available. If an item has many close substitutes, its demand is likely to be elastic, because if the price of the item rises, buyers will switch to some of the many close substitutes available. Hence, quantity demanded of that item will tend to fall significantly. Consider the case of a certain brand of coffee. If the price of that particular brand increases, consumers will buy other available brands instead. Thus, we find that the demand for products with many brands tends to be elastic. Conversely, if not many close substitutes exist, quantity demanded will still tend to fall as a result of the higher price, but not by much. Consider the case of a two-cent-per-litre increase in the price of gasoline at the pumps. We will probably observe no significant reduction in quantity demanded as a result of the price increase. Why? Substitution possibilities are limited.

> The greater the substitution possibilities, the more elastic the demand for an item is likely to be.

Number of Uses   In general, the greater the number of uses a commodity has, the more elastic the demand for that product is likely to be. Consider a fall in the price of a commodity (eggs, for example) that has many uses. As the price falls, more of it will be bought to be allocated to those different uses. Conversely, if the commodity has only one or two uses (for example, table salt), it is unlikely that a fall in its price will cause a significant increase in quantity demanded.

> If a product has a large number of uses, its demand is likely to be elastic; if it has only one or two uses, its demand is likely to be inelastic.

Share of the Item in the Budget   Another factor that is likely to affect elasticity of demand is the proportion of income spent on the commodity. If only a negligible percentage of consumers' income is spent on the commodity, the demand for that commodity is likely to be inelastic. An increase in the price of such a commodity has no appreciable effect on the consumer's budget. Hence, expenditure patterns will hardly be affected. As an example, consider the fraction of total income spent on matches. If the price of matches were to increase from five cents to eight cents (an increase of 60%), the resulting fall in quantity demanded is unlikely to be anywhere near 60%. As a matter of fact, the reduction in quantity demanded is likely to be minuscule. But consider the fraction of total income spent on a digital camera—a relatively costly item. An increase in the price of digital cameras will probably result in a significant reduction in quantity demanded. Similarly, a reduction in the price of digital cameras will probably result in a significant increase in quantity demanded; many people might then consider buying a second camera for a family member or as a gift.

> The larger the share of an item in the consumer's budget, the more elastic its demand is likely to be.

Luxury or Necessity   Whether the product is a luxury or a necessity has some effect on its price elasticity of demand. Most people consider milk a basic necessity in children's diets. If the price of milk increases by, say, 10%, quantity demanded will probably not fall by that proportion. Consumers will probably sacrifice some other commodity rather than allow their children to go without milk. The demand for an item that is considered to be a basic necessity is likely to be inelastic. Conversely, an increase in the price of a vacation package to Antigua (a small Caribbean island) is likely to cause a more than proportional decrease in the number bought—other things being equal, of course. In general, the demand for a luxury item is elastic. Luxury items that are also extremely expensive, however, may not quite fit into this general pattern. The demand for luxurious yachts is likely to be inelastic; the people in the market for them are so wealthy that a small increase in price is unlikely to cause any significant reduction in quantity demanded.

> The demand for necessities is likely to be inelastic, while the demand for luxuries is likely to be elastic.

Time The time period being considered will also have some effect on the elasticity of demand for a product. In general, the longer the period being considered, the more elastic the demand is likely to be. This is due largely to the fact that it takes time for people to adjust to new situations. If the price of gasoline rises, people will respond by buying less gasoline, but within a short time span, they are unlikely to buy a great deal less. As time goes by, however, they are likely to use public transportation more, make more use of car pools, and ultimately purchase smaller and more fuel-efficient cars.

> The price elasticity of demand is likely to increase as the time period expands. The longer the period, the more elastic the demand is likely to be.

Can we list some items with inelastic, unitary elastic, and elastic demands?

Studies of the elasticity of demand for various items by different researchers report the following estimates. The associated elasticity coefficients are in brackets after the good or service.

Table 4.7	Estimates of Coefficients of Price Elasticity of Demand (Selected Items)	
Inelastic Demand	**Near Unitary Elastic Demand**	**Elastic Demand**
Salt (0.1)	Movies (0.9)	Restaurant meals (2.3)
Matches (0.1)	Housing (1.2)	Foreign travel, long run (4.0)
Toothpicks (0.1)	Shellfish (0.9)	Airline travel, long run (2.4)
Airline travel, short run (0.2)	Oysters (1.1)	Fresh green peas (2.8)
Gasoline, short run (0.2)	Private education (1.1)	Chevrolet automobiles (4.0)
Gasoline, long run (0.7)	Tires, short run (0.9)	Fresh potatoes (4.6)
Natural gas, short run (0.1)	Tires, long run (1.2)	
Natural gas, long run (0.5)	Radio and TV sets (1.2)	
Coffee (0.25)		
Fish (0.5)		
Tobacco products (0.45)		
Legal services (0.4)		
Physicians' services (0.6)		
Taxi services (0.6)		
Automobiles (0.2)		

Reading Comprehension

The answers to these questions can be found on MyEconLab at **www.myeconlab.com.**   MyEconLab

1. What are the major factors that affect the degree of price elasticity of demand?

2. Would you expect the demand for electric lighting at current prices to be elastic or inelastic? Why?

3. Explain why you would expect the demand for an item to be more elastic in the long run than in the short run.

LO 4.7 Discuss cross-price elasticity and income elasticity

Other Demand Elasticity Concepts

Are there any other concepts of elasticity of demand?

Yes. At this point, we should consider two other important demand elasticity concepts:

- The concept of cross-price elasticity of demand
- Income elasticity of demand

Let us deal with each in turn.

Cross-Price Elasticity of Demand   In Chapter 3, we noted that changes in the prices of other commodities can have some effect on the quantity of a commodity demanded. A change in the price of limes affects the quantity of lemons demanded, and a change in the price of battery-operated toys affects the quantity of batteries demanded. (Remember substitutes and complements?) **Cross-price elasticity of demand** measures the degree of responsiveness in quantity demanded of one good to a change in the price of a related good.

cross-price elasticity of demand the degree of responsiveness in quantity demanded of one good to a change in the price of a related good

> The cross-price elasticity of demand for a product is the percentage change in quantity demanded of that product divided by the percentage change in the price of a related product.

Using the point formula and the notation introduced earlier in this chapter, we can express cross-price elasticity of demand symbolically as follows:

$$E_A P_B = \frac{\Delta Q_A}{Q_A} \div \frac{\Delta P_B}{P_B}$$

Or we can use the average formula and express cross-price elasticity as

$$E_A P_B = \frac{\Delta Q_A}{Q_{A0} + Q_{A1}} \div \frac{\Delta P_B}{P_{B0} + P_{B1}}$$

where $E_A P_B$ represents the cross-price elasticity between A and B, Q_A represents the quantity of product A demanded, P_B represents the price of product B, Q_{A0} and Q_{A1} are the two quantities, and P_{B0} and P_{B1} are the two prices. If A and B are substitutes, then an increase in the price of B causes an increase in the quantity of A demanded. Substitutes therefore show a positive cross-price elasticity of demand. If A and B are complementary goods, then an increase in the price of B causes a decrease in the quantity of A demanded. Complements therefore show a negative cross-price elasticity of demand. If A and B are independent goods (i.e., goods that are not related), then a change in the price of B will have no effect on the quantity of A demanded. Therefore, independent goods show a zero cross-price elasticity of demand. The foregoing discussion can be summarized as follows:

1. If A and B are substitutes, then their cross-price elasticity of demand is positive ($E_A P_B > 0$).
2. If A and B are complements, then their cross-price elasticity of demand is negative ($E_A P_B < 0$).
3. If A and B are independent, then their cross-price elasticity of demand is zero ($E_A P_B = 0$).

Income Elasticity of Demand   Other things being equal, an increase in income leads to an increase in quantity demanded if the good is a normal good. If the good is an inferior good, then an increase in income leads to a decrease in quantity demanded. But by how much will quantity increase or decrease? This depends on the income elasticity of demand. We can define **income elasticity of demand** as the degree to which quantity demanded responds to a change in income.

income elasticity of demand the degree to which quantity demanded responds to a change in income

Income elasticity of demand is measured by the percentage change in quantity demanded divided by the percentage change in income. If we use E_y to denote income elasticity of demand, then

$$E_y = \frac{\text{Change in quantity demanded}}{\text{Original quantity demanded}} \div \frac{\text{Change in income}}{\text{Original income}}$$

What about the sign of the income elasticity coefficient?

You will recall that in Chapter 3, we discussed normal goods and inferior goods. For most goods, as income rises, quantity demanded also rises. These are normal goods. The income elasticity of demand for normal goods will be positive. In some instances, however, smaller quantities of certain goods are demanded as income rises. These are inferior goods. The income elasticity of demand for inferior goods will be negative. We can summarize the foregoing discussion as follows:

1. For normal goods (and this includes most goods), the income elasticity of demand is positive ($E_y > 0$).

2. For inferior goods, the income elasticity of demand is negative ($E_y < 0$).

Can the average formula be used to calculate income elasticity of demand?

As in the case of price elasticity of demand, either of the two formulas can be used to compute income elasticity of demand. You simply substitute income for price.

Note: It is obviously of great importance for producers to have some idea of the effect of income changes on the sale of their products. In other words, they need to know something about income elasticity of demand for their products.

BUSINESS SITUATION 4.2

Farmers have been advised that the income elasticity of demand for wheat is 1.5. The price of wheat is fixed and, on average, people's incomes are expected to increase by 5%.

What change should wheat farmers make in their production of wheat?

The answer to this Business Situation can be found in Appendix A.

Reading Comprehension

The answers to these questions can be found on MyEconLab at www.myeconlab.com.   MyEconLab

1. What is cross-price elasticity of demand? How does it differ from own price elasticity of demand?
2. How can we use the sign of the coefficient of the cross-price elasticity of demand to determine whether two goods are substitutes, complements, or independent?
3. What is income elasticity of demand?
4. How can we use the sign of the coefficient of income elasticity of demand to determine whether a good is normal or inferior?
5. "People always buy more of an item when their income rises. Therefore, the income elasticity coefficient is always positive." Discuss this statement.

LO 4.8 Understand the concept of elasticity of supply and how to measure it

Elasticity of Supply

What is price elasticity of supply?

price elasticity of supply the degree to which quantity supplied responds to a change in price

The concept of elasticity of supply closely parallels that of elasticity of demand. For that reason, we need not devote a great deal of time to the elasticity of supply, but it should in no way minimize the importance of elasticity of supply. The degree to which quantity supplied responds to a change in price is known as the **price elasticity of supply**.

> Price elasticity of supply is the percentage change in quantity supplied divided by the percentage change in price.

If we follow the argument for the formula for the price elasticity of demand, and use E_s for the elasticity of supply, can we not deduce that the formula for price elasticity of supply is $E_s = \dfrac{\Delta Q}{Q} \div \dfrac{\Delta P}{P}$?

That is correct. The only difference between this formula and the price elasticity of demand formula is that Q here represents quantity supplied. By using the average formula, we can compute the coefficient of elasticity of supply as

$$E_s = \frac{Q_0 - Q_1}{Q_0 + Q_1} \div \frac{P_0 - P_1}{P_0 + P_1}$$

coefficient of elasticity of supply the number that measures the degree of elasticity of supply

The value obtained for E_s is the **coefficient of elasticity of supply**, which measures the degree of elasticity of supply. We say that supply is elastic if a given percentage change in price leads to a greater percentage change in quantity supplied. If a given percentage change in price leads to a smaller percentage change in quantity supplied, then we say that supply is inelastic. Note how closely the analysis parallels that of price elasticity of demand. Unlike own price elasticity of demand, however, the price elasticity of supply is positive. Why? Because of the direct relationship between price and quantity supplied.

We used graphs to illustrate various degrees of price elasticity of demand. Can the same be done for price elasticity of supply?

A linear supply curve indicates an elastic supply if it cuts the vertical (price) axis. If a linear supply curve passes through the origin, supply is unitary elastic regardless of its slope. If a linear supply curve cuts the horizontal (quantity) axis, supply is inelastic. Perfectly elastic supply is depicted by a horizontal supply curve and perfectly inelastic supply by a vertical supply curve. Figure 4.6 shows supply curves with different elasticities.

Figure 4.6	Supply Curves Showing Various Degrees of Elasticity

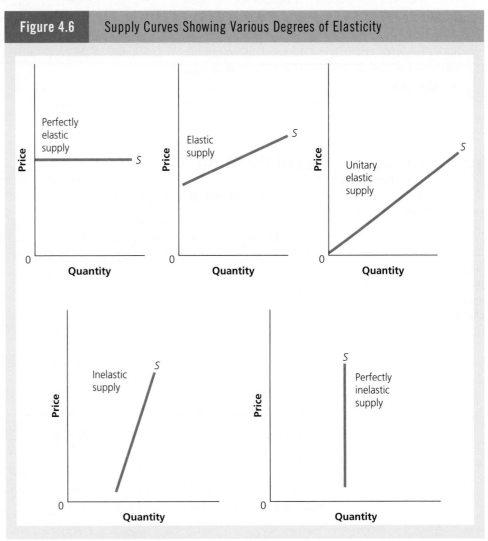

Reading Comprehension

The answers to these questions can be found on MyEconLab at **www.myeconlab.com.**   MyEconLab

1. Define elasticity of supply.
2. What does the coefficient of elasticity of supply measure?

3. What is the shape of the supply curve of a product with an elastic supply? With an inelastic supply?

LO 4.9 Identify the determinants of price elasticity of supply

Factors Affecting Price Elasticity of Supply

What are the factors that affect price elasticity of supply?

The major factors that affect price elasticity of supply are

- Time
- Storage cost and perishability
- Production substitutes and production complements
- The cost of increasing output

Let us consider how each of these factors affects the elasticity of supply.

Time   The period under consideration has a significant effect on the price elasticity of supply. Remember that we are discussing the extent to which producers can respond to a change in price. If the time being considered is very short, then an increase in price does not significantly affect the quantity offered for sale. If a certain quantity of a commodity has already been produced and brought to market, then an increase in price does not cause a larger quantity to be offered for sale, because the quantity is fixed. Producers do not have sufficient time to produce more and so cannot vary the quantity of goods placed on the market. We refer to this situation as the **very short period** or the **market period**. As the period under consideration becomes longer, supply tends to become more elastic. Sellers will be able to respond more easily to changes in the prices of their products. Note that even in the very short period, sellers may withdraw their products from the market rather than sell them below certain prices. This is likely to happen in the case of goods that are not perishable and that do not have high storage costs. The price below which sellers prefer to withdraw their products from the market is a **reservation price**.

very short period or market period a situation in which producers cannot vary the quantity of goods placed on the market

reservation price the price below which sellers prefer to withdraw their products from the market

> The price elasticity of supply is likely to increase as the period expands. The longer the period, the more elastic the supply is likely to be.

Storage Cost and Perishability   The elasticity of supply for goods that are not perishable and that can be stored at a relatively low cost tends to be greater than the elasticity of supply for perishables and goods with high storage costs. If an item can be stored cheaply and its price falls, sellers may respond to the fall in price by withdrawing the item from the market and storing it. If the price of such an item rises, suppliers may be in a position to release some extra quantities from storage onto the market. These options may not be feasible in the face of a high cost of storage. If an item is highly perishable, the supplier will prefer to receive something from it than to have it spoilt. Thus, if its price falls, the seller is unlikely to withdraw it from the market.

> The higher the storage cost, the less elastic the supply of an item is likely to be, and the more perishable an item, the less elastic its supply is likely to be.

Production Substitutes and Production Complements   If a product has a large number of substitutes in production, its supply is likely to be elastic. If the price of such a product falls, producers can shift resources into the production of any of the many substitutes. For example, if the price of cabbage falls, producers can easily switch to lettuce or cucumbers. Because of the ease with which producers can respond to a change in the price of cabbage, its supply is likely to be elastic.

Production complements, you will recall, are goods that are produced together. When one is produced, the other is produced as a direct result. These are joint products. The supply of a relatively minor joint product is likely to be inelastic. Consider again the case of beef and hides. A small increase in the price of hides is unlikely to induce farmers to butcher their cattle. Moreover, once cattle are slaughtered for beef, the hides will be sold at whatever the price may be. Therefore the supply of hides is likely to be inelastic.

> Goods with a large number of production substitutes are likely to have an elastic supply. The supply of a relatively minor joint product is likely to be inelastic.

The Cost of Increasing Output   Recall that price elasticity of supply indicates how sensitive suppliers are to a change in price. Their responsiveness depends on the ease or difficulty of altering output as a result of a change in price. If the cost of supplying each additional unit of an item rises sharply as the firm increases its output, then a higher price will not be much of an incentive to increase quantity supplied. In this case, supply will tend to be inelastic. If, however, the cost of supplying each additional unit rises very slowly as the firm increases its output, the enticement of a higher price will cause a large increase in output. In this case, supply will tend to be more elastic.

> The higher the cost of producing each additional unit of an item, the less elastic the supply is likely to be.

BUSINESS SITUATION 4.3

A retail outlet purchases winter gloves for $10 a pair. The store has a fixed quantity of these gloves, which it will not sell unless it can make a profit of at least 10%. There are no storage costs and the gloves are durable.

What will the retail outlet do (sell or not sell) if the market price is (a) $20, (b) $15, (c) $12, or (d) $10?

The answer to this Business Situation can be found in Appendix A.

Reading Comprehension

The answers to these questions can be found on MyEconLab at www.myeconlab.com.   MyEconLab

1. What are the main factors that affect the degree of price elasticity of supply?

2. Define each of the following terms:
    a) Very short period
    b) Reservation price

3. Explain why the supply of an item with a large number of production substitutes will likely have an elastic supply.

LO 4.10 Understand the uses
of the elasticity
concept

The Uses of the Elasticity Concept

Can you provide some examples of the application of the concepts of elasticity of demand and elasticity of supply?

The concept of elasticity of demand has important applications in business decisions and in public (government) policies. It will be helpful to refer to Table 4.6 on page 125. Suppose that farmers are contemplating increasing the price of tomatoes to increase their revenues from the sale of tomatoes. The success of such a move depends on the price elasticity of demand for tomatoes. As can be seen from Table 4.6, if the demand for tomatoes is price inelastic, then a small increase in price causes total revenue to increase. If the demand for tomatoes is elastic, an increase in price causes total revenue to fall. The farmers will then fail to achieve their objective.

The following example illustrates the importance of price elasticity of demand in government tax policy. Suppose the government of British Columbia wants to increase its revenue from taxation. What commodities can it tax to achieve this objective? Does a tax on gasoline, for example, increase tax revenues? The answer is most likely yes. A tax of two cents per litre on gasoline produces an increase in the government's tax revenues, because the demand for gasoline seems to be inelastic at current prices. If, however, the government increases the tax on a commodity with an elastic demand, the resulting fall in quantity demanded will be relatively greater than the increase in the tax. This implies a fall in tax revenues.

Let us now turn to the price elasticity of supply. We can learn a great deal about certain prices through the price elasticity of supply. Why, for example, are rare paintings so expensive? One answer, of course, is that there is a great demand for them. But that is only a part of the explanation. The other important aspect is that the supply of such paintings is, for all practical purposes, perfectly inelastic. A higher price will not cause another one to be produced. In such a case, the supply curve will be vertical, as shown in Figure 4.7.

Any increase in demand is reflected fully in an increase in price, because quantity supplied cannot increase to absorb or dampen the effect of the increase in demand.

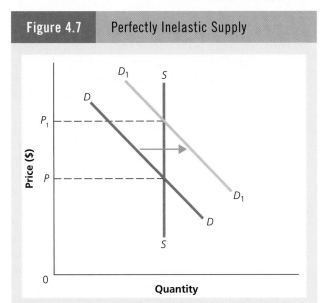

Figure 4.7   Perfectly Inelastic Supply

Reading Comprehension

The answers to these questions can be found on MyEconLab at **www.myeconlab.com.**   MyEconLab

1. Give one example of how a business could use the concept of price elasticity of demand.

2. Use the concept of elasticity of supply to explain why antique furniture is so expensive.

3. Explain why a tax on cigarettes is likely to increase the government's tax revenues.

Review

1. Review the learning objectives listed at the beginning of the chapter.
2. Have you accomplished all the objectives? One way to determine this is to answer the Reading Comprehension questions at the end of each section. They will help you assess the extent to which you have accomplished the learning objectives.
3. If you have not accomplished an objective, review the relevant material before proceeding.

Key Points to Remember

1. **LO 4.1** Elasticity refers to the extent to which one variable responds to a change in some other variable. Own price elasticity of demand is the degree to which buyers respond to a small change in the price of an item. It is measured by the percentage change in quantity demanded divided by the percentage change in price. The resulting value is the coefficient of elasticity of demand. Because of the inverse relationship between price and quantity demanded, the coefficient of own price elasticity of demand is always negative, but it is generally expressed as a positive number.
2. **LO 4.2** The demand for a product can be perfectly elastic (infinitely large response to a price change), elastic (relatively large response), unitary elastic (response proportionate to price change), inelastic (relatively small response), or perfectly inelastic (no response to price change). Perfectly elastic demand and perfectly inelastic demand are extreme cases. The demand for most goods and services is elastic, unitary elastic, or inelastic.
3. **LO 4.3** The elasticity coefficient is a measure of the degree of elasticity. An elasticity coefficient of zero means that the demand for the product is perfectly inelastic; a coefficient between 0 and 1 means that the demand for the item is inelastic; a coefficient of 1 means that the demand is unitary elastic; a coefficient between 1 and infinity means that the demand is elastic; and a coefficient that is infinitely large means that the demand for the product is perfectly elastic.
4. **LO 4.4** Although elasticity and slope are closely related, they are not identical concepts. The slope remains constant along a linear demand curve, but the elasticity varies, being higher at higher prices and lower at lower prices.
5. **LO 4.5** Total revenue is price times quantity. A change in price affects quantity demanded, but the degree to which quantity demanded is affected depends on the price elasticity of demand. If the demand for an item is elastic, a fall in its price, other things being equal, will cause total revenue to increase; an increase in its price will cause total revenue to decrease. If the demand for a product is inelastic, a fall in its price will cause total revenue to decrease; an increase in its price will cause total revenue to increase.
6. **LO 4.6** The main factors that affect own price elasticity of demand are the availability and kinds of substitutes, the number of uses to which the commodity can be put, the share of the commodity in the consumers' budget, the nature of the commodity (whether it is considered a luxury or a necessity), and the period under consideration.
7. **LO 4.7** Cross-price elasticity of demand measures the effect of a change in the price of one good on the quantity demanded of another good. If two goods are substitutes, their cross-price elasticity of demand will be positive. If they are complements, their cross-price elasticity will be negative. Income elasticity of demand refers to the extent to which quantity demanded changes as a result of a change in income. It is measured by the percentage change in quantity demanded divided by the percentage change in income. Normal goods have positive income elasticity of demand; inferior goods have negative income elasticity of demand.
8. **LO 4.8** Price elasticity of supply is the degree to which producers (sellers) respond to a small change in the price of an item. It is measured by the percentage change in quantity supplied divided by the percentage change in price. The resulting value is the coefficient of elasticity of supply. Because of the direct relationship between price and quantity supplied, the coefficient of price elasticity of supply is always positive.
9. **LO 4.9** Important determinants of price elasticity of supply are the period being considered, storage cost, and the existence of production substitutes and production complements.
10. **LO 4.10** The elasticity concept has important applications to decisions concerning pricing and output in business and in public policy. It also helps us to understand the behaviour of certain prices.

Economic Word Power

Problems and Exercises

Basic

1. **LO 4.1, 4.5** A DVD store raised the price of its DVDs from $12 to $16. Correspondingly, sales dropped from 1600 to 1000 per month.
   a. What can you conclude about the price elasticity of demand for DVDs at that store?
   b. What happened to total revenue?

2. **LO 4.5** A retailer noticed that by raising his price slightly, his total revenue increased. What can you conclude about the price elasticity of demand within the current price range?

3. **LO 4.2** Determine the degree of elasticity in each of the following cases:
   a. When the price of the only pill that soothes your headache rises from $4 to $8 per bottle, you buy it just the same.
   b. You would be willing to buy two tickets for $50 each to attend a rock concert; but at $75 each, you would not attend the concert.
   c. The price of coffee rose from $1.50 to $1.75 per cup, yet you buy the same number of cups of coffee as before.

4. **LO 4.1** A 5% increase in price results in a 7.5% decrease in quantity demanded. Calculate the coefficient of elasticity of demand.

5. **LO 4.3** If the coefficient of elasticity of demand is 2.1, what effect will a 4% rise in price have on quantity demanded?

6. **LO 4.1** When the price of an item rises from $45 to $55, quantity demanded falls from 65 000 to 35 000. Use the average elasticity formula to calculate the coefficient of elasticity of demand.

7. **LO 4.7** When the price of an item A increases from $100 to $110, quantity demanded of another item, B, rises from 800 to 900. Use the point elasticity formula to calculate the cross-price elasticity of demand between A and B. Are A and B substitutes or complements?

Questions in the Intermediate and Challenging Sections cover several different concepts, and have not been organized by learning objectives.

Intermediate

1. You went to an amusement park with $40, all of which you decided to spend on rides regardless of the price of tickets for the rides.
   a. Draw your demand curve for rides.
   b. What can you say about your elasticity of demand for rides?

2. It has been determined that the income elasticity of demand for big cars is 1.5. Over the past several years, income in general has risen, but the number of big cars bought has fallen. How can this fact be explained?

3. The price elasticity of demand for an item is 2.3 and the income elasticity of demand is 1.8. What effect will a 5% increase in price and a simultaneous 7% increase in income have on quantity demanded?

Challenging

1. A company is currently charging $10 for its product. It determines that near this price, the demand for its product is highly elastic, while below this price of $10, the demand for its product is highly inelastic.
   a. Draw the demand curve for this company's product.
   b. What price change should this company make to maximize its revenue?

2. When annual average income in a given community rises from $30 000 to $40 000, the demand for dishwashers increases from 80 000 to 120 000.
   a. Calculate the income elasticity of demand.
   b. What information can you gather from this elasticity coefficient?

3. A student accepts employment to sell a particular type of book door to door. Normally, the student sells 500 books per month at a price of $5 each. The company offers an incentive of one full week's pay if the student sells 1000 books per month. The student has the option of lowering the price by as much as $1.25. The price elasticity of demand for these books is 3. What price should this student charge to sell 1000 books per month? (Hint: Use the arc formula.)

MyEconLab Visit the MyEconLab website at www.myeconlab.com. This online homework and tutorial system puts you in control of your own learning with study and practice tools directly correlated to this chapter's content.

Study Guide

Self-Assessment

The answers to the Study Guide questions can be found in Appendix B.

What's your score?

Circle the letter that corresponds with the correct answer.

1. The concept of elasticity refers to
   a. The extent to which an item can be expanded
   b. The amount of elastic substances used to produce the item
   c. The degree of responsiveness to change
   d. The notion that people always prefer more to less

2. Elasticity of demand tells us
   a. How much people will buy at various prices
   b. The revenue that will be received from selling various quantities of an item
   c. The extent to which quantity demanded will change in response to a change in one of the determinants of quantity demanded
   d. All of the above

3. Own price elasticity of demand refers to
   a. A change in the price of a good resulting from a change in demand
   b. Buyers' demand for products that they are selling (that is, their own products)
   c. The sensitivity of the price of a product to changes in demand for that product
   d. The sensitivity of the quantity demanded of a product to a change in the price of the product

4. Price elasticity of demand measures
   a. The highest price that consumers are willing and able to pay for a good or service
   b. How much more consumers will buy as their incomes rise
   c. The effect of a change in price on the amount that consumers will be willing and able to buy
   d. The percentage change in price resulting from a given change in quantity demanded

5. The point elasticity formula for own price elasticity of demand is
   a. The change in price divided by the change in quantity demanded
   b. The change in quantity demanded divided by the change in price
   c. The percentage change in price divided by the percentage change in quantity demanded
   d. The percentage change in quantity demanded divided by the percentage change in price

6. Because price and quantity demanded are inversely related, the sign of the coefficient of price elasticity of demand
   a. Will be negative
   b. Can be either positive or negative
   c. Will be positive
   d. Is irrelevant

7. One advantage of the arc or average formula over the point formula is that the arc formula
   a. Is simpler and thus easier to use
   b. Gives the same value for the coefficient regardless of the direction of the price change
   c. Both (a) and (b)
   d. Neither (a) nor (b)

8. A 10% fall in the price of an item causes the quantity demanded to rise by 6%. This means that the demand for the item is
   a. Inelastic
   b. Unitary elastic
   c. Elastic
   d. Perfectly elastic

9. The coefficient of elasticity of demand for video games in a certain city is calculated to be −2.1, but we have agreed to express it as 2.1. If the price of video games increases by 10%, quantity demanded will fall by
   a. 12.1%
   b. 7.9%
   c. 5%
   d. 21%

10. The coefficient of price elasticity of demand for digital cameras is found to be 1.9. If sellers of digital cameras lower their prices, their revenues from the sale of digital cameras will
    a. Increase
    b. Decrease
    c. Remain constant
    d. Be indeterminate

11. A company that sells household products increases the price of one of its products in an attempt to increase its revenue from the sale of that product. This suggests that the company believes that the demand for that product is
    a. Elastic
    b. Inelastic
    c. Unitary elastic
    d. Perfectly elastic

12. Which of the following is a determinant of the degree of price elasticity of demand for an item?
    a. The number and closeness of substitutes
    b. The fraction of the budget spent on the item
    c. The number of uses the item has
    d. All of the above

13. A 5% increase in the price of beef causes the quantity of chicken demanded to increase by 8%. This implies that the cross-price elasticity of demand between chicken and beef is
    a. Elastic
    b. Inelastic
    c. Unitary elastic
    d. Unknown

14. The cross-price elasticity of demand between *A* and *B* is known to be positive. From this information, we can infer that
    a. *A* and *B* are substitutes
    b. *A* and *B* are complements
    c. *A* is an inferior good
    d. *B* is an inferior good

15. An increase in income from $7500 to $9000 causes an increase in purchases of a good from 3000 to 3500 units. The income elasticity of demand for that good must therefore be
    a. 1.20
    b. 0.83
    c. 3.60
    d. 0.61

16. If the income elasticity of demand for a product is negative, then we know that the product is
    a. A normal good
    b. Relatively scarce
    c. An inferior good
    d. None of the above

17. An important factor affecting price elasticity of supply is
    a. The ease with which buyers can obtain substitutes
    b. The number of uses the product has
    c. The length of time at the producers' disposal
    d. None of the above

18. Because price and quantity supplied are directly related, we would expect the sign of the coefficient for the price elasticity of supply to be
    a. Positive
    b. Positive then negative
    c. Negative
    d. Negative then positive

19. In the very short period (market period), supply is
    a. Perfectly elastic
    b. Unitary elastic
    c. Perfectly inelastic
    d. None of the above

20. Which of the following is likely to yield the highest tax revenue?
    a. A tax on a product with an elastic demand
    b. A tax on a product with an inelastic demand
    c. A tax on an inferior good
    d. A tax on a product with unitary elastic demand

Problems and Exercises (Use Quad Paper for Graphs)

Answers to these questions can be found on MyEconLab at www.myeconlab.com. MyEconLab

1. On Table 4.8, indicate the nature of demand (elastic, inelastic, etc.) for the commodity indicated and the reason for your answer. The first one is done as an example.

2. When the price of laptop computers falls from $1500 to $1200, quantity demanded increases from 20 000 to 27 000. Compute the coefficient of price elasticity of demand for laptop computers by using
    a. The point elasticity formula
    b. The arc elasticity formula

3. Repeat Exercise 2 but with a price change from $1200 to $1500 and a quantity change from 27 000 to 20 000.

Table 4.8	The Price Elasticity of Demand	
Commodity	**Nature of demand**	**Reason**
Prescribed drug	Inelastic	Necessity and its use is controlled
Bubble gum		
Beef		
Yachts		
Mint tea		
Vaseline® skin lotion		

Table 4.9	A Demand Schedule for a Commodity	
Price ($)	Quantity Demanded	Elasticity Coefficient
10	50	
		_____
8	60	
		_____
6	70	
		_____
4	80	
		_____
2	90	

Table 4.10	The Quantity of Wallets Bought at Different Prices		
Price ($)	Quantity Bought	Total Revenue ($)	Elasticity Coefficient
10	100	_____	
			_____
9	120	_____	
			_____
8	140	_____	
			_____
7	160	_____	
			_____
6	180	_____	
			_____
5	200	_____	

4. Table 4.9 shows the demand schedule for a certain commodity.
   a. Use the arc elasticity formula to compute the price elasticity coefficient at each price change, and complete the third column.
   b. From this exercise, what have you observed about the price elasticity of demand at higher prices compared with the price elasticity of demand at lower prices?
5. Table 4.10 gives data for the quantity of wallets bought during a period.
   a. Complete the total revenue column.
   b. Compute the price elasticity of demand for each price change and complete the elasticity coefficient column.
   c. Explain the relation that you observe between total revenue and price elasticity of demand.

6. When the price of x increases from $50 to $55, the quantity of y demanded rises from 400 to 450. Use the point elasticity formula to calculate the cross-price elasticity of demand between x and y.
7. When average income increases from $5000 to $8000, the quantity of automobiles demanded increases from 100 000 to 120 000.
   a. Calculate the income elasticity of demand.
   b. What information does this elasticity coefficient give?
8. Assume that Canadian wheat farmers face a price elasticity of demand for wheat of 0.65. How will a bad harvest that sends wheat harvest prices up by 15% affect wheat growers?

Chapter

5

Applications of Demand and Supply Analysis

Learning Objectives

After studying this chapter, you should be able to

5.1 Explain consumer surplus and producer surplus

5.2 Distinguish between price floors and price ceilings, and explain the effects of price ceilings and price floors

5.3 Analyze the effects of production quotas

5.4 Analyze the effects of excise taxes

5.5 Analyze the effect of a tax on buyers

Assess Your Knowledge

MyEconLab

Answers to these questions can be found on MyEconLab at **www.myeconlab.com**.

1. All provinces and territories in Canada have enacted minimum wage legislation. What do you think is the objective of minimum wage legislation?

2. Explain briefly why you think that a tax on the following items will or will not produce large tax revenues for the government:
   a. Food
   b. Prescribed medication
   c. Baby clothes
   d. Toilet paper

LO 5.1 Explain consumer surplus and producer surplus

Consumer Surplus and Producer Surplus

The market system is efficient. Why then does the government intervene in the market system?

Although the market mechanism encourages people to economize on the economy's scarce resources, it can produce results that most people consider to be unfair and unacceptable. For this reason, the government intervenes in the market system to alter the market-determined results and to produce effects that may be more politically and socially acceptable.

What is consumer surplus?

consumer surplus the difference between the amount that consumers would have paid for a commodity and the amount that they actually pay

Let us illustrate with an example. Suppose the price of apples is $0.50 per kilogram. Quite possibly, consumers might be willing to pay $0.85 for the first kilogram, but they pay only $0.50 because this is the market price. They thus enjoy a bonus or extra benefit of $0.35 on the first kilogram. We refer to this difference between the amount that consumers would have paid for a product and the amount that they actually pay as **consumer surplus**. Consumers might possibly be willing to pay $0.75 for the second kilogram, but they still pay only $0.50. So for the first two kilograms, consumers would have paid $1.60 ($0.85 for the first and $0.75 for the second), but they pay only $1.00 ($0.50 for each kilogram). The consumer surplus on the second kilogram would be ($0.75 less $0.50) = $0.25; and the consumer surplus on the first two kilograms would be $0.60 ($0.35 on the first plus $0.25 on the second). For the third kilogram, they might be willing to pay $0.70, but again, they pay only $0.50. The consumer surplus on the third kilogram is ($0.70 − $0.50) = $0.20. The consumer surplus on all three kilograms would therefore be ($0.60 + $0.20) = $0.80. They might be willing to pay $0.65 for the fourth kilogram, but once again they pay only $0.50, obtaining a consumer surplus of $0.15. The total consumer surplus on all four kilograms would be $0.95. Table 5.1 shows the relevant data.

So far, graphs have been used as visual aids in the understanding of many concepts. Can a graph be used to illustrate consumer surplus?

Consider Figure 5.1. The equilibrium price and the equilibrium quantity established by the market for this good or service are $0.50 and 6 kilograms, respectively. Many

Table 5.1	An Illustration of Consumer Surplus		
Apples (kg)	Total Amount Consumers Would Have Paid ($)	Total Amount Actually Paid ($)	Consumer Surplus ($)
1	0.85	0.50	0.35
2	1.60	1.00	0.60
3	2.30	1.50	0.80
4	2.95	2.00	0.95

Figure 5.1	A Graphical Illustration of Consumer Surplus

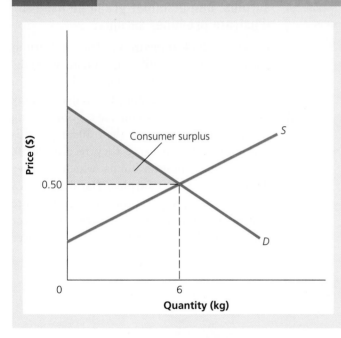

buyers would have been willing to pay a higher price than $0.50 to obtain this commodity. But because they have to pay only $0.50, they actually receive a bonus, which we have defined as consumer surplus.

Each consumer's surplus differs depending on the price that he or she is willing to pay. And this price depends on the consumer's evaluation of the benefits derived from this item. The shaded area in Figure 5.1 measures total consumer surplus. Note that an increase in price reduces the size of consumer surplus, while a fall in price increases consumer surplus.

Does consumer surplus have any particular economic significance?

Yes, it does. The economic significance of the concept of consumer surplus is that consumers often derive greater benefits from a good or service than is suggested by the price of the good or service.

Is there a concept that corresponds to consumer surplus on the producers' side?

Yes, and not surprisingly, it is referred to as producer surplus.

What is producer surplus?

The concept of producer surplus is analogous to that of consumer surplus. As we did in the case of consumer surplus, let us illustrate with an example. Suppose again that the price of apples is $0.50 per kilogram. Producers might be willing to sell the first kilogram for $0.25 (which would be at least equal to the cost of production), but they get $0.50—the market price. Thus, they derive a bonus of $0.25 on the first kilogram they sell. We refer to this difference between the amount that producers actually receive from selling an item and the amount they would have accepted for the item as **producer surplus**. Producers might possibly be willing to sell the second kilogram for $0.30, but they still receive $0.50, realizing a bonus or surplus of $0.20. So for the first two kilograms, producers would have accepted ($0.25 + $0.30) = $0.55, but they receive $1.00 ($0.50 for each kilogram). The producer surplus on the first two kilograms would be ($0.25 on the first plus $0.20 on the second) = $0.45. For the third kilogram, they might be willing to accept $0.35, but again they receive $0.50. The producer surplus on the third kilogram is ($0.50 − $0.35) = $0.15. The producer surplus on all three kilograms is ($0.45 + $0.15) = $0.60. Producers

producer surplus the difference between the amount that producers receive from selling an item and the amount they would have accepted for the item

might be willing to accept $0.40 for the fourth kilogram, but once again they receive $0.50, realizing a producer surplus of $0.10. The total producer surplus on all four kilograms would be $0.70. Table 5.2 shows the relevant data.

Table 5.2	An Illustration of Producer Surplus		
Apples (kg)	Total amount Producers Would Have Accepted	Total Amount Actually Received	Producer Surplus
1	0.25	0.50	0.25
2	0.55	1.00	0.45
3	0.90	1.50	0.60
4	1.30	2.00	0.70

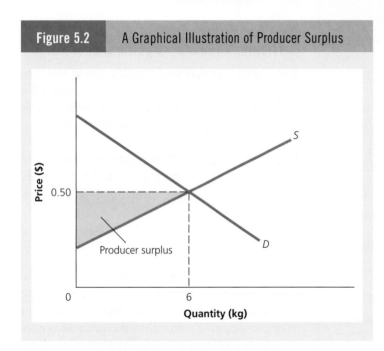

Figure 5.2 A Graphical Illustration of Producer Surplus

A graph was used to illustrate consumer surplus. Can a similar graph be used to illustrate producer surplus?

Let's take a look at Figure 5.2. The equilibrium price and the equilibrium quantity established by the market for this good or service are $0.50 and 6 kilograms, respectively. Many producers (sellers) would have been willing to accept a lower price than $0.50 for this commodity. But because they receive $0.50, they actually obtain a bonus, which we have defined as producer surplus. The shaded area in Figure 5.2 represents producer surplus. Note that an increase in price increases producer surplus, while a fall in price reduces producer surplus.

Reading Comprehension

The answers to these questions can be found on MyEconLab at www.myeconlab.com. MyEconLab

1. What is consumer surplus?
2. What is the economic significance of consumer surplus?

3. How does a change in price affect consumer surplus?
4. What is producer surplus?
5. How does a change in price affect producer surplus?

Price Ceilings and Price Floors

LO 5.2 Distinguish between price floors and price ceilings, and explain the effects of price ceilings and price floors

price ceiling the upper limit at which a seller is legally allowed to sell a commodity

What is a price ceiling?

A **price ceiling** is the upper limit at which a seller is legally allowed to sell a commodity. The law forbids the sale of the product above a certain price. For example, to prevent firms from charging what can be considered an exorbitant price for a product, and thus gouging consumers, a government can set an upper limit on the price that can be charged for that product.

What is the effect of a price ceiling?

We will use the example of rent control to show the effect of a price ceiling.

Rent Control   In an attempt to protect the interest of tenants, a government can pass legislation limiting the prices that landlords can charge for apartment rentals. Rent control means that a landlord is not permitted by law to charge his or her tenants a rent that is above what is prescribed by law. Rent control is an example of a price ceiling. Figure 5.3 is helpful in analyzing the effects of rent control. We will examine the issue both in the short run and in the long run.

In Figure 5.3, the demand for rented accommodation comes from tenants and is shown by the demand curve *DD*. The higher the rent, the smaller the quantity of rented accommodation demanded. The supply of rented accommodation comes from landlords. In the short run, because it takes landlords some time to respond to changes in price, the supply of rented accommodation is inelastic as shown by the short-run supply curve *SS*. The two curves intersect to determine the equilibrium rent and the equilibrium number of units that would be rented. The market-determined rent (the equilibrium rent) would be $600 per unit per month, and the equilibrium quantity of housing units would be 50 000.

If the maximum price permissible is set above the equilibrium price, say at a rent ceiling of $700 per month, landlords would charge the market-determined rent of $600 per month and be in compliance with the law, which stipulates that they cannot charge more than $700. In this case, the rent control would have no effect. Suppose now that the rent ceiling is set at $400, which is below the equilibrium price (rent). Landlords cannot legally charge the equilibrium price; to do so would be a violation of the law. At the government-determined price of $400, landlords are willing to offer only 25 000 units for rent, while tenants are willing to rent 75 000 units. A shortage of 50 000 (75 000 − 25 000) units results.

Figure 5.3	The Effect of a Price Ceiling (Rent Control)

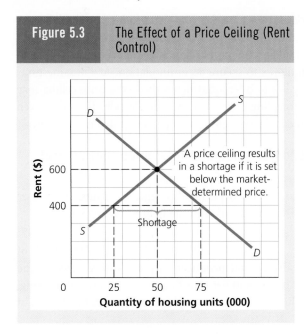

A price ceiling results in a shortage if it is set below the market-determined price.

So rent control causes a shortage. Is this in itself a problem?

A shortage in itself is not necessarily a problem in the market system. We have seen that in the absence of price control, a shortage will be eliminated by an increase in the price. But in the case of rent control, the price is not allowed to rise, and this indeed does create a problem. Note that those tenants who can find accommodation at this controlled rent derive some benefit. They obtain living accommodation at a lower rent.

What problem does a shortage cause?

To examine the effects of a shortage caused by rent controls, we must proceed to a long-run analysis. In the long run, landlords are able to respond to a greater extent to a change in price. They build fewer rental units or divert resources from the construction of new units to other uses. Often, they simply allow certain units to deteriorate. In the long run, the supply curve becomes more elastic. Note that in the long run, the shortage becomes greater.

When a shortage exists, some form of rationing must be instituted, if not by the government, then by the market.

black market a market in which products are sold illegally above the price prescribed by law

Black Markets   Quite often, a **black market**, a market in which products are sold illegally above the price prescribed by law, is the long-run result of price ceilings. In the case of rent control, tenants who are unable to find apartments because of the shortage, are willing to make secret deals (bribes) with landlords to secure accommodation. At the same time, landlords who are not permitted by law to offer apartments above the price ceiling may attempt to circumvent the law by accepting cash payments on the side. They may even require illegally large up-front payments before renting an apartment to a new tenant.

Besides the possible emergence of black markets, does rent control have any other effects?

Yes, it does. Rent control reduces consumer surplus and producer surplus, and causes resources to be lost. These effects can be analyzed with the help of Figure 5.4.

Loss of Consumer Surplus, Producer Surplus, and Deadweight Loss   In Diagram A of Figure 5.4, the sum of consumer surplus and producer surplus is maximized at the market-determined price and quantity of $600 per month and 50 000 units of housing. In Diagram B, both consumer surplus and producer surplus have shrunk by the area of

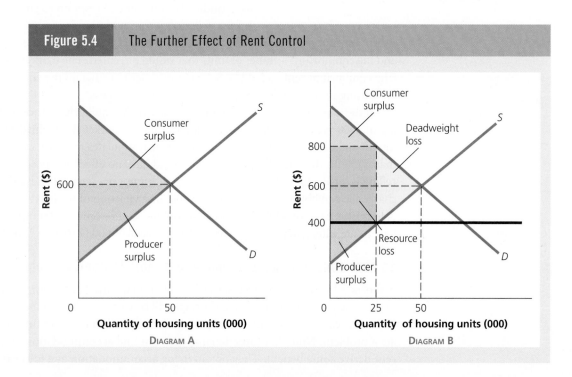

| Figure 5.4 | The Further Effect of Rent Control |

DIAGRAM A

DIAGRAM B

deadweight loss the loss in consumer surplus and producer surplus resulting from a switch from an efficient level of production to an inefficient level of production

the yellow triangle. This loss in consumer surplus and producer surplus resulting from a switch from an efficient level of production to an inefficient level of production is referred to as **deadweight loss**. It results from the reduction in the level of production from 50 000 units to 25 000 units—the effect of the $400 rent ceiling. Consumers and producers suffer this loss.

Part of the deadweight loss is borne by tenants who are unable to find housing because of the fall in the quantity supplied, and part is borne by landlords who are unwilling to offer housing at the rent ceiling.

Are there still additional losses?

Yes, there are additional losses.

Resource Loss Look again at Diagram B of Figure 5.4. You will notice an additional loss in consumer surplus and producer surplus that is not captured in the deadweight loss. Resources are used up in activities designed to evade the rent control. Resources are also used up in search cost—the time and energy expended in trying to find housing. These losses are represented in Diagram B by the green rectangle.

Are all the losses from rent control captured in Diagram B of Figure 5.4?

Unfortunately not. As time progresses and landlords have no motivation to provide additional housing at the price ceiling, or to spend money on building maintenance, not only the quantity of housing will diminish but the quality of housing will also decrease.

Rent control may result in the refusal of landlords to maintain their buildings. This may cause apartment buildings to be abandoned.

These losses are substantial. Does anyone benefit from price ceilings?

Some tenants do benefit from rent control. Those who are able to secure housing at the lower price of $400 per month obviously derive an increase in consumer surplus, and landlords who are able to circumvent the rent control law and charge a rent above $400 derive an increase in producer surplus.

BUSINESS SITUATION 5.1

Landlords in a Canadian city are charging $750 per month for each apartment. The city then introduces rent control, making it illegal for landlords to charge more than $650 per month for an apartment.

How might landlords react to this new business situation?

The answer to this Business Situation can be found in Appendix A.

What is a price floor?

price floor the lowest price at which a seller is legally allowed to sell a commodity

A **price floor** is the lowest price at which a seller is legally allowed to sell a commodity. The law forbids the sale of the good or service below a certain price. For example, to assist farmers, the government might enact legislation forbidding the sale of certain agricultural products below a certain price.

Table 5.3	Minimum Wage in Canada, March 2011

Province or Territory	Minimum Wage/Hour ($)
Alberta	8.80
British Columbia	8.00
Manitoba	9.50
New Brunswick	9.50
Newfoundland and Labrador	10.00
Northwest Territories	10.00
Nova Scotia	9.65
Nunavut	11.00
Ontario	10.25
Prince Edward Island	9.00
Quebec	9.50
Saskatchewan	9.25
Yukon	9.00

What is the effect of a price floor?

We will use the example of minimum wage legislation to show the effect of a price floor.

Minimum Wage Legislation   In an attempt to advance the interests of workers, a government can pass legislation making it illegal for employers to pay workers less than a certain wage. Employers can offer a wage rate that exceeds the minimum, but they cannot legally hire workers for less than the minimum wage. A minimum wage is an example of a price floor.

All provinces and territories in Canada have minimum wage laws. Table 5.3 records minimum wage rates in Canadian provinces and territories as of March 2011.

Figure 5.5 is helpful in analyzing the effects of minimum wage legislation. This time we are analyzing the market for a factor of production (labour). The demand for workers comes from employers (firms) and is shown by the demand curve *DD* in Figure 5.5. The higher the wage rate, the smaller the quantity of workers demanded. The supply of labour services comes from workers and is shown by the supply curve *SS* in Figure 5.5. The higher the wage rate, the greater the incentive to provide labour services. The two curves intersect to determine the equilibrium wage rate and the equilibrium number of workers that would be hired. The market-determined wage (the equilibrium wage) would be $5.00 per hour, and the equilibrium quantity of workers would be 50 000, as shown in Figure 5.5.

If the minimum wage is set below the equilibrium wage, say a minimum wage of $4.00 per hour, firms would pay the market-determined wage of $5.00 per hour and be in compliance with the law, which stipulates that they cannot pay less than $4.00. In this case, the minimum wage law would have no effect. Suppose now that the minimum wage is set at $7.00, which is above the equilibrium price (wage). Employers cannot legally pay the equilibrium wage; to do so would be a violation of the law. At the government-determined wage rate of $7.00 per hour, firms are willing to hire only 30 000 workers, while 75 000 workers are willing to offer their services at that wage rate. A surplus of 45 000 (75 000 − 30 000) workers results. This, of course, is unemployment. One result of the minimum wage law then is unemployment.

Figure 5.5	The Effect of a Price Floor (Minimum Wage)

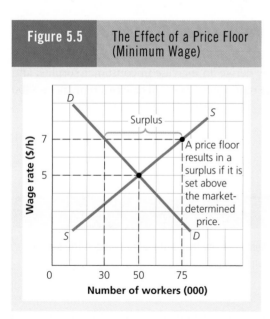

Does minimum wage legislation have other effects?

Yes. It results in a loss of employers' surplus, a loss of employees' surplus, a deadweight loss, and a loss of resources. Let's analyze these effects by using Figure 5.6. In Diagram A, at the market-determined wage rate of $5 per hour, employers' surplus (the blue triangle) and employees' surplus (the red triangle) are maximized when 60 000 workers are hired. This is shown by the sum of the red and blue areas in Diagram A.

Figure 5.6	The Further Effects of Price Floors

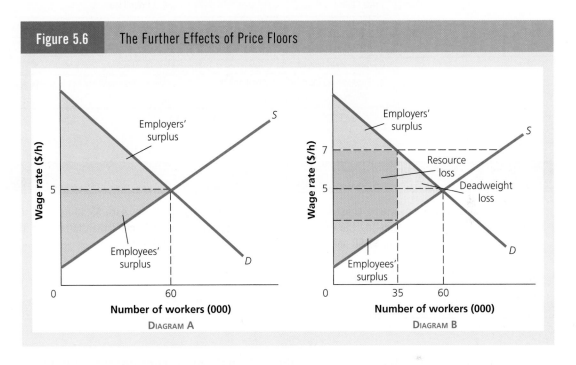

DIAGRAM A

DIAGRAM B

Loss of Employers' Surplus and Employees' Surplus   In Diagram B of Figure 5.6, employers' surplus (the blue area) and employees' surplus (the red area) have both shrunk. Employers and employees both suffer losses because of the minimum wage. Part of this loss is deadweight loss, shown by the area of the yellow triangle. This loss is borne by employers who reduce their workforce and by workers who cannot find employment at $7 per hour—the minimum wage.

Resource Loss   Look again at Diagram B. In addition to the deadweight loss, a further loss is represented by the area of the green rectangle. With only 35 000 jobs available at $7 an hour, people have to spend more time, energy, and other resources searching for scarce jobs. This search cost is a loss of resources. Black market transactions can also occur when some employers and employees engage in illegal deals—workers offer their services at rates below the minimum wage, and employees offer jobs below the minimum wage.

Does anyone benefit from a price floor?

Although a price floor results in a loss to society, not everyone loses. Those workers who are able to find employment at the higher minimum wage rate derive some employee surplus. But the loss exceeds this gain.

Can we summarize the effects of price ceilings and price floors?

Yes. We summarize the major effects of price ceilings and price floors in Table 5.4.

Table 5.4	The Summary of the Effects of Price Ceilings and Price Floors	
Price Ceiling		**Price Floor**
1. Shortages and black market activities occur.		1. Surpluses and black market activities occur.
2. Consumer surplus and producer surplus diminish.		2. Consumer surplus and producer surplus diminish.
3. Deadweight loss occurs.		3. Deadweight loss occurs.
4. Resources are lost in search cost and in circumvention of the price ceiling.		4. Resources are lost in search cost.

BUSINESS SITUATION 5.2

Claude Martin owns and operates a construction company. Several of his employees earn $5.50 per hour. Claude believes that he pays fair wages, considering the productivity of his employees. The government then introduces a law forbidding employers from paying less than $7.50 per hour. Claude now faces a new business situation.

How might Claude deal with this change?

The answer to this Business Situation can be found in Appendix A.

Are there any viable alternatives to rent control and minimum wage legislation?

Yes, there are. Market prices are a way of allocating society's scarce resources, and in most cases, they seem to do a reasonably good job. We will see later in this book that government intervention in the market process is sometimes desirable. The objective of rent control is to make housing more affordable, and the objective of minimum wage legislation is to help workers earn an acceptable living. These government policies are therefore designed to help low income groups.

Unfortunately, as we have seen, these policies often end up hurting the very people they are designed to help. Rent controls result in substandard housing and make it difficult for people to find living accommodation. Minimum wage legislation may result in unemployment for some workers.

Rent control and minimum wage laws are not the only ways to help tenants and workers. For example, instead of instituting a policy of rent control, the government can help poor families by providing financial assistance with their rent. One advantage of such rent subsidies is that they do not introduce distortion into the market process that results in housing shortages as do rent controls. Likewise, instead of instituting minimum wage laws, the government can provide low-income families with wage subsidies that increase their income without reducing the firms' incentive to employ them. The downside is that such subsidies cost the government money, which translates into higher taxes for tax payers.

Reading Comprehension

The answers to these questions can be found on MyEconLab at www.myeconlab.com.   MyEconLab

1. What is a price ceiling? Give an example of a price ceiling. Why might a government institute a price ceiling?
2. Summarize the effects of rent control.

3. What is a price floor? Give an example of a price floor. Why might a government institute a price floor?
4. Summarize the effects of a price floor.
5. What advantages do rent and wage subsidies have over rent controls and minimum wage laws?

LO 5.3 Analyze the effects of production quotas

Production Quotas

What exactly is a production quota?

production quota or quantity restriction the maximum quantity of an item that producers can legally produce

A **production quota** (or **quantity restriction**) is the maximum quantity of an item that producers can legally produce. In an attempt to increase the welfare of producers, a government can place a restriction on the quantity of a commodity that can be produced. In Canada, production quotas are prevalent in agriculture. For example, the production of chicken, dairy (milk and cream), eggs, and turkey are regulated by production quotas as part of the government's supply management program.

What are the effects of production quotas?

Let us answer this question with the help of Figure 5.7. The market demand and supply curves are shown as *DD* and *SS*, respectively. They intersect to determine an equilibrium price of $0.30 per unit and an equilibrium quantity of 6000 units. Now, let's assume that the government imposes a production quota of 3000 units. At this restricted quantity and at the initial equilibrium price of $0.30, a shortage exists. This shortage forces the price up from $0.30 to $0.40, as shown in Figure 5.7. Note that when the government sets a production quota, it does not set the price. Instead, the price is determined by demand and supply. The price of $0.40 is determined by the intersection of the demand curve *DD* and the restricted supply shown by the vertical line at 3000 units. We can conclude from this analysis that a quota, if set below the equilibrium quantity, raises the price above the free market equilibrium price.

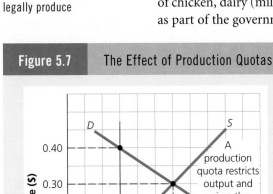

Figure 5.7 The Effect of Production Quotas

A production quota restricts output and raises the price.

How are consumers and producers affected by a production quota?

Figure 5.8 will help us to answer this question. The now familiar Diagram A shows consumer surplus (the blue triangle) and producer surplus (the red triangle). At the free market equilibrium price and quantity, the sum of consumer surplus and producer surplus is maximized. The effect of the quota on consumers and producers is shown in

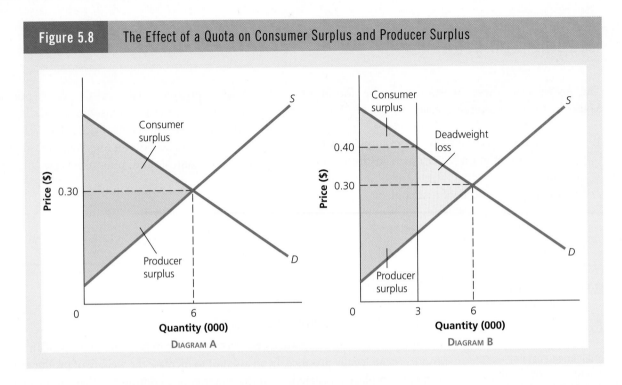

| Figure 5.8 | The Effect of a Quota on Consumer Surplus and Producer Surplus |

DIAGRAM A

DIAGRAM B

Diagram B. Because producers are not permitted to produce more than 3000 units and consumers cannot purchase more than 3000 at any price, there is a deadweight loss, shown by the yellow area. Consumer surplus diminishes substantially: compare the blue area in Diagram A with the blue area in Diagram B. Conversely, producer surplus increases, as shown by the red area in Diagram B.

Reading Comprehension

The answers to these questions can be found on MyEconLab at www.myeconlab.com.   MyEconLab

1. What is a production quota? Give an example of a production quota. Why might a government impose a production quota?

2. What is the effect of a production quota on the price of the product on which the quota is placed?

3. What is the effect of a production quota on consumer surplus? On producer surplus?

LO 5.4 Analyze the effects of excise taxes

Excise Taxes

What is an excise tax?

For a variety of reasons (for example, to raise revenue or to discourage consumption), a government may levy a tax on the sale of a specific commodity. Such a tax is referred to as an **excise tax**. It is actually a type of sales tax. Taxes imposed on gasoline and cigarettes are examples of excise taxes.

excise tax a tax levied on the sale of a specific commodity

Figure 5.9	The Effect of an Excise Tax

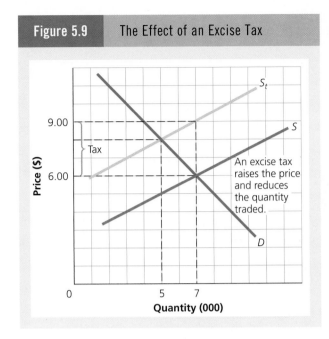

What effect does an excise tax have on equilibrium price and quantity?

Let us analyze the effect of an excise tax by using Figure 5.9.

Suppose a tax of $3 is imposed on each bottle of wine sold. The demand and supply curves before the imposition of the tax are shown D and S, respectively, and the equilibrium price and quantity are $6 and 7000 bottles of wine per month, respectively. The tax causes production costs to rise by $3 per bottle and thus reduces supply. The new supply curve with the tax is S_t. The supply curve shifts up by the amount of the tax, so the vertical distance between S and S_t represents the tax, shown in the figure by the green arrow.

Note that the new equilibrium price is not $9 per bottle but $8. The increase in price ($2) is less than the tax ($3). The quantity traded falls from 7000 bottles to 5000 bottles. The government's total revenue from the tax is ($3 × 5000) = $15 000. The consumers' share of the tax is $2, while the producers' share is $1 per bottle.

Is the burden of an excise tax always divided between consumers and producers?

No, it isn't. The distribution of the burden of a tax between consumers and producers is referred to as the **incidence of the tax**. The incidence of an excise tax depends on the elasticity of demand and the elasticity of supply of the item being considered. We have seen that if the demand curve is downward sloping and the supply curve is upward sloping, then the burden of the tax will be borne between consumers and producers. The less elastic the demand, the greater the tax burden on consumers. The less elastic the supply, the greater the tax burden on producers.

incidence of a tax the distribution of the burden of a tax

Under what conditions will consumers or producers bear the full burden of the tax?

Let us use Figure 5.10 to analyze the incidence of an excise tax in four scenarios:

- Demand is perfectly inelastic.
- Demand is perfectly elastic.
- Supply is perfectly inelastic.
- Supply is perfectly elastic.

Incidence of the Tax When Demand Is Perfectly Inelastic   In Diagram A of Figure 5.10, the demand for a prescribed drug is shown to be perfectly inelastic. The supply curve S intersects the vertical demand curve. In the absence of a tax, the equilibrium price and quantity are $0.60 and 5000 tablets per month, respectively. If a tax of $0.30 is imposed on this drug, the supply curve shifts up by $0.30 to S_t. The new equilibrium price rises to $0.90, but the quantity demanded remains unchanged at 5000 tablets per month, because the demand is perfectly inelastic. The increase in price is equal to the tax, so consumers pay the entire tax. Producers continue to receive $0.60 per tablet.

If the demand for an item is perfectly inelastic, the incidence of an excise tax will be borne entirely by consumers.

Figure 5.10   The Incidence of an Excise Tax

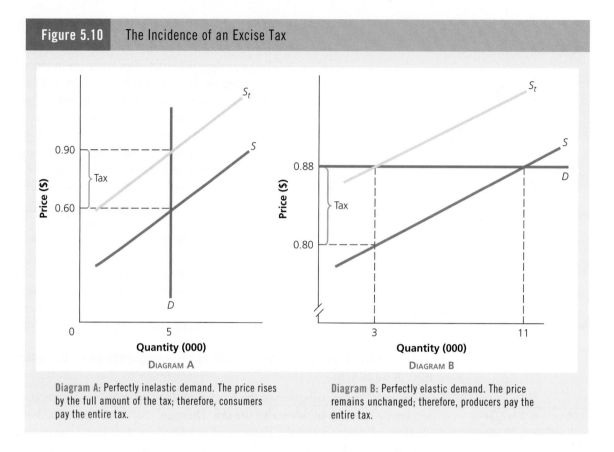

Diagram A: Perfectly inelastic demand. The price rises by the full amount of the tax; therefore, consumers pay the entire tax.

Diagram B: Perfectly elastic demand. The price remains unchanged; therefore, producers pay the entire tax.

Incidence of the Tax When Demand Is Perfectly Elastic   In Diagram B (Figure 5.10), the demand and supply curves for Diet Coke are D and S, respectively. D is a horizontal line because demand is assumed to be perfectly elastic. The equilibrium price and quantity are $0.88 per bottle and 11 000 bottles per week, respectively. A tax of $0.08 per bottle is imposed, which causes the supply curve to shift upward, as shown by the new supply curve S_t. The price remains at $0.88 per bottle, but the quantity falls from 11 000 to 3000 bottles per week. Producers receive $0.80 per bottle and pay the entire tax of $0.08 per bottle. Consumers purchase 3000 bottles at $0.88 per bottle, for a total expenditure of (3000 × $0.88) = $2640. The government receives (3000 × $0.08) = $240.00, and producers receive (3000 × $0.8) = $2400.

> If the demand for an item is perfectly elastic, the incidence of an excise tax will be borne entirely by the producers.

Incidence of the Tax When Supply Is Perfectly Inelastic   Diagram C of Figure 5.10 shows the demand and supply curves for trees. The supply is assumed to be perfectly inelastic—a change in price will not affect the quantity supplied in the short run. The equilibrium price is $60 per tree, and the equilibrium quantity is 140 000 trees per year. Let us assume that the government imposes a tax of $3 for every tree sold. Because the supply is perfectly inelastic, the tax does not affect the supply curve.

Figure 5.10   (*cont'd*) The Incidence of an Excise Tax

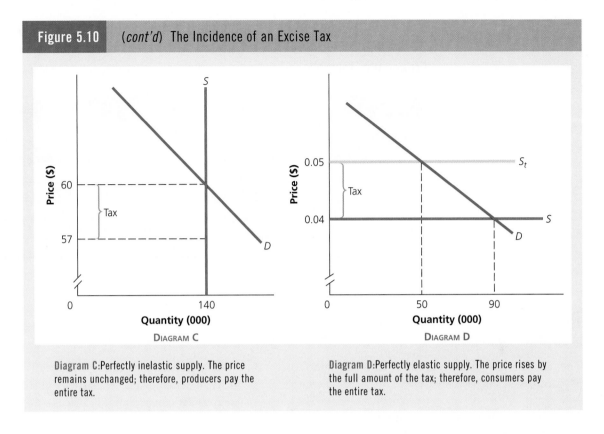

DIAGRAM C

DIAGRAM D

Diagram C:Perfectly inelastic supply. The price remains unchanged; therefore, producers pay the entire tax.

Diagram D:Perfectly elastic supply. The price rises by the full amount of the tax; therefore, consumers pay the entire tax.

Producers will grow 140 000 trees, with or without the tax. Consumers pay $60 per tree, while producers receive $57. They pay the entire $3 per trees. Consumers purchase 140 000 trees at $60 per tree for a total of (140 000 × $60) = $8 400 000. The government receives (140 000 × $3) = $420 000 in taxes. Producers receive (140 000 × $57) = $7 980 000.

> If the supply of an item is perfectly inelastic, the incidence of an excise tax will be borne entirely by producers.

Incidence of the Tax When Supply Is Perfectly Elastic   In a coastal community, producers use water from the sea to preserve meat. The supply of seawater is perfectly elastic at the current price. Diagram D shows demand and supply for seawater. The equilibrium price and equilibrium quantity before the tax are $0.04 and 90 000 barrels of sea water per month, respectively. The government imposes a tax of $0.01 per barrel of seawater. The supply curve shifts to S_t. The new equilibrium price and quantity are $0.05 and 50 000 barrels, respectively. Consumers of seawater pay the entire tax. Buyers of seawater spend a total of (50 000 × $0.05) = $2500. Sellers of seawater receive (50 000 × $0.04) = $2000. The government collects (50 000 × $0.01) = $500 in taxes.

> If the supply of an item is perfectly elastic, the incidence of the tax falls entirely on the consumers (buyers).

It seems like a good idea to summarize the results of our analysis of the incidence of an excise tax.

Let's do it in Table 5.5.

Table 5.5	The Summary of the Incidence of an Excise Tax
State of Elasticity	**Incidence of Tax**
1. Demand and supply are both elastic or inelastic but not perfectly so.	The tax is shared between consumers and producers.
2. Demand is perfectly inelastic.	The entire tax is paid by consumers.
3. Demand is perfectly elastic.	The entire tax is paid by producers.
4. Supply is perfectly inelastic.	The entire tax is paid by producers.
5. Supply is perfectly elastic.	The entire tax is paid by consumers.

Reading Comprehension

The answers to these questions can be found on MyEconLab at www.myeconlab.com.   MyEconLab

1. What is meant by the incidence of a tax?
2. What is an excise tax? Give two examples of excise taxes.

3. "The incidence of an excise tax depends on the elasticity of demand and the elasticity of supply for the item under consideration." Discuss.

LO 5.5 Analyze the effects of a tax on buyers

The Effect of a Tax on Buyers

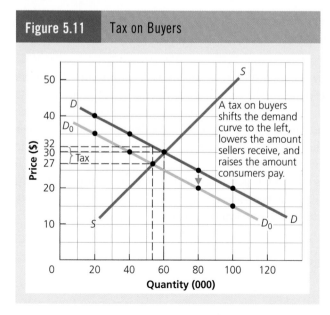

Figure 5.11   Tax on Buyers

A tax on buyers shifts the demand curve to the left, lowers the amount sellers receive, and raises the amount consumers pay.

We have talked about a tax on the sale of an item. Can we analyze the effect of a tax on buyers?

Up to this point we have looked at taxes that shift the supply curve. Now let's look at taxes that shift the demand curve. Let us assume that buyers of portable media players are required to pay a tax of $5.00 for each portable media player they buy. In this case, the demand for portable media players will be affected. Because of the tax, people will tend to buy fewer portable media players; thus, the demand curve shifts to the left.

Figure 5.11 will help to clarify the issue. The original demand and supply curves are *DD* and *SS*, respectively, and the equilibrium price before the tax is $30.00. Buyers respond to the tax as if the price were actually $5.00 higher than it is. Thus, the tax shifts the demand curve to the left by the amount of the tax. Before the tax was levied, the equilibrium price was $30.00. After the tax, with the reduced demand, the equilibrium price falls to $27.00. Buyers pay $27.00 to the sellers, but in addition, they pay the tax of $5.00; they pay a total of $32.00 ($27.00 + $5.00)—which is $2.00 more than they originally paid. We see, therefore, that the tax on buyers makes both buyers and sellers worse off. In this case, buyers pay $2.00 more while sellers receive $3.00 less. The burden of the tax is borne partly by the buyers and partly by the sellers.

> A tax imposed on buyers raises the price of the item for buyers and reduces the amount received by the sellers.

Reading Comprehension

The answers to these questions can be found on MyEconLab at **www.myeconlab.com.**   MyEconLab

1. Explain why a tax on buyers shifts the demand curve to the left.

2. "Sellers share no part of the burden of a tax imposed on buyers." Discuss briefly.

Review

1. Review the learning objectives listed at the beginning of the chapter.
2. Have you accomplished all the objectives? One way to determine this is to answer the Reading Comprehension questions at the end of each section. They will help you assess the extent to which you have accomplished the learning objectives.
3. If you have not accomplished an objective, review the relevant material before proceeding.

Key Points to Remember

1. **LO 5.1** Consumer surplus is the difference between the amount that consumers would have paid for an item and the amount they actually pay. Producer surplus is the difference between the amount that producers (sellers) actually receive from selling an item and the amount they would have accepted for the item.
2. **LO 5.2** A price ceiling is the legal upper limit at which a seller is permitted to sell a good or service. A price floor is the legal lower limit at which a seller is permitted to sell a good or service. Price ceilings reduce consumer surplus

and producer surplus, and result in a loss of resources. Price floors also reduce consumer surplus and producer surplus, and cause a loss of resources.

3. **LO 5.3** A production quota is the maximum quantity of an item that producers can legally produce. An effective production quota will raise the price of the item above the market equilibrium price. A production quota results in a loss of consumer surplus and a deadweight loss. Producer surplus increases.
4. **LO 5.4** An excise tax is a tax that is imposed on the sale of a specific commodity. An excise tax will generally raise the price of the item and reduce the quantity.
5. **LO 5.4** If demand is perfectly inelastic, the incidence of the tax will be borne by consumers. If demand is perfectly elastic, the incidence of the tax will fall entirely on producers. If supply is perfectly inelastic, the entire tax will be paid by producers. If supply is perfectly elastic, the entire tax will be paid by consumers.
6. **LO 5.5** A tax imposed on buyers raises the price of the item for buyers and reduces the amount received by the sellers.

Economic Word Power

Black market (p. 146)
Consumer surplus (p. 142)
Deadweight loss (p. 147)
Excise tax (p. 152)

Incidence of a tax (p. 153)
Price ceiling (p. 145)
Price floor (p. 148)
Producer surplus (p. 143)
Production quota or quantity restriction (p. 151)

Problems and Exercises

Basic

1. **LO 5.1** If the price of an item is $10 but consumers would be willing to pay $14, what is the consumer surplus?
2. **LO 5.1** Consider the demand schedule for chicken sandwiches shown in Table 5.6. Assume that the price of chicken sandwiches is $4 each.

Table 5.6	The Demand Schedule for Chicken Sandwiches
Price ($)	**Quantity**
6	0
5	5
4	10
3	15
2	20

   a. Plot the information from the demand schedule on a demand curve.
   b. What is the total expenditure on chicken sandwiches?
   c. Indicate this on your diagram.
   d. On your diagram, indicate the total amount that consumers would have paid.
   e. On your diagram, indicate the consumer surplus.
3. **LO 5.2** What is a black market? What might give rise to the development of a black market?
4. **LO 5.3** What effect does a production quota have on consumer surplus? on producer surplus?
5. **LO 5.4** What is the effect of an excise tax on the equilibrium price and quantity of the taxed item?
6. **LO 5.5** How does a tax on buyers hurt sellers?

Questions in the Intermediate and Challenging Sections cover several different concepts, and have not been organized by learning objectives.

Intermediate

1. Is there any relation between price and consumer surplus? What happens to consumer surplus if price increases?
2. With the help of an appropriate diagram, show that rent control actually reduces consumer surplus.
3. Show that minimum wage legislation reduces employee surplus.
4. Show that if the demand for an item is perfectly elastic, then the full burden of an excise tax will be borne by producers.
5. Under what condition will the incidence of an excise tax be borne partly by consumers and partly by producers?

Challenging

1. The government has placed a price ceiling on a particular pharmaceutical drug so that a shortage exists. The Pharmaceutical Association lobbies the government by claiming that the price ceiling is far below the equilibrium price. The government hires a consultant, who is not an economist, to investigate the situation. The consultant examines the situation and concludes that because the quantity bought at the ceiling price equals the quantity sold, the market is in equilibrium and a price change is unnecessary. What's wrong with the consultant's analysis?
2. A government, desiring to ensure that its citizens can afford adequate housing, considers two ways of achieving that objective. One approach is to institute rent control. The second approach is to subsidize home builders. What effect will each approach have on the price and quantity of rental housing in the short run and the long run?
3. To support domestic wine producers, the government imposes an import quota on French wines. What will be the likely effect of the quota if the elasticity of demand for French wines is quite inelastic?

MyEconLab Visit the MyEconLab website at www.myeconlab.com. This online homework and tutorial system puts you in control of your own learning with study and practice tools directly correlated to this chapter's content.

Study Guide

Self-Assessment
The answers to the Study Guide questions can be found in Appendix B.

What's your score?
Circle the letter that corresponds with the correct answer.

1. The government intervenes in the market system to
   a. Ensure that trading takes place only at the equilibrium price
   b. Ensure that neither consumers nor producers benefit
   c. Alter the market-determined results
   d. None of the above

2. Which of the following is correct?
   a. There can be no consumer surplus at the equilibrium price
   b. There can be no consumer surplus if the equilibrium quantity is produced
   c. Consumer surplus is the difference between what consumers receive and what producers receive
   d. None of the above

3. Consumer surplus is
   a. What consumers must give up to get something else
   b. The amount that consumers gain when items are sold at reduced prices
   c. The difference between the total amount spent by consumers and the amount spent by producers
   d. The difference between the amount that consumers would have paid for an item and the amount that they actually pay

4. Consumer surplus can increase
   a. Only if quantity demanded is greater than quantity supplied
   b. Only if producer surplus decreases
   c. Even without a decrease in producer surplus
   d. None of the above

5. Producer surplus is
   a. What producers must give up to produce a more profitable product
   b. The increase in quantity sold because of a fall in price

   c. The difference between the total amount received from selling an item and the total cost of producing the item
   d. The difference between the amount that producers actually receive from selling an item and the amount they would have accepted for the item

6. A price ceiling is effective
   a. Only if it is set at the equilibrium price
   b. Only if it is set above the equilibrium price
   c. Only if it is set below the equilibrium price
   d. No matter the price at which it is set

7. A black market is a(n)
   a. Legal device for dealing with shortages
   b. Illegal device for circumventing a price established by law
   c. Device for ensuring that a legally set price actually prevails in the market
   d. None of the above

8. In which of the following situations will a black market likely emerge?
   a. In a free market, when quantity demanded is less the quantity supplied
   b. In a free market, when quantity demanded equals quantity supplied
   c. In a free market, when quantity demanded is greater than quantity supplied
   d. When a price ceiling is set below the equilibrium price

9. Which of the following is a likely consequence of rent control?
   a. A shortage of housing
   b. The development of a black market
   c. A loss of producer surplus
   d. All of the above

10. Rent control benefits
    a. All landlords because demand increases
    b. All tenants because of lower rent
    c. Those tenants who secure housing at the lower rent control
    d. No one

11. A price floor will be effective
   a. Only if the minimum price is set below the market equilibrium price
   b. Only if the minimum price is set above the market equilibrium price
   c. Regardless of the level at which the minimum price is set
   d. Only if the minimum price coincides with the market equilibrium price

12. Minimum wage legislation is an example of
   a. A price ceiling
   b. A production quota
   c. A price floor
   d. None of the above

13. The effects of minimum wage legislation include
   a. Unemployment
   b. Loss of employers' surplus
   c. Loss of employees' surplus
   d. All of the above

14. A production quota is
   a. The highest price at which a producer can legally sell an item
   b. The lowest price at which a consumer can legally buy an item
   c. The equilibrium quantity determined by demand and supply
   d. The maximum quantity of an item that producers can legally produce

15. An effective production quota
   a. Raises the price above the free market equilibrium price
   b. Lowers the price below the market equilibrium price
   c. Has no effect on equilibrium price
   d. Must be set above the market equilibrium quantity

16. Which of the following is an example of an excise tax?
   a. A tax on gasoline
   b. A tax on alcohol
   c. A tax on cigarettes
   d. All of the above

17. The incidence of a tax refers to
   a. The probability that an item will be taxed
   b. How frequently a specific item is taxed
   c. The percentage of tax revenue accounted for by an excise tax
   d. None of the above

18. If the demand for an item is perfectly inelastic, the incidence of a tax is borne by
   a. Consumers only
   b. Producers only
   c. Consumers and producers equally
   d. Consumers mostly but partly by producers

19. If the demand for an item is perfectly elastic, the incidence of a tax is borne by
   a. Producers only
   b. Consumers only
   c. Producers and consumers equally
   d. Producers mostly but partly by consumers

20. If supply is perfectly elastic, the incidence of a tax is borne by
   a. Producers only
   b. Producers and consumers equally
   c. Consumers only
   d. Consumers mostly but partly by producers

Problems and Exercises (Use Quad Paper for Graphs)

Answers to these questions can be found on MyEconLab at www.myeconlab.com.   MyEconLab

1. The demand and supply schedules for a commodity are given below in Table 5.7.

Table 5.7	Demand and Supply Schedules	
Price ($)	Quantity Demanded	Quantity Supplied
8	60	140
7	80	120
6	100	100
5	120	80
4	140	60
3	160	40
2	180	20

   a. On quad paper, draw the demand and supply curves.
   b. On your graph, indicate the consumer surplus and the producer surplus.

2. The price of an item is $1.00. Consumers are willing to pay $1.85 for the first unit, $1.60 for the second, $1.35 for the third, and $1.10 for the fourth. On the basis of this information, complete Table 5.8.

Table 5.8	Consumer Surplus		
Quantity	Total Amount Consumers Would Have Paid ($)	Total Amount Actually Paid ($)	Consumer Surplus ($)
1	1.85	1.00	0.85
2	3.45	2.00	—
3	—	3.00	1.80
4	5.90	4.00	—

Table 5.9	Demand and Supply Schedules for Apartments	
Price ($)	Quantity Demanded (000)	Quantity Supplied (000)
1100	20	100
1000	30	90
900	40	80
800	50	70
700	60	60
600	70	50
500	80	40
400	90	30

3. The demand and supply schedules for apartments are given in Table 5.9. The Rental Board has set the maximum rent at $500 per month.
   a. On quad paper, graph the demand and supply curves for apartments.
   b. Indicate the rent control.
   c. Show that a rent control causes a shortage.
   d. What effect will a rent control of $900 per month have on the market for apartments? (How will equilibrium price and quantity be affected?)
4. a. Reproduce the demand and supply curves from Question 3.
   b. Indicate the consumer surplus and producer surplus before the rent control.
   c. On a separate diagram, draw the rent control of $500 per month and show the deadweight loss, the new consumer surplus, and the new producer surplus.
5. With the help of an appropriate diagram, show that minimum wage legislation can result in unemployment.
6. With the help of an appropriate diagram, show that a production quota raises the price of the item on which the quota is imposed.
7. Use a diagram to show that when the demand for an item is perfectly inelastic, an excise tax can be shifted totally to consumers.

Chapter 6

The Theory of Consumer Behaviour

Learning Objectives

After studying this chapter, you should be able to

6.1 Explain the concept of utility

6.2 Understand the principle of utility maximization

6.3 Explain the water-diamond paradox

6.4 Understand the relationship between utility and demand

6.5 Derive the market demand curve

Assess Your Knowledge

Answers to these questions can be found on MyEconLab at **www.myeconlab.com**.

1. Suppose you are playing a game that you really enjoy. What happens to the *extra* enjoyment you derive as you spend more and more time playing the game?

2. An extra dollar spent on apples gives you 10 units of satisfaction, while an extra dollar spent on oranges gives you 12 units of satisfaction. On which item would you spend the extra dollar and why?

3. Water is essential for life; diamonds are not. Why is water so inexpensive compared with diamonds?

LO 6.1 Explain the concept of utility

The Meaning of Utility

What is meant by utility?

utility the satisfaction derived from consuming goods and services

Economists use the term **utility** to refer to the satisfaction derived from consuming goods and services. Suppose we actually had a way to measure satisfaction in the same way that we can measure distances or weights. Then, after a very enjoyable meal, a consumer would be able to tell us exactly how many units of satisfaction he or she obtained from that particular meal.

Distance is measured in units called kilometres or miles, for example, and weight is measured in units called kilograms or pounds. Is there a name for a unit of satisfaction?

util the measure for a unit of satisfaction

Economists can be both ingenious and creative. Not surprisingly, therefore, they have invented a measure for a unit of satisfaction and have labelled it a **util**. So now you will be able to convince your friend that you derived 27 utils from that apple that you just ate and 23 utils from the headline story that you just read in this morning's newspaper.

> **Note:** The utility derived from the consumption of a good or service varies across individuals and from time to time for the same individual. Although satisfaction cannot actually be m easured objectively and is not subject to interpersonal comparison, the concept is nevertheless important in enabling us to understand how consumers exercise choice over the various commodities that they can purchase. The concept of making decisions *at the margin*, which we will present here, will help us in other areas of economics.

total utility total satisfaction derived from the consumption (or use) of a good or service

marginal utility the *extra* satisfaction derived from the consumption of additional units of a good or service

What is the difference between total utility and marginal utility?

Failure to distinguish between these two concepts can lead to serious confusion. **Total utility** is the total satisfaction derived from the consumption (or use) of a good or service. For example, if you are really fond of ice cream, the more you consume per week (within reason, of course), the greater will be your total utility. **Marginal utility** is the *extra* or *additional* satisfaction derived from the consumption of additional units of a good or service. If you derive 15 utils from the first cone of ice cream and 21 utils from the second cone,

Table 6.1	A Hypothetical Utility Schedule for Ice Cream	
Quantity of Ice Cream Consumed (cones per week)	Total Utility	Marginal Utility
0	0	
		40
1	40	
		30
2	70	
		25
3	95	
		20
4	115	
		15
5	130	
		10
6	140	
		5
7	145	
		2
8	147	
		0
9	147	
		−2
10	145	

then the marginal utility (the extra satisfaction) of the second cone is $21 - 15 = 6$ utils. We can express marginal utility as

$$MU = \frac{\Delta TU}{\Delta Q}$$

where MU is marginal utility, TU is total utility, and Q is quantity.

Can utility schedules (tables) be used to illustrate total utility and marginal utility?

Yes. In fact, Table 6.1 does exactly that. The first column shows quantities of ice cream that an individual consumes per week. The second column shows the total utility derived from different amounts of ice cream consumed, and the third column shows the extra satisfaction (marginal utility) derived from each additional cone of ice cream consumed per week.

Note that the marginal utility values are placed between the lines of the total utility values. Note also that by adding all of the marginal utilities in the third column of Table 6.1, we obtain the total utility derived from all 10 cones of ice cream.

What would the total utility and marginal utility curves look like if plotted on a graph?

Let's plot each one on a graph. Diagram A of Figure 6.1 shows the total utility curve that results from plotting columns 1 and 2 of Table 6.1. Diagram B is the result of plotting columns 1 and 3.

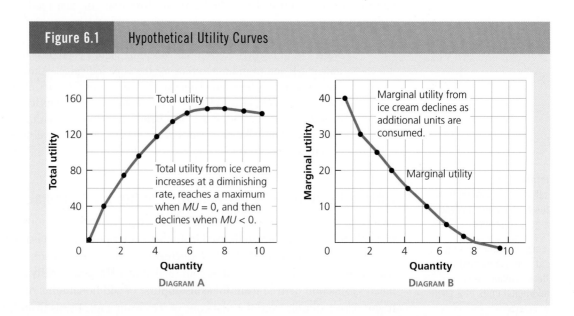

Figure 6.1   Hypothetical Utility Curves

How are total utility and marginal utility related?

It is important to understand the relation between total utility and marginal utility. In fact, the relation between the total and marginal concepts will be encountered again later in this book in a different context. But for now, let us focus on the relation between total utility and marginal utility. When we say that marginal utility is positive, we mean that if we consume an extra unit of a good or service, extra satisfaction will be added to what we are already deriving. Thus, the total utility will increase. This is the case up to eight cones of ice cream in Table 6.1.

When we say that marginal utility is negative, we mean that if we consume an extra unit of a good or service, it will take away from the amount of satisfaction that we are already deriving. Thus, the total utility will decrease. This is the case after the ninth cone of ice cream. Finally, when we say that the marginal utility is zero, we mean that if we consume an extra unit of a good or service, it will neither add to nor subtract from the satisfaction that we are already deriving. Thus, total utility will neither rise nor fall and must therefore be at its maximum. This is the case between the eighth and ninth cones of ice cream. Using TU to denote total utility and MU to denote marginal utility, we can summarize the foregoing discussion as follows:

1. If $MU > 0$, then TU will increase.
2. If $MU < 0$, then TU will decrease.
3. If $MU = 0$, then TU will neither rise nor fall but will be at its maximum.

Marginal utility gets smaller and smaller as the consumer consumes more and more ice cream. Is this significant?

It's good that you have observed that phenomenon. It is a fundamental hypothesis of the theory of consumer behaviour. Economists refer to it as the *law of diminishing marginal utility*. It can be stated as follows:

> As a consumer consumes more of a commodity, after a while, the utility or satisfaction derived from each additional unit diminishes. In other words, the marginal utility eventually diminishes.

Can you give an example to illustrate the law of diminishing marginal utility?

The following example should help to clarify the law. On a hot summer afternoon, you would probably really enjoy an ice cream cone. You might appreciate a second cone, though to a lesser extent than the first. You would likely enjoy a third cone even less than you enjoyed the second, and a fourth less than you enjoyed the third, and so on. Even though your total enjoyment increased, each additional cone of ice cream would give you less and less satisfaction. Stated in different words, the marginal utility would diminish.

Reading Comprehension

The answers to these questions can be found on MyEconLab at **www.myeconlab.com**.   MyEconLab

1. Distinguish between total utility and marginal utility. Give an example of each.

2. Do you think that the utility analysis of consumer behaviour is useful even though utility cannot be measured? Explain your answer.

3. Define *diminishing marginal utility* and state the law of diminishing marginal utility.

LO 6.2 Understand the principle of utility maximization

The Consumer's Problem and Utility Maximization

What is the objective of the consumer?

In economics, it is assumed that the consumer is trying to spend his or her budget in such a way as to derive as much satisfaction as possible. Stated differently, the consumer's objective is to maximize satisfaction subject to a budget constraint.

The consumer's problem, then, is how to maximize satisfaction given his or her budget and the prices of the goods and services that he or she wants to buy.

Yes.

If a consumer is maximizing his or her satisfaction and therefore has no desire to rearrange his or her purchases, can we then say that he or she is in equilibrium?

That is exactly the case. We assume that consumers behave in such a way as to ensure that they obtain maximum satisfaction from their purchases of goods and services. When this happens, consumers have achieved their objectives, and we say that they are in equilibrium. Consumers in equilibrium have no desire to rearrange their purchases of goods and services, because any rearrangement will only result in a lower level of satisfaction.

Consumers try to maximize their satisfaction when they purchase goods and services.

What condition must exist for the consumer to maximize his or her satisfaction?

Let us consider the case of Andrea, a consumer who has a given amount of money to spend (budget) on two commodities: novels and USB flash drives. Let us assume that Andrea has spent her budget in such a way that the last dollar spent on novels gives more satisfaction than the last dollar spent on flash drives. Let us assume, specifically, that the utility derived from the last dollar spent on novels is 15, while the utility derived from the last dollar spent on flash drives is 10. Obviously, because an extra dollar spent on novels yields greater satisfaction than an extra dollar spent on flash drives, Andrea can increase her total satisfaction by buying more novels and fewer flash drives. If the utility of the last dollar spent on flash drives were greater than the utility of the last dollar spent on novels, then Andrea could increase her satisfaction by buying more flash drives and fewer novels. As long as the utility of the last dollar spent on novels is different from the utility of the last dollar spent on flash drives, Andrea can increase her total satisfaction by rearranging her purchases of novels and flash drives. It is only when the utility of the last dollar spent on each commodity is equal that Andrea will be maximizing her satisfaction.

Let us return to the specific case in which the utility derived from the last dollar spent on novels is 15 and that derived from the last dollar spent on flash drives is 10.

As Andrea buys more novels and fewer flash drives, the marginal utility of novels will fall, while the marginal utility of flash drives will rise (remember the law of diminishing marginal utility). If the utility of the last dollar spent on novels falls to 12 while the utility of the last dollar spent on flash drives increases to 12, Andrea will maximize her satisfaction and therefore have no incentive to rearrange her purchases. When such a situation is attained, Andrea will be in equilibrium. Any change from this position will reduce Andrea's level of satisfaction.

What role do prices play in the analysis of the consumer's equilibrium?

So far, we have left the prices of novels and flash drives out of the analysis. But prices do play an important role. Andrea's equilibrium position can be restated in terms of marginal utility and price. The marginal utility per dollar of novels is the marginal utility of novels divided by the price of novels. Similarly, the marginal utility per dollar of flash drives is the marginal utility of flash drives divided by the price of flash drives. Thus, the condition to be met for Andrea (or any other consumer) to be in equilibrium can be formulated as follows:

> For a consumer purchasing two goods, A and B, to maximize satisfaction, the marginal utility of A divided by the price of A must equal the marginal utility of B divided by the price of B.

The utility maximization rule is often expressed in the following compact form:

$$\frac{MU_A}{P_A} = \frac{MU_B}{P_B}$$

equimarginal principle
the concept that a value is maximized (or minimized) by equating marginal values

where MU_A is the marginal utility of A, MU_B is the marginal utility of B, P_A is the price of A, and P_B is the price of B. This rule, known as the **equimarginal principle**, can also be expressed as

$$\frac{MU_A}{MU_B} = \frac{P_A}{P_B}$$

Expressed verbally, this formula says that a value is maximized (or minimized) by equating marginal values.

> The consumer will be in equilibrium (maximizing his or her satisfaction) when the ratio of the marginal utilities equals the ratio of the prices.

What would be the equilibrium condition if the consumer is purchasing more than two commodities?

The consumer is usually confronted with more than just two commodities. The equilibrium condition can be extended to cover the situation of many commodities. In such a case, the equilibrium condition for many goods from A to Z becomes

$$\frac{MU_A}{P_A} = \frac{MU_B}{P_B} = \frac{MU_C}{P_C} = \cdots = \frac{MU_Z}{P_Z}$$

Table 6.2		The Schedule of Marginal Utility	
$ Worth of A	MU_A	$ Worth of B	MU_B
1	80	1	58
2	70	2	56
3	60	3	52
4	50	4	48
5	40	5	44
6	30	6	40
7	20	7	35
8	10	8	30
9	5	9	25
10	1	10	20

Can you provide an example of how this principle can be applied?

The following example provides an opportunity to analyze the consumer's allocation problem. Consider the utility schedules of a consumer of two commodities, A and B, presented in Table 6.2. If the consumer, Marilyn Browne, has a budget of $11 to spend on A and B, how should she allocate her funds between A and B in order to maximize her satisfaction?

According to the information provided in the table, if Marilyn spends the first dollar on A, she obtains 80 utils but if she spends it on B, she obtains only 58 utils. The first dollar should therefore be spent on A. The second dollar spent on A will yield 70 utils, but if that dollar is spent on B, it will yield only 58 utils. It should therefore be spent on A. For the same reason, the third dollar should be spent on A.

Now, if the fourth dollar is spent on A, it will yield 50 utils as compared with 58 if it is spent on B. The fourth dollar should therefore be spent on B. By similar reasoning, the fifth and sixth should be spent on B, the seventh on A, and the eighth and ninth on B. When Marilyn reaches the 10th dollar, she can choose to spend it on either A or B, as both yield 40 utils. Marilyn will then spend the 11th dollar on the other commodity. We find that in the end, Marilyn will have bought $5 worth of A and $6 worth of B. Note that the allocation accords with the principle stated earlier: consumers will maximize their satisfaction when they allocate their incomes in such a manner that the utility of the last dollar spent on commodity A equals the utility of the last dollar spent on commodity B.

Can you provide another example?

Consider the information contained in Table 6.3 regarding the marginal utility of A and the marginal utility of B. The price of A is $5, and the price of B is $3. How should a consumer allocate a budget of $27 between A and B?

Table 6.3	The Marginal Utility of A and Marginal Utility of B					
	Commodity A				Commodity B	
Quantity	MU_A	MU_A/P_A	Quantity	MU_B	MU_B/P_B
1	130	26	1	90	30
2	120	24	2	84	28
3	115	23	3	75	25
4	100	20	4	69	23
5	80	16	5	60	20
6	65	13	6	54	18
7	50	10	7	45	15
8	40	8	8	39	13

It would be helpful to calculate the marginal utility per dollar of A (MU_A/P_A) and the marginal utility per dollar of B (MU_B/P_B). These values are shown in columns 3 and 6. Now we know that the consumer will maximize his or her satisfaction when

$$MU_A/P_A = MU_B/P_B$$

This equality occurs at 3 units of A and 4 units of B ($MU_A/P_A = MU_B/P_B = 23$), at 4 units of A and 5 units of B ($MU_A/P_A = MU_B/P_B = 20$), and again at 6 units of A and 8 units of B ($MU_A/P_A = MU_B/P_B = 13$). But only one of these possibilities amounts to $27, which is the consumer's budget. For example, 6 units of A and 8 units of B would cost $(6 \times \$5) + (8 \times \$3) = \$54$, which exceeds the consumer's budget. Similarly, 4 units of A and 5 units of B would cost $(4 \times \$5) + (5 \times \$3) = \$35$, which again exceeds the consumer's budget of $27. The consumer should buy 3 units of A and 4 units of B, which adds up to exactly $27.

Reading Comprehension

The answers to these questions can be found on MyEconLab at www.myeconlab.com.   MyEconLab

1. If a consumer purchasing apples and bananas finds herself in a position where the marginal utility per dollar of apples exceeds the marginal utility per

dollar of bananas, how should the consumer rearrange her purchases to maximize her satisfaction?

2. Explain the condition that must exist for a consumer to be in equilibrium (i.e., maximizing satisfaction).

 LO 6.3 Explain the water-diamond paradox

water-diamond paradox or paradox of value the apparent (superficial) contradiction in the fact that an absolute necessity, such as water, has a lower value than a luxury item, such as diamonds

The Water-Diamond Paradox: The Paradox of Value

What is the water-diamond paradox and what is the solution?

The **water-diamond paradox** or the **paradox of value** plagued numerous classical economists, including Adam Smith (1723–1790), the man considered to be the father of economics as a discipline. The paradox lies in the question "why is water so much cheaper than diamonds when water is so much more useful than diamonds?" One solution is that diamonds are relatively scarce while water is relatively abundant. In price determination, marginal utility—not total utility—is the relevant concept. Water is useful but its marginal utility is low, while the marginal utility of diamonds is high. And because price is proportional to marginal utility, the price of diamonds is higher than the price of water. The paradox of value can be defined as the apparent (superficial) contradiction in the fact that an absolute necessity, such as water, has a lower value than a luxury item, such as diamonds.

Reading Comprehension

The answers to these questions can be found on MyEconLab at www.myeconlab.com.   MyEconLab

1. What is the paradox of value?

2. What is the relationship between relative scarcity and the water-diamond paradox?

The Consumer's Demand Curve

Does any relationship exist between the consumer's demand curve and the consumer's attempt to maximize his or her satisfaction?

The analysis presented above can be used to determine how a change in the price of a commodity affects the quantity demanded. Let us assume again that the consumer can buy two goods: A and B. Let us assume also that the consumer is in equilibrium with $MU_A/P_A = MU_B/P_B$. If the price of A falls, then the marginal utility per dollar of A (MU_A/P_A) increases. This being the case, the consumer will buy more of A in an attempt to restore equilibrium. The following example will help to illustrate the point. Assume that the price of A (P_A) is \$10 and that the marginal utility of A (MU_A) is 40 when the consumer is in equilibrium. The marginal utility per dollar of A (MU_A/P_A) is $40 \div 10 = 4$.

Because the consumer is in equilibrium, we know that the marginal utility per dollar of A equals the marginal utility per dollar of B; that is,

$$\frac{MU_A}{P_A} = \frac{40}{10} = \frac{MU_B}{P_B} = 4$$

Now, if the price of A falls to \$8, then

$$\frac{MU_A}{P_A} = \frac{40}{8} = 5$$

which is now greater than

$$\frac{MU_B}{P_B}$$

To restore equilibrium, the consumer purchases more of A and less of B so that the MU_A falls while the MU_B rises until again

$$\frac{MU_A}{P_A} = \frac{MU_B}{P_B}$$

A fall in the price of A, therefore, causes the quantity of A that the consumer will buy to increase. In other words, the consumer's demand curve slopes downward from left to right.

We can use an alternative approach to demonstrate the relation between marginal utility and the consumer's demand curve. Consider the demand curve in Figure 6.2 for your favourite consumer, you, for oranges per month. We can interpret this demand curve as follows: for three bags of oranges, the maximum price you are willing to pay is \$18. If the price were higher than \$6 per bag, you would not buy the third bag of oranges.

Why are you not willing to pay more than \$6 for the third bag of oranges? The answer is that according to your subjective evaluation of the extra satisfaction derived from the third bag (i.e., its marginal utility), it is worth just \$6 but no more. Likewise, you will not buy the fifth bag for a price exceeding \$4 because that is your subjective evaluation of the marginal utility derived from the fifth bag. As we noted earlier in this chapter, the more of any item that

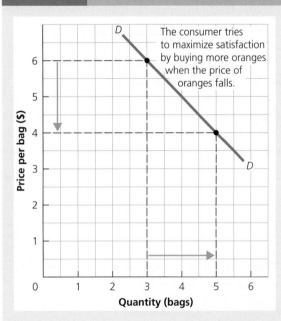

Figure 6.2 A Demand Curve for Oranges

The consumer tries to maximize satisfaction by buying more oranges when the price of oranges falls.

Price per bag (\$) / Quantity (bags)

you consume per month, the less satisfaction you derive from each additional unit and, hence, the less you are willing to pay for extra units of the item. This approach clearly brings out the relation between marginal utility and demand.

What is the difference between this demand curve (the consumer's demand curve) and the demand curve that we studied in Chapter3?

market demand curve the demand curve representing the demand of all the buyers in the market for an item

The demand curve that we have just derived is for an individual consumer. The consumer tries to maximize his or her satisfaction by buying more of an item as the price of the item falls. The demand curve that we studied in Chapter 3 was a **market demand curve**, that is, the demand curve representing the demand of all the buyers in the market for an item.

Reading Comprehension

The answers to these questions can be found on MyEconLab at **www.myeconlab.com.**   MyEconLab

1. Explain the relationship between marginal utility and consumer demand.

2. What does the demand curve for an individual consumer show?

3. What is the difference between the individual consumer demand curve and the market demand curve?

LO 6.5 Derive the market demand curve

Derivation of the Market Demand Curve

Is it possible to derive the market demand curve from the demand curves of the individual consumers in the market?

Once we obtain a demand curve for each consumer of a particular product, we simply add these individual demand curves to obtain the market demand curve discussed in Chapter 3. Let us assume, for the sake of simplicity, that there are only three consumers, Anita, Bob, and Claudia, in the market for a particular product. The individual demand schedules for these three consumers are given in Table 6.4.

At a price of $8, Anita will buy 2 units a week, Bob will buy 0, and Claudia will buy 3 units a week. Notice that at a price of $8, Bob is effectively out of the market. The total quantity demanded at $8 is therefore 5 units (2 for Anita and 3 for Claudia). This is shown in the market demand schedule. At a price of $6, Anita will buy 3 units a week; Bob will now enter the market and buy 2 units, while Claudia will buy 5 units. The total quantity demanded at a price of $6 is thus $(3 + 2 + 5) = 10$ units as shown

Table 6.4		Individual Demand and Market Demand Schedules					
Anita's Demand		Bob's Demand		Claudia's Demand		Market Demand	
P	*Q*	*P*	*Q*	*P*	*Q*	*P*	*Q*
8	2	8	0	8	3	8	5
6	3	6	2	6	5	6	10
4	4	4	4	4	7	4	15

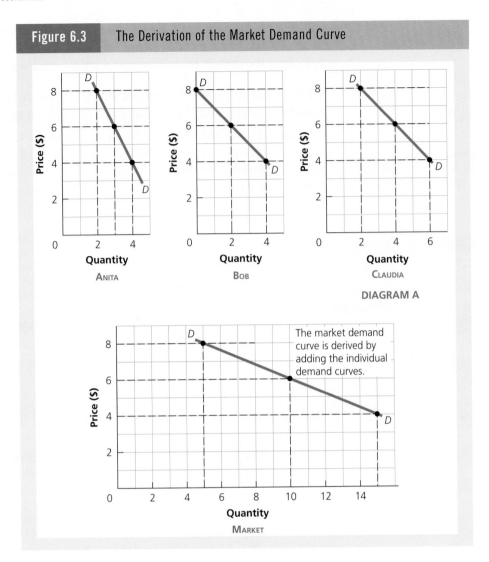

Figure 6.3   The Derivation of the Market Demand Curve

DIAGRAM A

The market demand curve is derived by adding the individual demand curves.

in the market demand schedule. At a price of $4, Anita will buy 4 units, Bob will buy 4, and Claudia will buy 7; together, they will buy 15 units at a price of $4. You can see, then, that the market demandis the sum of the individual consumers' demands in the market.

You asked whether we could derive the market demand curve from the individual demand curves, and we said yes. Let's investigate. Figure 6.3 shows the demand curves for Anita, Bob, and Claudia.

At a price of $8, the total quantity demanded by all three consumers is 5 units. This combination of price and quantity demanded gives one point on the market demand curve. At a price of $6, the total quantity demanded by all three consumers is 10 units per week. This combination of price and quantity demanded gives another point on the market demand curve. The third point on the market demand curve is obtained in a similar manner. Thus, we can draw the following conclusion:

> The market demand curve is the horizontal summation of the individual demand curves.

Note that the market demand curve is more elastic than any of the individual demand curves.

Reading Comprehension

The answers to these questions can be found on MyEconLab at www.myeconlab.com.　MyEconLab

1. Briefly outline the procedure for deriving the market demand curve from the individual consumers' demand curves.

2. If all consumers in a market don't buy more of an item when its price falls, one cannot derive the market demand curve. Is this true or false? Explain briefly.

Review

1. Review the learning objectives listed at the beginning of the chapter.
2. Have you accomplished all the objectives? One way to determine this is to answer the Reading Comprehension questions at the end of each section. They will help you assess the extent to which you have accomplished the learning objectives.
3. If you have not accomplished an objective, review the relevant material before proceeding.

Key Points to Remember

1. **LO 6.1** Utility refers to the amount of satisfaction derived from the consumption of goods and services. The utility approach to consumer behaviour assumes that consumers are able to measure the amount of satisfaction they receive from consuming a good or a service. In fact, however, utility is not measurable, and one person's utility cannot be meaningfully compared with that of another.
2. **LO 6.1** Total utility is the total amount of satisfaction derived from consuming goods and services. Marginal utility is the additional satisfaction derived from consuming an additional unit of a good or service. We can obtain total utility by adding all of the marginal utilities derived from each additional unit.
3. **LO 6.1** The law of diminishing marginal utility states that, as a consumer consumes more of a commodity, the utility or satisfaction derived from each additional unit diminishes.

4. **LO 6.2** In economics we assume that the objective of consumers is to maximize their satisfaction. They do this by equating the marginal utility of a dollar's worth of each of the commodities on which they spend their incomes (budget). In this position, consumers are said to be in equilibrium.
5. **LO 6.3** The water-diamond paradox refers to the apparent contradiction in the fact that an absolutely necessity, such as water, has a lower value than a luxury item, such as diamonds. The paradox is resolved when it is recognized that although water is so useful, its marginal utility is low, while the marginal utility of diamonds is high. Because price is proportional to marginal utility, the price of diamonds is higher than the price of water.
6. **LO 6.4** We can derive the consumer's demand curve from utility analysis. The consumer's demand curve reflects marginal utility.
7. **LO 6.5** The market demand curve for a particular commodity is the sum of the demand curves of the consumers in the market for that commodity.

Economic Word Power

Equimarginal principle　(p. 167)
Marginal utility　(p. 163)
Market demand curve　(p. 171)
Total utility　(p. 163)
Util　(p. 163)
Utility　(p. 163)
Water-diamond paradox or paradox of value　(p. 169)

Problems and Exercises

Basic

1. **LO 6.1** Table 6.5 shows data for total utility.
   a. Use the total utility values to calculate the marginal utility values and fill in the marginal utility column.
   b. Add up all the marginal utility values and compare your answer with the total utility derived from all 5 units of the good.

Table 6.5	Total Utility Data	
Marginal Utility	Quantity	Total Utility
0	0	
1	4	_____
2	7	_____
3	9	_____
4	10	_____
5	10	_____

2. **LO 6.1** Table 6.6 shows marginal utility values for units of an item consumed. Use the marginal utility (MU) data to derive the total utility (TU) data, and complete the TU column.

Table 6.6	Marginal Utility Values	
Quantity	MU	TU
0	6	
1	5	
2	4	
3	3	
4	2	
5	1	
6	0	

3. **LO 6.1, 6.2** The price of an item is $2. Table 6.7 contains total utility (TU) values. Complete columns 3 and 4.

Table 6.7	Total Utility Values		
Quantity (1)	TU (2)	MU (3)	MU per Dollar (4)
0	0		
1	10		
2	18		
3	24		
4	28		
5	30		
6	30		
7	28		

Table 6.8	Pravin's Utility	
Quantity	TU	MU
0	0	
1	8	
2	14	
3	18	
4	20	
5	20	
6	18	

4. **LO 6.1** Table 6.8 contains data for total utility that Pravin derives from a good.
   a. Complete the marginal utility (MU) column.
   b. If the good is free, how many will Pravin consume?
   c. On a graph, draw the TU and MU curves.
   d. What is the value of the MU when TU is at its maximum? Show this point on your graph.

5. **LO 6.2** Jing-Mei's MU curve for ice cream is given below in Figure 6.4. How many cups of ice cream should Jing-Mei consume to maximize her satisfaction?

6. **LO 6.2** Figure 6.5 shows MU for slices of pizza from Mr. Pizza, Pizza City, and Pizza Delite. Mr. Pizza claims, "You will want at least two slices."
   a. Explain what each graph shows.
   b. Is Mr. Pizza's claim justified?
   c. Who has the strongest case to make the claim?

Questions in the Intermediate and Challenging Sections cover several different concepts, and have not been organized by learning objectives.

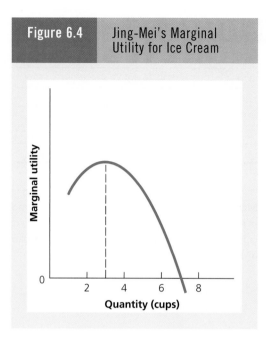

Figure 6.4 — Jing-Mei's Marginal Utility for Ice Cream

Table 6.9 — Utility Data for the Consumer

Unit of Item	MU_A/P_A	MU_B/P_B
First	10	12
Second	8	10
Third	7	9
Fourth	6	8
Fifth	5	6
Sixth	4	3
Seventh	3	2

Table 6.10 — Marginal Utility Values for Sam

Quantity	MU_H	MU_W	MU_M
1	10	50	60
2	9	40	40
3	8	30	32
4	7	20	24
5	6	16	20
6	5	12	16

Intermediate

1. A consumer has a budget of $10, which she wants to spend on two items: A and B. The price of A is $1 and the price of B is $2. Consider the data in Table 6.9.
   a. What quantity of each item should this consumer buy?
   b. If the consumer's budget increases to $19, what quantity of each should she buy?
2. Table 6.10 contains marginal utility values for Sam for hamburgers (MU_H), red wine (MU_W), and milkshakes (MU_M). The price of hamburgers is $1, the price of wine is $2, and the price of a milkshake is $4.
   a. Sam has $17. How much of each should he buy?
   b. If his budget increases to $25, how much of each should he buy?

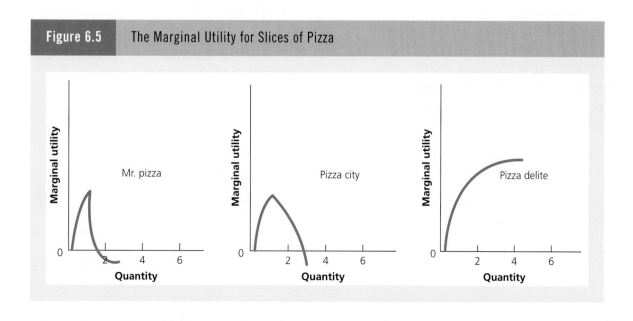

Figure 6.5 — The Marginal Utility for Slices of Pizza

3. Suppose it is known that the marginal utility of chicken is 100, that the price of chicken is $10 per box, and that the price of cheese is $5. If the consumer is in equilibrium, what must be the marginal utility of cheese?

4. Nora figures out that the marginal utility derived from *A* and *B* is as shown in Table 6.11. If the price of *A* is $2, the price of *B* is $3, and Nora's budget is $17 to spend on these two items, how much of each should Nora buy to maximize her total utility?

Table 6.11	Nora's Utility for *A* and *B*	
Units	*MU*$_A$	*MU*$_B$
1	10	5
2	8	4
3	2	3
4	2	2
5	1	2

Challenging

1. A progressive income tax system is one in which the percentage of income paid in taxes rises as income rises. For example, an income of $30 000 might be taxed at 15% while an income of $40 000 might be taxed at 20%. How might the hypothesis of diminishing marginal utility be used to justify a progressive income tax system?

2. Many restaurants offer an all-you-can-eat option. Use marginal utility theory to explain this practice. What conditions must such restaurants impose on patrons in order to make a profit?

MyEconLab Visit the MyEconLab website at **www.myeconlab.com.** This online homework and tutorial system puts you in control of your own learning with study and practice tools directly correlated to this chapter's content.

Study Guide

Self-Assessment
The answers to the Study Guide questions can be found in Appendix B.

What's your score?
Circle the letter that corresponds with the correct answer.

1. In economics, the term *utility* refers to
   a. The number of uses an item has
   b. Bills, such as electricity and telephone bills
   c. The satisfaction derived from goods and services
   d. The ease with which an item can be obtained

2. A util is
   a. A measure for a unit of satisfaction
   b. The maximum amount that a consumer is willing to pay for an item
   c. The minimum amount for which a consumer can obtain an item
   d. None of the above

3. In consumer theory, utility refers to
   a. The usefulness of a good
   b. The satisfaction derived from a good or service
   c. Large business enterprises producing electricity, gas, and telephone services
   d. None of the above

4. Economists refer to a unit of satisfaction as a
   a. Satisfit
   b. Unisat
   c. Util
   d. None of the above

5. Total utility refers to
   a. The total amount of use that can be obtained from a good or service
   b. The total amount of goods and services that can be bought with a given budget
   c. The additional amount of an item that a consumer buys as price falls

    d. The total amount of satisfaction derived from a good or service

6. Marginal utility is
   a. The minimum use expected from a good or service
   b. The minimum satisfaction derived from consuming a good or service
   c. The additional satisfaction derived from consuming an extra amount of a good or service
   d. Always positive or zero, never negative

7. On a graph with total utility on the vertical axis and quantity consumed on the horizontal axis, the total utility curve will be
   a. Vertical throughout
   b. Downward sloping, reaching a minimum and then upward sloping
   c. Downward sloping throughout
   d. Upward sloping, reaching a maximum, and then downward sloping

8. If marginal utility is positive, then total utility is
   a. Negative
   b. Increasing
   c. Zero
   d. Decreasing

9. When total utility is neither rising nor falling, then we know that marginal utility is
   a. Positive but falling
   b. Positive but rising
   c. Negative but rising
   d. Zero

10. In economics, it is assumed that consumers
    a. Try to buy as much of a good as they can afford
    b. Spend an equal amount of money on all goods and services
    c. Try to maximize their marginal utility
    d. Try to maximize their satisfaction

11. The law of diminishing marginal utility states that
    a. Total utility will always increase, while marginal utility will always diminish
    b. As more and more of a good or service is consumed, the total utility will diminish
    c. As additional units of a good or service are consumed, eventually, the marginal utility will diminish
    d. As additional units of a good or service are consumed, after a while, people will spend more for less

12. A consumer purchasing two goods, A and B, will maximize satisfaction when
    a. $MU_A > MU_B$
    b. $MU_A = MU_B$
    c. $MU_A/P_A > MU_B/P_B$
    d. $MU_A/P_A = MU_B/P_B$

13. If the utility derived from the last dollar spent on A is greater than that derived from the last dollar spent on B, the consumer can increase total utility by
    a. Buying more of A and less of B
    b. Buying more of B and less of A
    c. Making sure that the same amount of money is spent on A and B
    d. None of the above

14. Which of the following statements about utility is *incorrect*?
    a. If a good is wanted, it yields utility
    b. Total utility depends on price
    c. Utility is subjective
    d. Utility is a measure of satisfaction

15. If $MU_A/P_A > MU_B/P_B$
    a. The consumer is maximizing his or her satisfaction
    b. The consumer would purchase more of good A
    c. The consumer would purchase more of good B
    d. We cannot predict what the consumer would do

16. The consumption of a free good will continue until
    a. The marginal utility becomes positive
    b. The total utility is rising
    c. The total utility is falling
    d. The marginal utility is zero

17. The paradox of value
    a. Deals with the importance of paradoxes
    b. Relates to the apparent contradiction in the fact that some useful items have relatively low prices, while some less useful items have relatively high prices
    c. Is unrelated to total and marginal utilities
    d. None of the above

18. The market demand curve is
    a. The same as the consumer demand curve
    b. Unrelated to the individual consumers' demand curves
    c. The sum of the demand curves of all the consumers in the market
    d. None of the above

19. The consumer will be in equilibrium when she spends her budget in such as way that
    a. The marginal utility per dollar of A equals the marginal utility per dollar of B
    b. She cannot increase her satisfaction by rearranging her purchases
    c. The ratio of the marginal utilities of the items she buys equals the ratio of the prices of the items.
    d. All of the above

20. Which of the following is correct?
    a. We can derive the market demand curve for an item by adding the demand curves of all the buyers of the item
    b. The market demand curve is identical to the individual demand curve because consumers are assumed to have the same objective

c. The market demand curve can be derived from the individual demand curve only if all consumers have identical demand curves
d. None of the above

Problems and Exercises (Use Quad Paper for Graphs)

Answers to these questions can be found on MyEconLab at www.myeconlab.com.

MyEconLab

1. Table 6.12 contains data on the total utility (*TU*) derived from consuming various quantities of an item.

Table 6.12	The Total Utility Derived from an Item	
Quantity	**TU**	**MU**
0	0	
1	50	
2	95	
3	135	
4	170	
5	195	
6	210	
7	220	

a. Calculate the marginal utility (*MU*) values and complete the *MU* column.
b. Total the *MU* values and compare your answer with the *TU* derived from all seven units.
c. Graph the *TU* and the *MU* on two different graphs.

2. Based on the information you were given in Table 6.2 (page 168), how should Marilyn allocate a budget of $17 between commodities *A* and *B* in order to maximize her satisfaction?

3. Given the data shown in Table 6.13 on the utilities of *A* and *B*, and given that the price of *A* is $2 and the price of *B* is $3,
a. Fill in the MU_A/P_A and the MU_B/P_B columns.
b. How should a consumer allocate a budget of $12 between *A* and *B*?
c. What change should be made in the consumer's purchases if his or her budget increases to $22?

Table 6.13	The Utilities of A and B				
Quantity of A	**MU_A**	**MU_A/P_A**	**Quantity of B**	**MU_B**	**MU_B/P_B**
1	16		1	21	
2	18		2	24	
3	16		3	18	
4	14		4	15	
5	10		5	12	
6	6		6	6	
7	2		7	3	

Table 6.14	Demand Schedules for Disks				
Adam's Demand		**Barb's Demand**		**Connie's Demand**	
P	**Q**	**P**	**Q**	**P**	**Q**
10	8	10	6	10	5
8	10	8	8	8	7
6	12	6	10	6	9

4. The market for disks consists of three consumers: Adam, Barb, and Connie. Their demand schedules for disks are given in Table 6.14.
a. Construct the market demand schedule for disks.
b. Draw the demand curve for each consumer and then derive the market demand curve.

6A

Indifference Curve Analysis of Consumer Behaviour

Learning Objectives

After studying this appendix, you should be able to

6A.1 Discuss the advantage of the indifference curve approach over the cardinal utility approach

6A.2 Explain the budget line and illustrate how changes in income and prices affect it

6A.3 Discuss preference, indifference, and indifference curves

6A.4 Use indifference curve analysis to illustrate the consumer's equilibrium

6A.5 Show how changes in income and changes in prices affect the consumer's equilibrium

6A.6 Use indifference curve analysis to derive the consumer's demand curve

Assess Your Knowledge

MyEconLab

Answers to these questions can be found on MyEconLab at **www.myeconlab.com**.

1. To what extent do you think consumers are able to rank the amount of satisfaction they derive from consuming different goods and services?

2. What do you consider to be the main constraints on the amount of goods and services that a consumer can buy?

3. People buy more of most goods as their incomes rise. Can you think of a good that consumers buy less of as their incomes rise?

LO 6A.1 Discuss the advantage of the indifference curve approach over the cardinal utility approach

The Indifference Curve Approach

What are the advantages of the indifference curve approach over the cardinal or measurable utility approach?

One of the major problems with the analysis of consumer choice presented in Chapter 6 is that it assumes that the consumer is able to assign numbers, such as 1, 5, 9, and so on (called cardinal numbers), to the amount of satisfaction derived from consuming a unit of a commodity. These numbers that purport to measure satisfaction, you will recall, are in units called *utils*. With this approach (the *cardinal* or *measurable* utility approach) a consumer is presumed to be able to determine that he or she derives, say, 10 utils from consuming a unit of apple pie and 5 utils from consuming a unit of ice cream. On this basis, using the cardinal utility approach, we would conclude that the consumer likes apple pie twice as much as he or she likes ice cream.

Another problem with the approach presented in Chapter 6 is that it does not explicitly indicate the constraint under which the consumer chooses among the variety of goods to purchase. It is implied, of course, that if the consumer has a given budget to spend on A and B, more of A can be purchased only by sacrificing some of B. But the consumer's problem of choice is not explicitly indicated.

In this appendix, you will study an alternative to the cardinal utility approach. This more sophisticated approach to analyzing consumer behaviour avoids the highly suspect assumption that utility can be measured cardinally and assumes instead that consumers are able to rank or order their preferences. Thus, consumers can indicate their preference for commodity A over commodity B by ranking B at 6, for example, and ranking A at any level higher than 6 (say, 12). A ranking of 12 for A indicates only a

---

Reading Comprehension

The answers to these questions can be found on MyEconLab at **www.myeconlab.com**.   MyEconLab

1. What major advantage does the indifference curve approach hold over the cardinal utility approach in studying consumer behaviour?

2. What is the difference between cardinal numbers and ordinal numbers?

preference for *A*. It does not imply, for instance, that *A* gives twice as much satisfaction as *B*. The numbers have *ordinal* (not cardinal) significance. The ordinal utility approach also explicitly indicates the constraint under which the consumer exercises choices.

LO 6A.2 Explain the budget line and illustrate how changes in income and prices affect it

The Budget Line

What is the budget line?

Suppose a consumer, Mila Charles, has $24, which she will use to purchase novels and ice cream. We refer to the sum of $24 as her budget. Suppose also that the price of novels is $6 each and the price of ice cream is $3 per container. Table 6A.1 shows combinations of novels and ice cream that Mila can afford, given her budget of $24.

Such a table as Table 6A.1 is called a **purchase possibilities schedule** or a **consumption possibilities schedule**, which is a table showing various combinations of goods and services that a consumer can purchase for the same amount of money.

Table 6A.1	Alternative Purchases with a Given Budget	
Quantity of Novels	Quantity of Ice Cream	Amount ($)
0	8	24
1	6	24
2	4	24
3	2	24
4	0	24

purchase possibilities schedule or consumption possibilities schedule a table showing various combinations of goods and services that a consumer can purchase for the same amount of money

budget line or price line a graphical representation of all possible combinations of two commodities that a consumer can purchase for the same amount of money

Now, we can plot the information contained in Table 6A.1 on a graph. If Mila spends her entire budget of $24 on novels, she can purchase a maximum of 4 novels. This gives point *A* in Figure 6A.1. If she spends her entire budget on ice cream, she can purchase a maximum of 8 containers of ice cream. This gives point *E* on the diagram.

If we connect points *A* and *E* by a straight line, we obtain the **budget line** or the **price line** as it is sometimes called. All other combinations of novels and ice cream that Mila can obtain for $24 fall on this budget line. We can therefore define the budget line as a graphical representation of all possible combinations of two commodities that a consumer can purchase for the same amount of money, given the prices of the two commodities.

All combinations on or below the budget line are affordable. Such a point as *P*, which lies below the budget line, means that Mila is not spending her entire budget. All points, such as *Q*, that lie to the right of the budget line are unaffordable, given her budget and the prices of novels and ice cream. Mila is constrained by the budget line; she must confine her purchases to combinations that lie on or below the budget line. For this reason, the budget line is often referred to as the *budget constraint*.

Does a relationship exist between the slope of the budget line and the prices of the items under consideration?

Let us pursue this question. What does the slope of the budget line tell us? The slope of the budget line in Figure 6A.1 tells us the quantity of novels that must be given up in order to purchase one more container of ice cream. The slope of this budget line is

$$\frac{\text{Vertical distance}}{\text{Horizontal distance}} = -\frac{4}{8} = -\frac{1}{2}$$

Figure 6A.1	The Budget Line

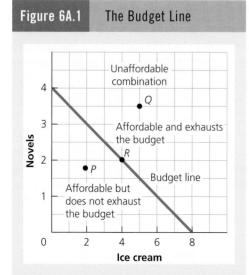

Note that this is the same as the ratio of the prices of the two goods, but with a negative sign.

$$\frac{\text{Price of ice cream}}{\text{Price of novels}} = \frac{3}{6} = \frac{1}{2}$$

Because this is so in all cases, we can draw the following conclusion:

> The slope of the budget line is the same as the ratio of the prices of the two items, but with a negative sign.

What would happen to the budget line if Mila's income increases?

Figure 6A.2	Effect on the Budget Line of a Change in Income

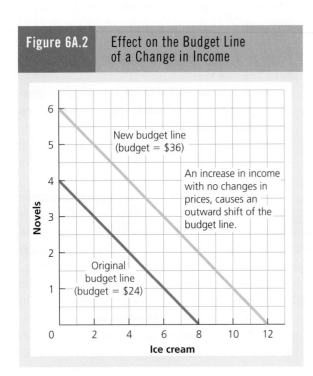

Let's assume that Mila's budget (income) increases from $24 to $36, while the prices of novels and ice cream remain unchanged at $6 and $3, respectively. Evidently, with a larger income, Mila can now afford more novels *and* more ice cream. Specifically, she can now afford to buy 6 novels if she buys 0 containers of ice cream, or 12 containers of ice cream if she buys 0 novels. Choices that were previously unattainable because of her income are now within her reach. The new budget line resulting from the increase in income is shown in Figure 6A.2. Note that the new budget line is parallel to the original budget line. An increase in income shifts the budget line to the right; a decrease in income shifts it to the left.

> Other things being equal, a change in consumer income results in a parallel shift in the budget line. An increase in income shifts the budget line to the right; a decrease in income shifts it to the left.

What would happen to the budget line if the price of one of the items (ice cream, for example) changes?

Figure 6A.3	Effect on the Budget Line of a Change in Price

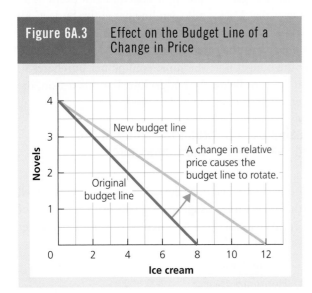

Suppose the price of ice cream falls from $3 per container to $2 per container, while the price of novels remains at $6 each. With a budget of $24, Mila can buy the same number of novels as before, namely, 4, if she buys no ice cream. But instead of 8 containers of ice cream, she can now afford 12 containers if she buys no novels. Figure 6A.3 shows how a fall in the price of ice cream affects the consumer's budget line. Note that a fall in the price of ice cream causes the budget line to move outward but not parallel to the original budget line. In other words, the budget line *rotates* rather than *shifts*. Because the price of novels did not change, Mila can still afford to buy 4 novels, as before. A change in the price of one of the items under consideration changes the price ratio and hence the slope of the budget line.

Other things being equal, a change in the price of one of the commodities that the consumer buys causes the slope of the budget line to change.

Reading Comprehension

The answers to these questions can be found on MyEconLab at www.myeconlab.com.   MyEconLab

1. What is a budget line? In what sense does a budget line represent a constraint on a consumer's purchases?

2. Explain how a change in income affects the budget line.

3. Explain how a change in price affects the budget line.

LO 6A.3 Discuss preference, indifference, and indifference curves

Preference, Indifference, and Indifference Curves

If utility cannot be cardinally measured, what alternative assumption is made in indifference curve analysis about the consumer?

In the indifference curve approach to consumer choice, the consumer is assumed to be able to state a preference for or indifference to the commodities that he or she consumes. Given three commodities, A, B, and C, for example, if a consumer prefers A to B, then that consumer will rank A higher than B. If the consumer is indifferent between B and C, then the consumer will rank B and C at the same level. Thus, the concepts of preference and indifference can be used to describe the consumer's tastes.

In any situation, if a consumer faces a choice between two goods or bundles of goods, that consumer will either express a preference for one over the other, or express indifference. Moreover, for any consumer, if A is preferred to B, and B is preferred to C, then A must be preferred to C. In other words, the consumer is assumed to have consistent preferences. We sometimes express this point by saying that the consumer's preferences are *transitive*.

What is an indifference schedule?

Let us answer this question by going through an example. Assume that you face six bundles—A, B, C, D, E, and F—each containing the combinations of apples and pears indicated in Table 6A.2.

Table 6A.2	An Indifference Schedule		
Bundle	**Apples**	**Pears**	**Total Utility**
A	40	29	S_1
B	32	30	S_1
C	26	31	S_1
D	23	34	S_1
E	21	39	S_1
F	20	46	S_1

Assume also that each bundle (combination) from A to F, according to your subjective evaluation, gives you the same level of satisfaction—namely S_1. It makes no difference to you whether you are given 40 apples and 29 pears, or 32 apples and 30 pears, or 26 apples and 31 pears, and so on; you feel equally well off with any of these combinations. Table 6A.2 is called an **indifference schedule**, a table showing various combinations of commodities that give a consumer the same level of satisfaction.

indifference schedule a table showing various combinations of commodities that give a consumer the same level of satisfaction

Can we construct an indifference schedule that shows a greater level of satisfaction than any of the combinations in Table 6A.2?

Of course this is possible. Consider the indifference schedule shown as Table 6A.3. Each combination from A to F is just as desirable as any other in this schedule; each gives a level of satisfaction of S_2.

But compare the schedule in Table 6A.2 with that in Table 6A.3. You will observe that each bundle in Table 6A.3 contains more than each bundle in Table 6A.2. Because we are assuming that consumers prefer more to less, then we conclude that a consumer will prefer any combination in Table 6A.3 to any combination in Table 6A.2. Therefore, S_2 represents a higher level of satisfaction than S_1.

Table 6A.3	An Indifference Schedule		
Bundle	Apples	Pears	Total Utility
A	58	29	S_2
B	51	30	S_2
C	46	31	S_2
D	42	34	S_2
E	39	39	S_2
F	38	46	S_2

indifference curve a graph that shows all combinations of two commodities (or groups of commodities) that yield the same level of satisfaction

What is an indifference curve?

Once you have grasped the meaning and significance of indifference schedules, it is an easy step to proceed to indifference curves. Let us begin by plotting on a graph the combinations of apples and pears shown in Table 6A.2, keeping in mind that many other combinations besides those shown in the table yield the same level of satisfaction. If we were to plot all the combinations that yield the same level of satisfaction, we would obtain a continuous curve like the one shown in Figure 6A.4.

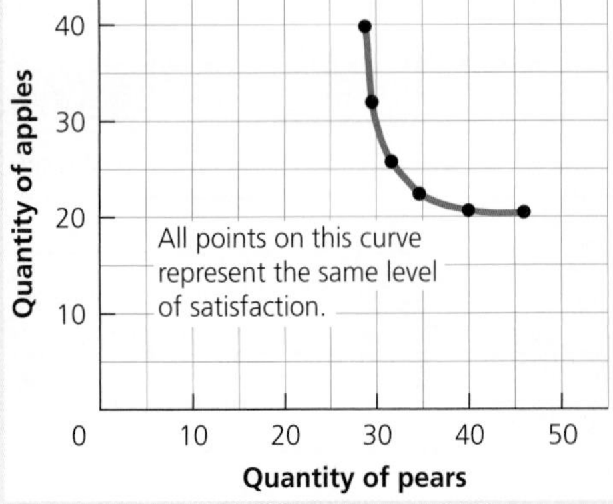

The curve shown in Figure 6A.4 is called an **indifference curve**, a graph that shows all combinations of two commodities (or groups of commodities) that yield the same level of satisfaction.

Figure 6A.4 An Indifference Curve

All points on this curve represent the same level of satisfaction.

What are the properties of indifference curves?

Indifference curves have three basic properties:

1. They slope downward.

2. They are convex (to the origin).

3. They do not intersect.

Let us examine each of these properties in turn.

Figure 6A.5	An Indifference Curve Assumed to Be Vertical

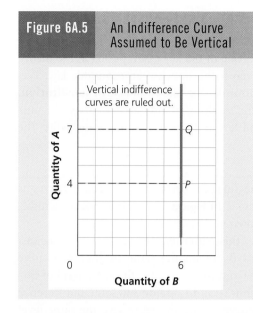

Downward Sloping Any curve must be vertical, horizontal, upward sloping, or downward sloping. There are no other possibilities. Let us suppose, for a moment, that indifference curves are vertical. What exactly would a vertical indifference curve mean? Let us investigate. Consider the indifference curve shown in Figure 6A.5.

Combination P represents 4 of A and 6 of B. Combination Q represents 7 of A and 6 of B. Clearly, because we are assuming that consumers prefer more of a commodity to less, it follows that P and Q do not yield the same level of satisfaction and cannot then be on the same indifference curve. This contradiction rules out the possibility of a vertical indifference curve. By analogous arguments, it can easily be shown that we can rule out horizontal and upward-sloping indifference curves. The downward-sloping indifference curve shown in Figure 6A.6 illustrates that if a consumer gives up 6 units of A ($10 - 4$), that consumer must be compensated with 5 units of B ($8 - 3$) in order to maintain the same level of satisfaction.

Figure 6A.6	A Downward-Sloping Indifference Curve

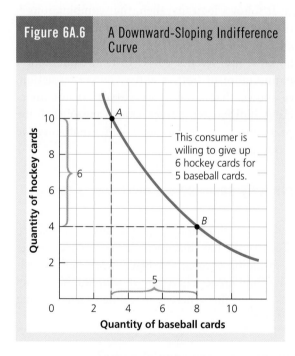

This consumer is willing to give up 6 hockey cards for 5 baseball cards.

Convex If a consumer has a large quantity of hockey cards, but only a small quantity of baseball cards, that consumer is likely to be willing to give up (trade off) some hockey cards for a given quantity of baseball cards. As the quantity of hockey cards diminishes, however, the consumer is likely to be willing to give up a smaller quantity of hockey cards for the same quantity of baseball cards. Similarly, starting with any quantity of baseball cards, a consumer is likely to be willing to give up an increasingly smaller quantity of baseball cards for hockey cards as the quantity of hockey cards diminishes. The more you have of anything, the more willing you are to trade for something of which you have only a small amount. This implies that indifference curves are *convex* to the origin (i.e., relatively steep at the upper portion and relatively flat at the lower portion, as shown in Figure 6A.6). The indifference curve shown in Figure 6A.6 is both downward sloping and convex.

Convexity of indifference curves may be explained this way, too: as the consumer moves along an indifference curve, that consumer is trading off one commodity for another. The rate at which this trade-off occurs is called the **marginal**

marginal rate of substitution
the rate at which a consumer is willing to trade off units of one commodity for units of another commodity so as to keep his or her level of satisfaction unchanged

rate of substitution (*MRS*), the rate at which a consumer is willing to trade off units of one commodity for units of another commodity so as to keep his or her level of satisfaction unchanged.

Note that the marginal rate of substitution is the slope of the indifference curve. As the consumer moves along an indifference curve, that consumer is willing to give up less and less of one commodity for another. In other words, the marginal rate of substitution diminishes (compare the slope of the indifference curve at point A with the slope at point B in Figure 6A.6). This is equivalent to saying that the indifference curve is convex to the origin.

principle of diminishing marginal rate of substitution the hypothesis that as a consumer moves along an indifference curve, consuming more and more of one commodity, and less and less of another commodity, the marginal rate of substitution diminishes

Is there a general tendency for the marginal rate of substitution to diminish?

Diminishing marginal rate of substitution is one of the key assumptions in the theory of consumer choice. Some writers have given it the status of an economic law. We, however, will refer to it as the **principle of diminishing marginal rate of substitution**, which is the hypothesis that as a consumer moves along an indifference curve, consuming more and more of one commodity, and less and less of another commodity, the marginal rate of substitution diminishes.

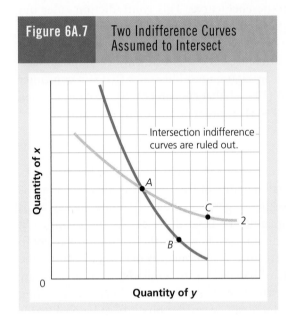

Figure 6A.7 Two Indifference Curves Assumed to Intersect

Intersection indifference curves are ruled out.

Quantity of x

Quantity of y

Non-intersecting The final property of indifference curves is that they do not intersect. In Figure 6A.7, two intersecting indifference curves are shown.

Let us examine this situation to see what it means. Combinations A and B are on the same indifference curve (indifference curve 1) and therefore give the same level of satisfaction. Combinations A and C are on the same indifference curve (indifference curve 2) and therefore give the same level of satisfaction. It follows logically, then, that combinations B and C yield the same level of satisfaction and must therefore, by definition, lie on the same indifference curve. But B and C are not on the same indifference curve. In fact, combination C clearly contains more of both x and y. By contradiction, then, we have shown that indifference curves do not intersect. Intersecting indifference curves would mean that the consumer's preferences are inconsistent—an eventuality we ruled out by assumption.

Does a single indifference curve fully describe the consumer's tastes and preferences?

No. An indifference curve simply tells us combinations of goods and or services to which the consumer is indifferent. To describe the consumer's tastes and preferences completely, we require an entire set of indifference curves. Figure 6A.8 shows a collection of indifference curves. Only five indifference curves are shown, but, in fact, an infinite number of indifference curves are possible. There is an indifference curve that passes through every point in the x-y frame.

Does the set of indifference curves have any special name?

A collection of indifference curves, such as is shown in Figure 6A.8, is referred to as an **indifference map** or an **indifference curve map** or a **preference map**.

indifference map or indifference curve map or preference map a collection of indifference curves

How does an indifference map describe the consumer's preference pattern?

The points on an indifference curve are points of equal satisfaction. Thus, all points on any particular indifference curve represent combinations that yield the same level

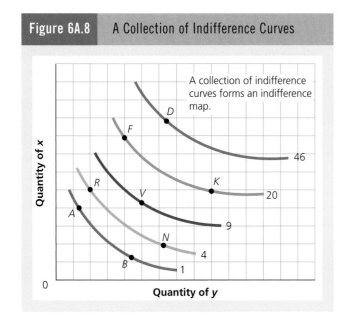

Figure 6A.8 A Collection of Indifference Curves

A collection of indifference curves forms an indifference map.

of satisfaction. Any combination on a higher indifference curve yields a higher level of satisfaction than any combination on a lower indifference curve.

Let us use the following notations to summarize the consumer's preferences:

  = denotes indifference

  > and < denote preference

Thus, $G = H$ means that G and H give equal satisfaction.

$G > H$ means that G is preferred to H.

$G < H$ means that G gives less satisfaction than H, or, alternatively, H is preferred to G.

In Figure 6A.8, the following would be true:

  $A = B$

  $D > N$

  $V < K$

  $D > F > R$

Reading Comprehension

The answers to these questions can be found on MyEconLab at **www.myeconlab.com.**   MyEconLab

1.   What are the properties of indifference curves?
2.   What is the significance of the convexity of indifference curves?

3.   Prove that indifference curves for the same individual do not intersect.
4.   What is an indifference map?

LO 6A.4 Use indifference curve analysis to illustrate the consumer's equilibrium

Equilibrium of the Consumer

Can we use the tools that we have developed so far to show how the consumer will maximize his or her satisfaction?

That was the whole purpose of developing those tools. Let us proceed now to solve the consumer's choice problem. The question we need to answer now is this: given the prices of two commodities and the consumer's budget, how much of each commodity will the consumer purchase in order to maximize his or her satisfaction? In Figure 6A.9 we show the indifference curves and the budget line for a consumer, Maurice.

Maurice can choose any combination of movies and dinners that lies on or below the budget line, and he wants to be on the highest attainable indifference curve. Maurice is going to spend his entire budget, so he can choose among points A, B, and C or any other points that lie on the budget line in Figure 6A.9. Points A and C are on a lower indifference curve than point B; hence, each yields a lower level of satisfaction than point B does. Maurice achieves maximum satisfaction at point B, where the

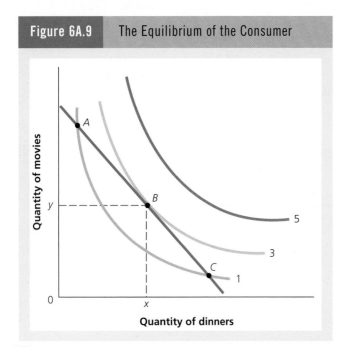

Figure 6A.9 The Equilibrium of the Consumer

budget line is just tangent to (that is, just touches) an indifference curve. Any move from this position will diminish Maurice's satisfaction. Experiment to see for yourself that this is true. Maurice is said to be in equilibrium at point *B*. He is maximizing his satisfaction or utility when he purchases *y* movies and *x* dinners. Generally, a consumer will choose the combination that maximizes his or her satisfaction. This will be the combination where the budget line is tangent to an indifference curve.

> A consumer maximizes his or her satisfaction by moving along his or her budget line to the highest indifference curve attainable. This occurs when the budget line is tangent to the indifference curve.

Some relationship seems to exist among the consumer's equilibrium, the marginal rate of substitution, and the prices of the items that the consumer buys. Is there any relationship?

To answer that question, let us examine the consumer's preferred position a little more closely. At the point of tangency between the budget line and an indifference curve, the slope of the indifference curve is the same as the slope of the budget line. The slope of the indifference curve, you recall, is the marginal rate of substitution (*MRS*). Recall also that the slope of the budget line is the ratio of the prices of the two items under consideration. We can therefore restate the consumer's equilibrium position in terms of the marginal rate of substitution and price ratios. The consumer is in equilibrium when the following condition holds:

$$MRS_{xy} = \frac{P_x}{P_y}$$

where MRS_{xy} is the marginal rate of substitution between two goods, *x* and *y*, and P_x and P_y are the prices of *x* and *y*, respectively.

Reading Comprehension

The answers to these questions can be found on MyEconLab at www.myeconlab.com. MyEconLab

1. The objective of the consumer is to maximize satisfaction. Frame this objective in terms of indifference curves.

2. What is your understanding of the equilibrium of the consumer?

3. Demonstrate that a consumer will be in equilibrium when he or she chooses a combination at which the budget line is tangent to an indifference curve.

The Effect of Changes in Income and Prices on the Consumer's Equilibrium

What effect will a change in income have on the consumer's equilibrium?

In Figure 6A.10, consumer Ken is in equilibrium at *A* on indifference curve 1. An increase in Ken's income will cause the budget line to shift out in a parallel manner. Because no change occurs in relative prices, the slope of the budget line will not change. The higher budget line will be tangent to a higher indifference curve, such as indifference curve 2. (Remember that the indifference map has an infinite number of indifference curves.) Ken is now in equilibrium at point *B*. Further increases in income cause further outward shifts in the budget line, which will be tangent to a higher indifference curve, such as indifference curve 3. This puts Ken in equilibrium at point *C*. Thus, as Ken's income increases, he attains higher and higher levels of satisfaction. You can quite easily work out the effect of a fall in income on the consumer's equilibrium position.

By joining points *A*, *B*, and *C* in Figure 6A.10, we obtain the **income consumption curve**. The income consumption curve is the line joining the points of tangency between budget lines and indifference curves as the consumer's income changes.

The income consumption curve shows how the consumer responds to changes in income. As Ken's income increases, he buys more of each good. Commodities that are bought in larger quantities as income increases are called *normal goods*. Wine and steak in Figure 6A.10 are normal goods.

It may happen that, as his income increases, Ken buys a smaller quantity of used clothing than he bought before the increase in his income. Such a commodity is called an *inferior good*, which we previously defined as a good for which demand decreases as income increases.

In Figure 6A.11, as Ken's income increases, he buys a smaller quantity of used clothing—two instead of five. Used clothing in Ken's case is an inferior good. Observe the shape of the income consumption curve in the case of an inferior good.

We have established a relationship between the consumer's income and his or her purchases of goods and services. Can this relationship be illustrated explicitly on a graph?

We can use graphs to illustrate how a consumer responds to changes in income. Let us assume that Ken's tastes and preferences, along with the prices of restaurant meals and used clothing, remain unchanged. His income, however, is

| Figure 6A.10 | Effect of an Increase in Income When the Good Is a Normal Good |

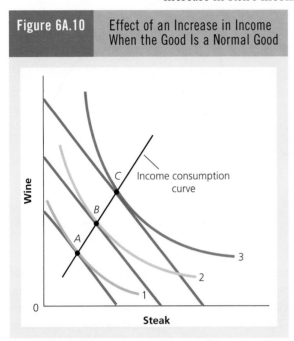

| Figure 6A.11 | Income Consumption Curve for an Inferior Good |

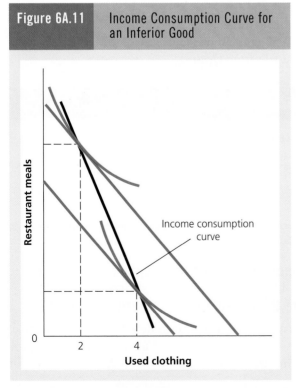

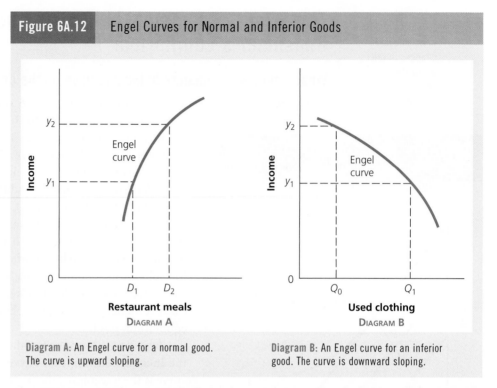

Figure 6A.12   Engel Curves for Normal and Inferior Goods

Diagram A: An Engel curve for a normal good. The curve is upward sloping.

Diagram B: An Engel curve for an inferior good. The curve is downward sloping.

income consumption curve the line joining the points of tangency between budget lines and indifference curves as the consumer's income changes

Engel curve a curve that shows the relationship between income and consumption

allowed to vary. In Figure 6A.11, we saw that as Ken's income increases, he buys a greater quantity of restaurant meals. He does, however, buy a smaller quantity of used clothing. This information is presented explicitly in Figure 6A.12 as a relation between income and quantity bought. The curves in Figure 6A.12 are called **Engel curves**, named after the nineteenth-century statistician Ernst Engel. An Engel curve shows the relationship between income and consumption.

Diagram A shows that as income rises from y_1 to y_2, the quantity of restaurant meals consumed increases from D_1 to D_2. Diagram B shows that as income rises from y_1 to y_2, the quantity of used clothing bought falls from Q_1 to Q_0.

BUSINESS SITUATION 6A.1

Conrad Jones opened his second-hand shop in a low-income part of town 25 years ago. He sells a wide variety of items. Over the years, the area in which Mr. Jones operates his shop has undergone significant change. The area has been transformed from a low-income area to an affluent area, and Mr. Jones's business has suffered substantial decline.

How might Mr. Jones deal with this new business situation?

The answer to this Business Situation can be found in Appendix A.

price consumption curve a line joining the points of tangency between budget lines and indifference curves as the price of one of the items changes

A change in the consumer's income allows the consumer to attain a higher indifference curve—a higher level of satisfaction. What effect will a change in price have on the consumer's equilibrium position?

Perhaps the best way to answer this question is to demonstrate with a specific example. Let us consider the case of Jennifer. Figure 6A.13 shows her in equilibrium at point A on indifference curve 1. She is purchasing patties and mints. A fall in the price of

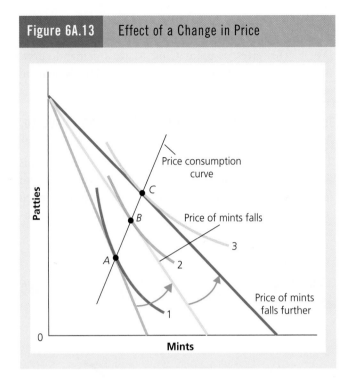

Figure 6A.13 Effect of a Change in Price

mints causes the slope of the budget line to change. The budget line rotates outward; it becomes flatter because Jennifer can now buy more mints while buying the same quantity of patties. This new budget line is tangent to a higher indifference curve—indifference curve 2 in Figure 6A.13. Jennifer is now in equilibrium at point *B*.

A further fall in the price of mints causes the budget line to become even flatter, and it is now tangent to indifference curve 3. Jennifer achieves equilibrium at point *C*. Clearly, a fall in the price of a commodity, other things being equal, allows the consumer to attain a higher level of satisfaction.

By joining points *A*, *B*, and *C* in Figure 6A.13, we obtain the **price consumption curve**, which we can define as a line joining the points of tangency between budget lines and indifference curves as the price of one of the items changes.

Reading Comprehension

The answers to these questions can be found on MyEconLab at **www.myeconlab.com.**   MyEconLab

1. What is the income consumption curve?
2. Use the indifference curve technique to demonstrate that an increase in income, other things being equal, increases consumer satisfaction.

3. What is a price consumption curve?
4. Show that a consumer buying two goods is made better off if the price of one of the goods falls, other things being equal.

LO 6A.6 Use indifference curve analysis to derive the consumer's demand curve

Derivation of the Consumer's Demand Curve

We were able to derive the consumer's demand curve from utility analysis. Can we derive the consumer's demand curve from indifference curve analysis?

Yes, the consumer's demand curve can be derived from indifference curve analysis. More specifically, it can be derived from the price consumption curve discussed above. We perform this exercise in Figure 6A.14. Diagram B shows changes in purchases made by Mario as the price of DVDs changes. As the price of DVDs falls, Mario increases his purchases from Q_1 to Q_2 to Q_3.

The graph in Diagram B is lined up with that in Diagram A. The price P_3 corresponds to the initial price. At that price, Mario purchases Q_1 DVDs. This gives us point *A* on the consumer's demand curve for DVDs. As the price falls to P_2, Mario purchases

| Figure 6A.14 | Derivation of the Consumer's Demand Curve |

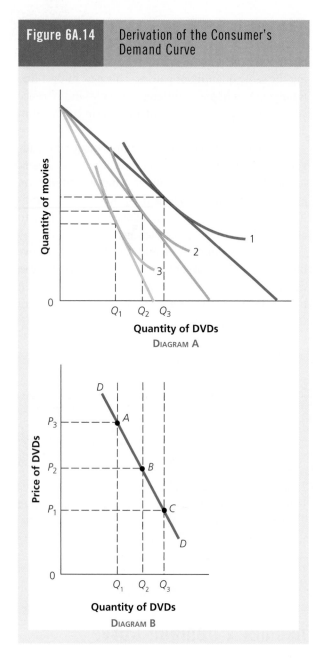

DIAGRAM A

DIAGRAM B

Q_2 DVDs. This gives us point B on Mario's demand curve. A further fall in price to P_1 causes Mario to purchase Q_3 DVDs. This gives us point C on Mario's demand curve. By joining points A, B, and C, we obtain Mario's demand curve.

Is it possible for a consumer's demand curve to be upward sloping?

The demand curves that we have studied up to this point are all downward sloping. As the price of an item falls, other things being equal, the quantity demanded increases. The demand curve in Figure 6A.14 is downward sloping.

| Figure 6A.15 | An Upward-Sloping Demand Curve |

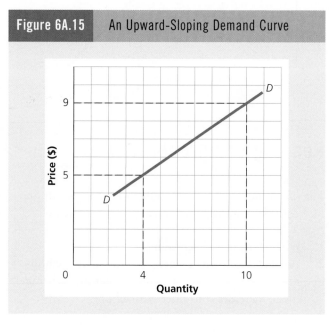

The Case of a Giffen Good   An economist of the Victorian era named Robert Giffen discussed the possibility of an upward-sloping demand curve. Consider a relatively inexpensive product, such as potatoes. If the price of potatoes falls, consumers' real incomes increase, so instead of buying more potatoes, consumers may substitute another product, such as steak, for potatoes. In this case, the quantity of potatoes demanded falls as the price of potatoes falls, and the demand curve will be upward sloping, as shown in Figure 6A.15. Specifically, as the price falls from $9 to $5, the quantity demanded also falls from 10 units to 4 units.

Such goods are referred to as Giffen goods. A **Giffen good** is a good whose quantity demanded rises as its price rises and falls as its price falls, other things being equal.

Giffen good a good whose quantity demanded rises as its price rises and falls as its price falls

Reading Comprehension

The answers to these questions can be found on MyEconLab at www.myeconlab.com.   MyEconLab

1. Describe the difference between the concepts in the following pairs:

a)   Normal goods and inferior goods
b)   Inferior goods and Giffen goods

2. What does an upward sloping demand curve for a consumer mean?

Review

1. Review the learning objectives listed at the beginning of the appendix.
2. Have you accomplished all the objectives? One way to determine this is to answer the Reading Comprehension questions at the end of each section. They will help you assess the extent to which you have accomplished the learning objectives.
3. If you have not accomplished an objective, review the relevant material before proceeding.

Key Points to Remember

1. **LO 6A.1** Problems with the cardinal approach to consumer behaviour are that it assumes that satisfaction can be measured cardinally, and it does not explicitly indicate the constraint under which the consumer chooses among the variety of goods and service to purchase. The indifference curve approach avoids these problems. It does not require cardinal measures of satisfaction, and it explicitly indicates the constraint under which the consumer exercises choices.)
2. **LO 6A.2** A change in income causes the budget line to shift parallel to the original budget line. A change in the price of one of the commodities causes the slope of the budget line to change.
3. **LO 6A.3** An indifference curve shows all possible combinations of two commodities that yield the same level of satisfaction. Indifference curves are downward sloping, convex to the origin, and do not intersect.
4. **LO 6A.3** The principle of diminishing marginal rate of substitution states that as the consumer moves along an indifference curve, consuming more and more of one

commodity, and less and less of another commodity, the marginal rate of substitution will diminish.
5. **LO 6A.4** Consumers achieve equilibrium (maximum satisfaction) by moving along the budget line until they arrive at a point at which the budget line is tangent to an indifference curve. In equilibrium, the marginal rate of substitution equals the ratio of the prices of the two commodities.
6. **LO 6A.5** A greater quantity of a normal good is bought as income increases. A smaller quantity of an inferior good is bought as income increases. The Engel curve for a normal good is positively sloped, whereas the Engel curve for an inferior good is negatively sloped.
7. **LO 6A.6** The consumer's demand curve can be derived from the price consumption curve.

Economic Word Power

Budget line or price line   (p. 181)
Engel curve   (p. 190)
Giffen good   (p. 192)
Income consumption curve   (p. 190)
Indifference curve   (p. 184)
Indifference map or indifference curve map or preference map   (p. 187)
Indifference schedule   (p. 184)
Marginal rate of substitution   (p. 185)
Price consumption curve   (p. 190)
Principle of diminishing marginal rate of substitution   (p. 186)
Purchase possibilities schedule or consumption possibilities schedule   (p. 181)

Problems and Exercises

Basic

1. **LO 6A.2** Mona Jarvis has $48 to spend on meals and novels. The price of a meal is $12 and novels are $6 each.
   a. Draw Mona's budget line.
   b. On your graph, show a combination of meals and novels that does not exhaust Mona's budget. Label it *E*.
   c. On your graph, show a combination of meals and novels that Mona cannot afford, given her current budget. Label it *U*.

2. **LO 6A.2** Use the data in Question 1 above to show the effect of an increase in Mona's budget from $48 to $60.

3. **LO 6A.2** A consumer has a budget of $24. The prices of novels and magazines are $6 and $3, respectively.
   a. Draw the consumer's budget line.
   b. If the price of magazines rises to $4, show the effect on the budget line.

4. **LO 6A.3** Dave Wong says that he is indifferent as to which of the following combinations of food and clothing shown in Table 6A.4 he will receive. On the basis of this information, draw Dave's indifference curve.

Table 6A.4	Combinations of Food and Clothing	
Combinations	**Food**	**Clothing**
A	1	6
B	2	3
C	3	2
D	4	1.5

5. **LO 6A.3** Figure 6A.16 illustrates Lydia's indifference map for restaurant meals and movies. Describe what happens to Lydia's total utility as she moves from point:
   a. *C* to *A*
   b. *B* to *C*
   c. *B* to *D*
   d. *C* to *D*
   e. *D* to *E*
   f. *A* to *B*

6. **LO 6A.2** Emiko has a budget of $12 a week to spend on drinks and burgers. The price of drinks is $1, and the price of burgers is $2.

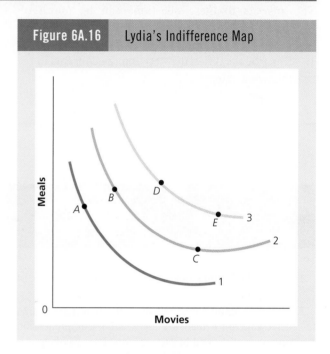

Figure 6A.16   Lydia's Indifference Map

a. Fill in the blanks in Table 6A.5 showing combinations of drinks and burgers that Emiko can purchase for $12.
b. With quantity of drinks on the vertical axis and quantity of burgers on the horizontal axis, draw Emiko's budget line.
c. If the price of burgers falls from $2 to $1.50 while drinks remain at $1, draw Emiko's new budget line on the same diagram.

Table 6A.5	Combinations of Drinks and Burgers
Drinks	**Burgers**
_____	6
2	_____
_____	4
_____	3
8	_____
10	_____
_____	0

7. **LO 6A.2** Vanessa has $40 to spend on scarves and gloves. The prices of scarves and gloves are $5 and $8, respectively.
   a. Draw Vanessa's budget line.
   b. If the price of gloves rises to $10 while the price of scarves remains at $5, draw Vanessa's new budget line on the same graph.
   c. Suppose Vanessa's budget increases from $40 to $60. With the prices of scarves and gloves at $5 and $10, respectively, draw Vanessa's new budget line.

Questions in the Intermediate and Challenging Sections cover several different concepts, and have not been organized by learning objectives.

Intermediate

1. A consumer has $36 to purchase two goods, A and B. The price of A is $4 and the price of B is $6.
   a. With A on the vertical axis and B on the horizontal axis, draw the consumer's budget line.
   b. Calculate the slope of the budget line.
   c. What is the ratio of the prices of A and B?

2. Use indifference curve analysis to show that a consumer is neither better off nor worse off if her income doubles while the prices of the items that she buys also double.

3. Table 6A.6 shows demand schedules for consumers A and B, the only buyers in the market.
   a. Fill in the quantities demanded by the market at the various prices.
   b. Draw each individual's demand curve on Figure 6A.17.
   c. Draw the market demand curve.

Challenging

1. If a consumer considers peaches and plums to be perfect substitutes, what would the indifference curve look like?

2. A consumer purchases two goods, A and B. Use indifference curve analysis to show that if the price of B falls, the consumer may purchase not just more of B but also more of A. How can this situation be explained?

Table 6A.6	Demand Curves for A and B		
Price ($)	**Consumer A**	**Consumer B**	**Market**
10	0	1	
8	1	2	
6	2	3	

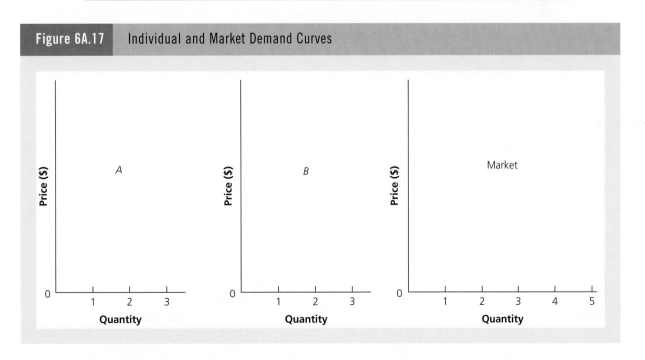

Figure 6A.17   Individual and Market Demand Curves

Study Guide

Self-Assessment

The answers to the Study Guide questions can be found in Appendix B.

What's your score?

Circle the letter that corresponds with the correct answer.

1. One advantage of the indifference curve approach over the cardinal utility approach is that
   a. The numbers used in the indifference curve approach have cardinal significance
   b. In the indifference curve approach, the consumer does not have to be rational
   c. In the indifference curve approach, there is no need to know the prices, while prices are needed in the cardinal utility approach
   d. None of the above

2. The budget line shows
   a. The relationship between price and quantity demanded
   b. The various quantities of a good or service that a consumer can buy with a given budget
   c. The various quantities that can be produced if all resources are employed
   d. The slope of the indifference curve

3. A budget line
   a. Defines the boundary between what is affordable and what is not
   b. Illustrates all combinations of a good or service that give the same level of satisfaction
   c. Depends only on the consumer's income
   d. Is usually upward sloping, showing that more will be bought as the budget increases

Questions 4 to 8 refer to Figure 6A.18. The price of A is $2 and the price of B is $1.

4. The consumer's budget is
   a. $5
   b. $50
   c. $20
   d. $10

5. Which of the following is correct?
   a. Point *P* represents a combination that the consumer cannot afford
   b. Points *H* and *R* give the same level of satisfaction
   c. Combination *R* costs more than combination *H*
   d. Point *P* represents a combination that the consumer can well afford

Figure 6A.18	A Budget Line

6. Combination *X* costs
   a. less than $5
   b. less than $10
   c. between $5 and $10
   d. more than $10

7. If the price of *B* rises, the budget line will
   a. Become steeper
   b. Become flatter
   c. Shift out in a parallel manner
   d. Shift in toward the origin but in a parallel manner

8. If the consumer's budget increases, while the prices of A and B remain at $2 and $1, respectively,
   a. The budget line will shift inward, but the slope will not change
   b. The budget line will shift outward, but the slope will not change
   c. The budget line will not be affected
   d. The budget line will rotate and become steeper

9. An indifference curve shows combinations of goods that
   a. Maximize the consumer's satisfaction
   b. The consumer can purchase for the same amount of money
   c. Give the consumer the same level of satisfaction
   d. None of the above

10. An indifference map
    a. Allows us to find the highest prices that the consumer would be willing to pay
    b. Is a collection of indifference curves
    c. Is a graph of intersecting indifference curves
    d. All of the above

11. Which of the following is a property of indifference curves?
    a. They are negatively sloped
    b. They do not intersect
    c. They are convex
    d. All of the above

Questions 12 to 14 refer to Figure 6A.19.

Figure 6A.19 Indifference Curves

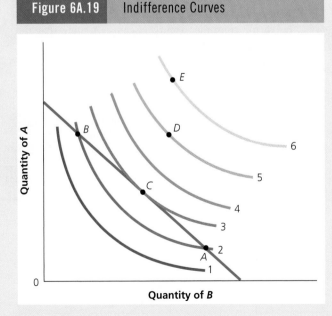

12. On the basis of the information contained in Figure 6A.19, the highest indifference curve attainable is
    a. indifference curve 1
    b. indifference curve 3

    c. indifference curve 4
    d. indifference curve 6

13. The consumer is in equilibrium at point
    a. E
    b. B
    c. C
    d. D

14. Which of the following is correct?
    a. B, C, and A give the same level of satisfaction
    b. B, C, and A cost the same, but C gives more satisfaction
    c. The consumer is in equilibrium at E because E is on the highest indifference curve
    d. B is preferred to A because it is higher up the budget line

15. Intersecting indifference curves would mean that
    a. Preferences cannot be ordered or ranked
    b. The law of diminishing marginal rate of substitution is not applicable
    c. The consumer was inconsistent
    d. All of the above

16. Which of the following is true about the marginal rate of substitution?
    a. It diminishes
    b. It is the slope of the indifference curve
    c. It is the rate at which one commodity is traded for another in order to keep the consumer's level of satisfaction unchanged
    d. All of the above

17. A change in the slope of the budget line means that
    a. Income has changed but not relative prices
    b. Prices have changed proportionally
    c. There has been a change in relative prices
    d. All of the above

18. A household maximizes satisfaction when
    a. The budget line ceases to move outward
    b. The indifference curve ceases to move outward
    c. The budget line is tangent to an indifference curve
    d. None of the above

19. Engel curves show the relationship between
    a. Price and quantity demanded
    b. Income and quantity demanded
    c. Normal goods and Giffen goods
    d. Price consumption curve and consumer equilibrium

20. Giffen goods are
    a. Goods that are bought in smaller quantities as their prices fall
    b. Goods whose demand curves slope downward
    c. Identical to inferior goods
    d. None of the above

Problems and Exercises (Use Quad Paper for Graphs)

Answers to these questions can be found on MyEconLab
at www.myeconlab.com.   MyEconLab

1. Janet's coffee and muffin budget is $10 a week. The price of a coffee is $2.00 and the price of a muffin is $1.00.
   a. Fill in the blanks in Table 6A.7 showing combinations of coffee and muffins that Janet can purchase for $10.

Table 6A.7	Combinations of Coffee and Muffins	
Coffee	**Muffins**	**Budget ($)**
0	___	10
___	8	10
2	___	10
3	___	10
___	2	10
___	___	10

   b. On quad paper, with quantity of muffins on the vertical axis and quantity of coffee on the horizontal axis, draw the budget line that results from Table 6A.7.
   c. Now suppose that Janet's budget increases from $10 to $16. Draw her new budget line on the same graph.

2. Consumer Evance's apple and hamburger budget is $15 a week. The price of an apple is $1.00, and the price of a hamburger is $1.50.
   a. On quad paper, draw Evance's budget line with the quantity of apples on the vertical axis and the quantity of hamburgers on the horizontal axis.
   b. On the same diagram, draw another budget line (dashed) that shows the effect of a fall in the price of hamburgers from $1.50 to $1.00.
   c. On your diagram, use U to indicate a combination of apples and hamburgers that Evance cannot afford.

3. Melissa has $40 to spend on scarves and novels. The prices of scarves and novels are $5 and $4, respectively.
   a. Draw Melissa's budget line.
   b. If the price of scarves rises to $8 while the price of novels remains at $4, draw the new budget line on the same graph.
   c. Suppose Melissa's budget increases to $56, the prices of scarves and novels being $8 and $4, respectively. Draw the new budget line.

4. A consumer has a budget of $40 to purchase goods x and y. The price of x is $2, and the price of y is $4. This consumer's budget constraint is shown in Table 6A.8.
   a. Draw the consumer's budget line.
   b. Calculate the slope of this budget line.

   c. What is the ratio of the prices of x and y?
   d. If the consumer's income increases to $60 while the prices of x and y remain constant, draw the new budget line.

5. Refer to Table 6A.8.
   a. Plot the budget line.
   b. If the price of x rises from $2 to $2.50 while other things remain the same, plot the new budget line.
   c. Calculate the slope of the new budget line.
   d. Calculate the new price ratio.

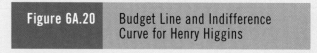

Table 6A.8	Budget Constraint		
Commodity Bundle	**Quantity of x**	**Quantity of y**	**Budget ($)**
A	20	0	40
B	16	2	40
C	12	4	40
D	8	6	40
E	4	8	40
F	0	10	40

6. Use an indifference curve diagram to show that a consumer can be made better off by reducing the price of one of the items that he or she buys while leaving the money income (budget) unchanged.

7. Figure 6A.20 depicts a budget line and an indifference curve for consumer Henry Higgins. Assume that the price of good x is $10.
   a. Calculate Henry's income (budget).
   b. What is the price of good y?

Figure 6A.20	Budget Line and Indifference Curve for Henry Higgins

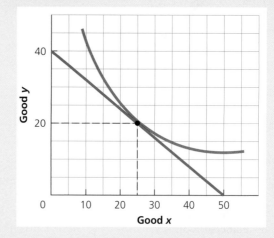

c. What is the marginal rate of substitution at the equilibrium point?

d. What is the ratio of the prices of x and y?

8. The price of A is $6 and the price of B is $10. The consumer has a budget of $60.

a. Draw the consumer's budget line.

b. If the prices of A and B and the consumer's income all double, draw the new budget line.

c. What can you deduce from this exercise about the effect of doubling all prices and income on the consumer's satisfaction?

9. Aletha has a budget of $6. Cucumbers are 30 cents and lettuce is 60 cents. Figure 6A.21 shows that Aletha will be in equilibrium when she buys 8 cucumbers and 6 heads of lettuce. If Aletha's budget and the prices of cucumbers and lettuce all double, how many of each item will Aletha now buy to maximize her satisfaction?

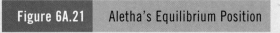

Figure 6A.21 Aletha's Equilibrium Position

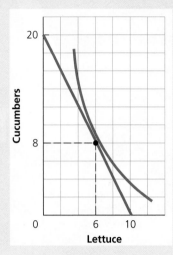

Chapter 7

The Theory of Production

Learning Objectives

After studying this chapter, you should be able to

7.1 Discuss the meaning of production and the objectives of the firm

7.2 Distinguish between economic efficiency and technological efficiency

7.3 Explain production runs (short run, long run)

7.4 Understand the production function

7.5 Understand the relationship among total, marginal, and average product

7.6 Discuss the effect of technology on the production function

7.7 Explain the law of diminishing returns

7.8 Explain the least-cost combination of inputs

7.9 Understand the principle of substitution

Assess Your Knowledge

MyEconLab

Answers to these questions can be found on MyEconLab at **www.myeconlab.com**.

1. Which of the following would you consider to be engaged in production?
   a. Your favourite radio station
   b. Your economics professor
   c. An employee in a Wal-Mart store
   d. All of the above

2. What legal forms of organization can an organization take?

3. What effect does technological advance have on a company's ability to convert inputs (resources) into output (goods and services)?

4. After a party at your house, some of your guests decide to help to clean up the kitchen. What will happen with the clean-up effort as more and more of your friends pour into the kitchen to help?

LO 7.1 Discuss the meaning of production and the objectives of the firm

The Meaning of Production

What is meant by production?

Production is an extremely important economic activity. It can be defined as follows:

production the process by which firms convert inputs into output

> **Production** is the process by which firms convert inputs (factors of production) into outputs (consumer and producer goods and services).

Example: Acme Chrome Furniture Ltd. purchases raw materials, hires workers, uses store and office space, and buys machinery. It uses these resources to make (produce) furniture for sale to retailers who, in turn, sell to the public. Acme Chrome Furniture is engaged in production. The retailers are also engaged in production.

It is worth noting that production is not limited to manufacturing activities. It includes other activities, such as providing consulting services, transportation, and banking services. A warehouse operator who stores goods so that they are available for distribution when needed is involved in production, as is the car manufacturer who uses labour, machines, and materials to produce automobiles.

What do economists mean by a firm?

We often hear such terms as "the law firm of . . . " or "the accounting firm of . . . ," so we associate the concept of a firm with these types of businesses. But the concept of a firm has a much wider meaning. Firms make up the economic unit that transforms inputs into output. They are business enterprises involved in producing goods and services, which may be consumer goods and services, such as microwave ovens, peanut butter, and haircuts; or they may be inputs, such as steel, bricks, and flour, that are used by other firms. A firm can be described as follows:

firms the economic unit that transforms inputs into output

> A **firm** is the economic decision-making unit that buys factors of production (inputs) and, through the production process, transforms these inputs into output for sale to other firms, consumers, and government.

What are the legal forms of business organization that a firm can take?

A firm can take one of several forms of business organization. Among the most popular, however, are the single proprietorship (also called sole proprietorship), the general partnership, the limited partnership, the corporation, and the cooperative.

Can we briefly outline the main features of each?

A single proprietorship is a business owned and managed by a single individual. The single proprietor is solely responsible for all aspects of the business, including its debts. This form of business organization is found mainly in small businesses, such as confectionaries and barbershops, and in certain professions, such as accounting and business and economic consulting.

A general partnership is a business owned by two or more people. Each owner (partner) is personally responsible for all the debts of the partnership. General partnerships are quite common among lawyers, doctors, business and management consultants, and small retail store owners.

A limited partnership is a business that is owned by two types of partners: general partners, who take part in running the business and are liable for all its debts, and limited partners, who play no role in running the business and whose liability is limited to their investment in the business.

A corporation is a business organization in which the owners are not personally responsible for decisions made in the name of the business. The corporation exists as a legal entity apart from its owners who are called shareholders. Not surprisingly, the corporation is the dominant form of business organization in large businesses.

A cooperative is a business owned, financed, and controlled by its members, who share in the profits and risks in proportion to their patronage of the business. Different types of cooperatives include consumer cooperatives, producer cooperatives, purchasing cooperatives, and marketing cooperatives.

Firms can be organized as single proprietorships, partnerships, corporations, or cooperatives.

What are the objectives of the firm?

To analyze the firm's behaviour and predict what course of action it will take under various circumstances, we must pinpoint its objectives. However, the question is not one that can be answered easily. In economic theory, we assume that the firm's objective is to maximize its profit.

profit the difference between total revenue and total cost

> The firm's **profit** is the difference between its total revenue and total cost.

Symbolically,

$$\pi = TR - TC$$

where π represents profit, TR denotes total revenue, and TC is total cost. (Recall that our concept of cost includes opportunity cost).

But not everyone accepts this position. When questioned, business owners and managers admit to pursuing goals other than profit maximization. Most critics of the profit-maximizing assumption agree that a certain level of profit must be achieved to provide earnings for the firm's owners. Once this level is reached, however, they claim that firms pursue other objectives, such as maximizing sales, creating and maintaining a certain public image, offering quality goods and services, maintaining or increasing market share, growing the business, satisfying consumers, looking after customers' general welfare, and charitable objectives. You might well ask, "Why do firms pursue these objectives?" And the answer might very well be that these are not really the firms' objectives. In fact, they are merely means whereby firms can achieve their fundamental objective of maximizing their profits, if not in the short run, then in the long run.

Despite the criticisms of the profit-maximizing assumption, we will accept this to be the firm's objective. The profit-maximizing assumption has served economists well; it has enabled them to analyze and predict the behaviour of firms with a great degree of success.

BUSINESS SITUATION 7.1

Mr. Allen Thomas owns a firm that produces hockey sticks. His objective is to maximize his profits from this business. He hires a competent business manager whose objective is to maximize the firm's revenue.

Is there any conflict between the manager and the owner?

The answer to this Business Situation can be found in Appendix A.

Reading Comprehension

The answers to these questions can be found on MyEconLab at **www.myeconlab.com.**   MyEconLab

1. What is production? Does production always result in some tangible output? Explain.

2. What is a firm? Give two examples of firms.

3. According to economic theory, what is the firm's objective? Mention three other objectives that firms might pursue.

4. How are profits calculated?

LO 7.2 Distinguish between economic efficiency and technological efficiency

Economic Efficiency versus Technological Efficiency

What is the difference between technical efficiency and economic efficiency?

One of the basic decisions that the firm has to make pertains to the method of production that it will employ. Usually, the firm has several ways of combining the factors of production to produce a given quantity of output. The method that uses the fewest inputs is said to be the most technically efficient. The concept of **technical or technological efficiency**, which is efficiency measured in terms of inputs, is illustrated by Table 7.1. Suppose A, B, and C are three methods by which a firm can produce 10 000 shirts per week. Method B uses more labour hours and more capital hours than do methods A and C. Method B is therefore least technically efficient. The firm will not use method B as long as methods A and C are available.

technical (technological) efficiency efficiency measured in terms of inputs

> Technical efficiency refers to efficiency in terms of input use, without reference to cost. The method that is most technically efficient is the one that uses the fewest inputs.

Table 7.1	An Illustration of Technological Efficiency		
Method	**Capital**	**Labour**	**Output**
A	100	500	10 000
B	180	900	10 000
C	50	800	10 000

But what of methods *A* and *C*? Method *A* uses more capital hours than method *C* does, but at the same time, it uses fewer labour hours than method *C* does. Both methods are technically efficient.

We have dealt with technical or technological efficiency; let us now turn to economic efficiency. In defining technical efficiency, we made no reference to cost. **Economic efficiency** is efficiency measured in terms of cost:

economic efficiency
efficiency measured in
terms of cost

> The method that is most economically efficient is the one that has the lowest cost.

Let us suppose that the prices of capital and labour are $40 and $5, respectively. Referring to Table 7.1, we can compute the cost associated with each method as follows:

$$C_a = (100 \times \$40) + (500 \times \$5) = \$6500$$
$$C_c = (50 \times \$40) + (800 \times \$5) = \$6000$$

where C_a is the cost associated with method *A*, and C_c is the cost associated with method *C*. Given the above prices, method *C* is more economically efficient than method *A*.

So when two methods are technically efficient, the firm can choose between them by using the one that is more economically efficient.

The firm will try to produce any given output at the lowest cost. Using method *A*, it would cost the firm $6500 to produce 10 000 shirts. Using method *C*, it would cost the firm $6000 to produce the 10 000 shirts. Clearly, it would be in the firm's best interest to use method *C*.

Does this mean that a change in the prices of capital and labour could change the economic efficiency of the methods?

Yes. Let's consider an example. Suppose the prices of capital and labour changed to $20 and $10, respectively. The cost associated with each method would be as follows:

$$C_a = (100 \times \$20) + (500 \times \$10) = \$7000$$
$$C_c = (50 \times \$20) + (800 \times \$10) = \$9000$$

In this case, method *A* would be more economically efficient than method *C*. Note that a method that is technically inefficient is also economically inefficient because the cost would be higher than with a method that is technically efficient. To choose the most economically efficient method is to choose from among the technically efficient methods the one with the lowest cost.

economic efficiency ratios
numbers that measure
the economic efficiency of
methods of production

What are economic efficiency ratios and when are they used?

Economic efficiency ratios (*EER*) are numbers that measure the economic efficiency of methods of production. We have seen that we can determine the most economically efficient method of production when the output produced by all methods is the same, as in the previous cases. In such cases, we need only compare costs. If, however, we are confronted with different costs for different output levels, then the problem of deciding on the most economically efficient method becomes a bit more difficult.

To choose the most economically efficient method in situations involving different costs and different output levels, we can use the concept of economic efficiency ratios. An economic efficiency ratio is calculated by dividing the value of the output by the cost of the input. If we use *EER* to denote economic efficiency ratio, then

$$EER = \frac{\text{Value of output}}{\text{Cost of inputs}}$$

A higher efficiency ratio implies a more efficient method.

Can you provide an example of how this ratio can be applied?

Consider Table 7.2. Let us assume that the prices of capital and labour are $20 and $10, respectively. The values of the inputs, using methods *A* and *C*, have already been calculated above as $7000 and $9000, respectively.

Table 7.2	Production Methods with Varying Output Levels		
Method	**Capital**	**Labour**	**Output**
A	100	500	10 000
C	50	800	11 000

The output level using method *A* is 10 000, while the output level using method *C* is 11 000.

If we assume that the price of each unit of output (shirts in this case) is $5, then the value of the output from method *A* is (10 000 × $5) = $50 000. The value of the output from method *C* is (11 000 × $5) = $55 000. Now we can calculate the economic efficiency ratios by using the *EER* formula given above.

$$EER \text{ (method } A) = \frac{50\ 000}{7000} = 7.1$$

$$EER \text{ (method } C) = \frac{50\ 000}{9000} = 6.1$$

Because method *A* has a higher economic efficiency ratio, it is more economically efficient than method *C*. Using method *A*, for every $1 of input, the firm receives $7.10 in output. Using method *C*, for every $1 of input, the firm receives $6.10 in output.

BUSINESS SITUATION 7.2

Penholders Inc. is a company that produces penholders. The company is faced with the methods of producing penholders shown in Table 7.3. The costs of capital and labour are $5 and $6, respectively, and the market price of penholders is $10 each.

Which method should the company choose?

Table 7.3	Methods of Producing Penholders		
Method	**Capital**	**Labour**	**Output**
1	10	6	24
2	15	2	25

The answer to this Business Situation can be found in Appendix A.

Reading Comprehension

The answers to these questions can be found on MyEconLab at **www.myeconlab.com.**   MyEconLab

1. Distinguish between technical efficiency and economic efficiency.

2. Define *economic efficiency ratio* (*EER*).

3. Use words to express how an economic efficiency ratio is calculated.

LO 7.3 Explain production runs (short run, long run)

Production Runs or Periods

What are fixed factors and variable factors?

An observation of the firm's inputs will reveal that some of them can be varied quite easily while others cannot be so easily varied. It is possible, then, to classify the firm's inputs (factors of production) into categories: fixed factors and variable factors.

fixed factors inputs that the firm cannot change during a given period

Fixed factors are inputs that the firm cannot change during a given period. A firm's fixed factors may be its land, its buildings, and its machinery.

variable factors inputs that the firm can change during a given period

Variable factors are inputs that the firm can change during a given period. A firm's variable factors may include its labour force and raw materials.

What do economists mean by short run and long run?

The firm's decisions regarding the efficient use of existing equipment and the expansion or contraction of its scale of operation can be grouped into short-run and long-run decisions, respectively. We define the **short run** and the long run as follows:

short run a situation in which the firm has a least one fixed factor

> The **short run** is a situation in which the firm has at least one fixed factor. It does not have sufficient time to vary all of its inputs.

long run a situation in which the firm has only variable factors

> The **long run** is a situation in which the firm has only variable factors. It is able to vary all of its inputs and has no fixed factors of production.

Example: You are operating a small photocopy business with two photocopy machines in a rented space near your college. After three years, you decide to get out of the photocopy business and move on to some more lucrative pursuit. Your lease on the space has just expired but you have two photocopy machines that you cannot get rid of for three weeks. Because it will take you three weeks to exit the business, the short run for you would be any time within three weeks. After three weeks, you are able to vary all your inputs—in this case getting rid of your machines—so your long-run situation would be any time after three weeks.

> **Note:** The definitions of the short run and the long run and the example just given make it quite clear that these time horizons (the short run and the long run) do not correspond to any specific period of calendar time. In some industries, the short run can be quite long, while in others, the long run can be quite short.

Example: The long run can be only a few hours for a shoeshine business. (How long does it take to vary all the inputs in that case?) But for a utility company, the long run can be several years.

Reading Comprehension

1. What is the difference between the items in each of the following pairs of concepts?

   a) Fixed factors and variable factors
   b) The short run and the long run

2. The short run and long run do not correspond to any specific period of calendar time. Explain.

| LO 7.4 | Understand the production function |

The Production Function

Table 7.4	The Relationship between Inputs and Output (Hypothetical Data)		
Units of Variable Factor (Labour) per Week	Total Product (units/week)	Marginal Product (units/week)	Average Product (units/week)
0	0		—
		15	
1	15		15
		19	
2	34		17
		23	
3	57		19
		31	
4	88		22
		22	
5	110		22
		16	
6	126		21
		14	
7	140		20
		4	
8	144		18
		0	
9	144		16
		−4	
10	140		14
		−19	
11	121		11
		−25	
12	96		8

production function the relation between inputs and output

What is a production function?

A firm uses factors of production (inputs) to produce its output of goods and services. A technological relationship exists between the firm's inputs and its output, which economists refer to as a **production function**.

> The production function is the technical relation between a firm's inputs and its output.

The production function defines the maximum possible output that the firm can produce with a given quantity of resources and a given level of technology. Looked at from another perspective, it specifies the minimum amount of inputs required to produce a given level of output.

To simplify the analysis, we will discuss a production scenario in which the firm uses only two inputs: labour and capital. We will also assume that land is a fixed factor while labour is a variable factor and that all workers are equally efficient. The technical (or engineering) relationship between the firm's inputs and its output can be expressed by using functional notation, as follows:

$$Q = Q(L, \overline{T})$$

where Q represents output, L represents the quantity of labour, and T represents the quantity of land. The bar over the T indicates that T is assumed to be fixed. Because this production function has a fixed factor, it is a short-run production function. Table 7.4 shows how output varies as units of labour are added to a fixed quantity of land.

Reading Comprehension

The answers to these questions can be found on MyEconLab at **www.myeconlab.com.** MyEconLab

1. What is a production function?

2. Use functional notation to express the production function.

LO 7.5 Understand the relationship among total, marginal, and average product

total product the maximum quantity of output that a firm can produce during a period

Total, Marginal, and Average Product

What is total product?

During any given period, a firm has a maximum quantity of output that it can produce. This is the firm's **total product** (*TP*). This definition makes it clear that total product is a flow, not a stock variable.

Column 2 of Table 7.4 shows how output (total output) changes with variations in the quantity of labour, the variable factor in column 1. Note that, as the number of units of the variable factor increases, total product increases, reaches a maximum of 144 units when eight or nine units of labour (workers) are hired, and then declines.

If all workers are assumed to be equally efficient, you would expect that each additional worker would contribute equally to total output. In the example in Table 7.4, the first worker hired added 15 units of output per week. You would probably expect the second worker to add another 15 units per week, but instead, that worker added 19 units. Why? One worker alone cannot take advantage of specialization and the division of labour. But when the second worker is hired, they can specialize and divide the labour, resulting in increased productivity.

What is marginal product?

marginal product the extra output derived from using one additional unit of a variable factor

Marginal product (*MP*) is the extra output derived from using one additional unit of a variable factor. We can express marginal product as follows:

$$MP = \frac{\Delta Q}{\Delta L}$$

where *L* is the quantity of the variable factor (labour in this case), and *Q* is the total product or output. Table 7.4 shows that the first unit of labour causes output to increase by 15 units. Thus, the marginal product is 15. Another unit of labour increases total output from 15 units to 34 units; thus, the marginal product at that point is 19.

Values of the marginal product of labour are given in column 3 of Table 7.4. Note that the values of the marginal product are placed in between the lines on which the total values are placed. We will pay special attention to the behaviour of marginal product as the quantity of the variable input is increased.

What is average product?

average product the output per unit of a variable factor

The concept of average product is easier to grasp than that of marginal product, probably because you are more familiar with averages. **Average product** (*AP*) is the output per unit of a variable factor. After a test, you ask to know the average mark. To arrive at the average mark, we add all the marks and then divide by the number of students who wrote the test. The average product is a similar concept. It is the total product divided by the number of units of the variable factor used.

If the total output produced by 15 workers is 255, then the average product is $255 \div 15 = 17$. We can express average product symbolically as

$$AP = \frac{Q}{L}$$

Values of the average product are calculated and recorded in column 4 of Table 7.4. Note that the average product rises, reaches a maximum at 22 units of output when four or five workers are hired, and then diminishes as more workers are hired.

Figure 7.1   Product Curves

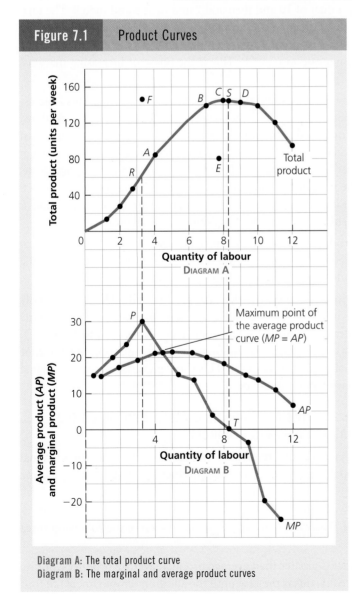

Diagram A: The total product curve
Diagram B: The marginal and average product curves

Is it possible to graph the total product, marginal product, and average product to see more clearly the relationship among them?

Let's begin with the total product curve. We plot the information in columns 1 and 2 of Table 7.4 to obtain the total product curve shown in Diagram A of Figure 7.1.

Let's examine the total product curve. First, we observe that it begins at the origin. If there are no workers, there will be no output. The curve rises quickly up to point *A*, where the number of workers is four and the total product is 88. Total product continues to rise after four workers are hired, but it does so at a slower rate, reaching a maximum between points *C* and *D*, where the number of workers is eight or nine and the total product is 144. Thereafter, it declines.

The total product curve defines the firm's production function. A point below the curve (such as *E*), represents inefficiency: with eight workers, the firm should produce 144 units of output instead of 80 units represented by point *E*. Any point that lies above the curve, such as *F*, is desirable but unattainable. When four workers are hired, the maximum quantity of output that the firm can produce is 88 (represented by point *A*) on the total product curve, not the 140 units represented by point *F*. Point *F* is currently beyond the firm's capability.

Let us now turn to the marginal and average product curves. The information contained in columns 1 and 3, when plotted on a graph, gives us the marginal product curve, while the information in columns 1 and 4 gives us the average product curve. These curves are shown in Diagram B of Figure 7.1. The marginal product rises, reaches a maximum of 31 units between the hiring of three and four workers, and then declines thereafter. The average product also rises, reaches a maximum of 22 units when four or five workers are hired, and then declines thereafter.

What is the relationship between marginal product and total product?

Now that we have drawn the graphs, we can more easily see the relationship between marginal product and total product.

Relationship between Marginal Product and Total Product   The following four points can be observed:

1. When the marginal product is rising, the total product increases at an increasing rate. That's because increasingly larger quantities are added to the total product. Suppose we start with a total product of 10 and then add 2 and then 5 and then 9. The total product will increase to 12, then to 17, and then to 26. In Diagram *B* of Figure 7.1, the marginal product rises to point *P*, and the total product shown in Diagram A increases at an increasing rate to point *R*. This is the phase of increasing marginal productivity.

2. When the marginal product is positive, the total product is increasing. This is necessarily so because the marginal product is the change in total product as an additional unit of the variable factor is used. If this number is positive, then the total product must increase. In Table 7.4 and Figure 7.1, the marginal product is positive up to the point at which the eighth worker is hired; hence, total product increases up to that point. Note, however, that when the marginal product is positive but declining (between points *P* and *T* in Diagram B), total product increases at a diminishing rate (between points *R* and *S* in Diagram A). This is the phase of diminishing marginal productivity.

3. When the marginal product is zero, the total product ceases to rise, but it does not fall either. It has reached its maximum. In Table 7.4 and Figure 7.1, this occurs at a total output of 144 units, when the firm hires nine workers.

4. When the marginal product is negative, the total product falls. This is necessarily so because a negative number is being added to the total product; that is, some quantity is being subtracted from the total product. In Table 7.4 and Figure 7.1, total product begins to decline after the employment of the ninth unit of labour. At that point, the marginal product is negative. This is the phase of negative marginal returns or negative marginal productivity.

The graph really illustrates the relationship clearly. Can we do the same with the marginal and average products?

Yes. To help you to understand and remember the relationship between marginal product and average product, think of the marginal product as a magnet that pulls the average product to it.

Relations between Marginal Product and Average Product   Observe the following three points:

1. When marginal product is greater than average product, average product will rise. In Table 7.4 and Figure 7.1, this is the case until the addition (employment) of four

workers. Note that when the marginal product curve is above the average product curve, it pulls the average product curve up, just like a magnet. To illustrate this relationship further, let us consider an example to which you can easily relate.

Example: Suppose that in a class of 30 economics students, the average mark on an economics test is 69%. A new student enters the class and gets a mark of 77%. The new mark (the marginal mark), being higher than the class average, will pull up the class average, right?

Example: Suppose your final grade is based on four tests written during the term. You have written three tests and your average mark is 70%. Your mark on the fourth test will be the marginal mark. If your mark on the fourth test is better than 70%, your average will increase. In the same way, a marginal product curve that is higher than the average product curve pulls up the average product curve.

2. When marginal product is less than average product, average product will fall. This can be seen in Table 7.4 and Figure 7.1 after the employment of the fifth worker. Note that in Figure 7.1, when the marginal product curve is below the average product curve, the average product curve falls. Can you explain why? Consider what would happen to your average grade if the mark on your fourth test were less than 70%.

3. When marginal product is equal to average product, average product is at its maximum. The marginal product curve shown in Figure 7.1 cuts the average product curve at the maximum point on the average product curve. In Table 7.4, this occurs when the average product is 22 units and between four and five units of labour are employed.

Reading Comprehension

The answers to these questions can be found on MyEconLab at **www.myeconlab.com.**   MyEconLab

1. What is total product? Describe the shape of the total product curve.
2. Describe the behaviour of total product when marginal product is
   a) Rising
   b) Positive
   c) Positive but falling
   d) Negative
3. Describe the behaviour of average product when marginal product is
   a) Greater than average product
   b) Equal to average product
   c) Less than average product
   d) Falling

LO 7.6 Discuss the effect of technology on the production function

Technology and the Production Function

What is the meaning of an improvement in technology?

We can view an improvement in technology in two ways. An improvement in technology occurs when a given quantity of output can be produced by fewer inputs, or when a given quantity of inputs can produce a greater quantity of output. A numerical example might be helpful. Suppose a firm was producing 2000 calculators per week, using 10 workers and 3 machines. Suppose it replaces the 3 machines with 3 new ones that are more efficient so that 10 workers and the 3 new machines now produce 2300 calculators per week. This would be considered an improvement in technology. Or suppose the firm finds a more efficient way of combining workers with the machines so that instead of using 10 workers and 3 machines to produce 2000 calculators per week, it can now use only 7 workers and 3 machines to produce the 2000 calculators. This also would be an improvement in technology.

Figure 7.2	The Effect of an Improvement in Technology on the Production Function

An increase in technology allows a firm to increase its output with a given quantity of inputs.

Earlier in this chapter, we defined the production function as a technological relationship between output and inputs. Does that mean that an improvement in technology affects the production function?

Yes. Let's take a look at Figure 7.2. *TP* is the initial total product curve. With five workers, the maximum quantity of output that the firm can produce is six units. An improvement in technology enables the firm to produce nine units of output with the same five workers. With total product *TP*, point *B* is unattainable. With total product TP_1, point B becomes attainable. We can conclude from this analysis that an improvement in technology shifts the total product curve upward.

Reading Comprehension

The answers to these questions can be found on MyEconLab at **www.myeconlab.com.**   MyEconLab

1. What is meant by an improvement in technology? What effect will an improvement in technology have on a firm's total product curve?

2. Give one example of an improvement in technology.

LO 7.7   Explain the law of diminishing returns

The Law of Diminishing Returns

In our analysis of the behaviour of total output, we noted that increasing the quantity of labour, after a while, causes the rate of increase of the total product to slow down. Does this phenomenon have a special name?

law of diminishing (marginal) returns the hypothesis that any increases in a variable factor, while holding one or more factors constant, will eventually cause marginal product to decline

The phenomenon to which you refer seems to be quite common in real-world production functions—so common, in fact, that the hypothesis is often referred to as the **law of diminishing (marginal) returns**. This is the hypothesis that any increases in a variable factor, while holding one or more factors constant, will eventually cause marginal product to decline.

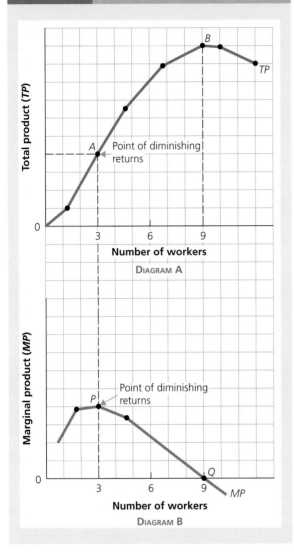

Figure 7.3 An Illustration of the Law of Diminishing Returns

DIAGRAM A

DIAGRAM B

The law of diminishing returns is the hypothesis that if increasing quantities of a variable factor are added to a fixed factor, after a while, the increase in the total product (i.e., the marginal product) will diminish.

The following example will help to illustrate the law of diminishing returns. Suppose Ms. Harris hires one gardener to mow her lawn. Think of what would happen if more and more gardeners were hired at the same time. Overcrowding would result in little or no lawn mowing.

The point of diminishing marginal returns or diminishing marginal productivity occurs at the level of output at which the marginal product is at a maximum. In Figure 7.3, it occurs at point *P* in Diagram B, which corresponds with point *A* in Diagram A. This means that after that point, the increase in total output will diminish. Note that when diminishing returns set in, the total product still increases but at a slower rate.

Observe that the law of diminishing returns states what will happen to physical returns rather than what will happen to monetary returns. In other words, the law deals with a physical rather than a monetary phenomenon. If diminishing returns were not a reality, then any firm could increase its output indefinitely by hiring more and more workers. The existence of the law of diminishing returns in reality presents a constant challenge to people to find more efficient methods of production.

Is there a name for the point at which the marginal product is zero and the total product is at its maximum?

You are referring to point *B* in Diagram A of Figure 7.3, or to point *Q* in Diagram B of Figure 7.3. This point is sometimes referred to as the **point of saturation** and is the point beyond which the marginal product is negative.

point of saturation the point beyond which the marginal product is negative

At this point and beyond, the fixed factors are saturated (swamped) with the variable factor to the extent that total productivity actually declines. Needless to say, no firm would deliberately use inputs up to that point.

BUSINESS SITUATION 7.3

We frequently observe firms changing their advertising messages. Instead of running one advertisement for a very long time (say, six months), they run two or three versions of the message for shorter duration (two months, for example).

Can any economic theory explain this behaviour?

The answer to this Business Situation can be found in Appendix A.

Reading Comprehension

The answers to these questions can be found on MyEconLab at www.myeconlab.com.　MyEconLab

1.　"Diminishing returns take effect only when the total product begins to decline." Discuss.

2.　State and explain the law of diminishing returns. How does the law pertain to rapid population growth?
3.　What is the point of saturation in production theory? Where does this point occur on the total product and marginal product curves?

LO 7.8 Explain the least-cost combination of inputs

Efficiency in the Use of Inputs

Given a certain budget, how does the firm decide on how much of each factor of production to buy to minimize cost?

The problem faced by the firm is similar in many ways to the problem faced by the consumer in deciding how to allocate a given amount of money among various commodities. To simplify our analysis, let us assume that the firm purchases only two factors of production: labour and capital. The firm's objective is to maximize its profits. It will therefore seek to produce any given volume of output at the lowest possible cost. To minimize cost, the firm must satisfy the following condition:

$$\frac{MP_K}{P_K} = \frac{MP_L}{P_L}$$

where MP_K is the marginal product of capital, that is, the extra output obtained by using an additional unit of capital; MP_L is the marginal product of labour, that is, the extra output obtained by using an additional unit of labour; P_K is the price of capital; and P_L is the price of labour.

If the last dollar spent on capital (MP_K/P_K) causes output to increase by 15 units, and the last dollar spent on labour (MP_L/P_L) causes output to increase by only 6 units, then it would benefit the firm to purchase more capital and less labour, provided that labour and capital are substitutable. Conversely, if the last dollar spent on capital causes output to increase by a lesser amount than the increase in output resulting from an extra dollar spent on labour, that is, if

$$\frac{MP_K}{P_K} < \frac{MP_L}{P_L}$$

then the firm would benefit by purchasing more labour and less capital. It follows that the firm will be in the best position (minimizing its costs) when

$$\frac{MP_K}{P_K} = \frac{MP_L}{P_L}$$

We can express this cost-minimizing condition as

$$\frac{MP_K}{MP_L} = \frac{P_K}{P_L}$$

In other words, the optimum input mix for the firm occurs when the ratio of the marginal product of capital to the marginal product of labour equals the ratio of the price of capital to the price of labour.

The least-cost combination of inputs is achieved when the ratio of the marginal products equals the ratio of the input prices.

Can you provide an illustration of this?

Let us assume that the firm has a budget of $1200 to purchase labour and capital. The price of labour is $2 per hour and the price of capital is $3 per hour. Table 7.5 contains information on the marginal product of labour and the marginal product of capital.

We are looking for quantities of labour and capital where $MP_L/P_L = MP_K/P_K$. We have several options and they are all highlighted in Table 7.5. For example, the cost minimization condition is satisfied if the firm buys 100 hours of labour and 200 hours of capital, where $MP_L/P_L = MP_K/P_K = 800$. The condition is met again when the firm buys 300 hours of labour and 200 hours of capital, or 500 hours of labour and 400 hours of capital, or 700 hours of labour and 700 hours of capital. But only one of these possibilities costs $1200.

Table 7.5	An Illustration of the Use of the Cost-Minimization Condition				
Quantity of Labour	MP_L	MP_L/P_L	Quantity of Capital	MP_K	MP_K/P_K
100	1600	800	100	2100	700
200	1800	900	200	2400	800
300	1600	800	300	1800	600
400	1400	700	400	1500	500
500	1000	500	500	1200	400
600	600	300	600	600	200
700	200	100	700	300	100

For example, 100 hours of labour at $2 per hour and 200 hours of capital at $3 per hour would cost $800. The firm wants to spend $1200. If the firm considers buying 700 hours of labour and 700 hours of capital, the cost would be $(700 \times \$2) + (700 \times \$3) = \$3500$. The firm has only $1200 to spend. If the firm buys 300 hours of labour and 200 hours of capital, the cost would be exactly $1200. This is the combination of labour and capital that the firm should buy.

Reading Comprehension

The answers to these questions can be found on MyEconLab at www.myeconlab.com.   MyEconLab

1. What incentive does the firm have to minimize the cost of producing any given volume of output?

2. In purchasing productive inputs with a given budget, how does the firm decide on how much of each input to buy to minimize cost?

LO 7.9 Understand the principle of substitution

The Principle of Substitution

How will a firm respond to a change in the prices of the inputs it purchases?

If the price of capital falls relative to the price of labour, and the two inputs are substitutable, the firm will tend to use more capital and less labour. But if the price of labour falls relative to the price of capital, then the firm will tend to use more labour and less capital.

Does this tendency have a name?

principle of substitution
the tendency for the firm to substitute a cheap factor for a more expensive factor

This tendency for the firm to substitute a cheap factor for the more expensive factor is called the **principle of substitution** and can be stated as follows:

> If two factors of production are substitutable and the price of one rises relative to the price of the other, the firm will tend to use less of the more expensive factor, substituting the less expensive factor for it.

BUSINESS SITUATION 7.4

A business enterprise can substitute labour for capital or capital for labour in its production process. Developments in the market for machinery have resulted in a significant reduction in the cost of machines in general.

If the objective of this business enterprise is to produce any given volume of output at minimum cost, how should the business respond to this reduction in the cost of machines?

The answer to this Business Situation can be found in Appendix A.

The principle of substitution relates to the cost-minimizing condition of the firm:

$$\frac{MP_K}{P_K} = \frac{MP_L}{P_L}$$

If the price of capital (P_K) falls, then

$$\frac{MP_K}{P_K} > \frac{MP_L}{P_L}$$

To maintain the cost-minimizing condition, the firm will use more capital. This then causes MP_K to fall and MP_L to rise, until equality between the two ratios is restored. Note that in the short run, the firm may not be able to substitute one factor for another, or may be able to do so only to a limited extent. In the long run, substitution of factor inputs is less difficult.

Reading Comprehension

The answers to these questions can be found on MyEconLab at **www.myeconlab.com.** MyEconLab

1. If labour and capital can be substituted and the wage rate rises, what adjustment will the firm likely make?

2. What is the principle of substitution? What is the relation between this principle and the cost-minimization condition?

Review

1. Review the learning objectives listed at the beginning of the chapter.
2. Have you accomplished all the objectives? One way to determine this is to answer the Reading Comprehension questions at the end of each section. They will help you assess the extent to which you have accomplished the learning objectives.
3. If you have not accomplished an objective, review the relevant material before proceeding.

Key Points to Remember

1. **LO 7.1** In economic theory, it is assumed that the firm's objective is to maximize its profits. Profit is the difference between total revenue and total cost.
2. **LO 7.2** Technological (or technical) efficiency refers to the use of inputs in physical terms, while economic efficiency refers to the use of inputs in terms of cost. A method of production that is technically inefficient is also economically inefficient. The method that is most technically efficient is the one that uses the fewest inputs. The method that is most economically efficient is the one with the lowest cost. The degree of economic efficiency can be measured by economic efficiency ratios.
3. **LO 7.3** The short run defines a situation in which the firm is unable to vary all its inputs. The long run is a situation in which the firm can vary all its inputs. These terms do not necessarily correspond to any particular periods of calendar time.
4. **LO 7.4, 7.5** A production function is the technological or engineering relationship between a firm's inputs and its output. Total product is the maximum quantity of output that a firm can produce during a period. Marginal product is the change in total product resulting from using an extra unit of a variable factor. Average product is output per unit of a variable factor. It is the total product divided by the quantity of the variable factor.
5. **LO 7.6** An increase in technology occurs when a firm is able to produce a greater output with the same inputs or the same level of output with fewer inputs.
6. **LO 7.7** The law of diminishing returns states that if additional quantities of a variable factor are added to a given quantity of fixed factors, a point will be reached eventually when the marginal product will diminish. This law is a short-run phenomenon. Also, it deals with the behaviour of physical output rather than with monetary returns.
7. **LO 7.8, 7.9** The least-cost combination of inputs is obtained by equating the ratio of the marginal products of the factors to the ratio of their prices. The principle of substitution states that if the price of a factor of production rises relative to the price of another factor, the firm will tend to substitute the less expensive factor for the more expensive factor.

Economic Word Power

Average product (p. 209)
Economic efficiency (p. 204)
Economic efficiency ratios (p. 204)
Firms (p. 201)
Fixed factors (p. 206)
Law of diminishing (marginal) returns (p. 212)
Long run (p. 306)
Marginal product (p. 208)
Point of saturation (p. 213)
Principle of substitution (p. 216)
Production (p. 201)
Production function (p. 207)
Profit (p. 202)
Short run (p. 206)
Technical (technological) efficiency (p. 203)
Total product (p. 208)
Variable factors (p. 206)

Problems and Exercises

Basic

1. **LO 7.2** Table 7.6 shows three methods of combining capital and labour to produce 5000 shirts. The costs of capital and labour are $2 and $5, respectively.
   a. Which method is technically inefficient?
   b. Which method is the most economically efficient?

Table 7.6	Production Methods for Shirts		
Method	Capital	Labour	Shirts
A	20	80	5000
B	30	100	5000
C	15	85	5000

2. **LO 7.2** Refer to Table 7.6. Assume that the costs of capital and labour are $5 and $2, respectively. Which method would be the most economically efficient?

3. **LO 7.5** Table 7.7 contains production data for a firm. *TP* is total product, *MP* is marginal product of labour, and *AP* is average product of labour.
   a. Calculate the marginal product and average product of labour and fill in the *MP* and *AP* columns.

Table 7.7	Production Data for a Firm		
Units of Variable Factor (Labour)	TP	MP	AP
0	0		
1	2		
2	5		
3	9		
4	12		
5	14		
6	15		
7	15		
8	14		

b. Draw the total product curve.

c. On the same graph, draw the marginal product (*MP*) and average product (*AP*) curves. **Note: The *MP* curve should cut your *AP* curve when *AP* is at its maximum.**

4. **LO 7.6** Draw a total product curve and then show the effect of technological advance on your total product curve.

5. **LO 7.3, 7.7** The data in Table 7.8 are for a firm.
   a. Is this a short-run or long-run situation? Justify your answer.
   b. Does this production schedule exhibit diminishing marginal returns?

Table 7.8	Production Data for a Firm	
Capital	Labour	Output
15	0	0
15	1	3
15	2	7
15	3	10
15	4	12
15	5	11

6. **LO 7.5** Table 7.9 shows a production schedule for a firm.
   a. Draw the *TP* curve.
   b. Complete the *MP* column and draw the *MP* curve on the same graph as the *TP* curve.

Table 7.9	A Production Schedule for a Firm	
Quantity of Labour	TP	MP
0	0	
1	3	
2	7	
3	10	
4	12	
5	13	
6	13	

Questions in the Intermediate and Challenging Sections cover several different concepts, and have not been organized by learning objectives.

Intermediate

1. Show that the costs of the inputs can influence the choice of technology (method of production) used by the firm.
2. Table 7.10 shows two methods of producing an item. The cost of capital is $2, the cost of labour is $4, and the price of the output is $10. Which of the two methods of production should the firm use?

Table 7.10	Two Methods of Producing an Item		
Method	Capital	Labour	Output
A	10	25	200
B	6	35	250

3. Draw the *MP* and *AP* curves for a hypothetical firm, and answer the following questions.
   a. When *AP* is rising, where is *MP* in relation to *AP*?
   b. What is happening to *AP* when *MP* is above it but falling? Is it rising, falling, or at its maximum?
   c. What is the relation between *MP* and *AP* when *AP* is at its maximum?
   d. When *AP* is falling, where is *MP* in relation to *AP*?
4. Table 7.11 contains production data for a firm that uses labour and capital to produce its output. Q_L = quantity of

Table 7.11	Production Data for a Firm		
Q_L	MP_L	Q_K	MP_K
1	16	1	21
2	18	2	24
3	16	3	18
4	14	4	15
5	10	5	12
6	6	6	6
7	2	7	3

labour, MP_L = marginal product of labour, Q_K = quantity of capital, and MP_K = marginal product of capital.
   a. If the costs of labour and capital are $2 and $3, respectively, and the firm has a budget of $12, what combination of labour and capital should this firm buy?
   b. If the firm's budget increases to $35, what combination of labour and capital should the firm then buy?

Challenging

1. The law of diminishing returns has a variety of real-world applications. Apply the law of diminishing returns to the concept of overpopulation.
2. Draw a total product curve and indicate the following regions on the curve:
   a. Increasing returns
   b. Diminishing returns
   c. Negative returns
3. Complete Table 7.12.

Table 7.12	A Production Schedule		
Units of Labour	TP	AP	MP
1		40	
			48
2			
3	138		
4		44	
			24
5			
6	210		
7		29	
			−27
8			

MyEconLab Visit the MyEconLab website at **www.myeconlab.com**. This online homework and tutorial system puts you in control of your own learning with study and practice tools directly correlated to this chapter's content.

Study Guide

Self-Assessment

The answers to the Study Guide questions can be found in Appendix B.

What's your score?

Circle the letter that corresponds with the correct answer.

1. Which of the following statements about production is correct?
   a. Production does not always involve the use of inputs
   b. The only evidence of production is a real physical tangible output
   c. Production involves the use of inputs to obtain output
   d. Because of the use of modern technology, production can never be inefficient

2. Which of the following would not be considered a firm?
   a. A corner grocery store
   b. The Bank of Montreal
   c. The Canadian Parliament
   d. General Motors of Canada

3. Some of the goals that firms claim to pursue include
   a. Maximizing sales
   b. Increasing market share
   c. Satisfying customers
   d. All of the above

4. In economic theory, we assume that the firm's objective is to
   a. Maximize sales
   b. Minimize cost
   c. Maximize profits
   d. All of the above

5. Profit is defined as
   a. The difference between total revenue and total cost
   b. The amount sold multiplied by the price at which it is sold
   c. Total cost minus total revenue
   d. Total cost minus taxes

6. Technological efficiency refers to
   a. Input use without reference to cost
   b. The lowest cost of producing a given output
   c. The maximum output that the firm can produce
   d. The maximum inputs required to produce a given output

7. Economic efficiency exists when the firm
   a. Uses many factor inputs
   b. Maximizes input cost
   c. Minimizes input cost
   d. Earns a profit

8. A method of production is technologically efficient if
   a. It uses more capital than labour
   b. It uses more labour than capital
   c. It uses equal amounts of capital and labour
   d. None of the above

9. The method of production that has the lowest cost associated with it is said to be
   a. Marginally efficient
   b. Economically efficient
   c. Technically inefficient
   d. None of the above

10. A fixed factor is
    a. One whose price remains constant
    b. One that cannot be transported from one place to another
    c. One whose quantity can be varied only to a limited extent
    d. One whose quantity cannot be varied within the time period being considered

11. Which of the following is likely to be a variable factor for a firm?
    a. Machinery
    b. Labour
    c. Land
    d. Buildings

12. In economics, the short run refers to
    a. A period not exceeding one year
    b. A situation in which the firm has at least one fixed factor
    c. A period shorter than three months
    d. None of the above

13. In economics, the long run refers to
    a. A situation in which the firm can vary all its inputs
    b. A period longer than one year
    c. A period longer than five years
    d. None of the above

14. Which of the following statements is correct?
    a. In the short run, all factors are fixed
    b. In the short run, all factors are variable
    c. In the long run, there are both fixed and variable factors
    d. In the short run, there are both fixed and variable factors

15. If total product is rising, then
    a. Average product must be falling
    b. Average product must be at its maximum
    c. Marginal product must be positive
    d. Marginal product must be rising
16. Total product will be at its maximum when
    a. Marginal product is at its maximum
    b. Marginal product is zero
    c. Average product is zero
    d. None of the above
17. If average product is rising, then
    a. Average product must be greater than marginal product
    b. Marginal product must be positive and rising
    c. Marginal product must be at its maximum
    d. Marginal product must be greater than average product
18. The law of diminishing returns states that as increasing quantities of a variable factor are added to a fixed factor,
    a. The increase in total product will eventually diminish
    b. The total product will diminish
    c. The total product will never reach its maximum
    d. None of the above
19. For a firm using two factors of production, capital and labour, its optimum input mix occurs when
    a. Labour and capital are used in equal amounts
    b. The ratio of the marginal product of capital to the marginal product of labour equals the ratio of the price of capital to the price of labour
    c. The prices of capital and labour begin to rise and the marginal products of capital and labour begin to fall
    d. None of the above
20. The principle of substitution states that
    a. Firms generally produce outputs that are substitutes
    b. It is always possible to substitute one factor for another
    c. On principle, firms should substitute labour for capital whenever it is possible to do so
    d. None of the above

Problems and Exercises (Use Quad Paper for Graphs)

Answers to these questions can be found on MyEconLab at www.myeconlab.com.

1. Table 7.13 shows the units of labour and capital required to produce 500 units of output. Labour costs $8 per unit and capital $5 per unit.
   a. Which of these methods is technically inefficient and why?
   b. Which method is most economically efficient?
   c. If the price of labour falls to $5 per unit, while the price of capital doubles, which method will be most economically efficient?

Table 7.13	The Labour and Capital Requirement for 500 Units of Output	
Combination	**Labour**	**Capital**
A	10	18
B	15	24
C	7	20

2. Table 7.14 shows the units of labour and capital required to produce 100 units of output.
   a. Which of these methods is technically inefficient and why?
   b. If labour costs $3 per unit and capital $5 per unit, which method is most economically efficient?
   c. If the price of labour doubles, while the price of capital remains the same, which method will be most economically efficient?

Table 7.14	The Combinations of Labour and Capital Required for 100 Units of Output		
Combination	**Labour**	**Capital**	**Output**
A	8	15	100
B	9	20	100
C	6	20	100

3. You are given the short-run production schedule shown in Table 7.15.
   a. Complete the marginal product column.
   b. Does this production schedule exhibit diminishing returns?

Table 7.15	A Short-Run Production Schedule	
Units of Variable Factor	**Total Product**	**Marginal Product**
0	0	
1	30	
2	65	
3	95	
4	120	
5	135	

4. You are given the production schedule in Table 7.16.
   a. Compute the marginal product of the variable factor and fill in the marginal product column.
   b. Does this production schedule exhibit diminishing returns?

Table 7.16	Production Data		
Units of Fixed Factor	Units of Variable Factor	Total Product	Marginal Product
20	0	0	
20	1	25	
20	2	45	
20	3	60	
20	4	70	
20	5	75	

5. Econoplex Ltd. has the production schedule shown in Table 7.17.
   a. Complete the marginal and average product columns.
   b. Does the production schedule exhibit diminishing returns?
   c. On quad paper, graph the total product, marginal product, and average product curves.

Table 7.18	Marginal Products of Capital and Labour, and Input Levels	
Level of Usage of Inputs	Marginal Product of Capital	Marginal Product of Labour
1	36	95
2	39	85
3	36	75
4	33	70
5	30	55
6	24	45

6. Table 7.18 shows the marginal product of capital and the marginal product of labour at various levels of capital and labour usage for a firm. The price of capital is $3 and the price of labour is $5. On the basis of this information, what is the optimal input mix for this firm?

7. A firm uses two variable inputs, labour and capital, to produce its output. The price of labour is $2 per hour and the price of capital is $5 per hour. The production schedules for the firm are set out in Table 7.19.
   a. Complete the table by filling in the marginal product of labour and the marginal product of capital columns.
   b. If the firm wants to spend $9 per hour on labour and capital, how much of each should it purchase?
   c. How should the firm allocate a total cost of $30 between labour and capital to minimize production cost?

Table 7.17	A Production Schedule for Econoplex Ltd.			
Capital	Labour	Output	Marginal Product	Average Product
40	0	0		
40	1	5		
40	2	11		
40	3	15		
40	4	18		
40	5	20		

Table 7.19		Production Schedules for Firm			
Labour			**Capital**		
Quantity per Hour	TP per Hour	MP$_L$ per Hour	Quantity per Hour	TP per Hour	MP$_K$ per Hour
0	0		0	0	
1	20		1	25	
2	30		2	40	
3	38		3	50	
4	43		4	55	
5	45		5	55	
6	45		6	50	

8. Table 7.20 shows variations in output as units of a variable factor are added to a fixed factor.

   a. Complete the table by filling in the marginal and average product columns.

   b. Graph the marginal and average product curves on the same diagram.

   c. Locate the maximum point on the average product curve and label it *M*. Compare the values of the average product and the marginal product at that point.

Table 7.20	Total Product Data		
Units of Variable Factor	Total Product	Marginal Product	Average Product
0	0		
1	12		
2	30		
3	51		
4	68		
5	80		
6	84		
7	84		
8	80		
9	72		

Chapter **8**

The Costs of Production

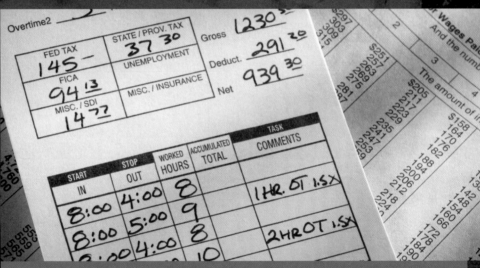

Learning Objectives

After studying this chapter, you should be able to

8.1 Distinguish between explicit cost and implicit cost

8.2 Analyze costs in the short run

8.3 Describe the relationship between marginal cost and marginal product, and between average variable cost and average product

8.4 Analyze costs in the long run

8.5 Understand returns to scale

8.6 Understand economies of scope

Assess Your Knowledge

MyEconLab

Answers to these questions can be found on MyEconLab at **www.myeconlab.com.**

1. A firm owns the building in which it operates. Does this firm incur a cost by using its building, even though it pays no rent?

2. Which of the following varies with the volume of output produced by a firm?
   a. Rent for the building it uses
   b. The salaries of the firm's top executives
   c. Property taxes
   d. None of the above

3. Why might a large department store chain, like Zellers, be able to sell women's pants at a lower price than that charged by a much smaller retail outfit, all else being equal?

LO 8.1 Distinguish between explicit cost and implicit cost

The Firm's Costs

What is meant by cost?

cost a payment for the inputs used to produce goods and services

Cost can be defined as a payment for the inputs used to produce goods and services. These payments include wages and salaries, rent for land and buildings, and expenditures for raw materials, fuel and electricity, and taxes.

What is a cost function?

cost function the mathematical expression of the relationship between cost and output

To produce its output, the firm uses inputs that involve a cost. The greater the output produced, the greater the cost is likely to be. It is this relation between cost and output that we refer to as a cost function. A **cost function** is the mathematical expression of the relationship between cost and output. The cost function can be expressed as

$$C = C(Q)$$

where C represents cost and Q represents output. The firm incurs cost by engaging in production. Therefore, a close relationship exists between production and cost.

What is the difference between explicit costs and implicit costs?

explicit costs or accounting costs direct payments to someone outside the firm for inputs

Such costs as wages, electricity bills, expenditures for raw materials, and telephone bills are known as **explicit costs** or **accounting costs**, which we can define as direct payments to someone outside the firm for inputs.

implicit costs or imputed costs opportunity costs that do not involve any direct payment to anyone outside the firm

In addition to these direct business outlays, the firm can use its own resources. In this case, opportunity costs that do not involve any direct payment to anyone outside the firm are incurred. Such costs are known as **implicit costs** or **imputed costs** and must be taken into account when calculating the firm's costs.

The concept of explicit cost is the usual way most people view cost, but the concept of implicit cost is new to most people. Can you provide some examples to further explain the concept?

The following examples should suffice.

Example: A hairdresser converted the family garage into a small salon from which she serves her customers. By so doing, she incurs a cost. This cost can be estimated by invoking the concept of opportunity cost. In this case, the opportunity cost would be the best possible alternative use to which the hairdresser could put the garage. Suppose the garage could be rented for $200 a month. Then the implicit cost would be $200 a month. Furthermore, suppose our hairdresser could have secured paid employment in another salon and earned $25 000 per year. The implicit cost of her being self-employed would be $25 000 per year.

To further illustrate the concept of implicit cost, consider the following example.

Example: Sam Richards invests $100 000 of his own money to start the Richards Bookbinding Company. The money is used to purchase machines for the business. Suppose Sam could have earned 8% interest annually by leaving his money in the bank. Then at the end of the year, Sam should include $8000 (i.e., 8% of $100 000) as a part of his costs (the implicit cost of capital). Moreover, during the year, Sam's machines would have suffered a certain amount of wear and tear through use. This **depreciation** of the machines, or loss of asset value through use or over time, also represents an implicit cost and should be considered as part of the cost of doing business.

depreciation a loss of asset value through use or over time

Is there a difference between costs as the economist sees them and costs as the accountant sees them?

Yes, there is, and the difference is important in understanding some of the conclusions that economists make regarding the behaviour of firms. To the accountant, costs are explicit costs and do not include implicit costs. To the economist, costs include both explicit and all implicit costs. Figure 8.1 illustrates the difference.

economic costs the sum of explicit and implicit costs; they include all opportunity costs

Explicit costs are indicated by the red rectangles in both columns, while implicit costs are indicated by the blue rectangle in the left column. **Economic costs**, which are the sum of explicit and implicit costs and include all opportunity costs, are the sum of red and blue rectangles in the left column, while accounting costs are represented by the red rectangle in the right column. The relationship between economic costs and accounting costs can be shown by the following equation:

Economic costs = Accounting costs + Implicit costs

What are sunk costs?

Sunk costs are costs that have already been incurred and cannot be recaptured. For decision-making purposes, they are irrelevant. If you bought a computer for $800 because someone promised to give you a part-time job working at home on the computer but that person changes his or her mind, the initial cost of the computer has nothing to do with whether you keep it or sell it.

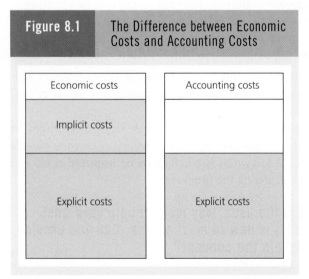

Figure 8.1   The Difference between Economic Costs and Accounting Costs

Economic costs	Accounting costs
Implicit costs	
Explicit costs	Explicit costs

BUSINESS SITUATION 8.1

Sam Baker owns and manages a bakery, supplying bread, cakes, and so on, to retail outlets. He operates from an old building that he converted into a bakery. He owns the building and therefore pays no rent. A similar building nearby is rented for $15 000 a year. A major bakery with business establishments from coast to coast has offered Sam a long-term contract to manage its national operation. If he accepts the offer, his salary will be $120 000 annually. Before making his decision, Sam sat down with his accountant to review his own business results, which are presented below and are typical of the last several years. Sam does not draw a salary, so he considers his profit of $120 000 to be his salary.

Total revenue	$320 000
Total expenses	$200 000
Total profits	$120 000

Assuming other things, such as taxes and job satisfaction, are equal, should Sam accept the offer?

The answer to this Business Situation can be found in Appendix A.

BUSINESS SITUATION 8.2

Suppose Tim Hortons buys a coffee machine for $600 with a no-return agreement. Three weeks later, Tim Hortons decides that the coffee machine is too small for the volume of coffee that it is making. A small diner offers to buy the coffee machine from Tim Hortons for $200—one-third of the price that Tim Hortons paid. Tim Hortons refuses the offer, claiming that it paid three times that much for the coffee machine.

Is that a good economic decision on the part of Tim Hortons?

The answer to this Business Situation can be found in Appendix A.

Reading Comprehension

The answers to these questions can be found on MyEconLab at **www.myeconlab.com.**   MyEconLab

1. What is the meaning of the term *cost function*?

2. What is the difference between explicit cost and implicit cost? Give an example of each.
3. What is the relationship between economic costs and accounting costs?

LO 8.2 Analyze costs in the short run

Costs in the Short Run

What are fixed costs?

Fixed costs, which in common business language are called **overhead costs**, are costs that do not vary with the volume of output. These costs remain the same whether the firm produces a little or a lot. They are incurred even if the firm temporarily suspends its operation.

fixed costs or overhead costs costs that do not vary with the volume of output

Can you give some examples of fixed costs?

Examples of fixed costs are insurance costs on the firm's property, interest payments on borrowed money, property taxes, rental payment on a factory or building, and management salaries. It must be emphasized that fixed costs apply only to the short run because fixed factors of production exist only in the short run.

> The firm will continue to incur fixed costs even during a temporary shut down. They are not affected by the quantity of output that the firm produces.

What are variable costs?

variable costs costs that are dependent on the volume of output

Variable costs are costs that are dependent on the volume of output. If the firm increases its output, its variable costs will increase. If it reduces its output, its variable costs will decrease. If the firm produces nothing at all (for example, if it ceases to operate temporarily), its variable costs will be zero. In other words, variable costs are the operating costs of production. Variable costs are incurred both in the short run and in the long run.

Can you provide some examples of variable costs?

Examples of variable costs are payments for raw materials, labour costs, sales taxes, fuel, and depreciation associated with production.

> Variable costs are directly related to the volume of output that the firm produces. They are incurred only if the firm produces some level of output.

Can we infer from the above discussion that the firm's total cost consists of fixed and variable costs?

That's correct. If we use TC to denote total cost, TFC to denote total fixed costs, and TVC to denote total variable costs, we can express the firm's total cost as follows:

$$TC = TFC + TVC$$

Should we become familiar with other short-run cost concepts?

The cost concepts that we have looked at so far are total cost concepts. Corresponding to these total cost concepts are the following average cost concepts: average total cost (ATC), average fixed cost (AFC), and average variable cost (AVC).

Can you define each of these average cost concepts?

average total cost the total cost per unit of output

Let's begin with **average total cost**, which is total cost per unit of output. Thus, if Q represents the quantity of output produced, we can express average total cost as follows:

$$ATC = \frac{TC}{Q}$$

Average total cost (also called unit cost) consists of average fixed cost (AFC) and average variable cost (AVC):

$$ATC = AFC + AVC$$

average fixed cost the total fixed cost per unit of output

Average fixed cost is total fixed cost per unit of output. Symbolically,

$$AFC = \frac{TFC}{Q}$$

average variable cost the total variable cost per unit of output

Average variable cost is the total variable cost per unit of output. That is,

$$AVC = \frac{TVC}{Q}$$

Note that we can obtain average total cost by dividing each component of total cost by quantity, as follows:

$$TC = TFC + TVC$$

$$ATC = \frac{TC}{Q} = \frac{TFC}{Q} + \frac{TVC}{Q}$$

$$ATC = AFC + AVC$$

What is marginal cost?

marginal cost or incremental cost the extra cost incurred by increasing output by one unit

This is another cost concept that we will use quite frequently. **Marginal cost** (*MC*), or **incremental cost**, is the extra cost incurred by increasing output by one unit. The concept is similar to the marginal utility and marginal product concepts encountered earlier. Symbolically, marginal cost can be expressed as

$$MC = \frac{\Delta TC}{\Delta Q}$$

Example: If the total cost of producing 9 units of output is $200, and the total cost of producing 10 units is $220, then the marginal cost of increasing output to 10 units (that is, the extra cost of producing one more unit—the 10th unit) is $20.

In many cases, computer technology has significantly reduced the cost of production.

Can you summarize the various cost concepts?

Summary of Cost Concepts

TC = total cost	$TC = TFC + TVC$
TFC = total fixed cost	$ATC = TC/Q = TFC/Q + TVC/Q$
TVC = total variable cost	$ATC = AFC + AVC$
ATC = average total cost	$MC = \Delta TC/\Delta Q$
AFC = average fixed cost	
AVC = average variable cost	
MC = marginal cost	

We used production schedules to show the relationship between total product, average product, and marginal product. Can we do the same for the short-run cost concepts?

Let us study Table 8.1. The various levels of output produced per period are given in column 1. Column 2 shows the firm's total fixed cost. This amount ($600 in the example) remains

Table 8.1		Hypothetical Cost Data for a Firm					
Quantity of Output (1)	TFC ($) (2)	TVC ($) (3)	TC ($) (4)	AFC ($) (5)	AVC ($) (6)	ATC ($) (7)	MC ($) (8)
0	600	0	600	—	—	—	
							400
1	600	400	1000	600.00	400.00	1000.00	
							200
2	600	600	1200	300.00	300.00	600.00	
							100
3	600	700	1300	200.00	233.33	433.33	
							100
4	600	800	1400	150.00	200.00	350.00	
							300
5	600	1100	1700	120.00	220.00	340.00	
							400
6	600	1500	2100	100.00	250.00	350.00	
							700
7	600	2200	2800	85.71	314.29	400.00	
							800
8	600	3000	3600	75.00	375.00	450.00	
							1000
9	600	4000	4600	66.66	444.44	511.10	
							2000
10	600	6000	6600	60.00	600.00	660.00	

unchanged for any level of output. Note that even when the firm produces no output at all ($Q = 0$), it still has to pay for its fixed factor inputs. Total variable cost is given in column 3. Total variable cost rises continuously as output expands: from $400 for the first unit to $6000 for 10 units of output. To produce a greater quantity of output, the firm must use more of its variable inputs (more labour, more raw materials, etc.) so its total variable cost increases. Column 4 shows total cost, which is obtained by adding total fixed cost and total variable cost. Total cost rises continuously because total variable cost rises continuously with increasing output.

What do total cost curves look like?

In Figure 8.2 we plot the total cost curves (*TFC*, *TVC*, and *TC*) from the data in Table 8.1. The *TFC* curve is the easiest to draw. It is a horizontal straight line, indicating that *TFC* is constant for any level of output ($600 in this example). The *TVC* curve rises continuously with increasing output. The *TC* curve is obtained by adding the *TFC* curve and the *TVC* curve. Because the *TFC* curve is a horizontal straight line, the *TC* curve will have the same shape as the *TVC* curve but will lie above the *TVC* curve. The vertical distance between the *TC* curve and the *TVC* curve at any level of output is the same: it is *TFC*.

| Figure 8.2 | Total Cost Curves |

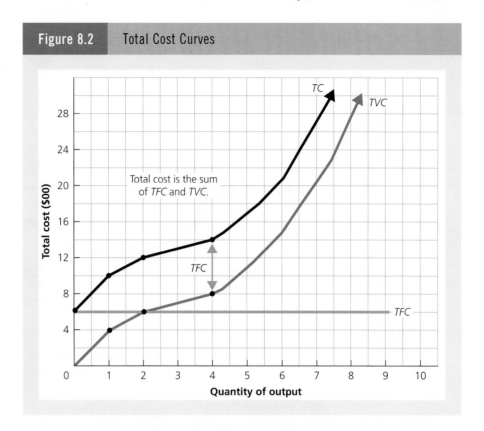

What about the remaining columns of Table 8.1?

Let's go back to the table. Column 5 of Table 8.1 shows the average fixed cost (*AFC*) of the firm, which is obtained by dividing column 2 by column 1. Average variable cost (*AVC*) is given in column 6 and is obtained by dividing column 3 by column 1. Column 7, the average total cost (*ATC*) column, is obtained by adding *AFC* to *AVC*. Alternatively, column 7 can be obtained by dividing column 4 by column 1. Column 8 gives marginal cost (*MC*), which can be obtained from column 3 or from column 4 by subtraction. Can you see why?

What do the "per unit" cost curves look like?

Figure 8.3 shows the unit cost curves (*AFC*, *AVC*, *ATC*, and *MC*). The figure helps to illustrate the relationship among these cost curves. The *AFC* curve declines continuously as output expands. This is so because as output expands, the fixed cost is spread over more and more units of output. The *AVC* curve first declines, reaches a minimum point (*K*, in this example), and then rises. The *ATC* curve also declines at first, reaches a minimum point (*L*, in this example), and then rises thereafter. The *MC* curve falls and then rises as output increases.

Note that the rising *MC* curve cuts the *AVC* curve and the *ATC* curve at their minimum points. It is easy to see why this is so. If *MC* is less than the average cost, the average cost will fall. If *MC* is greater than the average cost, the average cost will rise. When *MC* equals the average cost (at the point of intersection), the average cost ceases to fall and is about to rise. The average cost must therefore have reached its lowest point at its intersection with *MC*. Note also that *AVC* reaches its minimum point at a lower

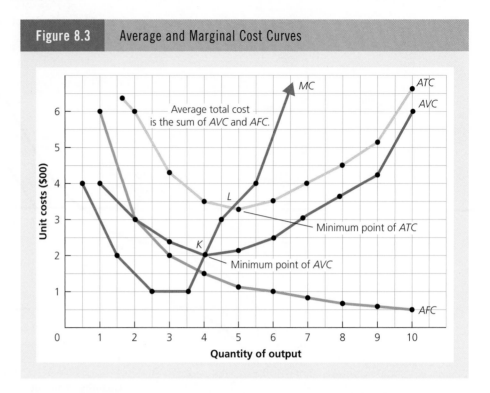

| Figure 8.3 | Average and Marginal Cost Curves |

level of output than *ATC* does. This is so because of the effect of the falling *AFC*, which is added to *AVC* to obtain *ATC*.

> The MC curve cuts the AVC curve and the ATC curve at their minimum points.
>   When the AVC curve has reached its minimum point, the declining AFC curve continues to exert a downward pull on the ATC curve. Thus, the minimum point of the AVC curve occurs at a lower level of output than that of the ATC curve.

Can we summarize the relations between marginal cost and average variable cost and between marginal cost and average total cost?

Let's present the summary in Table 8.2. In studying Table 8.2, remember the magnetic effect of the marginal on the average—the marginal pulls the average to it like a magnet.

| Table 8.2 | The Relations between *MC* and *AVC*, and *MC* and *ATC* |

Relations between *MC* and *AVC*	Relations between *MC* and *ATC*
1. When *MC* < *AVC*, *AVC* will fall (the marginal pulls the average down).This occurs over the range of output from 0 to 4 units in Figure 8.3.	1. When *MC* < *ATC*, *ATC* will fall (the marginal pulls the average down). This occurs over the range of output from 0 to about 5 units.
2. When *MC* > *AVC*, *AVC* will rise (the marginal pulls the average up).This occurs over the range of output above 4 units in Figure 8.3.	2. When *MC* > *ATC*, *ATC* will rise (the marginal pulls the average up). This occurs over the range of output above 5 units.
3. When *MC* = *AVC*, *AVC* will neither rise nor fall; it will be at its minimum. This occurs at 4 units of output.	3. When *MC* = *ATC*, *ATC* will be at its minimum. This occurs at about 5 units of output.

All the average cost curves are U-shaped except the average fixed cost curve. Can you explain the U-shape of the average variable cost and the average total cost curves?

To explain the U-shape of any curve, we must explain why the curve slopes downward initially and then eventually slopes upward. Let us begin with the *AVC* curve. Recall that the total product (*TP*) curve increases rapidly at first because of increasing marginal productivity resulting from specialization and the division of labour. Under conditions of increasing marginal productivity, increasingly fewer units of variable inputs are needed to increase output by an additional unit. This implies decreasing *AVC* and, hence, a downward-sloping *AVC* curve. We have explained why the *AVC* curve slopes downward initially. Let us now see why it slopes upward eventually.

Diminishing marginal returns imply that increasingly larger quantities of variable inputs are required for additional unit increases in output. Consequently, *AVC* rises, so the *AVC* curve slopes upward.

From this analysis, we can conclude that the *AVC* curve slopes downward initially but eventually slopes upward. In other words, it is U-shaped.

Now for the *ATC* curve. *ATC* consists of *AVC* and *AFC*. *AVC* and *AFC* both decline initially; hence, *ATC* declines initially. *AFC* continues to decline and exerts its downward pull on *ATC*. Eventually, diminishing returns will cause the increase in *AVC* to outweigh the decrease in *AFC*, resulting in an increase in *ATC*, so the *ATC* curve rises. This explains the U-shape of the *ATC* curve.

The marginal cost curve is also U-shaped. Why is this so?

The U-shape of the *MC* curve is the effect of increasing marginal returns and diminishing marginal returns. Initially, marginal product (*MP*) increases as output increases. This implies a decreasing *MC*, so the *MC* curve declines. Eventually, however, as output expands, diminishing returns set in; *MP* falls, so marginal cost rises and the *MC* curve slopes upward. This explains the U-shape of the *MC* curve.

All these cost curves seem to be interrelated. Is this so?

That is exactly the case. All these cost curves are different ways of looking at the same thing. Suppose you have data on *TC* at each level of output. You could draw the *TC* curve. Right? But you could also figure out *ATC*, *TFC*, *AFC*, *TVC*, *AVC*, and *MC*. It's really not as difficult as it may seem. Consider this for a moment:

1. The *TC* curve contains information about *TFC*. Just look at *TC* when the quantity of output is zero and you have *TFC* (*TC* = *TFC* when output = 0).

2. The *TC* curve also contains information about the variable cost. Just subtract *TFC* from *TC* and presto, you have *TVC* (*TC* − *TFC* = *TVC*).

3. *TC* contains information about *MC* as well. For any level of output, *Q*, *MC* is *TC* at *Q* − *TC* at *Q* − 1. Alternatively, *MC* is the change in *TC* that results from increasing output by one unit ($MC = \Delta TC/\Delta Q$).

OK. Total cost, total fixed cost, total variable cost, and marginal cost are all interrelated. But what about the average cost curves?

Averages are calculated the usual way. You can convert totals to averages simply by dividing by the quantity of output. If output is 15 units and the total cost is $240, then

ATC is $240 ÷ 15 = $16. If *TFC* is $105, then *AFC* is $105 ÷ 15 = 7. Now, suppose again that you have data on *TC*. You can easily figure out *AFC*, *AVC*, and *ATC* just by following the usual method of calculating averages (*AFC* = *TFC*/*Q*, *AVC* = *TVC*/*Q*, and *ATC* = *TC*/*Q*).

All these cost curves tie together quite neatly. We can go from average to total by multiplying by the quantity of output, and from total to average by dividing by the quantity of output. The interrelationship among these cost curves reinforces the point made earlier: these curves are just different ways of looking at the same thing.

Are some cost curves more helpful than others?

That really depends on what information you are looking for. If you are trying to find out *TC*, *TFC*, or *TVC* at each level of output, then the *TC* curves will give you the information instantly. If your objective is to find out the cost per unit of output, then the average cost curves will provide the information immediately. The average cost curves will also tell you instantly the lowest cost per unit, the amount of fixed cost per unit of output, and the amount of variable cost per unit of output.

Reading Comprehension

The answers to these questions can be found on MyEconLab at **www.myeconlab.com.**   MyEconLab

1. Distinguish between fixed costs and variable costs. Give an example of a cost that is likely to be fixed and one that is likely to be variable.
2. What is the relationship among *TC*, *TFC*, and *TVC*?
3. Briefly describe the shape of each of the following cost curves:
   a) The *TFC* curve
   b) The *TVC* curve
   c) The *TC* curve

4. What is the relationship between the *TC* curve and the *AC* curves?
5. What is the relationship between each of the following pairs of concepts?
   a) *MC* and average cost
   b) *MC* and *TC*
6. Explain why the *AFC* curve declines continuously.
7. Explain the U-shape of the *ATC*, *AVC*, and *MC* curves.

LO 8.3 Describe the relationship between marginal cost and marginal product, and between average variable cost and average product

The Relations between Marginal Cost and Marginal Product, and between Average Variable Cost and Average Product

We have a feeling that a close relationship exists between marginal cost and marginal product. Is this the case?

That is indeed the case. Let us explore this relationship. In Table 8.3, we present hypothetical cost and product data. Let us assume that each additional unit of the variable factor (each worker, if, for example, the variable factor is labour) is hired at a constant

Table 8.3	Hypothetical Cost and Product Data				
Quantity of Variable Factor (workers)	Total Product (units per week)	Marginal Product (units)	Average Product (units)	Marginal Cost per Unit of Extra Output ($)	AVC per Unit of Output ($)
0	0		—		—
		5		1.00	
1	5		5.0		1.00
		7		0.71	
2	12		6.0		0.83
		9		0.56	
3	21		7.0		0.71
		7		0.71	
4	28		7.0		0.71
		6		0.83	
5	34		6.8		0.74
		4		1.25	
6	38		6.3		0.79
		2		2.50	
7	40		5.7		0.88

price of $5 per unit of time. The marginal cost per unit of extra output is simply the extra cost ($5) divided by the extra output (marginal product) contributed by the worker. Thus, provided that the *MP* of each additional worker is rising, the marginal cost of each additional unit will fall.

In Table 8.3, the *MP* of the first worker is 5, but the extra cost of hiring this worker is $5, so *MC* per unit of extra output is $5/5 = $1. The *MP* of the second worker is 7, but the extra cost of hiring that worker is again $5, so *MC* per unit of extra output is $5/7 = $0.71. The other *MC* values are obtained in a similar manner.

Note, however, that after the third worker is hired, diminishing returns set in. Because *MP* is now falling, *MC* rises.

> Given the price of a variable factor, increasing *MP* (increasing returns) implies decreasing *MC*; diminishing *MP* (diminishing marginal returns) implies increasing *MC*.

Do similar relations exist between average product and average variable cost?

Yes! Similar relations exist between *AVC* and *AP*. *AVC* per unit of output is *AVC* divided by *AP*. In this case, *AVC* = $5, if we assume labour is the only variable input. The *AP* of the first worker is 5, so *AVC* per unit of output is $5/5 = $1. The average product of the second worker is 6, so *AVC* per unit of output is $5/6 = $0.83. The

Figure 8.4	The Relations between Marginal Product and Marginal Cost, and Average Product and Average Variable Cost

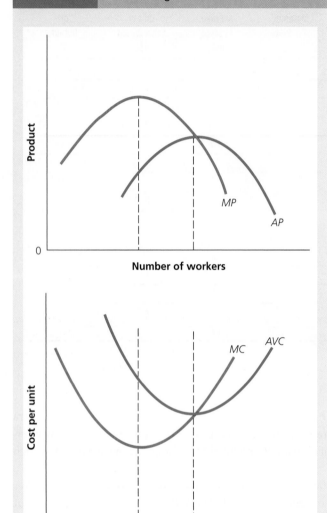

AP of the third worker is 7, so *AVC* per unit of output is $5/7 = 0.71. The other average cost figures are obtained similarly.

> Given the price of a variable factor, increasing *AP* implies decreasing *AVC*; diminishing *AP* implies increasing *AVC*.

Is it possible to illustrate these relations graphically?

Look at Figure 8.4. The top part of the diagram shows *MP* and *AP*. The bottom part of the diagram shows *MC* and *AVC*.

Can we summarize these relations?

The following six points provide a convenient summary of the relations discussed in this section.

Summary of Relations

1. When *MP* rises, *MC* falls.
2. When *MP* falls, *MC* rises.
3. When *MP* is at its maximum, *MC* is at its minimum.
4. When *AP* rises, *AVC* falls.
5. When *AP* falls, *AVC* rises.
6. When *AP* is at its maximum, *AVC* is at its minimum.

Reading Comprehension

The answers to these questions can be found on MyEconLab at www.myeconlab.com.

1. What is the relationship between *MP* and *MC*?
2. What is the relationship between *AP* and *AVC*?

LO 8.4 Analyze costs in the long run

Costs in the Long Run

Is this the same long run that we studied in the previous chapter?

Yes, it is. Recall that in the long run, all of the firm's factors of production can be varied. Up to this point in our analysis of the firm's costs, we have concentrated on the situation in which the firm had at least one fixed factor of production; our analysis dealt with a firm in the short run. We now turn our attention to the situation where the firm is able to vary all of its factor inputs; our analysis now turns to the firm in the long run.

Why is long-run cost analysis necessary?

Long-run cost analysis is necessary because the firm is in a different position from in the short run. The environment within which it makes its decisions is not the same as in the short run. In a long-run situation, the firm has no fixed factors of production and, hence, no fixed costs. In the long run, the firm can make any adjustment to the size of its plant and to its scale of operation that it deems necessary. The profit-maximizing firm will, of course, choose the minimum cost for each level of output.

How does the firm choose its plant size in the long run?

To illustrate how the firm chooses its plant size in the long run, let us assume that the firm has a choice of three plants of different sizes. Plant 1 is the smallest of the three; plant 2 is of medium size; and plant 3 is the largest of the three. Figure 8.5 shows the short-run average cost (*SRAC*) curves of the three plants and allows us to compare the average cost of producing any given level of output in each of the three plants.

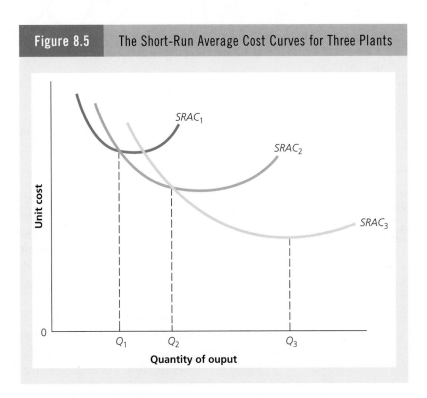

Figure 8.5 The Short-Run Average Cost Curves for Three Plants

$SRAC_1$ is the short-run average cost for plant 1, $SRAC_2$ is the short-run average cost curve for plant 2, and $SRAC_3$ is the short-run average cost curve for plant 3. If the firm contemplates a level of output less than Q_1 units, it will choose plant 1. This is so because plant 1 has the lowest average cost at that output level. If the firm contemplates an output between Q_1 and Q_2, it will choose plant 2. For an output level greater than Q_2, the firm will choose plant 3, which evidently has the lowest cost at that level of output. We can conclude, then, that for any desired level of output, the firm will choose the plant size for which the average cost is lowest.

What is long-run average cost?

long-run average cost the minimum cost per unit at which a firm can produce a given volume of output when its inputs are all variable

The **long-run average cost** (*LRAC*) is the minimum cost per unit at which a firm can produce each level of output when its inputs are all variable. In Figure 8.5, we have assumed that the firm has only three plant sizes from which to choose. Let us assume instead that the firm has an infinite number of plants of different sizes from which to choose. Figure 8.6 illustrates this situation.

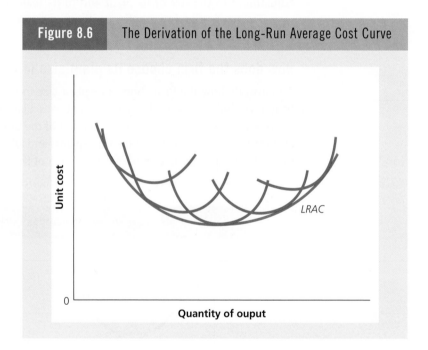

Figure 8.6   The Derivation of the Long-Run Average Cost Curve

long-run average cost curve, envelope curve, or planning curve the cost curve showing the minimum cost per unit at which a firm can produce a given volume of output when its inputs are all variable

Here, several *SRAC* curves are shown. The firm's **long-run average cost curve**, which is the cost curve showing the minimum cost per unit at which a firm can produce each level of output, is tangent to the infinite number of *SRAC* curves. For this reason, the *LRAC* curve is sometimes called the **envelope curve**—geometrically, the *LRAC* curve envelops the *SRAC* curves. Because the *LRAC* curve illustrates the firm's choices with respect to its long-run plans regarding plant size, it is referred to as the **planning curve**.

Note that when the *LRAC* curve is falling, the points of tangency with the *SRAC* curves lie to the left of the minimum points of the *SRAC* curves. When the *LRAC* curve is rising, the points of tangency lie to the right of the minimum points of the *SRAC* curves.

Figure 8.7 shows an *LRAC* curve without the associated *SRAC* curves.

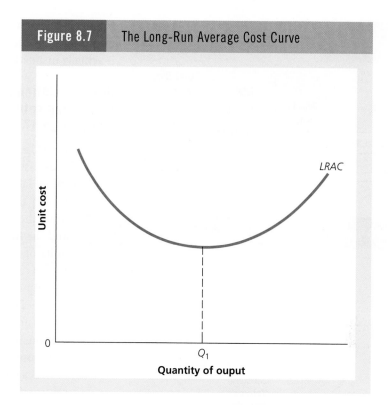

| Figure 8.7 | The Long-Run Average Cost Curve |

Reading Comprehension

The answers to these questions can be found on MyEconLab at **www.myeconlab.com.**   MyEconLab

1. What does the *LRAC* curve show?

2. "Long-run cost analysis is unnecessary if we really understand short-run cost analysis." Discuss briefly.

3. What is the relationship between the firm's choice of plant and its expected volume of output?

 LO 8.5   Understand returns to scale

Returns to Scale

What are returns to scale?

Returns to scale describe how the firm's total output responds to changes in all the firm's inputs, that is, to its scale of operation. Three cases are possible: increasing returns to scale, constant returns to scale, and decreasing returns to scale.

Can we discuss each of these cases?

Increasing Returns to Scale **Increasing returns to scale** refers to the condition that exists when a firm increases all its inputs by a certain proportion and, as a result, its output increases by a greater proportion.

If a firm doubles all its inputs and, as a result, its output more than doubles, then the firm is experiencing increasing returns to scale. The increase in its output is more than

increasing returns to scale, economies of scale, or decreasing (long-run average) cost the condition that exists when a firm increases all its inputs and, as a result, its output increases by a greater proportion than the increase in its inputs

Table 8.4		Production, Cost, and Increasing Returns to Scale		
Inputs		**Output (units)**	**Total Cost ($)**	**Long-Run Average Cost ($)**
L	**K**			
3	2	1	8	8/1 = 8
6	4	3	16	16/3 = 5.33

Figure 8.8	Returns to Scale

Quantity of ouput

proportional to the increase in its inputs; hence, the firm operating under conditions of increasing returns to scale is actually in an advantageous position.

Does a relationship exist between increasing returns to scale and long-run average cost?

The relationship can be illustrated as follows. For simplicity, let us assume that the firm uses only two factors of production: labour (L) and capital (K). Let us assume further that the price of labour is $2 per unit of time, the price of capital is $1 per unit of time, and the firm uses three units of labour and two units of capital to produce one unit of output. In this case, when the firm doubles all its inputs, its output more than doubles. In fact, its output triples. This is precisely the meaning of increasing returns to scale. Production and cost information are shown in Table 8.4. Note that $LRAC$ falls from $8 to $5.33.

As a consequence of this relation, increasing returns to scale and **decreasing cost** are used synonymously. Figure 8.8 shows decreasing costs or increasing returns to scale as the downward-sloping section of the $LRAC$ curve. The firm enjoys increasing returns to scale over the range of output from 0 to Q_1. A firm operating under conditions of decreasing cost is said to be enjoying **economies of scale**.

> Economies of scale describe a situation in which the firm's $LRAC$ falls as output increases.

constant returns to scale the condition that exists when a firm increases all its inputs by a certain percentage and, as a result, its output increases by the same percentage

Constant Returns to Scale **Constant returns to scale** refer to the condition that exists when a firm increases all its inputs by a certain percentage and, as a result, its output increases by the same percentage.

A firm operates under constant returns to scale if a given proportional increase in all of its inputs results in the same proportional increase in its output. Thus, under constant returns, if the firm doubles its inputs, its output doubles. Constant returns to scale imply that unit long-run cost remains unchanged as output increases. Consider the information given in Table 8.5.

In this case, as the firm doubles its inputs, its output also doubles. Note that $LRAC$ remains unchanged at $8. Figure 8.8 illustrates the case of constant returns to scale. The firm operates under constant returns to scale over the range of output from Q_1 to Q_2.

Table 8.5		Production, Cost, and Constant Returns to Scale		
Inputs		**Output (units)**	**Total Cost ($)**	**Long-Run Average Cost ($)**
L	**K**			
3	2	1	8	8/1 = 8
6	4	2	16	16/2 = 8

Does the level of output denoted by Q_1 have any significance?

Yes. The level of output at Q_1 has some significance. At this level of output, increasing returns to scale are exhausted and constant returns to scale begin. At a level of output less than Q_1, the firm is not taking full advantage of economies of scale, and no economies of scale can be gained at any level of output beyond Q_1. The point at which increasing returns to scale end and constant returns to scale begin (Q_1 in Figure 8.8) is referred to as the firm's **minimum efficient scale**. It is the minimum point of the *LRAC* curve.

minimum efficient scale the point at which increasing returns to scale end and constant returns to scale begin; the minimum point of the long-run average cost curve

Decreasing Returns to Scale   **Decreasing returns to scale** refer to the condition that exists when a firm increases all its inputs by a certain proportion and, as a result, its output increases by a smaller proportion. They are also referred to as **increasing (long-run average) cost**.

If a given proportional increase in all of the firm's inputs results in a less than proportional increase in the firm's output, then the firm is experiencing decreasing returns to scale. Thus, under decreasing returns to scale, if the firm increases its inputs by 50%, its output will increase by less than 50%.

Decreasing returns to scale imply that *LRAC* is increasing. This situation is illustrated in Table 8.6.

decreasing returns to scale, diseconomies of scale, or increasing (long-run average) cost the condition that exists when a firm increases all its inputs and, as a result, its output increases but by a smaller proportion than the increase in its inputs

Table 8.6		Production, Cost, and Decreasing Returns to Scale		
Inputs		**Output**	**Total Cost**	**Long-Run Average Cost**
L	*K*	(units)	($)	($)
3	2	1	8	8/1 = 8
6	4	1.5	16	16/1.5 = 10.67

In this case, when the firm doubles its inputs, the resulting output is less than double. Note also that decreasing returns to scale are illustrated graphically in Figure 8.8 by the rising portion of the *LRAC* curve. The firm faces increasing costs over the range of output beyond Q_2. At any point beyond Q_2, **diseconomies of scale** are said to be in effect.

> Diseconomies of scale describe a situation in which the firm's *LRAC* rises as output increases.

We discussed the reasons for the U-shape of the short-run average cost curves. Is the U-shape of the long-run average cost curve explained in the same way?

The *LRAC* curve is indeed U-shaped, but it cannot be because of the same factors that explain the U-shape of the *SRAC* curves. The reasons cited for the U-shape of the *SRAC* curves were diminishing returns and decreasing *AFC*. Diminishing returns and decreasing *AFC* both relate to the short run. In the long run, there are no fixed costs and no diminishing returns because there are no fixed factors in the long run. We must therefore seek other explanations.

Why then, does the long-run average cost have a U-shape?

The reason is not at all difficult to find. In fact, we have already discussed it. The reason relates to economies of scale, constant returns to scale, and diseconomies of scale. Let's look again at Figure 8.8 on page 240. When the firm is operating under conditions of economies of scale, *LRAC* declines. This occurs over the range of output from 0 to Q_1. When it is experiencing constant returns to scale, its *LRAC* is at its minimum. This occurs at any level of output between Q_1 and Q_2. Finally, when the firm is experiencing diseconomies of scale, the *LRAC* curve is rising. This occurs at levels of output beyond Q_2. This explains the U-shape of the *LRAC* curve.

Why do increasing returns to scale occur?

Increasing returns to scale occur for several reasons, but we will mention three of them.

Specialization   A large-scale operation has more opportunities to take advantage of specialization. For example, workers can concentrate on the performance of certain tasks, thereby increasing total output. This may not be practical in a smaller-scale operation.

Quantity Discounts   Decreasing cost (increasing returns to scale) can result from the firm's ability to purchase inputs in large quantities. They can take advantage of discounts for which smaller orders may not qualify.

Dimensional Relations   Suppose that a wooden storage room for a certain raw material has dimensions of 3 m by 3 m by 3 m, which gives a storage capacity of 27 m³. Doubling the dimensions of the room to 6 m by 6 m by 6 m may double the building materials used, and thus the cost, but it will more than double the capacity. The capacity will increase from 27 m³ to 216 m³ (i.e., $6 \times 6 \times 6$). Under these circumstances, the percentage increase in raw materials would be less than the percentage increase in the volume (storage capacity) of the room.

OK. That makes sense, but why do decreasing returns to scale occur?

The main reason generally given for decreasing returns to scale (diseconomies of scale or increasing costs) is inefficiency in management. As the size of the operation grows, management becomes increasingly complex and the decision-making process becomes ensnared in red tape.

> **Note:** We must point out that not all analysts believe that decreasing returns to scale exist. They contend that what is perceived as diminishing returns to scale is really the law of diminishing returns at work. Their argument is that when a firm claims to double all its inputs, even if it doubles the number of management personnel also, it does not really double managerial talent and skills. Thus, they claim, elements of fixed inputs remain.

BUSINESS SITUATION 8.3

Dollarama, a popular dollar store in Canada, operates a large number of outlets.

Why might it make good business sense for Dollarama to centralize its purchasing rather than having each outlet ordering its own supplies?

The answer to this Business Situation can be found in Appendix A.

Reading Comprehension

The answers to these questions can be found on MyEconLab at www.myeconlab.com.   MyEconLab

1. Explain each of the following terms:
   a) Increasing returns to scale
   b) Constant returns to scale
   c) Minimum efficient scale
   d) Decreasing returns to scale

2. What is the difference between diminishing returns and diminishing returns to scale?
3. Explain the U-shape of the *LRAC* curve.
4. What reasons can you give for the existence of increasing returns to scale and decreasing returns to scale?

LO 8.6   Understand economies of scope

Economies of Scope

What are economies of scope?

In our discussion of the costs of production up to this point, we have assumed that the firm produces only one product or service. In fact, many firms produce more than one product. One firm may produce radios, television sets, CD players, DVD players, and other electronic goods. Let us assume that one firm produces CDs and DVDs. It is quite likely that the production of CDs will affect the cost of producing DVDs, because in the production of each might be some common elements.

economies of scope the situation that exists when the costs of producing different goods together are less than they would be if the goods were produced separately

When the costs of producing different goods together are less than they would be if the goods were produced separately, **economies of scope** are said to exist.

Economies of scope help to explain why we find certain firms producing several different but closely related products at the same time. It should not be surprising to find the same firm producing refrigerators, washers, dryers, air-conditioning units, dishwashers, ovens, and even vacuum cleaners.

BUSINESS SITUATION 8.4

Panasonic produces TV sets, telephone systems, cameras, DVD players, VCRs, fax machines, home appliances, tools, computers, security products, and so on.

What economic concept can explain Panasonic's product offering?

The answer to this Business Situation can be found in Appendix A.

Reading Comprehension

The answers to these questions can be found on MyEconLab at **www.myeconlab.com.**   MyEconLab

1. Distinguish between economies of scale and economies of scope.

2. Why might a producer of television sets also produce radios?

Review

1. Review the learning objectives listed at the beginning of the chapter.

2. Have you accomplished all the objectives? One way to determine this is to answer the Reading Comprehension Questions at the end of each section. They will help you assess the extent to which you have accomplished the learning objectives.

3. If you have not accomplished an objective, review the relevant material before proceeding

Key Points to Remember

1. **LO 8.1** Explicit costs are those costs for which direct payment is made for inputs. Implicit costs or imputed costs are those costs for which no direct payment is made because the resources are already owned by the firm. Accounting costs are explicit costs. Economic costs include both explicit and implicit costs.

2. **LO 8.2** The firm's total cost in the short run consists of fixed costs and variable costs. Fixed costs are those costs incurred even if the firm suspends its operation temporarily. Variable costs are those costs that change with the level of output.

3. **LO 8.3** A close relationship exists between marginal cost (MC) and marginal product (MP), and between average variable cost (AVC) and average product (AP). Increasing MP implies decreasing MC; diminishing MP implies increasing MC. Increasing AP implies decreasing AVC; diminishing AP implies increasing AVC. When the MP is at its maximum, MC is at its minimum; when AP is at its maximum, AVC is at its minimum.

4. **LO 8.2** Average total cost (ATC) is total cost (TC) divided by the number of units produced. Average fixed cost (AFC) is total fixed cost (TFC) divided by the number of units produced. Average variable cost (AVC) is total variable cost (TVC) divided by the number of units produced. Average total cost (ATC) is the sum of average fixed cost and average variable cost. Marginal cost (MC) or incremental cost is the extra cost incurred by producing an additional unit of output.

5. **LO 8.2** Because total fixed cost does not vary with the volume of output, the total fixed cost curve is a horizontal straight line. The total variable cost curve and the total cost curve rise as the volume of output increases.

6. **LO 8.2** The average fixed cost curve declines continuously; the average variable cost and average total cost curves first decline, reach a minimum, and then rise. The marginal cost curve cuts the average variable cost and the average total cost curves at their minimum points. Like the average total cost and average variable cost curves, the marginal cost curve is U-shaped.

7. **LO 8.4** The long-run average cost ($LRAC$) is the lowest unit cost at which the firm can produce each level of output in a situation where the firm is able to vary all its inputs. The long-run average cost curve is also called the envelope curve and the planning curve.

8. **LO 8.5** Returns to scale can be increasing, constant, or diminishing. Increasing returns to scale exist when a given proportional increase in all of a firm's inputs leads to a more than proportional increase in its output. Constant returns to scale exist when a given proportional increase in all the firm's inputs results in the same proportional increase in its output. Diminishing returns to scale exist when a given proportional increase in all inputs leads to a less than proportional increase in output.

9. **LO 8.6** Economies of scope refer to the gain in economic efficiency that results from producing different products together rather than separately.

Economic Word Power

Average fixed cost   (p. 229)
Average total cost   (p. 228)
Average variable cost   (p. 229)
Constant returns to scale   (p. 240)
Cost   (p. 225)
Cost function   (p. 225)
Decreasing returns to scale, diseconomies of scale, or increasing (long-run average) cost   (p. 241)
Depreciation   (p. 226)

Economic costs   (p. 226)
Economies of scope   (p. 243)
Explicit costs or accounting costs   (p. 225)
Fixed costs or overhead costs   (p. 227)
Implicit costs or imputed costs   (p. 225)
Increasing returns to scale, economies of scale, or decreasing (long-run average) cost   (p. 239)
Long-run average cost   (p. 238)
Long-run average cost curve, envelope curve, or planning curve   (p. 238)
Marginal cost or incremental cost   (p. 229)
Minimum efficient scale   (p. 241)
Variable costs   (p. 228)

Problems and Exercises

Basic

1. **LO 8.2** Table 8.7 shows cost data for a firm.
   a. Complete the MC and ATC columns.
   b. Graph the MC and ATC curves.

Table 8.7	Cost Data		
Quantity	TC ($)	MC ($)	ATC ($)
0	20		
1	40		
2	58		
3	75		
4	92		
5	110		
6	132		
7	161		
8	192		

2. **LO 8.2** Given the TC data in Table 8.8,
   a. Complete the ATC and MC columns.
   b. Draw the ATC and MC curves.
   c. Is this a short-run or long-run situation? Why?

Table 8.8	Cost Data		
Quantity	TC ($)	MC ($)	ATC ($)
0	100		
1	110		
2	116		
3	132		
4	184		
5	250		
6	330		
7	420		

3. **LO 8.2** You are given the cost data shown in Table 8.9. Calculate TVC at each level of output and complete the TVC column.

Table 8.9		Cost Data	
Quantity	TFC ($)	TC ($)	TVC ($)
1	100	150	
2	100	195	
3	100	235	
4	100	270	
5	100	300	
6	100	330	
7	100	365	
8	100	400	
9	100	440	
10	100	490	

4. **LO 8.2** Figure 8.9 shows *TC* curves for two firms, *A* and *B*. Determine the fixed costs for firm *A* and firm *B*.

5. **LO 8.2** Indicate whether each of the following items is a fixed cost or a variable cost:

a. Power to run machines in a factory
b. Raw materials
c. Temporary office workers
d. Fire insurance
e. Rent
f. Gasoline for delivery trucks
g. Vehicle licences
h. Stocks of finished goods
i. Leased machinery
j. Wages of part-time labourers

6. **LO 8.5** Draw an *LRAC* curve showing increasing, constant, and decreasing returns to scale. Indicate each region on your graph.

Questions in the Intermediate and Challenging Sections cover several different concepts, and have not been organized by learning objectives.

Intermediate

1. Peter Simon lives in the country and owns a small lake. A family offers Peter $250 to rent his lake for the summer. Peter could fish from his lake instead of renting it out. He estimates that bait, fishing rods, hooks, and other fishing equipment would cost $200, and he expects to be able to sell his summer catch for $500.

a. What is Peter's explicit cost?
b. What is his implicit cost?
c. Should Peter rent out his lake?

2. An electric bulb manufacturing firm has an *AFC* of $0.75 per bulb at an output of 10 000 bulbs. If the firm expanded its output to 12 500 bulbs, what would be the *AFC*?

3. Table 8.10 shows *TC* data for a firm. Complete the *TVC*, *ATC*, *AVC*, and *MC* columns.

4. Indicate what is wrong (if anything) with the set of cost curves shown in Figure 8.10. Redraw the diagram as it should appear.

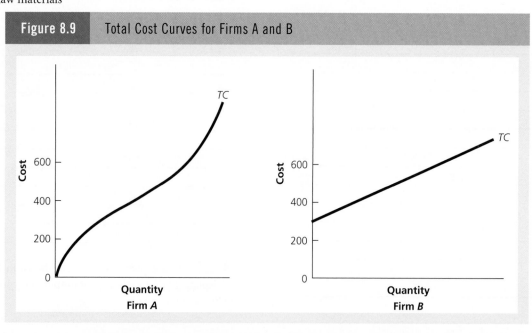

Figure 8.9 **Total Cost Curves for Firms A and B**

Table 8.10		Cost Data			
Output	**TC** ($)	**TVC** ($)	**ATC** ($)	**AVC** ($)	**MC** ($)
0	90				
1	95				
2	100				
3	105				
4	112				
5	120				
6	126				
7	147				
8	184				

Challenging

1. Use the concept of economies of scale to explain why industries with limited domestic markets might be interested in exporting.

Figure 8.10	A Set of Cost Curves

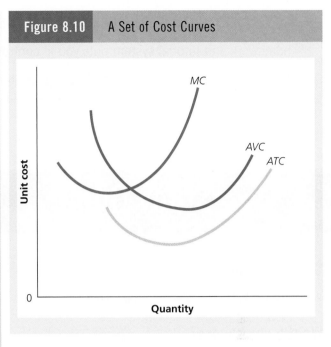

2. Explain how an increase in fixed costs will affect
   a. Total cost
   b. Average total cost
   c. Average variable cost
   d. Marginal cost
3. Figure 8.11 shows the *LRAC* curve. $SRAC_1$, $SRAC_2$, $SRAC_3$, and $SRAC_4$ are all short-run average cost curves. Could all these *SRAC* curves be associated with the *LRAC* curve? Explain.

Figure 8.11	Short-Run and Long-Run Average Cost Curves

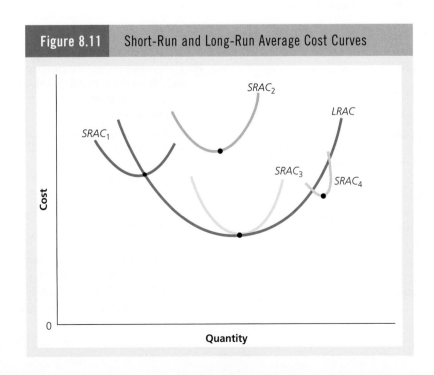

Study Guide

Self-Assessment

The answers to the Study Guide questions can be found in Appendix B.

What's your score?

Circle the letter that corresponds with the correct answer.

1. A firm's cost function states the relationship between
   a. Inputs and output
   b. Price and cost
   c. Cost and output
   d. None of the above

2. An implicit (imputed) cost is
   a. The cost of any input used by the firm
   b. Any cost that can never be estimated
   c. The difference between fixed cost and variable cost
   d. None of the above

3. Costs incurred by using factors of production already owned by the firm are called
   a. Uncollectible costs
   b. Implicit costs
   c. Explicit costs
   d. Marginal costs

4. Which of the following is correct?
   a. Economic costs = Accounting costs + Implicit costs
   b. Accounting costs = Implicit costs + Economic costs
   c. Accounting costs = All opportunity costs
   d. None of the above

5. Which of the following is most likely to be a fixed cost?
   a. Wages paid to unskilled workers
   b. Payment for raw materials
   c. Property taxes
   d. None of the above

6. Which of the following declines continuously?
   a. AFC
   b. MC

   c. ATC
   d. All of the above

7. Marginal cost is
   a. Total cost divided by the number of units produced
   b. The extra cost of producing an additional unit of output
   c. The average cost of the last unit produced
   d. Fixed cost divided by the number of units produced

8. When ATC has reached its minimum, we know that
   a. $ATC = TFC$
   b. $MC = AVC$
   c. $ATC = MC$
   d. None of the above

9. If we know TVC and TFC for various levels of output, then we can determine
   a. MC
   b. AFC
   c. ATC
   d. All of the above

10. The total cost of producing 10 units of a product is $120, and MC of the 11th unit is $34. Thus,
    a. ATC of 11 units is $14
    b. TFC is $86
    c. ATC of 11 units is $34
    d. We cannot determine ATC from the information given

11. If ATC is falling, then
    a. AFC must be rising
    b. $MC < ATC$
    c. $MC > ATC$
    d. MC must be falling

12. Which of the following is correct?
    a. The MC curve cuts the ATC curve and the AVC curve at the same level of output
    b. The MC curve always lies above the AVC curve

c. If *MC* is rising, then the average cost must also be rising

d. The *MC* curve cuts the *ATC* curve and the *AVC* curve at their minimum points

13. If *MC* is above *ATC*, then
    a. *AFC* will rise
    b. *AVC* is declining
    c. *ATC* will rise
    d. *ATC* is falling

14. In the long run,
    a. All costs are fixed
    b. All costs are variable
    c. Some costs are fixed while some are variable
    d. The firm can operate only at minimum cost

15. The *LRAC* curve represents
    a. The sum of all the firm's short-run cost curves
    b. The firm's cost structure for any period in excess of one year
    c. The lowest unit cost at which the firm can produce its output when all factors are variable
    d. All of the above

16. A firm is experiencing increasing returns to scale if
    a. Output more than doubles when all inputs are doubled
    b. *LRAC* increases as the firm expands its scale of operation
    c. Cost is proportional to output
    d. None of the above

17. Decreasing returns to scale can result from
    a. Greater specialization of labour and capital
    b. Large quantity input purchases resulting in quantity discounts
    c. The greater efficiency of larger plants
    d. Inefficiency in management as the operation expands

18. The minimum efficient scale for a firm occurs
    a. At the point where average cost begins to decline
    b. When the *AFC* curve begins to rise
    c. When *MC* is at its minimum
    d. None of the above

19. The *LRAC* curve is U-shaped because of
    a. The existence of fixed costs
    b. The effect of the law of diminishing marginal returns
    c. The effect of the declining *AFC* curve
    d. Increasing, constant, and decreasing returns to scale

20. Economies of scope exist when
    a. The production of complementary products together rather than separately reduces cost
    b. The firm pursues a narrow rather than a broad scope

c. The firm decides to take advantage of the opportunity to produce goods separately rather than together

d. None of the above

Problems and Exercises (Use Quad Paper for Graphs)

Answers to these questions can be found on MyEconLab at www.myeconlab.com.

MyEconLab

1. Table 8.11 shows cost data for a firm.
   a. Complete the table by filling in the remaining five columns.
   b. On graph paper, plot curves for *AFC*, *AVC*, *ATC*, and *MC*.
   c. At what levels of output does *MC* cut the *AVC* curve and the *ATC* curve?
   d. Compare these levels with the output levels at which the *AVC* curve and the *ATC* curve reach a minimum.

Table 8.11	Cost Data for a Firm						
Quantity	TFC ($)	TVC ($)	TC ($)	AFC ($)	AVC ($)	ATC ($)	MC ($)
1	100	25					
2	100	40					
3	100	48					
4	100	60					
5	100	80					
6	100	108					
7	100	140					
8	100	192					
9	100	270					
10	100	380					
11	100	550					
12	100	780					

2. You are given the data contained in Table 8.12 for a particular firm. Calculate each of the following at each level of output:
   a. *TFC*
   b. *TVC*
   c. *MC*

Table 8.12 Cost Data for a Firm

Quantity	AFC ($)	AVC ($)
0	—	—
1	20.00	30.00
2	10.00	28.00
3	6.67	27.00
4	5.00	26.00
5	4.00	24.00
6	3.33	23.00
7	2.86	24.00
8	2.50	26.00
9	2.22	29.00
10	2.00	32.00

3. Use your answer from Question 2 above to graph the *TFC*, *TVC*, and *TC* curves for the firm.
4. A firm has *TFC* amounting to $400. Draw the firm's *AFC* curve for output ranging from one unit to eight units.
5. Table 8.13 shows cost data for Memtech Corporation.
   a. Compute *MC*, *TVC*, *ATC*, and *AVC* and fill in the appropriate columns.
   b. Compute *AFC* values for Memtech Corporation.
   c. Graph Memtech's *AFC*, *AVC*, *ATC*, and *MC* curves all on the same diagram.
6. A textbook publisher finds that at an output of 10 000 books, its *AFC* (per book) is $5. What will the firm's *AFC* be if it increases its output to 15 000 books?
7. Table 8.14 contains data for T-shirt production.
   a. For what output range should the firm use plant 1?
   b. For what output range should the firm use plant 2?
   c. For what output range should the firm use plant 3?
   d. On the basis of the information given in Table 8.14, complete a table of the firm's *LRAC* curve for *Q* from 10 to 90 in increments of 10.

Table 8.13 Cost Data for Memtech Corporation

Output	TC ($)	MC ($)	TVC ($)	ATC ($)	AVC ($)
0	60				
1	65				
2	70				
3	75				
4	80				
5	85				
6	96				
7	112				
8	136				
9	162				
10	190				

Table 8.14 Short-Run Cost Schedules for the Production of T-Shirts

Plant 1		Plant 2		Plant 3	
Q	AC	Q	AC	Q	AC
10	20	10	30	10	35
20	18	20	25	20	32
30	17	30	16	30	23
40	19	40	13	40	16
50	25	50	12	50	13
60	40	60	18	60	10
70	65	70	27	70	15
80	102	80	46	80	25
90	150	90	78	90	45

Chapter **9**

The Firm in Pure Competition

Learning Objectives

After studying this chapter, you should be able to

9.1 Discuss the four market structures

9.2 Analyze short-run output decisions in a purely competitive firm

9.3 Discuss the firm's short-run shutdown decision, and derive the short-run supply curve of the purely competitive firm

9.4 Understand the short-run industry supply curve

9.5 Explain the long-run equilibrium position of a firm in pure competition

9.6 Discuss long-run industry adjustment in pure competition

9.7 Discuss the importance of the purely competitive model

Assess Your Knowledge

MyEconLab

Answers to these questions can be found on MyEconLab at **www.myeconlab.com**.

1. What is the difference between a firm and an industry?
2. How are total profits calculated?
3. If someone told you that a company is in a break-even position, how would you interpret the term *break-even*?

LO 9.1   Discuss the four market structures

Market Structures

What is meant by market structure?

market structure the competitive nature of the market environment in which firms make their pricing and output decisions

Firms operate in different types of markets, and these markets have different characteristics. The term **market structure** describes the environment in which firms make their pricing and output decisions. It emphasizes characteristics such as number of sellers and their ability to control price.

In discussing market structures, you will find the concept of an industry quite useful. A firm that is the only one in an industry will most likely behave quite differently from a firm that is just one among many in the industry.

What is an industry?

industry a group of firms that produce similar products

An **industry** is a group of firms that produce similar products. The one-firm industry (a monopoly) is an exception in that it operates alone. Thus, we talk about the furniture industry, the automobile industry, the insurance industry, the financial services industry, and so on.

What are the different types of market structures?

Different markets have different characteristics, but economists have managed to group these characteristics into four broad categories of market structures:

1. Pure or perfect competition
2. Monopoly
3. Monopolistic competition
4. Oligopoly

imperfect competition a collective term covering monopolistic competition and oligopoly

Note: As you will see shortly, pure competition and monopoly are at opposite ends on a continuum of market structures. Between these polar opposites are monopolistic competition and oligopoly, which economists frequently refer to as **imperfect competition**.

What is pure competition?

pure competition or **perfect competition** a market in which numerous firms produce identical products and to which there are no entry or exit barriers

The market structure termed **pure competition** or **perfect competition** refers to a market in which numerous firms produce identical products and to which there are no entry or exit barriers. Let us look at the characteristics of pure competition.

A Large Number of Firms   The purely competitive market consists of a large number of firms—so many that no single firm has any control over the price of its product. The purely competitive firm is therefore a **price-taker**. It has virtually no market power. Each firm in the industry produces such a tiny part of the entire industry output that total output is not noticeably affected by one firm producing and selling as much as it can or by ceasing production. Because each firm accounts for an extremely small fraction of the total output, the term **atomistic competition** is sometimes used to describe pure competition.

price-taker a firm with no control over the price of its product

atomistic competition a market in which each firm accounts for an extremely small fraction of the total output

Can you provide some examples of pure competition?

Agriculture, the stock market, and international money markets are usually cited as close approximations of perfect competition. It is not easy to find many good examples of purely competitive markets in the real world. Even in the case of agriculture, government programs influence the price at which the farmers sell their products, and marketing boards, for example, give farmers some degree of market power. Pure competition, therefore, does not really exist in these markets.

Homogeneous Products   The products of the firms in pure competition are homogeneous or standardized. Because the products are identical, buyers have no preference for purchasing from one firm rather than from another.

Freedom of Entry and Exit   A purely competitive market has freedom of entry into and exit from the industry. There are no entry or exit barriers, so resources are perfectly mobile in and out of the market.

Knowledge of Market Price   Buyers know the quality of the product and the price charged by each firm. If one firm attempts to charge a price higher than the market price, it will immediately lose all its customers.

Note 1: When a distinction is made between pure competition and perfect competition, the distinguishing feature is that in perfect competition, consumers have perfect knowledge regarding the prices charged by the firms in the market. In our analysis, we will make no distinction between pure competition and perfect competition; the two terms are used interchangeably.

Note 2: It is important to note that for competition to exist in a market, only two features are essential: numerous sellers (firms), and freedom of entry and exit. The conditions for the existence of pure competition are therefore more restrictive in scope than are the conditions for competition.

What is a monopoly?

In contrast to a purely competitive market, a monopoly is a one-firm industry. A **monopoly** is a market structure characterized by a single firm producing a product that has no close substitutes. The firm in monopoly has significant control over the price it charges for its product. The entry of other firms into the industry is precluded by a variety of entry barriers. Ontario Hydro, Hydro-Québec, and the Toronto Transit Commission are examples of monopolies.

monopoly a market structure characterized by a single firm producing a product that has no close substitutes

What is monopolistic competition?

In **monopolistic competition**, a large number of firms each sell differentiated products and exert some slight influence on the market price. Differentiated products are

monopolistic competition a market with a large number of firms selling differentiated products

products that are made to appear different from their rivals through certain characteristics, such as appearance, colour, shape, or brand. For example, Maxwell House, Taster's Choice, Nescafé, Folgers, and Starbucks are all differentiated products. Kobo and Kindle are differentiated ebook readers. Price differences are likely to be small among products sold by firms in monopolistic competition because although consumers acknowledge differences among the products, they perceive these differences as minor. For example, many different stores sell clothing, and we do observe differences in prices as we move from one retail outlet to the next. Not very often, however, do we observe startling differences in the prices of suits of similar quality.

What is an oligopoly?

In some markets, a few firms sell identical or differentiated products and produce a significant fraction of the total market output. We refer to such a market as an **oligopoly**. Because of the small number of firms in this type of market structure, each firm will take account of the policies and strategies adopted by its rivals. A firm in an oligopoly situation has considerable influence over the price of its product. If the firms happen to agree to act as a group to control price and output, their influence increases substantially.

oligopoly a market with few firms selling identical or differentiated products

Examples of oligopoly in Canada are the automobile industry, the brewing industry, the tobacco industry, and the pharmaceutical industry. The four largest firms in each of these industries produce more than 90% of the total output of these industries.

Can we summarize these market structures and their characteristics?

Table 9.1 does just that.

Table 9.1	Market Structures and Their Characteristics		
Pure Competition	**Monopolistic Competition**	**Oligopoly**	**Monopoly**
Large number of firms	Large number of firms	Few firms	Only one firm
Identical products	Differentiated products	Similar or differentiated products	Product has no close substitutes
No barriers to entry and exit	Freedom of entry and exit	Some barriers to entry and exit	Effective barriers to entry
No control over market price	Small control over market price	Substantial control over market price	Significant control over market price

BUSINESS SITUATION 9.1

Fashion Boutique is a small retail store that sells women's clothes. Fashion Boutique operates in an industry that is as close as possible to pure competition. For all practical purposes, it is a purely competitive firm. It is a price-taker and a quantity-adjuster. An advertising agency approaches Fashion Boutique and offers to advertise its products at a 40% discount on the regular advertising rate.

Should Fashion Boutique accept the agency's offer?

The answer to this Business Situation can be found in Appendix A.

Reading Comprehension

The answers to these questions can be found on MyEconLab at www.myeconlab.com   MyEconLab

1. What are the characteristics of each of the following market structures?
   a) Pure competition
   b) Monopoly
   c) Monopolistic competition
   d) Oligopoly
2. Why would you expect a single price to prevail in a purely competitive market?
3. Give an example of a firm that is a close approximation to a purely competitive firm.
4. What is meant by the term *price-taker*?

LO 9.2 Analyze short-run output decisions in a purely competitive firm

The Short-Run Output Decision in Pure Competition

How does the firm in pure competition decide how much to produce and what price to charge to maximize its profits?

Recall that a firm in pure competition has no control over the price at which it sells its output. Because the firm in pure competition must accept the market price as a given, such a firm must determine only what level of output to produce to maximize its profits. Actually, a firm can determine the level of output that will earn maximum profits in two ways: the total cost/total revenue method and the marginal method.

Can you demonstrate each of these approaches?

Yes. Let's begin with the total cost/total revenue approach.

The Total Cost/Total Revenue Approach to Profit Maximization Profit is the difference between total revenue and total cost. Let's use TR to denote total revenue, TC to denote total cost, and π to denote profit.

> If $TR > TC$, then $\pi > 0$.
> If $TR = TC$, then $\pi = 0$.
> If $TR < TC$, then $\pi < 0$.

To maximize its profits, the firm can choose that level of output at which the differences between TR and TC is greatest. The procedure for calculating maximum profit is outlined in Table 9.2.

Table 9.2	Revenue, Cost, and Profit for a Hypothetical Firm in Pure Competition			
Output (units) (1)	Price ($) (2)	Total Revenue ($) (3)	Total Cost ($) (4)	Profit ($) (5)
0	6	0	5	−5
1	6	6	9	−3
2	6	12	12	0
3	6	18	14	4
4	6	24	17	7
5	6	30	21	9
6	**6**	**36**	**26**	**10**
7	**6**	**42**	**32**	**10**
8	6	48	40	8
9	6	54	50	4
10	6	60	70	−10

| **Figure 9.1** | The Total Cost/Total Revenue Approach to Profit Maximization |

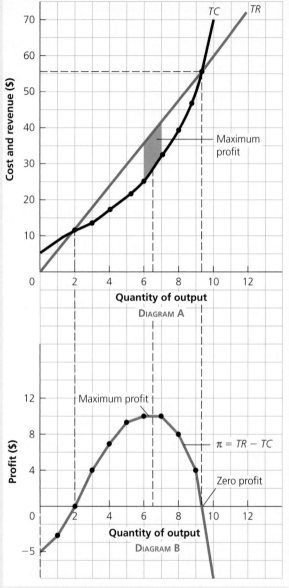

Diagram A: *TR, TC,* and profit
Diagram B: The total profit curve derived from plotting the difference between *TR* and *TC*

break-even point the point at which total revenue equals total cost

marginal revenue the extra revenue obtained by selling an additional unit of output

Column 1 of Table 9.2 shows various levels of output. The price of the product is $6, as shown in column 2. *TR* in column 3 is obtained by multiplying price by quantity of output. Column 4 gives *TC,* and column 5, the total profit column, is obtained by subtracting column 4 from column 3. As we can see from the table, total profit is at a maximum when the firm produces an output level between six and seven units.

Can the total cost/total revenue approach be illustrated graphically?

Yes. We illustrate the total cost/total revenue approach to profit maximization graphically in Figure 9.1. Diagram A plots the cost and revenue data shown in Table 9.2. The firm's *TR* is represented by a straight line through the origin. If there is no output, there will be no revenue. As output expands, *TR* rises in proportion to the increase in output—given a fixed price. *TC* rises as output increases. Note that a *TC* of $5 at zero output suggests a fixed cost of $5. The profit-maximizing output appears where the difference between *TR* and *TC* is greatest. The total profit curve is illustrated explicitly in Diagram B of Figure 9.1 by plotting the total profit data in column 5 of Table 9.2. The two diagrams are lined up for easy comparison.

At any level of output less than 2 units, the firm incurs losses. Profits are positive between 2 and 9.25 units of output. Beyond 9.25 units of output, the firm incurs losses. Profits are maximized when the firm produces 6 or 7 units of output. When *TR* and *TC* are equal, the firm earns zero profits. The point at which this occurs is referred to as the **break-even point**. In the diagrams, a break-even point occurs when the firm produces 2 units of output and again when the firm produces 9.25 units of output.

Marginal Approach to Profit Maximization Remember that marginal cost is the extra or additional cost incurred in producing one more unit of output. Before we can proceed to the marginal approach, we must first define **marginal revenue**, which is the extra revenue obtained from selling an additional unit of output. Symbolically, marginal revenue (*MR*) can be expressed as follows:

$$MR = \frac{\Delta TR}{\Delta Q}$$

Table 9.3	Revenue, Cost, and Profit Data for a Hypothetical Firm in Pure Competition					
Output (units) (1)	Price ($) (2)	TR ($) (3)	TC ($) (4)	Profit ($) (5)	MR ($) (6)	MC ($) (7)
0	6	0	5	−5		
					6	4
1	6	6	9	−3		
					6	3
2	6	12	12	0		
					6	2
3	6	18	14	4		
					6	3
4	6	24	17	7		
					6	4
5	6	30	21	9		
					6	5
6	6	36	26	10		
					6	6
7	6	42	32	10		
					6	8
8	6	48	40	8		
					6	10
9	6	54	50	4		
					6	20
10	6	60	70	−10		

Figure 9.2 Marginal Revenue/Marginal Cost Approach to Profit Maximization

MR and marginal cost (MC) are calculated in columns 6 and 7 of Table 9.3.

If the cost of producing an additional unit of output is less than the revenue obtained from that unit, then the firm will benefit from producing that additional unit. In other words, as long as MC is less than MR, the firm will expand its output. If, however, the cost of producing an additional unit of output is greater than the revenue obtained from that unit, then the firm will not produce the additional unit. To do so would reduce the firm's profits. In other words, as long as MC exceeds MR, the firm will reduce its output. It follows that when its MR equals its MC, the firm will be in the best profit position. In Table 9.3, this occurs at an output level between six and seven units where MR = MC = $6.

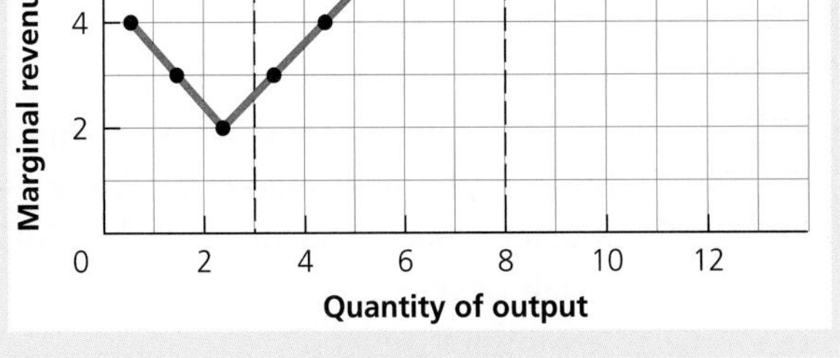

Can the marginal approach be illustrated graphically?

Let's take a look at Figure 9.2. It illustrates the marginal approach to profit maximization. The MR and MC data from Table 9.3 are plotted in Figure 9.2.

At a level of output of eight units, for instance, MC exceeds the MR. Hence, the firm will reduce its output.

At a level of output of three units, conversely, MR exceeds MC. Hence, the firm will increase its output. At an output level between six and seven units, the firm cannot increase its profits by changing its output. Hence, an output between six and seven units is the output level that maximizes the firm's profits. Note that the profit-maximizing level of output occurs where the rising MC curve cuts the MR curve.

You may ask, "Why increase output to the point where MR = MC? Why not stop at some level of output just before 6.5 units of output in Figure 9.2?" The reason for trying to operate where MR = MC will become much clearer if you think of the difference between MR and MC as extra profits. As long as MR > MC, the firm will earn extra profits by increasing its output. When no more extra profits can be made (i.e., when $MR = MC$), the firm will be in a profit-maximizing position.

The data in Table 9.3 seem to suggest that a relationship exists between price and the firm's marginal revenue in pure competition. Is this so?

The relationship among price, average revenue (AR), and marginal revenue (MR) in a purely competitive market structure is something you should understand. Let's investigate.

Recall that a purely competitive firm is a price-taker. The price at which it sells its output is given. Because variations in the output of a purely competitive firm have no appreciable effect on the market price of the product, the purely competitive firm faces a perfectly elastic demand curve. But let us study the information in Table 9.4, concentrating on the AR and MR columns. We assume that the price of the product is $6.

average revenue the revenue per unit of output sold; total revenue divided by quantity sold

Average revenue (AR) is the revenue per unit of output sold, or simply TR divided by quantity sold. It is what the firm receives when it sells one unit of output. But this is exactly the same as price. (See the AR column in Table 9.4.) The following simple algebraic exercise demonstrates that AR and price are identical:

$$TR = P \times Q$$

$$AR = \frac{TR}{Q} = \frac{P \times Q}{Q} = P$$

Therefore, $AR = P$.

Can we graph the demand, average revenue, and marginal revenue curves for a firm in pure competition?

The price and quantity columns in Table 9.4 will give us the firm's demand curve, while the AR and MR columns will give us the AR and MR curves, respectively. The information is plotted in Figure 9.3.

Table 9.4	Price, Average Revenue, and Marginal Revenue in Pure Competition			
Quantity	Price ($)	Total Revenue ($)	Average Revenue ($)	Marginal Revenue ($)
0	6	0	—	
				6
1	6	6	6	
				6
2	6	12	6	
				6
3	6	18	6	
				6
4	6	24	6	
				6
5	6	30	6	

Note that in Table 9.4, and in Figure 9.3, MR remains constant and equal to price or AR. This equality of MR and AR or price holds only in a situation of pure competition, where the firm has no influence on the price.

> The demand curve for a purely competitive firm coincides with its AR and MR curves.

The profit-maximizing condition for a purely competitive firm is often stated as

$$MR = MC = P$$

We will see later that pure competition is the only market structure in which profits are maximized when MC equals price.

Figure 9.3	Demand, Average Revenue, and Marginal Revenue Curves for a Firm in Pure Competition

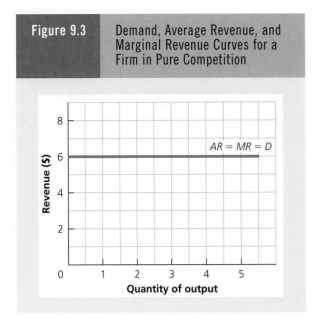

Can we analyze the competitive firm's short-run profit level?

The purely competitive firm maximizes its profits and will therefore be in equilibrium when it produces at an output level at which MC equals price. But how large or how small are these profits? A quick look at Figure 9.4 will reveal whether or not the firm is earning a profit and the size of the profit. For this purpose, you must remember that a firm's total profit is the difference between TR and TC. We can therefore determine the firm's profit per unit of output (i.e., average profit) by dividing its total profit by the number of units produced and sold.

$$\text{Profit per unit} = \frac{TR - TC}{Q}$$
$$= AR - ATC$$
$$= P - ATC$$

By comparing price and ATC, we can easily determine whether or not the firm is earning a profit:

$$\text{If } P > ATC, \text{ then } \pi > 0.$$
$$\text{If } P = ATC, \text{ then } \pi = 0.$$
$$\text{If } P < ATC, \text{ then } \pi < 0.$$

In Figure 9.4, if the price of the product is \$70, the profit-maximizing firm will produce an output of 50 units where $MR = P = MC$. At this level of output, $ATC = \$50$, so the firm makes a profit of \$70 − \$50 = \$20 on each unit of output. At a price lower than \$70, the firm's profit is reduced. In fact, it is possible for the price to be so low that the firm earns no profit at all and may even incur a loss. At a price of \$30, for example, the firm does not cover its ATC (the price is below the ATC curve); hence, the firm incurs losses.

Figure 9.4	The Purely Competitive Firm's Profit Level

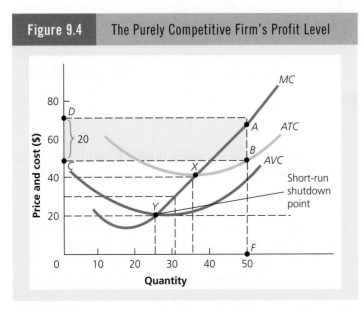

We can also use Figure 9.4 to determine the firm's TR, TC, and total profit at various price-output combinations. Let us assume that the price of the product is \$70. The firm seeking to maximize its profits will produce 50 units of output. The firm will receive a TR of \$70 × 50 = \$3500. This TR is illustrated by the rectangle 0DAF in Figure 9.4. The TC per unit when the firm produces 50 units is \$50, where the vertical line from 50 units crosses the ATC curve. The TC (or $ATC \times Q$) of producing an output of 50 units is \$50 × 50 = \$2500 and is illustrated by the rectangle 0CBF. The firm's total profit is the difference between its TR (0DAF) and its TC (0CBF). This is shown by the area of the shaded rectangle $ABCD$, which is \$20 × 50 = \$1000.

Reading Comprehension

The answers to these questions can be found on MyEconLab at **www.myeconlab.com.**   MyEconLab

1. Why are *MR* and price identical for a firm in pure competition?
2. With the help of a diagram, show that a firm will maximize its profits when it produces a level of output at which MR equals *MC*.

3. What is marginal revenue?
4. Define the break-even point.
5. What is average revenue and how is it related to price?

LO 9.3   Discuss the firm's short-run shutdown decision, and derive the short-run supply curve of the purely competitive firm

The Short-Run Supply Curve and Shutdown Point of the Firm in Pure Competition

Is it possible to derive the short-run supply curve from the analysis in the previous section?

The foregoing analysis provides a method of determining the short-run supply curve of the purely competitive firm. The firm is doing the best it can in the short run provided that it produces an output at which *MR* = *MC*. Figure 9.4 shows that at a price of $70, the firm earns a profit. In fact, the firm earns a profit if the price is anywhere above $40. At a price of $40, the firm makes neither a profit nor a loss; it just breaks even. The price equals its *ATC* (or its *TR* equals its *TC*). As discussed, this point is referred to as the break-even point. In Figure 9.4, point *X* is the break-even point, and the output of

break-even level of output the level of output at which total revenue equals total cost

35 units is the **break-even level of output**, or the output level at which *TR* = *TC*.

If the price falls below $40, the firm incurs losses. At a price of $30, for example, the firm is doing its best in the short run when it produces an output of 30 units (*MR* = *MC*), yet it is incurring losses. Any different level of output will merely increase the firm's losses. A firm in such a situation is said to be minimizing its losses.

A firm is minimizing its losses when its *MR* = *MC* and the price is between its average variable cost (*AVC*) and its average total cost (*ATC*).

Table 9.5	The Short-Run Supply Schedule for a Purely Competitive Firm

Price ($)	Quantity Supplied
70	50
60	45
50	40
40	35
30	30
20	25
Less than 20	0

Because the firm incurs losses when the price falls below $40, is it not better for the firm to close?

The answer is no. As long as the firm covers its average variable cost (*AVC*) in the short run, it should continue to operate. If it suspends its operation, it still has its fixed costs; if it continues to operate, its losses will be less than its *TFC*. The amount over its *AVC* can be used to defray a part of its fixed costs. When the price falls below $20, the

Figure 9.5	The Short-Run Supply Curve of the Purely Competitive Firm

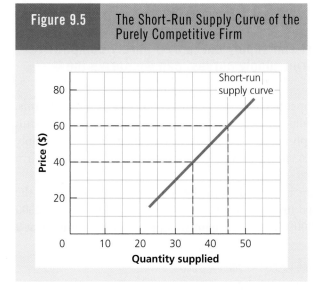

firm does not cover its variable costs and should therefore shut down. The point at which price equals the minimum *AVC* is called the **short-run shutdown point**.

In Figure 9.4, point *Y* is the short-run shutdown point. Points along the marginal cost curve show the various quantities that the firm will supply at various prices. Note, however, that no output will be supplied at prices below $20. The various quantities supplied at various prices are shown in Table 9.5.

This, of course, is the short-run supply schedule for a purely competitive firm. It corresponds with the marginal cost (*MC*) curve above the *AVC* curve in Figure 9.4. The section of the *MC* curve above the *AVC* curve is illustrated in Figure 9.5.

When will a firm that is minimizing its losses go out of business?

short-run shutdown point
the point at which price equals the minimum average variable cost

Let us return for a moment to Figure 9.4 on page 259. We said that in the short run, if the price of the product is between $20 and $40, the firm should continue to operate even though it is incurring losses. A firm will not continue to incur losses forever. In the long run, the firm has no fixed factors. In the long run, therefore, a firm that is incurring losses will leave the industry. We will study the firm's adjustment to the long run later in this chapter.

BUSINESS SITUATION 9.2

A certain firm is operating with fixed costs. The price of its product is $10 and it has no control over this price. The firm's *ATC* is below the given price of $10, thus the firm is earning a profit. Its lowest *AVC* is $6. Changes in the market for this firm's product suddenly cause the price to fall to $8, which is below the firm's *ATC*. The firm is now incurring losses.

Should the firm close down in light of this new business situation?

The answer to this Business Situation can be found in Appendix A.

Reading Comprehension

The answers to these questions can be found on MyEconLab at **www.myeconlab.com**.   MyEconLab

1. Explain how to derive the short-run supply curve for a firm trying to maximize its profits in pure competition.
2. Explain how a firm could be in equilibrium in the short run when it is incurring losses.

3. "The objective of the firm is to maximize its profits. If this objective is achieved, the firm is in equilibrium. The firm cannot, therefore, be in equilibrium if it is not making a profit." Discuss this statement.
4. Describe the short-run shutdown point for a purely competitive firm.

LO 9.4 Understand the short-run industry supply curve

The Short-Run Industry Supply Curve

We have discussed the short-run supply curve of a purely competitive firm. From the firms' short-run supply curves, can we derive the industry supply curve?

Yes. You know that a purely competitive industry consists of a large number of firms. However, to illustrate arithmetically and geometrically the derivation of the short-run industry supply schedule and supply curve, we will assume that an industry, D, has only three firms, A, B, and C. Table 9.6 shows the various quantities supplied by each firm at each possible price.

The industry supply function is derived from the horizontal summation of the supply functions of the individual firms. At a price of $3, firms A and C supply 2000 units each and firm B supplies 3000. The total quantity supplied by the industry at a price of $3 is

$$2000 + 3000 + 2000 = 7000$$

At a price of $6, firm A supplies 3000 units, firm B supplies 5000 units, and firm C supplies 4000. The total quantity supplied by the industry at a price of $6 is

$$3000 + 5000 + 4000 = 12\ 000$$

The other quantities supplied at other prices are obtained in a similar manner.

From the supply functions in Table 9.6, we can draw the supply curves for firms A, B, and C and for industry D. In Figure 9.6 we show how the short-run industry supply curve is derived from adding the supply curves of each firm horizontally. At a price of $6, the total quantity supplied by the industry is 12 000. This gives us point E in Figure 9.6. At a price of $15, the total quantity supplied by the industry is 27 000. This gives us point E_1 in Figure 9.6. In a similar manner, we can plot the other points in the industry supply function. By connecting these points, we obtain the short-run industry supply curve.

> The short-run industry supply curve is the horizontal summation of the individual short-run supply curves of all the firms in the industry.

Table 9.6	Derivation of the Short-Run Industry Supply Schedule			
Price ($)	Output Firm A	Output Firm B	Output Firm C	Output Industry D
3	2 000	3 000	2 000	7 000
6	3 000	5 000	4 000	12 000
9	4 000	7 000	6 000	17 000
12	5 000	9 000	8 000	22 000
15	6 000	11 000	10 000	27 000
18	7 000	13 000	12 000	32 000
21	8 000	15 000	14 000	37 000
24	9 000	17 000	16 000	42 000

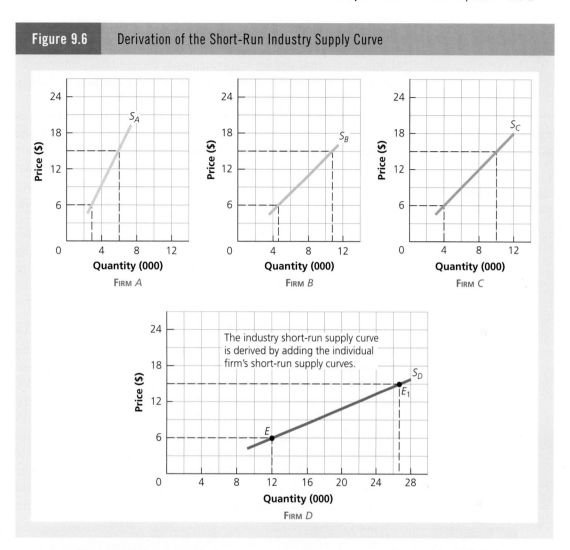

Figure 9.6 Derivation of the Short-Run Industry Supply Curve

Firm A

Firm B

Firm C

The industry short-run supply curve is derived by adding the individual firm's short-run supply curves.

Firm D

Reading Comprehension

1. What is the short-run industry supply curve?

2. Explain how to derive the industry short-run supply curve.

LO 9.5   Explain the long-run equilibrium position of a firm in pure competition

Long-Run Equilibrium of a Firm in Pure Competition

Can we discuss the long-run equilibrium position of a firm in pure competition?

In a purely competitive market structure, firms are free to enter or to leave the industry: the market has no barriers to entry or exit. If the firms in the industry earn profits in the short run, other firms will enter the industry. The entry of these new firms will increase total industry supply and, assuming no change in demand occurs, the price will tend to fall. New firms will tend to enter the industry provided that positive profits can be made. If firms in the industry are incurring losses, they will not remain in the industry in the long run. The exit of firms from the industry will cause total industry supply to fall and the price of the product will tend to rise.

Movement of firms into and out of the industry will cease when each firm in the industry is earning zero profit—sometimes referred to as **normal profit** or **zero economic profit**. You may wonder why a firm would stay in an industry if it were making zero profit, but the matter is easily clarified if we remind ourselves that profits are defined as *TR* minus *TC* and that total cost includes opportunity cost (that is, what the resources could earn in their best alternative uses). When a firm earns zero economic profit, it earns a profit that is just equal to the alternative (opportunity) cost of the resources used in production.

normal profit or zero economic profit a profit that is equal to the alternative (opportunity) cost of the resources employed in production

> A purely competitive firm in long-run equilibrium earns zero economic profit, called normal profit.

Can this long-run equilibrium position be illustrated diagrammatically?

Graphs do allow us to see certain situations more clearly than we can perceive through verbal explanations alone. If the price of the product is $14, as determined by the demand and supply curves for the industry shown in Figure 9.7, the firm will earn positive economic profits. New firms will enter the industry. As this happens, the industry supply curve shifts to the right, say, to S_1. This increase in supply causes the price to fall from $14 to $6. At this price, firms will incur losses and therefore leave the industry. This exit of firms from the industry causes industry supply to fall, and the industry supply curve shifts to the left (from $S_1 S_1$ to $S_0 S_0$ in Figure 9.7) resulting in an increase in price from $6 to $10. At this price, each firm in the industry earns zero economic profits. Note that this price equals average cost and that the firm is in equilibrium, because *MR* equals *MC*.

Figure 9.7	Long-Run Equilibrium of the Purely Competitive Firm

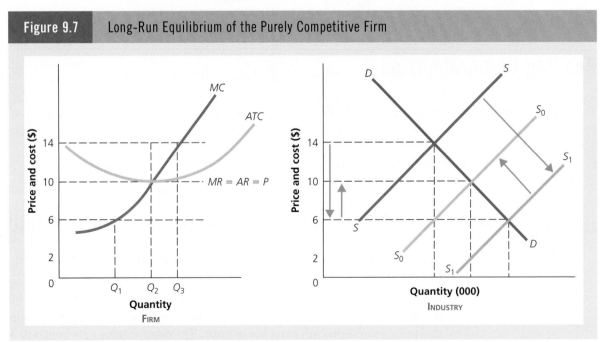

Note further that in equilibrium, price equals *MC*; but *MC* passes through the minimum point of the average cost curve, so the price equals minimum average cost, which is important. The purely competitive firm is in long-run equilibrium when

$$MR = MC = AC = P$$

When each firm in the industry is in long-run equilibrium, and when there is no incentive for firms to enter or leave the industry, the output of the industry will remain steady—the industry supply curve will not shift. In this case, we say that the industry is in long-run equilibrium.

> When the purely competitive industry is in long-run equilibrium, *MR* equals *MC*, and average cost equals *AR*, for each firm in the industry.

BUSINESS SITUATION 9.3

When Leonard Brooks opened his loose-leaf binding company, his was the only one in town. His business flourished, and profits were high. He charged a reasonable price. As the town's population grew, more loose-leaf-binding companies emerged. The increase in the number of companies forced the price down, but Mr. Brooks was still earning a profit. More firms entered the industry until no firm was making a profit, and no one had control over the price. They were all just breaking even. Mr. Brooks decided to stay in the business.

Did he make the right decision?

The answer to this Business Situation can be found in Appendix A.

Reading Comprehension

The answers to these questions can be found on MyEconLab at **www.myeconlab.com**.   MyEconLab

1. Describe the long-run position of a purely competitive firm in long-run equilibrium.

2. Why would a firm continue to operate in the long run if it is earning zero economic profits?

3. Explain why a purely competitive firm cannot earn positive economic profits in the long run.

LO 9.6 Discuss long-run industry adjustment in pure competition

Long-Run Industry Adjustment

What is the long-run supply curve of a purely competitive industry?

Remember that a supply curve shows various quantities of a good or service that will be supplied at various prices. Recall also that the industry consists of all the firms in the industry. We can therefore define the long-run supply (*LRS*) curve of a purely competitive industry as follows:

> The long-run supply (*LRS*) curve of a purely competitive industry is a graph that shows the various quantities of a good or service that all the firms in the industry will be willing to supply at various prices when the industry is in long-run equilibrium.

What is the shape of the long-run supply curve of a purely competitive industry?

It depends on whether the industry is a constant-cost industry, an increasing-cost industry, or a decreasing-cost industry. Some controversy exists as to whether an industry can experience increasing cost as it expands. However, we will not engage ourselves in that particular debate but will proceed as if increasing-cost industries do exist. Let us first discuss the long-run industry supply curve for a constant-cost industry.

What is a constant-cost industry?

constant-cost industry
an industry in which costs remain constant as the industry expands

In a **constant-cost industry**, costs remain constant as the industry expands. As new firms enter the industry, the prices of resources remain constant even as the supply of goods and services increases.

When the industry is in long-run equilibrium, the price equals minimum long-run average cost. In a constant-cost industry, the expansion of industry output by the entry of new firms has no effect on cost. The entry and exit of firms cause total industry output to change, but the price of the product always returns to the point at which it is equal to the minimum average cost. Thus, in the long run, the industry supplies various quantities at a constant price. Essentially, this means the following:

> The *LRS* curve of a constant-cost industry is horizontal (perfectly elastic) at the minimum average cost.

Can we use a diagram to help us with this analysis?

Figure 9.8 should help us. It shows a firm and an industry, both in equilibrium.

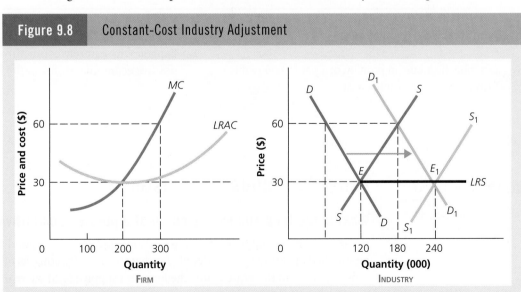

Figure 9.8 Constant-Cost Industry Adjustment

The firm shown in the diagram is representative of all the firms in the industry. It produces 200 units of output, and the price of the product is $30. The industry demand curve is *DD*, the supply curve is *SS*, and the quantity produced by the industry is 120 000.

Let us assume now that the demand for the product increases from *DD* to D_1D_1, as shown in Figure 9.8. This causes the price to rise from $30 to $60. The price is now above average cost, so the firms now earn positive economic profits. At a price of $60, the representative firm increases its output to 300 units, moving along its *MC* curve. The output of the industry increases along *SS* from 120 000 units to 180 000 units. Because profits are being earned in this industry, it attracts new firms. The entry of these new firms shifts the supply curve from *SS* to S_1S_1 and forces the price back to $30. With the price now back at $30, the initial firms reduce their output along their *MC* curves. Each firm in the industry now produces 200 units, but because there are now more firms, the industry output increases to 240 000. Profits are again zero; no firms move into or out of the industry. We started with an initial price of $30 and a total quantity of 120 000 units. We end up with a price of $30 and a total quantity supplied of 240 000 units. By joining points *E* and E_1, we obtain the *LRS* curve of the industry.

What is an increasing-cost industry?

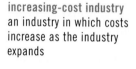

increasing-cost industry an industry in which costs increase as the industry expands

In an **increasing-cost industry**, costs increase as the industry expands with the entry of new firms. Hence, production costs go up. Although many industries seem to exhibit constant cost in the long run, it is reasonable to expect that as an industry expands, the increase in demand for increasingly scarce resources will raise the prices of inputs, and thus increase production costs.

The diagrams that we used to derive the long-run supply curve of a constant-cost industry in pure competition were very helpful. Can we use diagrams also to illustrate the case of increasing-cost industries?

Yes. Figure 9.9 will be helpful in our analysis. The firm and industry are in equilibrium at a price of $30. The representative firm produces 100 units of output. *DD* and *SS* are the initial demand and supply curves of the industry, and the total output of the industry is 50 000 units.

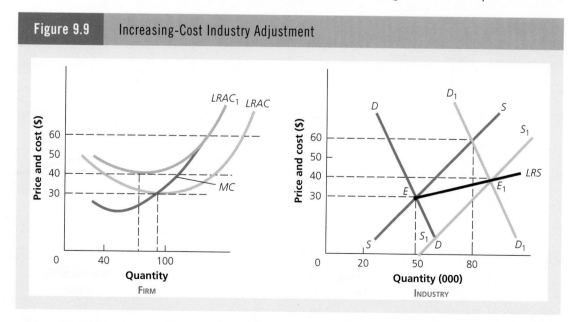

Figure 9.9 Increasing-Cost Industry Adjustment

Suppose that the demand for the industry's output increases from DD to D_1D_1. This causes the price to rise from $30 to $60. The existing firms increase their output, moving along their MC curves, and the industry output increases along SS from 50 000 to 80 000. Positive economic profits at a price of $60 induce new firms to enter the industry. As they do so, the supply curve shifts from SS to S_1S_1, but the cost rises, as shown by the shift of the long-run average cost curve from $LRAC$ to $LRAC_1$. Therefore, the increase in supply resulting from the entry of new firms does not force the price back to its initial level of $30, but only to $40. We obtain the LRS curve of the industry by joining points E and E_1. This analysis leads to the following conclusion:

> The LRS curve of an increasing-cost industry that is purely competitive is upward sloping.

What is a decreasing-cost industry?

decreasing-cost industry
an industry in which costs decrease as the industry expands

In a **decreasing-cost industry**, costs decrease as the industry expands with the entry of new firms. Hence, production costs are reduced. A decreasing-cost industry can be the result of conditions external to the firms in the industry. For example, improved transportation and communication facilities occur with industrial growth. Stated differently, the industry can experience economies of industry size, just as firms experience economies of scale, so that as the industry expands, its costs go down.

Can we use diagrams to illustrate the derivation of the long-run supply curve of a purely competitive industry with decreasing cost?

Figure 9.10 will help us to explain the derivation of the LRS curve of a decreasing-cost industry in pure competition. The industry and the firm are in equilibrium with a price of $50. The firm produces 100 units of output while the industry produces 50 000 units.

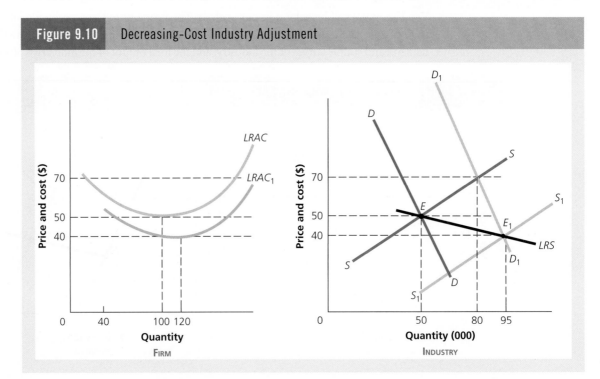
Figure 9.10   Decreasing-Cost Industry Adjustment

An increase in demand from *DD* to D_1D_1 causes the price to rise from $50 to $70. The existing firms increase their output in response to the higher price, moving along their *MC* curves (not shown), and the industry output increases along *SS* from 50 000 units to 80 000 units. The increase in price causes firms to move from a position of zero economic profits to a position of positive economic profits. Consequently, new firms are attracted into the industry, thus causing the supply curve to shift from *SS* to S_1S_1 in Figure 9.10. But in a decreasing-cost industry, the cost falls, as shown by the shift in the *LRAC* from *LRAC* to $LRAC_1$. Therefore, the increase in supply resulting from the entry of new firms does not send the price back to $50, but to $40. We obtain the *LRS* curve of the industry by joining points *E* and E_1. This analysis leads us to the following conclusion:

> The *LRS* curve of a decreasing-cost industry in pure competition is downward sloping.

Reading Comprehension

The answers to these questions can be found on MyEconLab at **www.myeconlab.com**.   MyEconLab

1. Describe the process by which a purely competitive industry reaches long-run equilibrium.
2. Define each of the following concepts:
   a) Constant-cost industry
   b) Increasing-cost industry
   c) Decreasing-cost industry
3. Why might a purely competitive industry experience (a) increasing cost and (b) decreasing cost as it expands in the long run?

LO 9.7 Discuss the importance of the purely competitive model

The Importance of the Purely Competitive Model

You mentioned earlier in this chapter that real-world examples of pure competition are not easy to find. Why then do we spend so much time analyzing behaviour in this type of market structure?

It is easier to understand the issue if you view pure competition as a model—an abstraction from reality. Let us remind ourselves first that the competitive solution occurs where price equals *MC*. This **marginal-cost pricing** (a characteristic feature of pure competition) implies that the firm establishes the equality of price and *MC*; that is, the firm sells its product at a price just equal to the opportunity cost. Let us also remind ourselves that long-run competitive equilibrium occurs where price equals minimum average cost. Hence, resources are efficiently employed in the purely competitive model.

marginal-cost pricing
the establishment of the equality of price and marginal cost

The purely competitive model serves as an ideal by which we can measure other market structures. We can, in fact, consider it a kind of measuring rod. Moreover, many of the predictions of the purely competitive model hold true even in situations where pure competition does not prevail.

What is Pareto efficiency?

Pareto optimality or Pareto efficiency the condition that exists when it is impossible to make someone better off without making someone else worse off

One objective of economic science is to allocate resources efficiently. But how do we know if resources are allocated efficiently? One way is to test for the presence of **Pareto optimality** or **Pareto efficiency**. Pareto optimality (named after the Italian-born economist Vilfredo Pareto) is the condition that exists when it is impossible to make someone better off without making someone else worse off.

Stated slightly differently, if it is possible to make someone better off without making someone else worse off, then Pareto efficiency does not exist.

What conditions are necessary for the existence of Pareto optimality?

The following conditions are necessary for the existence of Pareto efficiency:

1. Each consumer must have the opportunity to maximize his or her own satisfaction.
2. For each consumer, the ratio of the marginal utilities of any two goods must be the same. This means essentially that all consumers must pay the same price for each good or service.
3. Each firm must produce at an output level at which *MC* equals price.
4. The production of each good or service must be at the lowest possible cost.
5. Each factor of production must be employed in its most efficient use.
6. Each household must have the opportunity to supply as many factor services as it chooses.
7. People must be free to enter whatever occupation they choose.

It can be shown that if pure competition exists in all markets, all of the above conditions will prevail and Pareto efficiency will be attained. We can conclude, then, that the popular notion that competition is good has some basis.

Reading Comprehension

The answers to these questions can be found on MyEconLab at www.myeconlab.com.   MyEconLab

1. "The purely competitive model is completely useless in a world where pure competition rarely exists." Discuss.
2. How useful is the economic model of perfect competition?

3. What is Pareto optimality? Mention at least four conditions that are necessary for the existence of Pareto optimality.
4. Is there any relation between pure competition and Pareto optimality? Explain.

Review

1. Review the learning objectives listed at the beginning of the chapter.
2. Have you accomplished all the objectives? One way to determine this is to answer the Reading Comprehension questions at the end of each section. This will help you assess the extent to which you have accomplished the learning objectives.
3. If you have not accomplished an objective, review the relevant material before proceeding.

Key Points to Remember

1. **LO 9.1** In a purely competitive market, many firms sell a homogeneous product. Each seller (firm) is a price-taker. Firms are free to enter or to leave the industry. A monopoly exists when a single firm produces a product that has no close substitutes. In monopolistic competition, many firms each sell a differentiated product. In oligopoly, there are only a few sellers.
2. **LO 9.2** A firm's profit is the difference between its total revenue (TR) and its total cost (TC). The firm maximizes its profits by producing that output at which the difference between TR and TC is greatest, or by producing an output level at which marginal revenue (MR) equals marginal cost (MC).
3. **LO 9.2** A firm in pure competition earns positive profits in the short run, provided that the price at which it sells its product is above its average total cost (ATC). When the price is just equal to ATC, the firm is in a break-even position.
4. **LO 9.3** If the firm is covering its average variable cost (AVC) but not its total cost, and if it produces an output level at which MR equals MC, we say that it is minimizing its losses. The firm is better off doing this in the short run than closing down. The short-run shutdown point is the point at which the firm is just barely covering its variable cost with nothing left over.
5. **LO 9.3, 9.4** The competitive firm's short-run supply curve is the portion of its MC curve that lies above its AVC curve. We can obtain the short-run industry supply curve by adding horizontally the supply curves of the firms in that industry.
6. **LO 9.4** The short-run industry supply curve shows the various quantities of an item that will be supplied by all the firms in the industry at various prices. It is obtained by summing horizontally the short-run supply curves of all the firms in the industry.
7. **LO 9.5, 9.6** In long-run equilibrium, the purely competitive firm earns zero economic profits because of the effect of the entry and exit of firms into and out of the industry. The long-run equilibrium position is attained when $MR = MC = AC = P$. The industry is in long-run equilibrium when each firm is in equilibrium and when no firms enter into or exit from the industry.
8. **LO 9.7** Although examples of pure competition can be hard to find in the real world, the purely competitive model is useful as an ideal by which we can evaluate other types of market structures.

Economic Word Power

Atomistic competition   (p. 253)
Average revenue   (p. 258)
Break-even level of output   (p. 260)
Break-even point   (p. 256)
Constant-cost industry   (p. 266)
Decreasing-cost industry   (p. 268)
Imperfect competition   (p. 252)
Increasing-cost industry   (p. 267)
Industry   (p. 252)
Marginal revenue   (p. 256)
Marginal-cost pricing   (p. 269)
Market structure   (p. 252)
Monopolistic competition   (p. 253)
Monopoly   (p. 253)
Normal profit or zero economic profit   (p. 264)
Oligopoly   (p. 254)
Pareto optimality or Pareto efficiency   (p. 270)
Price-taker   (p. 253)
Pure competition or perfect competition   (p. 252)
Short-run shutdown point   (p. 261)

Problems and Exercises

Basic

1. **LO 9.1** In Table 9.7, fill in the market structure on the right that matches the description on the left.

Table 9.7	Market Structures
Description	**Market Structure**
a. The firm and the industry are identical.	a.
b. The demand curve is horizontal.	b.
c. The demand curve is relatively flat, products are differentiated, and the number of substitutes is very large.	c.
d. Collusion is possible and likely.	d.

2. **LO 9.2** The information in Table 9.8 refers to a firm in pure competition.
   a. Complete the *TR* and the profit columns.
   b. On a graph, draw the *TR* and *TC* curves.
   c. Indicate the break-even point on your graph.

Table 9.8	Data for a Firm in Pure Competition			
Price ($)	Quantity	TR ($)	TC ($)	Profit ($)
4	1		6	
4	2		9	
4	3		10	
4	4		12	
4	5		15	
4	6		21	

3. **LO 9.2** Price Right is a price-taker. Its *TC* schedule is shown in Table 9.9. The market price is $5.
   a. Complete the *TR* and profit columns.
   b. Draw the total profit curve.
   c. At what level of output is profit maximized?
4. **LO 9.4** Figure 9.11 shows short-run supply curves for firms *A* and *B*. Construct their total supply curves.
5. **LO 9.1** A firm has the record of output and *TR* shown in Table 9.10. Is this a purely competitive firm? Defend your answer.

Table 9.9	Cost Schedule for Price Right		
Quantity	TC ($)	TR ($)	Total Profit ($)
0	8		
1	12		
2	15		
3	17		
4	18		
5	19		
6	21		
7	24		
8	28		
9	35		
10	42		

Table 9.10	Output and Total Revenue for a Firm
Quantity	TR ($)
0	0
1	19
2	52
3	93
4	136
5	175
6	210
7	217
8	208

Questions in the Intermediate and Challenging Sections cover several different concepts, and have not been organized by learning objectives.

Intermediate

1. The data in Table 9.11 are given for a firm.
   a. Compute *TR*, *AR*, and *MR* and fill in the relevant columns.
   b. Draw the *TR*, *AR*, and *MR* curves.

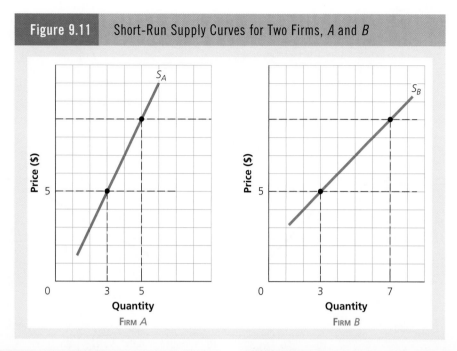

Figure 9.11 Short-Run Supply Curves for Two Firms, *A* and *B*

FIRM *A*

FIRM *B*

Table 9.11 Data for a Firm

Price ($) (1)	Quantity (2)	TR ($) (3)	AR ($) (4)	MR ($) (5)
6	1			
6	2			
6	3			
6	4			
6	5			
6	6			
6	7			
6	8			

Table 9.12 Total Revenue and Output for Firm in Pure Competition

Quantity	TR ($)
0	0
1	13
2	26
3	39
4	52
5	65
6	78
7	91

2. Table 9.12 contains information on *TR* and output for a firm in pure competition. Determine the price of the product.

3. Figure 9.12 shows price and cost data for a purely competitive firm.

a. If the market price of the product is $12, the profit-maximizing output will be _____ units. *TC* will be $_____, *TR* will be $_____, and total profits will be $_____.

b. If the price is $9, the equilibrium output will be _____ units. At this output, *TR* will be $_____, *TC* will be $_____, and total profits will be $_____.

c. If the price is $3, the equilibrium output will be _____ units.

d. This firm should shut down if the price falls below $_____.

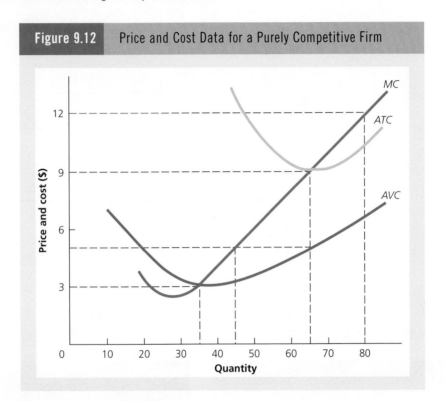

Figure 9.12 Price and Cost Data for a Purely Competitive Firm

4. For simplicity, let us assume that an industry consists of only three firms, each with identical cost curves. Figure 9.13 shows the cost curves for the firms.
   a. Use the data from Figure 9.13 to construct the industry supply schedule.
   b. Draw the industry supply curve.

5. In Figure 9.14, MC is the marginal cost for Perfcomp, a price-taker. The market price is P. If Perfcomp is a profit-seeking firm, why would it not produce quantities Q_0 or Q_2? Indicate the profit-maximizing output.

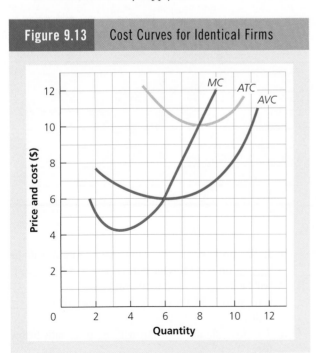

Figure 9.13 Cost Curves for Identical Firms

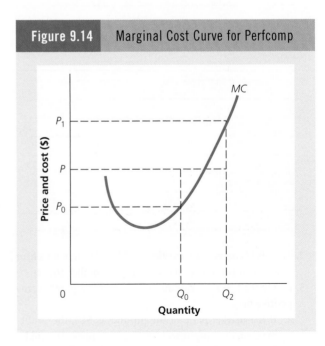

Figure 9.14 Marginal Cost Curve for Perfcomp

Challenging

1. The market demand curve is obtained by adding the individual demand curves horizontally. The summation of these individual demand curves produces a downward-sloping market demand curve. Given this fact, how can the addition of horizontal demand curves for purely competitive firms result in a downward-sloping demand curve?

2. A firm advertises mainly to increase its sales. Because a purely competitive market has so many firms, each firm will engage in competitive advertising to gain a larger share of the market. Do you detect any error in this argument?

MyEconLab Visit the MyEconLab website at **www.myeconlab.com.** This online homework and tutorial system puts you in control of your own learning with study and practice tools directly correlated to this chapter's content.

Study Guide

Self-Assessment

The answers to the Study Guide questions can be found in Appendix B.

What's your score?

Circle the letter that corresponds with the correct answer.

1. The competitive nature of the market environment in which firms make their price and output decisions is called
   a. Environmental market
   b. Market structures
   c. Competitive statute
   d. Economic competition

2. An industry is
   a. A company
   b. Any business that is not owned by the government
   c. A group of firms that produce similar products
   d. A group of firms that produce vastly different products

3. Which of the following is not a market structure?
   a. Monopoly
   b. Oligopoly
   c. Monopolistic competition
   d. Agriculture

4. Imperfect competition includes
   a. Pure and perfect competition
   b. Monopoly and pure competition
   c. Oligopoly and monopoly
   d. Oligopoly and monopolistic competition

5. Which of the following is true of pure competition?
   a. Each firm determines the price at which it sells its product
   b. Each firm tries to differentiate its product
   c. A few firms compete fiercely for customers
   d. Each firm is a price-taker and a quantity-adjuster

6. A monopoly is
   a. A market in which a single firm tries to dominate the other firms in the market
   b. A situation where a single firm controls more than 50% of the market
   c. A market structure with a single firm producing a product with numerous very close substitutes
   d. None of the above

7. Which of the following would you consider to be a firm in monopolistic competition?
   a. A furniture seller in Vancouver
   b. A clothing retail outlet in Montreal
   c. A pastry maker in Toronto
   d. All of the above

8. Which of the following is an example of an oligopoly in Canada?
   a. The tobacco industry
   b. The automobile industry
   c. The brewing (beer) industry
   d. All of the above

9. To maximize its profits, a firm in pure competition will
   a. Set its price low enough to attract customers
   b. Produce a level of output at which price equals marginal cost

c. Engage in competitive advertising to attract customers

d. Raise its price to increase its revenue

10. A firm in pure competition will maximize its profits by producing a volume of output where
    a. $MR > AR$
    b. $P > MC$
    c. $MR = MC$
    d. $P > AR$

11. The short-run supply curve of a purely competitive firm is
    a. The section of its MC curve that lies above its AVC curve
    b. The section of its AVC curve that lies above its MC curve
    c. The same as its AR curve
    d. The upward-sloping section of its AR curve

Questions 12, 13, and 14 refer to Figure 9.15. The price of the product is $7.

12. To maximize profits, the firm should
    a. Charge a price of $9 and produce nine units of output
    b. Charge a price above $9 and produce more than nine units
    c. Produce eight units of output
    d. Lower the price to attract more customers

13. At a price of $7, the firm should
    a. Shut down because price is less than ATC b. Raise the price to at least the break-even level
    c. Continue to operate because price is greater than AVC
    d. None of the above

14. The short-run shutdown point occurs at an output level of
    a. Seven units
    b. Eight units

c. Less than seven units

d. Nine units

15. In long-run competitive equilibrium,
    a. Each firm earns positive economic profits
    b. All firms incur slight losses
    c. Each firm operates where price equals average cost
    d. None of the above

16. If firms in a purely competitive market structure are earning positive economic profits, then in the long run
    a. Firms will leave the industry in search of even larger profits; hence, the market price will rise
    b. Firms will enter the industry, increasing total supply and causing price to fall
    c. Firms will raise their prices to earn even bigger profits
    d. Each firm will advertise to increase its market share

17. If firms in a purely competitive market structure are incurring losses, then in the long run
    a. Firms will leave the industry, causing the price to rise as industry output falls
    b. Firms will enter the industry to force out the inefficient ones
    c. Firms will lower their prices to keep out other firms
    d. Some firms will advertise to attract more customers

18. The LRS curve of a constant-cost industry is
    a. Upward sloping
    b. Horizontal
    c. Downward sloping
    d. Non-existent

Figure 9.15   Revenue and Cost Curves for a Purely Competitive Firm

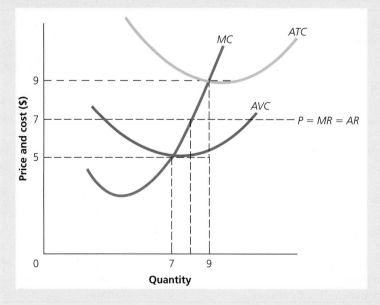

19. Which of the following is a plausible explanation of an increasing-cost industry?
    a. As firms leave the industry, demand for the industry's output falls
    b. As new firms enter the industry, the demand for resources causes the prices of factor inputs to rise and thus increases production costs
    c. Increases in demand for the industry's output raise the price of the product and increase costs
    d. None of the above
20. The *LRS* curve of a decreasing-cost industry is
    a. Upward sloping
    b. Horizontal
    c. Downward sloping
    d. Vertical

Problems and Exercises (Use Quad Paper for Graphs)

Answers to these questions can be found on MyEconLab   MyEconLab

1. The demand schedule facing a firm is shown below in columns 1 and 2 of Table 9.13.
    a. Compute *TR*, *AR*, and *MR*, and complete the table.
    b. Plot *AR* and *MR* on a graph.
    c. On the same graph, plot the demand curve.
    d. What do you notice about the demand curve and the *AR* curve?

Table 9.13	Demand and Revenue Data for a Firm			
Price ($) (1)	Quantity (2)	TR ($) (3)	AR ($) (4)	MR ($) (5)
5	1			
5	2			
5	3			
5	4			
5	5			
5	6			

2. Table 9.14 contains cost data for a firm in pure competition. The market price of the firm's product is $8.
    a. Complete the *TR* and profit columns.
    b. At what level of output does the firm earn maximum profits?
    c. Draw the firm's *TR* and *TC* curves.
3. The Perfect Print Company has the cost data shown in Table 9.15. The market price of the product is $5.

Table 9.14	Cost Data for a Firm		
Quantity	Total Cost ($)	Total Revenue ($)	Profit ($)
0	20		
1	24		
2	26		
3	27		
4	32		
5	38		
6	42		
7	60		
8	66		
9	82		
10	100		

Table 9.15	Cost Data for Perfect Print		
Quantity	Total Cost ($)	Total Revenue ($)	Profit ($)
0	10		
1	14		
2	17		
3	19		
4	20		
5	21		
6	23		
7	26		
8	30		
9	35		
10	44		

a. Calculate Perfect Print's *TR* at each level of output and complete the *TR* column.
b. Calculate Perfect Print's total profit and complete the profit column.

c. At what level of output does Perfect Print earn maximum profits?
d. Graph the *TR* and *TC* curves for Perfect Print and indicate the maximum profit.
4. Data for the Computex Corporation are given in Table 9.16. The market price of the product is $80.
  a. Complete the *TR* and total profit columns.
  b. At what level of output does Computex earn the highest profit?
  c. Complete the *MC* and *MR* columns and indicate the output level at which *MR* equals *MC*.
5. Table 9.17 refers to a purely competitive firm whose objective is to maximize is profits.
  a. Determine the price of the product.
  b. Complete the table.
  c. If the price were $80, should the firm continue to operate? Why or why not?
  d. If the price were to fall to $40, should the firm continue to operate? Why or why not?
  e. What is the minimum price this firm must receive to continue to operate in the short run?

Table 9.17		Cost and Revenue Data for a Purely Competitive Firm							
Output	TFC ($)	TVC ($)	TC ($)	AFC ($)	AVC ($)	ATC ($)	MC ($)	MR ($)	TR ($)
0	100	0	100						0
1	100	25							100
2	100	35							200
3	100	50							300
4	100	100							400
5	100	180							500
6	100	340							600
7	100	560							700

6. Use Table 9.17 to draw the firm's short-run supply curve.
7. Figure 9.16 shows cost curves for a purely competitive firm. Construct this firm's short-run supply schedule by completing the table below the figure.
8. The information in Table 9.18 is provided for the Best Hits Recording Company, which is a purely competitive firm. The price of its product is $20.

Table 9.16	Data for Computex Corporation				
Output	TC ($)	TR ($)	MC ($)	MR ($)	Total Profit ($)
0	180				
1	200				
2	220				
3	240				
4	268				
5	310				
6	372				
7	460				
8	580				
9	900				
10	1500				

Table 9.18	Cost Data for Best Hits Recording Company				
Quantity	TR ($)	MR ($)	TC ($)	MC ($)	Profits ($)
1			30		
2			40		
3			48		
4			58		
5			70		
6			90		
7			120		
8			160		

Figure 9.16	Price and Cost Curves for a Purely Competitive Firm

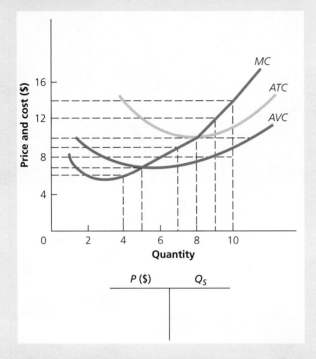

Figure 9.18	Cost and Revenue Curves for a Purely Competitive Firm

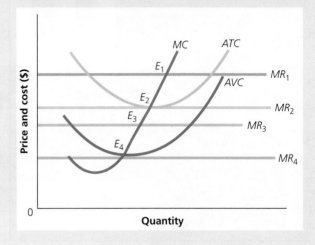

a. Complete the table and determine what level of output the firm should produce to maximize its profits.
b. On graph paper, draw the *TR* and *TC* curves. At what level of output is the difference between *TR* and *TC* greatest?
c. On graph paper, draw the *MR* and *MC* curves. At what level of output do these curves intersect?

9. Figure 9.17 illustrates a purely competitive firm.
a. If the price is $14, the profit-maximizing output will be _____ units. *TC* will be $_____, *TR* will be $_____, and total profits will be $_____.
b. If the price is $12, the equilibrium output will be _____ units. At this output, TR will be $_____, *TC* will be $_____, and total profit will be $_____.
c. If the price is $6, the equilibrium output will be _____ units.
d. This firm should shut down if the price falls below $_____.

10. Referring to Figure 9.18, describe the firm's position in terms of profitability for each *MR* curve shown.

Figure 9.17	Price and Cost for a Purely Competitive Firm

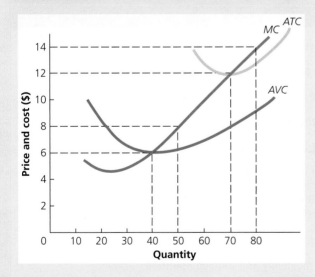

Chapter **10**
Monopoly

Learning Objectives

After studying this chapter, you should be able to

10.1 Understand the nature of monopoly

10.2 Discuss reasons for the existence of monopoly

10.3 Describe the demand and marginal revenue for a firm in monopoly

10.4 Understand the pricing and output decisions of a monopolist

10.5 Discuss the profit level of the monopolist

10.6 Understand the relation among elasticity, total revenue, and marginal revenue for a monopolist

10.7 Understand the long-run behaviour of a monopolist

10.8 Compare and contrast monopoly and pure competition

10.9 Understand monopoly regulation

10.10 Explain a monopolist's allocation of output among multiple plants

10.11 Understand price discrimination

10.12 Discuss the effects of taxes on a monopoly

Assess Your Knowledge

MyEconLab

Answers to these questions can be found on MyEconLab at **www.myeconlab.com**.

1. Can you think of a reason why we do not have several private train companies providing train services between Canadian cities?

2. Indicate whether each of the following statements is true or false:
   a. A monopoly can sell as much as it wants to sell at whatever price it wants to charge. (T, F)
   b. Monopolies have so much power that they never sustain losses. (T, F)

LO 10.1 Understand the nature of monopoly

The Nature of Monopoly

What problems are encountered in defining monopoly?

In the previous chapter, we defined a monopoly as a market structure in which a single firm produces a product that has no close substitutes. In pure monopoly, the firm and the industry are identical. That definition seems simple and straightforward enough, but it raises some important issues. First, the notion of close substitutes is subjective and arbitrary. Although most people may agree that the TomTom brand of GPS is a close substitute for the Garmin brand, they may not agree so easily on electricity and oil, or on microwave ovens and toaster ovens, for example. Electricity and oil can be considered close substitutes for heating purposes, but very poor substitutes, or not substitutes at all, for lighting purposes. Second (and this is related to the first), the definition of monopoly and the product that is monopolized are inseparable.

Is it easy to find good examples of monopoly?

Just as it is difficult to find real-world examples of pure competition, so too is it difficult to find examples of pure monopoly. The term *monopoly* often conjures up an image of a large firm that mercilessly takes advantage of consumers, controls price and output, and earns unconscionably large profits. But not all monopolies deserve this unscrupulous image. Public utilities are often monopolies. You may be able to think of some local monopolies in your area: the local public transit system or the water supply system, for example. Here are just a few of the monopolies operating in Canada today: Bank of Canada (monopoly on note issue); Canada Post (monopoly on delivery of first-class mail); Via Rail (monopoly on rail travel in Canada); and Société des alcools du Québec (monopoly on alcohol retail sale).

Reading Comprehension

The answers to these questions can be found on MyEconLab at **www.myeconlab.com**.   MyEconLab

1. What difficulty is involved in defining a monopoly?
2. Give an example of a firm that is a monopoly.

<table>
<tr><td>LO 10.2 Discuss reasons for the existence of monopoly</td><td></td></tr>
</table>

Barriers to Entry

How does a firm come to be the only one that serves a particular market?

For a monopoly to exist, circumstances must restrict the entry of other firms into the particular monopolized industry. Economists have discussed three main kinds of barriers, any one or combination of which can enable a firm to become a monopoly. Let us look at these barriers.

Barriers Created by the Government   You are a very enterprising student of economics and you have come up with an idea that you believe will earn you a great deal of money. You and your friends are going to pick up letters, mainly from businesses, and deliver them to their destination anywhere within a radius of 30 km from the downtown core. You know you can do this at a cost significantly below what the post office charges and still make a very good profit.

Hold it! You can't do it. The government won't let you. Sure, you can pick up and deliver letters, but it's illegal to do it for less than what the post office charges. You will have to dream up some other scheme for making your million dollars. The government prevents other firms from entering certain industries and competing with the existing firms. This type of legal barrier is quite common and quite effective in maintaining monopolies.

patent an exclusive right that a government grants a producer to produce a product

A **patent**, which is an exclusive right that the government grants to a producer to produce a product, is another legal device used to maintain monopolies. During the term of the patent, the firm is protected against potential competitors. Patents can often be circumvented, however, for although other firms are not allowed to produce an identical product or offer an identical service, they can produce a product or service that is quite similar.

BUSINESS SITUATION 10.1

Northern Pharmaceuticals, Inc. (a hypothetical company) has developed a drug that has proved to be successful in treating migraine headaches.

What can this company do to prevent other pharmaceutical companies from duplicating its product?

The answer to this Business Situation can be found in Appendix A.

---

franchise an exclusive right to operate a business in a certain geographical area

A government can also grant a producer a **franchise**, which is an exclusive right to operate a business in a certain area. The granting of a franchise means that no other firm can legally operate an identical business or provide an identical service in the same area. Canada Post, which has the exclusive right to deliver first-class mail in Canada, is an example of a public franchise.

Does this mean that only governments can grant franchises?

No. You should not interpret the foregoing to mean that only governments can grant franchises. Private concerns can also grant franchises. If you obtain a franchise from

McDonald's, you are protected against competition from any other McDonald's restaurant, because another one will not be established within the designated boundaries of your business area. You will enjoy a monopoly on McDonald's hamburgers, but you will face competition from Harvey's, Wendy's, Burger King, and other fast-food restaurants that will operate in close proximity to your restaurant.

Barriers Created by Ownership or Control of Essential Raw Materials   If a particular firm owns a raw material essential to the production of a certain product, and if the firm does not allow any other firm to use that essential material, then obviously a monopoly situation will develop. For example, bauxite is a necessary ingredient in the production of aluminum. If one company owns or controls all sources of bauxite in the country, and if the importation of bauxite or aluminum is strictly forbidden by law, then that company will have a monopoly in the domestic market for aluminum. One Johannesburg- and London-based diamond mining and trading corporation, the De Beers Group, has a virtual monopoly on the world's diamond market because it owns or controls most of the world's diamond mines. Using its monopoly power, De Beers has created an artificial scarcity of diamonds, thus keeping prices high.

Barriers Created by Economies of Scale   Because of substantial economies of scale, sometimes a single firm can satisfy the entire market demand more cheaply than two or more firms could. This is typically referred to as a **natural monopoly**. Often, the cost of establishing an efficient plant in this case is enormous, and the minimum average cost (*AC*) will be covered only at a level of output large enough to supply the entire market. If two or more firms are in this type of industry, the *AC* will be quite high because these firms divide the total market supply. Consider how much it would cost to start up a telephone company to provide telephone service to people in a certain area. Now compare that cost with the cost to an existing telephone company of providing the same service to those people. The case of a natural monopoly is analyzed with the help of Figure 10.1.

The downward-sloping long-run average cost (*LRAC*) curve in Figure 10.1 illustrates economies of scale. The total quantity demanded is 10 units, as shown by the demand curve *DD*. A single firm can produce the total quantity demanded at an *AC* of $3, while with two firms sharing the same market, each producing five units of output, *AC* rises to $6. When the *LRAC* curve is declining throughout (i.e., when economies of scale are present), it is always cheaper for a single firm to serve the entire industry. Examples of natural monopolies are telephone companies, gas companies, and electric power companies, like Hydro-Québec and Ontario Hydro.

natural monopoly a market in which a single firm can satisfy the entire market demand more cheaply than two or more firms could

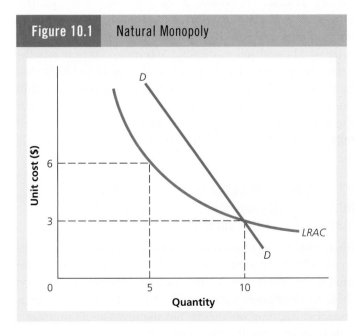

Figure 10.1   Natural Monopoly

Reading Comprehension

1. What is the difference between a patent and a franchise?

2. Define *natural monopoly*.

3. List and discuss factors that give rise to monopolies.

LO 10.3 Describe the demand and marginal revenue for a firm in monopoly

The Demand and Marginal Revenue Curves for a Firm in Monopoly

The demand curve for a firm in pure competition is a horizontal straight line. Is this the same for a firm in monopoly?

Not at all. A firm in pure competition faces a perfectly elastic demand curve. The firm has no control over the price. This is not the case in monopoly. Earlier in this book, we noted that the market demand curve slopes downward from left to right. Because the monopolist is the only firm in the industry, the demand curve is exactly the same as the industry or market demand curve. If the monopolist wants to sell a larger quantity, it can do so by lowering the price of its product. If it increases the price of its product, the quantity that it can sell will decrease.

Figure 10.2 shows the demand curve for a hypothetical monopolist. At a price of $11, the quantity demanded is 100 units; therefore, the monopolist can sell 100 units. When the price is $4, it can sell 200 units. Note that the monopolist is not a price-taker: it does have significant control over the price it charges for its product. However, it cannot completely control both price and quantity. If the monopolist has the demand curve shown in Figure 10.2, it cannot, for example, charge a price of $11 and sell more than 100 units. Once it sets the price, the quantity that it can sell at that price is determined by the demand curve. The monopolist must operate within the constraint imposed by its demand curve. The fact that the demand curve facing the monopolist slopes downward tells us that the demand for its product is not perfectly inelastic.

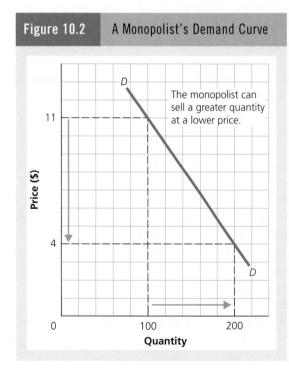

Figure 10.2   A Monopolist's Demand Curve

The monopolist can sell a greater quantity at a lower price.

OK. The demand curve for the monopolist is downward sloping. What is the shape of the marginal revenue curve?

Recall that under pure competition, demand (or average revenue, *AR*) and marginal revenue (*MR*) are identical. Under monopoly, however, this is not the case. It becomes necessary, then, to distinguish between *AR* (demand) and *MR*. *MR* is crucial in deciding whether or not the firm should produce a little more or a little less to maximize its profits. A declining *AR*

Table 10.1	Hypothetical Demand and Marginal Revenue for a Monopolist		
Price ($)	Quantity	TR ($)	MR ($)
10	1	10	
			8
9	2	18	
			6
8	3	24	
			4
7	4	28	
			2
6	5	30	
			0
5	6	30	
			−2
4	7	28	
			−4
3	8	24	

implies a declining *MR* (remember the magnetic effect of the marginal on the average). Moreover, the *MR* will fall at a faster rate than *AR*. This must be the case because to sell a larger volume of output, the monopolist receives a lower price on those units it could have sold at a higher price had it not chosen to increase its output. Table 10.1 helps to illustrate this idea.

Table 10.1 shows that the monopolist can sell one unit of output if the price is $10. The firm can sell two units only if it charges a price of $9. Total revenue (price × quantity) is now $18—an increase of $8 because of the sale of the additional unit. In other words, MR is now $8. The firm could have sold the first unit for $9, thus losing $1 of the sale price on that unit. Similarly, the firm can sell three units only if the price is $8. Total revenue (TR) is now 24 and MR is $6. The firm could also have sold the first two units for $9 each, thus losing $1 of the sale price on each of the first two units. This exercise shows the following:

> For a monopoly, *MR* is less than *AR* and falls at a faster rate than *AR*.

Note that price and *AR* are identical—a relation you learned in the previous chapter. Figure 10.3 shows the relation between *AR* and *MR*.

Note: If the demand and *MR* curves are both linear and downward sloping, then the *MR* curve will bisect any horizontal line between the vertical axis and the demand curve. In Figure 10.4, the *MR* curve bisects 0*Q* and *HK*.

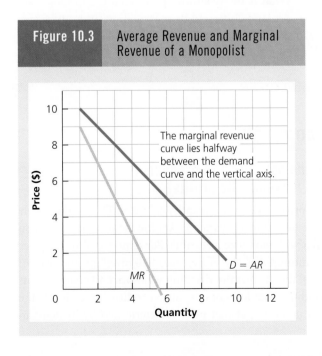

Figure 10.3 Average Revenue and Marginal Revenue of a Monopolist

The marginal revenue curve lies halfway between the demand curve and the vertical axis.

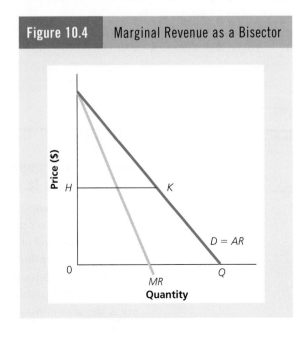

Figure 10.4 Marginal Revenue as a Bisector

Figure 10.5	The Total Revenue Curve of a Monopolist

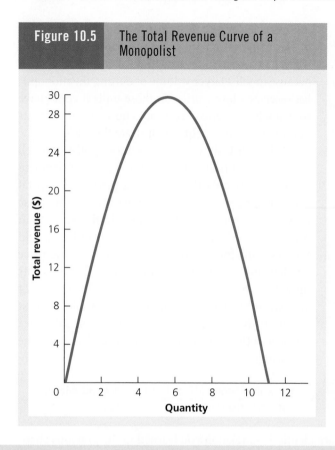

What does the monopolist's total revenue curve look like?

Clearly, if the monopolist produces nothing, its *TR* will be zero. Therefore, the *TR* curve starts at the origin. And if the price is zero, the monopolist's *TR* will also be zero. Table 10.1 and Figure 10.5 show that the monopolist's *TR* rises as price falls, reaches a maximum, and then falls.

We have seen that the concept of *MR* is important in determining the output level at which the firm maximizes its profits. (Recall the *MR* = *MC* rule for profit maximization.) We will use this profit maximization rule to analyze the pricing and output decision of the monopolist.

Reading Comprehension

The answers to these questions can be found on MyEconLab at www.myeconlab.com.   MyEconLab

1. Explain why a monopolist faces a downward-sloping demand curve.

2. What is the relationship between the monopolist's demand curve and its marginal revenue curve?

3. Describe the shape of the monopolist's total revenue curve.

LO 10.4	Understand the pricing and output decisions of a monopolist

Equilibrium under Monopoly

How does a monopolist decide how much to produce and what price to charge to maximize its profits?

The firm in pure competition is a price-taker and a quantity-adjuster. That is, the purely competitive firm accepts the price determined by the market for the product, and then decides on the level of output that will maximize its profits. For a monopolist, the price of the product is not given. The monopolist, therefore, faces two problems in terms of its profit-maximization objectives: the problem of deciding what price to charge for its product and the problem of deciding what level of output to produce. Once it sets the price, the maximum output that it can sell at that price is determined by its demand curve.

Price ($)	Total Quantity (units)	Marginal Cost ($)	Total Cost ($)	Marginal Revenue ($)	Revenue ($)	Profits ($)
11	0	10		0		−10
			2		10	
10	1	12		10		−2
			3		8	
9	2	15		18		3
			2		6	
8	3	17		24		7
			4		4	
7	4	21		28		7
			5		2	
6	5	26		30		4
			7		0	
5	6	33		30		−3
			10		−2	
4	7	43		28		−15
			17		−4	
3	8	60		24		−36

Table 10.2 Hypothetical Cost and Revenue Data for a Monopolist

For simplicity, we assume that the monopolist faces a cost situation similar to that faced by a firm in any other type of market structure. Table 10.2 contains hypothetical cost and revenue figures for a firm in a monopoly situation.

Profits are maximized at a level of output between three and four units, where the difference between *TR* ($24 or $28) and total cost ($17 or $21) is greatest at $7, and the price $8 or $7. Alternatively, using the *MR* = *MC* condition, we arrive at the same conclusion that the monopolist maximizes its profits by producing three or four units and selling at a price of $7 or $8.

Can the profit-maximizing position of the monopolist be illustrated graphically?

Yes. Figure 10.6 illustrates graphically the relations between the data shown in Table 10.2. In this figure, *MR* = *MC* at a level of output of three or four units. The maximum profit is shown in Diagram A as the greatest distance between *TR* and *TC* and as the shaded area in Diagram B, where the firm is shown to be producing 3.5 units at a price of $7.5. The per-unit profit is ($7.5 − $5.5) = $2; therefore, the total profit is (3.5 × $2) = $7. Diagram C shows the total profit curve, where the maximum profit is again $7.

We have determined the price-output combination that maximizes the profits of the monopolist. Given the conditions of demand and cost, any other price-output combination results in lower profits for the monopolist. But whether or not the monopolist will choose to charge the particular price at which profit is greatest is another question.

| Figure 10.6 | Profit Maximization for a Monopolist |

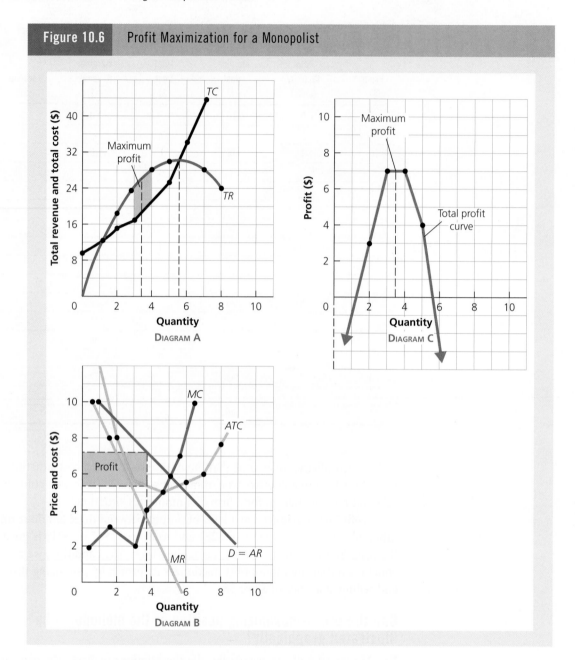

Are you suggesting that a monopolist may choose not to maximize its profits?

For several logical reasons, the monopolist may decide against earning maximum profits. First, extremely high profits provide incentive for other firms to attempt to break through the entry barriers and end the monopoly. Second, social conscience may prevent those who make the decisions in the monopoly from undertaking measures necessary to maximize profits. Public opinion may enter into such a decision, and the firm may want to *appear* to be acting in the public interest. In this case, the firm may decide to earn a satisfactory profit instead of trying to earn maximum profits. Third, the monopolist may want to avoid provoking the government to regulate its price and other profit factors.

The firm shown in Figure 10.6 is earning positive profits (its price is above its average total cost or *ATC*). This situation could continue even in the long run because barriers effectively block the entry of new firms into the industry. If potential firms are able to surmount the entry barriers and compete with the monopoly, the monopoly will be destroyed and the positive economic profits will dwindle in the long run.

BUSINESS SITUATION 10.2

All the electricity in a small town is provided by a private electricity generating company known as Total Electricity. Total Electricity charges a fixed price per day for its electricity. Through thorough economic analysis, Total Electricity has determined that its profit-maximizing price (rate) is $0.70 per day. Instead of charging $0.70 per day, the company charges $0.65 per day.

Is there any rationale in Total Electricity's pricing policy?

The answer to this Business Situation can be found in Appendix A.

Reading Comprehension

The answers to these questions can be found on MyEconLab at www.myeconlab.com.   MyEconLab

1. "Because of its tremendous market power, a monopolist can produce and sell any volume of output at any price it wants." Discuss briefly.

2. How does a monopolist decide how much to produce and what price to charge to maximize profits?
3. What considerations may lead a monopolist to seek less than maximum profits?
4. "A profit-seeking monopolist will always charge the highest possible price for its product." Discuss.

LO 10.5 Discuss the profit level of the monopolist

The Monopolist's Profit Level

Can a monopolist, with all its market power, incur losses?

Yes. A commonly held misconception is that monopolies always make huge profits. In fact, although some monopolies make huge profits, others incur losses. In some cases, excessively high production costs result in losses to the firm. Such a situation is illustrated in Figure 10.7.

At an output level of Q_1, this monopolist is doing the best it can under the existing circumstances. It is producing an output at which $MR = MC$. Nevertheless, the firm is incurring losses because the price, P, is below *ATC*. The price is, however, above the firm's average variable cost (*AVC*). The firm, then, will likely continue to operate in the short run to minimize its losses. These losses are shown in the shaded area in Figure 10.7. In the long run, however, the firm will likely shift its resources into more profitable uses.

Figure 10.7	A Monopoly Minimizing Its Losses

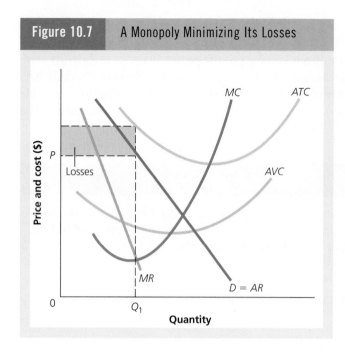

The firm can try to improve its profit position by increasing its *TR*. It would be possible to increase *TR* if the firm could raise its price by a certain percentage without reducing the quantity demanded by a similar or larger percentage. Quite often, this is easier said than done. The firm could try to shift its demand curve to the right. Advertising is one means of trying to shift the firm's demand curve to the right.

What effect will inefficiency have on the profit level of the monopolist?

The monopolist, being the only firm in the industry, may not feel the need to control cost adequately. It can adopt the attitude that customers have no alternative but to buy its product because there are no competing firms. Such inefficiency can destroy the profit potential of the monopoly. The term **X-inefficiency** is used to describe the condition that exists when a firm fails to use its resources in their most economically efficient way.

X-inefficiency a condition that exists when a firm fails to use its resources in their most economically efficient way

X-inefficiency can result from keeping on unproductive workers out of loyalty, putting unproductive relatives and friends on the payroll, or padding executives' expense accounts.

Can we use diagrams to illustrate the effect of X-inefficiency on the profit level of the monopolist?

Yes. Let's look at Figure 10.8. The figure shows the effect of X-inefficiency on the profit level of the monopolist. Diagram A shows an efficient monopolist, while Diagram B shows an inefficiently run monopolist.

Figure 10.8	The Effect of X-Inefficiency of the Monopolist's Profit

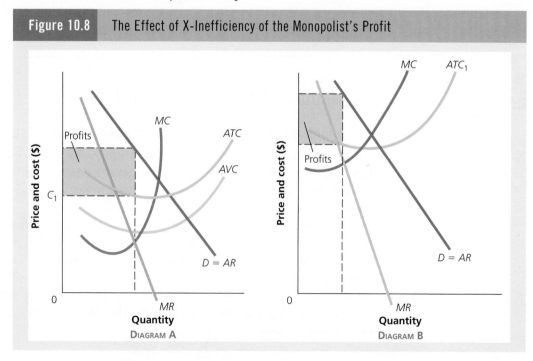

The demand and *MR* curves of both firms are identical. The efficient monopolist produces its output at an *ATC* of C_1. Note that the average total cost (ATC_1) of the inefficient monopolist is higher than that (*ATC*) of the efficient monopolist. This illustrates X-inefficiency. The smaller profit earned by the inefficient monopolist is due to X-inefficiency.

Reading Comprehension

The answers to these questions can be found on MyEconLab at **www.myeconlab.com**.   MyEconLab

1. Do monopolies always earn huge economic profits? Explain.

2. What is X-inefficiency? Mention two practices that might result in X-inefficiency.

3. How does X-inefficiency affect the monopolist's profit level?

LO 10.6 Understand the relation among elasticity, total revenue, and marginal revenue for a monopolist

Elasticity, Total Revenue, and Marginal Revenue

What is the relationship among elasticity, total revenue, and marginal revenue of a monopolist?

Remember that if the demand for a product is elastic, a reduction in price will cause *TR* to increase. But *TR* can increase only if *MR* is positive. It follows, therefore, that if *MR* is positive, the demand for the product in that range must be elastic.

When the price elasticity of demand is unitary, a reduction in the price of the product will not change *TR*. If *TR* is stable, then *MR* must be zero. Therefore, it follows that when *MR* is zero, the elasticity of demand for the product at that price must be one.

An inelastic demand implies that a reduction in price will cause *TR* to fall. But *TR* can fall only if *MR* is negative. Hence, when *MR* is negative, the demand for the product must be inelastic.

Can we summarize these relations?

Yes.

Summary of Relations among Elasticity, Total Revenue, and Marginal Revenue

1. If $MR > 0$, *TR* will rise, and demand is elastic.
2. If $MR = 0$, *TR* is at a maximum, and demand is unitary elastic.
3. If $MR < 0$, *TR* will fall, and demand is inelastic.

Can we show these relationships in a table or on a graph?

Table 10.3 shows the relation among demand, *TR*, and *MR* for a monopolist.

Table 10.3	Demand, Total Revenue, and Marginal Revenue for a Monopolist		
Quantity (units)	**Price** ($)	**Total Revenue** ($)	**Marginal Revenue** ($)
0	10.50	0	
			10
1	10.00	10	
			9
2	9.50	19	
			8
3	9.00	27	
			7
4	8.50	34	
			6
5	8.00	40	
			5
6	7.50	45	
			4
7	7.00	49	
			3
8	6.50	52	
			2
9	6.00	54	
			1
10	5.50	55	
			0
11	5.00	55	
			−1
12	4.50	54	
			−2
13	4.00	52	
			−3
14	3.50	49	
			−4
15	3.00	45	
			−5
16	2.50	40	
			−6
17	2.00	34	
			−7
18	1.50	27	
			−8
19	1.00	19	
			−9
20	0.50	10	

The relationship is also illustrated graphically in Figure 10.9. At an output level less than Q_1, MR is positive, TR is rising, and demand for the product is elastic in that range. At an output level of Q_1, MR equals 0, TR is at its maximum, and demand is unitary elastic at a price of P. At an output level greater than Q_1, MR is negative, TR is falling, and demand is inelastic at any price below P.

The monopolist incurs additional costs as it increases its output—that is, its marginal cost (MC) is positive. This implies that the MR and MC will intersect at some positive value. But if MR is positive, the demand is elastic. This leads to the following proposition:

A profit-maximizing monopolist will operate only within that range where the demand for its product is elastic.

Figure 10.9	Relations among Demand, Total Revenue, Marginal Revenue, and Elasticity

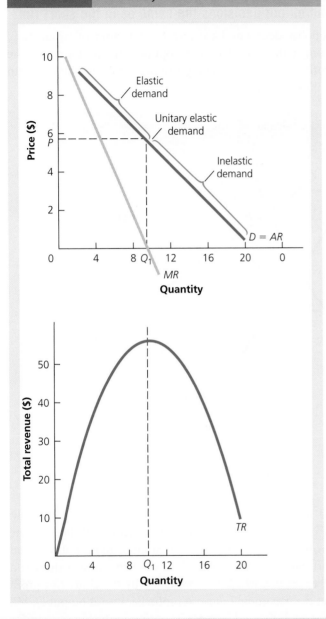

Reading Comprehension

The answers to these questions can be found on MyEconLab at www.myeconlab.com.

1. Explain why a profit-seeking monopolist will not operate at a level of output and price range at which the demand for its product is inelastic.

2. What can you say about total revenue and elasticity of demand when marginal revenue is zero?

Monopoly Behaviour in the Long Run

Does the firm in a monopoly situation have to adjust to the long-run situation? Are its price and output decisions the same as in the short run?

In the long run, the monopolist does not have any fixed factors of production. Compared with the short run, it therefore has more options. In the long run, the monopolist maximizes its profits when it equates long-run marginal cost (*LRMC*) with *MR*. Figure 10.10 helps us to illustrate the point.

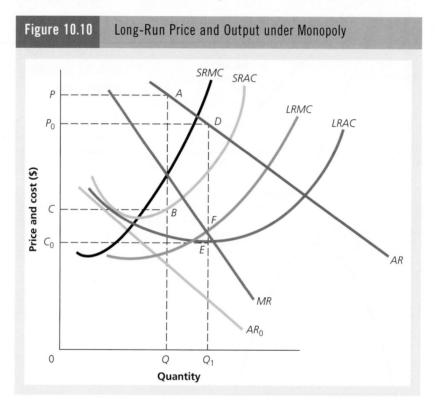

Figure 10.10   Long-Run Price and Output under Monopoly

The average revenue and marginal revenue curves are *AR* and *MR*, respectively. The short-run average cost is *SRAC* and the short-run marginal cost is *SRMC* in Figure 10.10. In the short run, the profit-seeking monopolist will produce an output of Q and charge a price of P. The short-run unit cost is QB; thus, the firm earns a short-run maximum total profit of BA times $0Q$, which is represented by the short-run profit rectangle $PABC$. But this is not the maximum long-run profit, because at output Q, MR is greater than *LRMC*. The monopolist would increase its output in the long run to Q_1, determined by the intersection of MR and *LRMC* at point F, and charge a price of P_0. At Q_1, the firm earns a per-unit profit of ED and a total profit of ED times $0Q_1$, which is equal to the rectangle P_0DEC_0. This is the maximum profit possible when the monopolist has sufficient time to vary all its inputs.

What will a monopolist do if it is incurring losses in the long run?

In the long run, the monopolist will exit the industry if it is operating at a loss. Referring to Figure 10.10, if the monopolist's *AR* curve, AR_0, is below its *LRAC* at all output levels, it will leave the industry.

Reading Comprehension

The answers to these questions can be found on MyEconLab at www.myeconlab.com.   MyEconLab

1. Compare the short-run equilibrium position of a monopoly with its long-run equilibrium position.

2. What will a monopolist do if its average revenue curve falls below its long-run average cost curve?

LO 10.8 Compare and contrast monopoly and pure competition

allocative efficiency the condition that exists when price equals marginal cost

Monopoly versus Pure Competition

What other comparisons can be made between monopoly and pure competition?

The model of pure competition serves as a convenient reference for the evaluation of other market structures. It is a useful exercise to compare the price and output behaviours of a purely competitive industry with those of a monopoly.

First, in a purely competitive market, each firm charges a price that just equals its MC. Economists refer to this situation as **allocative efficiency**, which is the condition that exists when resources are optimally allocated. This occurs when price equals MC.

In pure competition, resources are allocated efficiently. In a monopoly, the price is above MC. Therefore, resources are not allocated efficiently. This situation is illustrated graphically in Figure 10.11. We assume that the cost curves are the same in both market structures. AR represents the demand or average revenue of the monopolist, which is the same as the industry demand curve. For convenience, we show the position of one of the

| Figure 10.11 | Monopoly and Pure Competition Compared |

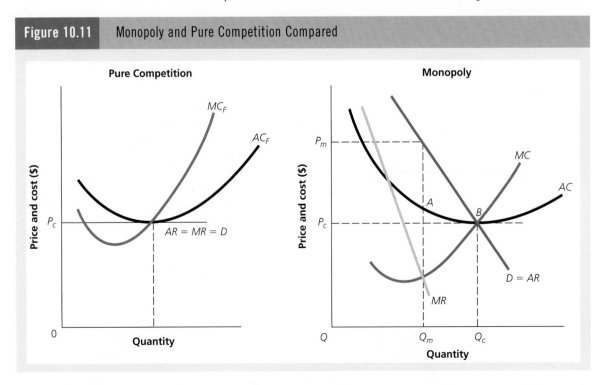

firms in the competitive industry in the diagram on the left. The subscript F indicates that the reference is to the firm. The comparison between monopoly and pure competition is illustrated in the diagram on the right.

To maximize profits, the monopolist produces an output of Q_m and charges a price of P_m, thus equating MR and MC. The purely competitive price will be P_c, which equals MC. Note that the monopoly price P_m is greater than MC.

Second, the purely competitive output is produced at a minimum unit cost. This is not the case under monopoly. The monopolist produces its output at a higher unit cost. Figure 10.11 shows that the profit-maximizing monopolist produces at point A on the AC curve. In the long run, however, production in a purely competitive industry occurs at point B, the minimum point on the AC curve.

Third, other things being equal, the monopolist produces less output than the competitive industry does. As illustrated in Figure 10.11, the monopolist produces an output of Q_m while the competitive industry produces an output of Q_c. This suggests that employment will be greater in the competitive industry than in the monopoly. The monopolist charges a higher price and supplies a smaller quantity than the purely competitive industry does.

Finally, if the monopolist's price is greater than its AC, it will earn positive economic profits. If the firms in a purely competitive industry earn positive profits in the short run, other firms will enter the industry and compete until profits settle down at zero in the long run. In the case of the monopolist, however, positive profits may remain because of barriers preventing other firms from entering the industry.

How does monopoly affect consumer surplus and producer surplus?

Let us answer this question with the help of Figure 10.12. Diagram A shows a purely competitive industry, while Diagram B shows a monopoly. The demand and cost curves are identical in each case.

Figure 10.12   Consumer Surplus, Producer Surplus, and Deadweight Loss under Monopoly

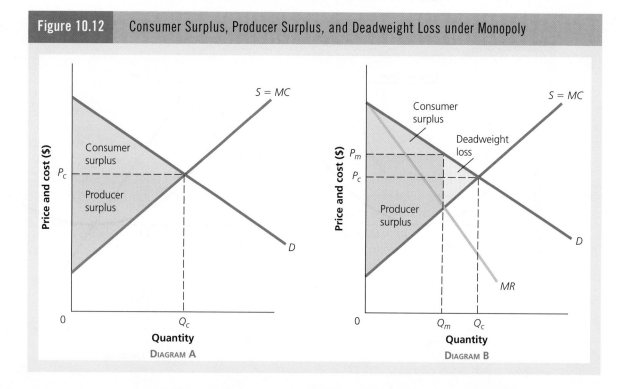

In Diagram A, the purely competitive industry produces an output of Q_c at a price of P_c. Consumer surplus is illustrated by the blue triangle, while producer surplus is represented by the red triangle. In Diagram B, the monopoly produces an output of Q_m at a price of P_m. The blue triangle represents consumer surplus while the red area represents producer surplus. Note that the consumer surplus under monopoly is less than that under pure competition. Note also that under monopoly, a deadweight loss occurs, represented by the yellow triangle in Diagram B. No deadweight loss occurs under pure competition. This analysis leads to the following conclusion:

> Monopoly reduces consumer surplus, increases producer surplus, and creates a deadweight loss.

Reading Comprehension

The answers to these questions can be found on MyEconLab at **www.myeconlab.com.**   MyEconLab

1. Define allocative efficiency.

2. From a societal point of view, what advantages does pure competition have over monopoly?

3. How does monopoly affect consumer surplus and producer surplus?

LO 10.9 Understand monopoly regulation

The Regulated Monopoly

What theoretical guidelines are available to a government for regulating monopoly behaviour?

The analysis presented in the previous section suggests that monopolies have certain economic and social consequences that are less desirable than those associated with pure competition. Compared with pure competition, for example, the monopolist produces a smaller output at a higher unit cost and sells at a higher price, other things being equal. This ability of a firm to exert control over price and output is called **monopoly power** or **market power**.

monopoly power or market power the ability of a firm to exert control over price and output

The misallocation of resources associated with monopolies has no parallel in the purely competitive market structure. The prices charged by many natural monopolies are determined by government regulatory agencies. Let us now answer the question by turning our attention to the ways in which a government or its regulatory agencies can regulate monopolies, and the consequences of such regulation. We will examine marginal-cost pricing, average-cost pricing, and minimum average-cost pricing. Let us discuss each in turn.

Marginal-Cost Pricing   We noted that a monopolist will operate at a point where price is greater than *MC*. Let us examine the consequences of a regulatory body setting the monopolist's price at a level equal to its *MC*. Figure 10.13 will help to clarify the effects of monopoly regulation.

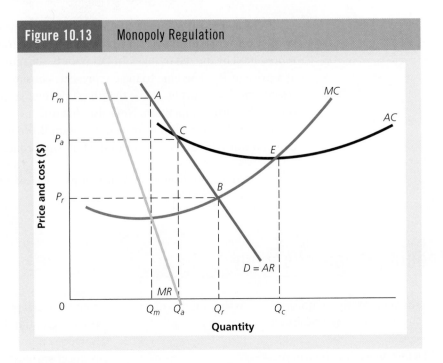

Figure 10.13 Monopoly Regulation

The diagram illustrates a natural monopoly. Note that because of huge fixed costs, the AR curve cuts the AC curve while the latter is still falling. The unregulated monopolist seeking to maximize profits produces an output of Q_m and sells at a price of P_m because, at this point, MR equals MC (position A in Figure 10.13). A regulation that sets price equal to MC will cause the monopolist to produce an output of Q_r at a price of P_r (position B). By setting a price of P_r, the regulatory agency prevents the monopolist from restricting output to exact a higher price. Marginal-cost pricing does not necessarily result in losses for the monopolist, but it sometimes does. The firm depicted in Figure 10.13 incurs a loss by operating where price equals MC. Because no firm wants to continue to incur losses indefinitely, this firm will have to take measures to survive, or leave the industry. If the monopoly is considered to be essential to society, the government could decide to take over its operation and endure the losses resulting from marginal-cost pricing, or it could subsidize the monopoly. But the notion of a government subsidizing a private monopoly is likely to incite public indignation.

Average-Cost Pricing If the regulatory agency considers marginal-cost pricing to be inappropriate, it can consider average-cost pricing as an alternative. Average-cost pricing regulation sets the price of the product equal to the AC (position C in Figure 10.13). Under average-cost pricing, the monopolist will produce an output of Q_a and charge a price of P_a. This alternative eliminates any monopoly profits that the monopolist would otherwise have made. Average-cost pricing is in accordance with the idea of a fair return on the owners' resources. Note that average-cost pricing results in a level of output of Q_a that, though greater than the unregulated monopoly output Q_m, is still less than the socially optimum output of Q_r, where price equals MC.

Minimum Average-Cost Pricing Finally, the regulatory agency can choose to have the monopolist operate at the lowest point on the AC curve (point E in Figure 10.13). If the AC curve declines over a large range of output, as in Figure 10.13, this minimum point could occur at a level of output too large for the market served by the monopolist.

To operate at the minimum point on the *AC* curve, this monopolist would have to produce a level of output of Q_c—just slightly less than the firm would be able to sell even at a very low price. The alternative chosen by the regulatory body ultimately depends on its objective. In any case, the regulated monopoly produces a larger output and sells at a lower price than if the monopoly were not regulated.

Reading Comprehension

The answers to these questions can be found on MyEconLab at www.myeconlab.com.   MyEconLab

1. Explain the term *monopoly power*. What actions might a government take to prevent the abuse of monopoly power?

2. What problem can result from marginal-cost pricing regulation of a monopoly?
3. In what way does monopoly regulation by government benefit the public?

LO 10.10 Explain a monopolist's allocation of output among multiple plants

The Multi-Plant Monopolist

How does a multi-plant monopolist decide how to distribute its output in each plant to maximize profits?

Up to this point in our analysis, we have assumed that the monopolist operates only one plant. It is quite possible that the monopolist will produce the output in more than one plant, and it is likely that cost conditions in each plant will differ. Let us consider the case where the monopolist produces its output in two plants. Figure 10.14 will help us with the analysis.

| Figure 10.14 | The Profit-Maximizing Multi-Plant Monopolist |

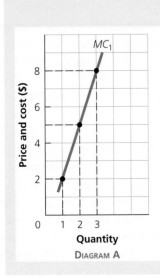
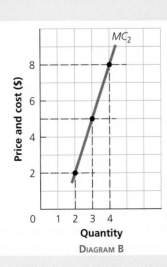
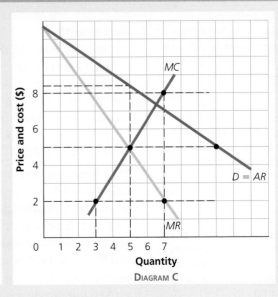

MC_1 in Diagram A is the MC curve for plant 1, while MC_2 in Diagram B is the MC curve for plant 2. For simplicity, we assume that the MC curves are linear. The monopolist achieves an MC of $2 when it produces one unit of output in plant 1 and two units in plant 2. This suggests that the monopolist's MC of producing $1 + 2 = 3$ units is $3. This is shown in Diagram C. The MC of producing three units in plant 1 and four units in plant 2 is $8, which means that the MC of producing $3 + 4 = 7$ units is $8. The MC curve of the multi-plant monopolist is the horizontal summation of the MC curves of each plant. The monopolist's MC curve is shown in Diagram C. Diagram C also shows the demand and MR curves of the monopolist. The profit-maximizing level of output occurs where the MR and MC curves intersect. The monopolist will produce a total of five units of output and sell at a price of $8.50, as shown in Diagram C. Of the five units, two will be produced in plant 1 and three in plant 2.

Reading Comprehension

The answers to these questions can be found on MyEconLab at **www.myeconlab.com.**   MyEconLab

1. For a multi-plant monopolist, explain how the monopolist's marginal cost curve is derived.

2. Explain how a profit-seeking monopolist will distribute the monopoly output between two plants.

LO 10.11 Understand price discrimination

The Discriminating Monopolist

What is price discrimination and why does a monopolist practise it?

In certain circumstances, the monopolist may find it profitable to charge different prices to different buyers for the same good or service. This practice of selling a product in different markets at different prices for reasons unrelated to cost is called **price discrimination**.

price discrimination the practice of selling a product in different markets at different prices for reasons unrelated to cost

Bell, for example, charges commercial users of its telephone service one price and residential users a different price. Many suppliers of electricity also have different rates for commercial and residential users. Similarly, lawyers may charge a wealthy client more than they charge a poor one for a similar case, or a company may sell exports in foreign countries more cheaply than the domestic price, which is referred to as **dumping**.

dumping the practice of selling exports in foreign countries more cheaply than the domestic price

Is price discrimination always possible?

Price discrimination is not always possible. To practise price discrimination, two conditions must be satisfied. First, the monopolist must be able to group the buyers of its product into different classes, such as rich and poor, adults and children, residential and commercial, or seniors and the rest of the population. Second, the monopolist must be able to maintain a separation between the markets in which the product is sold so that buyers will not be able to engage in **arbitrage transactions**. Arbitrage transactions refer to the purchase of products in a low-price market and their resale in a high-price market, thus producing a profit on the transactions.

arbitrage transactions the purchase of products in a low-price market and their resale in a high-price market

Those who buy in the market with the lower price must not be able to sell in the market with the higher price. If the monopolist cannot separate the markets in this way, the price will tend to rise in the cheaper market and fall in the more expensive market until the price differential is eliminated.

The monopolist practises price discrimination because it is profitable to do so. However, price discrimination will be profitable only if the price elasticity of demand in each market is different. The following example illustrates why price discrimination is profitable.

Suppose there are only two groups of people—students and professors—buying a certain product. Suppose also that students are willing to pay $10 per unit while the professors are willing to pay only $6. Obviously, the monopolist can increase its profits by charging a price of $10 to the students and a price of $6 to the professors. By not charging a single price of $6, the monopolist has succeeded in preventing the students from paying only $6 when they would be willing to pay $10. If, however, the monopolist charges a single price of $10, the professors will not purchase the product. We can use the concept of consumer surplus discussed earlier in this book to illustrate why the monopolist benefits from price discrimination. By charging each consumer the maximum amount that he or she is willing to pay, the monopolist captures the entire amount of the consumer surplus.

How does the monopolist determine the distribution of output between the separated markets?

The discriminating monopolist must decide how much to sell in each market and at what price. Figure 10.15 will help us to see how the decision is made. Diagrams A and B show the demand and *MR* curves in two markets, *A* and *B*, respectively.

Here, we assume, for simplicity, that the *MC* is constant in each market at 0*C*. To maximize profits, the monopolist will sell, in each market, an amount such that *MR* equals *MC*. The firm will therefore sell Q_a units in market *A* and Q_b units in market *B*.

Figure 10.15   The Distribution of Output by a Discriminating Monopolist

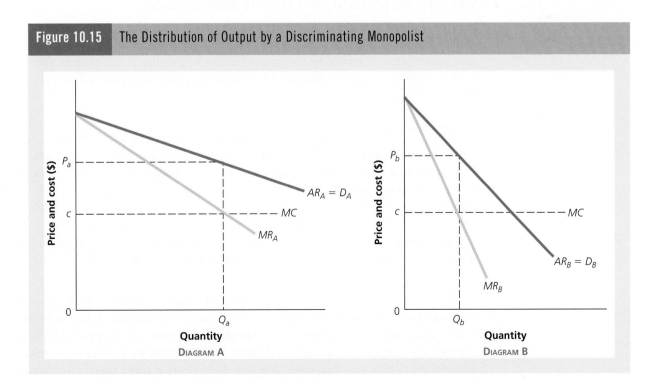

DIAGRAM A   DIAGRAM B

Figure 10.16	The Effect of Price Discrimination on Output

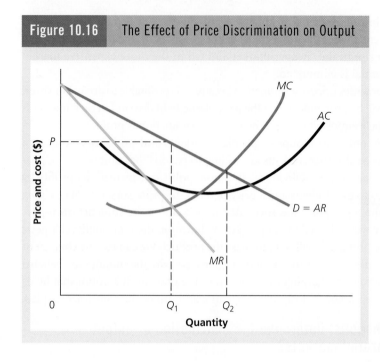

The price in market A will be P_a, while the price in market B will be P_b. Note that the higher price occurs in the market with the less elastic demand.

What are the effects of price discrimination?

We have already seen that by engaging in price discrimination, the monopolist can increase its profits. So that is one effect of price discrimination. Price discrimination also has an effect on the firm's output. Let's investigate with the help of Figure 10.16.

The graph illustrates that a non-discriminating monopolist will produce an output of Q_1, where MR equals MC. If it engages in complete price discrimination, selling each unit at the maximum price that a consumer is willing to pay, its demand curve will, in effect, become its MR curve. The discriminating monopolist will equate MR (its demand curve) and MC and thus produce an output of Q_2 units. It is unlikely that the monopolist will be able to practise complete price discrimination, because this would require the firm to know exactly the maximum price that each buyer is willing to pay. However, we can conclude that a discriminating monopolist will produce a greater output than a non-discriminating monopolist.

What are the pros and cons of price discrimination?

It is reasonable to conclude that many of those consumers who pay the higher prices under price discrimination consider the practice to be unfair. It is also clear that price discrimination is beneficial to the monopolists who practise it. Let us now proceed beyond these obvious conclusions and delve more deeply into the pros and cons of price discrimination.

The Pros On the positive side, many goods and services might not be produced at all if the monopolist were not allowed to engage in price discrimination. For example, the only lawyer in a small remote community may find it worthwhile to keep her practice in that community only if she can charge her wealthy clients a higher price than she can charge her less affluent clients. Similarly, where airlines and hotels enjoy monopoly power, price discrimination in airfares and hotel accommodation makes it possible for many parents to take their children on vacation. Price discrimination along these lines seems to be desirable and therefore should probably not be condemned.

The Cons On the negative side, the practice of price discrimination can be carried to the point where the price falls below MC. For example, price discrimination in electricity rates could result in such low rates to residential users that they end up wasting electricity. When price is allowed to fall below MC, a misallocation of resources results. The amount of resources that would flow into the industry is above the social optimum.

As another example, consider the case of a public transit system. Price discrimination is usually practised in favour of children and seniors. If price discrimination is carried too far in this case, taxpayers may have to subsidize the transit system. Resources that could be better allocated elsewhere would be diverted into this industry.

Reading Comprehension

The answers to these questions can be found on MyEconLab at **www.myeconlab.com.**   MyEconLab

1. Define each of the following terms:
   a) Price discrimination
   b) Dumping
   c) Arbitrage transactions
2. What is price discrimination?
3. What circumstances encourage a monopolist to practise price discrimination?

4. When is price discrimination possible? When is it profitable?
5. Explain how a discriminating monopolist allocates output between two markets with different price elasticities of demand to maximize profits.
6. What are the economic effects of price discrimination?
7. Do you think that we should always condemn price discrimination?
8. What are the pros and cons of price discrimination?

LO 10.12 Discuss the effects of taxes on a monopoly

Tax Applications

How do taxes affect a monopoly?

The analytical tools that we have introduced in this chapter can help us to organize our thinking on the effects of taxes on monopolistic behaviour. First, we will study the effects of an excise tax. We will then study the effect of a tax on the profits of the monopolist.

The Effect of an Excise Tax   Let us assume that a monopolist has to pay a tax on each unit of a product that it sells. Will the monopolist raise the price by the amount of the tax? Many people would probably answer yes to this question, but let us analyze the situation with the help of Figure 10.17.

We assume, for simplicity, that the demand and MR curves are linear, and that the monopolist has constant MC. AR and MR are, as usual, average revenue and marginal revenue, respectively, and MC is marginal cost before the imposition of the tax. To maximize profits, the monopolist produces a quantity of Q and charges a price of P, as shown in Figure 10.17. After the tax is imposed, the MC curve shifts up by the amount of the tax, to MC_t. The firm now produces an output of Q_0 and charges a price of P_t.

Figure 10.17   The Effect of a Sales Tax on a Monopolist

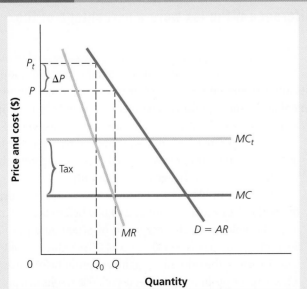

The increase in price from P to P_t is less than the tax (the vertical distance between MC and MC_t). We can therefore draw the following conclusion:

> If an excise tax is imposed on each unit of a commodity sold by a monopolist, the price will rise, but by an amount less than the tax. The tax alters the monopolist's behaviour in that it causes the monopolist to produce a smaller quantity and to charge a higher price.

Figure 10.18	The Effect of a Lump-Sum Tax on the Profit of a Monopolist

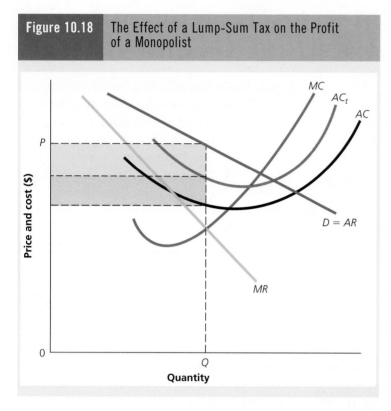

The Effect of a Tax on Profits   We turn now to an analysis of the effect of a tax on the profits of the monopolist. The demand ($D = AR$), MR, MC, and AC for a monopolist are shown in Figure 10.18. The firm is maximizing its profits by producing an output of Q and charging a price of P. The firm's maximum profit is illustrated by the sum of the red and blue rectangles.

Let us assume now that the government imposes a lump-sum tax on the monopolist's profit. The tax is actually a fixed cost that raises average cost from AC to AC_t, but leaves MC unchanged. MC is not affected because the fixed cost (the tax) does not affect the firm's variable cost. With the lump-sum tax, the profit-maximizing output remains at Q and the price remains at P. The lump-sum tax on profit does not affect the price-output decision of the monopolist. The only effect of the tax is that it reduces the monopolist's profit by the amount of the tax. The tax is represented by the red rectangle in Figure 10.18.

Would it have made a difference if the tax were a percentage of the monopolist's profit?

Not really. The monopolist would still maximize profits by producing the same level of output and charging the same price. Let's analyze the situation. Let us assume that a monopolist has to pay 30% of its profits in taxes. Should it change its price-output combination in response to the tax? Let's assume that the monopolist is maximizing its profits by equating its MR and its MC. If it raises its price, its profits will fall. It makes more sense to maximize profits and then pay the tax out of the maximum profits than out of reduced profits that would result from a change in price or output.

The data in Table 10.4 illustrate this point. At a price of $6, the firm earns a profit of $10 000 before taxes. A tax of 30% results in an after-tax profit of $7000. At a price of $4, profit before tax is $9500. A tax of 30% reduces profit to $6650. Clearly, the price that maximizes profit before taxes is $5, where the profit is $15 000. A tax of 30% results in a profit of $10 500 after tax, which is the maximum profit after tax.

Table 10.4	The Effect of a Percentage Tax on Profit

Price ($)	Profit before Tax ($)	30% Tax ($)	Profit after Tax ($)
6	10 000	3 000	7 000
5	15 000	4 500	10 500
4	9 500	2 800	6 650

BUSINESS SITUATION 10.3

Ben and Quan operate the only furniture manufacturing company in a town. The government has increased the tax on the company's profits by 1.5%. Ben argues that the company should raise the price of its furniture to compensate for the increase in the tax. Quan argues that raising the price will adversely affect the company's profit, which, at the present price, is at a maximum.

What is the right decision?

The answer to this Business Situation can be found in Appendix A.

Reading Comprehension

The answers to these questions can be found on MyEconLab at **www.myeconlab.com.**   MyEconLab

1. Discuss the effects of a sales tax on a monopolist.
2. Discuss the effects of a tax on the profits of a monopoly.

Review

1. Review the learning objectives listed at the beginning of the chapter.
2. Have you accomplished all the objectives? One way to determine this is toanswer the Reading Comprehension questions at the end of each section. They will help you assess the extent to which you have accomplished the learning objectives.
3. If you have not accomplished an objective, review the relevant material before proceeding.

Key Points to Remember

1. **LO 10.1** A monopoly is a market structure in which a single firm produces a product that has no close substitutes. Since the monopolist is the only producer of its product, the firm and the industry are identical. Because there are no close substitutes for the monopolized product, the monopolist has a deal great of market power. Unlike a firm in pure competition, the monopolist has a fair amount of control over the price of its product.
2. **LO 10.2** Monopolies exist because of barriers to entry into a market. Such barriers include legal barriers, such as patent rights, ownership of essential raw materials, and economies of scale.

3. **LO 10.3** Because the monopolist is the only firm in the industry, its demand curve is identical to the industry demand curve and slopes downward from left to right. Because the demand curve for the monopolist slopes downward, the marginal revenue (MR) curve must also slope downward. Marginal revenue will be less than demand or average revenue (AR) in the case of a monopoly.
4. **LO 10.4, 10.5** The monopolist maximizes profits at a level of output at which marginal revenue equals marginal cost (MC). However, the monopolist's price will exceed marginal cost. Fear of government regulation, fear of the entry of other firms into the market, and a desire not to incite public outcry are some of the factors that can prevent a monopolist from seeking maximum profits.
5. **LO 10.6** In a monopoly situation, if marginal revenue is positive, total revenue will rise, and demand will be elastic. If marginal revenue is zero, total revenue will be at its maximum, and demand will be unitary elastic. If marginal revenue is negative, total revenue will fall, and demand will be inelastic.
6. **LO 10.7** In the long run, the monopolist maximizes its profits when it equates its long-run marginal cost with marginal revenue. In the long run, if a monopolist is operating at a loss, it will leave the industry.

7. **LO 10.8** Compared with pure competition, a monopoly produces a smaller output and sells at a higher price. Also, the monopolist may earn positive economic profits even in the long run. Any positive profits that a competitive firm earns in the short run will disappear in the long run because of competition. A monopoly reduces consumer surplus, increases producer surplus, and creates a deadweight loss.

8. **LO 10.9** Because of some socially undesirable consequences associated with monopoly, the government may regulate certain monopolies. The regulated monopoly usually produces a greater output and sells at a lower price than would be the case if the monopoly were unregulated.

9. **LO 10.10** A multi-plant monopolist will maximize profits by producing that output at which marginal revenue equal marginal cost. The total output will be allocated in each plant so that marginal cost is the same in each plant.

10. **LO 10.11** Price discrimination is profitable only if the price elasticity of demand in each market is different. The discriminating monopolist tries to capture the consumer surplus. The discriminating monopolist will produce an output at which marginal revenue equals marginal cost and will distribute this output among the markets in such a way that marginal revenue equals marginal cost in each market.

11. **LO 10.12** A sales tax imposed on a monopoly increases its marginal cost. The tax raises the price, but by an amount less than the tax. The tax causes the monopolist to produce a smaller quantity and to charge a higher price. A tax imposed on the profit of a monopolist does not change the profit-maximization price and output, because the tax does not affect the firm's marginal cost. In the case of a tax on profit, the monopolist should maximize profit and pay the tax, rather than changing the profit-maximization price and output.

Economic Word Power

Allocative efficiency (p. 295)
Arbitrage transactions (p. 300)
Dumping (p. 300)
Franchise (p. 282)
Monopoly power or market power (p. 297)
Natural monopoly (p. 283)
Patent (p. 282)
Price discrimination (p. 300)
X-inefficiency (p. 290)

Problems and Exercises

Basic

1. **LO 10.3** Table 10.5 contains data for a monopolist.
   a. Compute the monopolist's *TR* at each price and complete the *TR* column.
   b. Draw the monopolist's *TR* curve.

Table 10.5	Data for a Monopolist	
Price ($)	Quantity	Total Revenue (*TR*) ($)
1	12	
2	11	
3	10	
4	9	
5	8	
6	7	
7	6	
8	5	
9	4	
10	3	

2. **LO 10.4** Table 10.6 contains data on demand and cost for a monopolist.
   a. Fill in the *TR*, *MR*, *MC*, and profit columns.
   b. On a graph, draw the monopolist's *TR* and *TC* curves.
   c. At what level of output is total profit maximized?
   d. On another graph, draw the monopolist's *MR* and *MC* curves.
   e. At what level of output do the *MR* and *MC* curves intersect?
   f. At what price should this firm sell its product?

3. **LO 10.3** Table 10.7 shows the demand schedule for a monopolist.
   a. Complete the *TR*, *AR*, and *MR* columns.
   b. Draw the demand and *MR* curves.

4. **LO 10.2** Table 10.8 contains data for a monopolist.
   a. Fill in the *TR*, *MR*, and *AR* columns.
   b. Draw the *MR* and *AR* curves.
   c. What is the relationship between *MR* and *AR* throughout the entire range of output?

5. **LO 10.4** Figure 10.19 represents a monopolist.
   a. What output should this firm produce and what price should it charge to maximize its profits?

Table 10.6	Demand and Cost Data for a Monopolist					
Quantity	Price ($)	TR ($)	MR ($)	TC ($)	MC ($)	Profit ($)
1	16			33		
2	15			34		
3	14			36		
4	13			39		
5	12			48		
6	11			58		
7	10			70		
8	9			84		

Table 10.7	Demand Schedule for a Monopolist			
Quantity	Price ($)	TR ($)	AR ($)	MR ($)
1	30			
2	26			
3	22			
4	18			
5	14			
6	10			

Table 10.8	Data for a Monopolist			
Quantity	Price ($)	TR ($)	MR ($)	AR ($)
2	20			
3	19			
4	18			
5	17			
6	16			
7	15			
8	14			
9	13			
10	12			
11	11			
12	10			

b. At the profit-maximizing price, what is the firm's *TR*?

c. If the firm produces 20 units of output, what will be its *TR*?

6. **LO 10.6** Table 10.9 shows price and quantity demanded for a monopolist. Is this demand elastic or inelastic at the price range of $10 to $9?

7. **LO 10.4** Figure 10.20 shows cost and revenue curves for a profit-maximizing monopolist.

a. This firm should produce an output of _____ units and charge a price of $_____. Its *TR* will be $_____, its *TC* will be $_____, and its total profit will be $_____.

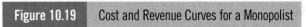

Figure 10.19 Cost and Revenue Curves for a Monopolist

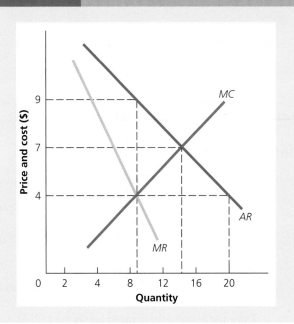

Table 10.9	Price and Quantity Demanded for a Monopolist	
Price ($)		Quantity
10		7
9		8

Figure 10.20   Marginal Revenue and Marginal Cost Curves for a Monopolist

Table 10.10	Data for a Monopolist			
Quantity	Price ($)	TR ($)	AR ($)	MR ($)
1	16			
2	14			
3	12			
4	10			
5	8			
6	6			
7	4			
8	2			

Table 10.11	Data for a Pure Competitor and a Monopolist		
	Firm A		Firm B
Quantity	Price ($)	Quantity	Price ($)
1	3	1	9
2	3	2	8
3	3	3	7
4	3	4	6
5	3	5	5

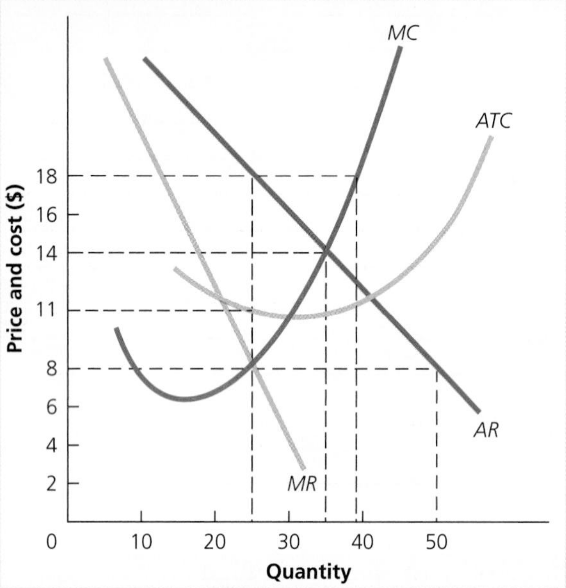

b. If this monopolist is forced to charge a price of $14, it will produce _____ units. Its *TR* will be $_____, its *TC* will be $_____, and its total profit will be $_____.

Questions in the Intermediate and Challenging Sections cover several different concepts, and have not been organized by learning objectives.

Intermediate

1. Table 10.10 shows data for a monopolist.
   a. Draw the monopolist's demand curve.
   b. Calculate the monopolist's *TR* at each level of output and fill in the *TR* column.
   c. Compute *AR* and *MR* for the monopolist and fill in the *AR* and *MR* columns.
   d. On the same graph, draw the *AR* and *MR* curves.
2. In Table 10.11, firm *A* is a pure competitor while firm *B* is a monopolist.
   a. Draw the *MR* and the demand curves for each firm.

b. Point out the difference shown between pure competition and monopoly.
3. Figure 10.21 shows the *MR* and *MC* curves for a monopolist.
   a. Draw the demand curve on the graph.
   b. Determine the equilibrium price and quantity for this monopolist.

Challenging

1. Assume that a government imposes a tax on a monopolist to acquire revenue to help clean up the environment. Describe how the profit-maximizing price and output would be affected if

a. The tax were imposed on each unit of output
b. The tax were a lump-sum tax without regard to output

2. You are given the demand and cost data for a monopolist shown in Table 10.12. Show that the *TC/TR* rule for profit maximization is the same as the *MR = MC* rule.

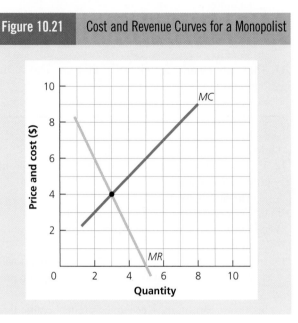

Figure 10.21 Cost and Revenue Curves for a Monopolist

Table 10.12 Demand and Cost Data for a Monopolist

Price ($)	Quantity	TC ($)
1	10	12
2	9	14
3	8	16
4	7	20
5	6	25
6	5	31
7	4	38
8	3	46

MyEconLab Visit the MyEconLab website at **www.myeconlab.com**. This online homework and tutorial system puts you in control of your own learning with study and practice tools directly correlated to this chapter's content.

Study Guide

Self-Assessment

The answers to the Study Guide questions can be found in Appendix B.

What's your score?

Circle the letter that corresponds with the correct answer.

1. A monopoly can be defined as
   a. A large number of firms producing the industry's output
   b. Few firms with significant control over price and output
   c. One firm selling a product that has no close substitutes
   d. A large number of firms producing differentiated products with many close, though not perfect, substitutes
2. Monopolies can arise because of
   a. Patents and franchises
   b. Control of essential raw materials
   c. Substantial increasing returns to scale
   d. All of the above
3. Monopolies can exist in the long run because
   a. There are barriers to entry into the industry
   b. They do not produce at the point where *MR = MC*.
   c. The long run is defined as a situation in which competition does not exist
   d. They minimize cost rather than maximize profits
4. In a monopoly,
   a. The firm's demand curve is perfectly elastic
   b. *MR* equals *AR*
   c. *MR* is less than *AR*
   d. *MR* is greater than *AR*

5. To maximize profits, a monopolist must produce where
   a. *MR* equals *MC*
   b. Price equals *MC*
   c. Price equals average *TC*
   d. All of the above

6. At its present level of output, a monopolist finds that its *MR* is greater than its *MC*. To maximize profits, the monopolist should
   a. Reduce price and leave output unchanged
   b. Increase price and leave output unchanged
   c. Continue to operate at current price and output levels
   d. Reduce price and increase output

7. The monopolist seeking to maximize profits will operate where its demand curve is
   a. Inelastic
   b. Elastic
   c. Unitary elastic
   d. Perfectly elastic

8. Which of the following is true for a monopoly?
   a. If *MR* > 0, demand is elastic
   b. If *MR* = 0, demand is unitary elastic
   c. If *MR* < 0, demand is inelastic
   d. All of the above

Questions 9–11 refer to Figure 10.22, which shows revenue and cost curves for a monopolist.

9. To maximize its profits, this firm should produce
   a. 60 units of output and charge a price of $12
   b. 85 units of output and charge a price of $9

Figure 10.22	Cost and Revenue Curves for a Monopolist

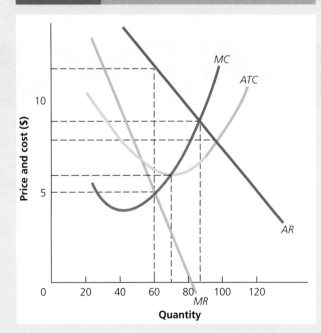

c. 85 units of output and charge a price of $12
d. 70 units of output and charge a price of $6

10. To maximize revenue, the firm should produce
    a. 60 units
    b. 120 units
    c. 80 units
    d. 85 units

11. The optimum price for this firm at the profit-maximizing output is
    a. $14
    b. $12
    c. $8
    d. $6

12. If in the long run a firm earns positive economic profits, then we know that
    a. The firm is not a profit maximizer
    b. The firm is definitely a pure competitor
    c. The industry must have barriers to entry
    d. Price equals *LRAC*

13. In the long run, the profit-maximizing monopolist will
    a. Maximize short-run profits and ignore long-run profits because they are identical
    b. Always earn positive economic profits because there are no competitors
    c. Operate where *MR* = *LRMC*
    d. None of the above

14. Allocative efficiency occurs when
    a. Price (*P*) > *MC*
    b. *MR* > *MC*
    c. *MR* = *MC*
    d. *P* = *MC*

15. Other things being equal, compared with pure competition, monopoly
    a. Produces a larger quantity of output at a higher price
    b. Produces a larger quantity of output at a lower price
    c. Produces a smaller quantity of output at a lower price
    d. Produces a smaller quantity of output at a higher price

16. Monopoly tends to
    a. Reduce consumer surplus and increase producer surplus
    b. Increase consumer surplus and reduce producer surplus
    c. Reduce both consumer and producer surplus
    d. Increase both consumer and producer surplus

17. Which of the following can be used to regulate a monopoly?
    a. Marginal-cost pricing
    b. Average-cost pricing
    c. Minimum average-cost pricing
    d. All of the above

18. Price discrimination is the practice of
    a. Refusing to sell to ethnic minority groups
    b. Adopting a very conservative approach to pricing

c. Setting price above *AR* for certain classes of buyers

d. None of the above

19. A discriminating profit-maximizing monopolist will charge a higher price in the market where
   a. The demand for the product is more elastic or less inelastic
   b. The demand for the product is less elastic or more inelastic
   c. The customers cannot be separated
   d. The output is greater

20. If a sales tax is imposed on each unit of a commodity sold by a profit-maximizing monopolist,
   a. The price will rise by an amount less than the tax
   b. The price will rise by an amount greater than the tax
   c. The *MC* will not be affected
   d. Neither the price nor the quantity sold will be affected

Problems and Exercises (Use Quad Paper for Graphs)

Answers to these questions can be found on MyEconLab at www.myeconlab.com.   MyEconLab

1. Table 10.13 shows a monopolist's demand and cost data.
   a. Draw the *TR* and total cost (*TC*) curves on a graph.
   b. Calculate the monopolist's *MR* and *MC* at each level of output. Complete the relevant columns in Table 10.13.

Table 10.13	Demand and Cost Data for a Monopolist				
Quantity	Price ($)	TR ($)	MR ($)	Total Cost ($)	MC ($)
1	15			30	
2	14			31	
3	13			32	
4	12			33	
5	11			34	
6	10			36	
7	9			39	
8	8			42	

c. On a new graph, draw the *MR* and *MC* curves.

d. What is the profit-maximizing output?

e. At what price should the firm sell this output?

2. Table 10.14 shows the demand schedule for a monopoly called Monoply Ltd.
   a. Compute *MR* for Monoply at each level of output.
   b. Graph the *AR* and the *MR* curves for Monoply.

Table 10.14	Demand Schedule for Monoply			
Quantity	Price ($)	TR ($)	AR ($)	MR ($)
1	20.00			
2	17.50			
3	15.00			
4	12.50			
5	10.00			
6	7.50			

3. Figure 10.23 shows the demand and *MC* curves for a monopolist.
   a. Draw the firm's *MR* curve on the graph.
   b. What is the profit-maximizing level of output?
   c. What is the profit-maximizing price for this output?

Figure 10.23	Demand and Marginal Cost Curves for a Monopolist

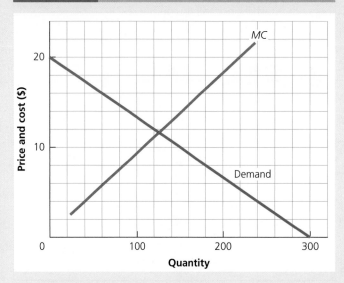

Figure 10.24	Revenue and Cost Curves for Power Plus

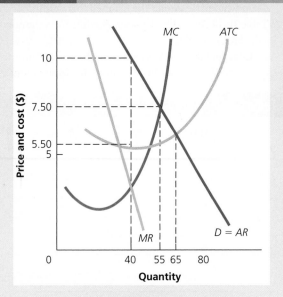

Figure 10.25	Cost and Revenue for Safe-T Transport

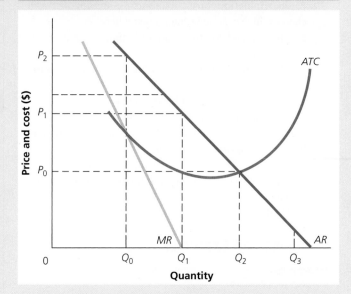

4. Figure 10.24 represents Power Plus, a monopolist.
   a. What output should Power Plus produce to maximize its profits?
   b. What price should it charge?
   c. What is the maximum total profit that this firm can earn?
   d. What is the firm's TR at the profit-maximizing output?
   e. What is the firm's TC when it is maximizing its profits?
5. The data presented in Table 10.15 refer to a monopoly called the Unifirm Corporation.
   a. Construct a table showing Unifirm's MC and MR.
   b. Draw Unifirm's MR and MC curves.
   c. What level of output should Unifirm produce so as to maximize profits?
   d. At what price will this output sell?

6. Figure 10.25 shows the revenue curves for the Safe-T Transport Company (a monopoly). The cost of transporting an additional passenger from point A to point B is practically zero.
   a. What price should this firm charge to maximize its profits?
   b. What level of output should it produce?

Table 10.16	Price and Cost Data for SIF				
P ($)	Q	TR ($)	MR ($)	TC ($)	MC ($)	Profit ($)
900	0			400		
800	1			500		
700	2			550		
600	3			650		
500	4			850		
400	5			1150		
300	6			1430		
200	7			1800		

Table 10.15	Cost and Revenue Data for Unifirm	
Quantity	Total Cost ($)	Total Revenue ($)
0	10	0
5	15	15.00
10	21	27.50
15	28	37.50
20	36	45.00
25	45	50.00
30	55	52.50
35	66	52.50

7. Table 10.16 contains data for a monopolist called SIF, which means Single-Industry Firm.
   a. Complete the table.
   b. What output should SIF produce to maximize its profits?
   c. What price will SIF charge?
   d. What will SIF's total profit be at this price?

8. A monopolist is maximizing its profits by producing 100 units of output and charging a price of $10. The government then levies a flat tax of $50 per month on the monopolist. Assume other things remain equal. Should the monopolist respond to the tax by changing its price and output? Why or why not?

9. A monopolist, Coverall Ltd., produces a particular type of garment. Coverall has to pay a tax of 40% on its profits. Should Coverall raise its price and thus try to pass the tax on to it customers? Explain.

10. The government imposes a tax of $2 on each unit of an item that a monopolist produces. Show that the profit-maximizing monopolist will raise the price, but by a smaller amount than the tax.

Chapter

11

Monopolistic Competition and Oligopoly

Learning Objectives

After studying this chapter, you should be able to

11.1 Understand the nature of monopolistic competition

11.2 Describe the demand and marginal revenue of the firm in monopolistic competition

11.3 Understand short-run equilibrium in monopolistic competition

11.4 Understand long-run equilibrium in monopolistic competition

11.5 Discuss the difference between monopolistic competition and pure competition

11.6 Discuss the effects of advertising

11.7 Understand the nature of oligopoly

11.8 Explain oligopoly pricing and output

11.9 Discuss the kinked demand curve model

11.10 Discuss cartels and other forms of collusion

11.11 Understand the basic concepts of game theory

11.12 Evaluate oligopoly and understand the concept of workable competition

11.13 Discuss the concept of contestable markets

Assess Your Knowledge

MyEconLab

Answers to these questions can be found on MyEconLab at **www.myeconlab.com**.

1. Many firms try to make their products appear different from similar products of other firms. What are some of the devices used to achieve this objective?

2. Sign Plus sells a product that is slightly different from those of its many competitors. Why might Sign Plus expect to sell significantly less by raising its price above that charged by its competitors?

3. Referring to Sign Plus above, why might the firm consider it important to advertise its product?

4. Why might a firm not raise its price in response to a small increase in cost?

LO 11.1 Understand the nature of monopolistic competition

The Nature of Monopolistic Competition

What do economists mean by imperfect competition?

As described in Chapter 9, economists often use the term imperfect competition to refer to a market structure that is neither purely competitive nor a pure monopoly. Hence, the term encompasses both monopolistic competition and oligopoly.

What are the main features of monopolistic competition?

As the name implies, monopolistic competition contains elements of both pure competition and monopoly. This type of market structure is characterized by a large number of firms, each selling differentiated products. The characteristics of monopolistic competition are set out below. As these characteristics are outlined, you will recognize the similarity between this market structure and pure competition. You may find it helpful to refer to Table 9.1 on page 254 to review the characteristics of the various market structures. The main features of monopolistic competition are (1) a relatively large number of firms, (2) differentiated products, and (3) freedom of entry and exit. Let us deal with each in turn.

A Relatively Large Number of Firms   The market structure characterized as monopolistic competition consists of a relatively large number of firms. The number is not as large as in pure competition. Although a specific number will be only arbitrary, most students still like to have an idea of what is "relatively large" when referring to monopolistic competition. For this purpose, a number between 30 and 100 will suffice. The essential point, however, is that because the number of firms is relatively large, each firm's share of the total market, though not negligible, is relatively small—just enough to cause each firm to have a slight influence on price. Also, the number of firms is sufficiently large to make it impractical for them to get together to act jointly to control price and output in the market. In this type of market structure, each firm acts independently of the others because the decision of any one firm will have a very small (almost unnoticeable) effect on the others.

product differentiation
the condition that exists when firms distinguish their products from those of their competitors

Differentiated Products   You will recall that in pure competition, the firms produce identical products. In monopolistic competition, the firms produce differentiated products. Indeed, **product differentiation**, the condition that exists when firms distinguish their products from those of their competitors, is a key feature of monopolistic competition. For example, one restaurant can differentiate itself from its competitors by the type of food it sells.

An important point to grasp here is that it does not matter much whether the products are different. What matters is whether buyers *perceive* them to be different. The true test of the existence of product differentiation is whether or not buyers prefer to purchase the item from one seller rather than from another.

The concept of product differentiation is clear, but how does a firm achieve product differentiation?

A firm can differentiate its product in many ways. First, the firm can achieve it through product characteristics, such as distinctive designs, packaging, trademarks, colour, durability, and brand names. Some trademark and brand names have become so popular with consumers that the product is often identified by the brand name or trademark. Examples include Kleenex (for tissues), Band-Aid (for plastic bandage strips), Xerox (for a photocopy), Scotch tape (for transparent adhesive tape), Q-tips (for cotton swabs), Vaseline (for white petroleum jelly), and iPod (for mini music players).

Second, a firm can differentiate its product through product image. The idea is to create a certain image of the product with the hope that it will appeal to certain buyers. For example, a product that has a conservative image will likely appeal to people who behave conservatively. A certain type of car, for example, may portray this conservative image.

Finally, a firm can achieve product differentiation by emphasizing certain of its features, which may include the convenient location, the attention given to customers by the firm's employees, and the services provided along with the product. A beauty salon may provide reading material or free coffee while its clients are waiting to be served. A furniture store may offer free delivery anywhere in the city and surrounding areas. These services differentiate the firms from those that offer no such services.

A car dealer can build a reputation on the basis of the service offered to its customers after they purchase a car. Product differentiation on the basis of service rendered is an attempt to compel consumers to view the product and the service offered with it as a single item. This type of product differentiation is particularly prevalent in retail outlets, where it is difficult or impossible to differentiate the physical characteristics of the product. The DVDs rented from one video outlet are identical to those of other outlets. The service, however, may vary from one outlet to another.

BUSINESS SITUATION 11.1

Cross-Town Taxi Service finds that increasing numbers of taxi companies have entered the industry.

How might Cross-Town Taxi set itself apart from other taxi companies in the field?

The answer to this Business Situation can be found in Appendix A.

In which industries is monopolistic competition usually found?

Monopolistic competition is prevalent in service industries. The many different beauty salons, barber shops, and restaurants operating in any large city are good examples of monopolistic competition. Other examples include bakeries, gasoline stations, shoe stores, men's and women's clothing stores, automotive garages, stationery stores, and florists.

Freedom of Entry and Exit   In pure competition, firms have freedom of entry into, and exit from, the industry. In the case of monopolistic competition, entry and exit are relatively easy also. Entry may not be as easy as in pure competition because of the need to differentiate the product in a monopolistically competitive market. Also, breaking into the monopolistically competitive industry may require significant advertising, the financial burden of which can be a factor limiting entry into the market.

Reading Comprehension

The answers to these questions can be found on MyEconLab at **www.myeconlab.com.**   MyEconLab

1. What are the main features of a monopolistically competitive market?

2. What do you understand by the term *product differentiation*? What devices are used to achieve product differentiation?

3. Give three examples of industries in Canada that are monopolistically competitive.

LO 11.2 Describe the demand and marginal revenue of the firm in monopolistic competition

Demand and Marginal Revenue of the Firm in Monopolistic Competition

What are the shapes of the average revenue and marginal revenue curves of a firm in monopolistic competition?

The firm in monopolistic competition is one among many. However, because its product is perceived to be different from those of its competitors, the monopolistic competitor is able to exercise some control over its price. If the firm in monopolistic

Figure 11.1	Demand and Marginal Revenue Curves for a Firm in Monopolistic Competition

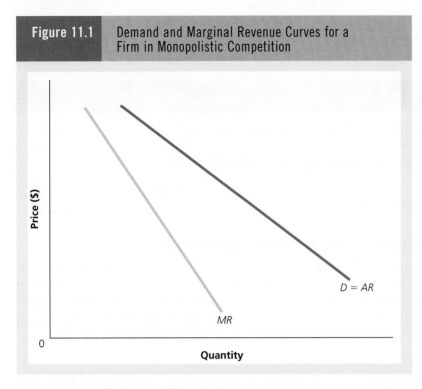

competition raises its price, it will lose some of its customers. But those who strongly prefer the product in question may remain; brand loyalty will cause them to stay with their preferred brand. If the firm lowers its price, it will attract some customers away from its competitors. Not all buyers will be attracted by the small reduction in price. This implies that the demand or average revenue (AR) curve for the monopolistic competitor slopes downward. Because so many substitutes for the product of any one firm are available in monopolistic competition, the demand for the product of any one firm is relatively elastic. The degree of elasticity will depend on the degree of product differentiation that the firm is able to achieve.

A downward-sloping demand curve implies a downward-sloping marginal revenue (MR) curve. The firm in monopolistic competition can sell a greater quantity only by lowering the price, other things being equal. Hence, each additional unit adds a smaller amount to total revenue (TR). Demand and MR curves for a firm in monopolistic competition are shown in Figure 11.1.

Reading Comprehension

The answers to these questions can be found on MyEconLab at **www.myeconlab.com.**   MyEconLab

1. Explain why a firm in monopolistic competition faces a relatively elastic downward-sloping demand curve.

2. Describe the marginal revenue curve of a firm in monopolistic competition.

LO 11.3 Understand short-run equilibrium in monopolistic competition

Short-Run Profit Maximization or Loss Minimization in Monopolistic Competition

How does the firm in monopolistic competition decide on its price and quantity of output?

The individual firm in a monopolistically competitive industry must decide on the price and output combination that will maximize its profits. The firm will earn maximum profits when it equates its MR and its marginal cost (MC). The short-run

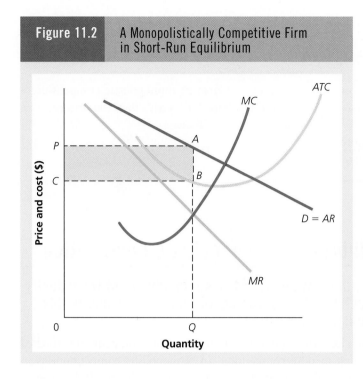

Figure 11.2   A Monopolistically Competitive Firm in Short-Run Equilibrium

(profit-maximizing) position of a firm in monopolistic competition is shown in Figure 11.2.

The firm illustrated in the diagram will produce an output of 0Q and charge a price of 0P to maximize its profits. The *TR* is represented by the area of the rectangle 0QAP, and the total cost (*TC*) is represented by the rectangle 0QBC. The total profit (*TP*) is shown by the area of the blue rectangle *CBAP*, which is the difference between 0QAP and 0QBC. For each unit sold, the firm receives QA (= 0P), but the unit cost is QB (= 0C). The average profit (profit per unit) is therefore BA (= CP).

Is it possible for the firm in monopolistic competition to operate where *MR = MC* and yet not earn any profits?

This is indeed possible. In such a situation, the firm would be minimizing its losses. A firm in monopolistic competition can incur losses in the short run. Figure 11.3 illustrates this situation.

We assume that this firm is covering its variable costs. The firm is doing the best it can in the short run by producing an output of 0Q and charging a price of 0P. It is, however, incurring losses because its price, 0P, is below its *ATC* at 0C. But it is minimizing its losses. The losses are illustrated by the blue area in Figure 11.3.

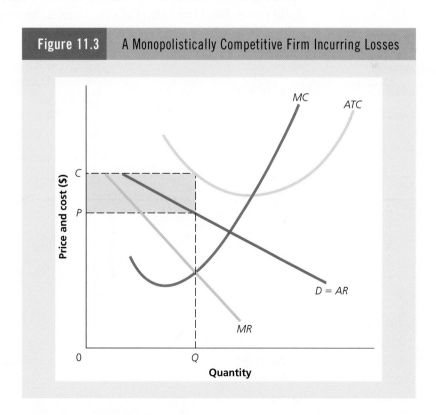

Figure 11.3   A Monopolistically Competitive Firm Incurring Losses

Reading Comprehension

The answers to these questions can be found on MyEconLab at **www.myeconlab.com.**   MyEconLab

1. With the help of an appropriate diagram, carefully explain the short-run profit-maximizing position of a firm in monopolistic competition.

2. As long as a firm in monopolistic competition is operating where $MR = MC$, then the firm must be earning profits. Discuss.

LO 11.4   Understand long-run equilibrium in monopolistic competition

Long-Run Equilibrium in Monopolistic Competition

In pure competition, the movement of firms into and out of the industry is the process through which long-run equilibrium is reached. Is this the same in monopolistic competition?

Yes. The process by which long-run equilibrium in monopolistic competition is reached is essentially similar to that in pure competition. In monopolistic competition, as in pure competition, entry into and exit from the industry are relatively easy. If the firms in the industry are earning positive economic profits, new firms will be attracted into the industry. As this happens, the demand curve for each firm will shift to the left, as shown in Diagram A of Figure 11.4, as each firm's share of the total industry demand falls. D is the original demand curve, representing the firm's share of the market demand, and D_0 is the new demand curve after the adjustment to the entry of new firms into the industry.

Figure 11.4   The Effects of Entry into and Exit from a Monopolistically Competitive Industry

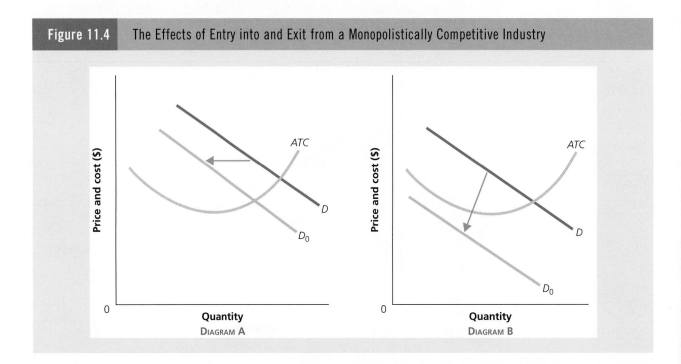

DIAGRAM A

DIAGRAM B

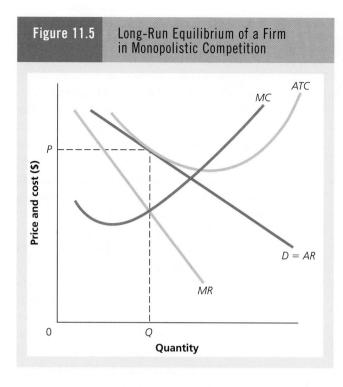

Figure 11.5 Long-Run Equilibrium of a Firm in Monopolistic Competition

The firm is still earning profits because its demand curve is still above its average total cost (*ATC*) curve.

If too many firms enter the industry, the demand curve will shift below the *ATC* curve. The firm will then incur losses. This occurrence is shown in Diagram B of Figure 11.4. Here, the demand curve has shifted from *D* to D_0, which is now below the *ATC* curve. This fall in demand will cause some firms to leave the industry, and as a result, the demand curve will shift back to the right.

When each firm in the industry is earning only normal profits (that is, when *P* = *ATC*), the entry and exit of firms will cease, and long-run equilibrium will be achieved. This situation is illustrated in Figure 11.5. The firm will produce an output of 0*Q* units at a price of 0*P*.

> In long-run equilibrium, a firm in monopolistic competition earns only normal profits.

Note that in long-run equilibrium, *MR* equals *MC*, and price equals *ATC*.

Reading Comprehension

The answers to these questions can be found on MyEconLab at www.myeconlab.com. MyEconLab

1. Explain the role of entry and exit of firms into and out of a monopolistically competitive industry on long-run equilibrium of a firm in monopolistic competition.

2. Why does a firm in monopolistic competition earn only normal profit (zero economic profit) in the long run?

LO 11.5 Discuss the difference between monopolistic competition and pure competition

Monopolistic Competition Compared with Pure Competition

We have seen that in pure competition, the firm in long-run equilibrium operates where price equals marginal cost. This means that resources are optimally allocated. We have also seen that in pure competition, the firm in long-run equilibrium operates where price equals minimum average cost. This means that consumers obtain the product at the lowest price. How does monopolistic competition compare with pure competition in terms of resource allocation and efficiency?

We can evaluate the efficiency of monopolistic competition relative to pure competition with the help of Figure 11.6.

This diagram shows that, in pure competition, price equals *MC*. In monopolistic competition, price exceeds *MC*. This means that resources are not optimally allocated in

| Figure 11.6 | A Comparison of Efficiency under Pure Competition and Monopolistic Competition |

monopolistic competition. An increase in output by the monopolistically competitive firm would benefit society. The firm in monopolistic competition is wasteful in the sense that it does not produce at the lowest point of its ATC curve as the purely competitive firm does. The fact that the monopolistic competitor does not produce at minimum average cost implies that the firm has excess or underutilized capacity. This concept has been termed the **excess capacity theorem**: in long-run equilibrium, a firm in monopolistic competition will operate with excess capacity; that is, it will operate at a point to the left of the minimum point on its long-run average cost curve ($LRAC$).

Figure 11.6 also shows that the purely competitive firm produces a greater output (Q_{pc}) than the monopolistically competitive firm does (Q_{mc}), and that the price charged by the monopolistically competitive firm (P_{mc}) is higher than the purely competitive price (P_{pc}).

excess capacity theorem
the hypothesis that firms in monopolistic competition will operate with excess capacity

That's clear so far. Considering the conclusions reached above, is the consumer then better off under pure competition than under monopolistic competition?

Actually, that question is asked quite frequently. It is true that under pure competition consumers pay a lower price, but their choices of products are limited. In a purely competitive industry, all of the firms in that industry produce (and sell) identical products. In a monopolistically competitive industry, consumers can choose from a wide variety of differentiated products. It can be argued that the higher price under monopolistic competition is offset by the greater choices available to consumers. Whether or not the greater variety of products sufficiently compensates for the higher price is a subjective matter and cannot be answered by economic analysis without additional data. The decision rests with the individual consumer.

Reading Comprehension

The answers to these questions can be found on MyEconLab at www.myeconlab.com. MyEconLab

1. How does the long-run equilibrium of a monopolistically competitive firm differ from that of a purely competitive firm? Illustrate with a diagram. Account for the difference.

2. State the excess capacity theorem.
3. Why might consumers be better off with monopolistic competition than with pure competition even though price is higher and output lower than in pure competition?

LO 11.6 Discuss the effects of advertising

Advertising

We know that a profit-seeking firm in pure competition will not advertise its product. Is this also true of a firm in monopolistic competition?

Advertising is, in itself, a form of non-price competition. A purely competitive firm need not spend money trying to increase the amount that it can sell. Why not? Because it can sell as much as it can produce at the going price. That is a characteristic of a purely competitive firm. But in the case of a monopolistic competitor, advertising may result in an increase in profits. It is obvious that for advertising to be profitable, it must add more to the firm's TR than it does to its TC. Successful advertising will increase the demand for the firm's product and will also make it less elastic or more inelastic. This will increase the monopolistically competitive firm's market power.

Is it possible for advertising to result in a reduction in the firm's profits?

That is a distinct possibility. If we assume that advertising outlay is a fixed cost, then it will have no effect on the firm's MC. And if advertising does not significantly affect demand for the firm's product, then the price and quantity at which $MR = MC$ will not change appreciably. In that case, advertising will simply push up the firm's TC and hence reduce the firm's profits.

That makes sense, but can that argument be illustrated graphically?

Figure 11.7 will help to illustrate the argument. If the firm's demand, MR, and MC curves are as shown in Figure 11.7, the firm will maximize its profits by charging a price of P and selling a quantity of Q units of output. The firm's profit is shown by the blue rectangle $PDFC$. If advertising is a fixed cost, the ATC curve will shift up to ATC_1, leaving the MC curve unchanged. If advertising is ineffective and does not affect the demand for the firm's product, the demand and MR curves will remain unchanged. The firm continues to produce Q units of output at a price of P. But because of the increase in cost, the firm's profit level is now reduced and is represented by rectangle $PDEC_1$. The firm's profit level falls by C_1EFC.

What are the pros and cons of advertising?

The issue of advertising has received a great deal of attention in economics and marketing literature. Does advertising increase or reduce prices? Is advertising wasteful? Does advertising hinder or promote competition? These issues are debatable. In this section, we will take a quick look at the main arguments in favour of and against advertising.

The Pros Those who argue in favour of advertising make the following claims:

1. Advertising creates employment and income for people in the advertising business and for people who work in the media. In addition, advertising increases the demand for goods and services, and

Figure 11.7   The Results of Ineffective Advertising

Ineffective advertising can reduce the firm's profit level.

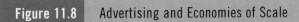

Figure 11.8   Advertising and Economies of Scale

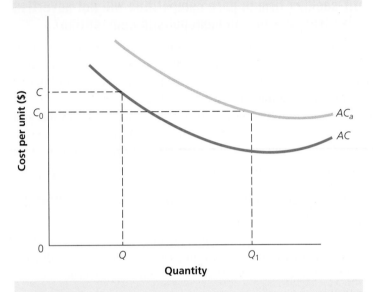

Advertising enables the firm to take advantage of economies of scale, which can reduce cost and price.

because the production of goods and services requires the use of resources, including labour, it increases employment in general.

2. Advertising enables firms to take advantage of economies of scale. This argument can be illustrated with the help of Figure 11.8. AC represents the firm's average cost without advertising. Suppose the quantity of the firm's product demanded without advertising is $0Q$. This quantity of output will be produced at an average cost of $0C$. Now, because of advertising, the firm's average cost curve shifts upward from AC to AC_a, and the quantity demanded now grows from $0Q$ to $0Q_1$. But the average cost of producing this greater output has fallen from $0C$ to $0C_0$. Hence, the benefits from economies of scale outweigh the increase in average cost resulting from advertising. Consumers benefit by obtaining the product at a lower price with advertising than without it.

3. Advertising provides consumers with valuable information that enables them to make better decisions in the marketplace. By informing consumers about new products, new locations, and new firms, advertising greatly reduces search costs to consumers.

4. Advertising leads to product improvement and development. When a firm advertises its product, it emphasizes some advantage of its product over the products of its competitors. A firm must therefore improve its product to justify its advertising claims. Moreover, the fact that its competitors are also advertising puts pressure on the firm to improve its product and its service.

5. Advertising increases competition. Advertising makes it easier to successfully launch new products that are close substitutes for existing products. Thus, advertising increases the number of firms in the industry and makes it more competitive.

BUSINESS SITUATION 11.2

In November 2006, Hershey Canada Inc. voluntarily recalled a wide range of its chocolate products nationwide after salmonella bacteria were detected in some of its candies. Doubtlessly, this recall adversely affected Hershey's candy sales in Canada.

What kind of advertising should Hershey have engaged in to attempt to rectify this business situation?

The answer to this Business Situation can be found in Appendix A.

The Cons   Those who argue against advertising raise the following points to support their case:

1. Advertising increases monopoly power. Firms in certain industries spend millions of dollars each year on advertising. To break into such industries, potential competitors must be willing to make those massive advertising outlays. This in itself can prove to be an effective barrier to new firms.

2. Advertising is wasteful. Resources that could be productively employed in other industries to produce goods and services to satisfy wants are wasted in advertising. Why, it is argued, use so much ink and paper in advertising, when those same resources could be used in producing educational books, which would improve society's well-being?

3. Advertising can increase costs and prices. A good portion of advertising simply causes consumers to switch from brand to brand. The output of the industry does not increase as a result of advertising, but costs rise, the market share of each firm hardly changes at all, and consumers end up paying higher prices.

4. Advertising is mainly persuasive, not informational. Many of the advertisements on radio and television give very little useful information to consumers in terms of helping them make rational choices. Some advertisements, it is claimed, may even give misleading or false information.

5. Advertising imposes indirect costs on society. Unsightly billboards that mar the beauty of the landscape, tons of advertising circulars that must be disposed of, and advertisements that are in bad taste are some examples of the costs imposed on society by advertising.

Reading Comprehension

The answers to these questions can be found on MyEconLab at **www.myeconlab.com.**   MyEconLab

1. Why might a firm in monopolistic competition advertise its product?

2. What arguments can you advance for and against advertising in monopolistic competition?

LO 11.7 Understand the nature of oligopoly

Oligopoly

What does the term *oligopoly* mean?

As described in Chapter 9, the term *oligopoly* has been applied to a market structure consisting of a few firms that recognize their interdependence. This type of market structure is typical of the petroleum industry, the automobile industry, the steel industry, the tobacco industry, and the brewing industry. If an industry consists of only two firms, the term **duopoly** is generally used.

duopoly an industry consisting of only two firms

The brewing industry in Canada is an example of an oligopoly.

What are the main features of oligopoly?

The main features of oligopoly are outlined below.

Few Firms   The industry consists of only a few firms—so few that each produces a relatively large share of the total output of the industry. As in the case of monopolistic competition, any specific number given must be quite arbitrary, but we typically think of an oligopoly as consisting of 2 to 15 firms.

Interdependence Recognized   As a consequence of the small number of firms in an oligopoly, the actions taken by any one firm have a noticeable effect on the other firms. Acknowledging this interdependence is crucial in understanding the behaviour of firms in oligopoly.

Barriers to Entry   An oligopoly has barriers to entry. These barriers often include the huge capital investment necessary to establish a firm in an oligopoly, and the enormous advertising necessary to capture a worthwhile share of the market.

Identical or Differentiated Products   Firms in oligopoly may produce identical products or they may produce differentiated products. For example, the cement produced by one firm is similar to that produced by the other firms. An obvious difference exists, however, between General Motors's compact cars and Ford's compact cars. The term **differentiated oligopoly** is used when the products of the firms in an oligopoly are differentiated.

differentiated oligopoly an oligopoly in which the firms' products are differentiated

---

BUSINESS SITUATION 11.3

In November 2006, Canada's largest grocery chain (Loblaw) announced that it was closing several of its stores that were operating under the Loblaw, Provigo, and Maxi banners. Before that decision by Loblaw, Wal-Mart had announced plans to significantly expand its sale of groceries in superstores.

To what extent might Loblaw's decision have been influenced by Wal-Mart's plans?

The answer to this Business Situation can be found in Appendix A.

Is there any measure that can be used to determine the extent of market power?

Two measures have been used to determine the extent to which a market is dominated by a few firms (i.e., an oligopoly). These measures are concentration ratios and the Herfindahl-Hirschman Index.

What are concentration ratios?

concentration ratio the percentage of total market share accounted for by a few of the largest firms in the industry

Concentration ratios show the percentage of total market share accounted for by a few of the largest firms in the industry. For example, a two-firm concentration ratio for the beer industry would tell you what percentage of the beer industry's business is done by the two largest breweries. A four-firm concentration ratio for the auto industry would tell you what percentage of the auto industry's total output is accounted for by the four largest automakers. The larger companies in highly concentrated industries usually have branches in several provinces and sell their output from coast to coast.

Does this mean that the higher the concentration ratio, the less competitive the industry is?

That's right. In monopolistic competition, the concentration ratio will be relatively low. In oligopoly, it will be relatively high. In pure monopoly, the concentration ratio will be 100% because a single firm produces 100% of the total output.

What is the Herfindahl-Hirschman Index?

Herfindahl-Hirschman Index (HHI) an index of industry concentration derived from summing the squares of the market shares of the firms in the industry

The **Herfindahl-Hirschman Index (HHI)** is a commonly used index of industry concentration derived from summing the squares of the market shares of the firms in the industry. For example, let us assume that there are only four firms in the industry and that their market shares are 40%, 30%, 20%, and 10%, respectively. Then the HHI would be

$$HHI = 40^2 + 30^2 + 20^2 + 10^2 = 3000$$

How is the Herfindahl-Hirschman Index generally interpreted?

The interpretation of the HHI is somewhat arbitrary, but the general guideline is offered in Table 11.1.

Note that a concentration ratio does not necessarily include all the firms in the industry, whereas the HHI does.

Table 11.1	Herfindahl-Hirschman Index Interpretation
HHI	**Interpretation**
Less than 1000	Unconcentrated
1000–1800	Moderately concentrated
More than 1800	Highly concentrated

Reading Comprehension

The answers to these questions can be found on MyEconLab at **www.myeconlab.com.**   MyEconLab

1.   What are the main characteristics of oligopoly?

2.   Define each of the following terms:
  a)   Duopoly
  b)   Differentiated oligopoly
  c)   Concentration ratio
  d)   Herfindahl-Hirschman Index

LO 11.8 Explain oligopoly pricing and output

Oligopoly Pricing and Output

How does a firm in oligopoly decide on its profit-maximizing price and output?

Figure 11.9 Price and Output for a Firm in Oligopoly

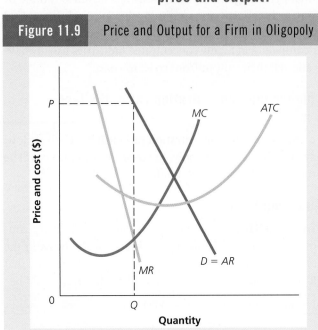

The firm in oligopoly produces a substantial portion of the total industry output and therefore has some control over the price of its product. Product differentiation by the firm in oligopoly can also increase its market power. The demand curve for the firm in oligopoly therefore slopes downward. Like firms in other market situations, the firm in oligopoly is assumed to be a profit maximizer. The firm in oligopoly will therefore produce an output at which *MR* equals *MC*. In Figure 11.9, the profit-maximizing output is $0Q$, and the price charged is $0P$.

An increase in the cost of production will normally lead a firm to increase the price of its product. If a firm in oligopoly increases its price, however, some buyers will probably switch to substitutes offered by other firms. Such substitution can result in an increase in the prices of the substitutes.

Reading Comprehension

The answers to these questions can be found on MyEconLab at **www.myeconlab.com**   MyEconLab.

1. Describe the shapes of the demand and marginal revenue curves for a firm in oligopoly.

2. How does a firm in oligopoly decide on its profit-maximizing price and output?

LO 11.9 Discuss the kinked demand curve model

The Kinked Demand Curve

What is a kinked demand curve and what does it illustrate?

It has been observed that prices tend to remain relatively stable in oligopoly markets. One explanation for the relative price stability is that firms in oligopoly realize that a price cut by one firm can cause other firms to retaliate by cutting their prices also. Instead of engaging in a price war, which will hurt every firm, each firm tacitly agrees to live and let live by sharing the market—and the profits. This, of course, is a result of the strong interdependence of firms in oligopoly markets, which is absent in other market structures.

The **kinked demand curve** is a demand curve with a kink resulting from the assumption that firms will follow the lead of a price reduction but not of a price increase; it is used to explain price rigidity in oligopolies. The model was advanced

kinked demand curve
a demand curve with a kink resulting from the assumption that firms will follow the lead of a price reduction but not of a price increase; used to explain price rigidity

independently but almost simultaneously in 1939 by Paul Sweezy in the United States and by Robert Hall and Charles Hitch in Britain. The theory is based on two basic assumptions about firms' reactions to price changes by their rivals:

1. A price increase by one firm will not be matched by similar increases in other firms.

2. A reduction in price by one firm will be matched by similar reductions in other firms.

Firms in oligopoly are assumed to behave in this manner to keep their customers or to capture a larger share of the market. If, for example, Minute Maid increases the price of its orange juice, we can assume that Tropicana, to attract customers from Minute Maid, will leave its price unchanged. But if Minute Maid reduces its price, it is assumed that Tropicana will follow suit so as not to lose customers to Minute Maid.

This situation is illustrated in Figure 11.10. Consider an oligopolist selling a product at price P. If the firm raises its price above P, its rivals, by assumption, will not raise their prices. Thus, the quantity of the firm's product demanded can be expected to fall significantly as buyers switch to the firm's rivals. This implies that the demand curve is relatively elastic at prices above P.

If the oligopolist lowers its price from P, its rivals will, by assumption, follow its lead and lower their prices so as not to lose their customers. Thus, the quantity of the firm's product demanded as a result of lowering its price will not increase significantly. Buyers will have no price incentive to switch from the firm's rivals. This implies that the demand curve is relatively inelastic at prices below P. The demand curve is relatively elastic at prices above P and relatively inelastic at prices below P.

Thus, the demand curve has a kink or a bend at point A in Figure 11.10. The MR curve associated with such a demand curve is also illustrated in the diagram. Note that the MR curve has a discontinuous section.

Figure 11.10 shows that if the MR and the MC curves intersect within the range of the vertical section of the MR curve, an appreciable shift in the MC curve will have no effect on the profit-maximizing price and output for the firm. For example, an increase from MC_1 to MC_2 leaves price and output unchanged at 0P and 0Q, respectively. Changes in cost will affect price and output only when they are very substantial.

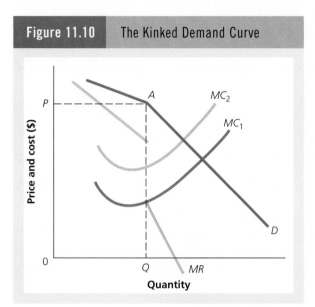

Figure 11.10   The Kinked Demand Curve

The kinked demand curve model explains why price may remain constant even when cost increases. But what determines where the kink occurs, and how is the rigid price established in the first place?

The model of the kinked demand curve explains how a kink occurs in the demand curve, but it does not explain where the kink occurs. Once the price is known, we can use the model to explain price rigidity, but it does not tell us anything about the determination or the establishment of the rigid price in the first place.

Does price rigidity have other explanations?

The model of the kinked demand curve is one explanation of relative price rigidity in oligopolies, but it is not the only explanation, and it cannot be regarded as a general theory of price and output determination in oligopoly markets. In fact, other explanations of rigid prices exist.

The kinked demand curve model does a good job of explaining "sticky" (inflexible) prices. We will here examine two other explanations of sticky prices that have been advanced: long-term contracts and small menu costs.

Long-Term Contracts   Many firms enter into long-term agreements with their suppliers to provide inputs at pre-arranged prices. This is one way to insulate themselves against price increases and the uncertainly of supplies. Many companies also enter into contracts to provide retail outlets with a certain amount of output at some pre-negotiated prices. Such arrangements obviously contribute to price rigidity as they ensure that prices will not respond to short-run changes in demand and supply. Such contracts protect market players against the vagaries of market forces.

Small Menu Costs   Changing the prices of items is not a costless exercise—costs are involved. The firm that is changing its prices has to pay employees to remove old price tags and add new ones, or to place new price tags over old ones. New catalogues and price lists may have to be printed and distributed to customers and potential customers. The costs incurred when changing prices are referred to as **menu costs**, because they are similar to the costs incurred by a restaurant changing its menu when its prices change.

menu costs the costs incurred in changing prices; may explain price rigidity

The existence of these menu costs may cause a firm to hesitate to change its prices.

Reading Comprehension

The answers to these questions can be found on MyEconLab at www.myeconlab.com.   MyEconLab

1. What does the model of the kinked demand curve explain?
2. What are some of the difficulties associated with the kinked demand curve model of oligopoly behaviour?

3. The kinked demand curve model provides one explanation for price rigidity. Discuss other explanations that have been offered for sticky prices.
4. Give three examples of small menu costs.

LO 11.10 Discuss cartels and other forms of collusion

Other Models of Oligopoly

Are there other models of the behaviour of firms in oligopoly markets?

Because of the interdependence of firms in oligopoly, and the huge range of tactics firms can employ, it is virtually impossible to develop a single model that explains the various possible decisions that each firm can make. Therefore, numerous models have been developed to explain behaviour under particular assumptions.

What are some of these models?

Other models of the behaviour of firms in oligopoly are

- Limit or predatory pricing
- Price leadership
- Cost-plus pricing
- Cartels
- Game theory

These models explain different pricing strategies that can be used by firms in oligopoly. Let us examine each in turn.

Limit or Predatory Pricing   In cases where significant economies of scale exist and initial capital outlays are high, the firms in an oligopoly situation may deliberately set their prices so low that new entrants into the market will make no profits. This pricing strategy is known as **limit pricing** or **predatory pricing**.

limit pricing or predatory pricing a pricing strategy in which firms set their prices so low that new entrants into the market will make no profits

Can this concept of predatory pricing be illustrated graphically?

Yes. Figure 11.11 illustrates how predatory pricing works. Assume that the demand, *MR*, *AC*, and *MC* curves are as shown in Diagram A of Figure 11.11.

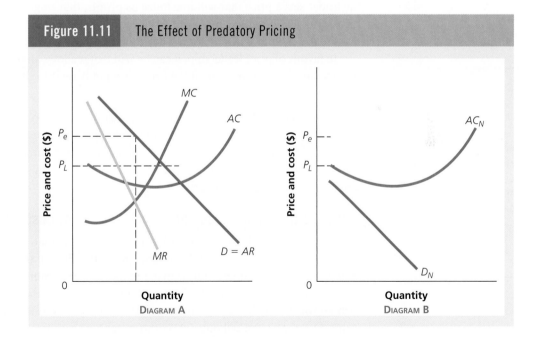

| Figure 11.11 | The Effect of Predatory Pricing |

The profit-maximizing price shown in Diagram A is P_e. If the existing firms set a price of P_L, they will earn a profit at this low price because they control such a large share of the market. When the existing firms charge a price of P_L, the share of the market that can be captured by any potential competitor is represented by the demand curve D_N in Diagram B of Figure 11.11. This price is too low for any new firm to make a profit. At any level of output, the new firm's demand curve lies below its *AC* curve,

AC_N. The potential firm's share of the market, therefore, will be too small for profitable operation.

Price Leadership   The firms in an oligopoly may refrain from engaging in price competition. Consequently, a situation of **price leadership** can emerge in which one firm in an industry takes the lead in changing prices and the other firms follow suit.

price leadership the condition that exists when one firm in an industry takes the lead in changing prices and the other firms follow suit

Two types of price leadership exist: dominant price leadership and barometric price leadership. Dominant price leadership exists when the industry consists of a few smaller firms and a single firm that dominates the industry. Price changes are initiated by the dominant firm, and the smaller firms simply follow the leader.

In a situation of *barometric price leadership*, the industry may not be dominated by any single firm. Any firm can be the leader, or the leadership role may rotate in a rather orderly manner. Changes in demand and cost conditions in the industry may cause one firm to initiate a price change that is followed by the other firms in the industry.

What are the advantages and disadvantages of price leadership?

Price leadership can prevent the dangerous problems (for the firms) of a price war, in which all the firms lose, but the arrangement is unlikely to benefit all firms equally. As you know, a firm maximizes its profits by setting a price at which its *MR* equals its *MC*. Because all the firms in the industry are unlikely to have the same cost, it follows that if the leader sets a price that will maximize its profits, that single price will not benefit all firms equally. To reduce the risk of a price war, the price leader must take the situation of its followers into consideration when initiating price changes for the industry.

In favour of price leadership, it can be said that it allows an orderly change from one price to another, noting that all the firms may not benefit to the same extent.

Cost-Plus Pricing   It is believed that many firms in oligopoly markets determine the prices of their products by adopting a method of pricing known as **cost-plus pricing** or **markup pricing**, a pricing strategy in which a firm determines price simply by adding a certain percentage markup to its *AC*. For example, if the firm's *AC* is $12, it may choose a markup of 25% and set its price at $15.

cost-plus pricing or markup pricing a pricing strategy in which firms determine price by adding a certain percentage markup on cost

What are the advantages and disadvantages of cost-plus pricing?

The advantage of this method of price determination is that it is easy to calculate and easy to understand. But it does have some problems. First, if the firm is trying to maximize its profits, how does it know that a markup of 25% rather than a markup of 20% or 30% will equate MR and MC? Second, the cost-plus method is practical only if the firm knows exactly how much it can sell at various prices. If it puts its markup at 25%, it may find that it can sell only 70% of its output at that price. It may then be forced to lower its markup.

collusion firms that unite to control price and output in particular markets

unwritten agreements agreements reached by handshake only, with no formal written document

Cartels   It is certainly not uncommon for firms in oligopoly to act in unison to control price and output of a particular product. **Collusion**, as such practices are called, is illegal in Canada. Nevertheless, firms still seem to get together informally and enter into **unwritten agreements** (agreements reached by handshake only, with no formal written document) to control price and market shares. Tacit agreements among firms are more likely to occur when the industry consists of only a few firms.

BUSINESS SITUATION 11.4

The Canadian brewing industry comprises two giants: Labatt and Molson, and several microbreweries. Molson and Labatt account for about 90% of the Canadian beer market. The microbreweries have alleged that Labatt and Molson have engaged in anti-competitive practices that have adversely affected the microbreweries. Some of the practices alluded to include special agreements with licensed establishments (retailers of beer).

How might the microbreweries be disadvantaged by these practices?

The answer to this Business Situation can be found in Appendix A.

cartel a formal agreement among independent firms to act in concert to control price and output in a particular industry

The best-known form of collusion among firms in oligopoly is probably a **cartel,** which is a formal agreement among independent firms to act in concert to control price and output in a particular industry.

In many international markets, agreements to control prices and output are legal. Therefore, many cartels operate in international markets. Cartels are quite common in markets for natural resources. The International Bauxite Association, the Organization of the Petroleum Exporting Countries (OPEC), and the International Air Transport Association (IATA) are examples of cartels.

Cartels can be perfect or imperfect. In a perfect cartel, all decisions regarding price and output are surrendered to a central decision-making body, and the profits are distributed to each firm according to the terms of the cartel agreement. In an imperfect cartel, each firm reserves some decision-making powers and may be allowed to keep whatever profits it earns. This is the type of cartel likely to be found in practice.

Do cartels face any particular problems?

Cartels face a variety of problems. However, we will focus our attention on three common problems that plague cartels. First, individual independent firms are unlikely to be willing to surrender their decision-making powers to the central body. Second, each firm in the cartel has a strong temptation to cheat and produce more than its quota with the prospect of earning greater profits. Whether other cartel members cheat or not, any individual firm faces a strong profit incentive to cheat.

Third, the cartel faces the problem of the entry of new firms into the industry. If a new firm enters the cartel, and the total demand for the industry's product does not increase, the optimum output for the cartel remains unchanged but the given profits of the group must now be shared among a greater number of members. If the new firm enters the industry but is not admitted into the cartel, then the survival of the cartel is threatened.

Can you provide an example to show why the incentive to cheat is so strong?

Consider the following example. Suppose that the cartel has decided that Firm A should produce an output of 400 units per period at the cartel price of $500. Suppose Firm A could produce an extra unit at a *MC* of only $200. Firm A could break the cartel rule (i.e., cheat) and produce the additional unit and sell it for $500, thus increasing its profit by $300.

Collectively, the firms in a cartel arrangement have an interest in restricting output to maintain price at a given level. However, individually, each of the member firms can benefit by producing more than its allotted share. Clearly, if each firm cheats, industry output will increase, the price will fall, and the existence of the cartel will be threatened. The cartel may have to resort to industrial surveillance (spying) because of the enormous incentive to cheat.

How are prices and output determined in cartels?

It is reasonable to assume that a cartel will attempt to adopt a price and output policy that maximizes joint (collective) profits. If that is the case, then the cartel will choose a price-output combination that equates *MR* with *MC*. In other words, the cartel will behave exactly like a monopolist producing its output in different plants, as discussed in Chapter 10.

So the cartel chooses a price-output combination that maximizes the total profits of the group. But this output is produced by different members of the cartel. How does the cartel allocate output and profits among cartel members?

The allocation of output and profits is another problem that a cartel faces. Once it decides on its price-output combination, it must decide on the allocation of that output and profits among its members. The allocation of output can be done in any of several ways, including the assignment of exclusive territories and the establishment of output quotas for members. The output quota approach is followed by OPEC—perhaps the best-known cartel.

The allocation of profits can be done by negotiation, taking into consideration the contribution of each member to the generation of total profits. Clearly, this is not a simple problem, and it helps to explain the instability observed in many cartel arrangements.

Reading Comprehension

The answers to these questions can be found on MyEconLab at www.myeconlab.com.　　MyEconLab

1. Why do you think there are so many different models of oligopoly behaviour? Do you think it would be easy to develop a general model of oligopoly? Why or why not?
2. What is the difference between each of the following pairs of concepts?
   a) Dominant price leadership and barometric price leadership

   b) Cartel and unwritten agreement
   c) Perfect cartel and imperfect cartel
3. What is cost-plus pricing? Will cost-plus pricing automatically generate maximum profits?
4. Explain how predatory pricing can be used to prevent potential competitors from entering an industry.
5. What are some of the problems faced by cartels?
6. Why is the incentive to cheat so strong among cartel members?

Game Theory

Game theory is a method of analysis used by economists (and others) to study strategies in situations in which the interdependence of decisions is recognized. Recall that firms in oligopoly markets recognize their interdependence. For this reason, game theory is ideally suited for oligopoly behaviour.

The idea of game theory can be illustrated by what has come to be popularly known as the prisoner's dilemma.

game theory a method of analysis used by economists (and others) to study strategies in situations in which the interdependence of decisions is recognized

> The **prisoner's dilemma** occurs when two prisoners are caught in a situation in which it is difficult to cooperate even when cooperation is beneficial to both prisoners.

prisoner's dilemma what happens when two prisoners are caught in a situation in which it is difficult to cooperate even when cooperation is beneficial to both prisoners

Two criminals, Bonnie and Clyde, we'll call them, commit a crime. The prosecutor has enough evidence to convict them of a minor offence for which the penalty is a year in prison. Here comes the dilemma. Separated from each other, each prisoner is told that if one confesses while the other does not, the one who confesses will be set free, while the other will get a 10-year jail sentence. If Bonnie and Clyde both confess, they will each get a sentence of five years. If neither confesses, they will each get a sentence of one year. The outcomes of each prisoner's decision are shown in Figure 11.12.

Here, there are two decision makers (players), Bonnie and Clyde, and each can make one of two decisions, which are strategies—confess or don't confess. The outcomes (payoffs) are their sentences.

What are the rudiments of game theory?

All games have the following elements:

- *Players:* The players are the parties involved in playing the game. In the case of oligopoly, the players are the firms.
- *Strategies:* The strategies are the various options (or moves) that are available to each player. In the game of baseball, a batter's strategy might be to bunt. In

Figure 11.12	The Prisoner's Dilemma

oligopoly, a firm's strategy might be to lower its price. Another firm's strategy might be to offer free samples of a product for a time.

- *Rules:* The rules of the game outline the strategies that the players may or may not employ. To continue with our baseball analogy, one of the rules is that a batter is out if he or she gets three strikes. In oligopoly, a rule might be that firms are not allowed to collude and fix the price. In this case, the rules are established by laws and regulations.

- *Outcome:* The result, outcome, or **payoff** in a game is the result of the moves or strategies adopted by the players. The outcome resulting from lowering the price might be more customers being drawn away from a competitor.

payoff the result or outcome of a strategy in a game

Nash equilibrium the condition that exists when each player in a game selects the best possible strategy, given the strategies of the other players

payoff matrix a table that shows the outcomes of various strategies in a game

The concept of equilibrium has been prominent in our analyses of the behaviour of firms in various situations. Does the concept of equilibrium have any meaning in game theory?

In fact, a concept of equilibrium does pertain to game theory. If each player in a game selects the best possible strategy, given the strategy of his or her opponent, then equilibrium is achieved. This concept of equilibrium is called **Nash equilibrium**, named after the economist John Nash, who introduced it. Nash equilibrium is the condition that exists when each player selects the best possible strategy, given the strategies of the other players.

Figure 11.13	A Payoff Matrix for Duopolists

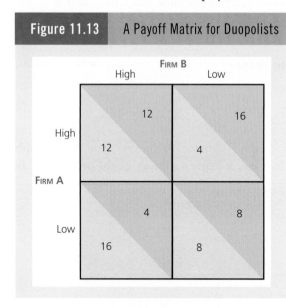

Can a diagram be used to explain the basic idea behind game theory?

The outcomes of the various strategies in a game are usually presented in a table called a **payoff matrix**. To illustrate the payoff matrix, let us consider the case of only two firms in an industry (duopoly). Each has to decide on a pricing strategy that will result in the highest monetary outcome or payoff. Figure 11.13 shows the consequences of employing a particular pricing strategy.

If both firms choose a high-price strategy, each will earn $12 million. If both choose a low-price strategy, each will earn $8 million. If Firm *A* chooses a low price and *B* doesn't, *A* will earn $16 million. If *B* chooses a low price and *A* doesn't, *B* will earn $16 million. Thus, if they do not collude, each will choose the low-price strategy. The equilibrium of this game is that each firm will select the low-price strategy.

Reading Comprehension

The answers to these questions can be found on MyEconLab at **www.myeconlab.com**.   MyEconLab

1. What is game theory?

2. Define Nash equilibrium.
3. What is a payoff matrix?
4. Explain why game theory is so useful in oligopoly.

LO 11.12 Evaluate oligopoly and understand the concept of workable competition

Evaluation of Oligopoly

What are some of the disadvantages associated with oligopoly?

Like monopoly, oligopoly has certain undesirable social consequences. Barriers to the entry of new firms into the industry can result in a price that exceeds *ATC* in most firms in oligopoly. Thus, firms in oligopoly are likely to earn excess profits. Also, the price established in an oligopoly is likely to be above *MC*. This inequality between price and MC implies a misallocation of resources. Furthermore, firms in oligopoly tend to spend huge amounts of money on advertising in an attempt to maintain or increase their share of the market. Many people consider this enormous advertising outlay to be wasteful.

Does this mean that oligopoly is socially undesirable?

workable competition the condition that exists when competition is sufficient to ensure that market power is not excessive

Not necessarily. Despite the disadvantages listed above, oligopoly is not always socially undesirable. If the industry has **workable competition**—that is, if competition in the industry is sufficient to ensure that market power is not excessive—oligopoly may not be totally undesirable.

We can even argue that economies of scale under oligopoly can lead to lower cost and hence lower prices. Moreover, many firms in oligopoly do undertake a significant amount of research and development (R&D). New and important products are developed, and new techniques are discovered and introduced—often with significant benefits to society.

A large percentage of the goods and services produced in the Canadian economy are produced by firms in oligopoly; therefore, an understanding of the theories that attempt to explain the behaviour of firms in oligopoly contributes to our understanding of the Canadian economy.

Reading Comprehension

The answers to these questions can be found on MyEconLab at **www.myeconlab.com.** MyEconLab

1. What are some of the undesirable social consequences associated with oligopoly?

2. What is workable competition?

LO 11.13 Discuss the concept of contestable markets

Contestable Markets

Will any other factor besides the number of firms in the industry influence the behaviour of the firms?

Yes. Your question suggests that you have observed our concentration on the number of firms in the industry. In some cases, however, the number of firms might not provide a proper indication of how the firms in the industry will behave.

Let us assume that Ms. Lillian Lovelaw is the only lawyer in a small town. There is not another lawyer within a 15-kilometre radius of Ms. Lovelaw. For all practical purposes, Lillian Lovelaw is a monopoly. She will charge a price that equates *MR* and *MC*. She may even be able to practise price discrimination and thus increase her profits by capturing more of the consumer surplus.

Consider now the case of Harry Hedgetrimmer Enterprises, a firm that specializes in trimming hedges for private homes. Like Lillian Lovelaw, Harry Hedgetrimmer is a monopoly. However, the pricing behaviour of the two firms will likely be quite different. Whereas Lillian may set a price that results in positive economic profits, Harry Hedgetrimmer may behave more like a pure competitor than like a monopolist and deliberately earn only normal profit (zero economic profit).

Now why would these two firms adopt different pricing strategies?

contestable market a market into which entry is so easy that the threat of entry by potential competitors prevents the existing firms from exercising any monopoly power

The reason is as follows. Entry into Lillian Lovelaw's market requires legal training and the passing of special examinations. Thus, her market is not easily contestable. Conversely, it is relatively easy to enter Harry Hedgetrimmer's industry. His is a **contestable market**. A market is said to be contestable if entry into the industry is easy so that the threat of entry by potential competitors prevents the existing firms from exercising any monopoly power.

The concept of contestable markets suggests that looking at the number of firms in an industry is not enough to determine the extent of market power. The ease of entering the industry, thus creating potential competitors, must also be considered.

Reading Comprehension

The answers to these questions can be found on MyEconLab at **www.myeconlab.com**.   MyEconLab

1. When is a market contestable?

2. "Any firm with market power will never behave like a pure competitor." Discuss.

Review

1. Review the learning objectives listed at the beginning of the chapter.
2. Have you accomplished all the objectives? One way to determine this is to answer the Reading Comprehension questions at the end of each section. They will help you assess the extent to which you have accomplished the learning objectives.
3. If you have not accomplished an objective, review the relevant material before proceeding.

Key Points to Remember

1. **LO 11.1** Monopolistic competition is a market structure in which a large number of firms produce differentiated products. In this market structure, it is relative easy for firms to enter or leave the industry, and each firm has a slight control over its price. Because of the large number of substitutes available, the demand for the product of a firm in monopolistic competition is relatively elastic.

2. **LO 11.2** The demand curve for a firm in monopolistic competition is relatively elastic because of the large number of close substitutes. Recall that the demand curve is the average revenue curve. Since the demand curve is downward sloping, the marginal revenue curve is also downward sloping and is below the average revenue or demand curve.

3. **LO 11.3** The firm in monopolistic competition maximizes profits when its marginal revenue (*MR*) equals its marginal cost (*MC*). The price charged exceeds marginal cost.

4. **LO 11.4** Entry into an industry that is monopolistically competitive is relatively easy. Therefore, if a monopolistically competitive firm is earning positive economic profits in the short run, new firms will enter the industry and compete, and those profits will dwindle away. In long-run equilibrium, price equals average cost (*AC*).

5. **LO 11.5** Several important differences exist between monopolistic competition and pure competition. Among them are the following: (1) In pure competition, the firms sell identical products whereas in monopolistic competition they sell differentiated products. (2) In pure competition, price equals marginal cost whereas in monopolistic competition, price exceeds marginal cost. Thus, resources are not optimally allocated in monopolistic competition. (3) In pure competition, firms operate at minimum average cost in the long run. In monopolistic competition, they operate with excess capacity. (4) In the long run, firms in pure competition produce a larger quantity of output at a lower price than do firms in monopolistic competition.

6. **LO 11.6** Firms in monopolistic competition often engage in advertising to increase the demand for their products or to maintain their share of the market. If advertising is successful, it will shift the demand curve to the right and make it less elastic.

7. **LO 11.7** An oligopoly is a market structure in which there are only a few firms. Because of the small number of firms, they all recognize their interdependence. In an oligopoly market structure, the behaviour of one firm depends critically on how it believes the others will react to any move that it might make.

8. **LO 11.8** The demand and marginal revenue curves of a firm in oligopoly are downward sloping. The firm in oligopoly maximizes profits by equating marginal revenue and marginal cost.

9. **LO 11.9** The kinked demand curve is an oligopoly model designed to explain price rigidity in oligopoly markets. The model is based on two basic assumptions about competitors' reactions to price changes. The model assumes that a price increase by one firm will not be matched by similar increases in other firms; but a reduction in price by one firm will be matched by a similar reduction in other firms. These assumptions give rise to a kink in the demand curve. In such a case, a small change in cost will not result in a change in price.

10. **LO 11.10** A cartel maximizes joint (collective) profits by choosing a price-output combination that equates marginal revenue and marginal cost. In determining the output that should be produced by each cartel member, the cartel behaves like a multi-plant monopolist, allocating output to each member so that the marginal cost is the same for each member. This marginal cost must equal the marginal revenue of the cartel.

11. **LO 11.11** Game theory is a tool used to analyze the behaviour of firms in a situation where the strategies of the firms are interdependent. Nash equilibrium is the condition that exists when each player selects the best possible strategy given the strategy of the opponent.

12. **LO 11.12** Oligopoly has certain undesirable social consequences. Firms usually charge a price that exceeds average cost, which leads to excess profits; price is likely to exceed marginal cost, which means that resources are likely to be misallocated; and firms in oligopoly tend to collude to control the market. If however, workable competition exists, then oligopoly might provide some advantages.

13. **LO 11.13** Contestable markets prevent firms in a monopolistically competitive industry or in an oligopoly from exercising monopoly power.

Economic Word Power

Cartel (p. 333)
Collusion (p. 332)
Concentration ratio (p. 327)
Contestable market (p. 338)
Cost-plus pricing or markup pricing (p. 332)
Differentiated oligopoly (p. 326)
Duopoly (p. 325)
Excess capacity theorem (p. 322)
Game theory (p. 335)
Herfindahl-Hirschman Index (HHI) (p. 327)
Kinked demand curve (p. 328)
Limit pricing or predatory pricing (p. 331)
Menu costs (p. 330)
Nash equilibrium (p. 336)
Payoff (p. 336)
Payoff matrix (p. 336)
Price leadership (p. 332)
Prisoner's dilemma (p. 335)
Product differentiation (p. 316)
Unwritten agreements (p. 332)
Workable competition (p. 337)

Problems and Exercises

Basic

1. **LO 11.1** List five firms that are likely to operate in monopolistic competition.
2. **LO 11.1** Product differentiation is a key factor in monopolistic competition. List at least three ways whereby a firm might differentiate its product.
3. **LO 11.2** Table 11.2 shows data for a firm in monopolistic competition.
   a. Fill in the TR and MR columns.
   b. Graph the demand and MR curves.
   c. From your graph, determine the level of output at which TR is at its maximum.
   d. What is the value of MR when TR is at its maximum?

Table 11.2	Data for a Firm in Monopolistic Competition		
Quantity	Price ($)	TR ($)	MR ($)
1	55		
2	50		
3	45		
4	40		
5	35		
6	30		
7	25		

4. **LO 11.2** Figure 11.14 shows cost and revenue curves for a firm in monopolistic competition. Label the curves.
5. **LO 11.3** Table 11.3 contains data for a firm in monopolistic competition.
   a. Complete the table by filling in TR, MR, TC, MC, and profit for this firm.
   b. How many units of output should this firm sell to maximize its profits?

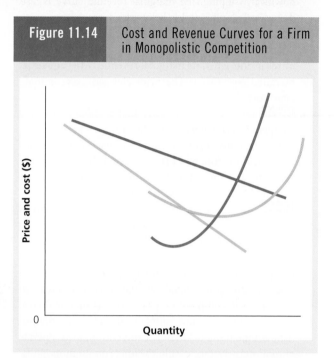

Figure 11.14	Cost and Revenue Curves for a Firm in Monopolistic Competition

Table 11.3	Data for a Firm in Monopolistic Competition					
Price ($)	Quantity	TR ($)	MR ($)	ATC ($)	TC ($)	MC ($)	Profit ($)
20	1			21			
19	2			17			
18	3			16			
17	4			15			
16	5			18			
15	6			20			
14	7			24			

c. What price should the firm charge?
d. What is the maximum profit that this firm can earn?

6. **LO 11.3** Table 11.4 presents revenue and cost data for a firm in monopolistic competition.
   a. Fill in the *TR*, *MR*, *TC*, *MC*, and profit columns.
   b. Plot the *ATC*, *AR*, *MR*, and *MC* curves.
   c. From your graph, estimate the output level at which *MR* = *MC*.

Table 11.4	Revenue and Cost Data for a Firm in Monopolistic Competition						
Quantity	AR ($)	ATC ($)	TR ($)	MR ($)	TC ($)	MC ($)	Profit ($)
20	16	15					
40	14	13					
60	12	14					
80	10	17					
100	8	22					
120	6	28					

7. **LO 11.7** Table 11.5 shows data for an industry consisting of six firms.
   a. Calculate the four-firm concentration ratio.
   b. Calculate the Herfindahl-Hirschman Index (HHI).
   c. On the basis of the HHI, is this industry highly concentrated, moderately concentrated, or unconcentrated?

Table 11.5	Sales Data for a Six-Firm Industry
Firm	Value of Sales ($ mil)
A	60
B	50
C	40
D	30
E	10
F	10

Questions in the Intermediate and Challenging Sections cover several different concepts, and have not been organized by learning objectives.

Intermediate

1. Draw a diagram for a firm in monopolistic competition showing *MC*, *ATC*, *MR*, and *AR*. Show what the profit-maximizing price and output will be.
2. Figure 11.15 represents a firm in oligopoly. Fill in the blanks.
   a. To maximize profits, this firm will produce _____ units of output and charge a price of $_____. Its *TR* will be $_____.
   b. *MC* can vary between $_____ and $_____ without causing a change in the equilibrium price.
   c. To maximize its *TR*, this firm will produce _____ units and charge a price of $_____.

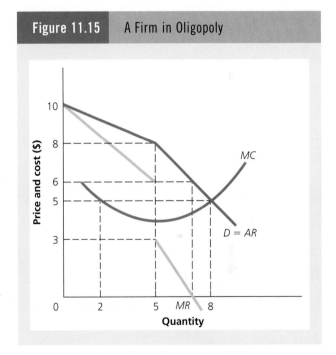

Figure 11.15	A Firm in Oligopoly

3. The payoff matrix shown in Table 11.6 represents outcome for two rival oligopolists, *A* and *B*, vying for the largest market share. In this situation, what is the Nash equilibrium?

Table 11.6	Payoff Matrix for Two Firms			
	Firm *B*'s Strategies			
	B_1	B_2	B_3	B_4
Firm *A*'s Strategies A_1	48	93	16	22
A_2	30	3	7	99
A_3	60	37	6	33

Challenging

1. "In monopolistic competition, product differentiation is key. Without it, monopolistic competition does not exist." Present an argument against the view expressed in the above statement. (Hint: Make the case that it is possible for many firms to sell exactly identical products and still be in monopolistic competition).
2. Figure 11.16 represents a firm in monopolistic competition.
   a. Label the curves and the axes.
   b. How much should this firm produce?
   c. What price should it charge?
   d. Indicate the excess capacity.

| Figure 11.16 | A Firm in Monopolistic Competition |

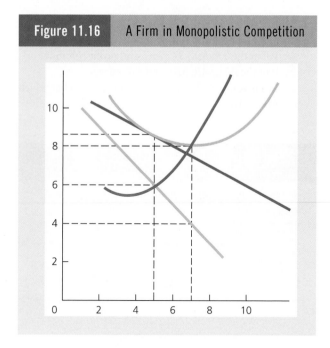

MyEconLab Visit the MyEconLab website at **www.myeconlab.com.** This online homework and tutorial system puts you in control of your own learning with study and practice tools directly correlated to this chapter's content.

Study Guide

Self-Assessment

The answers to the Study Guide questions can be found in Appendix B.

What's your score?

Circle the letter that corresponds with the correct answer.

1. Economists use the term imperfect competition to refer to
   a. Competition that is spoiled by government intervention
   b. The situation where rivalry among firms is almost non-existent
   c. Monopolistic competition and oligopoly
   d. None of the above
2. In monopolistic competition, there are
   a. A few competitive firms that have formed a monopoly
   b. Several monopolies competing for a larger share of the market
   c. Many pure competitive firms that have agreed not to compete
   d. Many firms producing differentiated products
3. In the market structure labelled monopolistic competition,
   a. Two monopolists compete against each other
   b. Some firms in the industry are monopolies while others are purely competitive
   c. The firms interchange their roles as pure competitors and pure monopolists
   d. Many firms produce differentiated products
4. Which of the following is not an example of a firm in monopolistic competition?
   a. General Motors
   b. A retail boutique in Toronto
   c. A barber shop in Montreal
   d. A used car dealer in Victoria

5. In short-run equilibrium, a firm in monopolistic competition, seeking to maximize profits, will operate where
   a. MR exceeds MC
   b. MR equals MC
   c. Price equals MC
   d. Price is less than ATC

6. In long-run equilibrium, a monopolistic competitor will have
   a. Price equal to MC
   b. Price equal to AC
   c. Price greater than AC
   d. Price less than AC

7. Successful advertising by a firm in monopolistic competition will
   a. Shift the firm's demand curve to the right
   b. Shift the firm's demand curve to the left
   c. Make the firm's demand curve more elastic or less inelastic
   d. Cause kinks in the MR curve

8. In long-run equilibrium, a firm in monopolistic competition will
   a. Earn positive economic profits
   b. Operate at the minimum point of its AC curve
   c. Earn zero economic profit
   d. Operate where MC equals AR

9. The excess capacity theorem relates to the fact that a profit-maximizing monopolistic competitor will produce
   a. An output level where $LRAC$ equals zero
   b. An output level less than the level that minimizes $LRAC$
   c. Its output with excess capacity no matter what output level is chosen
   d. None of the above

10. One major characteristic of firms in oligopoly is that
    a. They produce identical products
    b. They all have kinked demand curves
    c. They always collude to control price and output
    d. They recognize their interdependence

11. In Canada, which of the following would not be considered a firm in oligopoly?
    a. General Motors
    b. Esso
    c. Molson
    d. A farm in Saskatchewan

12. An industry with only two firms is called
    a. A double monopoly
    b. A duopoly
    c. A cartel
    d. None of the above

13. The model of the kinked demand curve
    a. Is based on the assumption that a price increase by one firm will not be matched by similar increases by other firms
    b. Is based on the assumption that a price reduction by one firm will be matched by similar reductions by other firms
    c. Explains relative price rigidity in oligopoly
    d. All of the above

14. Which of the following is a possible explanation of rigid (inflexible) prices?
    a. A kinked demand curve
    b. Small menu costs
    c. Long-term contracts
    d. All of the above

15. Limit pricing is
    a. A pricing strategy designed to serve as an effective barrier to entry
    b. The practice of raising prices to the highest limit
    c. A decision by government not to place any limit on prices charged by firms
    d. Price control by a government agency

16. Concentration ratios show
    a. The percentage of total industry supply accounted for by a few of the largest firms in the industry
    b. The ratio of TR to TC
    c. The profit ratio within an oligopoly
    d. None of the above

17. Which of the following is a problem typically faced by a perfect cartel?
    a. The tendency for individual members to cheat
    b. The problem of deciding how production quotas should be set
    c. The problem of deciding how profits should be distributed
    d. All of the above

18. Game theory is most applicable to
    a. Monopoly
    b. Monopolistic competition
    c. Oligopoly
    d. None of the above

19. Oligopoly can be advantageous because it can lead to
    a. Perfectly competitive behaviour
    b. Marginal-cost pricing
    c. Lower prices resulting from economies of scale
    d. All of the above

20. A market is said to be contestable when
    a. It is monopolized
    b. The firms in the industry are all oligopolists
    c. Entry into the industry is easy
    d. None of the above

Problems and Exercises (Use Quad Paper for Graphs)

1. Table 11.7 shows data for a firm in monopolistic competition.
   a. Complete the table by filling in *TR*, *MR*, *TC*, *MC*, and profit for this firm.

   b. How many units should the firm sell to maximize profits?
   c. What should the price of each unit be?
   d. What will the firm's total profit be?

2. Table 11.8 contains data for a firm in monopolistic competition.
   a. Complete the table.
   b. On quad paper, plot the *ATC*, *AR*, *MR*, and *MC* curves.
   c. At what output level do *MR* and *MC* intersect?
   d. What is the total profit at this output?

Table 11.7			Demand and Cost Data for a Firm in Monopolistic Competition			
P ($)	Q	TR ($)	MR ($)	ATC ($)	TC ($)	MC ($)	Profit ($)
200	1			210			
190	2			175			
180	3			160			
170	4			155			
160	5			155			
150	6			165			
140	7			170			
130	8			180			

Table 11.8			Revenue and Cost Curves for a Firm in Monopolistic Competition				
Q	AR ($)	ATC ($)	TR ($)	MR ($)	TC ($)	MC ($)	Total Profit ($)
200	20	19					
400	18	17					
600	16	15					
800	14	18					
1000	12	21					
1200	10	24					

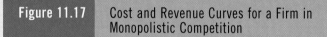

Figure 11.17	Cost and Revenue Curves for a Firm in Monopolistic Competition

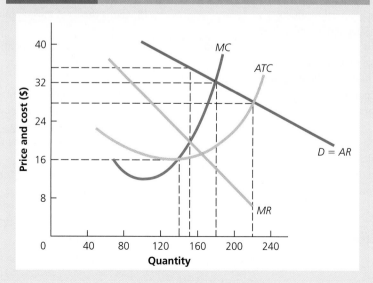

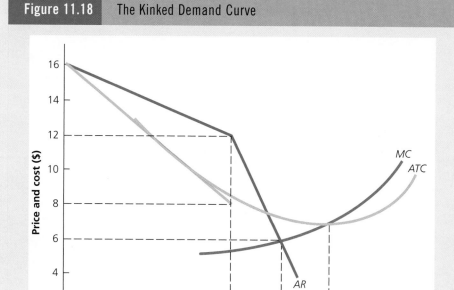

Figure 11.18 The Kinked Demand Curve

3. Figure 11.17 shows a monopolistically competitive firm.
   a. What level of output should this firm produce to maximize profits?
   b. What price should the firm charge for its product?
   c. What is the maximum total profit that this firm can earn?
4. Draw a demand curve for a firm in monopolistic competition, and then draw another demand curve to show the effect of a successful advertising campaign on the firm's demand curve. Explain your diagram.
5. Two brothers, Frank and Paul, decide to start a business that is in monopolistic competition. They have carefully calculated their costs, and they know the demand for their product. Their objective is to maximize their profits. Paul, who has a degree in marketing, suggests that they take a sample of the prices being charged by their competitors, and then set their prices as the average of their sample prices. Do you agree with Paul that this is the best pricing decision? Explain.
6. Answer the following questions on the basis of Figure 11.18.
   a. What output should this firm produce to maximize its profits?
   b. What price should this firm charge?
   c. What is the firm's *TC* at the profit-maximizing output?
   d. Calculate the firm's total profit at the price and output in parts (a) and (b).

7. Figure 11.19 represents a firm in oligopoly. The firm's objective is to maximize profits.
   a. What output should the firm produce?
   b. What price should it charge?
   c. What price-quantity adjustment should the firm make following a $2 increase in *MC*?
8. Table 11.9 contains data for an industry consisting of seven firms.
   a. Compute the four-firm concentration ratio.
   b. Compute the five-firm concentration ratio.
   c. Compute the Herfindahl-Hirschman Index
   d. On the basis of the HHI calculated in (c), how would you describe concentration in this industry?

Table 11.9 Sales Data for Seven-Firm Industry

Firm	Value of sales ($ mil)
A	30
B	25
C	23
D	20
E	15
F	15
G	10

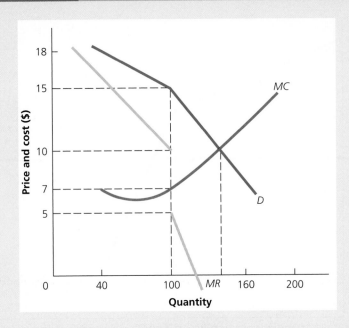

Figure 11.19 Cost and Revenue Curves for a Firm in Oligopoly

9. Table 11.10 is a payoff matrix showing payoffs for two firms, *A* and *B*, depending on whether they open four or five days a week. On the basis of the payoff matrix, find the equilibrium of the game and explain how you arrive at the equilibrium.

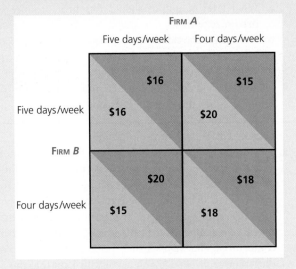

Table 11.10 Payoff Matrix for Two Firms

Chapter

12

The Market for Resources

Learning Objectives

After studying this chapter, you should be able to

12.1 Explain the demand for labour services

12.2 Explain the supply of labour services

12.3 Explain and use the model of competitive wage determination

12.4 Discuss the collective bargaining process

12.5 Discuss the factors in wage negotiations

12.6 Analyze the effects of labour unions in the labour market

12.7 Understand the nature of rent

12.8 Explain the model of rent determination

12.9 Distinguish between rent and transfer earnings

12.10 Explain how interest rates are determined

12.11 Understand the nature of profits

12.12 Discuss the economic role of profits

Assess Your Knowledge

MyEconLab

Answers to these questions can be found on MyEconLab at **www.myeconlab.com**.

Indicate whether each of the following is true or false:

1. If the wage rate rises, firms will tend to hire more workers.
2. If there is a shortage of labour, the wage rate will tend to rise.
3. The profitability of businesses has no bearing on wage negotiations.
4. All types of land generate the same rent.
5. The greater the degree of risk associated with a loan, the higher the rate of interest is likely to be.
6. Profits can be viewed as a reward for taking risks.

LO 12.1 Explain the demand for labour services

The Demand for Labour Services

Is there a difference between the demand for a factor of production, such as labour, and the demand for a consumer good or service?

direct demand the demand for final goods and services as opposed to the demand for factor inputs

Consumers buy goods and services in the product market because they derive utility (satisfaction) directly from goods and services. The demand for final goods and services is therefore a **direct demand**. In contrast, producers buy factors of production in the factor market to produce goods and services. In that sense, factor inputs do not give satisfaction directly as consumer goods and services do. The demand for factors of production (such as labour services) depends on the demand for the goods and services that the factors of production are used to produce. If the demand for goods and services increases, then more factors of production are required to produce them. The demand for inputs that is due to the demand for goods and services produced by the inputs is therefore a **derived demand**.

derived demand the demand for inputs that is due to the demand for the goods and services produced by the inputs

Where does the demand for labour services come from?

In addition to firms that demand labour services to be combined with other productive factors in the production of goods and services, the various levels of government demand labour services to offer the wide variety of services that governments provide. The government's use of labour services has some effect on the availability of workers for the private sector.

How does a firm decide on the number of workers that it will hire?

If the firm hires too many workers, then it is spending more money than it needs to. If the firm hires too few workers, then it is losing out on additional output that it could profitably produce. Fortunately, there is a way for the firm to determine the optimal number of workers to hire. The principle of substitution (see Chapter 7) indicates that if the price of an input falls, the firm will tend to use more of that input. Thus, if the price of labour (the wage rate) falls, the firm will tend to use more labour. The following analysis helps to determine how a firm decides on the number of workers it will hire. We assume that the firm is operating in a purely competitive industry and that it buys its inputs in a purely competitive market.

marginal physical product of labour the extra output derived from using an additional unit of labour

The marginal product of labour (MP_L) is the extra output derived from using an additional unit of labour input. If this value is expressed in physical terms, economists call it the **marginal physical product of labour** (MPP_L). That is,

$$MPP_L = \frac{\Delta TP}{\Delta L} \text{ where } TP \text{ is total product and } L \text{ is quantity of labour.}$$

marginal revenue product (of labour) the additional revenue contributed by the last unit of labour

The additional revenue contributed by the last unit of labour is called the **marginal revenue product (of labour)** (MRP_L).

The marginal revenue product, then, is simply the value of the marginal physical product ($VMPP$). We can calculate the $VMPP$ by multiplying the marginal physical product by the market price of the product. That is,

$$MRP_L = VMPP_L = MPP_L \times P$$

where P is the price of the product.

If an additional worker will contribute more to total revenue than to total cost, then it will benefit the firm to hire the extra worker. Hence, if the marginal revenue product (MRP_L) is greater than the wage rate (W), the firm will likely employ additional units of labour. If the marginal revenue product is less than the wage rate, then the firm will likely reduce its employment of labour. It follows that the firm seeking to maximize its profits will employ labour up to the point where $MRP_L = W$.

Figure 12.1	The Firm's Demand Curve for Labour

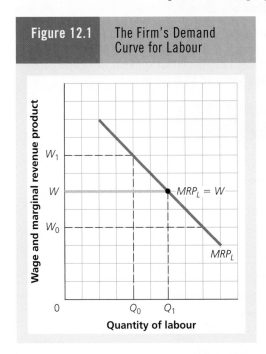

Can this argument be illustrated with the help of a graph?

Figure 12.1 will illustrate the point.

Because marginal product declines as additional units of labour are employed (diminishing returns), the marginal revenue product curve slopes downward, as shown in Figure 12.1. The market wage rate is assumed to be $0W$. If the firm were hiring $0Q_0$ units of labour at a wage rate of $0W$, the marginal revenue product $0W_1$ would be greater than the wage rate, and the firm would benefit by hiring more labour. If it were hiring $0Q_1$ units of labour at a wage rate of $0W$, the marginal revenue product $0W_0$ would be less than the wage rate ($0W$), and the firm would benefit by hiring fewer units of labour. At a wage rate of $0W$, the firm will hire $0Q$ units of labour because, with that amount of labour, the MRP_L equals the wage rate. This concept, known as the **marginal productivity theory of wages**, can be stated as follows: under purely competitive conditions, a profit-maximizing firm will hire labour up to the point at which the wage rate equals the value of the marginal product of labour.

marginal productivity theory of wages the theory that under purely competitive conditions a profit-maximizing firm will hire labour up to the point at which the wage rate equals the value of the marginal product of labour

A close relationship seems to exist between the marginal revenue product of labour and the firm's demand curve for labour. Is there?

Let's take a moment to examine that relationship. Look again at Figure 12.1. Note that if the wage rate were $0W_1$ instead of $0W$, the firm would employ $0Q_0$ units of labour instead of $0Q$. As the wage rate falls, the firm employs more units of labour. The MRP_L curve, therefore, is the firm's demand curve for labour.

The MRP_L curve is the firm's demand curve for labour.

Observe that a change in the wage rate causes a movement along, not a shift in, the firm's demand curve for labour. Such factors as changes in income, changes in tastes, and changes in market size, which affect the demand for the firm's product, will change the quantity of labour demanded by the firm at any given wage rate, and will thus shift the firm's demand curve for labour.

Is the market demand curve for labour derived by adding the demand curves for labour of all the firms in the industry?

On the surface, this seems logical. However, a complication does arise if we attempt to derive the market demand curve for labour by adding the individual firm's demand curves for labour. This complication arises because as the wage rate falls, the increased employment of labour by all firms in the industry is likely to increase the supply of the product. For this reason, the market demand curve for labour will be less elastic than that derived by adding the demand curves of the individual firms. If we assume, for analytical purposes only, that the price of the product is not affected by the firm's employment of labour, then we can derive the market demand curve for labour by adding the demand curves of all the firms in the industry.

BUSINESS SITUATION 12.1

Total Fitness manufactures a particular type of exercise machine. The company hires workers in a competitive labour market and pays each worker a wage of $300 per week. The market price of the machine is $100 each. Information on the firm's marginal product (*MP*) and its marginal revenue product (*MRP*) is given in Table 12.1. The firm is currently hiring five workers. The government then passes legislation making it illegal for firms to pay less than $400 per week.

Table 12.1	Marginal Product and Marginal Revenue Product for Total Fitness	
Number of Workers	*MP*	*MRP* ($)
0		
	5	500
1		
	6	600
2		
	5	500
3		
	4	400
4		
	3	300
5		
	1	100
6		

How should Total Fitness respond to this new business situation?

The answer to this Business Situation can be found in Appendix A.

Reading Comprehension

The answers to these questions can be found on MyEconLab at www.myeconlab.com.   MyEconLab

1. How does the demand for an input, such as labour, differ from the demand for a product, such as bread?
2. What is the difference between MPP_L and MRP_L?
3. Explain why the MRP_L curve slopes downward.
4. What is the relationship between MRP_L and the firm's demand curve for labour?
5. Briefly explain the marginal productivity theory of wages. Do you think that the theory is relevant to Canada today?

LO 12.2 Explain the supply of labour services

The Supply of Labour

Is there a difference between the supply of labour facing the firm and that facing the industry of which the firm is a part?

Yes, and it is an important difference. In a purely competitive market, the firm can purchase all the labour services it wants at the going wage rate. Such a firm therefore faces a perfectly elastic supply curve for labour services. The industry, however, faces a market supply curve that is upward sloping. Let's investigate. The labour supply curve shows the number of units of labour offered at each possible wage rate. Of course, it is the households that supply labour services to the labour market. We assume that at low wage rates, only small quantities of labour services are offered. Households regard both income and leisure as being desirable. As the wage rate increases, households will be more willing to sacrifice leisure and offer more labour services. We assume also that there is labour mobility between industries. One industry may attract workers by offering higher wage rates than those offered in other industries. The market supply curve of labour, then, slopes upward, as shown in Figure 12.2.

At a wage rate of $0W_1$, the quantity of labour supplied is $0Q_1$. At the higher wage rate of $0W_2$, a larger quantity of labour ($0Q_2$) is offered for hire. Observe also that the change in the wage rate causes a *movement along*, not a *shift in*, the labour supply curve.

> The supply of labour refers to the various quantities of labour services that will be offered for sale at various wage rates, during a period. The higher the wage rate, other things being equal, the greater the quantity of labour offered by households.

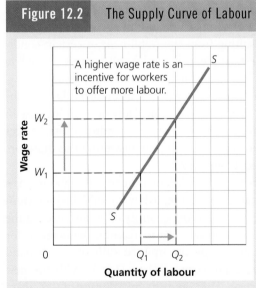

Figure 12.2   The Supply Curve of Labour

A higher wage rate is an incentive for workers to offer more labour.

Reading Comprehension

The answers to these questions can be found on MyEconLab at www.myeconlab.com.   MyEconLab

1. Explain the shape of the supply curve for labour.
2. How does an increase in the wage rate affect the supply curve of labour?
3. Who supplies labour services to the labour market?

LO 12.3 Explain and use the model of competitive wage determination

Wage Determination in a Competitive Labour Market

Is the equilibrium wage rate determined in a similar manner to the equilibrium price of a good or service in the product market?

Yes, market forces work in essentially the same way. We can determine the equilibrium wage rate and the amount of labour employed in a competitive labour market by bringing together demand for and supply of labour. Figure 12.3 shows the demand curve for labour (D_L) and the supply curve for labour (S_L).

At a wage rate of $0W_1$, the quantity of labour supplied is $0Q_1$, while the quantity demanded is $0Q_0$. Therefore, at a wage rate of $0W_1$, the quantity of labour supplied exceeds the quantity demanded. This surplus of labour will tend to force down the wage rate. At a wage rate of $0W_0$, the quantity of labour demanded exceeds the quantity supplied. At a wage rate of $0W_0$, there is therefore a shortage of labour that will tend to bid up the wage rate. At a wage rate of $0W$, the quantity of labour demanded equals the quantity supplied. The labour market clears and the wage rate stabilizes. The equilibrium wage rate is $0W$, and the quantity of labour hired at that wage rate is $0Q$.

Figure 12.3 Equilibrium in the Labour Market

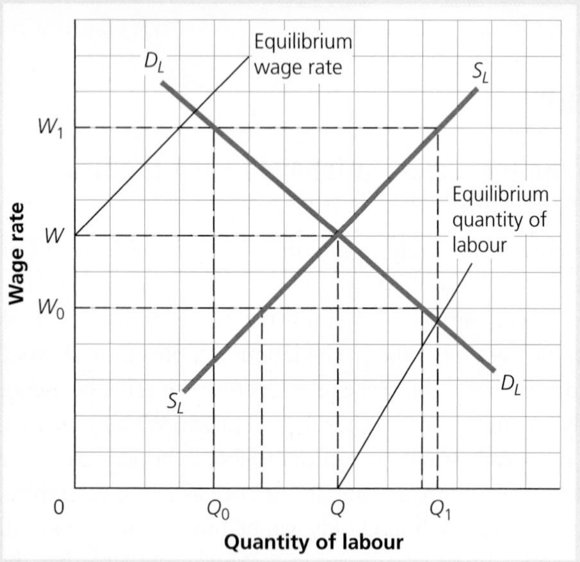

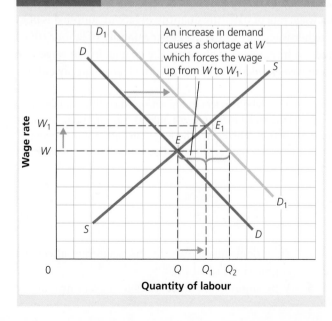

Can we use this model of wage determination to make any predictions?

As you know, one of the purposes of an economic model is to help us to predict the general direction of events resulting from the fulfillment of certain conditions. For example, this model will help us to analyze the effect of a change in the demand for labour in a particular industry on wages in that industry. Let us consider the following question: "How does an increase in demand for labour in a particular industry affect wages in that industry?" For help in answering this question, let us look at Figure 12.4.

DD is the original demand curve for labour, SS is the original supply curve, $0W$ is the initial equilibrium wage rate, and $0Q$ is the quantity of labour hired at the equilibrium wage rate. An increase in the demand for labour is shown by the upward shift of the demand for labour curve (from DD to D_1D_1). With the new demand curve D_1D_1 and the initial wage of $0W$, there is a shortage of $Q_2 - Q$ units of labour. This shortage forces the wage rate up from W to W_1. The quantity of labour employed increases from $0Q$ to $0Q_1$. From this analysis, we can make the following prediction:

Figure 12.4 Effect of an Increase in the Demand for Labour

An increase in the demand for labour, other things being equal, will cause a rise in the wage rate and an increase in the quantity of labour hired.

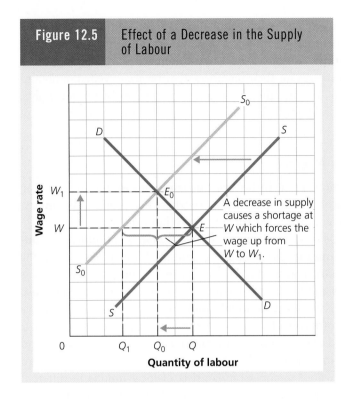

Figure 12.5 Effect of a Decrease in the Supply of Labour

Note that although there is an increase in the quantity of labour hired, there is no increase in the supply of labour. The labour supply curve does not shift. Instead, households respond to the higher wage rate by offering a greater quantity of labour, moving along the labour supply curve from E to E_1 in Figure 12.4.

We can also use this simple model of wage determination to predict the effect in a change in the supply of labour. Let us suppose that the supply of labour falls. Figure 12.5 shows such a fall as a shift in the supply curve from SS to S_0S_0.

With the initial wage rate of $0W$ and the new supply S_0S_0, there is a shortage of labour represented by $Q - Q_1$. This shortage forces the wage rate up from W to W_1. The quantity of labour hired falls from Q to Q_0. This analysis leads to the following prediction:

> A reduction in the supply of labour, other things being equal, will cause an increase in the equilibrium wage rate and a fall in the equilibrium quantity of labour.

Note that although there is a fall in the quantity of labour hired, there is no reduction in the demand for labour. The demand curve does not shift. Instead, firms respond to the higher wage rate by moving along the demand for labour curve from E to E_0 in Figure 12.5.

Reading Comprehension

The answers to these questions can be found on MyEconLab at **www.myeconlab.com.**　　MyEconLab

1. Explain how the wage rate and the number of workers employed are determined in a purely competitive labour market.

2. Explain how an increase in the wage rate could result in unemployment. Draw a diagram to illustrate this.

3. If a provincial or territorial government sets the minimum wage significantly higher than those in other provinces and territories, what economic consequences (for labour) would you expect?

LO 12.4 Discuss the collective bargaining process

Unions and Collective Bargaining

What exactly is a union?

It is assumed that most of us know what unions are, but to answer the question, let us define a **union** as an association of workers organized to promote the interests of its members in negotiations with their employers.

union an association of workers organized to promote the interests of its members in negotiations with their employers

What role have unions played in the labour market?

Unions have played, and continue to play, an important role in the labour market. We have come to accept labour unions as quite normal in our society, but this was not always the case. The rights now enjoyed by labour unions were won only after bitter struggles. The union movement has contributed significantly to the pleasant working conditions that modern workers (unionized and non-unionized) now enjoy. Unions have won important wage increases for their members, they have succeeded in obtaining a certain measure of job security, they have prevented abuses of human rights, and they have lobbied successfully for legislation and programs to improve the lives of ordinary workers.

Are there different types of unions?

craft union or trade union a union of workers in a single occupation

Indeed, different types of unions exist. In the **craft or trade union**, the membership comprises workers in a single occupation irrespective of where they work. In the **industrial union**, the membership comprises workers in a given industry.

industrial union a union of workers in a given industry

local union the lowest level of a union and the one to which a worker belongs directly

Perhaps we can get a deeper understanding of the various types of unions by examining their structure and organization. Unions are organized at four levels. First is the **local union**, to which the individual worker belongs directly. The local union holds meetings to discuss problems and to decide on courses of action. The local union also collects membership dues. Second is the **national union**, of which the local union is a member. The national union often does the bargaining and sets broad policy outlines. It receives a part of the dues paid to the locals. The Canadian Labour Congress (CLC) and the Confederation of Canadian Unions (CCU) are examples of national unions. Third is the **international union**, whose membership consists of local unions in different countries. The American Federation of Labor and Congress of Industrial Organizations (AFL-CIO) is an example of an international union. Fourth is the **federation**, which is an association of national unions. The Confédération des syndicats nationaux (CSN), based in Quebec, is an example of a federation of unions.

national union a national association of local unions, which usually sets policy and does the bargaining for the associated unions

international union a union whose membership consists of local unions in different countries

federation (of unions) an association of national unions

What tactics do unions use to secure their position?

Unions try to secure their positions by a variety of methods.

open shop a workplace in which union membership is not a prerequisite for employment

Union Security   The methods or tactics unions use include the closed shop and the union shop. The concept of an open shop helps to explain how a closed shop or union shop arrangement helps to secure the union. In an **open shop** workplace, union membership is not a prerequisite for employment; in a **closed shop** workplace, jobs are given only to union members. Between these two practices is the **union shop**, in which workers who are not union members can be hired, provided that they become union members within a specified period. It should be obvious that unions are least likely to support open shops. A union is most powerful when all of the workers at an establishment are unionized.

closed shop a workplace in which jobs are given only to union members

union shop a workplace in which workers who are not union members can be hired, provided that they become union members within a specified period

What is featherbedding?

featherbedding the practice of providing workers with unnecessary work to keep them on the payroll

Featherbedding is a technique that a union might use to increase the job security of its members and strengthen its own position. **Featherbedding** is the practice of providing workers with unnecessary work to keep them on the payroll. For example, a union of musicians in a province might succeed in getting music halls in that province to hire orchestras from another province or country only if a local orchestra is allowed to play. Such an agreement provides work for local musicians. As another example, in the railroad industry, trains still had firemen long after steam engines had been replaced.

Featherbedding represents an inefficient use of labour resources, but it also protects workers who might otherwise experience great difficulty in finding another job. The issue therefore involves a trade-off between economic efficiency on one hand and humanitarianism on the other.

What is the Rand formula that is often talked about in union circles?

An important development in Canadian labour practice was the introduction in 1945 of the **Rand formula**, the legislation that made it compulsory for a worker who is a member of a unit for which a union is the bargaining agent to pay union dues even if not a union member. Of enormous support to union security, the Rand formula was named after Mr. Justice Ivan Rand, who passed an arbitration decision in a labour dispute at the Ford Motor Company of Canada. According to that decision, Ford workers were to pay union dues whether or not they were members of the union. These dues were to be deducted from the workers' pay by the company's administrators and then handed over to the union. Canadian industries commonly use the Rand formula or some version of it.

> **Rand formula** the legislation that made it compulsory for a worker who is a member of the unit for which a union is the bargaining agent to pay union dues even if not a union member

What is collective bargaining?

A union is expected to represent its members and protect their interests. It is the collective voice of its members.

The Collective Bargaining Process   Instead of individual employees negotiating directly with their employer, the union negotiates on behalf of all employees. Sometimes, several different unions unite to form a common front when negotiating with a common employer. This often happens with public-sector unions negotiating with the government. Negotiations constitute **collective bargaining**, the process by which wages and other working conditions are negotiated between a union and an employer.

The contract that results from the collective bargaining process is called a **collective agreement**. This contract specifies the responsibilities of employers and employees concerning wages and salaries; vacation; safety on the job; non-monetary benefits, such as maternity leaves and training; job security; and other employment-related issues.

> **collective bargaining** the process by which wages and other working conditions are negotiated between a union and an employer
>
> **collective agreement** the contract that results from the collective bargaining process

What are the main factors that determine the outcome of labour-management negotiations?

The wage and other conditions of work determined by the collective bargaining process depend on the relative strengths of the bargaining parties and on the skills of the negotiators. In a period of severe unemployment, the employer tends to have greater market power. In a period of general labour shortage and rising demand for labour services, the unions enjoy greater market power. Another factor that seems to have some effect on the outcome of labour-management negotiations is public opinion. If the union has the support of the public, the outcome is likely to be in its favour. If public opinion comes down on the side of the employer, then the outcome is likely to favour the employer.

What mechanisms exist for the settlement of disputes between employers and employees?

It is reasonable to expect disputes between employers and employees. In cases in which a compromise cannot be reached, the two parties have several ways to attempt to settle

conciliation or mediation the process of submitting a dispute to a mediator for recommendations for settlement

voluntary arbitration the voluntary submission of a dispute to a third party whose decision on the matter is binding

compulsory arbitration the compulsory submission of a dispute to a third party whose decision on the matter is binding

strike a work stoppage by a union in an attempt to exert pressure on the employer

lockout a temporary closing of a plant by the employer to win or end a dispute

such disputes. One approach is to submit a dispute to a mediator for recommendations for settlement in a process called **conciliation** or **mediation**. Neither party is obligated to accept the conciliator's suggestion.

Another approach used in settling labour-management disputes is **voluntary arbitration**, in which each party voluntarily submits the dispute to a third party whose decision on the matter is binding. Yet another technique used to settle labour-management disputes is **compulsory arbitration**. In this case, the government compels the disputing parties to submit their dispute to a third party whose decision on the matter is binding.

Strikes and Lockouts   As a means of obtaining its demands, a union may resort to strike action.

What is the difference between a strike and a lockout?

A **strike** is a temporary work stoppage by a union in an attempt to exert pressure on the employer to grant its demands. From the employer's side, the equivalent of a strike is a **lockout**, which is a temporary closing of a plant by an employer to win or end a dispute.

How frequently do strikes and lockouts occur in Canada?

Contrary to popular belief, strikes and lockouts occur relatively infrequently in Canada. In most years, the working time lost because of strikes and lockouts amounts to only a very small percentage of overall working time. This suggests that the vast majority of collective agreements are reached without resorting to strikes and lockouts.

How costly are strikes?

Strikes are expensive. We are fortunate that they do not occur more frequently in this country. A proper analysis of the costs of strikes requires that these costs be grouped into at least two categories: direct costs and indirect costs.

Direct Costs of a Strike   It is relatively easy to pinpoint the direct costs of a strike. The cost to workers is lost wages. The cost to employers is lost production, lost sales, and lost profits. A strike can also have emotional costs to workers and employers, although this type of cost can be difficult to measure in terms of dollars and cents.

Indirect Costs of a Strike   A strike in one industry affects other industries and the general public. For example, a strike by truckers affects grocery stores and other retail outlets, because they may not be able to obtain supplies during the strike. And if they can, it may be at additional cost. This is an indirect cost. If workers in the steel industry go on strike, the auto industry may have to shut down because of a shortage of steel, which is an important input in the auto industry. In many cases, strikes cause a great deal of inconvenience to the public—as, for example, when a public transportation company goes on strike. These indirect costs often outweigh the direct costs of the strike.

Do strikes necessarily result in a reduction of total output in the economy?

Many strikes do result in a loss in total output as plants close, but not all strikes do. A strike in a certain factory at a certain time may mean simply that the factory has to work harder and longer at the end of the strike to compensate for the loss of production during the strike. In this case, the strike results in a shifting of the timing of production rather than in the volume of output.

Reading Comprehension

The answers to these questions can be found on MyEconLab at **www.myeconlab.com**.   MyEconLab

1. Distinguish among an open shop, a closed shop, and a union shop.
2. What is featherbedding?

3. What is a collective agreement?
4. Strikes are costly. What are some of the costs of strikes? (Discuss both direct and indirect costs.)

 Discuss the factors in wage negotiations

Factors in Wage Negotiations

What are some of the important factors in wage negotiations?

In the early stages of negotiation, both parties consider a variety of factors when drawing up their lists of proposals. In deciding on wage demands and wage offers, one factor that is likely to be particularly significant is the cost of living. Workers try to protect their purchasing power against a rising cost of living. The employer cannot easily ignore such a consideration. Unions try to protect their members' purchasing power by building an **escalator clause** into their contracts, a stipulation in a labour contract that future wages and salaries will be adjusted to reflect changes in the price level. Other devices used to protect purchasing power are **indexation**, the adjustment of wages to the rate of price increase, and a **cost-of-living adjustment** (COLA), which allows for the adjustment of wages to the cost of living.

Another factor likely to carry some weight in wage negotiations is productivity. Workers will naturally expect to share in any increase in their productivity. And employers are less likely to resist demands for wage increases in the face of productivity increases. Similarly, a fall in the productivity of workers is likely to result in the refusal of employers to grant anything but modest wage increases.

A third factor likely to feature significantly in wage demands and offers is the profitability of the business. If the firm has had a substantial increase in profits, the union will certainly use that fact as justification for higher wage demands. Conversely, if the firm has undergone a period of declining profits, the employers will likely refuse to agree to higher wages.

escalator clause a stipulation in a labour contract that future wages and salaries will be adjusted to reflect changes in the price level

indexation the adjustment of wages to the rate of price increase

cost-of-living adjustment (COLA) the adjustment of wages to the cost of living

---

BUSINESS SITUATION 12.2

Kim and Sabine operate the Starlight Bakery in the west end of the city. They hired 12 employees, who are unionized. The time for labour negotiations arrived. The union claimed that an increase in wages should be given on the basis of the size of an employee's family. Sabine, who grew up in a large family, is sympathetic to the union's position and wants to concede. Kim, however, is against the union's view, claiming that family size is totally unrelated to a worker's wage.

Who is right?

The answer to this Business Situation can be found in Appendix A.

Reading Comprehension

The answers to these questions can be found on MyEconLab at **www.myeconlab.com.**

MyEconLab

1. Discuss some of the factors that union leaders and employers consider when deciding on wage demands and offers.

2. What are some devices used by union negotiators to protect the purchasing power of their members?

LO 12.6 Analyze the effects of labour unions in the labour market

Effects of Labour Unions in the Labour Market

How do unions attempt to influence market outcomes in the labour market?

One of the objectives of a union is to secure higher wages for its members. Economic theory predicts that higher wages will result from an increase in the demand for labour services or a decrease in the supply of labour services. A union may therefore attempt to shift the equilibrium wage rate upward by shifting the labour demand curve to the right or by shifting the labour supply curve to the left.

Increasing the Demand for and Reducing the Supply of Labour   Recall that the demand for labour services is a derived demand. That is, if the demand for a certain product increases, the demand for the inputs (including labour) used to produce that product also increases. This relationship suggests that one way in which unions can increase the demand for labour is to increase the demand for the products of unionized workers. This increase in the demand for labour services will likely increase the wage rate, other things being equal.

Many unions encourage their members to purchase union-made products. The effect of this practice is illustrated in Figure 12.6.

DD and SS are the initial demand and supply curves for labour. The equilibrium wage rate is W. A campaign to encourage people to buy union-made products, if successful, will increase the demand for labour. This increase in demand is shown by the new demand curve D_1D_1. Assuming that the supply does not change, the wage rate increases to W_1, and the quantity of labour hired increases from L to L_1.

A union can shift the supply curve of labour upward and to the left by restricting the entry of newcomers into certain occupations and professions. The effect of this practice on the wage rate is illustrated in Figure 12.7.

The initial demand curve for labour in the particular occupation or profession is DD. The initial supply curve is SS. The initial wage rate is $0W$.

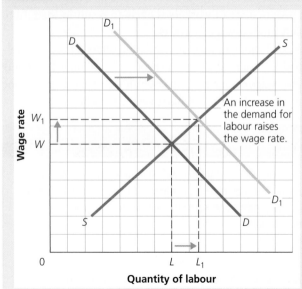

Figure 12.6   Effect of Increasing the Demand for Labour

An increase in the demand for labour raises the wage rate.

Wage rate

Quantity of labour

Figure 12.7	Effect of a Decrease in the Supply of Labour

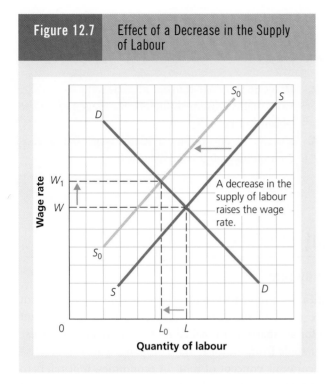

Figure 12.8	Effect of a Negotiated Wage Rate That Exceeds the Market Equilibrium Wage Rate

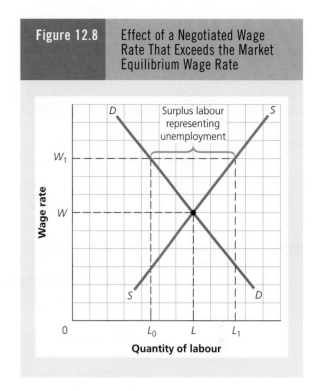

By limiting new entrants into the occupation or profession, the union shifts the supply curve from SS to S_0S_0. This has the effect of raising the wage rate from $0W$ to $0W_1$, but it reduces the quantity of labour from L to L_0.

Does an increase in wages and salaries in one occupation or profession affect wages and salaries in other occupations and professions?

An increase in wage rates in one occupation or profession can spark demands for wage increases in other occupations and professions, leading to higher wages. The process by which changes in wages in one occupation are transmitted to other occupations is referred to as the **wage transfer mechanism**.

Wage rates have undoubtedly increased significantly in the various industries. Whether these higher wages result from union activities, however, is still a matter of considerable debate among economists. It is suspected that unions have played a role but that other factors have also contributed.

wage transfer mechanism
the process by which changes in wages in one occupation are transmitted to other occupations

Effect of a Negotiated Wage   A union may succeed in obtaining a wage that is higher than the market equilibrium wage. We can analyze the effect of such an outcome. Let us consider Figure 12.8.

DD and SS are the demand and supply curves for labour, respectively. The equilibrium wage rate is $0W$, and the equilibrium quantity of labour demanded and supplied is $0L$. Let us assume now that a union enters the picture and succeeds in negotiating a wage rate of $0W_1$, which exceeds the market equilibrium wage. This higher wage rate results in a surplus of labour on the labour market, represented by $0L_1 - 0L_0$. Those who are employed do enjoy the higher wage rate, but unemployment results.

Reading Comprehension

The answers to these questions can be found on MyEconLab at www.myeconlab.com.   MyEconLab

1. How can unions increase the demand for labour? What effect does an increase in the demand for labour have on the wage rate?

2. Describe the wage transfer mechanism.
3. How might a union influence the wage rate in the labour market?
4. Discuss the effect of a negotiated wage that exceeds the market equilibrium wage rate.

LO 12.7 Understand the nature of rent

The Meaning of Rent

What do economists mean by rent?

When economists speak technically of rent, they refer to a concept that is different from the ordinary usage of the term. In ordinary language, the monthly payment made by a tenant to a landlord for an apartment is called rent. You can also rent a car for a weekend. Or you can rent tools from a tool rental company. These notions of rent, however, differ from the economic concept of rent. In economics, rent refers to the return on a productive factor whose supply is fixed. The income derived from a factor of production whose supply is completely price inelastic is referred to as **pure economic rent**. Land is often used as the best example of a factor of production that generates pure economic rent because, for practical purposes, the total quantity of land in existence is fixed.

pure economic rent the income derived from a factor of production whose supply is completely price inelastic

Can we briefly examine the notion of a fixed quantity of land?

Physically, the supply of land available to society is fixed. Only so much land is available to society, and offers of higher prices will not induce a greater quantity. The fertility of land, however, can be increased or reduced. Moreover, land can undergo a variety of improvements, such as drainage of swamps. But these improvements do not actually create new land. We can view these improvements to land as increasing capital rather than creating new land. It is important to note also that the quantity of land available for one use can be increased by reducing the quantity available for some other use. For example, farmland can be converted into land for residential purposes.

Reading Comprehension

The answers to these questions can be found on MyEconLab at www.myeconlab.com.   MyEconLab

1. What do economists mean by rent?

2. Discuss the notion of a fixed quantity of land.

LO 12.8 Explain the model of rent determination

Rent Determination

How is rent determined in a competitive market for land?

Rent is determined in the market like any other price: by demand and supply. The quantity of land demanded is inversely related to the price of land (rent). Other things being equal, the higher the rent, the smaller is the quantity of land demanded. In Figure 12.9, *DD* is the demand curve for land in a particular area.

The quantity of land is fixed. The quantity of land available in a given area cannot be increased or decreased in response to any factor. In other words, the total supply of land is perfectly inelastic. A perfectly inelastic supply curve is illustrated by a vertical line, as shown by *SS* in Figure 12.9. Equilibrium occurs at a rent of *r*, where the quantity of land demanded equals the quantity supplied.

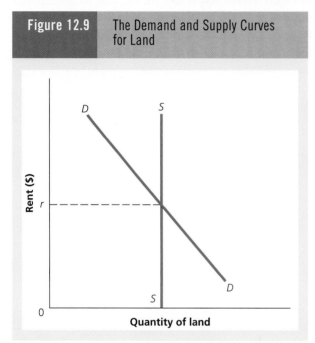

Figure 12.9 The Demand and Supply Curves for Land

What are the factors that will affect the demand for land?

The demand for land will be affected mainly by the following factors:

- *Population growth:* Population growth increases the demand for all goods and services and, as a result, the demand for land used in the production of goods and services increases.
- *Technology:* The introduction of new technology can increase or decrease the demand for land. For example, if a new low-cost wind-powered machine is invented, some manufacturers will install the machine. This will increase the demand for land, as land will be required to accommodate the new machine. Conversely, a new technology that significantly increases the yield from land will likely reduce the demand for land for certain purposes.
- *Expected yield:* Other things being equal, the higher the yield per hectare of land, the greater the demand for land will be.
- *Resource content:* We can expect the demand for a parcel of land that is rich in mineral deposits to be greater than the demand for a parcel that is lacking in any such deposits.
- *Location:* The location of a parcel of land will have some effect on its demand. Compare the demand for land in the heart of a large city, such as Montreal, Toronto, or Vancouver, with the demand for land in a more remote area.

How will an increase in the demand for land affect rent?

We know that, other things being equal, an increase in the demand for an item will increase the price of the item. Rent is the price of land. Therefore, an increase in the

Figure 12.10

Figure 12.10 | The Effect of an Increase in the Demand for Land

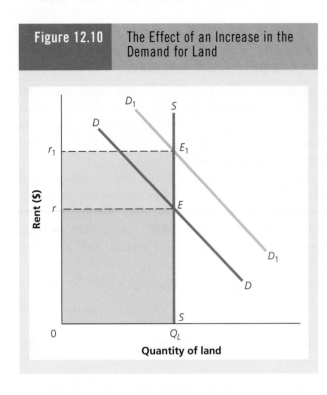

demand for land will result in an increase in rent. Figure 12.10 will help to illustrate the point.

The initial demand for land is *DD* and the supply is *SS*. The equilibrium rent is *r*, and the quantity of land is *QL*. The total economic rent will be the area shaded red in Figure 12.10 ($0Q_L \times 0r$). An increase in the demand for land from *DD* to D_1D_1 will cause the rent to increase from *r* to r_1, and the additional economic rent will be the area shaded blue in Figure 12.10.

Reading Comprehension

The answers to these questions can be found on MyEconLab at **www.myeconlab.com**. MyEconLab

1. What are the main factors that will affect the demand for land?

2. How will an increase in the demand for land affect rent, other things being equal?

3. What are the main determinants of rent differentials?

 LO 12.9 Distinguish between rent and transfer earnings

Economic Rent and Transfer Earnings

Can the concept of economic rent help us understand the huge salaries earned by some people?

We defined rent as the income earned by a factor of production whose supply is perfectly price inelastic. Another way of understanding rent is to view it as a return on a factor of production over and above its opportunity cost. Many superstars in music, sports, and entertainment earn what appear to be exceptionally high incomes, and many people openly express dissatisfaction with the huge incomes earned by these individuals. Criticism of superstar salaries, however, is actually aimed at the rent portion of their incomes.

What is the rent portion of the income of a hockey player who earns $450 000 per season? To answer this question, we must determine the next-best employment alternative for this hockey player. In other words, what is the opportunity cost? Or what is the minimum that this hockey player must earn playing hockey to decide not to quit hockey and take up some other job? This minimum is sometimes called **transfer earnings**, a term used to describe the amount that a factor of production can earn in the next-best employment alternative.

transfer earnings the term used to describe the amount that a factor of production can earn in the next-best employment alternative

Let us assume that the best employment this hockey player could get outside of hockey is a job that pays $30 000 a year. Then the excess ($450 000 2 $30 000 5 $420 000) is the rent portion of the hockey player's income. Superstars are paid very high salaries because the market judges their marginal revenue products to be very high. Note that resources other than land can be fixed in supply in the short run. Incomes or the return on a factor of production whose supply is fixed only in the short run are usually called **quasi-rent** to distinguish them from pure economic rent.

quasi-rent the return on a factor of production whose supply is fixed only in the short run

What would be the economic effect of taxing the rent portion of income?

This issue has been hotly debated. Some people argue that taxing away the rent portion of income does not affect incentives or resource use. For example, if the rent portion of a hockey player's income is taxed, that person will likely continue to be a hockey player. Hockey players are unlikely to quit hockey for other careers, because their incomes as hockey players are higher than the incomes that they could earn in other occupations.

However, if the rent portion of income is taxed away, will individuals still push themselves to achieve that rare quality that makes them superstars? Will they still take the time and trouble to develop and maintain those talents and skills that contribute to their exceptionally high incomes? How many would continue to strive for perfection? These questions are not easy to answer. We could conclude that rents are essential because they provide incentives for certain resources to be maintained.

What would be the economic effect of taxing the economic rent from land?

The incomes of superstars can be explained, at least in part, by their practice and hard work to excel at what they do. Can the same argument be applied to land? Consider the owner of a piece of land in some isolated area. Population growth or a population shift could increase the demand for the land, thus raising its price twenty-fold within a relatively short time. This massive economic rent on the land would be a matter of luck rather than exerted effort or diligent work. For this reason, many argue that the economic rent from land should be taxed. Such a tax, it is argued, is neutral in that it affects neither the incentive to produce nor the allocation of resources. The landowner simply pays the tax and that's it. The incidence (burden) of the tax falls entirely on the landowner.

In practice, however, a land tax as suggested above may have some difficulties. Rarely is the payment for land limited to the land itself. It often includes payment for investment made to improve the land, and it may not be easy to separate the improvements made to the land from the land itself. Taxing the economic rent from land under such circumstances would adversely affect investment, such as land clearing, drainage, and other infrastructure provided on the land.

Reading Comprehension

The answers to these questions can be found on MyEconLab at **www.myeconlab.com.** MyEconLab

1. Define each of the following terms:
   a) Transfer earnings
   b) Quasi-rent

2. Justify the high salaries earned by superstars.
3. Would you support a proposal to tax away the rent portion of income? Defend your position.

LO 12.10 Explain how interest rates are determined

Interest

What is interest?

Quite simply stated, interest is the payment for the use of money for a specified time. To purchase capital (machines, buildings, tools, equipment, etc.), many firms borrow money and pay interest to those who lend these funds. Households also borrow money from financial institutions, such as banks and finance companies, to purchase certain items, such as cars, furniture, and appliances, and pay interest to these lenders. People lend money directly to corporations by purchasing corporate bonds or indirectly by depositing funds in banks and other deposit-taking institutions. People lend money to the federal government by purchasing Canada Savings Bonds. To the lenders, interest represents income, while to the borrowers, it represents a cost. We can look at interest in a slightly different way. If you lend your friend $500, you are foregoing consumption that you could have had by spending your money. To induce you to forego that consumption, your friend must pay you something. That payment is interest.

interest rate or rate of interest the price paid for the use of money

Is there a difference between interest and the rate of interest?

Yes, there is a difference, and it is important to distinguish between the two concepts. Interest, as noted earlier, is a sum of money. It is income derived from money capital. The **interest rate** (or the **rate of interest**) is the price paid for the use of money. The amount of money lent or borrowed is called the principal. The rate of interest is the ratio of the interest to the principal, expressed as a percentage:

$$\text{Rate of interest} = \frac{\text{Interest}}{\text{Principal}} \times 100$$

Chartered banks are a major source of finance for consumers and businesses.

For example, if you borrow $5000 for one year and you pay $600 interest, then the rate of interest on your loan is

$$\frac{600 \times 100}{5000} = 12\% \text{ per year}$$

Interest income depends on the amount of funds a factor owner has lent out and on the rate of interest. If you lend $1000 at an interest rate of 5% per year, your interest income will be 5% of $1000 = $50 a year. If the interest rate were 10% a year, your interest income would be $100 a year. Clearly, then, the rate of interest is important in determining the return on loans.

loanable funds theory of the rate of interest a theory that the rate of interest is determined by the demand for and supply of loanable funds

Is the rate of interest determined in the market like any other price?

Yes. The rate of interest is a price—the price of loans. This price is determined in the market by the demand for and supply of borrowed funds or loanable funds. In Figure 12.11, the demand for loanable funds is shown by *DD*.

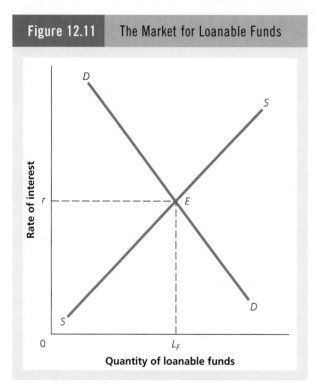

Figure 12.11   The Market for Loanable Funds

This demand is assumed to come from firms that want to borrow money for investment purposes, from consumers who want to purchase certain consumer items, and from governments that want to spend more than their revenues, that is, to finance their deficits. The demand curve slopes downward, indicating that a greater amount of money will be borrowed as the rate of interest falls. The supply of loanable funds is shown by *SS* in Figure 12.11. This supply comes from the savings of households, businesses, and governments who have money to lend. The demand and supply curves intersect at point *E* to give the equilibrium rate of interest, r, and the equilibrium quantity of loanable funds, *LF*. This model of interest rate determination is called the **loanable funds theory of the rate of interest**, which states that the rate of interest is determined by the demand for and supply of loanable funds.

BUSINESS SITUATION 12.3

John Dawson, owner and operator of J. D. Printing, Inc., is contemplating a bank loan to purchase some new printing equipment. The situation is not critical at the moment, so waiting for six months or a year will not be problematic. John's business adviser has informed him that the government has announced that it will shortly borrow a significant amount of money from the commercial banks. In addition, mortgage loans are expected to increase dramatically in the very near future.

How might this information influence John's decision?

The answer to this Business Situation can be found in Appendix A.

What are the main factors that account for differences in interest rates?

The following are three main factors that explain interest rate differentials:

risk premium an addition to the interest rate to compensate for the risk of default

- *Risk:* Interest rates vary according to the borrower and type of loan. All loans carry a certain amount of risk, but the risks associated with different types of loans vary. One reason for interest rate differentials is the degree of risk associated with loans. The probability of defaulting on a loan varies from borrower to borrower. Those borrowers likely to default will be charged a **risk premium**—an addition to the interest rate to compensate for the risk of default. For example, the prime lending rate (the rate of interest banks charge their most creditworthy corporate customers) is lower than the rate charged to less creditworthy borrowers.

maturity the length of time before a loan is supposed to be paid off

- *Maturity:* **Maturity** is the length of time before a loan is supposed to be paid off. Generally, the interest rate on a long-term loan is higher than that on a short-term loan. This assertion is based on the assumption that people prefer to have their money now rather than later. In other words, people have a preference for liquidity: they like to have ready access to their money. Because short-term loans are more liquid than long-term loans, higher interest rates induce lenders to lend funds for longer periods.

- *Stage of market development:* The stage of development of the market for a specific credit instrument helps to explain differences in interest rates. If the market for a specific credit instrument (evidence of debt, such as a bond) is well developed, the transaction cost of buying or selling that instrument will be relatively low; hence, the rate of interest will tend to be low. In places where financial markets are not well developed, it is relatively difficult to negotiate loans, and often the very few lenders that operate in such places charge exorbitant interest rates.

Does a relationship exist between interest rates and inflation?

In fact, a close relationship exists between interest rates and inflation. This relationship can best be illustrated by using the concepts of real and nominal interest rates.

real rate of interest the interest rate that would be charged if the rate of inflation were zero

Real versus Nominal Interest Rates Economists usually distinguish between the real rate of interest and the nominal rate of interest. The **real rate of interest** is the interest rate that would be charged if the rate of inflation were zero (or in the absence of inflation). The **nominal rate of interest** is the rate quoted for a loan or a deposit, which includes a premium for inflation.

nominal rate of interest the rate quoted for a loan or a deposit, which includes a premium for inflation

Let us illustrate the relation between the real and nominal rates of interest with the following example. Assume that the annual rate of inflation is 5%. This means that at the end of the year, a given sum of money will purchase only 95% of what it could purchase at the beginning of the year. If a person borrows $1000 for a year, when he or she repays the loan at the end of the year, the $1000 will be worth only $950 in terms of what it can buy. Without making any allowance for inflation, the lender would have lost 5% purchasing power over the year. An increase in prices lowers the value (purchasing power) of money. Thus, if lenders expect a rate of inflation of 5% per year, they will likely protect themselves from loss caused by inflation by adding 5 percentage points to the rate of interest. If lenders would normally have charged 7% interest in the absence of inflation, they would now charge 12% (7% + 5% = 12%) because of inflation. The following equation expresses the relation between interest rates and inflation:

$$NR = RR + e$$

where *NR* is the nominal rate, *RR* is the real rate, and *e* is the rate of inflation.

Reading Comprehension

1. Distinguish between *interest* and the *rate of interest*.
2. How is the equilibrium rate of interest determined in a purely competitive market for funds?

3. How would an increase in government borrowing affect the rate of interest?
4. Interest rates tend to be high during inflationary times. Explain why this is so.
5. Why are some groups able to borrow money at lower rates of interest than other groups?

LO 12.11 Understand the nature of profits

Profits

Is there a difference between economic profits and accounting profits?

It is important to understand the difference between the accountant's notion of profits and the economist's concept of profits. Accounting profits refer to the difference between the revenues obtained from the sale of goods and services and the expenses incurred in producing the goods and services. Economic profits, however, refer to the difference between the revenues obtained from the sale of goods and services and the total cost, including opportunity cost, of producing the goods and services. The following example will help to illustrate the difference. The revenues and expenses of Joe Pine, the owner of pine cabinet shop, are shown in Table 12.2. Such a statement is referred to as an **income statement** or a **profit and loss statement**, which is an accounting device for reporting revenues, expenses, and net income. Note that accounting profits are also referred to as **net income**, which is the difference between total revenue and total expenses.

income statement or profit and loss statement an accounting device for reporting revenues, expenses, and net income

net income the difference between total revenue and total expenses

To calculate economic profits, however, we would need to know not just the expenses incurred by Joe Pine but also how much Joe could have earned in the next-best alternative job. In other words, what is Joe's opportunity cost? Let us assume that Joe could have earned $20 600 instead of running his own business. Then we would have the following situation:

Total revenue .... = $50 000
Total cost = ($29 400 + $20 600) .... = $50 000
Profit ($50 000 − $50 000) .... = $ 0

Table 12.2   An Income Statement

Revenue:		
Sales		$50 000
Expenses:		
Rent	$ 2 500	
Utility	600	
Wages	15 000	
Transportation	800	
Materials and supplies	10 000	
Miscellaneous	500	
Total expenses		$29 400
Net income ($50 000 − $29 400)		$20 600

In this case, Joe is earning zero economic profit, or normal profit—returns that just equal the opportunity cost of the resources used. If, however, Joe can earn only $18 000 instead of operating his shop, then the situation would change as follows:

Total revenue .... = $50 000
Total cost = ($29 400 + $18 000) .... = $47 400
Profits ($50 000 − $47 400) .... = $ 2 600

Joe would then earn positive economic profit of $2600.

> Normal profits are returns that just equal the opportunity cost of the resources used.

Can profits be viewed from other perspectives?

Yes, there are other ways of looking at profits. Profits can be viewed as a return on innovation, as a reward for taking risks, or as the result of market power. It's a good idea for us to examine profits from each of these different perspectives.

Profit as a Return on Innovation and Entrepreneurial Ability Why do people decide to own their own business enterprises rather than sell their factor services to others? One reason is the prospect of greater profits. Another is that they prefer the independence. Presumably, many people feel that they have better insight, more imagination, and are more adventurous than anyone they have worked for or can work for. If these people are indeed as innovative as they think and their innovations succeed, then they are compensated with profits. If they fail, they suffer losses.

Profit as a Reward for Taking Risks No matter how shrewd businesspeople may be, they must confront the risk involved in owning their own businesses. Profits are sometimes viewed as a reward for bearing the risks of business ownership—a sort of risk premium. In the absence of this risk premium, many people would not consider it worthwhile to bear the risks associated with business ownership.

Profit from Market Power We have already seen that a firm in pure competition can earn positive economic profits in the short run, but in the long run, because of competition, such profits will dwindle away. A firm with significant market power may be able to earn positive economic profits even in the long run because of effective barriers to entry, such as patent rights, economies of scale, and limit-pricing techniques.

Reading Comprehension

The answers to these questions can be found on MyEconLab at www.myeconlab.com.   MyEconLab

1. Differentiate between accounting profits and economic profits.

2. What is an income statement?

3. Define normal profits.

LO 12.12 Discuss the economic role of profits

Economic Role of Profits

What economic functions do profits perform?

Basically, profits perform three economic functions:

1. They serve as a signal to resource owners.
2. They provide a motive or incentive for efficiency.
3. They reward the resourceful or enterprising.

Profit as a Signal to Resource Owners   The existence of profits in any industry or sector of the economy is a clear signal that price exceeds average cost of production and that resources should be shifted into that industry or sector. Likewise, the existence of losses in an industry is a loud and clear signal that resources should be shifted out of that industry and put to more productive uses.

Profit as a Motive for Efficiency   The desire for profits serves as an incentive for producers to cut production costs where possible. In the face of competition, high-cost firms will lose their market shares to low-cost firms. Unless high-cost firms can increase their efficiency, they will ultimately be forced out of the market.

Profit as Reward   Profits serve as a reward for the resourceful, the imaginative, the innovative, and the enterprising. The prospect of earning profits is often the driving force behind the development and maintenance of special resources and talents.

Reading Comprehension

The answers to these questions can be found on MyEconLab at **www.myeconlab.com.**   MyEconLab

1. Do profits perform any economic functions?

2. Explain how profits serve as a signal for resource allocation.

Review

1. Review the learning objectives listed at the beginning of the chapter.
2. Have you accomplished all the objectives? One way to determine this is to answer the Reading Comprehension questions at the end of each section. They will help you assess the extent to which you have accomplished the learning objectives.

3. If you have not accomplished an objective, review the relevant material before proceeding.

Key Points to Remember

1. **LO 12.1** Labour is not a good, such as milk or coffee, that consumers buy in the product market. Instead, it is demanded because it can be used to produce other

resources or the consumer goods and services required to satisfy people's wants. If the demand for consumer goods and services increases, then more labour services are required to produce them. Because the demand for labour is derived from the demand for goods and services produced with the help of labour, the demand for labour is a derived demand. It comes from firms who use labour services to produce goods and services.

2. **LO 12.2** The supply of labour services refers to the various quantities of labour services that will be offered for sale in the labour market at various wage rates. The supply of labour services comes from workers. The higher the wage rate, the greater the quantity of labour services that will be offered for sale; the lower the wage rate, the smaller the quantity of labour services that will be offered for sale.

3. **LO 12.3** The equilibrium wage rate is determined by the intersection of the demand and supply curves for labour. An increase in the demand for labour, other things being equal, results in an increase in the equilibrium wage rate. An increase in the supply of labour results in a fall in the equilibrium wage rate.

4. **LO 12.4, 12.5** Collective bargaining refers to the whole process whereby union and management arrive at an agreement about the terms of employment. The contract agreement deals with wages, vacation, safety, and other non-monetary matters, such as job security. Among the factors considered by the negotiating parties when deciding on wage demands and offers are productivity, profitability, and the cost of living.

5. **LO 12.6** Unions can shift the wage rate up by increasing the demand for union-made products and by restricting the entry of newcomers into certain occupations and professions. Union activity may result in higher wages, but it may also cause unemployment.

6. **LO 12.7** *Rent* is the term used to refer to income from a factor of production whose supply is fixed. Land is often used as the best example of a factor of production from which rent is derived. For practical purposes, the quantity of land in existence is fixed.

7. **LO 12.8** Rent is determined in the market by demand for and supply of land. Changes in demand for land explain changes in rent.

9. **LO 12.9** It is important to distinguish between rent and transfer earnings. Rent is income derived from a factor of production whose supply is fixed. The term transfer earning is used to describe the amount that a factor of production can earn in the next best employment alternative.

10. **LO 12.10** The demand for and supply of loanable funds determine the equilibrium rate of interest. The demand for loanable funds comes from firms, households, and government. The supply comes from savers.

11. **LO 12.11, 12.12** Profits can be viewed as a return on entrepreneurial ability or a reward for taking risks. Profits serve as a signal for resource movement, a motive for efficiency, and a reward for enterprise.

Economic Word Power

Closed shop   (p. 354)
Collective agreement   (p. 355)
Collective bargaining   (p. 355)
Compulsory arbitration   (p. 356)
Conciliation or mediation   (p. 356)
Cost-of-living adjustment (COLA)   (p. 357)
Craft union or trade union   (p. 354)
Derived demand   (p. 348)
Direct demand   (p. 348)
Escalator clause   (p. 357)
Featherbedding   (p. 354)
Federation (of unions)   (p. 354)
Income statement or profit and loss statement   (p. 367)
Indexation   (p. 357)
Industrial union   (p. 354)
Interest rate or rate of interest   (p. 364)
International union   (p. 354)
Loanable funds theory of the rate of interest   (p. 365)
Local union   (p. 354)
Lockout   (p. 356)
Marginal physical product of labour   (p. 349)
Marginal productivity theory of wages   (p. 349)
Marginal revenue product (of labour)   (p. 349)
Maturity   (p. 366)
National union   (p. 354)
Net income   (p. 367)
Nominal rate of interest   (p. 366)
Open shop   (p. 354)
Pure economic rent   (p. 360)
Quasi-rent   (p. 363)
Rand formula   (p. 355)
Real rate of interest   (p. 366)
Risk premium   (p. 366)
Strike   (p. 356)
Transfer earnings   (p. 363)
Union   (p. 353)
Union shop   (p. 354)
Voluntary arbitration   (p. 356)
Wage transfer mechanism   (p. 370)

Problems and Exercises

Basic

1. **LO 12.1** Table 12.3 shows information about a purely competitive firm operating in a purely competitive labour market. The price of the product is $10 and the wage rate is $50. TPP_L = total physical product of labour, MPP_L = marginal physical product of labour, and MRP_L = marginal revenue product of labour.

Table 12.3	Data for a Purely Competitive Firm in a Purely Competitive Labour Market		
Number of Workers	TPP_L	MPP_L	MRP_L
1	15		
2	25		
3	33		
4	38		
5	42		

a. Fill in the MPP_L and the MRP_L columns.
b. Draw the firm's demand curve.
c. How many workers should this firm hire?
d. If the wage rate rises from $50 to $80, how many workers will the firm hire?

2. **LO 12.1** Figure 12.12 shows the MRP_L.
a. If the wage rate is $40, how many workers will this firm hire?

Figure 12.12	Marginal Revenue Product of Labour

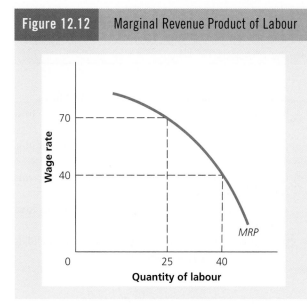

b. If the wage rate increases to $70, how many workers will be hired?

3. **LO 12.2** Figure 12.13 shows two supply curves for labour in a competitive labour market. Indicate which supply curve is for the firm and which is for the industry.

Figure 12.13	Supply Curves for Two Firms

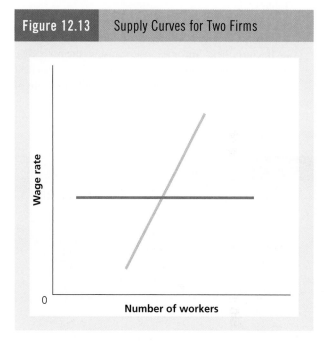

4. **LO 12.3** Table 12.4 shows the demand and supply curves for labour services in a competitive labour market.
a. Draw the demand and supply curves for labour services.
b. Indicate the equilibrium wage rate and the equilibrium quantity of labour services.

Table 12.4	Demand and Supply Schedules for Labour Services	
Wage Rate	**Quantity Demanded** (000)	**Quantity Supplied** (000)
6	5	1
7	4	2
8	3	3
9	2	4
10	1	5

c. Suppose that the government legislates a minimum wage of $9. What quantity of labour will be demanded and what quantity will be supplied?

d. How would you describe the effect of the minimum wage legislation?

5. **LO 12.8** Assume that the supply of land is perfectly inelastic.

a. Draw the supply and demand curves for land.

b. Indicate the equilibrium price (rent).

c. Show the effect of an increase in the demand for land on the price of land and on the quantity demanded.

6. **LO 12.10** The demand and supply for loans are shown in Table 12.5.

a. Graph the demand and supply curves for loans.

b. What is the equilibrium rate of interest?

c. If consumers' incomes rise, causing them to save more money at each rate of interest, show the effect of this increase in saving on the equilibrium rate of interest.

Table 12.5	Demand and Supply for Loans	
Rate of Interest	Quantity Demanded ($000)	Quantity Supplied ($000)
16	50	140
14	60	120
12	70	100
10	80	80
8	90	60
6	100	40
4	110	20

Questions in the Intermediate and Challenging Sections cover several different concepts, and have not been organized by learning objectives.

Intermediate

1. A union can increase the wage rate by increasing the demand for labour or by reducing the supply of labour. Which of these two techniques is preferable from the union's point of view? Illustrate graphically.

2. The information in Table 12.6 is provided for Pavel's Photo Studio. Pavel has refused a job that would have earned him $1500 per month. Determine the following:

a. Pavel's monthly profit (in an accounting sense)

b. Pavel's monthly profit (in an economic sense)

Table 12.6	Monthly Revenue and Cost Data for Pavel's Photo Studio	
Revenue:		
	Sale of goods..............................	$ 200
	Sale of services..........................	3 000
	Total.........................	$3 200
Cost:		
	Rent...	$ 500
	Materials....................................	150
	Telephone..................................	50
	Utilities......................................	40
	Wages..	600
	Other expenses...........................	20
	Total.........................	$1 360

3. The data in Table 12.7 refer to a purely competitive firm that buys labour services in a competitive labour market. The wage rate is $50 and the price of the product is $10.

Table 12.7	Production Data for a Purely Competitive Firm		
Quantity of Labour	TPP_L	MPP_L	MRP_L
2	80		
3	90		
4	98		
5	103		
6	105		
7	106		
8	104		

a. Draw the demand for labour curve for this firm.

b. How many units of labour services will this firm buy?

c. What is the total wage bill (labour cost) for this firm?

4. Use graphs to explain how each of the following events will affect the market rate of interest:

a. A government borrows $1.5 billion on the loan market.

b. A successful advertising campaign causes households and firms to increase their saving.

c. Firms and households become pessimistic about the future of the economy.
d. Unemployment increases substantially.
e. There is a sudden loss of confidence in financial institutions.

Challenging

1. The labour supply curve shown in Figure 12.14 is referred to as a backward-bending supply curve. Explain the meaning of the shape of this labour supply curve.
2. Explain why the options available to a union to increase the demand for labour are limited.

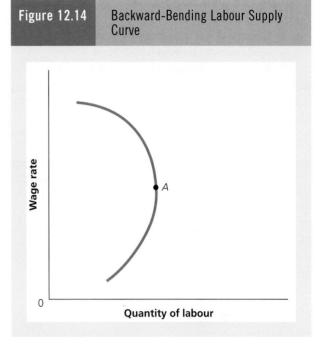

Figure 12.14	Backward-Bending Labour Supply Curve

MyEconLab   Visit the MyEconLab website at **www.myeconlab.com.** This online homework and tutorial system puts you in control of your own learning with study and practice tools directly correlated to this chapter's content.

Study Guide

Self-Assessment

The answers to the Study Guide questions can be found in Appendix B.

What's your score?

Circle the letter that corresponds with the correct answer.

1. The demand for labour services is derived from
   a. The demand for the goods and services to be produced with the use of labour
   b. The demand for other factor inputs
   c. The satisfaction derived from using labour services
   d. All of the above
2. The MRP_L curve is
   a. The firm's demand curve for labour
   b. The firm's supply curve for labour
   c. Always above the firm's demand curve
   d. None of the above

3. The MRP_L is obtained by
   a. Dividing the total output by the change in the number of workers
   b. Multiplying the total cost of labour by the wage rate
   c. Adding the change in total product and the additional revenue from labour input
   d. Multiplying the MPP_L by the price of the product
4. The marginal productivity theory of wages states that the firm will employ labour up to the point at which
   a. The wage rate equals the value of the marginal product of labour
   b. The wage rate exceeds the marginal revenue product
   c. The wage rate falls below the marginal revenue product, thus increasing profits
   d. Productivity decisions cannot be made at the margin

5. Other things being equal, an increase in the demand for labour will
   a. Lower the equilibrium wage rate and increase the equilibrium quantity of labour hired
   b. Raise the equilibrium wage rate and lower the equilibrium quantity of labour hired
   c. Lower the equilibrium wage rate and the equilibrium quantity of labour hired
   d. Raise the equilibrium wage rate and the equilibrium quantity of labour hired

6. An increase in the supply of labour (a shift in the labour supply curve to the right) can result from all of the following except
   a. An increase in the wage rate
   b. An increase in the number of immigrants coming to Canada
   c. A reduction in the need for leisure time
   d. A reduction in the rate of income taxes

7. If a union succeeds in negotiating a wage increase for its members,
   a. All workers will benefit
   b. Some workers may benefit while others lose
   c. Only the union leaders will benefit
   d. None of the above

8. Which of the following arrangements provides the greatest security for a union?
   a. A closed shop
   b. A union shop
   c. An open shop
   d. The Rand formula

9. Collective bargaining refers to
   a. A legislation ordering striking employees back to work
   b. Negotiations among employees to determine who should perform certain functions
   c. The collective distribution of income for bargaining purposes
   d. The process by which labour and management reach a negotiated agreement regarding the terms of employment

10. A union may shift the equilibrium wage upward by
    a. Reducing the demand for goods and services produced by unionized workers
    b. Restricting the entry of newcomers into certain occupations
    c. Encouraging the entry of newcomers into certain occupations
    d. None of the above

11. The income earned by a factor of production whose supply is completely price inelastic is referred to as
    a. Normal profit
    b. Pure economic rent

    c. Economic profit
    d. Pure economic profit

12. Willie Homerun earns $650 000 annually as a baseball player. He could earn $50 000 annually as a manager of the All Pro Sport Shop. Willie's transfer earning is
    a. $650 000
    b. $600 000
    c. $700 000
    d. $50 000

13. Referring to Question 12, the rent portion of Willie's earnings from baseball is
    a. $650 000
    b. $600 000
    c. $700 000
    d. $50 000

14. Interest is
    a. The income earned from the ownership of capital
    b. The income that lenders derive from loans
    c. The payment made for using someone's money
    d. All of the above

15. The nominal rate of interest is
    a. The minimum rate of interest that banks must pay their depositors
    b. The rate of interest on loans with a maturity date less than one year
    c. The rate of interest adjusted for inflation
    d. None of the above

16. The loanable funds theory of the rate of interest states that
    a. Banks often charge the highest possible interest on their loans
    b. The equilibrium rate of interest is determined by the demand for and supply of loans
    c. Because of inflation, the real rate of interest will always be higher than the nominal rate
    d. The nominal rate of interest is the real rate adjusted for inflation

17. Which of the following does the economist consider to be a cost?
    a. Dividends paid out to shareholders
    b. Positive economic profits
    c. Normal profits
    d. All of the above

18. Usually, accounting profits will be
    a. Greater than economic profits
    b. Less than economic profits
    c. Equal to economic profits
    d. The same as normal profits

19. Which of the following is a way of looking at profit?
    a. As a return on innovation
    b. As a reward for taking risks
    c. As a result of market power
    d. All of the above

20. Which of the following is not an economic role of profits?
    a. To support a government deficit
    b. To serve as a signal for resource allocation
    c. To provide a motive for efficiency
    d. To serve as a reward for the enterprising

Problems and Exercises (Use Quad Paper for Graphs)

Answers to these questions can be found on MyEconLab at www.myeconlab.com.   MyEconLab

1. Table 12.8 contains data for a hypothetical firm in pure competition. The labour market is also purely competitive, and the price of the firm's product is $2.

Table 12.9	Data for a Firm in Pure Competition			
Quantity of Labour	Total Product	MPP$_L$	Price of Product ($)	MRP$_L$
0	0		6	
1	8		6	
2	23		6	
3	44		6	
4	60		6	
5	70		6	
6	78		6	
7	84		6	
8	88		6	

Table 12.8	Wage and Employment Data for a Firm		
Units of Labour	Wage Rate ($)	MPP$_L$	MRP$_L$
0	10	4	
1	10	6	
2		5	
3		4	
4		3	
5		3	
6		1	
7			

Table 12.10	Production Schedule for a Firm	
Number of Workers		Total Product
0		0
1		25
2		35
3		43
4		48
5		52
6		52
7		50

a. Complete the table.
b. On a graph, draw this firm's demand curve for labour.
c. How many units of labour will this firm hire?
d. Now, suppose that the wage rate falls to $6. How many units of labour will the firm hire?

2. The data in Table 12.9 are for a firm in pure competition. The wage is $60 per period of time.
   a. Complete the table.
   b. Graph the marginal revenue product (MRP_L) curve and the wage rate.
   c. How many units of labour will this firm employ?
   d. If the wage falls to $48, how many units of labour will be hired?

3. The information in Table 12.10 is given for a firm that operates in a purely competitive market. The firm sells its product for $10, and pays workers a wage of $50 per day.
   a. How many workers should this firm hire?
   b. How many workers should this firm hire if the wage rate rises to $80 per day?

4. The production schedule for the Minilite firm, which uses labour as the only variable input, is given in Table 12.11. Workers are paid $50 a day and Minilite's product sells for $5 each in a purely competitive market. What is the optimum number of workers for Minilite to employ?

Table 12.11	Production Schedule for Minilite	
Number of Workers		Total Product
0		0
5		100
10		175
15		235
20		285
25		325
30		350

Table 12.12	Data for a Purely Competitive Firm			
Number of Workers	Total Product	MPP	MRP (p = $3)	MRP (p = $5)
8	80			
9	100			
10	118			
11	134			
12	148			
13	160			
14	170			
15	178			

5. Table 12.12 is for a purely competitive firm.
   a. Complete the table.
   b. Graph the demand curve for labour when the price of the product is $3. Label it *D*.
   c. On the same diagram, graph the demand curve for labour when the price of the product is $5. Label it D_1.
   d. Given a daily wage of $42 per worker and an output price of $3, how many workers should the firm hire?
   e. If the price of the product rises to $5 and the wage increases to $50, how many workers should the firm now employ?
6. Table 12.13 shows the demand and supply of labour.
   a. Draw the demand and supply curves on a graph.
   b. What is the equilibrium wage rate?
   c. How many workers will be hired at this wage rate?

Table 12.13	Demand and Supply of Labour	
Wage Rate ($)	Quantity of Labour Demanded	Quantity of Labour Supplied
4	11	1
5	9	4
6	7	7
7	5	10
8	3	13

7. Based on the information given in Question 6, suppose the government legislates a minimum wage rate of $7. How many units of labour will be unemployed?
8. With the help of diagrams, explain how each of the following will affect the labour market, other things being equal (ignore long-term effects):

   a. An increase in the labour force because of immigration
   b. A more optimistic economic outlook on the part of firms
   c. An increase in the demand for Canadian goods because of the free-trade arrangement between Canada and the United States
   d. An increase in the tax rate, which reduces work incentive
9. It is sometimes argued that labour unions, by demanding higher wages for their members, may end up hurting them. Discuss.
10. Use diagrams to illustrate the difference in demand for a hectare of swampland in a remote area, and a hectare of prime commercial real estate in the heart of a thriving metropolis.
11. Table 12.14 shows the demand schedule for a certain type of land. The total quantity available is 500 000 hectares.

Table 12.14	Demand and Supply Schedules for Land	
Rent per Hectare ($)	Quantity Demanded (ha)	New Quantity Demanded (ha)
1 000	250 000	300 000
900	300 000	
800	350 000	
700	400 000	
600	450 000	
500	500 000	
400	550 000	
300	600 000	
200	650 000	
100	700 000	

   a. What will be the equilibrium rent for this land?
   b. What quantity of land will be rented at this price?
   c. On quad paper, graph the demand and supply curves for this land.
   d. If the quantity of land bought at each price increases by 50 000 hectares, complete the third column of the table and draw the new demand curve on your graph.
   e. What will be the equilibrium rent for this land now?
   f. What quantity will be rented at this new price?
12. Alonso earns a salary of $650 000 for playing football. Outside of football, he could earn a maximum of $100 000 as the proprietor of a sporting goods store. Apart from the money, it makes no difference to Alonso whether he plays football or whether he owns the store.

What portion of Alonso's salary can be considered rent?

13. An actor earns $600 000 a year. She could have earned $70 000 at best as a public relations consultant. What part of her earnings is economic rent and what part is transfer earnings?

14. Your friend borrows $200 from you. Because she is your friend, you do not want to benefit financially from the loan transaction; therefore, you do not charge her interest. Is this a rational decision?

15. Table 12.15 shows the demand and supply schedules for loans.
    a. Graph the demand and supply curves for loans.
    b. Indicate the equilibrium rate of interest and the equilibrium quantity of loans.
    c. If the rate of interest rises by 2 percentage points, a _____ (shortage, surplus) of $_____ million will exist. The amount of loans _____ (demanded, supplied) at this interest rate would have to _____ (rise, fall) by $_____ million to clear the market.

16. Pierre Gunter is the proprietor of a photography studio. His typical monthly expenses are shown in Table 12.16.

Pierre has been offered as much as $1500 per month to work for other companies. Compute the following:
    a. Pierre's monthly profit (in an accounting sense)
    b. Pierre's monthly profit (in an economic sense)

17. Jasmine operates a small retail outlet. Her total revenue last year was $150 000. Her expenses were as outlined in Table 12.17. In the same year, Jasmine refused an offer of a job that pays $50 000. Calculate Jasmine's economic profit for last year.

Table 12.16	Cost and Revenue Data for Pierre Gunter	
Revenue:		
	Sale of goods...	$ 150
	Sale of services...	2 500
	Total...	$ 2 650
Cost:		
	Rent	200
	Materials	50
	Telephone	40
	Utilities	30
	Wages	500
	Other expenses...	25
	Total..	$ 845

Table 12.15	Demand and Supply Schedules for Loans	
Interest Rate (%)	**Amount of Loans Demanded ($ mil)**	**Amount of Money Lent ($ mil)**
15	8	23
14	10	20
13	12	17
12	14	14
11	16	11
10	18	8
9	20	5
8	22	2

Table 12.17	Jasmine's Expenses
Rent	$ 6 000
Wages	24 000
Utilities...	1 000
Transportation	1 000
Materials	40 000
Other expenses	800
Total expenses	72 700

13

Income Distribution and Poverty

Learning Objectives

After studying this chapter, you should be able to

13.1 Discuss the criteria for distributing income

13.2 Discuss income distribution and inequality

13.3 Understand the meaning of poverty

13.4 Understand the dimensions of poverty

13.5 Discuss the incidence of poverty

13.6 Explain the causes of low income

13.7 Discuss various measures to alleviate poverty

13.8 Discuss Canada's income security programs

13.9 Explain the negative income tax

Assess Your Knowledge

MyEconLab

Answers to these questions can be found on MyEconLab at **www.myeconlab.com**.

1. List three causes of income inequality.

2. How would you determine whether or not a family is poor?

3. Name three causes of low income among Canadians.

4. Describe two ways in which the problem of poverty could be alleviated.

LO 13.1 Discuss the criteria for distributing income

market income the sum of earnings from employment and self-employment, investment income, private retirement income, and other incomes, excluding government transfers

Criteria for Income Distribution

What are the criteria for distributing income?

The concept of **market income** is used to approximate the sum of earnings from employment and self-employment, investment income, private retirement income, and other incomes, excluding government transfers.

Most people in our society seem to agree that income and wealth should be shared in some manner that is fair. No general agreement exists, however, on what constitutes fairness or equity, or how to distribute income equitably. But to answer the question, we will briefly examine three views about the equitable distribution of income.

Distribution According to Contributions   The first view is that income should be distributed according to productivity. Supporters of this view claim that it is only fair to reward people according to their contribution to total output. They see certain advantages to this criterion. First, it provides incentives for greater productivity. Second, the system works automatically through the market system.

Distribution According to Need   Another view of income distribution is that income should be distributed according to need. This criterion has found expression in the popular saying of the early French revolutionary Louis Blanc: "From each according to his ability, to each according to his needs." This approach, however, has obvious problems. First, how are needs to be determined? This, in itself, presents an almost insurmountable problem. Second, if income is distributed according to need, does anyone have any incentive to work? That's a question that is well worth pondering.

Equal Distribution to All   According to this view, income should be distributed equally to all. The simplicity of this criterion is appealing. To arrive at the amount of income to be distributed to each, we simply divide the total income by the population. The problem with this approach to income distribution is that it fails to provide incentives for economic activity; and without incentive for economic activity, the level of economic activity will fall, resulting in an undesirable decline in income and output.

Reading Comprehension

The answers to these questions can be found on MyEconLab at **www.myeconlab.com.**   MyEconLab

1. What criteria have been suggested for an equitable distribution of income?

2. Of the three criteria suggested for an equitable distribution of income, which do you consider to be the best? Support your choice.

3. What problems could be expected from using the need approach to income distribution?

 LO 13.2 Discuss income distribution and inequality

Income Distribution and Inequality

How is income inequality measured?

A measure that is frequently used to determine how evenly total income is distributed among individuals and households is the **size distribution of income**.

size distribution of income the distribution of income among individuals and households

If 5% of the households control more than 90% of the total income and wealth in a society, most people would conclude that the income disparity was too large and would probably grumble about social injustice.

Lorenz curve a graphical device for measuring income inequality

An important graphical device for measuring income inequality is the **Lorenz curve**, named after an American-born economic statistician, Max Otto Lorenz (1880–1962), who introduced the device in 1905. The construction of a Lorenz curve is a relatively simple matter and is illustrated in Figure 13.1. On the vertical axis we measure the cumulative percentage of income, and on the horizontal axis we measure the cumulative percentage of families. The diagonal straight line 0A in Figure 13.1 represents an even distribution of income or perfect equality. Ten percent of families receive 10% of the total income, 20% receive 20% of income, 30% receive 30% of the income, and so on.

In Canada, the distribution of income has remained fairly constant over the past 20 years, with the distribution of income among families as shown in Table 13.1.

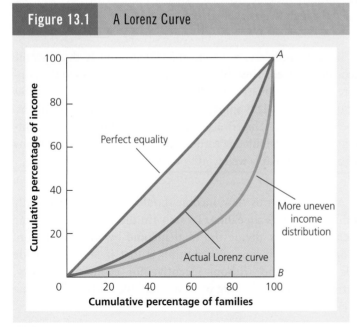

Figure 13.1	A Lorenz Curve

Table 13.1	Distribution of Income
Families	**Income**
Lowest 20%	6% approximately
Lowest 40%	18% approximately
Lowest 60%	36% approximately
Lowest 80%	60% approximately
All families	100%

The actual Lorenz curve for Canada is shown in Figure 13.1 as a blue curve. A Lorenz curve shown by the green curve in Figure 13.1 would represent a case where income is more unevenly distributed than in Canada. The greater the distance between the Lorenz curve and the line of perfect equality, the greater the inequality in income distribution.

An even more precise measure of the degree of income inequality is the ratio known as the **Gini coefficient**, named after the Italian statistician Corrado Gini (1884–1965), who introduced the concept in 1912. The Gini coefficient is the area enclosed by the Lorenz curve and the line of perfect equality in income distribution (that is, the area shaded in blue) expressed as a proportion of the area of triangle $0AB$ in Figure 13.1. In other words, the Gini coefficient is the area shaded in blue divided by the total of the areas shaded in blue and red. For example, if the area of the area shaded in blue is F and the area of the triangle is H, then the Gini coefficient is F/H. The larger the Gini coefficient, the greater the inequality in the distribution of income. If income distribution is perfectly equal, the Gini coefficient will be zero.

Gini coefficient a ratio that measures the degree of income inequality

What are the main causes of income inequality?

Inequality in the distribution of income has many causes, but among the main ones are education, productivity, age, discrimination, sex, and social connections. Let us examine each of these in turn.

Education   In our society, other things being equal, people are paid on the basis of their education. People with university degrees tend to earn significantly more than people who have completed only high school. The reason for this difference in income is the belief that people with higher levels of education contribute more to their employers than do people with lower levels of education.

Productivity   The marginal productivity theory of wage determination suggests that workers will be paid the value of their marginal physical product. On this premise, then, workers with higher marginal physical productivity will tend to be paid more than workers with lower marginal physical productivity.

Age   Age is closely related to experience and on-the-job training, both of which affect income. Think of a typical individual. Between the ages of 20 and 24, he or she may be just entering the workforce, with little or no experience or on-the-job training. Earnings at that age are usually low. As the employee advances in years, he or she tends to gain experience and job-related training. Accordingly, earnings tend to increase, reaching a peak at about age 55 to 60. Earnings tend to decrease as the employee reaches retirement. This life-cycle earning pattern is illustrated in Figure 13.2.

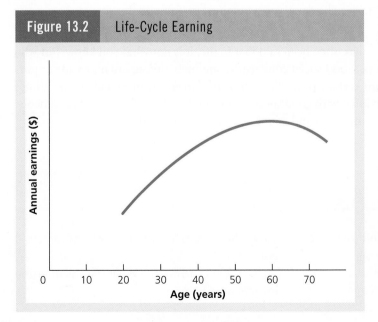

Figure 13.2	Life-Cycle Earning

Table 13.2	Average Earnings by Sex, 1999–2008		
Year	Women	Men	Women as % of Men
	Earnings in terms of 2008 dollars		
1999	27 000	43 000	62.6
2000	27 500	44 500	61.7
2001	27 600	44 000	62.1
2002	27 900	44 400	62.8
2003	27 600	43 800	62.9
2004	27 900	44 000	63.5
2005	28 600	44 700	64.0
2006	29 000	44 800	64.7
2007	29 900	45 500	65.7
2008	30 200	46 900	64.5

Source: Statistics Canada, Summary Tables, "Average Earnings by Sex and Work Pattern." Available online at www40.statcan.gc.ca/l01/cst01/labor01a-eng.htm. Extracted March 23, 2011.

Discrimination   Because of discrimination, many people are denied opportunities that could enable them to earn a reasonable income. Some may be denied access to educational opportunities, while others may be passed over for promotions because of their sex, age, or ethnicity. Discriminatory practices result in certain groups being disadvantaged in the workplace, and consequently, members of these groups end up with lower incomes than members of other groups.

Sex   Even before the advent of feminism, people spoke out against prejudicial treatment of women. It was claimed that income has always been distributed in favour of men. In 1999, average earnings by women were $27 000, while the average for men was $43 000. In percentage terms, a woman earned only 62.6% of a man's earnings. By 2008, the percentage was 64.5%. The details are contained in Table 13.2.

Social Connections   It has often been said that in life, it is not what you know, but who you know that matters. Good social connections and networking often provide opportunities for entry into certain professions and for career advancement. Other things being equal, the individual with good social connections will get the edge over someone without those vital connections and will thus earn a higher income.

Reading Comprehension

The answers to these questions can be found on MyEconLab at www.myeconlab.com.   MyEconLab

1. What do you understand the term *size distribution of income* to mean?

2. What is the Lorenz curve? Is it of any practical importance?

3. What is the Gini coefficient? What is its relationship to income distribution?

The Meaning of Poverty

How is poverty defined?

We can define poverty in either an absolute sense or a relative sense. We can say that an individual or family is living in **absolute poverty** when it lacks the financial resources required for the basic necessities of life. The individual or family's income is so low that it cannot afford the goods and services that most people in the society would consider to be just enough to enable them to live in minimum comfort.

absolute poverty the condition that exists when an individual or a family lacks the financial resources required for the basic necessities of life

But what is minimum comfort?

This concept has obvious problems. How is minimum comfort defined? Who decides what minimum comfort is? The amount required to achieve this minimum comfort will vary from family to family and from individual to individual. The definition obviously has a certain amount of subjectivity and arbitrariness. However, despite these problems, it is clear that poverty is the condition of not having enough money to afford the basic needs as society views these needs.

Poverty is often discussed in terms of what has become known as the **poverty line**, an arbitrary level of income below which poverty is said to exist and below which an individual or a family is unable to maintain a satisfactory standard of living.

Statistics Canada has established a **low income cut-off**, which most people consider to be a poverty line, based on the size of the area of residence and on the size of the family unit. For example, the low income cut-off for an unattached person living in a rural area will be much lower than the low income cut-off for a couple with three children living in a large urban area. This difference, of course, reflects the fact that the latter would require a larger sum of money to be able to afford the basic necessities of food, shelter, and clothing. According to this criterion, any family or unattached individual whose income is below the low income cut-off is considered to be living in poverty. Statistics Canada, it should be noted, stresses that the low income cut-off is not considered a poverty line by government.

Statistics Canada defines its low income cut-offs (LICOs) as "income thresholds at which a family would typically spend 20 percentage points more of its income than the average family on the necessities of food, shelter and clothing."

Based on the LICOs established by Statistics Canada, approximately 2 725 000 people in families and 1 701 000 unattached individuals, totalling an estimated 4 426 000 people or about 13.6% of the Canadian population, were living below the poverty line in 2008. In 2004, the comparable figure was 15.8%.

poverty line or low income cut-off an arbitrary level of income below which poverty is said to exist

Do we have any other way of determining whether or not people are poor?

Yes. Another way of determining poverty is to consider the proportion of income spent on food, shelter, and clothing—the so-called basic necessities. Statistics Canada has established that families who on average spend 56.2% or more of their income on food, shelter, and clothing are considered to be in straitened circumstances.

We have discussed absolute poverty. Is there another concept of poverty?

Yes. There is the concept of **relative poverty**, the condition that prevails when an individual or family has a standard of living that is far below that enjoyed by others in society. Thus,

relative poverty the condition that prevails when an individual or a family has a standard of living that is far below that enjoyed by others in society

according to this concept, an unattached individual with an annual income of $100 000 would be considered to be relatively poor if the vast majority of people in the society have annual incomes in excess of $350 000. Viewed in this way, any substantial unequal distribution of income will give rise to poverty, regardless of the absolute size of the income.

Reading Comprehension

The answers to these questions can be found on MyEconLab at **www.myeconlab.com.**   MyEconLab

1. What is the difference between absolute poverty and relative poverty?

2. How does Statistics Canada define its low income cut-off?

3. "Poverty is a phenomenon of poor countries. It does not exist in a rich country like Canada." Discuss.

LO 13.4 Understand the dimensions of poverty

Dimensions of Poverty

What are some of the more serious effects of poverty?

Poverty imposes severe hardships on individuals. The poor are barred from enjoying the good things in life that many people take for granted. They are deprived of good homes and even good health sometimes, and their children may be deprived of a good education. As a result, they may turn to various forms of criminal activities in an attempt to escape the harsh realities of poverty. Thus, not only the individual but also the society suffers as a result of poverty.

In addition to the loss of property (and possibly life) that can result from poverty are other economic disadvantages that define its dimensions. Because the poor are likely to have low levels of education and skills, their productivity is likely to be low. This low productivity prevents the economy's output of goods and services from reaching its full potential. Hence, the population as a whole must accept a lower standard of living.

Reading Comprehension

The answers to these questions can be found on MyEconLab at **www.myeconlab.com.**   MyEconLab

1. How does poverty affect the individual and his or her family? How does it affect the economy and society?

2. Write a short paragraph describing the dimensions of poverty.

LO 13.5 Discuss the incidence of poverty

The Incidence of Poverty

Are specific groups more likely to be poor than other groups?

Yes. Poverty is not confined to any one region, age group, sex, or ethnicity. It is found among the young and the old, in rural areas and large urban centres, among men and women. The distribution of low-income families and unattached individuals roughly follows the distribution of the population. Yet, in general, certain groups are more likely to be poor than other groups.

incidence of poverty the likelihood of being poor

The Incidence of Poverty   The incidence of poverty is the likelihood of being poor. We will discuss the **incidence of poverty** by identifying groups with a high likelihood of being poor.

- *Families with many children:* Families with a large number of young children have a high incidence of poverty. For example, the incidence of low income for a family with three or more children under 16 years old is significantly higher than that for a family with only one or two children under the age of 16.
- *Families in certain provinces:* The incidence of low income among households in Quebec, Newfoundland and Labrador, British Columbia, and Manitoba is higher than that in the other provinces. It must be understood, however, that this is not a permanent state. For a variety of reasons, economic and social conditions change, and a province or territory with a relatively high incidence of low income at one time could have a relatively low incidence of low income at some other time.
- *Families in rural areas:* The incidence of poverty is usually high among families in rural areas. Low income in rural areas is usually less visible than in urban areas. For instance, the urban poor may live in rundown houses, while the rural poor may not. The prospects of finding jobs that offer high remuneration in rural areas are usually not very good and, in general, the incomes of farm operators and farm workers tend to be substantially below incomes earned by families in urban areas. Expectations of a better life in the city can attract some people (especially young adults) into the city, where, unable to find jobs, they are simply added to the list of the urban poor. This fact partly explains the poverty observed in many large metropolitan areas.
- *Families headed by females:* Low income is prevalent among families headed by females. A family headed by a female is three times as likely (or more) to be poor as a family headed by a male. This is related to the observation that 13% of females in families have low incomes; the comparable figure for males is 11.5%.
- *Young families:* The incidence of low income is high among families whose heads are 24 years old or younger. Such families are at least four times as likely to be poor as families whose heads are between 45 and 54 years old. One reason for low income among young families is that they often lack education, valuable marketplace skills, and working experience.
- *Senior families:* Female heads of families and unattached individuals who are 65 years and older have a high incidence of poverty. These are mostly retired people who live on pension income.
- *Families headed by individuals not in the labour force:* Families headed by individuals who are not in the labour force have a high incidence of low income. The heads of such families are usually of poor health or injured and must therefore look for ways of sustaining themselves other than employment income.
- *Unattached individuals:* In general, the incidence of low income among unattached individuals is much higher than that among families. The incidence of low income is particularly high among unattached individuals who are not in the labour force, who are 70 years or older, who have low levels of education, who are self-employed, or who are females.

Reading Comprehension

The answers to these questions can be found on MyEconLab at **www.myeconlab.com.**   MyEconLab

1. What is meant by the *incidence of poverty*?

2. Write a short paragraph describing the incidence of poverty.

LO 13.6 Explain the causes of low income

Causes of Low Income

What are the causes of poverty?

It is impossible to identify any single cause of poverty or to attribute poverty to one major cause. The causes of poverty are numerous and no one cause can claim supremacy over the others. We can, however, discuss some of the prime causes of poverty.

Low Productivity   One cause of poverty is low productivity. We know that in a purely competitive labour market, each worker will be paid the value of his or her marginal product. Even in an imperfect market setting, workers with high productivity tend to be paid higher wages than workers with low productivity. Workers with low productivity, then, will likely have low incomes.

Low Economic Growth   Poverty can be caused by the inability of the economy to expand fast enough to keep pace with a growing population. In such a situation, an increasing number of people will be among the unemployed and, consequently, among those considered to be in straitened circumstances.

Quantity and Quality of Resources   Individuals earn income from the natural, human, and financial resources at their command: rent from land, wages and salaries from labour services, interest and dividends from money and physical capital, and profits from entrepreneurial services. Families and unattached individuals with very small quantities and low quality of natural resources and physical and human capital will tend to have low incomes.

Physical and Mental Disabilities   Another cause of poverty is having a physical or mental disability. Individuals who have a disability may have trouble competing with others for a share of the output of the economy. They are quite often the victims of discrimination and may have to depend on charitable organizations and government assistance programs for their survival.

economic discrimination the situation in which certain groups are targeted for different treatment in the labour market

Discrimination   **Economic discrimination** occurs when certain groups are targeted for different treatment in the labour market, although there are no differences in their output. Economic discrimination comes in several forms: employment discrimination, wage discrimination, and occupational discrimination. Let us briefly define each of these forms of economic discrimination.

> Employment discrimination is a situation in which particular groups are denied employment on the basis of their identification with those groups.
>
> Wage discrimination is a situation in which particular groups are paid lower wages and salaries than others are paid for similar work.
>
> Occupational discrimination is a situation in which particular groups are prevented from entering certain occupations.

Discrimination in its various forms is one of the major causes of poverty. Because of discrimination, certain groups can be prevented from taking advantage of opportunities that are open to others. They may be denied access to certain schools, or they may be prevented from entering certain occupations. Reports abound of visible minorities being paid lower wages than others, and women earning lower wages than men, not because of any difference in productivity among the groups, but because of prejudice against them. Numerous accounts also exist of promotions being given on the basis of ethnicity and sex rather than on the basis of merit as demonstrated by qualification, competence, or experience, or a combination of all three.

Reading Comprehension

The answers to these questions can be found on MyEconLab at **www.myeconlab.com.**   MyEconLab

1. What are some of the major causes of poverty?

2. Define each of the following concepts:
    a)   Employment discrimination
    b)   Wage discrimination
    c)   Occupational discrimination

LO 13.7 Discuss various measures to alleviate poverty

Measures to Alleviate Poverty

Can anything be done to alleviate poverty?

Some people believe that poverty is self-perpetuating. That is, the very existence of poverty is itself a cause of poverty. According to this view, people who are born and raised in poverty tend to develop a "culture of poverty." For people who have inherited a culture of poverty, it is extremely difficult to break the poverty cycle. A few might escape, but the majority will remain to perpetuate the vicious cycle.

This view notwithstanding, the foregoing discussion of the causes of poverty points to some approaches whereby this problem can be alleviated. First, increase the productivity of the working poor by providing education and training so that workers can improve their skills. Second, an increase in the rate of economic growth and policies to promote employment will do much to reduce poverty. Third, legislation forbidding discrimination, though it will not eliminate discrimination, may help to lessen the misery of those who face discriminatory practices. Fourth, the provision of certain goods and services free or at greatly reduced cost to the poor will help to reduce poverty. An example of this approach is the provision of subsidized housing. Finally, the government can provide employment for people with disabilities in special government-operated workshops. In this way, people with disabilities will make a positive contribution to society's output of goods and services. The workshops would also provide on-the-job training and serve as transitions to regular work in the private or public sector.

Reading Comprehension

The answers to these questions can be found on MyEconLab at www.myeconlab.com.   MyEconLab

1. Explain the "self-perpetuating" view of poverty.

2. What are some of the measures that can be taken to alleviate poverty?

 LO 13.8 Discuss Canada's income security programs

Canada's Income Security Programs

What are Canada's income security programs?

government transfer payments payments from the government that do not represent payments for productive services; they include such items as employment insurance and welfare payments

Government transfer payments are money from the government that does not represent payment for productive services; they include such items as employment insurance and welfare payments.

In an attempt to alleviate the problems of low-income families and unattached individuals and to provide income security for Canadians, the federal, provincial, and territorial governments in Canada have instituted certain programs. Provincial and territorial governments have social assistance programs that provide minimum levels of income to those in need. The provincial and territorial governments are also responsible for Workers' Compensation plans that provide benefits to workers who sustain injury or death on the job. We will look at a few of the federal government's programs. Specifically, we will discuss the Old Age Security (OAS) program, the Canada Pension Plan (CPP) and the Quebec Pension Plan (QPP), and the Employment Insurance (EI) program.

Human Resources and Skills Development Canada (HRSDC) administers the OAS programs and CPP, and through the Canada Employment Insurance Commission, it is responsible for the EI program.

Old Age Security Program   The OAS program incorporates the (1) OAS pension, (2) Guaranteed Income Supplement (GIS), and (c) Allowance and Allowance for the Survivor. The legislation that established the OAS program was enacted in 1952 and has seen many amendments since then. The OAS program is funded by the federal government, and benefits are indexed to the cost of living.

- *Old Age Security Pension:* The OAS Pension is paid monthly to eligible Canadian citizens or legal residents who have reached the age of 65 years. The pensioner's duration of residence in Canada determines the amount of OAS pension received, and OAS pension benefits are subject to federal and provincial or territorial income tax.
- *Guaranteed Income Supplement:* The GIS is paid to recipients of OAS benefits who have little or no other income. Unlike the OAS benefits, GIS payments are made on the basis of need. Recipients of the GIS apply for it once and then are awarded it based on their income tax returns. Unlike the OAS pension, the GIS is not subject to federal, provincial, or territorial income tax.

■ *Allowance and Allowance for the Survivor:* Many Canadians face difficult economic circumstances because they are widowed or because they are married and living on the pension of only one spouse. The Allowance and Allowance for the Survivor are designed to provide assistance for such people. These allowances are monthly payments made to the spouse of an OAS pensioner or to a survivor who is between the ages of 60 and 64 and who has lived in Canada for at least 10 years after the age of 18. Recipients of these allowances must apply annually, and to qualify for benefits under this scheme, the applicant's annual income cannot exceed certain limits. These allowances are not subject to income tax, but they must be reported when the recipients file their income tax returns.

The Canada Pension Plan   CPP and its counterpart in Quebec, QPP, provide benefits to people who have contributed to the plan. Contributors are eligible to receive monthly retirement pension after their 60th birthday. Almost all employed and self-employed persons between the ages of 18 and 70 who earn more than a minimum level of income yearly are covered by the CPP/QPP. The plan is funded through contributions from employees, employers, and self-employed persons, and from interest from the Canada Pension Plan Fund. The CPP and QPP are indexed to the cost of living.

Employment Insurance   Established in 1940, the Unemployment Insurance program was intended to insure workers against loss of income during periods of unemployment. Employees contribute a certain percentage of their income to the plan while they are employed. Once they become unemployed and they qualify for benefits under the plan, they can draw benefits. This program was replaced by the new EI system, the stated objective of which is to encourage people to return to the job market. In fact, the system emphasizes the merits of a rapid return to work. The EI system extends temporary income support or income benefits to a large number of Canadians.

Reading Comprehension

The answers to these questions can be found on MyEconLab at **www.myeconlab.com.**   MyEconLab

1. Define *government transfer payments* and give an example.

2. What are the elements of Canada's income security program?

LO 13.9 Explain the negative income tax

The Negative Income Tax

What is a negative income tax?

Most people would probably agree that families and individuals ought to be guaranteed some minimum income. They would also agree that it is desirable to provide this minimum income without at the same time destroying the incentive to work. To accomplish both, however, is easier said than done. A negative income tax is one scheme proposed to deal with this situation.

Table 13.3	Operation of a Negative Income Tax	
Earned Income ($)	Government Payment (a negative tax) ($)	After-Tax Income ($)
0	4 000	4 000
1 000	3 500	4 500
2 000	3 000	5 000
3 000	2 500	5 500
4 000	2 000	6 000
5 000	1 500	6 500
6 000	1 000	7 000
7 000	500	7 500
8 000	0	8 000
9 000	−500	8 500
10 000	−1 000	9 000

negative income tax
a system whereby the government makes payments to people whose incomes are below the taxable level

Under a **negative income tax** (NIT) system, the government makes payments to people whose incomes are below the taxable level. The amount of payment varies with an individual's income. The payment by the government can vary with the individual's income in many ways. Table 13.3 illustrates one way in which an NIT program might work.

Suppose the government decides to guarantee a minimum annual income of $4000 and that thereafter for every extra dollar earned up to, say, $8000, the government subsidy will be reduced by $0.50. Thus, the government pays an individual who has earned no income for a year a subsidy—a negative income tax—of $4000. As Table 13.3 shows, for an income of $1000, the subsidy of $4000 will be reduced by $500 ($0.50 for every dollar of income), so the individual receives a payment of $3500 from the government, making a total after-tax income of $4500. If the individual earns $8000, the subsidy of $4000 is reduced by a half of that income (that is, by $4000) so no payment is received from the government. It is important to note that, under the NIT scheme, the income subsidy is reduced but not taken away entirely if the individual earns an income below $8000.

That sounds like a good scheme! Can we itemize the advantages of such a plan?

Proponents of the NIT claim the following advantages:

1. Under the NIT, the incentive to work is not destroyed. Under some welfare programs, the individual may be better off not working because the reduction in the subsidy may be greater than any extra income that could be earned by working. This is not the case with the NIT.

2. Individuals are left to spend their income as they see fit. They are not told how they should spend their income as is the case, for example, with subsidized housing. Thus, under the NIT, individuals have a greater freedom of choice.

3. The administration of an NIT is relatively simple. It should require a smaller bureaucratic structure than that required for many other programs because for the most part, it would be administered by Canada Revenue Agency personnel.

Does the negative income tax have opponents?

Yes. The arguments in favour of the NIT have been countered by critics. The opponents of the NIT scheme advance the following arguments:

1. The NIT would not be less expensive than the programs now in existence, and the cost would also escalate.

2. The establishment of a national low income cut-off is impractical. An established poverty line may be too low for Ontario but too high for Newfoundland and Labrador. So it may be necessary to establish poverty lines on a regional, provincial, or territorial basis.

3. The NIT is politically problematic, because many voters vehemently oppose the idea of making direct cash payments to people for staying at home and doing nothing.

Has Canada ever experimented with the NIT?

An experimental NIT program was introduced in Manitoba in the 1970s. No conclusive statement can be made about the effects of the NIT on the basis of that experiment. However, evidence seems to suggest that less social stigma is attached to people who quit their jobs to accept an NIT than to those who quit to go on welfare, as the term is traditionally understood. This implies that the NIT has an adverse effect on incentives to work. This view is supported by results from similar experiments in the United States, where the NIT, aimed at encouraging people to work, seemed to have a disincentive effect on work effort.

Is there any other scheme that might alleviate poverty?

guaranteed annual income proposal a proposal for the government to give everyone a grant of a certain amount of money; any income above that level would be subject to tax

Yes. Another scheme has been proposed, called the **guaranteed annual income proposal** (GAIP). According to this proposal, everyone in Canada could be given a certain sum of money (say $2000) annually. This would be referred to as taxable income. People who had no other income from any source would be exempt from paying income tax, but those with incomes in excess of the $2000 grant would have to pay some of it in income tax. A guaranteed income scheme could require grant recipients who are able to engage in gainful employment or to undergo job training to improve their job skills. This way, the government grant would not be seen as merely a handout to people who are staying at home. The GAIP seems to have some merit, but its practicality is questioned on political grounds.

Reading Comprehension

The answers to these questions can be found on MyEconLab at www.myeconlab.com.   MyEconLab

1. What is a negative income tax system?

2. What are the main issues in the NIT debate?
3. What is the guaranteed annual income proposal? What major problem might it encounter in practice?

Review

1. Review the learning objectives listed at the beginning of the chapter.
2. Have you accomplished all the objectives? One way to determine this is to answer the Reading Comprehension questions at the end of each section. They will help you assess the extent to which you have accomplished the learning objectives.
3. If you have not accomplished an objective, review the relevant material before proceeding.

Key Points to Remember

1. **LO 13.1** Three competing schools of thought about the equitable distribution of income are the productivity approach, the need approach, and the equality approach. The need and equality approaches can adversely affect work incentive.
2. **LO 13.2** The Lorenz curve is a useful graphic device for measuring and illustrating the degree of income inequality. The Gini coefficient expresses income inequality as a

ratio. The larger the ratio, the greater the degree of income inequality.

3. **LO 13.3** Absolute poverty is the condition that exists when an individual or a family lacks the financial resources required for the basic necessities of life. Statistics Canada has established a low income cut-off that is regarded as the poverty line. Relative poverty is the condition that exists when an individual or family has a standard of living that is significantly below that enjoyed by others in society.

4. **LO 13.4** Poverty causes severe hardship for individuals. The poor are often deprived of good homes, good education, good health, and many of the other things that others take for granted. The poor may turn to various criminal activities in an attempt to avoid the harsh realities of poverty. Society, as well as the poor individual, suffers from poverty. Poverty is also related to low productivity.

5. **LO 13.5** Although poverty is not confined to any particular group, some groups are more likely to be poor than others. Groups with high incidence of low income include families with many young children, families in rural areas, families with female heads, young families, senior families, families with self-employed heads, families whose heads are not in the labour force, and unattached individuals.

6. **LO 13.6** Some of the causes of low income are low productivity, low economic growth, lack of large quantities of valuable resources, physical and mental disabilities, and discrimination.

7. **LO 13.7** Suggestions to alleviate poverty include increasing the productivity of the working poor, accelerating the rate of economic growth, making laws forbidding discriminatory practices, assisting the poor, and providing employment for people with disabilities in special government-operated workshops.

8. **LO 13.8** Through various income security programs, Canada offers assistance to people in difficult economic circumstances and provides income security for its citizens and legal residents.

9. **LO 13.9** A negative income tax is a plan whereby the government pays a subsidy to low-income people to provide a guaranteed minimum income. Although a negative income tax has some appealing advantages, it does suffer from problems.

Economic Word Power

Absolute poverty (p. 383)
Economic discrimination (p. 386)
Gini coefficient (p. 381)
Government transfer payments (p. 388)
Guaranteed annual income proposal (p. 391)
Incidence of poverty (p. 385)
Lorenz curve (p. 380)
Market income (p. 379)
Negative income tax (p. 390)
Poverty line or low income cut-off (p. 383)
Relative poverty (p. 383)
Size distribution of income (p. 380)

Problems and Exercises

Basic

1. **LO 13.1** The information in Table 13.4 is available for Mark Hector. Calculate Mark Hector's market income.

Table 13.4	Information for Mark Hector
Item	Amount ($)
Labour income	30 000
Investment income	500
Government transfers	2 000
Private retirement income	5 000
Other income	1 000

2. **LO 13.1** Referring to Table 13.4, if government transfer payments increase to $2500, what will be Mark's market income?

3. **LO 13.1** The left column of Table 13.5 contains criteria for income distribution. Fill in the right column by inserting at least one problem associated with each criterion.

4. **LO 13.2** Draw a Lorenz curve and indicate
   a. The curve of equal income distribution
   b. A curve of very unequal income distribution
   c. A curve of moderately unequal income distribution

5. **LO 13.2** Figure 13.3 shows a Lorenz curve.
   a. Calculate the Gini coefficient.
   b. If the Gini coefficient increases after 10 years, what has happened to income distribution?

Table 13.5	Criteria for Income Distribution
Criteria	**Associated Problem**
1. According to contribution	1.
2. According to need	2.
3. Equal distribution	3.

Table 13.6	Hypothetical Government Guaranteed Income Program	
Earned Income ($)	**Government Subsidy ($)**	**After-Tax Income ($)**
0	5 000	5 000
1 000		
2 000		
3 000		
4 000		
5 000		
6 000		
7 000		
8 000		
9 000		
10 000		

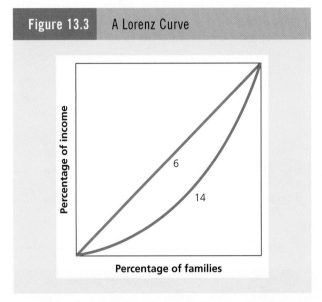

Figure 13.3	A Lorenz Curve

Table 13.7	Hypothetical Government Guaranteed Income Program	
Earned Income ($)	**Government Subsidy ($)**	**After-Tax Income ($)**
0	5 000	5 000
1 000		
2 000		
3 000		
4 000		
5 000		
6 000		
7 000		
8 000		
9 000		
10 000		

6. **LO 13.9** The government decides to guarantee a minimum annual income of $5000. Thereafter, for every extra dollar earned up to $10 000, the government subsidy is reduced by $0.50. There is no tax on an income of $10 000 or less. On the basis of this program, complete Table 13.6.

7. **LO 13.9** Refer to Table 13.6. Suppose the government decides to reduce the subsidy by $0.40 for every dollar earned up to $10 000. Complete Table 13.7.

8. **LO 13.2** Table 13.8 gives information on income distribution in a hypothetical economy.
   a. Draw the Lorenz curve for this economy.
   b. Indicate the line of absolute equality in income distribution.

Table 13.8	Income Distribution in a Hypothetical Economy
Household Income	**Percentage share of Income**
Lowest 20%	10
Second 20%	10
Third 20%	15
Fourth 20%	25
Fifth 20%	40

Questions in the Intermediate and Challenging Sections cover several different concepts, and have not been organized by learning objectives.

Intermediate

1. In a certain country, 50% of the population has no wealth, while wealth is equally distributed among the remaining 50%. Draw the Lorenz curve for this country.

2. Consider Figure 13.4 which shows Lorenz curves for two countries, *A* and *B*.

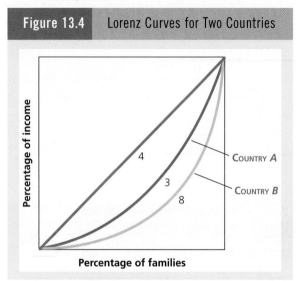

Figure 13.4	Lorenz Curves for Two Countries

a. Explain why the straight line illustrates an equal distribution of income.

b. In which country is income more evenly distributed?

c. Calculate the Gini coefficient for each country.

Challenging

1. Postsecondary tuition fees in Quebec have been kept low for several years. Students in Quebec have demonstrated against any increase in tuition fees and have requested greater government transfer payments to students on the basis that they are among the lowest income groups.

a. Present an argument in support of the students.

b. Present an argument against the students' request for larger government transfers and maintenance of the low tuition fees.

2. The story is told of a mythical character named Robin Hood, who stole from the rich and gave to the poor. Use the concept of the Lorenz curve to show and explain the effect of the activities of Robin Hood.

MyEconLab Visit the MyEconLab website at **www.myeconlab.com.** This online homework and tutorial system puts you in control of your own learning with study and practice tools directly correlated to this chapter's content.

Study Guide

Self-Assessment
The answers to the Study Guide questions can be found in Appendix B.

What's your score?
Circle the letter that corresponds with the correct answer.

1. Market income is
   a. Income generated by the stock market
   b. Total income from all sources minus government transfer payments
   c. The total revenue that firms receive from selling goods and services on the market
   d. None of the above

2. Government transfer payments include
   a. Taxes collected by the government
   b. Payments made by the government to its employees
   c. Government payments to individuals that do not represent payments for services rendered or for goods purchased
   d. Interest payments by the government

3. Which of the following is a suggestion for an equitable distribution of income?
   a. Income should be distributed according to the recipient's contribution to total income
   b. Income should be distributed according to need

   c. Income should be distributed equally to all

   d. All of the above

4. The distribution of income among individuals and households is called

   a. The size distribution of income

   b. The functional distribution of income

   c. The factor-share distribution of income

   d. The Lorenz curve factor

5. The Lorenz curve is

   a. A curve showing how fast income rises as people become wealthier

   b. Always a straight line

   c. Used to show how income is distributed

   d. None of the above

6. The Gini coefficient is

   a. The same as the Lorenz curve

   b. Unrelated to the Lorenz curve

   c. The vertical distance between two Lorenz curves

   d. None of the above

7. The Gini coefficient of a society with perfect equality in income distribution is

   a. 0

   b. 1

   c. 0.50

   d. 0.10

8. Income inequality can be caused by differences in

   a. Education

   b. Productivity

   c. Age

   d. All of the above

9. Absolute poverty is

   a. A figment of economists' imaginations

   b. Non-existent in a rich country like Canada

   c. A lack of financial resources to acquire the basic necessities of life

   d. None of the above

10. The poverty line

   a. Measures relative poverty

   b. Measures absolute poverty

   c. Decreases as the society becomes more wealthy

   d. Is unrelated to the cost of living

11. Relative poverty depends on

   a. A comparison of incomes in a society

   b. An individual's absolute income only

   c. A given poverty line

   d. None of the above

12. John has an annual income of $80 000. From this we can conclude that John is

   a. Relatively poor

   b. Absolutely poor

   c. Above the poverty line

   d. It is impossible to tell

13. Which of the following is among the more serious effects of poverty?

   a. Inability to enjoy the good things in life

   b. The possibility of anti-social behaviour

   c. Economy-wide loss of productivity

   d. All of the above

14. The incidence of poverty refers to

   a. The reduction of poverty by government programs

   b. The actual number of poverty cases identified each year

   c. The difference between the highest and lowest income in a given society

   d. The likelihood of being poor

15. Who of the following has the highest incidence of poverty?

   a. Males between 35 and 45 years old

   b. Families with few children over the age of 18 years

   c. Families with female heads and many children under 16 years old

   d. People who are employed by companies

16. Occupational discrimination occurs when

   a. Workers in one occupation are paid a different wage from workers in another occupation

   b. Particular groups are prevented from entering certain occupations

   c. Particular groups are denied employment

   d. All of the above

17. Which of the following would tend to alleviate poverty?

   a. An increase in the productivity of the working poor

   b. An increase in the rate of economic growth

   c. Subsidies to the poor

   d. All of the above

18. Which of the following is *not* included in Canada's income security programs?

   a. The Guaranteed Income Supplement

   b. The Old Age Security pension

   c. Employment Insurance

   d. Reduced goods and services tax for the poor

19. An NIT guarantees a minimum annual income of $5000. The government subsidy is reduced by $0.40 for every extra dollar earned. A person who earns $3000 will receive a total income of

   a. $5000

   b. $8000

   c. $6800

   d. $6200

20. Critics of the NIT argue that

   a. It is too costly to operate

   b. A national low income cut-off is impractical

   c. Many people would oppose it

   d. All of the above

Problems and Exercises (Use Quad Paper for Graphs)

Answers to these questions can be found on MyEconLab at www.myeconlab.com.

MyEconLab

1. On a graph, draw four Lorenz curves, ranging from equal income distribution to most unequal distribution. Label the curves as follows:
   a. Equal distribution
   b. Unequal distribution
   c. More unequal distribution
   d. Most unequal distribution

2. The data in Table 13.9 are given for a hypothetical country.
   a. Complete the last two columns of the table.
   b. On the basis of the data in Table 13.9, draw the Lorenz curve for the hypothetical country.
   c. Draw the line of perfect income equality.
   d. Shade the area that represents the degree of income inequality in income distribution.

Table 13.9	Income Distribution			
Income Group ($)	Percentage of Families in Group	Percentage of Income Received	Cumulative Percentage of Families	Cumulative Percentage of Income Received
Under 5 000	3	0	3	0
5 000–11 999	14	4		
12 000–15 999	8	3		
16 000–19 999	10	5		
20 000–24 999	13	11		
25 000–29 999	14	13		
30 000–34 999	11	13		
35 000–39 999	9	11		
40 000–44 999	6	9		
45 000 and more	12	31		

3. Figure 13.5 shows Lorenz curves for two countries, A and B. The numbers in the diagram are for the areas indicated.
   a. Compute the Gini coefficient for countries A and B.
   b. What do these coefficients tell you about income distribution in A relative to B?

4. Figure 13.6 shows Lorenz curves for two countries. The area of triangle $0AB$ is 50.
   a. In which country is income more evenly distributed?
   b. Calculate the Gini coefficient for country A.
   c. Calculate the Gini coefficient for country B.

Figure 13.5	Lorenz Curves for Two Countries

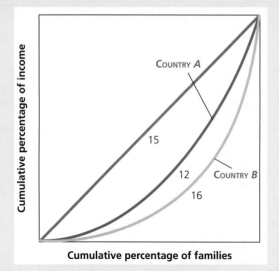

Cumulative percentage of families

Figure 13.6	Lorenz Curves for Two Countries

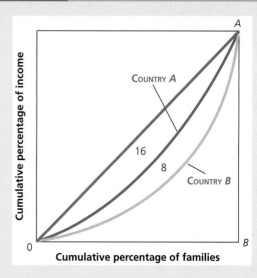

Cumulative percentage of families

5. A government guarantees a minimum annual income of $6000 for each adult citizen by giving a subsidy. The subsidy is reduced by $0.40 for every extra dollar earned. The relevant data are contained in Table 13.10.
   a. On the basis of this information, complete the table.
   b. At what level of earned income will an individual neither get a subsidy nor pay income tax?

6. The government establishes a guaranteed annual income of $2000 and decides to reduce the income subsidy (negative tax) by 40% of each extra dollar of earned income. Complete Table 13.11.

Table 13.10	Negative Income Tax	
Earned Income ($)	Government Subsidy (negative tax) ($)	After-Tax Income ($)
0	6 000	6 000
1 000		
3 000		
5 000		
7 000		
9 000		
11 000		
13 000		
15 000		
17 000		

Table 13.11	Earned Income and Negative Income Tax	
Earned Income ($)	Negative Income Tax ($)	Total Income ($)
0	2 000	2 000
1 000		
2 000		
3 000		
4 000		
5 000		

Chapter

14

The Economics of International Trade and Trade Policy

Learning Objectives

After studying this chapter, you should be able to

14.1 Explain the basis for international trade

14.2 Identify the gains from trade

14.3 Discuss the factors that determine comparative advantage

14.4 Describe further gains from trade

14.5 Discuss Canada's exports and imports

14.6 Discuss tariffs and trade policy issues

Assess Your Knowledge

MyEconLab

Answers to these questions can be found on MyEconLab at **www.myeconlab.com**.

1. Why does Canada not produce (grow) oranges?
2. How have you, personally, benefited from international trade?
3. List three items that Canada exports.
4. List three items that Canada imports.
5. Which country is Canada's largest trading partner?

LO 14.1 Explain the basis for international trade

international trade the exchange of goods, services, and resources between nations

The Basis for International Trade

What is international trade?

The term **international trade** is used in two ways. It is used to describe the study of the import and export of goods, services, and resources between countries, and of the effects of these flows on the economy. It is also used to refer to the actual exchange of goods, services, and resources between nations.

What is the basis for international trade?

The basis for international trade is the fact that different countries are differently endowed with resources and technical expertise. Some countries, for instance, are heavily endowed with natural resources, while others are less favourably endowed. Some nations are rich in capital. Others suffer from a lack of capital relative to other resources. Human resources vary among countries. Some countries have more highly skilled labour forces than others. Some countries have larger populations than others. Moreover, technological capabilities are not evenly distributed across nations. Country *A* may have a technological edge over country *B* in the production of telecommunication equipment while country *B* may have a technological advantage over country *A* in the production of books.

A country well endowed with labour can be expected to have lower wage rates than a country with scarce labour resources. Consequently, we can expect the cost of manufacturing a product requiring a large amount of labour to be lower in a labour-abundant country than in a labour-scarce country. Similarly, we would expect the cost of growing tropical fruits, such as oranges and bananas, in a tropical climate to be much lower than it would be in a temperate climate. Consider the amount of resources that would have to be used to grow citrus fruits in northern Canada! It makes good economic sense to import citrus fruits and to pay for them with the export of apples, for example.

BUSINESS SITUATION 14.1

WebPro designs webpages for Canadian businesses. In a recent visit to India, the owner of WebPro discovered that webpage designers in India could design webpages to his specifications at a fraction of the cost that he paid in Canada.

How might WebPro benefit from this new information?

The answer to this Business Situation can be found in Appendix A.

Reading Comprehension

The answers to these questions can be found on MyEconLab at **www.myeconlab.com.**   MyEconLab

1. What is the importance of international trade to the Canadian economy?

2. How would you respond to the question "Why do nations trade?"

3. Why does Canada import oranges from Florida instead of producing them itself?

LO 14.2 Identify the gains from trade

Gains from Trade

What is the principle of absolute advantage?

absolute advantage
the ability to produce a commodity by using fewer resources than another country

A country is said to have an **absolute advantage** over another country in the production of a commodity if it has the ability to produce the commodity more efficiently. It can produce the commodity by using fewer resources than the other country would use. In other words, if country A is more efficient than country B in the production of a certain commodity, country A has an absolute advantage in the production of that commodity.

Can the idea of absolute advantage be illustrated with a numerical example?

Yes. A numerical example will help to illustrate the concept. Suppose that a Canadian worker can produce five cars per year, while a worker in Mexico can produce only two cars per year. Suppose also that a Mexican worker can produce 10 metric tons of grain per year, while a Canadian worker can produce only eight metric tons of grain per year. Table 14.1 contains the relevant data.

A Canadian worker is 2.5 times as efficient as a Mexican worker in the production of cars, but a Mexican worker is 1.25 times as efficient as a Canadian worker in grain production. In this case, Canada has an absolute advantage in the production of cars, while Mexico has an absolute advantage in the production of grain.

Table 14.1	Hypothetical Output per Worker in Canada and Mexico	
Country	**Cars** (units)	**Grain** (metric tons)
Canada	5	8
Mexico	2	10

How does the existence of absolute advantage influence trade between countries?

The existence of absolute advantage makes trade beneficial to both countries. The following example illustrates how the combined output of cars and grain in both countries (Canada and Mexico) will increase if Canada specializes in the production of cars and Mexico specializes in the production of grain. Suppose a Canadian worker is transferred from grain production into car production. The output of cars in Canada would increase by five while the output of grain would fall by eight metric tons. If, at the same time, a Mexican worker is transferred from car production into grain production, the output of cars in Mexico would fall by two, but the output of grain would increase by 10 metric tons. The net effect then would be an increase in cars by three and an increase in grain by two metric tons.

We have shown that two countries can gain by trading if each specializes in the production of the commodity in which it has an absolute advantage. But what if one country has an absolute advantage in the production of both commodities? Will trade still benefit both countries? The principle of comparative advantage provides the answer.

But what is comparative advantage?

comparative advantage the ability to produce a commodity at a lower opportunity cost than another country can

Comparative advantage is the ability of one country to produce a commodity at a lower opportunity cost than another country can.

Can this concept be illustrated with a numerical example?

Let us assume that a Canadian worker can produce either 10 cars or five metric tons of grain per year, while a Mexican worker can produce either three cars or three metric tons of grain per year. Table 14.2 contains the data.

In this example, a Canadian worker is more efficient than a Mexican worker in the production of cars and in the production of grain.

Instead of producing 10 cars, a Canadian worker could have produced five metric tons of grain. Hence, the opportunity cost of a car in Canada is 0.5 metric tons of grain. That is, to produce one car, Canada must sacrifice 0.5 metric tons of grain. Conversely, instead of producing three cars, a Mexican worker could have produced three metric tons of grain. Hence, the opportunity cost of a car in Mexico is one metric ton of grain. Because the opportunity cost of a car in Canada is less than the opportunity cost of a car in Mexico, Canada is said to have a comparative advantage in the production of cars.

Table 14.2	Hypothetical Output per Worker in Canada and Mexico	
Country	Cars (units)	Grain (metric tons)
Canada	10	5
Mexico	3	3

Let's now examine the situation in Mexico. The opportunity cost of a metric ton of grain in Canada is two cars, while the opportunity cost of a metric ton of grain in Mexico is one car. Because the opportunity cost of grain in Mexico is less than the opportunity cost of grain in Canada, Mexico has a comparative advantage in the production of grain.

Will countries benefit from trade when comparative advantage exists?

Yes. And we can demonstrate the mutual gain from trade when comparative advantage exists. In the absence of international trade, in the example immediately above, Canada must give up 0.5 metric tons of grain for one car while Mexico must give up one metric ton of grain for a car. Let us assume that Canada and Mexico can exchange cars for grain at a rate somewhere between the ratios 1:0.5 and 1:1; let us say 1 car for 0.75 metric tons of grain (1:0.75). The actual rate at which cars will exchange for grain (called the **terms of trade**) is determined by cost and by demand for these two commodities in both countries. The terms of trade are the rates at which a country's exports are exchanged for its imports.

For every worker transferred from grain production into car production in Canada, the output of grain falls by five metric tons, but the output of cars rises by 10. Each of those cars can now be exported to Mexico for 0.75 metric tons of grain, resulting in a net gain of (0.75 − 0.5 =) 0.25 metric tons of grain per car for Canada. Does Mexico also gain from this transaction? Let's investigate. To produce one car, Mexico would have to give up one metric ton of grain. By trading with Canada, Mexico obtains the car for only 0.75 metric tons of grain—a clear gain of 0.25 metric tons of grain. This analysis leads to the following principle of comparative advantage:

> The principle of comparative advantage states that if each country has a comparative advantage in the production of a commodity, both countries will benefit if each specializes in the production of the commodity in which it has a comparative advantage, and then trades with the other.

Note that trade between the two countries is mutually beneficial only because of a difference in opportunity cost between the two countries. If the opportunity cost were identical in both countries, neither would have a comparative advantage and therefore no gain from trade.

Can comparative advantage be illustrated graphically?

The principle of comparative advantage and the gains from trade can be illustrated graphically. For simplicity, let us assume that Canada and Mexico each have only one worker and that production in both countries takes place under conditions of constant opportunity cost, so that the production possibility (p-p) curves are linear, as shown in Figure 14.1.

Canada's p-p curve shows that if Canada uses all its resources to produce grain, it can produce five metric tons of grain. Alternatively, if it uses all its resources to produce only cars, it can produce 10 cars. Conversely, with full utilization of its resources, Mexico can produce six cars or six metric tons of grain. Note that as before, Canada has a comparative advantage in the production of cars while Mexico has a comparative advantage in the production of grain.

Let us assume that both countries want both grain and cars. In the absence of international trade, each country would have to produce some quantities of both goods. Suppose that Canada decides to produce two cars and four metric tons of grain, thus operating at point *A* on its p-p curve. Suppose also that Mexico decides to produce four cars and two metric tons of grain, thus operating at point *B* on its p-p curve. The total output of both countries is six cars and six metric tons of grain. Note that each country is operating efficiently because each is operating on its p-p curve.

Now let us introduce specialization and trade. Suppose that Canada specializes in the production of cars (in which it has a comparative advantage) and Mexico specializes in the production of grain (in which it has a comparative advantage). With Canada

terms of trade the rate at which a country's exports exchange for its imports

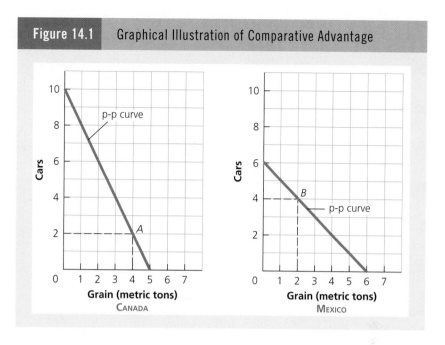

Figure 14.1 Graphical Illustration of Comparative Advantage

producing only cars and Mexico producing only grain, the combined output would be 10 cars and six metric tons of grain. Because of specialization, the output of cars increases from six to 10 while the output of grain remains unchanged at six metric tons. But Canada has only cars and Mexico has only grain. Here, trade can be beneficial to both countries.

Recall that in the absence of international trade, Canada would operate at point A on its p-p curve (Figure 14.1), producing two cars and four metric tons of grain. Mexico would operate at point B on its p-p curve, producing four cars and two metric tons of grain. Note that Canada must sacrifice one metric ton of grain to produce two cars. For Canada, one metric ton of grain costs two cars. However, Canada would like to obtain one metric ton of grain for less than two cars.

Recall that for Mexico, one car costs one metric ton of grain. Therefore, two cars cost two metric tons of grain. Suppose Canada offers to pay Mexico one car for 0.75 metric tons of grain (that is, two cars for 1.5 metric tons of grain) and Mexico accepts the offer. The terms of trade (one car for 0.75 metric tons of grain) would mean that Canada would obtain a metric ton of grain more cheaply (for 1.33 cars instead of two cars), and Mexico would obtain a car more cheaply (for 0.75 metric tons of grain instead of one metric ton of grain). Figure 14.2 shows the gain from specialization and trade.

The p-p curves for Canada and Mexico are the same as in Figure 14.1. With trade and specialization, Canada can specialize in car production, but now it can trade 10 cars, at the terms of trade, for 7.5 metric tons of grain. Canada's trading curve is illustrated in Figure 14.2. Mexico can specialize in grain production, but now it can trade six metric tons of grain, at the terms of grain, for eight cars. Mexico's trading curve is also shown in Figure 14.2. Note that because the trading curve is above the p-p curve, any point on the trading curve is preferable to any point on the p-p curve. A **trading curve** is a graphical depiction of all combinations of goods and services available through specialization and trade.

It would be inefficient for Canada and Mexico to remain on their p-p curves when international trade is possible. Canada can produce 10 cars and then trade (export) six

trading curve a graphical depiction of all combinations of goods and services available through specialization and trade

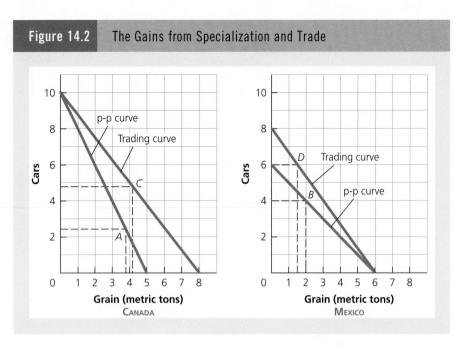

Figure 14.2   **The Gains from Specialization and Trade**

cars to Mexico for 4.5 metric tons of grain, thus moving to point C on its trading curve. Canada is unambiguously better off at C than at A. But what about Mexico? If Mexico specializes in the production of grain, it can sell 4.5 metric tons of grain to Canada for six cars, thus moving to point D on its trading curve. Mexico is definitely better off at point D than at point B.

Reading Comprehension

The answers to these questions can be found on MyEconLab at **www.myeconlab.com.**   MyEconLab

1. Assume that Canada is the most efficient country in the world in the production of agricultural goods. Could Canada still benefit from importing food? Explain.
2. Carefully explain the principle of comparative advantage.

3. Explain the difference between absolute advantage and comparative advantage.
4. Explain why energy (crude petroleum, natural gas), industrial goods (metals and alloys, chemicals, plastics, and fertilizers), and agricultural and fishing products are major export items for Canada.

LO 14.3 Discuss the factors that determine comparative advantage

Factors That Determine Comparative Advantage

Why might one country have a comparative advantage over another country in the production of an item?

The factors that account for the existence of comparative advantage are natural endowment, acquired advantage, and special knowledge. Let us discuss each of these factors in turn.

Natural Endowment   The Caribbean islands have numerous white sandy beaches and a warm (sometimes hot) climate all year round, naturally. They therefore are an attraction for Canadian tourists who want to get away for a week or two between December and March, when it is cold and snowing in Canada. The comparative advantage enjoyed by the Caribbean islands in this field is a matter of natural endowment. In this case, the comparative advantage is geographically determined—hence the concept of **geographical determinism**, the theory that comparative advantage is determined by natural endowment.

geographical determinism
the theory that comparative
advantage is determined
by natural endowment

This theory has been around for a long time; despite its age, it still has relevance in explaining comparative advantage in some instances.

Acquired Advantage   In the same way that some individuals work hard to develop and improve whatever abilities have been bestowed on them, so too can nations, by their own efforts, acquire comparative advantage in certain lines of production. Japan is often cited as the classic example of a nation that has compensated for its lack of natural resource endowment by saving and making huge investment in capital, both physical and human.

Special Knowledge   Whether by accident or design, some countries have special knowledge that gives them a comparative advantage in the production of certain products. A country that comes to mind in this regard is Switzerland, with its reputation for watchmaking. Switzerland's expertise in watchmaking is undoubtedly partly a result of many years of concentration on that activity.

Reading Comprehension

The answers to these questions can be found on MyEconLab at **www.myeconlab.com.**   MyEconLab

1. Discuss the major factors that determine comparative advantage.

2. Explain the concept of geographical determinism as it pertains to international trade.
3. Explain how investment in physical and human capital might result in comparative advantage.

LO 14.4   Describe further
gains from trade

Further Gains from Trade

We have seen that absolute advantage and comparative advantage make it possible for nations to gain from international trade. Do any other factors make trade beneficial?

Yes. Further gains from trade can result from increased efficiency and economies of scale. Let us explore these ideas.

Increased Efficiency   We can reasonably expect that as Canada specializes in the production of cars and Mexico specializes in the production of grain, Canadian workers will acquire greater skills and expertise in the production of cars. Mexico will likewise acquire greater skills and expertise in the production of grain. Thus, each country, by specializing, will experience an increase in worker productivity.

Table 14.3	Products Requiring High and Medium Levels of Electricity	
High	**Medium**	
Newsprint	Other pulp and paper	
Aluminum	Titanium	
Magnesium	Steel works	
Zinc and cadmium	Carbon steel mill	
Silicon carbide	Copper	
Chlorine and sodium hydroxide	Glass	
Phosphorus	Melted alumina—95%	

Economies of Scale   Production costs may fall as the volume of output increases. If this is the case, then the average cost of producing cars in Canada will fall, because specialization in car manufacturing will have increased the volume of output. Similarly, the average cost of producing grain will fall in Mexico, because specialization in grain manufacturing will have increased the volume of output.

In what activities does Canada have a comparative advantage?

Canada has a comparative advantage in a number of economic activities. Among these are the production of electricity, certain agricultural items, forestry items, certain minerals, and certain kinds of technology, such as communication. Canada's large supply of electric power attracts industries that require large amounts of electricity. Table 14.3 lists products whose manufacture requires high and medium levels of electricity.

BUSINESS SITUATION 14.2

Canadian producers of electricity have developed a new technology that cuts the cost of generating electricity by 50%. A Canadian manufacturer of newsprint has found that its cost has decreased substantially, mainly because of the fall in its electricity bill.

How might this newsprint manufacturer use this newly acquired advantage to expand its business?

The answer to this Business Situation can be found in Appendix A.

Reading Comprehension

The answers to these questions can be found on MyEconLab at www.myeconlab.com.   MyEconLab

1.   Briefly explain how international trade might result in increased efficiency.

2.   Explain how international trade might lead to a fall in the average cost of producing an item.

LO 14.5   Discuss Canada's exports and imports

Canada's Exports

How important are exports in the Canadian economy and what are Canada's main export items?

Exports are very important to the Canadian economy. In 2009, exports of goods and services from Canada amounted to $438.6 billion, accounting for 28.7% of the total amount of goods and services produced in Canada.

Table 14.4	Value and Percentage of Export Items, 2009	
Item	**Value ($ mil)**	**Percentage**
Agricultural and fishing products	37 260.2	10.1
Energy products	79 854.9	21.6
Forestry products	19 500.9	5.3
Industrial goods and materials	79 172.4	21.4
Machinery and equipment	80 438.0	21.8
Automotive products	43 815.2	11.8
Other consumer goods	17 934.8	4.9
Special transactions trade	6 411.8	1.7
Unallocated adjustments	5 140.5	1.4
Total	**369 528.8**	**100.0**

Source: Data are from Statistics Canada Summary Tables, "Exports of Goods on a Balance-of-Payments Basis, by Product." Available online at www40.statcan.gc.ca/l01/cst01/gblec04-eng.htm. Extracted March 23, 2011.

Canada undertakes trade missions to encourage trade with the rest of the world.

Major export items include machinery and equipment, automotive products, industrial goods and materials, and energy products. You will notice from Table 14.4 that a significant part of Canada's exports consists of raw materials and that only a few items, such as paper, automobiles, and some machinery and equipment, undergo extensive processing before being exported. However, one of the largest single export items (automobile products) undergoes complete processing in Canada. Table 14.4 shows the value and percentage of Canadian export items in 2009.

In 2005, exports of automotive products were $87 994.4 million. In 2009, this value fell to $43 815.2 million, a decline of 50.2%. There were also significant decreases in the export of energy products, forestry products, industrial goods and materials, and machinery and equipment. These declines were most likely a reflection of the effects of the 2007−2009 global recession.

Which countries are Canada's major trading partners?

In 2009, almost 75% of Canada's merchandise exports went to the United States. Canada's largest export market is the United States for two main reasons. First, the proximity of the United States to Canada makes trade between the two countries relatively easy. Transportation is a major cost of trading, and the nearness of the two countries to each other greatly reduces transportation cost. Second, the economic size of the United States gives it the ability to purchase goods and services from Canada.

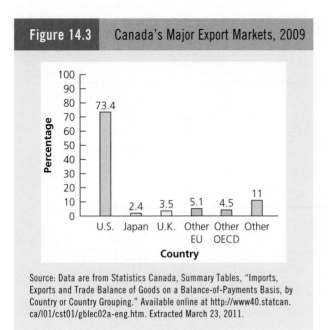

Figure 14.3   Canada's Major Export Markets, 2009

Percentage

- U.S.: 73.4
- Japan: 2.4
- U.K.: 3.5
- Other EU: 5.1
- Other OECD: 4.5
- Other: 11

Country

Source: Data are from Statistics Canada, Summary Tables, "Imports, Exports and Trade Balance of Goods on a Balance-of-Payments Basis, by Country or Country Grouping." Available online at http://www40.statcan.ca/l01/cst01/gblec02a-eng.htm. Extracted March 23, 2011.

Other important export markets are Japan, the United Kingdom, Germany, the Netherlands, China, and France. Figure 14.3 shows Canada's leading export markets along with the percentage of total exports destined for each.

In 2009, Canadian merchandise exports to the countries constituting the European Union (excluding the United Kingdom) amounted to $19.0 billion or just over 5% of Canada's total merchandise exports. Trade was also lively between Canada and Japan. Canada's exports of goods and services to Japan in 2009 totalled $8.8 billion, accounting for 2.4% of Canada's total merchandise exports. Canada sold $13 billion worth of goods to the United Kingdom and $16.7 billion to countries composing the Organisation for Economic Co-operation and Development (OECD), excluding the United States, Japan, the United Kingdom, and the other European Union countries.

Reading Comprehension

The answers to these questions can be found on MyEconLab at www.myeconlab.com.   *MyEconLab*

1. What are some of Canada's main exports?

2. List the major countries to which Canada exports goods. Which of these is the major buyer of Canada's exports? Explain why this is so.

LO 14.5 Discuss Canada's exports and imports

Canada's Imports

What is the dollar value of Canada's imports, and what are Canada's main import items?

In 2009, Canada imported $374.1 billion worth of goods and services. Table 14.5 provides information on Canada's imports.

From which countries does Canada purchase most of its imports?

Not surprisingly, most of Canada's imports come from the United States. In 2009, imports from that country accounted for almost 63.2% of Canada's total imports. Figure 14.4 shows the major countries that supply Canada's imports.

In 2009, Canada purchased $8.5 billion worth of goods from the United Kingdom. Canada's imports from Japan were valued at more than $9 billion—just about 2.5% of Canada's merchandise imports. Imports from other countries in the European Union amounted to $30.2 billion or 8.1% of imports from all countries. Other OECD countries supplied Canada with over $26.0 billion worth of goods.

Table 14.5	Value and Percentage of Import Items, 2009	
Item	**Value ($ mil)**	**Percentage**
Agricultural and fishing products	29 343.9	7.8
Energy products	33 954.9	9.1
Forestry products	2 385.3	0.6
Industrial goods and materials	75 078.0	20.0
Machinery and equipment	107 933.7	28.9
Automotive products	55 325.0	14.8
Other consumer goods	57 486.1	15.4
Special transactions trade	4 756.3	1.3
Unallocated adjustments	7 833.7	2.1
Total	**374 096.8**	**100.0**

Source: Statistics Canada Summary Tables, "Imports of Goods on a Balance-of-Payments Basis, by Product." http://www40.statcan.gc.ca/l01/cst01/gblec05-eng.htm. Extracted March 23, 2011.

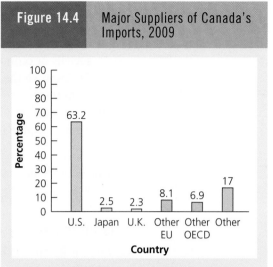

Figure 14.4 Major Suppliers of Canada's Imports, 2009

Source: Data are from Statistics Canada, Summary Tables, "Imports, Exports and Trade Balance of Goods on a Balance-of-Payments Basis, by Country or Country Grouping." Available online at http://www40.statcan.ca/l01/cst01/gblec02a-eng.htm. Extracted March 23, 2011.

Reading Comprehension

The answers to these questions can be found on MyEconLab at www.myeconlab.com.

MyEconLab

1. What are some of Canada's main imports?

2. List the major trading partners from which Canada imports goods. Which of these is the main supplier of Canada's imports?

LO 14.6 Discuss tariffs and trade policy issues

Tariffs and Trade Policy Issues

What are tariffs and why do nations impose them?

No nation is so self-sufficient that it is completely independent of any other country. Trading among nations is the rule rather than the exception. When we import goods from France or another country, we pay a tax or duty on those goods. Similarly, when Canadian exporters sell their goods to foreign countries, those countries impose a tax or duty on the goods coming from Canada. This duty or tax on foreign goods is called a **tariff**.

tariff a tax imposed on imported goods

> A tariff is a tax imposed on imported goods.

Why do nations impose tariffs?

That's a good question. There are many reasons why nations impose tariffs. The list is not exhaustive, but it gives an idea of the wide range of arguments used to defend tariffs:

- To support certain industries considered to be vital from an economic, a military, or a political point of view
- To raise revenue for the government

- To improve the country's balance-of-payments position
- To reduce unemployment in the country
- To restrict the consumption of certain foreign goods that may be considered socially or economically undesirable
- To improve the country's terms of trade and thus increase its share of the gains from trade
- To protect certain industries from the full force of international competition
- To redistribute income from one group to another

Clearly, nations have no shortage of reasons for imposing tariffs. A tariff can usually be defended (correctly or incorrectly) on one or more of the grounds listed above.

Is there any way of classifying tariffs?

Yes. Tariffs can be classified according to their main objectives. If the main objective of the tariff is to raise revenue for the government, then the tariff is called a **revenue tariff**. If the objective is to product domestic industries or producers, then the tariff is called a **protective tariff**.

revenue tariff a tariff aimed at raising revenue

protective tariff a tariff aimed at protecting domestic industries

> A revenue tariff is a tariff whose main objective is to raise revenue for the government.
>
> A protective tariff is a tariff whose main objective is to protect domestic industries or producers.

Protective tariffs are much more common in Canada than are revenue tariffs. In 2009, customs duties in Canada accounted for less than 0.5% of the total revenue of the federal government.

Tariffs can also be classified as specific, ad valorem, or compound. A **specific tariff** is expressed as so much per unit of the imported item. Thus, a tariff of $0.60 imposed on each litre of a certain chemical imported would be an example of a specific tariff. An **ad valorem tariff** is expressed as a fixed percentage of the value of the imported item. Thus, a tariff of 35% of the value of textiles imported into Canada would be an example of an ad valorem tariff. A **compound tariff** is a combination of specific and ad valorem tariffs. A tariff expressed as $0.30 per kilogram for the first 50 kilograms and 10% of the value of any amount over 50 kilograms is an example of a compound tariff.

specific tariff a tax or duty specified as a fixed amount per unit of the imported item

ad valorem tariff a tax or duty levied on an imported item, expressed as a fixed percentage of its value

compound tariff a combination of specific and ad valorem tariffs

> A specific tariff is a tax or duty specified as a fixed amount per unit of the imported item.
>
> An ad valorem tariff is a tax or duty levied on an imported item, expressed as a fixed percentage of its value.
>
> A compound tariff is a tax or duty on an imported item that combines both a specific tariff and an ad valorem tariff.

What arguments are used to support the use of tariffs?

Several arguments have been used to support the use of tariffs. These include both economic and non-economic arguments. Let us discuss the economic arguments.

The Infant Industry Argument   One very popular argument put forward by supporters of tariffs is the so called **infant industry argument**. The infant industry argument can be explained as follows. New domestic industries cannot compete with those that are older and better established in foreign countries; hence, new domestic industries, especially those that show great promise of success, need to be protected by tariffs. New domestic industries, moreover, may have the potential to develop a comparative advantage, if given a chance. This potential may never be realized unless such industries are allowed to grow to maturity with the assistance of tariffs.

infant industry argument the argument that tariffs are necessary to protect infant industries

> The infant industry argument is the argument in favour of using tariffs to protect young domestic industries from competition from similar foreign industries.

Are there any concerns about this argument?

Yes, two main concerns exist. First, for the infant industry argument to carry much weight, the tariff would have to be temporary—in place only until the industry matures. In practice, however, an industry is often protected for such a long time that one wonders whether the tariff is not preventing the industry from maturing. Constantly sheltering the infant might preventing it from "growing up." Second, protection is valid only if the gains from such protection cannot be claimed exclusively by the firms' owners in the form of eventual profits. In other words, the infant industry argument is significantly strengthened when external economies, in the form of benefits to the society, are present.

The Employment Argument   Another argument often used to support the use of tariffs is that they help to create jobs. The imposition of tariffs, it is argued, keeps out foreign goods and thus increases domestic production. The increase in employment in domestic industries competing with the imported goods will spread to other industries. For example, increased employment in the communications industry will increase total income in that industry. This increase in income will increase demand for goods produced by other industries and thus increase employment in those industries. Additional investment may also be undertaken to produce domestic substitutes.

> The employment argument in favour of tariffs is the case that is sometimes made that tariffs create and protect jobs by keeping out foreign goods.

That sounds like a solid argument. Does it raise any concerns?

Indeed, it does sound like a convincing argument. However, when considering this argument, it is important to realize that the reduction of our imports because of tariffs means a reduction of exports from our trading partners, which may result in unemployment, lower incomes, and reduced imports abroad. Our exports will then also be reduced, and we, too, may suffer unemployment and falling incomes.

The Terms of Trade Argument   A third argument advanced in support of tariffs is that a country can improve its terms of trade by imposing tariffs on goods imported from other countries. Recall that the phrase *terms of trade* refers to the rate at which a country's exports can be exchanged for its imports. The imposition of a tariff means that a larger quantity of imports will be required for any given quantity of exports. Improvement in a country's terms of trade can make the country better off.

> The terms of trade argument is the claim that tariffs improve the country's terms of trade and thus make the country better off.

Is the terms of trade argument foolproof?

This argument is sound up to a point. It is true that a tariff can improve a country's terms of trade. But it is not necessarily true that the country will be better off as a consequence of higher tariffs. If the tariff is so high that it chokes off all imports, then the country may be worse off than if the tariff had not been imposed. There is therefore some level of tariff that is optimal in terms of increasing the benefits derived from the terms of trade.

The Diversification and Industrialization Argument   This diversification and industrialization argument is somewhat akin to the infant industry argument. The argument is that protection of domestic industries by tariffs is necessary to promote diversification and industrialization. The argument seems to rest on the assumption that industrialization and diversification are desirable because they result in an increase in real income. If industrialization and diversification are desirable for their own sake, then protection by tariffs is one way (though not necessarily the most efficient way) of achieving these ends.

> The diversification and industrialization argument for tariffs is the argument that tariffs are necessary to protect domestic industries to allow for the promotion of industrialization and diversification.

Does the diversification and industrialization argument have problems too?

Yes, we must understand that diversification and industrialization do not necessarily lead to an increase in real income, that is, purchasing power. Indeed, the pursuit of industrialization and diversification may lead to severe misallocation of an economy's scarce resources and, consequently, to a reduction in real income.

How about anti-tariff arguments? Are there arguments against tariffs?

Yes, there are two powerful economic arguments against tariffs. Let us discuss each briefly.

Comparative Advantage   The main economic argument against tariffs is that they interfere with the principle of comparative advantage. Thus, they reduce or negate the gains from specialization and trade. We have seen that international trade benefits each trading partner and increases total production. The imposition of tariffs, conversely, can result in each trading partner being worse off.

Efficiency   Another argument against tariffs is that the objectives that they are designed to achieve can, in most cases, be achieved by other, more efficient means. For example, the objective of industrialization can be achieved more efficiently by subsidization than by the imposition of tariffs. This occurs because if, for example, the objective of the tariff is to increase the production of a certain item, a subsidy will likely produce the desired result without discouraging the total consumption of the item by raising its price as a tariff does. Also, when a temporary tariff may achieve a specific objective, it becomes extremely difficult to remove the tariff once the objective has been achieved; tariffs tend to become permanent once they are imposed.

Can we use graphs to analyze the effects of tariffs?

We certainly can. Let us use simple demand and supply graphs to help us analyze the effects of a tariff. To avoid unnecessary complications, we assume that there are only two countries in the world: Canada and Rest of the World (ROW). To simplify the analysis even further, we assume that Canada and ROW use a common currency called the dollar ($). Diagram A of Figure 14.5 shows the demand and supply curves for wheat in Canada, and Diagram B shows the demand and supply curves for wheat in ROW.

The world price of wheat is P. At that price, Canadian wheat producers supply X units to the Canadian market, but the quantity demanded at that price is X_2. At the world price of P, there is a shortage of $X_2 - X$ units of wheat in Canada.

What's happening in ROW? Let's take a look. The quantity demanded at the world price of P is Y, while the quantity supplied by ROW producers is Y_2 units. Therefore, a surplus of $Y_2 - Y$ occurs in ROW. This surplus is exactly equal to the shortage in Canada. Is this a coincidence? Not really. The total quantity of wheat demanded in both countries must be equal to the total quantity supplied at the world price. If Canada and ROW are allowed to trade freely, Canada will import $X_2 - X$ units of wheat from ROW, and ROW will export $Y_2 - Y$ units of wheat to Canada.

Let's assume now that Canada imposes a tariff of on wheat imported from ROW. The Canadian price of wheat is now P_t. Canadian wheat growers increase the quantity supplied from X to X_1 units, and Canadian consumers reduce the quantity demanded from X_2 to X_1. ROW has lost its export market. This loss of the Canadian market forces

---

Figure 14.5   The Effects of Tariffs

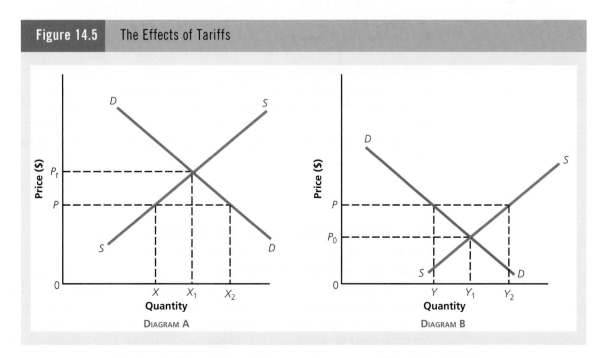

DIAGRAM A

DIAGRAM B

the ROW price down from P to P_0 in Diagram B. ROW wheat growers reduce the quantity supplied from Y_2 to Y_1 while ROW consumers increase their purchases of ROW wheat from Y to Y_1.

What is the effect of the tariff? Canadian consumers are paying a higher price and getting a smaller quantity of wheat. They can't be too happy. But Canadian wheat farmers are happy. They are getting a great deal more money: (P_t, X_1) instead of (P, X) in Diagram A. And what has happened in ROW? Wheat farmers there cannot be too happy. They are selling less wheat at a lower price.

Are tariffs the only restrictions on trade?

No, a tariff is not the only device that restricts the volume of trade between countries. Other such devices include import quotas, export subsidies, and voluntary restrictions and are referred to as non-tariff barriers. Let us look briefly at each.

Import Quotas   For one reason or another, a country might limit the quantity of an item that is imported into the country. Such a limitation is referred to as an import quota, which can be defined as follows:

> An import quota is the maximum amount of a commodity that may be permitted to enter the country during a given period of time.

To ensure that the quota is adhered to, the government requires each importer to obtain an import licence for the amount to be imported.

export subsidies devices used by a government to help exporters

Export Subsidies   A government may offer assistance to its exporters by giving them a subsidy. Such **export subsidies** reduce the exporters' costs, thus enabling them to reduce their prices and so compete more effectively with foreign producers.

> An export subsidy is any of the variety of means used by a government to help exporters.

Some countries use export subsidies rather liberally to promote their industries.

Voluntary Export Restraints   Imports from a certain country may adversely affect a domestic industry. In this case, a government may ask the exporting country to cooperate by voluntarily restricting its exports. Voluntary export restraints (VER) or voluntary restraint agreements (VRA), as this type of trade restriction is called, may prevent a flood of low-priced goods on the market, enabling domestic industries to compete.

> Voluntary export restraints (VER) are non-tariff barriers in which an importing country persuades another country to voluntarily reduce its exports of a commodity.

How are tariffs and quotas different in their effects?

Both tariffs and quotas raise the domestic price of the product and reduce the volume of trade. There are, however, differences in the effects of tariffs and quotas.

First, import quotas are likely to be more effective than tariffs in limiting the quantity of imports entering a country. If the preference for an imported good is very strong, some amount of that good is likely to be imported in spite of a high tariff. Some consumers may be willing and able to pay the price to have the item. But in the case of an import quota, the quota establishes the limit and it cannot be exceeded. The government may even place a ban on the importation of certain goods.

Second, a tariff, as we have seen, raises the price of the imported product and thus reduces the quantity demanded of that product. The proceeds from the tariff accrue to the government as added tax revenues. The tax burden is borne by Canadian consumers of the imported product in the form of increased prices, and also by the foreign exporters in the form of reduced quantities demanded. Domestic producers of the product are thus at an advantage, because the tariff does not apply to their product. A quota, conversely, reduces the supply of the product on the domestic market, and hence pushes up its price. The higher prices are paid to foreign exporters of the product and also to domestic producers. They do not accrue to the government as tax revenues as in the case of a tariff.

Finally, a tariff is non-discriminatory in the sense that it applies equally to all foreign exporters. Thus, all domestic importers of the product pay the same tariff. On the other hand, import licences may be awarded on the basis of criteria that have nothing to do with efficiency. For example, import licences may be granted to some importers for political reasons, while more efficient importers may be denied import licences. In such cases, the consumers will be the main losers.

Reading Comprehension

The answers to these questions can be found on MyEconLab at **www.myeconlab.com**.   MyEconLab

1. What is the difference between a revenue tariff and a protective tariff? What kind of tariffs does Canada usually impose?
2. List some techniques used to restrict imports. Do these restrictions benefit the domestic industries?

3. List the main features of the infant industry argument in favour of tariffs. Is there a problem with this argument? If so, what is it?
4. List the main arguments against restricting trade through tariffs.
5. Compare and contrast tariffs and quotas as restrictive devices.

Review

1. Review the learning objectives listed at the beginning of the chapter.
2. Have you accomplished all the objectives? One way to determine this is to answer the Reading Comprehension questions at the end of each section. They will help you assess the extent to which you have accomplished the learning objectives.
3. If you have not accomplished an objective, review the relevant material before proceeding.

Key Points to Remember

1. **LO 14.1, 14, 2** International trade can mutually benefit two or more trading partners if each specializes in the production of the commodity in which it has an absolute advantage. Absolute advantage is the ability to produce an item by using fewer resources than another country can.
2. **LO 14.2** International trade will also mutually benefit trading partners if each specializes in the production of the commodity in which it has a comparative advantage. Thus, trade

can benefit partners even in cases where one trading partner has an absolute advantage in the production of all goods. Comparative advantage is the ability to produce a commodity at a lower opportunity cost than another country can.

3. **LO 14.3, 14.4** Comparative advantage can result from natural endowment, acquired advantage, or from special knowledge. Gains from international trade can also include increased efficiency and economies of scale.

4. **LO 14.5** Canada's major export items include motor vehicles and parts, newsprint paper, energy products, machinery, and equipment. Canada's largest export market is the United States, which buys about 75% of Canada's merchandise exports.

5. **LO 14.5** Canada imports a wide variety of products, including motor vehicles and parts, machinery and equipment, and industrial goods and materials. The United States is Canada's largest supplier of imports. Japan, the United Kingdom, and other European Union countries are also important suppliers of imports.

6. **LO 14.6** A tariff or duty is a tax imposed on goods from foreign countries. Tariffs may be revenue tariffs or protective tariffs. Arguments exist for and against tariffs. A tariff raises the price of the item on which it is imposed and reduces the quantity demanded. Non-tariff barriers to trade include import quotas, export subsidies, and voluntary export restraints.

Economic Word Power

Absolute advantage   (p. 400)
Ad volarem tariff   (p. 410)
Comparative advantage   (p. 401)
Compound tariff   (p. 410)
Export subsidy   (p. 414)
Geographical determinism   (p. 405)
Infant industry argument   (p. 411)
International trade   (p. 399)
Protective tariff   (p. 410)
Revenue tariff   (p. 410)
Specific tariff   (p. 410)
Tariff   (p. 409)
Terms of trade   (p. 402)
Trading curve   (p. 403)

Problems and Exercises

Basic

1. **LO 14.2** With given resources, country *A* can produce either 30 units of corn or 30 units of copper, while country *B* can produce either 20 units of corn or 10 units of copper. The relevant data are shown in Table 14.6.

Table 14.6	Production of Corn and Copper in Countries *A* and *B*	
Country	**Units of Corn**	**Units of Copper**
A	30	30
B	20	10

a. Which country has an absolute advantage in both corn and copper production?
b. Which country should specialize in copper production?
c. Which country has a comparative advantage in corn production?

2. **LO 14.2** Agricounty can produce 80 metric tons of wheat or 2000 computers with a given quantity of resources. Electrocounty can produce 50 metric tons of wheat or 3000 computers with the same quantity of resources.

a. What is the opportunity cost of one metric ton of wheat in Agricounty?
b. What is the opportunity cost of one metric ton of wheat in Electrocounty?
c. Which county should concentrate on wheat production?
d. Which county should concentrate on computer production?

3. **LO 14.2** Country *A* can produce 8000 houses or 80 000 automobiles. Country *B* can produce 5000 houses or 100 000 automobiles. Assume that both countries operate under conditions of constant opportunity cost.

a. Graph each country's p-p curve.
b. Which country should specialize in house production?
c. Which country should specialize in automobile production?
d. Without knowing the terms of trade for houses and automobiles between these countries, show how international trade could benefit both countries.

4. **LO 14.1** Table 14.7 contains demand and supply data for Canada and Mexico for printer cartridges.

a. Draw the demand and supply curves for cartridges in Canada and indicate the equilibrium price and quantity.
b. Draw the demand and supply curves for cartridges in Mexico and indicate the equilibrium price and quantity.

c. Draw the demand and supply curves for Canada and Mexico combined and indicate the equilibrium price and quantity.

Table 14.7	Demand and Supply Data for Printer Cartridges in Canada and Mexico			
	Canada		**Mexico**	
Price ($)	Q_d	Q_s	Q_d	Q_s
20	60	30	80	20
25	55	40	70	25
30	50	50	60	30
35	45	60	50	35
40	40	70	40	40
45	35	80	30	45

5. **LO 14.1** Refer to Table 14.7 and your graphs.
   a. Given the demand and supply curves for Canada and the post-trade price of cartridges, determine whether Canada has a surplus or a shortage. How much is this surplus or shortage?

b. Given the demand and supply curves for Mexico and the post-trade price of cartridges, determine whether Mexico has a surplus or a shortage. How much is this surplus or shortage?

6. **LO 14.5** Refer to Table 14.4 on page 407. Provide an explanation for Canada's exports of
   a. Agriculture and fishing products
   b. Energy products (petroleum, natural gas, etc.)
   c. Forestry products

7. **LO 14.5** Refer to Table 14.5 on page 409. Provide an explanation for Canada's imports of
   a. Fruits and vegetables
   b. Energy products
   c. Forestry products

Questions in the Intermediate and Challenging Sections cover several different concepts, and have not been organized by learning objectives.

Intermediate

1. By completing Table 14.8, show how each of the events in Canada and the United States will affect exports from and imports into Canada.

Table 14.8	Influences on Canada's Exports and Imports	
Event	**Effect on Canada's Exports**	**Effect on Canada's Imports**
1. An increase in income in the United States	1.	1.
2. A fall in income in Canada	2.	2.
3. An increase in prices in the United States	3.	3.
4. A fall in prices in the United States	4.	4.
5. An increase in prices in Canada	5.	5.
6. A fall in prices in Canada	6.	6.
7. A fall in income in the United States	7.	7.
8. An increase in income in Canada	8.	8.

2. Refer to Table 14.7 again.
   a. Assume that no trade occurs between Canada and Mexico. What will be the equilibrium price of cartridges in Canada?
   b. What will be the equilibrium price in Mexico?
   c. Now, suppose trade opens up between Canada and Mexico. What will be the price of printer cartridges in both countries?
   d. Which country will export cartridges?
   e. How many cartridges will the exporting country export?
3. Consider two countries: Terredonia and Capitalia. Terredonia is well endowed with land but has very little capital. Capitalia, conversely, is well endowed with capital but has very little land.
   a. Which country would you expect to export capital goods, such as machines?
   b. Which country would you expect to export agricultural goods, such as corn?

c. What would you expect to happen to the prices of capital and land in both countries as international trade progresses?

Challenging

1. In an industrial country, capital is abundant. In a rural country, land is abundant. If these two countries establish trading relations, each specializing in the good in which it has a comparative advantage, explain what will happen to the prices of the factors of production (capital and land) in the two countries.
2. Assume that all countries in the world have identical opportunity costs so that no country has a comparative advantage in any line of production. Show that gainful trade is still possible.
3. "Tariffs always benefit the country that imposes them." Discuss.

MyEconLab   Visit the MyEconLab website at **www.myeconlab.com.** This online homework and tutorial system puts you in control of your own learning with study and practice tools directly correlated to this chapter's content.

Study Guide

Self-Assessment

The answers to the Study Guide questions can be found in Appendix B.

What's your score?

Circle the letter that corresponds with the correct answer.

1. International trade is
   a. The flow of people between countries through immigration and emigration
   b. The exchange of goods, services, and resources between nations
   c. Negotiations between sovereign states regarding trading policies
   d. All of the above
2. The main reason for international trade is
   a. The desire to help poor countries
   b. Economic self-sufficiency

c. The fact that trade is beneficial to the participants in trade
   d. None of the above
3. The basis for international trade is the fact that
   a. Some nations are rich while others are poor
   b. Some countries operate under a free enterprise system while others do not
   c. Countries are differently endowed with resources
   d. Some countries are large while others are small
4. Country A has an absolute advantage over country B if country A can
   a. Produce a good by using fewer resources than can country B
   b. Produce a good by using more resources than can country B
   c. Sell a good at a higher price than can country B
   d. None of the above

5. The principle of absolute advantage states that
   a. No country can ever have an absolute advantage in anything
   b. A country should specialize in the production of the commodity in which it has an absolute advantage
   c. Absolute advantage is irrelevant as far as international trade is concerned
   d. None of the above

6. Comparative advantage is
   a. The ability to produce a commodity at a lower opportunity cost than another country can
   b. The ability to produce a commodity with fewer resources than another country can
   c. The advantage derived by producing a higher-quality commodity than that produced by another country
   d. All of the above

7. A country is said to have a comparative advantage in those products
   a. That it can sell more cheaply
   b. In which its efficiency relative to other countries is highest
   c. In which its efficiency relative to other countries is lowest
   d. None of the above

8. Which of the following statements is correct?
   a. Only comparative advantage can result in benefits from trade
   b. Only absolute advantage can result in trade benefits
   c. Both absolute advantage and comparative advantage can result in benefits from trade
   d. Trade cannot result in mutual benefits to trading partners: if one gains, someone must lose

9. Specialization and trade lead to
   a. Higher prices and higher output
   b. Higher prices and lower output
   c. Lower prices and lower output
   d. Lower prices and higher output

10. Country *A* can produce 5 units of tea or 18 units of clothing with 1 unit of resources. Country *B* can produce 10 units of tea or 20 units of clothing with 1 unit of resources. We would expect
    a. Country *A* to specialize in producing tea
    b. Country *A* to produce neither tea nor clothing
    c. Country *B* to export tea and import clothing
    d. Country *B* to import tea and export clothing

11. If country *C* can produce 50 metric tons of corn or 30 books with 1 unit of resources, and country *D* can produce 10 metric tons of corn or 20 books with 1 unit of resources, then
    a. Country *C* should specialize in the production of books
    b. Country *C* has a comparative advantage in the production of books

    c. Country *D* has a comparative advantage in the production of corn
    d. Country *C* has a comparative advantage in the production of corn

12. Which of the following is *not* an economic reason for specialization and trade?
    a. Self-sufficiency
    b. Increased efficiency
    c. Economies of scale
    d. All of the above

13. The terms of trade refer to
    a. The conditions and terms governing the export of goods from a country
    b. The conditions that must be met before importers can bring goods into the country
    c. The rate at which exports are exchanged for imports
    d. The regulations governing trade between countries

14. Geographical determinism explains
    a. Country location
    b. Population growth
    c. Country size
    d. Comparative advantage

15. The trading curve is a curve that shows
    a. The pattern of exports from a country
    b. The pattern of imports from other countries
    c. Items that can be traded and items that cannot be traded
    d. All combinations of goods and services made possible through specialization and trade

16. Which of the following is a determinant of comparative advantage?
    a. Natural endowment
    b. Acquired advantage
    c. Special knowledge
    d. All of the above

17. In which of the following does Canada not have comparative advantage?
    a. The production of cane sugar
    b. The production of electricity
    c. The production of energy products
    d. The production of metals and alloys

18. What percentage of its output of goods and services does Canada export?
    a. 2%−7%
    b. 10%−17%
    c. 30%−40%
    d. 50%−60%

19. Major exports from Canada include
    a. Machinery and equipment
    b. Automotive products
    c. Energy products
    d. All of the above

20. Which of the following is Canada's most important trading partner, in terms of volume of trade?
    a. The United Kingdom
    b. The United States
    c. Japan
    d. France
21. Which of the following is a reason for imposing a tariff?
    a. To protect certain domestic industries
    b. To create employment
    c. To improve the terms of trade
    d. All of the above
22. Which of the following is not an argument in favour of a tariff?
    a. It lowers prices
    b. It protects infant industries
    c. It increases domestic production
    d. It improves the terms of trade.

Problems and Exercises (Use Quad Paper for Graphs)

1. Table 14.9 shows hypothetical demand and supply schedules for desk sets in Canada and Japan.
   a. Without trade between the two countries, what will be the price in Canada?
   b. Without trade between the two countries, what will be the price in Japan?
   c. Now, suppose free trade exists between Canada and Japan. What will be the price of desk sets?
   d. Which country will export desk sets?
   e. How many desk sets will the country selected in (d) export?
2. Country A can produce 1 typewriter or 20 pairs of shoes. Country B can produce 1 similar typewriter or 80 pairs of shoes.
   a. Which of these countries has an advantage in the production of typewriters?
   b. Is this advantage absolute or comparative?
   c. Which country has an advantage in the production of shoes?
   d. Is this advantage absolute or comparative?
   e. Would international trade benefit these countries?
3. Suppose that, per year, country A can produce 75 000 typewriters and 100 000 pairs of shoes, while country B can produce 1500 typewriters and 500 000 pairs of shoes.
   a. On the basis of this information, complete Table 14.10.

Table 14.10	Production of Typewriters and Shoes	
Country	**Typewriters**	**Pairs of Shoes**
Country A		0
Country B	0	
Total		

b. Now, suppose that country A specializes in the production of typewriters while country B specializes in the production of shoes. Use the figures in Question 2 above to complete the post-specialization Table 14.11.

Table 14.11	Post-Specialization Production of Typewriters and Shoes	
Country	**Typewriters**	**Pairs of Shoes**
Country A		0
Country B	0	
Total		

Table 14.9	Hypothetical Demand and Supply for Desk Sets in Canada and Japan				
	Canada			**Japan**	
Price ($)	**Quantity Demanded (000)**	**Quantity Supplied (000)**	**Quantity Demanded (000)**	**Quantity Supplied (000)**
10	14	5	7	4
12	12	6	6	6
14	10	7	5	8
16	8	8	4	10
18	6	9	3	12

4. *A* and *B* are two neighbouring countries. A worker in country *A* can produce either six units of clothing or three units of food. A worker in country *B* can produce either four units of clothing or one unit of food.
   a. Does either country have an absolute advantage in the production of both products? If so, which country?
   b. The production of clothing and food in country *A* and country *B* is shown in Table 14.12.

Table 14.12	Production of Clothing and Food in Countries *A* and *B*	
Country	**Clothing** (units)	**Food** (units)
Country *A*	5 000	15 000
Country *B*	50	10 000
Total	5 050	25 000

If country *A* specializes in the production of clothing while country *B* specializes in the production of food, use the opportunity cost figures given above to complete post-specialization Table 14.13.

Table 14.13	Post-Specialization Production of Clothing and Food	
Country	**Clothing** (units)	**Food** (units)
Country *A*		0
Country *B*	0	
Total		

5. Country *A* can produce 40 clocks or 2000 units of clothing with a certain amount of resources. Country *B* can produce 20 clocks or 1500 units of clothing with the same amount of resources.
   a. Is this an example of absolute advantage or comparative advantage?
   b. Will free trade between these countries be beneficial to them?
   c. If these countries engage in free trade, which country should specialize in clothing?

6. Electroland and Agroland are two hypothetical countries. They use a common currency. Electroland can produce 50 000 TV sets and 10 000 metric tons of wheat per year. Agroland can produce 10 000 TV sets and 30 000 metric tons of wheat per wheat.
   a. Complete Table 14.14.

Table 14.14	Production of TV Sets and Wheat	
Country	**TV Sets**	**Wheat**
Electroland		
Agroland		
Total		

   b. Production costs in Electroland are $200 to produce a TV set and $300 to produce a metric ton of wheat. Production costs in Agroland are $800 to produce a TV set and $200 to produce a metric ton of wheat. Suppose Electroland specializes in TV sets while Agroland specializes in wheat. Complete Table 14.15.

Table 14.15	Post-Specialization of TV Sets and Wheat	
Country	**TV Sets**	**Wheat**
Electroland		
Agroland		
Total		

15

The Economics of Environment and Government Regulation

Learning Objectives

After studying this chapter, you should be able to

15.1 Discuss the main sources of market failure

15.2 Explain the nature of economic externalities

15.3 Discuss the concept of a public good

15.4 Explain the need for environmental protection

15.5 Discuss the concept of open-access resources and the common-pool problem

15.6 Explain how economic analysis can help to arrive at an appropriate level of pollution

15.7 Discuss measures to deal with the problem of pollution

15.8 Discuss Canada's role in environmental protection

15.9 Understand the main elements of the Copenhagen Accord

15.10 Discuss the Cancun Agreement

Assess Your Knowledge

MyEconLab

1. Do you think society would be better off if education were provided only by private institutions for profit?

2. Name three consequences of pollution.

3. State *briefly* (one or two sentences) what you know about the Kyoto Protocol. Is Canada a signatory to this protocol?

4. What do you know about the Copenhagen Accord?

LO 15.1 Discuss the main sources of market failure

market failure the inability of the price system to achieve an efficient allocation of resources

Sources of Market Failure

What do economists mean by market failure?

Economists use the term **market failure** to refer to the inability of the price system to achieve an efficient allocation of resources. These malfunctions in the market mechanism lead to inefficient outcomes.

Why does the market fail to achieve an efficient allocation of resources?

Economists have analyzed market failure and have identified its four main causes: imperfections in the market, inadequate information, the existence of externalities, and the existence of public goods. We will discuss market imperfections and inadequate information here, and externalities and public goods in the sections that follow.

Market Imperfection A market is considered to be imperfect if individual buyers and sellers have so much power in the market that they can influence the prices of inputs and outputs. This is the situation described earlier in this textbook as imperfect competition. Market imperfections lead to a misallocation of society's resources or to their unproductive use. The freedom of entry that is characteristic of a purely competitive industry ensures that other firms will enter the industry if profits can be gained. Their entry will reduce the price of the product to the point at which economic profits are zero. In the case of a monopoly or oligopoly, effective barriers to entry prevent firms from entering the industry. Such firms will tend to set the prices of their products to earn maximum profits. These firms may deliberately restrict output to keep price above average total cost.

In monopolistic competition, even though there is freedom of entry and exit, the firms acquire some degree of market power through product differentiation. In the long run, firms in monopolistic competition earn zero economic profit, but the price of the product is above the purely competitive price, and there is underproduction of the product. Allocative efficiency does not exist in this case.

Inadequate Information In the purely competitive model, buyers and sellers are assumed to have full knowledge of the market. In making their decisions, they possess full knowledge of the products and prices. Lack of adequate information can cause market players to make decisions that do not maximize their profits or their satisfaction.

Quite often, households may not have the expertise to be able to judge the quality of a product. The complexity of some products requires specific knowledge on the part of buyers to enable them to evaluate the products—knowledge that many buyers just do not possess. We may conclude, erroneously, that a stereo system or a television set with a $1500 price tag is better than one with a $1000 price tag. But the price may not always send the right signal about quality. Also, buyers often purchase items on the basis of information contained in advertisements. If the advertisement lacks truth, then buyers' decisions will be based on false advertising, resulting in inefficient outcomes.

Reading Comprehension

The answers to these questions can be found on MyEconLab at **www.myeconlab.com.**   MyEconLab

1. What is market failure?
2. What are some of the sources of market failure?

LO 15.2 Explain the nature of economic externalities

Economic Externalities

How are economic externalities related to market failure?

The existence of external costs and benefits is another source of market failure. We can discuss the concept of economic externality by first introducing the concept of private costs and social costs. When a firm decides to produce a product, the costs considered include the costs of such items as labour and raw materials. When an individual decides to take a vacation in a foreign country, the costs considered include the costs of air travel, accommodation, local transportation, and entertainment. Such costs are called **private costs**, and they are borne solely and directly by the individuals or firms making the decision to acquire inputs or purchase goods and services.

private costs costs borne solely and directly by the individuals or firms making the decision

Some costs, however, are not borne solely by the individuals or by the firms, but by society as a whole. Consider the case of a chemical manufacturer that dumps wastes into a river. The river becomes polluted, the fish population in the river is destroyed, and the river can no longer be used for swimming and recreational activities. Moreover, property values along the riverside decrease. These are costs that have to be borne not just by private firms and households but also by society as a whole, in terms of the total sacrifice made when resources are used. When these costs are added to private costs, we obtain what economists call **social costs**, the total costs to society of decisions made and actions taken by individuals and firms.

social costs the total costs to society of decisions made and actions taken by individuals and firms

Social costs = Private costs + External costs

economic externality a cost or benefit that accrues to persons not directly involved in the actions or decisions made by firms and individuals

Very often, we encounter situations in which private costs conflict with social costs. For example, a chemical manufacturer that pollutes the environment bears only a part of the cost of production: the private costs. Such divergences between private costs and social costs are called **economic externalities**. They are *external* in the sense that the firm or the individual does not take them into consideration when calculating costs. Society bears these costs in the form of a less healthy population, higher medical bills, the loss of animal life, the loss of good recreational areas, the loss of aesthetic value, and higher taxes to pay for the cleaning up of the environment. Economic externalities are costs (or benefits) that accrue to persons not directly involved in the actions or decisions made by firms and individuals.

As just noted, an economic externality need not be a cost; it can also be an external benefit. For example, the development of a resort area will increase property values in that area. If the externality results in some benefit, we refer to it as an **external economy** or a **positive externality**. If it results in a cost, as in the case of pollution, we refer to it as an **external diseconomy** or a **negative externality**.

> **external economy or positive externality** an economic externality that results in a benefit

> **external diseconomy or negative externality** an economic externality that results in a cost

What is the effect of a positive externality on the optimal level of consumption of a good?

Let us look again at the idea of a positive externality. Positive externalities occur when production or consumption by particular firms or consumers results in benefits to other firms or other consumers. For example, if you are inoculated against the flu, the risk of your contracting it is greatly reduced; but others also benefit from your inoculation because the chance of your transmitting the flu to them is also reduced. In this way, vaccinations provide positive externalities (external benefits) to others.

Let us answer the question by using health as an example of a good that creates a positive externality. We can use Figure 15.1 to illustrate the effect of external benefits on the optimal level of consumption of health services.

The demand curve D_p represents the private demand for health. The demand curve shows the various quantities of health care that would be demanded by individuals at various prices for health. The demand curve D_p reflects the marginal private benefit derived by those who directly acquire the health services. Note that a greater quantity of health care is demanded as the price of health care falls.

The benefits of health, however, are not confined only to the individuals who purchase health services. They extend to others in society. By adding these positive externalities (or marginal external benefit) to the marginal private benefit of health, we obtain the marginal social benefit of health. All the benefit that society derives from health is included in the marginal social benefit. The marginal social benefit curve D_s in Figure 15.1 lies above the private demand curve D_p. This means that at each level of health care, the marginal social benefit exceeds the marginal private benefit. The difference is the marginal external benefit generated by that unit of health care.

The supply curve S in Figure 15.1 shows the marginal cost of producing each unit of health. The intersection of the private demand curve D_p with the supply curve S at point E_p gives the equilibrium quantity of health, Q_p, that would be demanded privately. Here, the marginal cost of health equals the marginal private benefit.

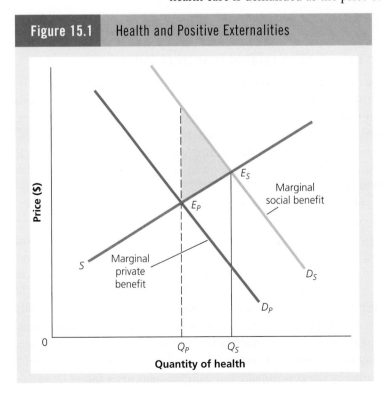

Figure 15.1   Health and Positive Externalities

Note, however, that at this level of health care, the marginal social benefit exceeds the marginal cost. Therefore, the society would benefit from an expansion of health services beyond Q_p. Society would benefit from an expansion of health services as long as the marginal social benefit of health care exceeds its marginal cost. The social equilibrium quantity of health is determined by the intersection of the marginal social benefit curve D_s and the supply curve at point E_s. The social equilibrium quantity of health care is indicated as Q_s in Figure 15.1. Here, the marginal social benefit equals the marginal cost, and social benefit is maximized. The blue triangle represents the increase in social benefit that results from increasing the quantity of health care from Q_p to Q_s.

Clearly, society is better off if the quantity of health provided exceeds the private equilibrium level. Because of a positive externality, private decisions lead to market failure. Here is a justifiable case for the government to get involved in providing health services. The existence of external benefits requires public policy to expand output beyond the private equilibrium level.

Reading Comprehension

The answers to these questions can be found on MyEconLab at **www.myeconlab.com.**   MyEconLab

1. Distinguish between private costs and social costs.

2. What are economic externalities? How is the concept of economic externality related to environmental pollution?

LO 15.3 Discuss the concept of a public good

Public Goods

How are economic externalities related to market failure?

public goods goods or services that are consumed collectively; no one can be excluded from their consumption

We have seen that the unregulated market system can lead to the production and distribution of harmful products. It can also lead to the underproduction of some goods that society values but that may not be produced by private, profit-seeking enterprise. Such goods are known as **public goods**—goods or services that are consumed collectively. Once such a good or service is produced, it is generally impossible to exclude anyone from enjoying its benefits. Its consumption by one person does not diminish the amount available to others.

Classic examples of public goods are police protection, public health services, national defence, and education.

The production of public goods presents a difficulty for the unregulated market mechanism. Private goods present no such difficulty. Automobile producers, for example, can earn a profit by producing cars because people cannot obtain the services of these cars without someone purchasing them. But let us now consider the case of national defence. If a private firm were to provide this service, you would personally benefit from it and so would every other person living in Canada. The firm, however, would not be in a position to enforce payment from you or from anyone else; hence, a private, profit-seeking firm is not likely to produce a public good. This explains why public goods are provided by the government and paid for collectively out of taxes.

merit goods goods or
services that the government
has determined to be
necessary and therefore
mandatory for society

The government can enact legislation making the consumption of certain goods mandatory. Education is a case in point. In Canada (as in many other countries) children must attend school up to a certain age. Goods or services that the government has determined to be necessary and therefore mandatory for society are referred to as **merit goods**.

Reading Comprehension

The answers to these questions can be found on MyEconLab at www.myeconlab.com.   MyEconLab

1. What is the difference between public goods and merit goods? Give an example of a good that is both a public good and a merit good.

LO 15.4 Explain the need for
environmental
protection

Environmental Protection

What are some of the environmental effects of rapid economic growth?

Industrial nations, such as Canada, the United States, and Japan, have undoubtedly made a significant amount of economic progress. Unfortunately, along with this progress comes a variety of problems; progress comes with a cost. In our attempt to maximize our total output of goods and services, we have seriously damaged our environment. For example, as the national output of goods and services rises, so does the national output of garbage. One question that our society must answer is whether progress is worth the associated sacrifice. Because rapid economic progress is a major cause of environmental problems, should we not therefore have zero economic growth? This is exactly what some people have advocated. The fact is, however, that economic growth is essential if we are to meet the challenges that face our economies and our societies.

Economic growth involves a cost. Smog, water pollution, and acid rain threaten our environment. Greenhouse gases are causing global warming with potentially disastrous consequences. Our ecosystems are less productive and our health, our lifestyles, our economy, and our society are all at risk because of pollution. We must protect our environment, and by doing so, we will be protecting ourselves.

The United Nations Climate Change Conferences, such as those held in Kyoto, Japan, in December 1997; in Montreal from November 28 to December 9, 2005; in Copenhagen from December 7 to December 18, 2009; and in Cancun, Mexico, from November 29 to December 10, 2010, are a clear sign that environmental issues are still of enormous global significance.

Reading Comprehension

The answers to these questions can be found on MyEconLab at www.myeconlab.com.   MyEconLab

1. What is the relationship between rapid economic growth and environmental decay?

2. What are some of the visible signs of environmental pollution?

LO 15.5 Discuss the concept
of open-access
resources and the
common-pool
problem

open-access resources
resources that are difficult
or costly to exclude
individuals from using

common-pool problem
the overuse of open-access
resources that occurs
because of unrestricted
access

The Common-Pool Problem

What is the common-pool problem?

In some cases, it is difficult or prohibitively costly to exclude individuals from the use of certain resources. Such resources (for example, the sea, the atmosphere, clean water, and wildlife) are referred to as **open-access resources**. All have unrestricted access to such resources.

Open-access resources give rise to what has been labelled the **common-pool problem**, because open-access resources tend to be in "common" use. The common-pool problem is the overuse of open-access resources that occurs because of unrestricted access.

Because no direct private cost is associated with the use of open-access resources, their use will continue up to the point at which the marginal benefit is zero. An example of this problem is overfishing that depletes the stock of fish.

Does the common-pool problem have a solution?

The obvious solution to the common-pool problem is the imposition of restrictions on the use of open-access resources. For example, a government might restrict hunting to a certain time of the year, or it might impose a quota on the size and quantity of fish that can be caught. These restrictions allow stocks to be replenished.

Reading Comprehension

The answers to these questions can be found on MyEconLab at **www.myeconlab.com.**   MyEconLab

1. What are open-access resources? Give two examples.

2. What is the common-pool problem? What, if any, is the relationship between open-access resources and the common-pool problem?

LO 15.6 Explain how economic
analysis can help to
arrive at an
appropriate level of
pollution

The Optimal Level of Envrionmental Protection

Because the environment is so important for our very existence, shouldn't we protect the environment by totally eliminating environmental pollution?

If the cost of eliminating pollution were zero, the answer to the question would be emphatically yes! And perhaps the question would not even be asked. But the cost of achieving a zero level of pollution, and hence total environmental protection, would be prohibitive. Economic analysis, however, can help us to determine what amount of pollution we should allow. If society considers the level of pollution to be sufficiently serious, then society should be willing to sacrifice some goods and services to attain a lower level of pollution. If the benefits derived from further pollution abatement (i.e., more environmental protection) exceed the costs,

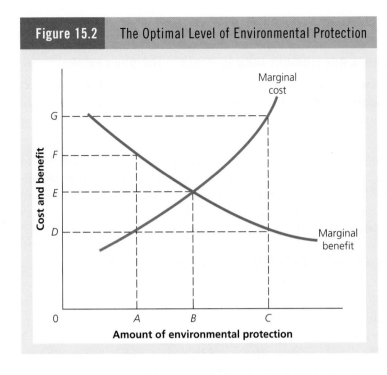

Figure 15.2 The Optimal Level of Environmental Protection

then additional resources should be allocated to environmental protection. Conversely, if the costs of additional pollution abatement exceed the benefits, then the extra costs should not be incurred.

These trade-offs are illustrated in Figure 15.2. As more and more abatement is undertaken, the extra benefit declines. Figure 15.2 shows this decline as a downward-sloping marginal benefit curve. Conversely, as more pollution abatement is undertaken, the extra cost increases. The upward-sloping marginal cost curve depicts this increase. At a pollution abatement level of 0C, the extra benefit (0D) is less than the extra cost (0G). Therefore, at 0C, there is too much environmental protection. At an abatement level of 0A, additional benefit (0F) exceeds the extra cost (0D). Hence, more environmental protection should be undertaken. At an environmental protection level of 0B, the marginal cost equals the marginal benefit, represented by 0E. Hence, 0B is considered to be the optimal level of environmental protection.

BUSINESS SITUATION 15.1

The New Line Paper Mill emits large quantities of toxic waste into the environment annually. The chair of the board, the president, and the chief financial officer (CFO) meet to discuss the situation. The president is very pro-environmental protection, while the chair and the CFO are more concerned with the company's profit margin.

The president argues that New Line Paper Mill should aim to reduce its pollution to the bare minimum possible to protect the environment. The chair and the CFO disagree, stating that the company should focus on its operations and just ignore the environment.

Whose position is economically correct?

The answer to this Business Situation can be found in Appendix A.

Reading Comprehension

The answers to these questions can be found on MyEconLab at www.myeconlab.com.   MyEconLab

1. "Society should aim for a zero level of pollution." Discuss.

2. Under what condition might a zero level of pollution be an appropriate target?

LO 15.7 Discuss measures to deal with the problem of pollution

Measures to Protect the Environment

What measures can a government take to protect the environment?

A government has a few options available to protect the environment. These are direct regulation, the imposition of effluent fees, the granting of tax incentives, the establishment of property rights, and moral appeal. Let us deal with each in turn.

Direct Regulation   One way in which the government can protect the environment is to prohibit the dumping of waste in certain areas and to prohibit the use of certain chemicals. Regulations forbidding the use of certain pesticides that damage the environment and the setting and enforcement of emission standards for automobiles and certain manufacturing plants that pollute the environment are examples of direct regulation.

This seems rather straightforward. Does this approach have any problems?

Yes. One problem with direct regulation is the difficulty of enforcing it. For direct regulation to be effective, an effort must be made to detect the offenders; this involves a substantial cost. The offenders, if caught, must then be prosecuted. This can also be a very costly process. The detection of an offence can be quite difficult. Some polluters, therefore, find it less expensive to continue to pollute and pay the penalty (if caught) than to install expensive anti-pollution equipment. Many individuals also may continue to dump waste into the environment in spite of the regulation, if the probability of being caught is low.

Another problem with direct regulation is that of determining the permissible level of pollution for each polluter. If the government aims to reduce pollution levels by say, 20% during a period, should all polluters be required to reduce their pollution levels by 20%, regardless of cost and the amount of pollution caused? Or should pollution levels be reduced by more than 20% in some plants and by less than 20% in others? Clearly, the decision is not an easy one.

Effluent Fees   Another approach to environmental protection is to charge the polluter a fee for polluting the environment. This charge, known as an **effluent fee**, forces polluters to consider the social costs rather then just the private costs of their decisions. In other words, they are forced to *internalize* their costs.

effluent fee a fee that is imposed on a polluter for polluting the environment

According to this approach, the fee charged would vary directly with the level of pollution caused by each polluter.

How do economists, in general, respond to this approach to environmental protection?

This approach to environmental protection has strong appeal among economists because it works through the market mechanism. Polluters are left free to pursue their objectives of profit maximization (in the case of firms) or utility maximization (in the case of consumers). Effluent fees provide polluters with an economic incentive to refrain from polluting the environment. We can expect this method, therefore, to result in greater protection of the environment. The higher the level of the effluent fee, other things being equal, the lower the level of pollution and the greater the protection of the environment.

Tax Incentives   Anti-pollution devices impose a substantial cost on those who buy them. If tax relief is given to people who incur the cost of purchasing and installing anti-pollution equipment, the level of pollution is likely to decrease as more and more of these anti-pollution devices are installed.

Does this approach to environmental protection have any problems?

Yes. One objection to tax incentives as a method of protecting the environment is that the practice of giving tax incentives may become widespread. If tax incentives are given for anti-pollution equipment, then why not for other types of investment that may be considered by some groups to be equally important? We may find ourselves in a situation where tax incentives are given for just about anything. The question can be asked: Is this the best use of taxpayers' money?

Another problem with tax incentives is the tendency for the recipients to abuse them. For example, a producer could buy some equipment, state that it is to be used for pollution abatement, claim the tax credit, and then use the equipment for some other purpose.

Property Rights   One reason that polluters abuse the environment is that no single individual or firm owns it. For example, no single individual or firm owns the air around v, so we can dump all kinds of poisonous gases into it without paying anything. Some people have suggested that the assignment of private property rights to individuals and firms can lead to a reduction in the overall level of pollution. Let us illustrate with the following example. Suppose a lake is owned by no one and a firm uses the lake for waste disposal. In the absence of government regulation forbidding the dumping of waste into the lake, the firm will use the lake for waste disposal. Let us now suppose that the government offers to sell the lake or to sell exclusive rights to use it for any purpose.

If individuals or groups of individuals value the purity of the lake for recreational purposes above the value placed on it by the firm for waste disposal, then they will be willing to buy the lake and keep it free from pollution. If the value of the lake to the firm as a place for waste disposal is greater than its value to those people who want to use it for recreation, then the firm will acquire the rights to the lake and use it for waste disposal. Note that the firm will purchase the lake for waste disposal only if the cost is lower than the cost of any alternative way of disposing of its waste.

Does the "private property rights" approach have any problems?

Critics of this approach point out the fact that some resources cannot meaningfully be owned as private property because it is practically impossible to enforce some property rights. For example, how could private individuals or firms own the air, or the right to fish in the ocean? No private property rights to such resources exist because an individual or a firm cannot prevent others from using such resources and cannot realize the value of such resources by using them all or selling them all.

Moral Appeal   An appeal to producers and consumers may help to reduce the level of pollution. Consumers can be persuaded to use public transportation and to organize car pools rather than to drive millions of air-polluting cars into the city. An appeal to firms to develop cleaner methods of production can also help to win the battle against pollution. Moral appeal is most effective where polluters are convinced that a polluted environment is against their own interests.

What about a carbon tax as a means of reducing pollution?

carbon tax a tax imposed on items that emit carbon dioxide

A **carbon tax** is being proposed as an effective device for reducing the level of pollution. Before moving further into a discussion of carbon tax, let us define the concept.

> A carbon tax is a tax imposed on items (called fossil fuel) that emit carbon dioxide, such as gasoline, natural gas, and coal.

A carbon tax is considered to be effective in reducing pollution because it provides an economic incentive for everyone to reduce the use of the items on which the tax is imposed. Also the carbon tax is considered to be fair in the sense that the tax one pays is proportional to the amount of emission caused.

Is there a carbon tax in Canada?

Canada does not have a national carbon tax. However, on October 1, 2007, Quebec made history when it became the first North American province, territory, or state to levy a carbon tax. On July 1, 2008, British Columbia imposed a carbon tax that was hailed as the most significant carbon tax in the western hemisphere.

Can we analyze the effect of a carbon tax?

We can do so using a simple demand and supply graph. A carbon tax is an example of an indirect tax. It is imposed on a transaction as opposed to a direct tax that is imposed directly on income. A carbon tax forces society to internalize the cost of producing fossil fuel such as gas, oil, and coal that emit carbon dioxide into the atmosphere. Let us now perform the economic analysis.

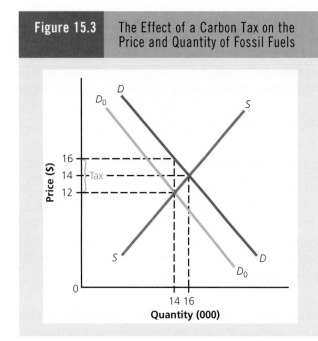

Figure 15.3	The Effect of a Carbon Tax on the Price and Quantity of Fossil Fuels

A tax on an item raises the price of the item to its users and reduces the quantity of the item used. Figure 15.3 illustrates the point.

The following analysis assumes that the tax is imposed on the users (buyers) of fossil fuel. The pre-tax demand and supply curves for fossil fuel are shown as DD and SS, respectively, in Figure 15.3. The equilibrium price and quantity are \$14 and 16 000 respectively. Now, suppose a tax of \$4 is imposed on fossil fuel. The tax serves as an incentive for users of fossil fuel to reduce their consumption of fossil fuel. The demand curve therefore shifts from DD to $D_0 D_0$. Consequently, the quantity demanded falls from 16 000 to 14 000 and the price falls from \$14 to \$12. But a tax of \$4 pushes the price to \$16. Sellers receive a price of \$12, which is \$2 less than the \$14 that they initially received. Users of fossil fuel pay \$16 instead of the initial pre-tax price

Figure 15.4	The Effect of a Carbon Tax Imposed on Producers of Fossil Fuels

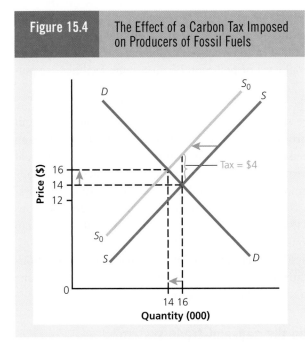

of $14. The effect of the carbon tax is to raise the price of fossil fuel to users and reduce the quantity used.

What if the carbon tax is imposed on producers of fossil fuel?

Well, let's see what would happen. Figure 15.4 will be helpful.

DD and *SS* represent the demand and supply curves respectively. The initial equilibrium price and quantity are $14 and 16 000 respectively, as before. Now suppose a tax of $4 is imposed on the producers of fossil fuel. This tax is a cost to the producers and therefore shifts the supply curve to the left from *SS* to S_0S_0, as shown in Figure 15.4. Consequently, the price rises from $14 to $16 and the quantity falls from 16 000 to 14 000. Consumers of fossil fuel now pay $16 instead of the initial price of $14. They pay $2 of the tax. What about the producers? From the new price of $16, producers have to pay $2 of the tax, leaving them with $14. As in the previous case where the tax is imposed on consumers, the effect is a higher price for fossil fuel and a reduction in the quantity bought and sold.

Do other countries have a carbon tax?

Yes, in some countries, such as those listed in Table 15.1, a carbon tax has been imposed on fossil fuel. It should be noted that the tax is structured differently in different jurisdictions.

Table 15.1	Some Countries In Which a Carbon Tax Has Been Imposed

Country	Year of Introduction of a Carbon Tax
Finland	1990
Denmark	1990
Sweden	1991
Norway	1991
Great Britain	2001
Canada	
Quebec	2007
British Columbia	2008
United States	
Boulder, Colorado	2007
California	2008
Ireland	2010

Sources: Data are from Carbon Tax Center, "Where Carbon Is Taxed." Available online at http://carbontax.org/progress/where-carbon-is-taxed; and Wikipedia, "Carbon Tax." Available online at http://en.wikipedia.org/wiki/Carbon_tax.

There is much discussion about cap and trade. What exactly is cap and trade?

Discussion of carbon tax often leads to at least a mention of **cap and trade**. Without going into a detailed discussion of the cap-and-trade system, we can outline its main features or elements. The cap-and-trade system is a free market approach to controlling and reducing pollution. Under this system, the government establishes pollution limits or "caps" on specific sources of pollution such as factories, power plants, etc. by giving a certain number of allowances or pollution credits. These allowances set the amounts of pollutants that the facility or organization is allowed to emit.

A cap-and-trade system is a market-oriented approach to pollution control that involves the sale of pollution credits on the open market.

cap and trade a system for reducing pollution by selling pollution credits on the open market

Facilities and organizations that control their pollution, perhaps through the implementation of technology, may not use up all their pollution credits. Other polluters may have difficulty operating under the established cap. This creates a market for pollution credits. Polluters that cannot meet their pollution allowances can buy pollution credits from those who have left over credits. In this way, some polluters are able to pollute more without increasing the overall level of pollution because some facilities are polluting less.

The cap-and-trade system is good in that it does result in a reduction in pollution. It also rewards polluters who are successful in coming in under the allowable limit through the use of effective control devices. Additionally, cap and trade provides an opportunity for polluters who need a longer adjustment time to buy some adjustment time. Supporters of cap and trade note that it provides strict environmental accountability without restraining economic growth. One problem with the cap-and-trade system is that it allows one area to become much more polluted than is desirable. Regions that purchase pollution credits so that they can "feed" their pollution habits will tend to be more polluted than other regions.

Note that the cap-and-trade system can be applied internationally as well as nationally. One country may be able to buy or sell pollution credits from another in the same way that domestic polluters can trade pollution allowances.

Has any country implemented the cap-and-trade system?

Yes. Table 15.2 contains a list of countries where the cap-and-trade system has been implemented or is being contemplated.

Table 15.2	Some Jurisdictions In Which a Cap-and-Trade System Has Been Implemented or Contemplated
Country or Jurisdiction	**Name of System**
Australia	Australian Trading Scheme
European Union	European Union Emission Trading Scheme
New Zealand	New Zealand Emissions Trading Scheme
United States	American Clean Energy and Security Act

Reading Comprehension

The answers to these questions can be found on MyEconLab at **www.myeconlab.com.**   MyEconLab

1. Briefly discuss the measures that can be taken to reduce the level of pollution.
2. Do you think that tax incentives are effective in reducing the level of pollution?

3. What is a carbon tax? How can such a tax reduce the level of pollution?
4. Briefly explain how a system of cap and trade works.
5. List one advantage and one problem with the cap-and-trade system.

LO 15.8 Discuss Canada's role in environmental protection

Environmental Round-Up

What is the current state of Canada's environment?

We will answer this question by evaluating some of the critical components of Canada's environment: air and water pollution, ecosystems and habitats, and climate change. We will examine the threats to our health, our economy, and our lifestyles, and we will pay some attention to efforts that are being made to deal with the problem. Let us begin with air pollution.

Air Pollution   The importance of clean air is obvious. Without it, our environment and our health suffer. Because of the fuels we burn in our vehicles, in our homes, and in our factories, the air is polluted. The air is further polluted by the use of solvents and cleaners, pesticides, and even our barbecues. Smog signals the presence of air pollution. The term "smog" was originally coined from a combination of smoke and fog in the air:

$$\text{Smoke} + \text{Fog} = \text{Smog}$$

It is the most visible form of air pollution. Ontario, the southern Atlantic region, and British Columbia are susceptible to smog. It is said that the region from Windsor, Ontario, to Quebec City has the worst air quality in Canada. Vigorous economic activity in Ontario and air pollution from the United States account for almost all of the smog in Ontario. Much of the smog in parts of New Brunswick and Nova Scotia can be attributed to air pollution from the eastern United States, while British Columbia itself generates the major part of its smog.

What are some of the effects of smog?

Air pollution is a serious matter. Because of smog, people may suffer temporary or long-term health effects. Seniors, small children, and people with respiratory or cardiovascular disease are more susceptible to the health effects of smog. It is claimed that thousands of Canadians die prematurely each year from air pollution, as ground-level ozone (the major component of smog) and other pollutants are inhaled into the lungs. An analysis by Health Canada of the relationship between air pollution and mortality concluded that about 5900 deaths per year in eight Canadian cities (Quebec City, Montreal, Ottawa, Toronto, Hamilton, Windsor, Calgary, and Vancouver) were attributable to air pollution. Studies on vegetation show leaf damage and lower yields resulting from smog. Estimates in southern New Brunswick show crop losses reaching millions of dollars per year as a result of smog. Smog can inhibit plant growth and can cause damage to crops and forests.

Additionally, because of air pollution, hundreds of thousands of lakes are vulnerable to acid rain and several thousands are acidified. The benefit of reducing smog in our major cities is evaluated at several billion dollars annually. Thanks to government action, our cars are now equipped with mechanical devices to reduce harmful emissions, our gasoline is cleaner, and harmful emissions from factories are lower.

Water Pollution   Canada is blessed with an abundance of fresh water; and that is good news because Canada is one of the highest water users per capita in the world. Unfortunately, some of the waters are polluted to the extent that they are unsafe for swimming, and the fish they contain cannot be eaten. One of the main sources of water pollution is toxic waste from industrial, agricultural, and domestic activities. Chemical spills, chemical production, municipal waste, and acid rain all contribute to water pollution.

One of the problems with water pollution is that it may be difficult to discern, and its effects may not be immediate. Clearly, water pollution affects both our health and our economy. Toxic substances in our water are injurious to our health and are damaging to our environment. Some of these substances are carcinogenic (cancer causing), and some are harmful to the reproductive and immune systems. Toxic substances are adversely affecting beluga whales in the St. Lawrence River, and acid rain continues to threaten thousands of lakes in Eastern Canada.

The Government of Canada and the Government of Ontario have entered into the Canada–Ontario Agreement (COA) Respecting the Great Lakes Basin Ecosystem several times over the past 40 years. The objective of the COA is to clean up the Great Lakes. The current agreement was signed in 2007.

What progress has Canada made in the fight against water pollution?

Canada has made significant progress in reducing water pollution. Lake Erie, for example, that was considered dead about 35 years ago, now sustains commercial fishing and sport fishing. Tougher federal and provincial regulations have significantly reduced overall emissions of certain toxic substances. Reductions of pollution in the St. Lawrence River, the Great Lakes, and the Fraser River are success stories for Canada. Through the continued work of the Department of the Environment, more success stories can be expected.

Nature Our consumption, commercial, and industrial activities are putting nature to the test. Many species of birds, mammals, and other creatures are disappearing or are threatened globally and here in Canada. Rapid industrial and urban development is threatening and destroying habitats. Our ecosystems are under attack and their ability to maintain environmental balance is weakened. Urban development and resource-based industries, such as mining and forestry, have exerted severe strains on natural habitats.

We have much to gain by protecting nature. Nature provides many health benefits through the development of new sources of food and medicines. Many drugs used to treat diseases are derived from living organisms. Many economic benefits are also derived from nature. For example, agriculture, forestry, and fishing provide employment for many Canadians and make significant contributions to the total value of goods and services produced in Canada annually.

Federal, provincial, territorial, and community efforts and initiatives have reduced the threats to our ecosystems. The Atlantic Coastal Action Program, the St. Lawrence Action Plan, the Northern Rivers Ecosystem Initiative, and the Fraser River Action Plan/ Georgia Basin Ecosystem Initiative have protected a significant amount of Canadian wildlife habitat. Ecologically sensitive lands are also being protected.

BUSINESS SITUATION 15.2

What opportunities does pollution provide for business enterprises?

The answer to this Business Situation can be found in Appendix A.

Climate Change   Climate change is a pressing environmental problem. It can affect our economy and our way of life. Climate change is closely related to greenhouse gases (water vapour, carbon dioxide, methane, nitrous oxide, ozone, and fluorocarbons). These gases keep the earth's temperature at comfortable levels. Without them, the average temperature on earth would be –18°C, instead of the current 15°C. The heating of the earth by these greenhouse gases is referred to as the **greenhouse effect**.

greenhouse effect the heating of the earth by greenhouse gases

Human activities seem to be increasing the amount of greenhouse gases in the atmosphere and, hence, global average temperature. An increase in global temperatures results in climate change. Major human causes of climate change are the burning of fossil fuels and deforestation.

The consequences of climate change for Canada are new infectious diseases, pollution, increased health problems from heat stress, reduced capability to grow crops, severe droughts, flooding, more frequent forest fires, and more severe weather disturbances. Climate change will adversely affect fishing, forestry, lakes, rivers, coastal communities, and the North. Climate change could indeed have serious consequences for our environment, our economy, and our lifestyles.

How is Canada responding to climate change?

In 1995, the federal, provincial, and territorial governments approved a National Action Program on Climate Change. Through this initiative, many companies have developed action plans to reduce their greenhouse gas emissions, and many Canadian municipalities joined the **20% club**, the objective of which was to reduce local greenhouse gas emissions from 1990 levels by 20% by 2005. They did not succeed. The various levels of government are involved in other programs to reduce greenhouse gas emissions.

20% club a group of municipalities whose objective was to reduce greenhouse gas emissions by 20% by 2005

What is the Kyoto Protocol and what is Canada's role in this accord?

The **Kyoto Protocol** is a treaty signed by about 180 countries at Kyoto, Japan, in December 1997. The Kyoto Protocol committed Canada and 37 other industrialized countries to reducing their emissions of greenhouse gases below the 1990 levels between 2008 and 2012. Canada's target was to reduce its greenhouse gases to 6% below 1990 levels.

Kyoto Protocol a treaty signed by about 180 countries at Kyoto, Japan, to reduce greenhouse gas emissions

Did Canada meet its target?

Unfortunately not! From 1990 to 1996, total greenhouse gas emissions *increased* between 10% and 13%. And Canada's greenhouse gas emissions are projected to keep rising unless drastic measures are taken to reverse the trend. It is indeed a challenge of mammoth proportions for Canada to meet its Kyoto commitment.

LO 15.9 Understand the main elements of the Copenhagen Accord

The Copenhagen Accord

Copenhagen Accord a non-binding agreement that endorsed the continuation of the Kyoto Protocol

Representatives from about 170 countries met in Copenhagen, Denmark, for a United Nations Climate Change Conference from December 6 to December 18, 2009. The **Copenhagen Accord** was the document outlining the agreement reached at the Copenhagen Conference. The main elements of the Copenhagen Accord were the following:

- The goal of limiting global temperature increase to 2°C
- A process whereby countries could enter their mitigation pledges by January 31, 2010

- Provision for countries to report and verify their actions
- A commitment by developed countries to provide $30 billion between 2010 and 2012 to assist developing countries in reducing emission levels, preserve forests, and adapt to climate change.
- The goal of mobilizing $100 billion annually by 2020 to meet the needs of developing countries

The Canadian government has affirmed its commitment to the Copenhagen Accord.

<table>
<tr><td>LO 15.10</td><td>Discuss the Cancun Agreement</td></tr>
</table>

The Cancun Agreement

Cancun Agreement an agreement signed by more than 190 countries at Cancun, Mexico, to continue efforts to reduce greenhouse gas emissions

Between November 29 and December 10, 2010, at the United Nations Climate Change Conference held at Cancun, Mexico, more than 190 countries supported the **Cancun Agreement**. The Agreement has the following main objectives:

- Set peak emissions and an overall 2°C target to limit temperature rise
- Assess each country's actions to tackle climate change through the UN system
- Adhere to a system whereby it can be determined whether countries are living up to their promises to take action on emissions
- Establish the Green Climate Fund to help developing countries use low-carbon technology and adapt to climate impacts
- Slow, halt, and reverse destruction of trees and comply with the rules for monitoring progress
- Set up the mechanism to help developing countries access low-carbon technology and adapt to climate change

Canada is a signatory to the Cancun Agreement.

Reading Comprehension

The answers to these questions can be found on MyEconLab at www.myeconlab.com.   MyEconLab

1. What regions of Canada are most susceptible to smog, and what accounts for the smog in each of these regions?
2. Provide some indication of the seriousness of air pollution in Canada.
3. What are some of the main causes of water pollution in Canada, and what progress has Canada made in dealing with water pollution?

4. "We have much to gain by protecting nature." Discuss this statement.
5. What are some of the consequences of climate change? How is Canada responding to climate change?
6. What is the Kyoto Protocol, and what is Canada's role in it?
7. What is the Copenhagen Accord?
8. What is the general idea of the Cancun Agreement?

Review

1. Review the learning objectives listed at the beginning of the chapter.
2. Have you accomplished all the objectives? One way to determine this is to answer the Reading Comprehension questions at the end of each section. They will help you assess the extent to which you have accomplished the learning objectives.
3. If you have not accomplished an objective, review the relevant material before proceeding.

Key Points to Remember

1. **LO 15.1** Sources of market failure include market imperfection, inadequate information, economic externalities, and the existence of public goods.
2. **LO 15.2** Economic externalities are the divergences between private costs and social costs and between private benefits and social benefits. If the economic externality results in some benefit, we call it an external economy or a positive externality. If it results in a cost, we call it an external diseconomy or a negative externality.
3. **LO 15.3** A public good is a good that is provided by the government for the benefit of society. Its consumption by one person does not diminish the amount available to others. Goods for which consumption is mandatory are called merit goods.
4. **LO 15.4** Pollution causes a variety of problems. It affects our health, our economy, and our way of life. Numerous benefits are to be derived from environmental protection.
5. **LO 15.5** Open-access resources are resources from whose use it is difficult or costly to exclude individuals. Examples of open-access resources are the atmosphere, the sea, and wildlife. The common-pool problem is the problem of overuse of open-access resources. The solution to the common-pool problem is the imposition of restrictions on the use of open-access resources.
6. **LO 15.6** Because pollution abatement involves substantial costs, the optimal level of pollution abatement is not the one that reduces the level of pollution to zero, but the level at which the marginal cost of pollution abatement equals the marginal benefit.
7. **LO 15.7** Measures to deal with the problem of pollution include using direct regulation, charging effluent fees, providing tax incentives, selling property rights, and using moral appeal.
8. **LO 15.8** Through the Kyoto Protocol, Canada committed to reducing its greenhouses gas emissions to 6% below the 1990 level. However, the greenhouse gas emissions have been rising and are projected to keep rising unless effective measures are taken to reverse the trend.
9. **LO 15.9** The Copenhagen Accord calls for limiting global temperature increase to 2°C, having countries report their actions with respect to reaching this goal, committing $30 billion from developed countries to help developing countries with environmental protection, and creating other devices to face the challenge of climate change.
10. **LO 15.10** The Cancun Agreement represents an important step toward seriously dealing with the problem of climate change internationally.

Economic Word Power

Cancun Agreement   (p. 438)
Cap and trade   (p. 433)
Carbon tax   (p. 432)
Common-pool problem   (p. 428)
Copenhagen Accord   (p. 437)
Economic externality   (p. 424)
Effluent fee   (p. 430)
External diseconomy or negative externality   (p. 425)
External economy or positive externality   (p. 425)
Greenhouse effect   (p. 437)
Kyoto Protocol   (p. 437)
Market failure   (p. 423)
Merit goods   (p. 427)
Open-access resources   (p. 428)
Private costs   (p. 424)
Public goods   (p. 426)
Social costs   (p. 424)
20% club   (p. 437)

Problems and Exercises

Basic

1. **LO 15.1** Indicate whether each of the following is a private cost or a social cost:
   a. Josh pays $8500 in tuition fees.
   b. Mary pays $5000 to take her two children on vacation during spring break.
   c. Pleasure boating on Lake Clarion pollutes the lake.
   d. Gloria and Michael throw loud parties that disturb their neighbours.

2. **LO 15.1** Indicate whether each of the following bestows private or social benefits:
   a. Your brand new car
   b. My beautifully kept lawn
   c. Your efforts to practise basic hygiene
   d. Manon's new extra-fast computer

3. **LO 15.3** Provide arguments in favour of the government providing the following:
   a. Free primary and secondary education
   b. Sanitation services
   c. Inoculation against infectious diseases

4. **LO 15.3** Table 15.3 shows the demand and supply schedules for education.

Table 15.3	Demand and Supply Schedules for Education		
Price ($000)	Quantity Demanded (000)	Quantity Supplied (000)	Marginal Social Benefit (000)
10	3	9	4
8	4	7	5
6	5	5	6
4	6	3	7
2	7	1	8

   a. What is the relationship between the quantity of education demanded and the marginal private benefit of education?
   b. Without considering the positive externalities of education, determine the equilibrium price and quantity of education.
   c. Explain the marginal social benefit column.
   d. What quantity of education is in society's best interest?

5. **LO 15.6** Many Canadians regard environmental pollution as a serious problem. Does this mean that the government should aim for a zero level of pollution? Explain your answer with the help of an appropriate diagram.

Questions in the Intermediate and Challenging Sections cover several different concepts, and have not been organized by learning objectives.

Intermediate

1. Refer to Table 15.3.
   a. Draw the demand and supply curves for education.
   b. Which of these curves reflects the marginal cost of education?
   c. Draw the marginal social benefit curve on your graph.
   d. On your graph, indicate the quantity of education that maximizes social well-being.

2. You overhear the following conversation between Kai and Anna:

   Kai: Poor air quality is bad for everyone; therefore, it is in society's interest to make the air perfectly clean.

   Anna: Not necessarily! That would be the case only if the cost of making the air perfectly clean were zero.

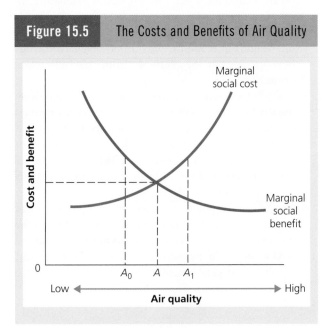

Figure 15.5	The Costs and Benefits of Air Quality

Use Figure 15.5 to illustrate Anna's point of view that unless no cost is involved in achieving perfect air quality, perfectly clean air is not socially optimum.

3. Show graphically that the imposition of a tax on polluters will reduce the level of pollution.

4. Figure 15.6 shows the marginal benefits derived from fishing. Consider fishing as a common-pool problem.

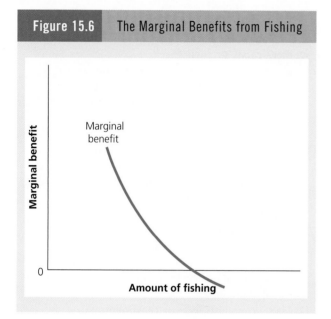

Figure 15.6 The Marginal Benefits from Fishing

a. Indicate the amount of fishing that will be done in the absence of any restrictions. Explain your answer.

b. Now suppose the government imposes a limit on the amount of fishing that can be done. On the graph, show the effect of such a restriction.

5. Figure 15.7 shows the demand for a lake as an outlet for pollution.

a. In the absence of any environmental control, what quantity of pollution will occur?

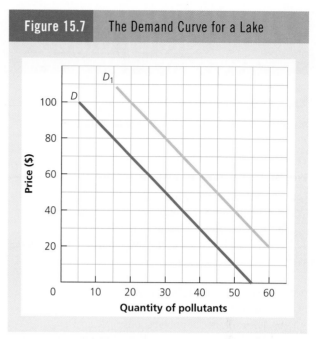

Figure 15.7 The Demand Curve for a Lake

b. Suppose the government establishes 30 as the maximum allowable quantity of pollutants and then sells the rights to pollute. At what price will these rights sell?

c. If the demand for pollution rights increases to D_1, what will be the market-clearing price for pollution rights?

Challenging

1. Use the concept of externality to make the case for subsidized education.

2. Explain why you would support each of the following:
   a. Restrictions on deer hunting
   b. A ban on smoking in restaurants
   c. The prohibition of temporary snow shelters (tempos) by a municipality
   d. A law forbidding large airplanes from landing or taking off between 12:01 a.m. and 4:59 a.m.

MyEconLab Visit the MyEconLab website at **www.myeconlab.com**. This online homework and tutorial system puts you in control of your own learning with study and practice tools directly correlated to this chapter's content.

Study Guide

Self-Assessment

The answers to the Study Guide questions can be found in Appendix B.

What's your score?

Circle the letter that corresponds with the correct answer.

1. Market failure refers to
   a. The inability of firms to control the market
   b. A lack of sales resulting from too small a market
   c. The malfunctions in the market system that produce inefficient outcomes
   d. All of the above

2. Sources of market failure include
   a. Limited information
   b. The existence of public goods
   c. The presence of monopolistic elements in the market
   d. All of the above

3. Which of the following would be considered a private cost?
   a. The cost to a family of a new car
   b. The cost to a company of installing air conditioners in its offices
   c. The cost of groceries for a family for a whole year
   d. All of the above

4. Social costs are
   a. The costs of joining social organizations
   b. The costs of providing social facilities
   c. The total costs to society of decisions made and actions taken by individuals and firms
   d. All of the above

5. The social cost of an action is equal to the
   a. Private costs associated with the action
   b. Private costs plus the external costs resulting from the action
   c. External costs associated with the action
   d. Difference between external costs and private costs associated with the action

6. Which of the following is an example of an economic externality?
   a. The benefit you derive from your neighbour's music
   b. The loss of property value because of criminal activities
   c. The benefit society derives from the good health practices of individuals
   d. All of the above

7. Which of the following is an example of a negative externality?
   a. The advertising costs of a firm
   b. The increased sales resulting from an advertising campaign
   c. The dumping of toxic waste near a residential area
   d. The money a firm pays out to ship its exports

8. Public goods are goods
   a. That are produced by private firms for the public
   b. That are cherished so much by the public that they are not consumed
   c. That bestow collective benefits on society
   d. None of the above

9. Merit goods are goods that
   a. Are good on their own merit and thus are costly
   b. Have won merits in competitive markets
   c. Are determined by the government to be good for people
   d. None of the above

10. The existence of external benefits will lead to
    a. Less than the socially optimal quantity of the good
    b. More than the socially optimal quantity of the good
    c. The socially optimal quantity of the good
    d. A ban on the good

11. Which of the following is a cost of pollution?
    a. The amount spent to reduce pollution
    b. The destruction of rivers and lakes by pollution
    c. The loss of fish stocks and birds because of pollution
    d. All of the above

12. Many economists argue that environmental quality could be improved by
    a. Direct regulation
    b. Moral appeal
    c. Effluent fees
    d. All of the above

13. Open-access resources are
    a. Resources that are sold on the open market
    b. Resources that are difficult or costly to exclude individuals from using
    c. Resources to which free access must be given by the government
    d. None of the above

14. Which of the following is an open-access resource?
    a. The sea
    b. Wildlife
    c. The atmosphere
    d. All of the above

15. The optimal level of environmental protection is
    a. One hundred percent protection (zero pollution)
    b. The level at which the marginal cost of protection equals the marginal benefit
    c. The level at which the marginal cost of protection exceeds the marginal benefit
    d. The level at which the marginal cost of protection is less than the marginal benefit

16. By charging polluters effluent fees, they will
    a. Internalize the costs of their polluting activities
    b. Pollute more, because they own the right to pollute
    c. Deduct the charge from their direct costs to arrive at a total cost
    d. None of the above

17. The establishment of property rights will
    a. Reduce the level of pollution
    b. Increase the level of pollution
    c. Have no effect on the level of pollution
    d. Make all firms more profitable

18. Which of the following is a disadvantage of the use of direct regulation to reduce pollution?
    a. The difficulty of enforcing the regulation
    b. The problem of determining an equitable way of applying the regulation
    c. Both (a) and (b) are disadvantages
    d. Neither (a) nor (b) is a disadvantage

19. Which of the following is not a method of reducing the level of pollution?
    a. Using direct regulation
    b. Lowering taxes on goods that pollute
    c. Establishing property rights
    d. Using moral appeal

20. By the Kyoto Protocol, Canada is committed to a reduction of greenhouse gas emissions between 2008 and 2012 to below 1990 levels by
    a. 1.5%
    b. 6%
    c. 15%
    d. 20%

Problems and Exercises (Use Quad Paper for Graphs)

Answers to these questions can be found on MyEconLab at www.myeconlab.com.

MyEconLab

1. An electric generating plant located in a hypothetical city uses gasoline to propel its turbines. This plant emits large quantities of smoke that pollutes the air. Devise a market-oriented program that will cause this plant to reduce its level of air pollution.

2. Table 15.4 shows the demand for pollution rights.
    a. On a graph, draw the demand curve for pollution rights.
    b. If firms do not have to pay to pollute the environment, how many metric tons of pollution will they dump into the environment?
    c. If the government charges $1600 per pollution right, how many metric tons of pollution will be dumped into the environment?
    d. If the price of pollution rights increases to $2000, show how many metric tons of pollution will now be dumped into the environment.

Table 15.4	The Demand for Pollution Rights
Price per Pollution Right ($)	**Amount of Pollution (metric tons)**
2 600	400
2 400	600
2 200	800
2 000	1 000
1 800	1 200
1 600	1 400
1 400	1 600
1 200	1 800
1 000	2 000
800	2 200

    e. What have you learned from this exercise about a possible means of controlling pollution?

3. Table 15.5 contains cost and benefit data for a hypothetical economy.
    a. Draw the demand and supply curves on a graph.
    b. What is the external cost per unit of production?
    c. At what level will the economy produce if the externality is not regulated?
    d. At what level should the economy produce to achieve economic efficiency?
    e. Calculate the dollar value of the net gain to society from correcting the externality.
    f. Indicate this social gain on your diagram.

Table 15.5	Cost and Benefit Data for a Hypothetical Economy		
Quantity	**Marginal Private Benefit (demand) ($)**	**Marginal Private Cost (supply) ($)**	**Marginal Social Cost ($)**
1	20	4	8
2	18	6	10
3	16	8	12
4	14	10	14
5	12	12	16
6	10	14	18
7	8	16	20
8	6	18	22
9	4	20	24
10	2	22	26

Chapter

16

The Economics of Information

Learning Objectives

After studying this chapter, you should be able to

16.1 Define the concept of information

16.2 Explain search costs

16.3 Discuss the informational content of advertising

16.4 Understand asymmetric information

16.5 Discuss adverse selection and moral hazard

16.6 Explain the concept of market signalling

16.7 Discuss the principal-agent problem

Assess Your Knowledge

MyEconLab

Answers to these questions can be found on MyEconLab at **www.myeconlab.com**.

1. List two sources of information that you consult on a regular basis.

2. Would you spend as much time searching for an item that is relatively inexpensive as you would searching for a relatively expensive item?

3. Why do auto insurance policies often contain a "deductible" clause?

LO 16.1 Define the concept of information

Information Defined

What is information?

Information is defined differently in different disciplines. Some see information as anything that reduces uncertainty. In this view, information illuminates a situation and reduces the magnitude of the unknown. Some regard information as the meaning derived from facts, that is, data. Thus, if the receiver or observer of data does not derive any meaning from the data, then the data do not constitute information. Still another conception of information is useful facts or data for a particular analysis or decision. According to this view, if the data are not useful for the particular purpose at hand, then it does not constitute information.

information knowledge of specific events or situations derived from study, experience, or instruction

Most definitions of information make reference to knowledge in some form or another. The link between information and knowledge is undeniable. For our purpose, we define **information** as knowledge of specific events or situations derived from study, experience, or instruction.

This definition of information is simple and distinguishes it from other concepts and ideas. Some people have suggested that the knowledge that is communicated or received must be true; otherwise, it is *mis*information rather than information.

In today's world, it is hardly necessary to stress the importance of information as an economic resource. Without it, decision making becomes quite difficult. Without adequate information, it is difficult, if not impossible, to exercise choice. Usually, before a firm decides to hire an employee, the firm collects relevant information. What are the employee's qualifications? What skills does he or she possess? Does he or she work well with other employees? Answers to such questions provide information on which the firm can base its hiring decision.

Given the prevalence of information, and the relative ease with which individuals may access it, should information be considered an economic good or a free good?

economic good a tangible or an intangible thing that is scarce and satisfies people's wants

Let us begin the answer by defining an **economic good**, which is a tangible or an intangible thing that is scarce and satisfies people's wants. A good is scarce if people want more of it than would be available if it were free. A good is described as an economic good if the quantity of the good demanded exceeds the quantity supplied at a price of zero.

Let us see whether information qualifies as an economic good. A plethora of information is available, but it would seem that the quantity of information demanded, in general, exceeds the quantity supplied, even if it were free. That explains why house-holds, firms, and governments are willing to pay for information. Information does command a positive price in the marketplace; therefore, it is indeed an economic good.

Reading Comprehension

The answers to these questions can be found on MyEconLab at www.myeconlab.com.   MyEconLab

1. Define *information*.

2. What is an economic good? Given two examples of economic goods.
3. Information is everywhere. Does this mean that information is not an economic good?

LO 16.2 Explain search costs

The Economics of Search

What are search costs?

search costs the costs, such as search time, incurred in searching for information about a product

The costs incurred in searching for information about a good or service are known as **search costs**. They can include the time spent reading advertisements, telephoning, inspecting, and travelling to acquire relevant information.

The sight of shoppers reading labels on products to find out the attributes is quite common in stores. We try to get enough information about the product before we actually purchase it: Is this product good? How does the price in this store compare with the price of a similar product in another store? What are the safety features of this product? Consumers might spend a considerable amount of time on the internet searching for information about the product and doing comparison shopping. They might purchase newspapers and trade magazines and read advertisements about the product. Before purchasing a car, many people may read new and used car reports on the internet.

The government often provides a great deal of information, such as safety standards, weather reports, and information about new automobiles—information that reduces search costs and improves purchasing decisions.

When should a consumer abandon the search for lower prices?

Search has both benefits and costs. We discussed the costs above, but what about the benefits? The benefit derived from the search is the lower price that the consumer finds as a result of the search. Because consumers do not have perfect information, the market will have price differentials, even in the case of homogeneous products. Of course, a rational consumer will not continue to search for a lower price if he or she knows that the price quoted by the first seller is lower than any other price in the market. Initially, as the consumer begins the search for a lower price, the marginal benefit will be relatively large, but as he or she continues the search and obtains more information, additional information provides less and less extra benefit. Generally then, the extra benefit derived from searching declines as additional searches are made.

A rational consumer in search of information will first gather the information that is most easily available. But as the search intensifies, the consumer is forced to make

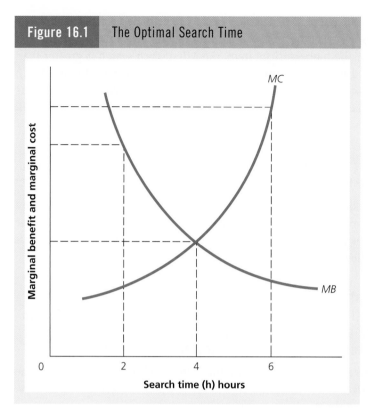

Figure 16.1 The Optimal Search Time

(y-axis: Marginal benefit and marginal cost; x-axis: Search time (h) hours; with MC curve sloping upward, MB curve sloping downward, intersecting at 4 hours; gridlines at 2, 4, 6)

increasingly greater sacrifice in terms of both time and money. The consumer's opportunity cost increases as more and more time is spent acquiring information. In general, the extra cost associated with additional search will tend to rise.

The optimal search for lower prices and good quality follows the usual marginal cost (*MC*) = marginal benefit (*MB*) rule established earlier in this textbook. If the *MB* from continuing the search exceeds the *MC*, then the search should continue. If the *MB* is less than the *MC*, search time should be reduced. The optimal search occurs at the point where *MB* equals *MC*. At this point, the consumer should abandon the search for a lower price.

So here is yet another case of decision at the margin! Can this decision rule for the optimal search be illustrated graphically?

Let us look at Figure 16.1. The *MB* curve slopes downward, reflecting the fact that the consumer derives less and less benefit from additional search. The *MC* curve slopes upward, reflecting the fact that the *MC* of acquiring additional information increases as the consumer extends his or her search.

As shown in Figure 16.1, if the consumer searches for two hours, the *MB* will be more than the *MC*; therefore, the consumer should continue the search for a lower price. If the consumer searches for six hours, the *MC* will be greater than the additional benefit from the search. The consumer should reduce the search time. If the consumer searches for four hours, the point will be reached where *MB* = *MC*. At that point, the consumer should end the search. Because nothing can be gained by curtailing or extending the search, four hours is the optimal search time.

Does the price of the product have any effect on search time?

First, we can provide an intuitive answer. Let us suppose that you are considering purchasing an item whose price is $5. Would you spend as much time searching for lower prices as you would for an item whose price is $100? Probably not! But why? The higher the price of an item, the greater is the *MB* of each search. You have more to gain by conducting an additional search. This conclusion can also be illustrated with the help of Figure 16.2.

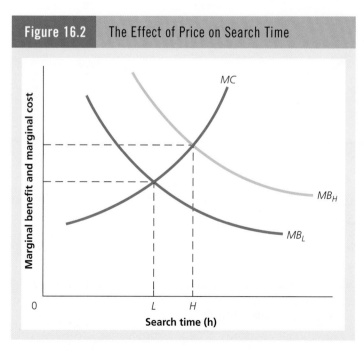

Figure 16.2 The Effect of Price on Search Time

(y-axis: Marginal benefit and marginal cost; x-axis: Search time (h); with MC curve sloping upward, two MB curves MB_H and MB_L sloping downward, intersecting MC at points L and H)

The marginal benefit curve for the lower-priced item is depicted by MB_L. The marginal cost curve is MC. The optimal search time for the lower-priced item is $0L$, where $MB_L = MC$. For the higher-priced item, the MB of each search is greater than that of the lower-priced item. Thus, the MB curve for the higher-priced item (MB_H) is above that of the lower-priced item, as shown in Figure 16.2. We assume that the MC is the same in each case. The optimal search time for the higher-priced item is $0H$, where $MB_H = MC$.

Does this mean that if all consumers follow the same rule, they will end up paying the same price?

Not at all! The MC of search for each consumer is different; consumers will abandon the search for a lower price at different times and end up paying different prices for the item. Sellers offering the product at a higher price will sell to consumers who have less information because they abandon the search for a lower price.

The opportunity cost of search is the income that the searcher could have earned if the time had not been spent in searching. This seems to suggest that as the market wage increases, less time will be spent on search. Is this correct and can it be illustrated graphically?

Your conclusion is correct. Let us analyze with the help of a graph. In Figure 16.3, the marginal benefit is MB and the marginal cost is MC_W when the market wage is W.

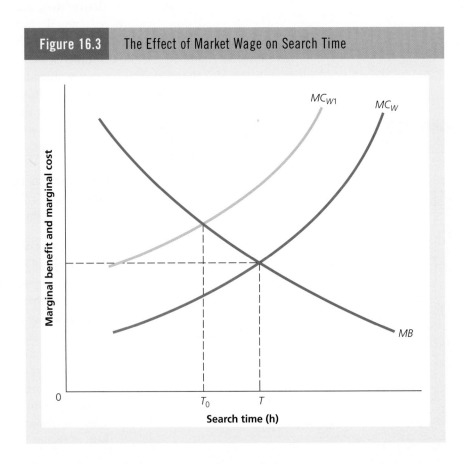

| Figure 16.3 | The Effect of Market Wage on Search Time |

If the market wage of the searcher rises, the marginal cost curve will shift up to MC_{w1}. As a result, the search time falls from T to T_0. This implies that a high-wage earner will be willing to pay a higher price for an item than will a low-wage earner, and that it is possible for similar items of equal quality to be sold at different prices.

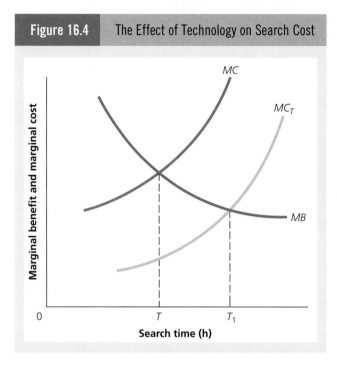

Figure 16.4	The Effect of Technology on Search Cost

What effect does technology have on search cost?

Technology, particularly information technology, such as computers, faxes, and the internet, has greatly increased the efficiency of search time. Through technology, a great deal of information about price and product characteristics can be collected, processed, and transmitted at incredible speeds. Technology thus reduces search cost. Figure 16.4 illustrates the effect of technology on search cost.

The now familiar marginal benefit and marginal cost of search are depicted by the MB and MC curves, respectively. The optimal search time is T. Because technology reduces search cost, the MC curve shifts down to the right, as shown by MC_T in Figure 16.4. The optimal search time increases from T to T_1. Now what does this imply? It implies that as buyers extend their search for lower prices, they acquire more information. As a result, price differentials decrease.

Reading Comprehension

The answers to these questions can be found on MyEconLab at www.myeconlab.com.

1. What are some of the costs involved in searching for lower prices of better-quality goods?
2. Explain the following:
   a) Why does the MC of search rise with additional search?
   b) Why does the MB of search diminish with additional search?
3. Comment on the following statement: "A consumer should continue the search for a lower price until the lowest price is found."

4. Explain why the optimal search occurs at the point where the MB of the search equals the MC of the search.
5. On which of the following items do you think consumers spend more time searching for lower prices: a pair of shoes or a computer? Why?
6. Why would you expect the price differential for hand cream to be greater than the price differential for refrigerators?

Advertising as a Source of Information

What effect does advertising have on search cost?

A great deal of advertising is persuasive or even manipulative. This is not at all surprising because the main objective of advertising is to increase the sale of the commodity that is advertised. But we must not forget that advertising often contains a fair amount of information. It informs us of the availability of products; it informs us of the features of the products; it informs us of the various stores that sell the products; it informs us of the uses of the products; and it informs us of the prices of the products. All of this is extremely useful information to consumers. Just imagine that you are contemplating purchasing an MP3 player. You are watching television when a commercial suddenly appears on the screen informing you of a sale on MP3 players. The advertisement explains the properties of the MP3 player, the location of the retail outlet where the MP3 players are available, clear directions as to how you can get to the store, the price at which the MP3 players are sold, and the warranty that covers the MP3 players. Having this information has taken a tremendous burden off your shoulders. This advertising has just reduced your search cost significantly. Advertising often results in increased competition among sellers and lower prices as they make their pitch for the consumers' dollar.

Does any relationship exist between the type of good that is advertised and the informational content of advertising?

search goods goods whose quality can be evaluated by inspection at the time of purchase.

Goods have different properties. The quality of some goods can be determined by inspection at the time of purchase, while the quality of other goods can be known only after using them. Goods whose quality can be evaluated by inspection at the time of purchase are called **search goods**. When most people purchase greeting cards, they take a long time, reading different cards to ensure that the words on the card convey their sentiments. By carefully inspecting the card, they are able to assess its quality before purchasing it. Thus, greeting cards are an example of search goods. Other examples of search goods are shoes, fish, ties, and fresh fruits. Some people actually taste grapes before purchasing them. Goods whose quality can be known only after using them are called **experience goods**. If you were about to purchase a computer system, you could spend a great deal of time asking the sales clerk questions about it and reading about its features, but you would not really be able to judge the system before using it. Thus, computers are an example of experience goods. Other examples of experience goods are TV sets, automobile tires, packaged rice, cars, and batteries.

experience goods goods whose quality can be known only after using them

A discussion of search goods and experience goods does not answer the question of the relationship between the type of good that is advertised and the informational content of advertising. Does it?

No. But it paves the way for an answer. We can now classify the good that is advertised either as a search good or as an experience good. And we can examine the relationship between these types of goods and the informational content of advertising. Because the quality of search goods can be determined on the spot before purchasing them, advertisements of such goods must be packed with information. Because the product can be evaluated by inspection, the seller cannot easily convey misinformation. Persuasive and manipulative advertisements of search goods are unlikely to be very effective when buyers can easily evaluate the quality of such goods before purchasing them. This is not the case with experience goods, where consumers cannot determine their real properties before using them. Although advertisements of experience goods will contain some information about the goods, sellers will tend to focus on persuading customers and potential customers of the admirable and desirable features of the goods. Notice how advertisements for automobiles attempt to convince potential buyers to choose one type of car over another.

BUSINESS SITUATION 16.1

The manager of a shoe store is contemplating a campaign to advertise her shoes.

Would you expect her advertising messages to be largely manipulative or largely informative?

The answer to this Business Situation can be found in Appendix A.

Reading Comprehension

The answers to these questions can be found on MyEconLab at www.myeconlab.com.   MyEconLab

1. Distinguish between search goods and experience goods. Give an example of each.

2. Explain why advertisements of search goods tend to have a relatively large informational content, while advertisements of experience goods tend to have a relatively large manipulative content.

LO 16.4 Understand asymmetric information

Asymmetric Information and the Market for Defective Goods

Is there a name for the situation that exists when an imbalance of information exists between buyers and sellers?

asymmetric information
information that is known to one party to a transaction but not to the other

Yes, the situation that you have described is referred to as **asymmetric information**, which is information that is known to one party to a transaction but not to the other. Asymmetric information results in a price that is higher or lower than the product would command if all parties to the transaction had equal information.

Usually, it is the seller who has the information advantage, but it is possible for the opposite to be true. Asymmetric information can lead to market distortions and can result in inefficiencies.

Can you provide an example of the effect of asymmetric information?

Yes. The market for "lemons" is a good example, and by "lemons" we mean defective products. To simplify our analysis, let us assume that the market for used cars consists of two types: high-quality used cars and lemons (defective used cars). In this case asymmetric information exists because the sellers of used cars have more information than do the buyers. The market price for used cars will be based on the average quality of used cars. Lemons would sell for a higher price than they are worth, and good used cars would sell for a lower price than they are worth. Knowing that they are receiving a lower price than their cars are worth, sellers of high-quality cars will tend to withdraw their cars from the market, leaving a high percentage of lemons on the market. The better-quality cars among the lemons will likewise be withdrawn from the market for the same reason that high-quality cars were withdrawn. This process continues until only the lowest-quality cars (the real lemons) are left on the market to be sold at the appropriate low price. The following general principle emerges:

> When asymmetric information exists, low-quality products will drive high-quality products out of the market. The market will then be dominated by defective products.

lemon problem when asymmetric information exists, low-quality products will drive high-quality products out of the market., leaving the market to be dominated by defective products

This principle is sometimes referred to as the **lemon problem**.

Does the lemon problem have a solution?

Because the problem stems from lack of information, one obvious solution is for the party lacking information to acquire more information. In our used-car example, the prospective buyer can arrange to have a competent and impartial mechanic examine the car before it is purchased. If the car can be ascertained as being of higher quality, then the buyer would be willing to pay a higher price for higher quality, and the problem can be overcome or reduced.

Reading Comprehension

The answers to these questions can be found on MyEconLab at www.myeconlab.com.   MyEconLab

1. What is asymmetric information?

2. Explain why asymmetric information leads to adverse selection.

3. What is the lemon problem? How can it be solved?

LO 16.5   Discuss adverse selection and moral hazard

Adverse Selection and Moral Hazard

What is adverse selection?

adverse selection a situation in which the informed party to a transaction uses its information advantage to act in a way that benefits it at the cost of the uninformed party

In a transaction, the party with the information (such as the used-car dealer in the used-car example) could use it to act in a way that benefits him or her and harms the uninformed party. Note that the informed party may not intend to harm the uninformed party. This is the problem of **adverse selection**. An example of adverse selection is having low-risk clients pay a higher premium for insurance because of high-risk clients.

Adverse selection can also be observed in the markets for loans and credit cards. For example, because of adverse selection, high-risk borrowers pay higher interest rates on loans than they would in the absence of adverse selection. The lender may not have adequate information to be able to properly assess the risk of default. Therefore, a rate is charged that is high enough to cover the relatively high risk of certain types of borrowers.

Do any other problems result from asymmetric information?

moral hazard the lack of any incentive on the part of a party to protect itself from a risk when it is insulated against it

Yes, other problems do result from asymmetric information, but here we will discuss only the problem of **moral hazard**. Moral hazard is the lack of any incentive on the part of a party to protect itself from a risk when it is insulated (by insurance, for example) against it. An example of moral hazard is the behaviour of a motorcyclist wearing a helmet, who drives recklessly because of the feeling that the helmet offers additional security. In this case, the motorcyclist behaves differently from the way he or she would behave if he or she were fully exposed to the risk of injury.

The insurance market provides a good example of moral hazard. Some people may purchase auto insurance against theft. Once the contract (policy) is signed, they fail to take adequate precaution to protect their automobiles from theft. The same may occur for other types of insurance. For example, a homeowner who purchases home insurance may not be as careful as he or she ought to be in preventing exposure of the home to risk. In this case, the homeowner's insurance serves as an incentive for the homeowner to be careless.

Note that in the case of insurance, if the insurer could accurately predict the behaviour of the insured after the contract is made, the insurer would change the premium to match the risk.

Can an insurance company, for example, take any steps to reduce the problem of moral hazard?

Certainly! And they have. Life insurers usually require applicants to complete a lengthy form with questions about their medical history. In addition, they are required to submit to a medical examination by a medical practitioner often chosen by the insurer. The "deductible" clause in an automobile policy, in which the insured is required to pay, say, the first $500 of a claim, is a way of reducing moral hazard for auto insurers. Another method that insurance companies use to reduce moral hazard is to require the insured to pay higher premiums as more claims are made.

Reading Comprehension

The answers to these questions can be found on MyEconLab at www.myeconlab.com.   MyEconLab

1. Briefly explain the concept of adverse selection.

2. What is moral hazard? How can the problem of moral hazard be reduced?

LO 16.6   Explain the concept of market signalling

Market Signalling

What is market signalling?

market signalling the transmission of information, by the use of proxy measures, about unobservable characteristics

Market signalling is the transmission of information, by the use of proxy measures, about unobservable characteristics. The information is communicated from the party with the information to the party that lacks it. For example, an applicant for a job can somehow send a signal to a potential employer that he or she is more productive than can be gathered from the information available. Likewise, a borrower can send a signal to a lender that he or she is a lower-risk borrower than might be suggested by the loan application.

What is the effect of such signals, and how are they sent?

If the market signals are true, they reduce the problem of adverse selection. For example, market signalling by an applicant for a job could result in the right selection and an appropriate salary. Market signals can be sent in many ways. A seller can signal product quality by offering warranties and by adopting a policy of easy exchange of, or refunds for, defective products. A purchaser of automobile insurance, for example, can signal to the insurer that he or she is a low-risk by providing information on his or her safe-driving record.

Reading Comprehension

The answers to these questions can be found on MyEconLab at **www.myeconlab.com**.   MyEconLab

1.   What is market signalling? Give an example.

2.   Explain how market signalling can reduce the problem of adverse selection.

LO 16.7   Discuss the principal-agent problem

The Principal-Agent Problem

In the context of principal and agent, who is the principal and who is the agent?

principal the main party in a contractual agreement

agent the party chosen to act on behalf of the principal

The **principal** is the main party in a contractual agreement. The **agent** is the party chosen to act on behalf of, and in the interest of, the principal. For example, if you purchase a business and hire a manager to run it, you are the principal and the manager is the agent. A professional singer could hire someone to take care of bookings, travel arrangements, contract negotiations, promotional activities, financial arrangements, and other associated activities. In this case, the singer would be the principal while the agent would be the person hired to take care of the bookings, and so on.

What problem arises when the principal's objectives conflict with those of the agent?

Let us refer to the example of the professional singer. Suppose the agent is paid a fixed monthly salary regardless of the number of engagements the singer receives. Suppose also that the objective of the singer is to maximize net income, while the agent has a hidden agenda, which is to maximize his or her reputation. In this case, the agent could book only those engagements that accomplish his or her hidden objective. By pursuing his or her hidden agenda, the agent's actions adversely affect the principal. The problem that arises when the agent can take hidden actions that accomplish his or her objectives to the detriment of the principal is referred to as the **principal-agent problem**.

principal-agent problem
the problem that arises when the agent can take hidden actions that accomplish the agent's objectives to the detriment of the principal

Can the principal-agent problem be overcome?

Yes, it can. One way is to provide incentives for the agent to pursue the objectives of the principal. For example, instead of paying the agent a fixed monthly salary, the agent could be paid a salary that is based on the income of the principal. Another way is to offer substantial bonuses to the agent based on the extent to which the principal's objectives have been achieved. Yet another way is to set up a monitoring system to exercise some kind of control over the actions of the agent to ensure that he or she is not pursuing a hidden agenda that is incompatible with the principal's objectives. Such devices would induce the agent to act in the interest of the principal.

Reading Comprehension

The answers to these questions can be found on MyEconLab at **www.myeconlab.com**.   MyEconLab

1. An insurance company hires a consultant to develop a marketing plan for its products. In this relationship, who is the principal and who is the agent?

2. State the principal-agent problem. How can this problem be overcome?

BUSINESS SITUATION 16.2

The Outfitting Factory is planning to renovate its premises. It can hire a contractor to do the job. The contractor, in turn, usually hires subcontractors to perform the actual renovation. It is usually cheaper to hire the subcontractors directly.

What problem might result from hiring the subcontractors directly?

The answer to this Business Situation can be found in Appendix A.

Review

1. Review the learning objectives listed at the beginning of the chapter.
2. Have you accomplished all the objectives? One way to determine this is to answer the Reading Comprehension questions at the end of each section. They will help you assess the extent to which you have accomplished the learning objectives.
3. If you have not accomplished an objective, review the relevant material before proceeding.

Key Points to Remember

1. **LO 16.1** Information is knowledge of specific events or situations derived from study, experience, or instruction. Although we are often bombarded with tons of information, it is still considered an economic good because the quantity demanded, in general, exceeds the quantity supplied even if it were free. Since information commands a positive price in the marketplace, it is an economic good.

2. **LO 16.2** Search costs are the costs incurred in searching for information about a good or service. Search costs include the time spent reading product labels, reading and listening to advertisements and commercials about a product, and telephoning, and the time and cost of travelling to acquire information about the product.

3. **LO 16.2** If the marginal benefit (*MB*) of the search exceeds the marginal cost (*MC*) of the search, the search should continue. If the marginal benefit of the search is less than the marginal cost, the search should be curtailed. The optimal search occurs when the marginal benefit equals the marginal cost.

4. **LO 16.3** Advertising is a tremendous source of information, which reduces search cost. The quality of search goods can often be determined by on-the-spot inspection. The quality of experience goods can be determined only after using them. Advertisements of search goods tend to be informational, while advertisements of experience goods tend to be persuasive and manipulative.

5. **LO 16.4** Asymmetric information is information that is known to one party in a transaction but not to the other. Asymmetric information results in a variety of problems in the marketplace. The existence of asymmetric information can cause low-quality products to drive high-quality products out of the market. The phenomenon is referred to as the lemon problem.

6. **LO 16.5** Adverse selection is a situation in which the party with the information uses his or her information advantage to make decisions in a manner that places the uninformed party at a disadvantage. Moral hazard is the lack of any incentive on the part of a party to protect itself from a risk when it is insulated against it.

7. **LO 16.6** Market signalling is the use of indirect measures to transmit information about unobservable or hidden characteristics. Market signalling can resolve or reduce the problem of adverse selection.

8. **LO 16.7** Because of differences in the objectives of parties to a contractual agreement, a principal-agent problem arises. The agent may pursue a hidden agenda that impedes the attainment of the principal's objective. The principal-agent problem can be overcome by careful monitoring of the actions of the agent, or by providing incentives for the agent to promote the principal's interests.

Economic Word Power

Adverse selection (p. 452)
Agent (p. 454)
Asymmetric information (p. 451)
Economic good (p. 445)
Experience goods (p. 450)
Information (p. 445)
Lemon problem (p. 453)
Market signalling (p. 454)
Moral hazard (p. 452)
Principal (p. 454)
Principal-agent problem (p. 455)
Search costs (p. 446)
Search goods (p. 450)

Problems and Exercises

Basic

1. **LO 16.1** You are thinking of purchasing winter tires for your car. Make a list of information that you will need to make a good purchasing decision.

2. **LO 16.2** Make a list of the search costs associated with shopping for a vacation in Antigua.

3. **LO 16.2** Which of the following are considered search costs in the decision to take a course with a particular professor?
   a. The time spent talking to students who have taken the course with the professor
   b. The price of the textbook for the course
   c. The number of students taking the course

d. The number of hours spent in reading students' evaluation of the professor

e. The knowledge you expect to gain from the course

f. The time spent in doing assignments in the course

g. Attempts made to find out the failure rate in this professor's course

4. **LO 16.2** Figure 16.5 shows the optimal amount of information that a firm will gather to make a decision.

   a. If information is free, how much information will this firm gather?

Figure 16.5	**The Marginal Benefit and Marginal Cost of Information**

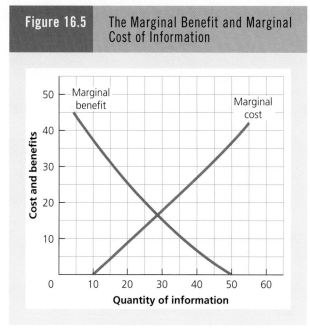

b. At a quantity of information of 20, will the firm gather additional information? Why or why not?

c. At a quantity of information of 40, will the firm gather more information? Why or why not?

d. What quantity of information will optimize the firm's search for information?

5. **LO 16.4** Lack of information can cause buyers of used cars to pay more than the cars are worth. Name two precautions that buyers can take to protect themselves from this mistake.

6. **LO 16.7** Indicate the principal and the agent in each of the following situations and complete Table 16.1.

7. **LO 16.4** In each of the following situations, identify the party with the information advantage:

   a. A consumer buys insurance

   b. A corporation hires a manager

   c. A top-ranking school accepts you as a student

   d. A family agrees to pay a contractor $20 an hour to do repairs

Questions in the Intermediate and Challenging Sections cover several different concepts, and have not been organized by learning objectives.

Table 16.1	**Identification of Principal and Agent**
Principal	**Agent**
a. You take your car to a mechanic shop for repairs	
b. You hire a retired professor to tutor you in economics	
c. Your dentist calls you for your annual check-up	
d. A young artist hires you to do her public relations work	
e. You accept an assignment to mow your neighbour's lawn	
f. Luke and Leonie sign a contract with Mr. Barthley, the butcher, to supply them with meat	

Intermediate

1. Sellers of used cars usually have more information about the cars than do buyers of these cars. Explain how this asymmetric information might result in bad cars (lemons) driving good cars out of the market.

2. New employees usually have to go through a probationary period before they are given permanent employment. Explain the moral hazard problem that might arise because of this practice. What can an employer do to reduce this moral hazard?

3. Certain professionals, such as lawyers, doctors, dieticians, and consultants, often display their credentials in their offices where clients and prospective clients can see them. Use the concept of market signalling to explain this practice.

Challenging

1. A finance company has repossessed a car because of payment default on the part of the owner. The finance company holds an auction at which Anwar Thomas wins the bid. Explain how Anwar is likely to be a loser even though he wins the bid.

2. You suddenly discover that you possess a tremendous musical talent. You hire an agent to manage you as a performer. You realize from having taken this course in economics that a principal-agent problem could develop. Design a strategy to deal with this potential problem.

┌───┐
│ MyEconLab Visit the MyEconLab website at www.myeconlab.com. This online │
│ homework and tutorial system puts you in control of your own learning with study and practice │
│ tools directly correlated to this chapter's content. │
└───┘

Study Guide

Self-Assessment

The answers to the Study Guide questions can be found in Appendix B.

What's your score?

Circle the letter that corresponds with the correct answer.

1. Information can be viewed as
   a. Something that reduces uncertainty
   b. Meaning derived from data
   c. Facts that are useful for analysis or decision making
   d. All of the above

2. Which of the following is a necessary feature of an economic good?
   a. It must command a high price in the market
   b. It must be available in large quantities
   c. It must be relatively scarce
   d. None of the above

3. Information cannot be considered an economic good because
   a. It is available for free
   b. It cannot yield any profit
   c. It is impossible to control it
   d. None of the above

4. Which of the following would constitute a search cost?
   a. The time spent gathering information about the product
   b. The actual amount paid for the product
   c. The amount saved by searching for a lower price
   d. The satisfaction derived from knowing that the purchase is a good one

5. At the optimal search level
   a. *MB* exceeds *MC*
   b. *MC* exceeds *MB*
   c. *MB* equals *MC*
   d. *MC* must be falling

6. If the *MB* is greater than the *MC* of the search,
   a. The search should be extended
   b. The search should be curtailed

   c. The search is optimal
   d. The search should be abandoned because the benefit is too great

7. The higher the price of an item,
   a. The greater the search and the greater the price differential
   b. The greater the search and the smaller the price differential
   c. The shorter the search and the smaller the price differential
   d. The shorter the search and the greater the price differential

8. The effect of an increase in the market wage is to
   a. Reduce search time
   b. Increase search time
   c. Reduce price differentials
   d. Leave search time and price differentials unchanged

9. Technology
   a. Reduces search cost and increases price differentials
   b. Reduces search cost and reduces price differentials
   c. Increases search cost and increases price differentials
   d. Increases search cost and reduces price differentials

10. Advertising could
    a. Reduce search cost
    b. Increase competition
    c. Lower prices
    d. All of the above

11. Search goods are goods that
    a. Require a great deal of search time
    b. Can be easily evaluated by inspection before purchase
    c. Must be aggressively advertised so that their characteristics can be known
    d. None of the above

12. Which of the following would you consider to be an experience good?
    a. Fresh fruits and vegetables
    b. A birthday card

c. A pair of shoes

d. A brand new car

13. Asymmetric information can result in
    a. A price that is different from the price that would prevail in the absence of asymmetric information
    b. Significant price differences
    c. Adverse selection
    d. All of the above

14. The lemon problem refers to the fact that
    a. Some lemons are not suited for lemonade
    b. Lemons will sell for lower prices when they are scarce
    c. Defective products will tend to drive better-quality products out of the market
    d. None of the above

15. Adverse selection
    a. Always results in mutual benefit to the parties to a transaction
    b. Always harms both parties to a transaction
    c. Usually results in one party to a transaction being disadvantaged
    d. None of the above

16. Which of the following can result from asymmetric information?
    a. Adverse selection
    b. The lemon problem
    c. Moral hazard
    d. All of the above

17. Moral hazard occurs
    a. Only in the insurance business, where risk is prevalent
    b. In insurance as well as other businesses
    c. Only in markets with perfect information
    d. Only in the market for search goods

18. Which of the following would constitute market signalling?
    a. A two-year warranty on a used car
    b. The offer of a full refund on any product found to be defective
    c. Information about a job applicant's educational attainment and training
    d. All of the above

19. When a principal-agent problem exists, the agent will succeed only if
    a. The objectives of the principal and the agent are compatible
    b. The true intentions and actions of the agent can be hidden
    c. The agent possesses skills lacking in the principal
    d. The principal is dependent solely on the agent

20. The principal-agent problem can be overcome by
    a. Revealing the objective of the principal to the agent
    b. Hiding the objective of the principal from the agent

c. Providing incentives for the agent to pursue the principal's interests and making it difficult for the agent to pursue his or her hidden agenda

d. Making it easy for the agent to accomplish his or her personal objective so that there will be sufficient time left over to promote the interest of the principal

Problems and Exercises (Use Quad Paper for Graphs)

Answers to these questions can be found on MyEconLab at www.myeconlab.com.   MyEconLab

1. Indicate which of the following would be considered a search cost in the case of the decision to purchase a computer:
   a. The time spent reading newspapers and magazines about the particular computer
   b. The number of hours you spend at work
   c. The prices of laptops and computer programs
   d. The time spent driving around in search of relevant information
   e. The satisfaction you expect to derive from the computer
   f. The time spent on the internet reading about the particular computer

2. a. Draw a diagram showing the optimal search for a lower price of a particular type of car.
   b. On your diagram, show the effect of an increase in search technology on the optimal search.

3. Classify each of the following items as a search good or an experience good, and complete Table 16.2.
   a. Fresh vegetables
   b. Socks
   c. Books

Table 16.2	Search Goods and Experience Goods
Search Goods	**Experience Goods**

d. A lounge chair
e. A TV set
f. An eyeglass frame
g. Automobiles
h. Canned foods
i. Tires
j. An electric guitar

4. Suppose you were writing two advertisements: one for a bicycle, the other for fresh celery. How would the content of the advertisements differ in terms of information and manipulation?

5. A professor enters into an agreement with her students that as long as they attend classes, they will pass the course. Because attendance is the only requirement for passing the course, what will some students do that will constitute a moral hazard problem? How could the professor-student contract be modified to overcome the moral hazard problem?

6. Your parents hire a carpenter to build a fence around their property, and agree to pay him by the hour. State the moral hazard problem that could arise. How can the moral hazard problem be overcome?

7. Refer to Question 6 above. Suppose your parents had agreed to pay the carpenter a fixed sum of money to build the fence. What moral hazard problem could arise? How could that problem be overcome?

8. Place yourself in the position of an employer who is selecting an employee to fill a certain position in the company. Compose a short list of three proxies that you could use as signals to help you make a decision on the expected performance of the applicant.

Chapter 1

1.1 John Adams faces the economic problem of scarcity. He has limited resources ($25 000), and he must decide whether he should use the money to increase his stock or do something else, such as buying a used delivery van.

1.2 The price at which the product would be sold and the quantity of the product to produce are microeconomic considerations. The others are macroeconomic considerations.

Chapter 1A

1A.1 A line graph would be appropriate to show the direct relationship between the number of calls and sales. She could put quarterly sales on the vertical axis and the number of calls per quarter on the horizontal axis, and then plot the points. The resulting upward-sloping line would illustrate her point.

1A.2 The 7% interest on $100 000 amounts to $7000. If he purchases inventories, he earns ($107 500 − $100 000) = $7500. He is better off using the money to purchase inventories.

Chapter 2

2.1 A production possibility curve is ideal for this illustration. It can be easily shown that a movement from one point on the curve to another involves giving up one type of ties for another.

2.2 If Maple Leaf Foods sells its products in the U.S. market, then a strong Canadian dollar would mean that Maple Leaf Foods products would become more expensive to Americans. Thus, sales in the U.S. market would decline and that could adversely affect Maple Leaf Foods profits.

Chapter 3

3.1 The consultant could have been thinking that the observed increase in the number of persons buying laptop computers could have been due to a lowering of the prices of laptops, and would therefore be an increase in quantity demanded rather than an increase in demand. To increase stock on the basis of a fall in price could be a mistake indeed. It is possible that the entrepreneur would be able to sell his increased stock only at greatly reduced prices—probably even at a loss.

3.2 Computers and flash drives are complements. By selling the computers at significantly reduced prices, the store will attract more people who want to purchase computers. As they purchase more computers, they will likely buy more flash drives as well.

Chapter 4

4.1 Because the demand for her product is highly elastic, lowering the price will result in a large increase in quantity demanded. Total revenue is the price times the quantity sold. In this case, the increase in quantity sold more than compensates for the lower price. Thus, total revenue will increase.

4.2 Because the income elasticity of demand for wheat is 1.5, an increase in income of 5% causes the demand for wheat to increase by 7.5% (5 × 1.5). Farmers should therefore increase their production of wheat by 7.5%.

4.3 The retail outlet has incurred a cost of $10 for each pair of winter gloves purchased for resale. The minimum acceptable profit is 10%. That means that the store must make at least $1 (10% of $10) on each pair of gloves sold. The reservation price is therefore $11. For (a), (b), and (c), the market price is above the reservation price, so the retail outlet will sell. But a market price of $10 is below the reservation price, so the store will withdraw the gloves from the market.

Chapter 5

5.1 The rent control law will cause a shortage of apartments. Landlords will not be inclined to provide the same quantity (and quality) of apartments at this lower price. They will likely seek other investment opportunities, and will be unwilling to spend money on repairs, renovations, and general maintenance of their apartment buildings.

5.2 Since Claude considers $5.50 an hour to be a fair wage, he will not be inclined to pay $7.50 to his employees who now earn $5.50; but he has to comply with the law. He will tend to lay off some workers and perhaps use machines instead of labour, where possible.

Chapter 6A

6A.1 Mr. Jones's problem seems to be a decline in patronage for his shop. The affluent community in which his shop is located may not be interested in his second-hand goods. Mr. Jones might respond to this situation by changing his product offering from used goods to new goods. Alternatively, he might consider moving his shop from its present location to a low-income area where there may be a greater demand for his goods.

Chapter 7

7.1 Profit maximization and sales maximization may not be consistent objectives. The manager wants to sell as much as possible and may be less inclined to control cost than is the owner, who wants to maximize profits. For example, lowering the price of the product may increase revenue, but it may also reduce profits.

7.2 The choice between methods 1 and 2 will be made on the basis of their relative economic efficiency. Using method 1, the cost of the inputs is $(10 \times \$5) + (6 \times \$6) = \$86$. The value of the output is $(24 \times \$10) = \$240$. Therefore, the economic efficiency ratio is $240 \div 86 = 2.79$. Using method 2, the cost of the inputs is $(15 \times \$5) + (2 \times \$6) = \$87$. The value of the output is $(25 \times \$10) = \$250$. Therefore, the economic efficiency ratio is $250 \div 87 = 2.87$. Method 2 should be chosen, because it is more economically efficient.

7.3 The longer an advertisement runs, the greater the chance that it will become less and less effective. This, of course, is an instance of the law of diminishing returns at work. To avert diminishing returns, advertisers can change their advertisements and run them for shorter periods.

7.4 Here is a splendid opportunity to apply the principle of substitution. As the cost of capital (machines) falls, the last dollar spent on capital increases productivity more than if that dollar were spent on labour. Thus, to minimize cost, the enterprise should buy more capital and less labour.

Chapter 8

8.1 Sam's profit of $120000 is accounting profit (total revenue less total expenses). The analysis does not account for implicit costs. The implicit costs are $120000 that he could earn elsewhere and $15000 for which his building could be rented. Sam's total cost of operating his bakery is as follows:

Explicit cost (total expenses)	$200 000
Implicit cost ($120 000 + $15 000)	$135 000
Total cost	$335 000

His total revenue is $320000; therefore, Sam is actually losing $15000. He should accept the job offer.

8.2 The $600 that Tim Hortons paid for the coffee machine is irrelevant. The real choice Tim Hortons has to make is whether it prefers to have the coffee machine or the $200 offered by the diner. The cost of the coffee machine to Tim Hortons is the $200 it could have received from the diner. Tim

Hortons is wrong to base its decision on the original cost of the machine. It is sunk cost.

8.3 By centralizing its purchases, Dollarama can take advantage of huge quantity discounts that might not be available on smaller quantities to individual outlets. Also, by being a large-volume buyer, Dollarama might be able to exercise some strength in negotiations with its suppliers.

8.4 Panasonic's product offering is truly extensive. However, the products are all related to electronics. Economies of scope can likely fully explain Panasonic's product offering.

Chapter 9

9.1 Advertising costs money, even with a 40% discount. Fashion Boutique must weigh the cost of advertising against the benefits. Because the store is considered a purely competitive firm, it can sell as much as it can place on the market at the given price. Therefore, advertising will not benefit Fashion Boutique. Why should the firm incur costs when there are no associated benefits? Fashion Boutique should decline the agency's offer.

9.2 The fall in price results in losses for the firm. But the price ($8) is still higher than the AVC ($6), so the firm is covering its AVC, with money left over to pay some of its fixed costs. If it closes down, it makes no money at all but still has to pay its fixed costs. Clearly, this firm should continue to operate as long as these fixed costs exist.

9.3 This situation is similar to the theoretical long-run equilibrium of a firm in pure competition. Mr. Brooks's resources, including his entrepreneurial skills, were earning as much as they could earn in the next-best alternative use. That being the case, Mr. Brooks had no reason to leave the industry and made the right decision.

Chapter 10

10.1 Northern Pharmaceuticals can protect its product by obtaining a patent from the federal government. This patent will provide some measure of protection from potential competitors.

10.2 Total Electricity's pricing policy might be quite rational. By deliberately charging a

price that is less than the profit-maximizing price, the company could be acting in a manner that would avoid it being regulated or even nationalized, that is, being taken over by the government. Also, the company could be creating a "caring company" image that could be beneficial in terms of customer loyalty.

10.3 Quan is correct. Raising the price will result in marginal revenue and marginal cost no longer being equal. It makes more sense to make as much profit as possible by charging the price that maximizes total profits, and then pay the tax.

Chapter 11

11.1 Cross-Town Taxi must differentiate its product and publicize its differences from its competitors. It can do this by emphasizing its experience in the business, the quality of its services, the reliability of its services, and so on. These measures could set Cross-Town Taxi apart from its competitors.

11.2 Hershey's customers must have been wary about the health risk involved in eating Hershey's candies. Some may even have switched to some of Hershey's competitors. An informative advertising campaign aimed at educating and convincing customers of the safety of Hershey's candies could help to rectify the situation and regain many of the lost customers.

11.3 Oligopoly theory deals largely with firms reacting to decisions made by other firms. Canada's grocery chain stores operate in an oligopolistic market. The largest chains dominate the industry. Wal-Mart's decision to significantly increase its grocery operation will mean increased competition for the consumer's grocery dollar. To meet this competition, Loblaw has to ensure that its operation is efficient. The closure of several of its stores can be seen as an attempt to attain that efficiency. The decision is most likely a direct reaction to Wal-Mart's plan.

11.4 This is a classic case of an oligopoly market. If the microbreweries' claim is true, then it means that Labatt and Molson are using their market power to secure preferential treatment from the licensed establishments. If these establishments carry only Molson and Labatt products, and give special shelf space to these products, then the microbreweries would not be playing on a level field.

Chapter 12

12.1 Total Fitness should hire workers up to the point at which the wage equals the marginal revenue product. The legislated wage is $400 per week. This wage and the marginal revenue product are equal when Total Fitness hires four workers. The firm's reaction to the legislated wage should be to lay off one worker.

12.2 Although we can be sympathetic toward workers with large families, Kim's view is correct. Wage negotiations should be based on such factors as the worker's productivity, the profitability of the business, and the cost of living—not on family size.

12.3 The increase in demand for loans and mortgages will exert upward pressure on interest rates. John should take out the loan now before interest rates rise, rather than later, after interest rates rise. This decision could save him a good amount of money in interest charges.

Chapter 14

14.1 WebPro can take advantage of the relatively cheap labour in India by having its webpages designed there and then "exporting" them to Canada via the internet.

By so doing, WebPro would significantly reduce cost and thus increase its profits.

14.2 The substantial reduction in the cost of producing newsprint presents a tremendous opportunity for this newsprint manufacturer to expand its market beyond Canada's borders. It can export relatively cheap newsprint to countries that cannot produce newsprint at such a low cost.

Chapter 15

15.1 This business situation involves a decision regarding the appropriate level of pollution abatement. For the New Line Paper Mill, pollution abatement has costs and benefits. A cost could be the money spent on pollution abatement equipment, while a benefit could be a healthier workforce. The president's position could easily result in too much pollution abatement, while the position of the chair and the CFO could result in too little pollution abatement. The appropriate level of pollution abatement for New Line is not necessarily the one that results in minimum pollution, but the one that equates the marginal benefit and the marginal cost of pollution abatement.

15.2 Given the seriousness of the pollution problem, any development that reduces the level of pollution holds out promise of substantial profits. For example, a

company that develops a technology to reduce poisonous emissions into the atmosphere will likely earn huge profits, provided that the cost makes it economically feasible. As another example, consider a company that develops a cost-effective method of treating waste that is dumped into rivers and lakes. Such a business could, indeed, earn huge profits.

Chapter 16

16.1 Because shoes are search goods, the store's manager is likely to use informative messages in her advertisements. By pointing out the desirable qualities of the shoes, the messages will likely have a greater impact on buyers than would messages that tend to be manipulative.

16.2 The Outfitting Factory may not have the expertise to properly evaluate the qualifications of the subcontractors. Also, it may not be able to adequately monitor their performance. Even though subcontractors may charge a lower rate, the renovation job could end up costing a great deal more than the contractor charges. The information imbalance between the contractor and the subcontractors is likely to be less than that between the Outfitting Factory and the subcontractors. Hiring the contractor seems to be the better decision.

Answers to Study Guide Questions

Score:

Give yourself one mark for each correct answer.

Interpretation

If you obtained a score of 80% or higher, you have a good understanding of the material covered in the chapter. However, you should review the sections dealing with the questions that you missed. If you obtained a score between 60% and 75%, you have a fair understanding of the material. You should study those sections dealing with your incorrect answers. A score below 60% means that you need to study the material again, paying special attention to your incorrect answers.

Chapter 1

Answers

1. c	2. d	3. b	4. b
5. b	6. b	7. c	8. b
9. b	10. d	11. c	12. c
13. b	14. b	15. b	16. c
17. c	18. d	19. d	20. c
21. a	22. d	23. c	24. a
25. a	26. c	27. c	28. d

Appendix 1A

Answers

1. b	2. c	3. d	4. d
5. c	6. c	7. c	8. d
9. a	10. b	11. a	12. d
13. c	14. c	15. c	16. a
17. b	18. c	19. b	20. b

Chapter 2

Answers

1. c	2. d	3. c	4. d
5. d	6. a	7. d	8. a

9. d	10. b	11. d	12. c
13. c	14. d	15. a	16. d
17. b	18. a	19. d	20. b

Chapter 3

Answers

1. d	2. c	3. b	4. a
5. c	6. d	7. c	8. b
9. c	10. d	11. c	12. b
13. a	14. c	15.b	16. c
17. a	18. d	19. d	20. a

Chapter 4

Answers

1. c	2. c	3. d	4. c
5. d	6. a	7. b	8. a
9. d	10. a	11. b	12. d
13. a	14. a	15. b	16. c
17. c	18. a	19. c	20. b

Chapter 5

Answers

1. c	2. d	3. d	4. c
5. d	6. c	7. b	8. d
9. d	10. c	11. b	12. c
13. d	14. d	15. a	16. d
17. d	18. a	19. a	20. c

Chapter 6

Answers

1. c	2. a	3. b	4. c
5. d	6. c	7. d	8. b
9. d	10. d	11. c	12. d
13. a	14. b	15. b	16. d
17. b	18. c	19. d	20. a

Appendix 6A

Answers

1. d	2. b	3. a	4. d
5. d	6. d	7. a	8. b
9. c	10. b	11. d	12. b
13. c	14. b	15. c	16. d
17. c	18. c	19. b	20. a

Chapter 7

Answers

1. c	2. c	3. d	4. c
5. a	6. a	7. c	8. d
9. b	10. d	11. b	12. b
13. a	14. d	15. c	16. b
17. d	18. a	19. b	20. d

Chapter 8

Answers

1. c	2. d	3. b	4. a
5. c	6. a	7. b	8. c
9. d	10. a	11. b	12. d
13. c	14. b	15. c	16. a
17. d	18. d	19. d	20. a

Chapter 9

Answers

1. b	2. c	3. d	4. d
5. d	6. d	7. d	8. d
9. b	10. c	11. a	12. c
13. c	14. a	15. c	16. b
17. a	18. b	19. b	20. c

Chapter 10

Answers

1. c	2. d	3. a	4. c
5. a	6. d	7. b	8. d

9. a	10. c	11. b	12. c
13. c	14. d	15. d	16. a
17. d	18. d	19. b	20. a

Chapter 11

Answers

1. c	2. d	3. d	4. a
5. b	6. b	7. a	8. c
9. b	10. d	11. d	12. b
13. d	14. d	15. a	16. a
17. d	18. c	19. c	20. c

Chapter 12

Answers

1. a	2. a	3. d	4. a
5. d	6. a	7. b	8. a
9. d	10. b	11. b	12. d

13. b	14. d	15. c	16. b
17. c	18. a	19. d	20. a

Chapter 13

Answers

1. b	2. c	3. d	4. a
5. c	6. d	7. b	8. d
9. c	10. b	11. a	12. d
13. d	14. d	15. c	16. b
17. d	18. d	19. c	20. d

Chapter 14

Answers

1. b	2. c	3. c	4. a
5. b	6. a	7. b	8. c
9. d	10. c	11. d	12. a
13. c	14. d	15. d	16. d

17. a	18. c	19. d	20. b
21. d	22. a		

Chapter 15

Answers

1. c	2. d	3. d	4. c
5. b	6. d	7. c	8. c
9. c	10. a	11. d	12. d
13. b	14. d	15. b	16. a
17. a	18. c	19. b	20. b

Chapter 16

1. d	2. c	3. d	4. a
5. c	6. a	7. b	8. a
9. b	10. d	11. b	12. d
13. d	14. c	15. c	16. d
17. b	18. d	19. b	20. c

GLOSSARY

Note: This comprehensive glossary lists the key terms and definitions included in the text and provides definitions for additional economic terms that you will encounter in your studies.

Ability-to-pay principle The idea that people should be taxed according to their ability to pay; the rich should pay more in taxes than the poor

Absolute advantage The ability to produce a commodity by using fewer resources than another producer (or country) can

Absolute poverty The condition that exists when an individual or a family lacks the financial resources required for the basic necessities of life

Absolute price The monetary price of a good or service; the amount of money that must be spent to obtain one unit of a good or service

Accounting costs See *explicit costs*

Ad valorem tariff A tariff expressed as a fixed percentage of the value of an imported item

Administered price A price that is controlled rather than determined exclusively by demand and supply

Adverse selection A situation in which the informed party to a transaction uses his or her information advantage to act in a way that benefits the informed party at the cost of the uninformed party

Agent The party chosen to act on behalf of the principal

Aggregate output The total amount of goods and services produced in an economy

Air pollution Smog caused mainly by burning fuels

Allocative efficiency The condition that exists when price equals marginal cost

Arbitrage transactions The purchase of products in a low-price market and their resale in a high-price market

Arbitration A mechanism for settling disputes in the collective bargaining process whereby a decision is made by an independent person or persons

Arc elasticity (of demand) A measure of elasticity for a segment of a demand curve

Assumptions Statements of the conditions under which a model will work

Asymmetric information Information that is known to one party to a transaction but not to the other

Atomistic competition See *pure competition*

Average cost (*AC*) Total cost divided by the number of units produced; it represents the cost *per unit* of output

Average cost pricing A pricing strategy in which price and average cost are equated; often used by regulatory agencies in regulating monopolies

Average fixed cost (*AFC*) The total fixed cost per unit of output; total fixed cost divided by the number of units produced

Average product (*AP*) The output per unit of a variable factor; total product divided by the quantity of the variable factor employed

Average revenue (*AR*) The revenue per unit of output sold; total revenue divided by quantity sold

Average total cost (*ATC*) The total cost per unit of output; the sum of average fixed cost and average variable cost

Average variable cost (*AVC*) The total variable cost per unit of output; total variable cost divided by the quantity produced

Backward-bending labour supply curve A negatively sloped supply curve illustrating that higher wages can result in a decrease in the number of hours worked

Bads Things that are unwanted and do not give any satisfaction

Bar graph A vertical or horizontal graph with categories on one axis and the value assigned to each category measured on the other axis

Barometric price leadership The situation that exists when any of a few firms takes the lead in setting the price while the others follow

Barriers to entry Obstacles preventing firms from entering an industry

Basic economic problem The scarcity of resources relative to wants

Basic sectors of the economy Household sector, producing sector, and government sector

Beggar-thy-neighbour policy A policy of trade protectionism that restricts the flow of imports

Benefit principle (of taxation) The idea that people should be taxed in proportion to the benefits received from goods and services provided by the government

Black market A market in which products are sold illegally above the price prescribed by law

Bond Interest-earning evidence of debt issued by a government or corporation, which pays interest to the lender for a specified period and the principle when the loan matures

Boycott An effort to persuade consumers not to purchase certain goods or services, or not to deal with certain firms

Break-even level of output The level of output at which total revenue equals total cost; profit is zero

Break-even point The point at which total revenue equals total cost

Budget line A graphical representation of all possible combinations of two commodities that a consumer can purchase for the same amount of money; also called *price line*

Canadian International Development Agency (CIDA) Government agency that dispenses foreign aid to less developed countries

Cancun Agreement An agreement signed by more than 190 countries at Cancun, Mexico, to continue efforts to reduce greenhouse gas emissions

Cap and trade A system for reducing pollution by selling pollution credits on the open market

Capital Produced means of production; the productive factor of production defined as all human-made means of production; it includes the stock of machinery, equipment, buildings, human skills, and so on

Capital market A factor market in which stocks and bonds are traded and in which businesses can obtain funds for investment purposes

Capital stock The total amount of capital (machinery, equipment, buildings, infrastructure, etc.) in existence at a particular time

Capitalism An economic system characterized by free enterprise and that emphasizes private ownership of resources; also called *free enterprise system*

Carbon tax A tax imposed on items that emit carbon dioxide

Cardinal utility A concept that assumes that individuals are able to measure (cardinally) the amount of satisfaction derived from consuming goods and services

Cartel A formal agreement among independent firms to act in concert to control price and output in a particular industry

Central planning The mechanism whereby decisions about what to produce, how to produce it, and for whom to produce it are made by central authorities in a command economy

Ceteris paribus Other things being equal; allows for the investigation of the effects of one variable while assuming that others remain constant; also called *other things being equal assumption*

Change in demand A shift in a given demand curve caused by a change in one of the determinants of demand for the good; a change in the price of the item will not change the demand

Change in quantity demanded A movement along the demand curve for a good in response to a change in the price of the good

Change in quantity supplied A movement along the supply curve for a good in response to a change in the price of the good

Change in supply A shift in a given supply curve caused by a change in one of the determinants of the supply of the good; a change in the price of the item will not change the supply

Choice The ability to decide between one thing and another when the means to obtain both are not available

Circular flow An economic model that shows the flow of resources, goods and services, expenditures, and income between sectors of the economy

Closed shop A workplace in which jobs are given only to union members

Coefficient of elasticity of demand The number that measures the degree of elasticity of demand

Coefficient of elasticity of supply The number that measures the degree of elasticity of supply

COLA clause Cost-of-living adjustment clause often found in labour agreements

Collective agreement The contract that results from the collective bargaining process

Collective bargaining The process by which wages and other working conditions are negotiated between a union and an employer

Collusions Firms that unite to control price and output in particular markets

Command economy An economy in which economic decisions are made mainly by central authorities; also called *socialistic system*

Commodities Goods and services together

Common market An arrangement between nations to allow the free movement of goods and resources between them

Common-pool problem The overuse of open-access resources that occurs because of unrestricted access

Communism The economic and political system in which there is little private ownership and most of the production and distribution choices are made by the government

Comparative advantage The ability to produce a commodity at a lower opportunity cost than another producer (or country) can

Comparative statics (or comparative static analysis) An analysis that involves comparing one equilibrium condition with another after a change has occurred

Competition Interaction among sellers of a product, which tends to keep prices low and which promotes efficiency

Competitive capitalism The free enterprise economic system

Complements (complementary goods) Goods that are consumed (used) together

Complements (in production) Goods such that the production of one implies the production of the other; also called *joint products*

Compound tariff A combination of specific and ad valorem tariffs

Compulsory arbitration The compulsory submission of a dispute to a third party whose decision on the matter is binding

Concave curve A curve bowed outward from the origin

Concentration ratio The percentage of total market share accounted for by a few of the largest firms in the industry

Conciliation The process of submitting a dispute to a mediator for recommendations for settlement; also called *mediation*

Conspicuous consumption The practice of buying consumer goods for the purpose of impressing others

Constant Anything that remains unchanged

Constant returns to scale The condition that exists when a firm increases all its inputs by a certain percentage and, as a result, its output increases by the same percentage

Constant-cost industry An industry in which costs remain constant as the industry expands

Consumer cooperative A cooperative formed by consumers to promote their interests

Consumer durables Consumer goods intended to last for a long time (arbitrarily, more than a year)

Consumer equilibrium The condition that exists when a consumer has arranged his or her purchases in a way that maximizes total satisfaction

Consumer sovereignty The notion that consumers have the power to decide, by their purchases, what goods and services will be produced

Consumer surplus The difference between the amount that consumers would have paid for a commodity and the amount that they actually pay

Consumption The use or purchase of consumer goods and services to satisfy wants

Consumption possibility curve A curve on a graph showing various combinations of two different goods that a consumer can buy with a given amount of money; also called *purchase possibility curve*

Consumption possibility schedule See *purchase possibility schedule*

Consumption tax Taxes on goods and services, such as sales tax and excise tax

Contestable market A market into which entry is so easy that the threat of entry by potential competitors prevents the existing firms from exercising any monopoly power

Convex curve A curve bowed toward the origin

Cooperative A business owned, financed, and controlled by its members, who share in the profits and risks in proportion to their patronage; each member has only one vote regardless of the number of shares owned

Copenhagen Accord A non-binding agreement that endorsed the continuation of the Kyoto Protocol

Corporation A business in which all owners have limited liability; a form of business organization that is a legal entity apart from its owners

Correlation A relationship between variables; variables are correlated if they change together

Cost A payment for the inputs used to produce goods and services

Cost function The mathematical expression of the relationship between cost and output

Cost of living The amount of money that must be paid to obtain goods and services

Cost-benefit approach An analysis in decision making that involves the comparison of costs and benefits

Cost-of-living adjustment (COLA) The adjustment of wages to the cost of living

Cost-plus pricing A pricing strategy in which firms determine price by adding a certain percentage markup on cost; also called *markup pricing*

Craft union A union of workers in a single occupation; also called *trade union*

Cross-price elasticity of demand The degree of responsiveness in quantity demanded of one good to a change in the price of a related good

Crown corporation A corporation owned by the government

Customs duties Taxes levied on imported goods

Customs union An arrangement between nations to eliminate tariffs on goods traded between them and to maintain a common tariff with the rest of the world

Deadweight loss The loss in consumer surplus and producer surplus resulting from a switch from an efficient level of production to an inefficient level of production

Debt capital Capital (funds) raised through bonds or credit

Decreasing (long-run average) cost See *increasing returns to scale*

Decreasing returns to scale The condition that exists when a firm increases all its inputs and, as a result, its output increases but by a smaller proportion than the increase in its inputs; also called *increasing (long-run average) cost* and *diseconomies of scale*

Decreasing-cost industry An industry in which costs decrease as the industry expands

Deficiency payments A subsidy to farmers given at a certain amount per unit

Definition A set of words that explain the meaning of a term or concept

Demand The various quantities of a good or service that people are willing and able to buy at various prices during a specific period

Demand curve A downward-sloping curve showing the inverse relationship between price and quantity demanded

Demand function An equation expressing the relationship between price and quantity demanded

Demand schedule A table showing the inverse relationship between price and quantity demanded

Demand shifters The non-price determinants that shift the demand curve

Dependent variable The variable that is being explained; a variable whose value is determined by the value of some other variable

Depreciation A loss of asset value through use or over time

Derived demand The demand for inputs that is due to the demand for the goods and services produced by the inputs

Differentiated oligopoly An oligopoly in which the firms' products are differentiated

Differentiated products Products that are similar in many respects yet sufficiently different that the sellers are able to charge prices different from those charged by their competitors

Diminishing marginal utility The decrease in satisfaction experienced as additional units of a commodity are consumed

Diminishing returns A situation in which output increases less than the increase in the variable factor when at least one factor remains constant

Direct demand The demand for final goods and services as opposed to the demand for factor inputs

Direct relation The relation that exists between variables that increase or decrease together; the variables move in the same direction

Diseconomies of scale See *decreasing returns to scale*

Dividends Payments made to shareholders of corporations; the reward for capital

Division of labour A situation in which a task is broken up into a number of operations, each of which is performed by a different worker

Dominant price leadership The situation that exists when a dominant firm takes the lead and setting the price while the other firms follow

Dual economy The coexistence of an advanced sector and an underdeveloped sector in the same economy; found in many less developed countries

Dumping The practice of selling exports in foreign countries more cheaply than the domestic price

Duopoly An industry consisting of only two firms

Durable good A good that is intended to last for a long time (arbitrarily, more than a year)

Econometrics The use of statistical methods to test economic hypotheses

Economic cooperation An arrangement among countries to reduce certain forms of trade discrimination among them

Economic costs The sum of explicit and implicit costs; they include all opportunity costs

Economic discrimination The situation in which certain groups are targeted for different treatment in the labour market

Economic efficiency Efficiency measured in terms of cost; a situation in which the least costly method of production is attained

Economic efficiency ratios Numbers that measure the economic efficiency of methods of production

Economic externality A cost or benefit that accrues to persons not directly involved in the actions or decisions made by firms and individuals

Economic forecast The assignment of a future value to a variable

Economic good A tangible or an intangible thing that is scarce and satisfies wants

Economic growth An increase in a country's real GDP

Economic integration An arrangement among countries to abolish certain trade discriminatory practices among them

Economic model A simplification of economic reality

Economic prediction A statement of the general direction of a variable resulting from the fulfillment of certain conditions

Economic profits The difference between total revenue and the opportunity cost of the factor inputs

Economic regulation Government measures directed at controlling certain prices, output, and other economic activities to effect certain desired objectives

Economic rent A payment to a factor input in excess of what is required to supply the factor

Economic system A set of mechanisms by which a society accomplishes the task of producing goods and services to satisfy wants

Economic theory (model) A simplified version of reality designed to capture the important features of the relationship being studied

Economic union An arrangement among countries to abolish restrictions on the free movement of goods and resources and to harmonize economic policies

Economics The social science that studies how people use limited means to satisfy their unlimited wants

Economies of scale See *increasing returns to scale*

Economies of scope The situation that exists when the costs of producing different goods together are less than they would be if the goods were produced separately

Economy An entity within which production, consumption, and exchange take place

Efficiency wage A wage that is kept relatively high to attract high-quality workers and improve productivity

Effluent fee A fee that is imposed on a polluter for polluting the environment

Elastic demand A given percentage change in price causes a more than proportional change in quantity demanded; the situation in which a change in the price of an item produces a relatively large change in the quantity of the item demanded; the percentage change in the quantity demanded is greater than the percentage change in price

Elasticity A measure of the sensitivity of one variable to a change in some other variable

Elasticity of demand A measure of the extent to which quantity demanded changes as a result of a change in price; it is the percentage change in quantity divided by the percentage change in price

Elasticity of supply A measure of the extent to which quantity supplied changes as a result of a change in price; it is the percentage change in quantity supplied divided by the percentage change in price

Empirical Descriptive, as in observed, measured, and recorded

Endogenous variable A variable whose value is determined within a given model

Engel curve A curve that shows the relationship between income and consumption

Engel's law The hypothesis that as income increases, the percentage spent on food will diminish

Entrepreneur An individual who assumes the risk of organizing resources into production with the objective of producing a good or service for sale at a profit

Entrepreneurship The organization of land, labour, and capital into production; the risk-taking aspect of business decision making

Envelope curve See *long-run average cost curve*

Equalization payments Transfer payments from the federal government to the provinces to reduce economic inequality among the provinces

Equilibrium A situation in which change in unlikely to occur; a state of balance

Equilibrium price The price at which quantity demanded equals quantity supplied; there is no tendency for this price to change

Equilibrium quantity The quantity traded (bought and sold) at the equilibrium price

Equimarginal principle The concept that a value is maximized (or minimized) by equating marginal values

Equity capital Capital raised from issuing shares

Escalator clause A stipulation in a labour contract that future wages and salaries will be adjusted to reflect changes in the price level

Euro The official currency of the Euro Area; now used by 15 European Union countries

Excess capacity theorem The hypothesis that firms in monopolistic competition will operate with excess capacity

Excess quantity demanded See *shortage*

Excess quantity supplied See *surplus*

Excise tax A tax levied on the sale of a specific commodity

Exogenous variable A variable whose value is determined by factors outside a given model l

Experience goods Goods whose quality can be known only after using them

Explicit costs Direct payments to someone outside the firm for inputs, such as wages, rent, and utility bills; also called *accounting costs*

Export subsidies Assistance offered to exporters by the government to help them compete in world markets

External diseconomy An economic externality that results in a cost; also called *negative externality*

External economy An economic externality that results in a benefit; also called *positive externality*

Externalities Costs or benefits that accrue to persons not directly involved in the production or consumption of a commodity

Factor market The market in which factors of production are bought and sold; also called *resource market*

Factors of production Resources used to produce goods and services

Featherbedding The practice of providing workers with unnecessary work to keep them on the payroll

Federation (of unions) An association of national unions

Financial capital Money, as opposed to real capital (machinery, equipment, tools, etc.)

Financial market The market in which funds are lent and borrowed

Firms The economic sector that makes decisions about what resources to purchase and how the resources will be used to produce goods and services; the economic unit that transforms inputs into output

Fixed costs Costs that do not vary with the volume of output; they exist even when output is zero; also called *overhead costs*

Fixed factors Inputs that the firm cannot change during a given period; factors of production whose quantity does not vary with the volume of output

Flow A change in a stock over time

Flow variable The change in a stock variable during a period

Franchise An exclusive right to operate a business in a certain geographical area

Free enterprise system See *capitalism*

Free good A good that is so plentiful that even at a price of zero, the quantity available exceeds the quantity demanded

Free lunch Additional output produced without sacrificing the production of any other good or service

Free trade area An arrangement among countries to eliminate tariffs among them; each member, however, maintains its own tariffs on goods from non-member countries

Free trade Trade between countries that is unimpeded by tariffs or other trade restrictions

Function An expression of a relation among variables

Functional distribution of income Income distribution on the basis the ownership of the factors of production

Functional notation A mathematical tool for expressing relations among variables

Functional relationships Cause-effect relationships among variables

Gains from trade The increased output and income generated by specialization and trade

Game theory A method of analysis used by economists to study strategies in situations where the interdependence of decisions is recognized

General Agreement on Tariffs and Trade (GATT) An international tariff reduction treaty adopted in 1947

General equilibrium analysis A method of analysis that studies the effects of a variable in different markets

General partnership A business owned by two or more people, without limited liability

Geographical determinism The theory that comparative advantage is determined by natural endowment

Giffen good A good whose quantity demanded rises as its price rises and falls as its price falls

Gini coefficient A ratio that measures the degree of income inequality

Goods Tangible things that satisfy wants

Goods and services market See *product market*

Goods and services tax (GST) A consumption tax imposed on the final sale of goods and services

Government sector The sector of the economy that involves government purchases of goods and services; production decisions are made by government or government agencies; also called *public sector*

Government transfer payments Payments made by the government that do not represent payments for productive services (e.g., employment insurance payments, welfare payments, old age security payments)

Graph A geometric (diagrammatic) representation of information

Greenhouse effect The heating of the earth by greenhouse gases

Guaranteed annual income proposal A proposal for the government to give everyone a grant of a certain amount of money; any income above that level would be subject to tax

Herfindahl-Hirschman Index (HHI) An index of industry concentration derived from summing the squares of the market shares of the firms in the industry

Homogeneous products Products that are so similar that no one firm can profitably charge a different price from that charged by other firms

Households The economic sector that makes decisions about what resources to sell and what goods and services to buy

Human capital Education, training, skills, health, and so on, that improve the quality of labour

Hypothesis A statement of suspected relationships among two or more variables

Imperfect competition A collective term covering monopolistic competition and oligopoly

Implicit costs Opportunity costs that do not involve any direct payment to anyone outside the firm; also called *imputed costs*

Import quotas Restrictions on the quantity of a good that can be imported

Imputed costs See *implicit costs*

Incentive A motivation to do or not to do something

Incidence of a tax The distribution of the burden of a tax

Incidence of poverty The likelihood of being poor

Income and employment theory See *macroeconomic theory*

Income consumption curve The line joining the points of tangency between budget lines and indifference curves as the consumer's income changes

Income effect The effect on quantity demanded caused by the change in purchasing power resulting from a change in price

Income elasticity of demand The degree to which quantity demanded responds to a change in income; it is the percentage change in quantity divided by the percentage change in income

Income statement An accounting device for reporting revenues, expenses, and net income; also called *profit and loss statement*

Increasing (long-run average) cost See *decreasing returns to scale*

Increasing returns to scale The condition that exists when a firm increases all its inputs and, as a result, its output increases by a greater proportion than the increase in its inputs; also called *economies of scale* and *decreasing (long-run average) cost*

Increasing-cost industry An industry in which costs increase as the industry expands

Incremental cost See *marginal cost*

Independent goods Goods that are not related

Independent variable The variable that provides the explanation; it causes changes in the dependent variable

Indexation The adjustment of wages to the rate of price increase

Indexation clause A clause in a contract that calls for adjustment in wages as prices rise

Indifference curve A graph that shows all combinations of two commodities (or groups of commodities) that yield the same level of satisfaction

Indifference curve map See *indifference map*

Indifference map A collection of indifference curves; also called *indifference curve map* or *preference map*

Indifference schedule A table showing various combinations of commodities that give a consumer the same level of satisfaction

Industrial union A union of workers in a given industry

Industry A group of firms that produce similar products

Industry equilibrium A situation in which all firms in the industry are in equilibrium; industry output remains stable

Inelastic demand A given percentage change in price causes a less than proportional change in quantity demanded

Infant industry argument (for tariffs) The argument that tariffs are necessary to protect new domestic industries from foreign competition so that they can develop their potential

Inferior goods Goods for which demand decreases as income increases and for which demand increases as income falls

Information Knowledge of specific events or situations derived from study, experience, or instruction

Inheritance (bequest) saving Saving motivated by the desire to leave an inheritance to children or grandchildren

Innovation The introduction of new techniques of production

Input Any resource used in the process of production

Institution of private property The right of individuals to own things

Interest The reward for capital; the payment for borrowed money

Interest and dividends Income from capital

Interest rate The price paid for the use of money; the ratio of interest to the amount borrowed; also called *rate of interest*

Internalize The act of taking into consideration for decision-making purposes a previously external factor

International economy The economy considered from a global or international perspective

International trade The exchange of goods, services, and resources between countries

International union A union whose membership consists of local unions in different countries

Inverse relation The relation that exists between variables such that as one increases, the other decreases, and vice versa; the variables move in opposite directions

Isocost line A downward-sloping straight line on a graph that indicates the various combinations of two inputs that the firm can purchase for the same amount of money

Isoquant A curve showing the various combinations of inputs that can produce the same quantity of output

Job An obligation to provide labour services for pay

Joint products See *complements (in production)*

Kinked demand curve A demand curve with a kink resulting from the assumption that firms will follow the lead of a price reduction but not of a price increase; used to explain price rigidity

Kyoto Protocol A treaty signed by about 180 countries at Kyoto, Japan, to reduce greenhouse gas emissions

Labour Human physical and mental efforts

Labour market The market in which labour services are bought and sold

Labour mobility program A program designed to reduce unemployment by encouraging the relocation of unemployed persons

Labour union See *union*

Land All natural resources

Law of demand A statement of the inverse relationship between price and quantity demanded

Law of diminishing (marginal) returns The hypothesis that any increases in a variable factor, while holding one or more factors constant, will eventually cause marginal product to decline; also called *law of variable proportion*

Law of diminishing marginal utility The hypothesis that, as increasing quantities of a good or service are consumed, the increase in total satisfaction (i.e., extra satisfaction) decreases

Law of increasing opportunity cost The phenomenon of increasing unit cost as an economy increases its production of a commodity

Law of supply A statement of the direct relationship between price and quantity supplied other things being equal, as the price of an item falls, the quantity supplied will also fall, and vice versa

Law of variable proportion See *law of diminishing (marginal) returns*

Lemon problem When asymmetric information exists, low-quality products will drive high-quality products out of the market., leaving the market to be dominated by defective products

Life-cycle saving Saving that is motivated by the desire to maintain a certain level of consumption during retirement

Limit pricing A pricing strategy in which firms set their prices so low that new entrants into the market will make no profits; also called *predatory pricing*

Limited liability A provision that makes investors in a corporation liable only up to the amount of money they invested in the business

Limited partners Partners who have limited liability

Limited partnership A business owned by two or more people, one or more, but not all, of whom have limited liability

Loanable funds Money available for loans or required by borrowers

Loanable funds theory of the rate of interest A theory that the rate of interest is determined by the demand for and supply of loanable funds

Local union The lowest level of a union and the one to which a worker belongs directly

Lockout A temporary closing of a plant by the employer to win or end a dispute

Long run A situation in which firms are unconstrained by fixed factors and therefore can vary all their inputs and adjust fully to market conditions

Long-run average cost curve The cost curve showing the minimum cost per unit at which a firm can produce a given volume of output when its inputs are all variable; also called *envelope curve* and *planning curve*

Long-run average cost The minimum cost per unit at which a firm can produce a given volume of output when its inputs are all variable

Long-run supply curve A curve showing supply conditions after the economy has adjusted to change

Lorenz curve A graphical device for measuring income inequality

Low-income cut-off See *poverty line*

Macroeconomics The branch of economics that studies the behaviour of broad economic aggregates

Marginal A concept widely used in economics to mean incremental, extra, or additional

Marginal cost The extra cost incurred by increasing output by one unit; also called *incremental cost*

Marginal cost pricing A pricing strategy that involves setting price equal to marginal cost; it is intended to force optimal resource use

Marginal physical product of labour The extra output derived from using an additional unit of labour

Marginal (physical) product (*MPP*) See *marginal product (MP)*

Marginal product (*MP*) The extra output derived from using one additional unit of a variable factor; also called *marginal (physical) product (MPP)*

Marginal productivity theory of wages The theory that under purely competitive conditions a profit-maximizing firm will hire labour up to the point at which the wage rate equals the value of the marginal product of labour

Marginal profit The extra or additional profit that is realized from a one-unit increase in output

Marginal rate of substitution (*MRS*) The rate at which a consumer is willing to trade units of one commodity for units of another commodity so as to keep his or her level of satisfaction unchanged

Marginal revenue product (of labour) (*MRP*) The additional revenue contributed by the last unit of labour; it is the marginal physical product multiplied by the price of the product or the value of the marginal physical product

Marginal revenue The extra revenue obtained by selling an additional unit of output

Marginal utility The *extra* satisfaction derived from the consumption of additional units of a good or service

Marginal-cost pricing The establishment of the equality of price and marginal cost

Market The mechanism that facilitates the buying and selling of resources and goods and services

Market condition The relationship between quantity demanded and quantity supplied

Market demand curve The demand curve representing the demand of all the buyers in the market for an item

Market economy An economy in which the market forces of demand and supply play a prominent role

Market failure The inability of the price system to achieve an efficient allocation of resources

Market income The sum of earnings from employment and self-employment, investment income, private retirement income, and other incomes, excluding government transfers

Market mechanism The complicated network of markets and prices found in most Western countries

Market period See *very short period*

Market power See *monopoly power*

Market quotas Limits placed on the amount of a product that producers can market

Market share The fraction of the total output of goods and services accounted for by a firm or a group of firms

Market signalling The transmission of information, by the use of proxy measures, about unobservable characteristics

Market structure The competitive nature of the market environment in which firms make their pricing and output decisions

Marketing cooperative A cooperative whose objective is to take advantage of large-volume selling

Market-size effect The effect on quantity demanded caused by a change in the number of buyers in the market as a result of a change in price

Markup pricing A pricing formula in which firms charge consumers the cost of production plus an additional amount—a mark up—to cover profit; see *cost-plus pricing*

Maturity The length of time before a loan is supposed to be paid off

Mediation See *conciliation*

Mediator An impartial third party who tries to find a solution to a dispute between two parties

Menu costs Costs incurred when changing prices, such as updating catalogues and changing labels; may explain price rigidity

Merit goods Goods or services that the government has determined to be necessary and therefore mandatory for society

Microeconomics The branch of economics that studies the behaviour of individual economic units; also called *price theory*

Midpoint formula (for elasticity) A formula that calculates elasticity by using the average of the quantities and the average of the prices

Minimum efficient scale The point at which increasing returns to scale end and constant returns to scale begin; the minimum point of the long-run average cost curve

Mixed economy An economy that has a mixture of free enterprise and central decision making

Mixed private enterprise economy A free enterprise economic system with some government intervention

Model A simplified version of a more complex system of relationships; sometimes called a theory

Money flows Flows of income and expenditures in monetary terms

Monopolistic competition A market with a large number of firms selling differentiated products

Monopolized market A market in which sellers have significant control over price or output

Monopoly power The ability of a firm to exert control over price and output; also called *market power*

Monopoly A market structure characterized by a single firm producing a product that has no close substitutes

Moral hazard The lack of any incentive on the part of a party to protect itself from a risk when it is insulated against it

Nash equilibrium The condition that exists when each player in a game selects the best possible strategy, given the strategies of the other players

National energy policy The federal government program for energy self-sufficiency

National union A national association of local unions, which usually sets policy and does the bargaining for the associated unions

Natural monopoly A market in which a single firm can satisfy the entire market demand more cheaply than two or more firms could

Negative externality See *external diseconomy*

Negative income tax A system whereby the government makes payments to people whose incomes are below the taxable level

Negative slope The slope of a declining curve

Net income The difference between total revenue and total expenses

Nominal rate of interest The rate quoted for a loan or a deposit, which includes a premium for inflation

Normal goods Good for which demand increases as income increases and for which demand falls as income falls

Normal profit A profit that is equal to the alternative (opportunity) cost of the resources employed in production; also called *zero economic profit*

Normative economics Explains how the economy should work

Normative statements Statements about what ought to be

Occam's razor The idea of stripping away unnecessary details from what is being studied and focusing only on what is immediately relevant

Offers to purchase See *price supports*

Oligopoly A market with few firms selling identical or differentiated products; a market structure in which there are only a few firms, all recognizing their interdependence

Open shop A workplace in which union membership is not a prerequisite for employment

Open-access resources Resources that are difficult or costly to exclude individuals from using

Openness the extent of involvement in international trade

Opportunity cost The alternative that is sacrificed when a choice is made

Optimum tariff The tariff that maximizes the country's welfare

Optimum tax rate For a revenue tax, the rate that maximizes tax revenue

Ordinal utility A concept based on the assumption that individuals are able to rank their preferences in relation to the consumption of goods and services

Origin The point of intersection of the vertical and horizontal axes

Other things being equal assumption See *ceteris paribus*

Outputs The goods and services produced by the factors of production

Overhead costs See *fixed costs*

Paradox of value See *water-diamond paradox*

Pareto efficiency See *Pareto optimality*

Pareto optimality The condition that exists when it is impossible to make someone better off without making someone else worse off; also called *Pareto efficiency*

Partial equilibrium analysis A method of analysis that studies the behaviour of variables in individual markets in isolation from other markets

Partnership agreement An oral or a written agreement governing the partners in a business

Partnership A non-incorporated business formed by two or more partners

Patent An exclusive right that a government grants a producer to produce a product; it is not extended to any other producer for the duration of the patent; it serves as an effective barrier to entry

Payoff The result or outcome of a strategy in a game

Payoff matrix A table that shows the outcomes of various strategies in a game

Perfect competition See *pure competition*

Perfectly elastic demand A change in price causes an infinitely large change in quantity demanded

Perfectly inelastic demand A change in price has no effect on quantity demanded

Physical capital Manufactured resources used to produce goods and services

Pie chart A circular graph whose pieces add up to 100%

Planning curve See *long-run average cost curve*

Point elasticity of demand A measure of elasticity of demand derived by measuring elasticity at a point on the demand curve

Point elasticity of supply A measure of elasticity of supply derived by measuring elasticity at a point on the supply curve

Point of saturation The point beyond which the marginal product is negative

Positive economics Explains or describes how the economy works

Positive externality See *external economy*

Positive slope The slope of a rising curve

Positive statements Statements about what is

Post hoc fallacy The erroneous conclusion that one event causes another simply because it precedes the other

Poverty line An arbitrary level of income below which poverty is said to exist; also called *low income cut-off*

Precautionary saving motive The incentive to save to provide for illness and emergencies

Predatory pricing See *limit pricing*

Preference map See *indifference map*

Price Value expressed in terms of money; the amount of money paid for a unit of a commodity

Price ceiling The upper limit at which a seller is legally allowed to sell a commodity

Price consumption curve A line joining the points of tangency between budget lines and indifference curves as the price of one of the items changes

Price controls Government restrictions on prices that sellers are allowed to charge

Price discrimination The practice of selling a product in different markets at different prices for reasons unrelated to cost

Price elasticity of demand The degree to which quantity demanded responds to a change in price; it is the percentage change in quantity demanded divided by the percentage change in price

Price elasticity of supply The degree to which quantity supplied responds to a change in price; it is the percentage change in quantity supplied divided by the percentage change in price

Price floor The lowest price at which a seller is legally allowed to sell a commodity

Price leadership The condition that exists when one firm in an industry takes the lead in changing prices and the other firms follow suit

Price line See *budget line*

Price mechanism The market system in which prices determine the production and distribution activities in an economy

Price supports A system established by government to prevent the prices of certain farm products from falling below a desired level; also called *offers to purchase*

Price system A system of prices and markets that determines what to produce, how to produce, and for whom to produce

Price theory See *microeconomics*

Price-taker A firm with no control over the price of its product; it cannot, by itself, affect the market price at which it sells its product by varying its level of output; a firm in pure competition is a price-taker

Principal (with reference to contractual agreement) The main party in a contractual agreement

Principal (with reference to loans) The amount lent or borrowed on which interest is normally paid

Principal-agent problem The problem that arises when the agent can take hidden actions that accomplish the agent's objectives to the detriment of the principal

Principle of diminishing marginal rate of substitution The hypothesis that as a consumer moves along an indifference curve, consuming more and more of one commodity, and less and less of another commodity, the marginal rate of substitution diminishes

Principle of substitution The tendency for the firm to substitute a cheap factor for a more expensive factor

Prisoner's dilemma What happens when two prisoners are caught in a situation in which it is difficult to cooperate even when cooperation is beneficial to both prisoners

Private costs Costs borne solely and directly by the individuals or firms making the decision

Private sector The household sector and the private business sector; the non-public sector

Producer cooperative A cooperative formed by producers to promote their interests

Producer sovereignty The concept that producers decide what to produce and then convince consumers to buy it

Producer surplus The difference between the amount that producers receive from selling an item and the amount they would have accepted for the item

Producers See *firms*

Product differentiation The condition that exists when firms distinguish their products from those of their competitors

Product market The market in which goods and services (products) are bought and sold; also called *goods and services market*

Production The process by which firms convert inputs into output

Production function The relation between inputs and output

Production possibilities (p-p) curve A graph showing all combinations of goods and services that can be produced if all resources are fully employed and technology is constant; also called *production possibility (p-p) boundary*, *production possibility (p-p) frontier*, and *transformation curve*

Production possibilities (p-p) schedule A table showing various combinations of goods and services that can be produced with full utilization of all resources and a given state of technology

Production possibility (p-p) boundary See *production possibility (p-p) curve*

Production possibility (p-p) frontier See *production possibility (p-p) curve*

Production possibility (p-p) point A combination of goods or services that an economy can produce

Production quota The maximum quantity of an item that producers can legally produce; also called *quantity restriction*

Productive efficiency The situation that exists when an economy cannot increase its production of one commodity without reducing its production of some other commodity

Productive inefficiency The situation that exists when it is possible to produce more of one commodity without reducing less of some other commodity

Productivity A measure of output per unit of a specified input

Profit Income from entrepreneurship; the difference between total revenue and total cost

Profit and loss statement See *income statement*

Property right the right of individuals to own property and legally use their resources as they see fit

Property tax A tax levied on property, usually on real estate

Proportional tax system A system in which the tax *rate* remains constant as income rises

Protective tariff A tariff whose main objective is to protect domestic industries

Psychic income Non-monetary rewards, such as the satisfaction derived from a job

Public finance The study of the microeconomic aspects of government spending and taxation

Public goods Goods or services that are consumed collectively; no one can be excluded from their consumption

Public sector See *government sector*

Purchase possibility curve See *consumption possibility curve*

Purchase possibility schedule A table showing various combinations of goods and services that a consumer can purchase for the same amount of money; also called *consumption possibility schedule*

Purchasing cooperative A cooperative whose objective is to take advantage of large-scale purchasing

Purchasing power The ability to purchase goods and services

Pure competition A market in which numerous firms produce identical products and to which there are no entry or exit barriers; also called *atomistic competition* and *perfect competition*

Pure economic rent The income derived from a factor of production whose supply is completely price inelastic

Pure monopoly A market structure in which a single firm sells a product a product that has no substitutes

Quality competition Competition by a firm attempting to make its products appear to be superior to the competitors'

Quantity demanded The quantity that people will be willing and able to buy at a specific price

Quantity restriction See *production quota*

Quantity supplied The quantity of a product that sellers (firms) are willing to offer for sale *at a particular* price

Quasi-rent The return on a factor of production whose supply is fixed only in the short run

Quota A limit imposed on quantity

Rand formula The legislation that made it compulsory for a worker who is a member of the unit for which a union is the bargaining agent to pay union dues even if not a union member

Rate of interest See *interest rate*

Real capital Capital goods, such as buildings, tools, and equipment; not money capital

Real flows Flows of real, physical goods, services, and resources

Real rate of interest The interest rate that would be charged if the rate of inflation were zero

Regional specialization A situation in which different regions of a country concentrate on the economic activity in which each has an advantage

Regressive tax system A system in which the tax *rate* decreases as income increases

Regulated monopoly A monopoly that is controlled by government legislation

Relative poverty The condition that prevails when an individual or a family has a standard of living that is far below that enjoyed by others in society

Relative price The ratio of two absolute prices; the price of one good expressed in terms of the price of another good

Rent Income from land

Reservation price The price below which sellers prefer to withdraw their products from the market

Resource market See *factor market*

Resources The things used to produce goods and services

Revenue tariff A tariff with the main objective of raising revenue for the government

Risk premium An addition to the interest rate to compensate for the risk of default

Sales tax A percentage tax imposed on the selling price of a wide range of commodities

Scarcity The situation that exists when resources are inadequate to produce all the goods and services that people want

Science A particular method of acquiring knowledge that involves observation, measurement, and testing; also refers to the knowledge acquired through the process; see also *scientific method*

Scientific method See *science*

Search costs The costs, such as search time, incurred in searching for information about a product

Search goods Goods whose quality can be evaluated by inspection at the time of purchase

Services Intangible things that satisfy wants

Shortage A situation in which quantity demanded exceeds quantity supplied; also called *excess quantity demanded*

Short run A situation in which firms cannot vary all their inputs or productive resources; thus, they operate with some fixed costs

Short-run industry supply curve A curve that shows the various quantities of an item supplied by all firms in the industry at various prices in the short run; it is the horizontal summation of the short-run supply curves of all the firms in the industry

Short-run shutdown point The point at which price equals the minimum average variable cost

Short-run supply curve (in pure competition) The portion of the firm's marginal cost curve that lies above its average variable cost curve

Single proprietorship A business owned by a single individual, without limited liability; also called *sole proprietorship*

Size distribution of income The distribution of income among individuals and households

Slope (of a curve) The steepness or flatness of a curve; the upward or downward inclination of a curve

Slope of a linear curve The vertical distance divided by the horizontal distance; slope is $\Delta Y/\Delta X$

Slope of a non-linear curve (at a point on the curve) The slope of the line drawn tangent to the curve at the given point

Social costs The total costs to society of decisions made and actions taken by individuals and firms

Social science Any discipline that studies human behaviour

Socialism An economic system in which the state owns and controls the resources of the economy

Socialistic system See *command economy*

Sole proprietorship See *single proprietorship*

Specialization Concentration on a particular occupation or task

Specific tariff A tariff expressed as a fixed amount per unit of an imported item

Stock A quantity existing at a particular time

Stock market The market in which shares of companies are traded

Strike A work stoppage by a union in an attempt to exert pressure on the employer

Subsidy A payment made by the government to a producer of a good or service; it reduces the price to the consumer

Substitute A good that can be used in place of another

Substitutes (in production) Goods that are produced as alternatives to each other

Substitution effect The effect on quantity demanded caused by people switching to or from a product as its price changes

Sunk cost A cost that cannot be recovered and thus cannot be considered when making a choice

Supply The various quantities of a good or service that sellers are willing and able to offer for sale (place on the market) at various prices during a specific period

Supply curve An upward-sloping curve showing the direct relationship between price and quantity supplied

Supply function Equation expressing the relationship between price and quantity supplied

Supply schedule A table showing the direct relationship between price and quantity supplied

Supply shifters The non-price determinants that shift the supply curve

Surplus A situation in which quantity supplied exceeds quantity demanded; also called *excess quantity supplied*

Target saving Saving for a specific purpose

Tariff A tax on imported goods

Tariff evasion Avoidance of tariffs by, for example, re-routing goods through other countries

Tax A compulsory payment imposed by a government

Technical (technological) efficiency Efficiency measured in terms of inputs

Technology A method of doing things, often applied to production

Terms of trade The rate at which a country's exports exchange for its imports

Theory A testable hypothesis about the way in which variables are related; sometimes called a model

Total cost (*TC*) The sum of all costs incurred in producing a given output of goods and services; the sum of total fixed cost and total variable cost

Total product (*TP*) The maximum quantity of output that a firm can produce during a period

Total revenue (*TR*) The total amount received from the sale of goods and services; it is the quantity sold multiplied by the price

Total utility Total satisfaction derived from the consumption (or use) of a good or service

Trade creation A situation in which economic integration leads to a change in the direction of trade from a higher-cost supplier to a lower-cost supplier

Trade diversion The volume of trade that moves from a lower-cost supplier to a higher-cost supplier because of economic integration

Trade union See *craft union*

Trading curve A graphical depiction of all combinations of goods and services available through specialization and trade

Transfer earnings The term used to describe the amount that a factor of production can earn in the next-best employment alternative

Transformation curve See *production possibility (p-p) curve*

20% club A group of municipalities whose objective was to reduce greenhouse gas emissions by 20% by 2005

Unemployment An economic condition that exists when workers are without jobs even though they are willing and able to work

Union An association of workers organized to promote the interests of its members in negotiations with their employers; also called *labour union*

Union shop A workplace in which workers who are not union members can be hired, provided that they become union members within a specified period

Unit elasticity of demand A given percentage change in price causes the same percentage change in quantity demanded

Unwritten agreements Agreements reached by handshake only, with no formal written document

Util The measure for a unit of satisfaction

Utility The satisfaction derived from consuming goods and services

Variable Anything that changes

Variable costs Costs that are dependent on the volume of output

Variable factors Inputs that the firm can change during a given period

Very long run A situation in which a firm can vary all its inputs and its technology

Very short period A situation in which producers cannot vary the quantity of goods placed on the market; also called *market period*

Voluntary arbitration The voluntary submission of a dispute to a third party whose decision on the matter is binding

Voluntary restrictions A situation in which one government asks another to restrict its exports to that country

Wage rate The price of labour per unit of time

Wage transfer mechanism The process by which changes in wages in one occupation are transmitted to other occupations

Wages and salaries Income from labour

Wagner's law The statement that government spending will grow at a faster rate than the rate of increase in output

Water pollution The toxic waste, chemical spills, chemical production, municipal waste, and acid rain that contaminate water systems

Water-diamond paradox The apparent (superficial) contradiction in the fact that an absolute necessity, such as water, has a lower value than a luxury item, such as diamonds; also called *paradox of value*

Workable competition The condition that exists when competition is sufficient to ensure that market power is not excessive

X-inefficiency A condition that exists when a firm fails to use its resources in their most economically efficient way

Zero economic profit See *normal profit*

Photo Credits

Index

Key terms and their page references are in boldface.